Introduction to
SOCIAL WELFARE INSTITUTIONS

Social problems, services,
and current issues

The Dorsey Series in Social Welfare

Introduction to

SOCIAL WELFARE INSTITUTIONS

Social problems, services, and current issues

CHARLES ZASTROW

Social Welfare Department
University of Wisconsin—Whitewater

REVISED EDITION   1982

THE DORSEY PRESS
Homewood, Illinois
60430

COVER PHOTO: Jean-Claude Lejeune

ISBN 0-256-02676-9
Library of Congress Catalog Card No. 80–71058
Printed in the United States of America

5 6 7 8 9 0 MP 9 8 7 6 5 4

To Chellie and Ross

This book is designed to stimulate students' interests in social welfare and to provide an experiential "flavor" of what the fields of social welfare and social work are really like. A social problems approach describes how people are affected by such problems as poverty, child abuse, emotional difficulties, sexism, alcoholism, crime, mental retardation, racism, overpopulation, and sexual dysfunctions. Information on the nature, extent, and causes of such problems is also presented. In teaching introductory courses in social welfare, a number of my colleagues and I have found that presenting material on social problems tends to arouse students' interests as it confronts them face-to-face with tragic social conditions encountered by people. This book also presents a number of case examples through which the reader is able to identify with people in need of help.

With this information on social problems, the reader is then prepared and motivated to read additional material covered in the text on current services, merits and shortcomings of current services, and new programs that are needed to meet service gaps and shortcomings.

Additional emphases in *Introduction to Social Welfare Institutions: Social Problems, Services, and Current Issues* are to:

a. Provoke the reader's thinking about some of the controversial, contemporary issues in social welfare—I believe developing the student's reasoning capacities is much more important than learning unimportant facts to be recited on exams.
b. Convey material on counseling techniques and on how to analyze policy issues that the reader will find usable in working with people and in arriving at policy decisions.
c. Provide case examples of the functions, roles, responsibilities, gratifications, and frustrations of social workers that will assist the student who is considering a social work major in making a career decision.
d. Provide a brief historical review of the development of social welfare, social work, and various social services.
e. Help the reader "sort out" his or her value structure toward welfare recipi-

Preface

ents, single parents, ex-convicts, the mentally ill, the divorced, abusive parents, minority groups, those who are prejudiced, and so on. The aim is not to sell any particular set of values, but to help the reader arrive at a value system that he/she will be comfortable with and find functional in interacting with others.

PLAN OF THE BOOK

Part One introduces the student to the fields of social welfare, social work, and human services. These terms are defined, and their relationships to sociology, psychology, and other disciplines are described. A brief history of social welfare and social work is provided, and the future is also looked at. A wide variety of human services are described, and the location of social work within the network of human services is discussed. Social work as a career and a profession are also discussed. This section is written with an emphasis on providing material that will help the reader in deciding whether to pursue a career in social work.

Part Two focuses on the most common social problems served by the field of social welfare. This part constitutes the main emphasis of the text and describes:

a. The 16 prominent social problems in our society.
b. Current social services to meet these problems.
c. Gaps in current services.
d. Controversial issues in each service area.
e. Proposed new programs to meet current gaps in services.

Numerous case examples are given to provide the reader with a "feeling" awareness of how the problems affect people, and to convey what it is really like to be a social worker.

Part Three focuses on social work practice and describes the three practice areas of casework, group work, and community organization. This part provides considerable usable information on how to counsel individuals, on how to work with groups, and on how to be a community organizer.

This second edition updates information in all of the chapters, and several chapters have been extensively revised in accordance with the suggestions received from a number of faculty members who have reviewed and commented on the first edition. In addition two new chapters have been added on sexism and on physical/mental handicaps. The chapter on sexism was included to be consistent with the Council on Social Work Education's recently approved accreditation standard involving women's issues and sex discrimination. The chapter on physical/mental handicaps was added to cover rehabilitative services—an important field of service in social welfare.

With the above objectives and approach, the book is intended for use in introductory social welfare courses. For prospective social work majors, it is designed to introduce them to the field of social welfare, to assist them in arriving at a career decision, and to prepare them for future social work courses. For nonmajors, it is designed to inform them of available social services, to provide a framework for analyzing policy issues and for making citizenship decisions, and to further their liberal arts education.

ACKNOWLEDGMENTS

I wish to express my deep appreciation to the following people and organizations who made this book possible:

The contributing authors.
The illustrator, Robert Gustafson.

The following who gave special permission to reprint material:

Warren B. Armstrong, President of Eastern New Mexico State University

Dae H. Chang, Chairperson of the Department of Administration of Justice at Wichita State University

Marlene A. Cummings, Human Relations Coordinator for Madison Public Schools

Galen Janeksela, Assistant Professor in the Department of Administration of Justice at Wichita State University

John Howard Association in Chicago, Illinois

National Association of Social Workers, Inc., New York, New York

Prentice-Hall, Inc., Englewood Cliffs, New Jersey

Racine County Department of Social Services, Racine, Wisconsin

Warren Shibles, Assistant Professor at the University of Wisconsin-Whitewater

Time Magazine, New York City

Shel Trapp, National Coordinator for the National Training and Information Center, Chicago, Illinois

Wisconsin Council on Criminal Justice (associated with Law Enforcement Assistance Administration)

Wisconsin Department of Health and Social Services

The following who gave special permission to reproduce photographs:

The Capital Times, Madison, Wisconsin

The Christian Science Monitor

Corrections Division, Wisconsin State Department of Health and Social Services

Curative Rehabilitation Center, Milwaukee, Wisconsin

Division of Family Services, Wisconsin State Department of Health and Social Services

Lakeland Counseling Center, Elkhorn, Wisconsin

Lutheran Social Services of Wisconsin and Upper Michigan

Madison General Hospital in Madison, Wisconsin

Madison Opportunity Center, Inc., Madison, Wisconsin

Methodist Hospital, Madison, Wisconsin

Military Science Department, University of Wisconsin-Whitewater

Racine County Department of Social Services, Racine, Wisconsin

Rock County Health Care Center, Janesville, Wisconsin

United Way of Dane County in Wisconsin

Wisconsin State Department of Health and Social Services

Wisconsin State Journal, Madison, Wisconsin

A sincere thank you to Linda Brown, Kay Guler, Debra Parkin, Ralph Navarre, Nancy Tobiason, and Vicki Vogel who were "alter egos" for conceptualizing various chapters and helped in a number of ways with the writing of this text.

C. Z.

CONTRIBUTING AUTHORS

TIM BLISS
Former Director, Alcoholism/Drug Abuse Program,
Rock County Health Care Center, Janesville, Wisconsin

MAUREEN O'GORMAN FOSTER
Executive Director
Dane County Hospice, Inc.
Madison, Wisconsin

URSULA SENNEWALD MYERS
Executive Director
Rock County Department of Social Services, Janesville, Wisconsin

DON NOLAN
Social Worker, Jefferson County Public School System, Wisconsin

ROBERT SCHEURELL
Associate Professor and Coordinator,
Undergraduate Social Work Program,
University of Wisconsin—Milwaukee

LLOYD G. SINCLAIR
Sex Therapist, Midwest Center for Sex Therapy
Madison, Wisconsin;
Instructor, University of Wisconsin—Whitewater

xiii

Contents

part one

Introduction: Social welfare, social work, and human services

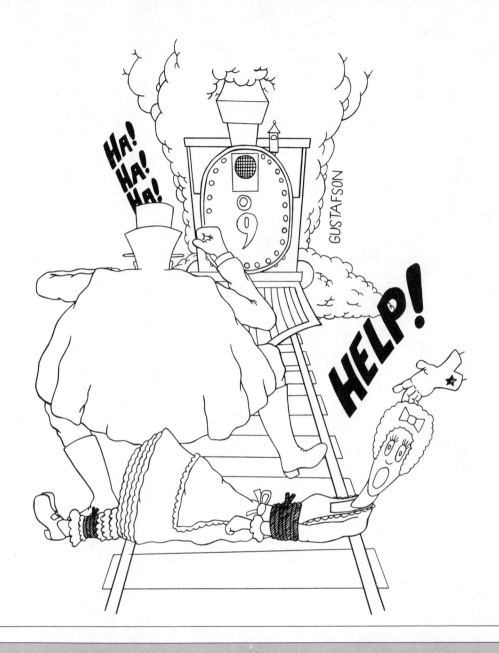

chapter 1

BUSINESS OF SOCIAL WELFARE

The goal of social welfare is to fulfill the social, financial, health, and recreational requirements of all individuals in a society. Social welfare seeks to enhance the social functioning of all age-groups, both rich and poor. When other institutions in our society, such as the market economy and the family, fail at times to meet the basic needs of individuals or groups of people, then social services are needed and demanded.

In more primitive societies, people's basic needs were fulfilled in more direct and informal ways. Even in this country, less than 150 years ago, most Americans lived on farms or in small towns with extended families and relatives close by. If financial or other needs arose, relatives, the church, and neighbors were there to "lend a helping hand." Problems were visible and personal; everyone knew everyone else in the community. When a need arose, it was taken for granted that those with resources would do whatever they could to alleviate the difficulty. If, for example, the need was financial, personal acquaintance with the storekeeper or banker usually was sufficient to obtain needed goods or money. Needless to say, we are now living in a different era. Our technology, economic base, social patterns, and living styles have changed dramatically. Our commercial, industrial, political, educational, and religious institutions are considerably larger and more impersonal. We tend to live in large urban communities, away from families or relatives, frequently without even establishing acquaintances with neighbors. We have become much more mobile, often having few roots and limited knowledge of the community in which we live. Vocationally, we also have specialized and become more interdependent on others, and thereby we have diminishing control over large aspects of our lives. Our rapidly changing society is a breeding ground for exacerbating former social ills and creating new problems, such as the eruption of our inner cities, higher rates of crime, energy crises, and the destruction of the quality of our environment. Obviously, the old rural-frontier methods of meeting social welfare needs are no longer viable. In our industrialized, complex, and rapidly changing society, social welfare activities have become one of the most important functions in terms of the money spent, the human misery treated, and the number of people served.[1]

Social welfare: Its business, history, and future

It is the business of social welfare:

To find homes for parentless children.

To rehabilitate people who are addicted to alcohol or drugs.

To treat those with emotional difficulties.

To make life more meaningful for the aged.

To provide vocational rehabilitation services to the physically and mentally handicapped.

To meet the financial needs of the poor.

To rehabilitate juveniles and adults who have committed criminal offenses.

To end racial and religious discrimination.

To provide child care services for working mothers.

To counteract problems and violence in families, including child abuse and spouse abuse.

To fulfill the health and legal requirements of those in financial need.

To counsel individuals and groups having a wide variety of personal and social difficulties.

To provide recreational and leisure-time services to all age-groups.

To educate and provide socialization experiences to children who are mentally retarded or emotionally disturbed.

To serve families struck by such physical disasters as fires and tornadoes.

To provide vocational training services and employment opportunities to the unskilled and unemployed.

To meet the special needs of Indians, migrant workers, and other minority groups.

WHAT IT'S ALL ABOUT

Shortly after their marriage Frank Lund, age 24, and his wife, Jean, age 22, moved from their rural farm background in northern Wisconsin to a large midwestern city in the fall of 1947. They had bright hopes for their future. Frank obtained a good-paying job on the assembly line of an auto manufacturing company. Jean worked part-time as a file clerk until her first pregnancy in the spring of 1949. In the next four years they had three children, and also purchased a three-bedroom home in a suburb. Then in 1954, while on a hunting trip, Frank was accidentally killed. Mrs. Lund was never quite the same. She had periodic moods of depression, and had considerable difficulty in finding the energy to care for her three young children.

In 1955 the Lunds' financial resources were depleted. Unable to make the payments on the house, they were forced to move to a rundown two-bedroom apartment closer to the center of the city. In the winter of 1955 Mrs. Lund applied for financial assistance under the Aid to Dependent Children program. The community in which the Lunds lived had negative attitudes toward welfare, and consequently the monthly payments the Lunds received were barely sufficient to meet their basic needs. In addition, the neighbors never attempted to understand the Lunds' plight. They were more concerned about their tax dollars being spent for "such people." Mrs. Lund felt she was a second-class citizen and stigmatized because she was a "charity" case. She also soon became aware that some of her neighbors would not permit their children to play with her children. When the children entered school, they began to feel they were different from other children; they were poorly dressed, the lunch they brought from home usually consisted of cheese sandwiches, and they had no father. A few years later Mrs. Lund dated a salesman for awhile; being lonely she permitted him to stay over some evenings at the apartment. The neighbors frowned about this and made moral accusations. Several months later Mrs. Lund ended this relationship when she became aware she would be unable to change the man's drinking problem (when intoxicated he was sometimes abusive to Mrs. Lund and the children).

When the oldest child, Tom, was 15 he was arrested for starting three fires in the neighborhood. Perhaps he just wanted attention, or maybe it was his way of demonstrating he needed help. Anyway, he was judged to have emotional difficulties and was sent to a residential treatment center. At the age of 20 he was released. He applied for several semi-skilled jobs, but partly because of potential employers' concerns about his past, someone else was always hired. He therefore obtained a series of odd jobs as maintenance man, dishwasher, store clerk, and so forth. Not finding more stimulating work, he began drinking, sometimes to excess. At 25 he married and within the next few years fathered four children. Because of his family responsibilities, low-paying job, and drinking problem, he and his family are now locked into poverty.

The second child, Corine, wanted to escape from her home and from school when she became a teenager. She ran away several times but was always returned by the police. At 16 she became involved with Mike, a high school dropout, and became pregnant. Mike's parents would not give their consent to a marriage. Corine dropped out of school, delivered, and decided to keep the baby. For the next six years she continued to live with her mother, even though there were frequent arguments. At 22 she met and within a year married Bill Loomans, a seasonal construction worker and a widower with three children. Already Bill and Corine were close to being locked into poverty for the rest of their lives. The two additional children they had after marriage did not help.

The youngest child, Dave, was also a problem for Mrs. Lund. In the early years of school he had considerable difficulty learning to read. He soon fell behind the rest of his classmates. By the fourth grade he felt self-conscious about being unable to read. In class he no longer would put forth much of an effort to do academic work, and instead spent most of his time clowning around. Psychological testing indicated Dave had average mental ability, and suggested he had developed an "emotional block" to academic work that appeared to be related to his home environment. Upon entering the fifth grade, he was placed in a special class for the retarded. Dave was very sensitive about this, and became involved in several fights when referred to as a "dummy" by his peers. At age 16 he dropped out of school and was fortunate to obtain a job pumping gas. Two years later he was "forced" to marry. Terri and Dave had a stormy marriage, with frequent disputes. Within a year and a half they had two children. Six months later they separated, and Dave was required by the court to pay child support until the children were 18. Two years later, upon being named as the father of another child delivered by an unmarried mother, Dave was required by the court to make monthly support payments for this child. He tried to meet these responsibilities, but his income would not stretch, and therefore he wrote some checks that "bounced." Recently he was arrested and placed on probation for two years. He now appears to be solidly locked into poverty for the remainder of his life. His chances of securing a better paying job are slight, because of his past, his lack of training for a skilled job, and his inability to read.

The story of the Lund family raises a number of questions for social welfare. Who is to "blame" for the difficulties of this family—or is no one at fault? Is this cycle of poverty which has been transmitted from one generation to another, and the social difficulties associated with it, likely to be continued among the grandchildren of Frank and Jean Lund? What should be done, now, to help the members of the Lund family? Who should pay for the help provided? What kind of help (both services and money), if provided to Jean Lund when her husband was accidentally killed, would probably have prevented the social difficulties experienced by her children and likely to be faced by her grandchildren?

SOCIAL WELFARE'S RELATIONSHIP TO SOCIOLOGY AND TO SOCIAL WORK

Along with many other concepts, social welfare has not been precisely defined. The National Association of Social Workers (a professional group) states:

Social Welfare generally denotes the full range of organized activities of voluntary and governmental agencies that seek to prevent, alleviate, or contribute to the solution of recognized social problems, or to improve the well-being of individuals, groups or communities. Such activities use a wide variety of professional personnel such as physicians, nurses, lawyers, educators, engineers, ministers, and social workers. . . .[2]

Examples of social welfare programs and services are foster care, adoption, day care, Headstart, probation and parole, public assistance programs such as Aid to Families with Dependent Children, public health nursing, sex therapy, suicide counseling, recreational services such as Boy Scouts and YWCA programs, services to minority groups, services to veterans, school social services, medical and legal services to the poor, family planning services, meals on wheels, nursing home services, shelters for battered spouses, protective services for child abuse and neglect, assertiveness training programs, encounter groups and sensitivity training, public housing projects, family counseling, Alcoholics Anonymous, runaway services, services to the developmentally disabled, and sheltered workshops.

One difficulty with the above definition of social welfare is that it does not mention the knowledge base of social welfare. It is at this level that social welfare relates to sociology. Sociology is the scientific study of the social behavior of human beings. It is concerned with social interaction within and between groups; it takes for analysis groups ranging in size from two people to whole societies, with one focus being to examine the effects of these groups on individuals. The knowledge base of social welfare overlaps with sociology, and with other disciplines such as psychology, cultural anthropology, social psychology, economics, psychiatry, and po-

FIGURE 1–1 Overlap of knowledge base of social welfare with other disciplines

litical science. (See Figure 1–1.) Theories and research in these disciplines may or may not, depending on the nature of the content, be considered part of the knowledge base of social welfare. When theories and research in these other disciplines have direct applications to the social welfare goal of enhancing the social functioning of people, then this material is also part of the knowledge base of social welfare.

A few examples may be useful in illustrating this overlap. Sociological research on, and conceptualization of, the causes of social problems (for example, juvenile delinquency, mental illness, poverty, and racial discrimination) may also be considered part of the knowledge base of social welfare; only through an understanding of such problems can social welfare effectively prevent and control such problems. Sociological studies on the effects of institutions (for example, mental hospitals and prisons) on individuals currently has considerable interest and application in social welfare. Other sociological

investigations of such subjects as mobility, urbanization, secularization, formation of groups, race relations, prejudice, and the process of assimilation have also become part of the knowledge base of social welfare because such investigations have direct applications to enhancing the social well-being of people. However, other subject interests of sociology, such as studies of social organizations among primitive tribes, are usually considered outside the knowledge base of social welfare since such research usually does not have direct applications to the social welfare goal of enhancing the social functioning of people.

Comparable overlap occurs between social welfare and the other previously mentioned disciplines. Using psychology as an example, studies and theory development in such areas as personality growth and therapeutic techniques would be considered part of the knowledge base of social welfare as it has direct social welfare applications. On the other hand, experimental investigations of perception and thinking processes of animals does not, at least at the present time, have direct social welfare applications, and would not therefore be considered part of the knowledge base of social welfare.

In the past social welfare has been more of an applied science than a pure science. It has primarily formed its knowledge base from the theories and research of other disciplines, and focused on applying such knowledge through social programs.

On a different level, a functional level, social welfare overlaps with such institutions as the family, education, religion, and politics. One of the functions of the family is raising and caring for children. Social welfare assists families by providing such services as counseling, day care, foster care, and adoption. Certain educational courses have both educational and social welfare aspects; for example, social science and physical edu-

1
2

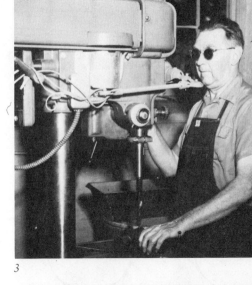

3

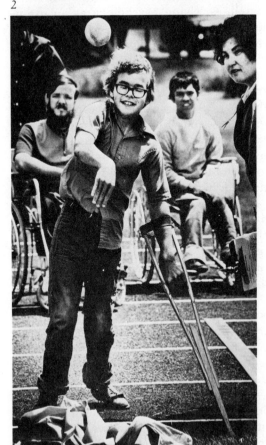

4
5

6

7

8

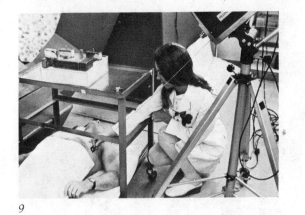

9

10

12

11

13

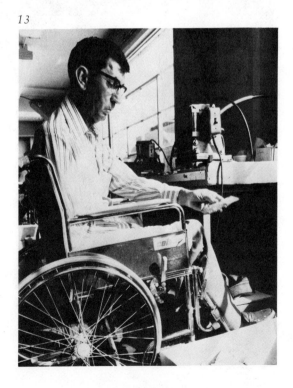

14

15

People helped by social welfare services

1. *Day-care center for migrant workers*

2. *A handicapped person learning to play baseball*

3. *Vocational rehabilitation for the blind*

4. *Occupational therapy*

5. *A "big brother-little brother" pair*

6. *Red Cross first aid*

7. *Learning to read braille*

8. *A physical handicap does not stand in the way of making a living*

9. *Radiotherapy for cancer*

10. *Headstart program*

11. *Learning sign language*

12. *A handicapped child learning to walk down a flight of stairs*

13. *A handicapped person at a sheltered workshop*

14. *A home damaged by a tornado: The family needs emergency housing and financial help*

15. *A foreign-born baby adopted a few years ago*

cation courses provide socialization experiences and are important in the social development of youth. Religion has long been interested in the social well-being of people, and has provided such social welfare services as counseling, financial assistance, day care, and recreation. The overlap between politics and social welfare occurs primarily at the stage of development of new social service programs where out political leaders must decide whether expenditures of tax dollars for such programs are warranted. Some social welfare programs, for example, public assistance, have long been a controversial political topic.

The term *social welfare* is frequently confused not only with sociology, but also with social work. Social welfare is a more global term which encompasses social work. Social welfare and social work are primarily related at the level of practice. *Social work* has been defined by the National Association of Social Workers (the professional social work organization) as follows:

> Social work is the professional activity of helping individuals, groups, or communities to enhance or restore their capacity for social functioning and to create societal conditions favorable to their goals.
>
> Social work practice consists of the professional application of social work values, principles, and techniques to one or more of the following ends: helping people obtain tangible services; providing counseling and psychotherapy for individuals, families, and groups; helping communities or groups provide or improve social and health services and participating in relevant legislative processes.
>
> The practice of social work requires knowledge of human development and behavior; of social, economic, and cultural institutions; and of the interaction of all these factors.[3]

The term *social worker* is generally applied to graduates (either with bachelor's or master's degrees) of schools of social work who are employed in the field of social welfare. A social worker is a "change agent." As a change agent a social worker is expected to be skilled at working with individuals, groups, and families, and in bringing about community changes. Almost of all social workers are employed in the field of social welfare. There are, however, many other professional and occupational groups that may be employed in the field of social welfare, as illustrated in Figure 1–2.

FIGURE 1–2 Examples of professional groups within the field of social welfare

Illustrations of professional people staffing social welfare services include attorneys providing legal services to the poor, urban planners in social planning agencies, physicians in public health agencies, teachers in residential treatment facilities for the emotionally disturbed, psychologists, nurses, and recreational therapists in mental hospitals, and psychiatrists in mental health clinics.

SOCIAL WELFARE INSTITUTIONS

Social welfare institutions are composed of social service programs (public assistance, foster care, probation and parole, for example) and social service organizations (Planned Parenthood, Alcoholics Anonymous, U.S. Department of Health and Human Services,* for example). The purposes of social welfare institutions are to prevent, alleviate, or contribute to the solution of recognized social problems so as to improve the well-being of individuals, groups, and communities directly. Social welfare institutions are established by policies and laws, with the programs and services being provided by voluntary (private) and governmental (public) agencies.

The term *social welfare institution* is applied to various levels of complexity and abstraction. The term may be applied to a single program or organization—for example, day-care services for the mentally handicapped or Planned Parenthood may be called a "social welfare institution." The term may be applied to a group of services or programs—for example, social welfare institutions for children include adoption, foster care, juvenile probation, runaway services, day care, school social services, and residential treatment. The highest aggregate level to which "social welfare institution" is applied includes *all* of the social programs and organizations that are designed to prevent, alleviate, or contribute to the solution of recognized social problems.

HISTORY OF SOCIAL WELFARE

Two conflicting views

The present social welfare scene is substantially being influenced by the past. Currently there are two conflicting views of the role of social welfare in our society.[4] One of these roles has been termed *residual;* a gap-filling or first-aid role. This view holds that social welfare services should only be pro-

vided when an individual's needs are not properly met through other societal institutions, primarily the family and the market economy. With the residual view, it is thought that social services and financial aid should not be provided until all other measures or efforts have failed, after the exhaustion of the individual's or his/her family's resources. In addition, this view asserts that funds and services should be provided on a short-term basis (primarily during emergencies), and are to be withdrawn when the individual or the family again becomes capable of being self-sufficient.

The residual view has been characterized as being "charity for unfortunates."[5] Funds and services are not seen as a right (something which one is entitled to), but as a gift, with the receiver having certain obligations; for example, in order to receive financial aid, recipients may be required to perform certain low-grade work assignments. Associated with the residual view is the belief that the causes of social welfare clients' difficulties are rooted in their own malfunctioning; that is, that clients are to blame for their predicaments because of personal inadequacies, or ill-advised activities or sins.

Under the residual view there is usually a stigma attached to receiving services or funds. The prevalence of the residual stigma can be shown by asking, "Have you ever in the past felt a reluctance to seek counseling for a personal or emotional situation that you faced because you were wary of what others might think of you?" For almost everyone the answer is "yes," and the reluctance to seek help is due to the residual stigma. The prevalence of this stigma in American society was dramatically shown in 1968 when Senator Thomas Eagleton was dropped as a vice presidential candidate on the Democratic ticket after it became known that he had once received psychiatric counseling.

---

* In May 1980 the U.S. Department of Health, Education and Welfare became the U.S. Department of Health and Human Services. The U.S. Department of Education is a new agency.

BLAMING THE VICTIM

Jerry Jorgenson and Joyce Mantha decided to get married after dating for three years. Both looked forward to a big wedding and a happy future. They had met in college, and now both were working in Mayville, a small town that Jerry had grown up in. Joyce was a kindergarten teacher, and Jerry was manager of an A&P grocery store. Against Jerry's wishes, Joyce drove one weekend to a nearby city to attend a premarriage party with some of her college women friends. The party was still going strong at 2:00 A.M., but Joyce thought it was time to return to her motel in order to return to Mayville early on Sunday. In the parking lot Joyce was sexually assaulted. She tried to fight off the assailant and suffered a number of bruises and abrasions. After the assault, a passerby called the police and an ambulance. Joyce called Jerry the next day. At first he was angry at the rapist. But the more he thought about it, the more he assigned blame to Joyce—she went to the party against his wishes, and he thought that she probably dressed and acted in such a way to interest the rapist, especially since he further assumed she was high on alcohol.

The weeks that followed became increasingly difficult for Jerry and Joyce. Joyce sensed that Jerry was blaming her for being raped. She tried to talk it out with Jerry but it did not help. Their sexual relationship became practically nil, as Jerry felt his "sexual rights" had been violated, and the few times he made sexual advances he had images of Joyce being attacked by a stranger. They postponed the marriage.

Many townspeople when they first heard about the rape, also thought that Joyce had "asked for it" while partying in the big city. Postponing the marriage was interpreted by the townspeople as evidence for this belief, and they began shunning Joyce. After several months of such treatment Joyce began to believe that she was at fault and increasingly blamed herself for her predicament. She became despondent, and moved back with her parents for refuge.

This story is only one illustration of the tendency in American culture to blame the victim. Others abound. If an adult is unemployed for a long time, often that person is believed to be "lazy" or "unmotivated." AFDC mothers (mothers receiving Aid to Families of Dependent Children) are *erroneously* stereotyped as being promiscous, irresponsible, and desirous of having more children in order to increase their monthly grant. When a marriage breaks up, either the husband or wife or both are blamed, rather than viewing the relationship as having deteriorated. When unfortunate circumstances occur (e.g., lightning striking one's home) some people believe it is a punishment for sinful activity. Slapping one's wife is justified by some segments of the population as being a way to "keep her in line" and to "show her who's boss." People living in poverty are often erroneously viewed as being personally inadequate, incompetent, lazy, or as having a culture that holds them in poverty. The problems of slum housing in inner cities are sometimes traced to the characteristics of "southern rural migrants" not yet "acculturated" to life in the big city. Such blaming of the victim sometimes sadly leads to acceptance by the general public of the victimization, with few efforts then being made to make constructive changes.

But perhaps the saddest feature of victim blaming is that the erroneous explanation often becomes a self-fulfilling prophecy. Tell a teacher a child is a poor learner, that teacher will interact with the child as if the child were a slow learner. Unfortunately the child will eventually come to believe the teacher is correct, and is likely to learn little. Labeling people as lazy, criminal, immoral, or mentally ill strongly influences the expectations people hold for them, and simultaneously influences the victims themselves in their expectations and self-definition.

The opposing point of view, which has been coined the *institutional view*,* holds that social welfare programs are to be "accepted as a proper, legitimate function of modern industrial society in helping individuals achieve self-fulfillment."[6] Under this view there is no stigma attached to receiving funds or services; recipients are viewed as being entitled to such help. Associated with this view is the belief that an individual's difficulties are due to causes largely beyond his/her control (for example, the reason a person is unemployed may well be due to a lack of employment opportunities). With this view, when difficulties arise, causes are sought in the environment (society), and efforts are focused on improving the social institutions within which the individual functions.

The residual approach characterized social welfare programs from our early history to the Depression of the 1930s. Since the Great Depression, both approaches have been applied to social welfare programs; some programs being largely residual in nature, while others being more institutional in design

and implementation. Social insurance programs, such as Old-Age, Survivors, and Disability Insurance (described in Chapter 4) are examples of "institutional" programs.

Early European history

One of the problems faced by all societies is to develop ways to meet the needs of those who are unable to be self-sufficient; the orphaned, the blind, the physically disabled, the poor, the mentally handicapped, and the sick. Prior to the Industrial Revolution, this responsibility was largely met by the family, the church, and by neighbors. One of the values of the Judean-Christian religion throughout history having considerable relevance for social welfare is humanitarianism; that is, ascribing a high value to human life and benevolently helping those in need.

With the development of the feudal system in Europe, when a tenant family was unable to meet a relative's basic needs, the feudal lord usually provided whatever was necessary.

The Elizabethan Poor Law

In the Middle Ages, for such reasons as famines, wars, crop failures, recurrences of

_____

* The term *institutional view of social welfare* is distinctly different from, and not to be confused with, the term *social welfare institutions*.

pestilences, and the breakdown in the feudal system, there were substantial increases in the number of people in need. Former approaches, primarily through the church and the family, were not capable of meeting the needs of many who were unable to be self-sufficient. As a result, many of these people were forced to resort to begging. To attempt to meet this social problem, England passed several poor laws between the mid-1300s to the mid-1800s. The most significant of these was the Elizabethan Poor Law of 1601, enacted during the reign of Queen Elizabeth. The fundamental provisions of this Poor Law were incorporated into the laws of the American colonies, and have had an important influence on our current approaches to public assistance and other social legislation.

The Elizabethan Poor Law established three categories of relief recipients:

1. The able-bodied poor. This group was given low-grade employment, and citizens were prohibited from giving them financial help. Anyone who refused to work was placed in stocks or in jail.

2. The impotent poor. People unable to work composed this group—the elderly, the blind, the deaf, mothers with young children, and the physically and mentally handicapped. They were usually placed together in an almshouse (institution). If the impotent poor had a place to live and if it appeared less expensive to maintain them there, they were permitted to live outside the almshouse where they were granted "outdoor relief," usually "in kind," (food, clothing, and fuel).

3. Dependent children. Children whose parents or grandparents were unable to support them were apprenticed out to other citizens. Boys were taught the trade of their master and had to serve until their 24th birthday. Girls were brought up as domestic servants and were required to remain until they were 21 or married.

This Poor Law did not permit the registra-tion of a person as being in need of charity whenever his/her parents, spouse, children or other relatives were able to provide support. Although the law was passed by the English Parliament, the parish (town or local community) was assigned the responsibility of implementing the provisions of the law, with the program expenses to be met by charitable donations and a tax in the parish upon lands, houses, and tithes. The Poor Law also stated that the parish's responsibility only extended to those who had legal residence in the parish, which was variously defined as having been born in the parish to having lived in the parish for three years. Residency requirements are still part of current public assistance programs. The Poor Law of 1601 set the pattern of public relief under governmental responsibility in Great Britain and this country for the next 300 years.

Most of the provisions of the Elizabethan Poor Law were incorporated into the social welfare policies of colonial America. Towns were assigned the responsibility of providing for the needy, almshouses were built to house the unemployables, orphaned children were apprenticed out, and a system of legal settlement was established which made it clear that towns were not responsible for meeting the needs of destitute strangers. Conditions in almshouses, it should be noted, were unbelievably deplorable. Into almshouses were packed not only the poor but also the sick, the emotionally disturbed, the blind, the alcoholic, and dependent children. Straw and old cots served for beds, there were no sanitary facilities, and the dilapidated buildings were barely heated in winter.

The Industrial Revolution

In the 17th, 18th, and 19th centuries the Industrial Revolution flourished in Europe and America. A major reason for its development was technological advances, such as the development of the steam engine. But the Revolution was also made possible by the *protestant ethic* and the *laissez-faire economical view.* These two themes also had important effects on social welfare. The protestant ethic emphasized *individualism,* the view that one is master of one's own fate. Hard work and acting in one's own self-interest were highly valued. An overriding goal for human beings set by the protestant ethic was to acquire material goods. People were largely judged not so much on the basis of their personalities and other attributes, but on how much wealth they had acquired. To be poor was thought to be due to one's own moral fault.

The laissez-faire economical theory asserted that the economy and society in general would best prosper if businesses and industries were permitted to do whatever they desired to make a profit. Any regulation by the government of business practices (for example, setting safety standards, minimum wage laws, prohibiting child labor) was discouraged. The protestant ethic and laissez-faire economical view, together, justified such business practices as cutthroat competition, formation of monopolies, deplorable safety and working conditions, and exploitation of the working class through low pay, long hours, and child labor.

The social welfare implications of the protestant ethic reached its most inhumane declarations in the theory of *Social Darwinism* which was based on Charles Darwin's theory of evolution. Darwin theorized that higher forms of life evolved from lower forms by the process of survival of the fittest; he had seen in the animal world a fierce struggle for survival that destroyed the weak, rewarded the strong, and produced evolutionary change. Herbert Spencer extended this theory to humanity; struggle, destruction, and

survival of the fit were thought to be essential to progress in human society as well. The theory stated in its most inhumane form that the strong (the wealthy) survived because they were superior, while the weak (the needy) deserved to perish and that it would be a mistake to help the weak survive. Although leaving the weak to perish was never advocated on a wide scale, the theory did have a substantial influence in curbing the development of innovative and more human social welfare programs.

Prior to the Industrial Revolution there were few communities in Europe or America with a population larger than a few thousand. One of the consequences of the Revolution was the development of large urban areas close to where factories were located. Since employment opportunities were limited in rural areas, many workers moved to cities. With such movement, family and kinship ties were broken, and those who were unable to adapt faced a loss of community identity, alienation, and social breakdown. To attempt to meet the needs of people living in urban areas, private social welfare services began to be developed in the 1800s—primarily at the initiation of the clergy and religious groups. (A public social welfare agency receives its funds through tax dollars, while a private or voluntary agency generally receives a large part of its funds from charitable contributions.)* Because of the lack of development of public social services, private agencies provided most of the funds and services to the needy until the 1930s. In the 1800s social services and funds were usually provided by upper middle-class volunteers

---

* Some private agencies are now contracting with public agencies to receive public funds to provide services to certain clients. Public agencies are established and administered by governmental units, while private agencies are established and administered by nongovernmental groups or private citizens.

who combined "charity" with religious admonitions.

Turn of the 20th century

Around 1880 various segments of the population became aware of the evils of unlimited competition, and abuses by those with economic power. It became clear that a few captains of industries were becoming very wealthy, while the standard of living for the bulk of the population was remaining static and only slightly above the subsistence level. One of the leaders of this new social view was Lester Ward who in *Dynamic Sociology* (1883) drew a sharp distinction between purposeless animal evolution and human evolution.[7] By manipulating the environment, and by social and economic controls, Ward asserted that all men could benefit. This new thinking was in direct opposition to the Social Darwinism and laissez-faire economical views. It called upon the federal government to take on new functions; to establish legislation to regulate business practices, and to provide social welfare programs. As a result, around 1900 there was an awakening to social needs, with the federal government beginning to place some, although limited, funds into such programs as health, housing, and slum clearance.

In the early 1900s social welfare became more professionalized. Prior to this time such services were generally provided by well-meaning, but untrained volunteers (do-gooders) from the middle and upper socio-economic groups. At this time people with more formalized training were employed in some positions, and there was an increased interest in developing therapeutic skills and methods in counseling clients. In this era some of our present patterns of specialization also developed, such as family services and probation and parole. It was also at this time that the first schools of social work and social welfare were founded in universities.

The Great Depression

The Depression of the 1930s brought about profound changes in social welfare. Until this time there was still largely the belief in individualism, that one is master of one's fate. The Depression shattered this myth. With an estimated 15 million people unemployed in the middle and upper classes, it became clear that causes and effects beyond individual control could cause deprivation, misery, and poverty. In addition, it became obvious that private social work agencies, which up until this time had distributed most of the financial assistance to the poor, did not have the resources to meet the needs of the large number who were now unemployed and poor.

Therefore, the federal government was called upon to fill this new role. In the early 1930s some temporary financial relief programs were established which provided grants-in-aid to states for financial relief. The experience during the Depression years with emergency relief and work programs demonstrated the need for more permanent federal efforts for dealing with some of the critical problems of unemployment, aging, disability, illness, and dependent children. As a result, in 1935 the Social Security Act was passed which formed the basis of many of our current public social welfare programs. Although there have been a number of amendments to the Social Security Act, the basic programs that were established in 1935 still remain. There were three major categories under the act.

1. Social insurance. This category was set up with an "institutional" orientation and provided insurance for unemployment, retirement, or death. There are two main

programs under this category: (*a*) Unemployment Compensation which provides weekly benefits for a limited time for workers who become unemployed; and (*b*) Old-Age, Survivors, and Disability Insurance which provides monthly payments to individuals and their families when the worker retires, becomes disabled, or dies. In everyday conversation this program is generally referred to as *social security.*

2. Public assistance. This category has many "residual" aspects. To receive benefits an individual must undergo a "means test" in which one's assets and expenses are reviewed to determine if there is a financial need. There were several programs under this category with the titles indicating eligible groups; Aid to the Blind (people of any age whose vision is 20/200 or less with correction), Aid to the Disabled (people between 18 and 65 years of age who are permanently disabled), Old Age Assistance* (people 65 years and older) and Aid to Families with Dependent Children (primarily mothers with children under age 18 where the father is out of the home). Public assistance programs incorporated several features of the English Poor Laws: for example, residence requirements, means test, some of the aid being "in kind" such as food, and the benefits being viewed as "charity" rather than aid which recipients are entitled to. Public assistance, particularly the Aid to Dependent Children program, is frequently criticized and stigmatized by politicians and the general public. An inaccurate public stereotype is that "welfare" is only public assistance. In actuality, public assistance is only one of more than a hundred social welfare programs. A frequent complaint is that too

much money is being spent on public assistance; yet it is generally unknown that five to six times as much money is spent annually on social insurance programs than on public assistance![8] Another erroneous public stereotype is that public assistance recipients are immoral, shiftless "chiselers" who would rather be on "welfare" than work. The truth is only a small percentage of the people receiving public assistance are able to work; less than 1 percent are able-bodied fathers over 80 percent of the welfare rolls are composed of children, the elderly, the blind, and the disabled, with the remainder being primarily mothers with young children.[9] Unfortunately, stigmatizing recipients lowers their self-image and tends to perpetuate their financial dependency. Instead of criticizing recipients of public assistance; a more productive topic would be to discuss what can be done for the estimated 25 million people in this country who are living in poverty.[10]

3. Public health and welfare services. While the first two categories provided financial benefits, this category established the role of the federal government in providing social services, for example, adoption, foster care, and services to crippled children.

Following the enactment of the Social Security Act, public social welfare services became dominant in terms of expenditures, people served, and personnel. The private role shifted from financial aid to certain specialized service areas. One of the roles of private agencies has been to test the value of new services and approaches, which if successful, it is hoped public social services will take on and provide on a large-scale basis.

RECENT YEARS

Following World War II and the Korean War there was optimism that we were on our

---

* In January 1974 the following three programs (Aid to the Blind, Aid to the Disabled, and Old Age Assistance) were combined into one program entitled Supplemental Security Income.

way to a golden era in which poverty would gradually disappear, racial integration would occur, and other social problems would also be smoothly and painlessly met. This optimism was exemplified in the early 1960s in President Lyndon Johnson's War on Poverty programs and the Great Society theme of his administration. The late 60s were therefore a shock; with the inner cities erupting, substantial increases in crime, student discontent on campuses with the Vietnam War and other issues, racial minorities and poor people organizing to demand their piece of the national financial pie, and recognition of new social ills such as the drug problem and preserving the environment. In the social welfare field in the late 60s there was a renewed interest in changing the environment or the system to better meet the needs of clients (sociological approach) rather than the psychological approach of enabling clients to better adapt and adjust to their life situations. Social action again became an important part of social work, with some social workers becoming active as advocates of clients, community organizers, and political organizers for social reform.

After the end of the Vietnam War in the early 1970s, the turmoil of the late 60s was replaced for several years with an atmosphere of relative calm on both foreign and domestic levels. In contrast to the hope in the 60s that governmental programs could cure our social ills, an opposing philosophy emerged which assumed many problems were beyond the capacity of the government to alleviate. The liberalism of the 60s which resulted in the expansion and development of new social programs was replaced by a more conservative approach in the 1970s. Practically no new, large-scale social welfare programs were initiated in the 1970s. Constitutionally, this country survived a political crisis during these years in which both the president and the vice president were forced to resign. Unfortunately other crises (including Vietnam, Watergate, inflation, the Israeli-Arab conflict, energy crises, political turmoil in Iran) in the last 15 years have received more attention than the handling of our ongoing social problems which may again soon erupt; for example, living conditions in the inner cities, high unemployment rates, racial discrimination, increasing rates of crime, conditions within prisons, violence in families, increasing divorce rates, and overpopulation concerns.

The election of President Ronald Reagan, along with the defeat of many other liberal political leaders by conservatives in 1980, could result in a cutback in allocations for social welfare programs in the next few years.

There are currently a number of important issues in social welfare, such as: Should a guaranteed annual income program be enacted to replace the Aid to Dependent Children program? Should drug laws be less restrictive? How can crime be curbed more effectively and the correctional system made more rehabilitative? What measures should be taken to eliminate racial discrimination? How to meet the problems of our inner cities? Should black children-white parents transracial adoptions be encouraged? Should abortion laws be made more or less restrictive? Should a national health insurance program be established? How can child pornography be prevented? How to help the physically impaired? How to prevent the social security system from going bankrupt? How to curb fraud in Medicaid, AFDC, and other social welfare programs? How can child abuse, incest, and spouse abuse be curbed? How to reduce the rapidly increasing illegitimacy rate? How to prevent suicides, especially the increasing number among teenagers? Should prostitution be legalized? What should be done about the teenage runaway problem? How can alcohol

A home in Mexico: Poverty is rampant throughout the world

and drug abuse be curbed? What programs are needed to prevent rape? How can retirement living be made more meaningful? Do we really want to provide the funds and services that are necessary to break the cycle of poverty, or do we still believe that many poor people are undeserving, in the sense that they would rather be on welfare than working?

The future

The future direction and nature of social services will largely be determined by technological advances, primarily technological advances in other areas. Changes in our lifestyles are primarily determined by technological advances.[11] In the past 50 years the

following advances have resulted in dramatic changes in our lifestyles: auto and air travel, nuclear power, television, birth control devices, automation, new electrical appliances, shopping centers, and the discovery of penicillin and other wonder drugs.

The relationship between technological breakthroughs and changes in social welfare programs generally follows this format: *technological advances largely determine changes in our lifestyles; lifestyle changes largely determine changes in our future social, financial, health, and recreational needs; and the latter changes largely determine what changes will be demanded in social service programs.*

Predicting what technological breakthroughs will occur, and how these advances will affect our lifestyles is difficult and undoubtedly filled with error. A number of advances are being predicted: robots that talk and act like humans, space travel, solar energy, computers capable of thinking, shopping from the home with two-way cable television, weather and climate control, minicomputers in autos that tell the driver how each part of the car is working, lawn mowers and vacuum cleaners with a memory that are programmed to follow a route of mowing or cleaning, visual telephones, 20-hour workweeks. A remarkable fact is that 90 percent of all scientists who ever lived are now alive.[12] This statistic suggests that future technological breakthroughs are apt to occur even more rapidly than has occurred in the past. In fact, Alvin Toffler in *Future Shock* asserts that adjusting psychologically to rapid lifestyle changes is currently a major problem, and will become the most difficult adjustment people will have to make in future years.[13]

In spite of predicted technological advances, it should be noted that environmentalists are predicting our civilization is in serious danger due to overpopulation, depletion of energy resources, likelihood of mass famines and starvation, and dramatic declines in the quality of life.

A home in Georgia: What impact will the New South have on the Old?

What the future will hold is difficult to accurately predict. The worst mistake, however, is to take the "ostrich head in the sand" approach in which no effort is made to plan and control the future.

To assist the reader in looking at the future, predicted changes in the American family will be summarized. This area is being selected because it is a key area for social welfare, when there is family breakdown, then social services are generally needed, and as the needs of families change, there is a corresponding demand to change social services.

Dramatic changes foreseen in the American family

In viewing the future of the American family, it is helpful to gain a perspective by taking a quick glance at some of the changes that have occurred in the past. Two hundred years ago marriages were primarily arranged by parents, with economic considerations being the most important determinant of who married whom. Two hundred years ago divorce was practically unheard of; now more than one out of three marriages ends in divorce or annulment.[14] Two hundred years ago women did not work outside the home and children were an economic asset; now nearly 50 percent of married women work outside the home, and children are a financial liability.[15] Since colonial days the family has lost (or there has been a sharp decline in) a number of functions: educational, economic production, religious, protective, recreational, and combative.[16] Today, the two main functions that remain are the affectional or companionship and the child-rearing functions.

In our fast-paced society the family is likely to change even more dramatically in the future. As in the past, the family is likely to be affected significantly by technological changes.[17] Laborsaving devices in the home (for example, electrical appliances) have in the past and currently are an important factor in making it possible for both spouses to work outside the home. Birth control devices have undoubtedly been an important factor in leading to an increase in premarital sexual relationships and in the recent development of mate-sharing arrangements. Abortions now are important in leading to current reductions in illegitimate and unwanted pregnancies. This reduction has been a factor in sharply reducing the number of children available for adoption. A number of adoption agencies have temporarily suspended taking applications from couples desiring healthy white infants. Now, an ethically questionable business has developed where women are paid to deliver and give up their babies for adoption in order to meet the demands of infertile couples who want a child.[18] Women willing to bypass the normal adoption channels may sell an unwanted infant for as much as $20,000.[19]

In the future the American family is likely to be substantially affected by technological breakthroughs in biology and medicine. A few illustrations of scientific developments in these areas will be presented—developments that are as alarming as they are intriguing.

Artificial insemination. In 1979 there were an estimated 20,000 babies born through the process of artificial insemination, with the usage expecting to continue to increase in the future.[20] Artificial insemination is used widely in livestock breeding because it eliminates all the problems that can be associated with breeding. A breeder can transport a prized animal's frozen sperm across the world and raise a whole new herd of animals almost effortlessly. The fact that human sperm can be frozen, thawed, and used to impregnate for long periods of time (the length of time has not been determined, it is generally acknowledged that five years would be safe with close to 100 percent assurance) has led to the development of an unique new institution, the private sperm bank. The sperm bank is usually a private institution that has a couple of functions. It collects and maintains sperm for private citizens for a fee depending on length of time. The sperm is then usually withdrawn at some later date to impregnate (with a physician's assistance) a woman.

The sperm used in artificial insemination may be the husband's (called AIH). There may be several reasons for using AIH. It is possible to pool several ejaculations from a man with a low sperm count and to inject them simultaneously into the vaginal canal of his spouse, thus vastly increasing the chance of pregnancy. AIH may also be used for family planning purposes—for example, a man might deposit his sperm in the bank, then receive a vasectomy, and then later withdraw the sperm to have children. High-risk jobs might prompt a man to make a deposit in case of untimely death or sterility.

A second type of artificial insemination is called AID, and involves the donor of the sperm being someone other than the husband, AID has been used for several decades to circumvent male infertility, and also used when it is known that the husband is a carrier of a genetic disease (for example, a condition such as hemophilia). In recent years an increasing number of single women are requesting the services of a sperm bank. The usual procedure involves the woman requesting the general genetic characteristics she wants from the father, and the bank then trying to match such requests from the information known about their donors.

There have been a number of ethical, social, and legal questions raised about artificial insemination. There are the objections from religious leaders that this practice is wrong, that God did not mean for people to reproduce this way. In the case of AID, there are certain psychological stresses placed on husbands and on marriages, as the procedure emphasizes the husband's infertility, and involves having a baby that he is not the biological father of. On a broader dimension, artificial insemination raises such questions as: What are the purposes of marriage and of sex, and what will happen to male/female relationships if we do not have to even see each other to reproduce?

There have also been some very unusual court cases which suggest whole new books on laws will have to be rewritten. For instance, there is the case of Mr. and Mrs. John M. Prutting. He was medically determined to be sterile as a result of radiation he received at work. Without her husband's knowledge, she was inseminated. After the birth of the baby, he sued her for divorce on the grounds of adultery.[21]

In another case a wife was inseminated with the husband's consent by a donor. The couple later divorced. When he requested visiting privileges, she took him to court on the grounds that he was not the father and thus had no right. In New York he won, but she moved to Oklahoma, where the decision was reversed.[22] And finally, there was a reported case of an engaged couple who were discovered to have had the same donor through artificial insemination, and were thus related. The marriage was called off.[23]

There are other possible legal implications. What happens if the sperm at a bank is not paid for? Would it become the property of the bank? Could it be auctioned off? If a woman was artificially inseminated by a donor and the child was later found to have genetic defects, could the parents bring suit against the physician, the donor, or the bank? Does the child have a right to know his/her real father?

Sperm banks can be used in genetic engineering movements. In the spring of 1980 it was disclosed that Robert Graham had set up an exclusive sperm bank to produce exceptionally bright children. Graham stated that at least five Nobel Prize winners had donated sperm to inseminate women. Three women were said to have already become pregnant through the services of this bank.[24] This approach raises questions whether reproductive technology should be used to produce "superior" children, and what characteristics should be defined as superior?

Test-tube babies. On July 24, 1978 Mrs. Lesley Brown in England gave birth to the first test-tube baby. The baby had been externally conceived, and then implanted in Mrs. Brown's uterus to complete the normal process of pregnancy. The technique called embryo transfer was developed by gynecologist Patrick Steptoe and physiologist Robert Edwards. This technique was developed for women whose Fallopian tubes are so damaged that the fertilized egg cannot pass through the tubes to the womb to grow until birth. Following the announcement of this birth there was a surge of applications from thousands of childless couples to fertility experts asking for similar implants.[25]

The next step, yet to come in the embryo-transfer technique, will probably soon arrive. This is the use of surrogate mothers to bear children, a modern-day twist on the wet nurse of earlier times. The scientific tools are available, medical researchers point out.

Surrogate pregnancies can, on one hand, be seen as the final step in the biological liberation of women. Like men, women could "sire" children without the responsibility of pregnancy and childbirth.

On another level surrogate pregnancies promise to create a legal nightmare. Does the genetic mother and father have any binding legal rights? Can the genetic mother place reasonable restrictions on health, medical care, and diet during the pregnancy? Can the genetic mother require the surrogate mother not to smoke or drink? Could the genetic mother require the surrogate to abort? Could the surrogate abort despite the mother's consent? Whose child is it—what if both the genetic mother and the surrogate mother legally wanted to be recognized as the "mother" after the child is born? Will the lower class and minorities serve as "holding tanks" for upper class women's children?

Legal experts see far-reaching changes in family law, inheritance, and the concept of legitimacy if laboratory fertilization and child rearing by surrogate mothers become accepted practices.

Human embryo transplants, when combined with principles of genetic selection, would also allow people who want "superhuman" children to select embryos in which the resultant infant would have a high probability of being free of genetic defects, and allow parents to choose with a high probability the genetic characteristics they desired—such as the child's sex, color of eyes and hair, skin color, probable height, probable muscular capabilities, and probable IQ. This breakthrough will raise a number of personal and ethical questions. Couples desiring children may face the decision of having a child through natural conception, or selecting in advance supernormal genetic characteristics through embryo transplants. Another question that will arise is whether our society will attempt to use this new technology to control human evolutionary development. If the answer is affirmative, decisions will need to be made about which genetic characteristics should be considered as being desirable, and questions will arise about who should have the authority to make such decisions. Although our country may not desire to control human evolutionary development in this manner, will we not feel a necessity to do so

if a rival nation begins a massive evolutionary program? In addition, will parents have the same, or somewhat different, feelings toward children who are the result of embryo transplants as compared to children who result from natural conception.

Genetic screening. Forty-six states now require mandatory genetic screening programs for various disorders.[26] There are about 2,000 human disorders caused by defective genes, and it is estimated that each of us carries 2 or 3 of them.[27] Mass genetic screening could eliminate some of these disorders. One screening approach that is increasingly being used with pregnant women is amniocentesis, which is used to determine chromosomal abnormality. (Amniocentesis is discussed in Chapter 14.) More and more pregnant women are being pressured to terminate the pregnancy of a high-risk or proven genetically inferior fetus. Also, some genetic disorders can be corrected if caught in time.

Fortune magazine carried a recent article with the heading "How to Save $100 Billion" which urged genetic screening be used much more extensively to reduce the incidence of persons with genetic diseases. One quote follows:

> . . . if we allow our genetic problems to get out of hand by not acting promptly . . . we can run the risk of overcommitting ourselves to the care of and maintenance of a large population of mentally deficient patients at the expense of other urgent social problems.[28]

Genetic screening programs raise serious questions whether our society wants to increasingly become involved in deciding such questions as: Who shall live? Who shall be allowed to have children? Who shall make such decisions? Is this a direction which our country ought to head?

The eugenics movement was proposed

late in the 19th century and embraced by many scientists and government officials. Similar to today, eugenics was designed to improve humanity or individual races by encouraging procreation by those deemed most desirable and discouraging those judged as "deficient" from having children. The movement fell into disfavor for a while when Adolf Hitler used it to justify the Holocaust, which exterminated millions of Jews, Gypsies, mentally retarded people, and others. Are we headed in a similar direction again?

Cloning. This term refers to the process whereby a new organism is reproduced from the nucleus of a single cell. The resultant new organism has the same genetic characteristics of the organism contributing the nucleus; that is, it probably will be possible to make biological carbon copies of humans from a single cell. Biologically, each cell is a blueprint containing all the genetic code information for the design of the organism. Cloning has already been used to reproduce frogs, mice, and other lower animals.[29]

One type of cloning amounts to a nuclear transplant. The nucleus of an unfertilized egg is destroyed and removed. It is then injected with the nucleus from body cell by one means or another. It should then begin to take orders from the new master, and manufacture a baby with the same genetic features as the donor. The embryo would need a place to develop into a baby—either an artificial womb or a woman willing to supply her own. The technology for a complete artificial womb is not yet in sight. The resultant clone would start life with a genetic endowment identical to that of the donor, although learning experiences may alter the physical development or personality. The possibilities are as fantastic as they are repulsive. Denlinger dreams, "Imagine a basketball team of two Kareem Abdul-Jabbars and

three Jerry Wests. Or a football team with three Jim Browns in the backfield and four Alan Pages on the defensive line."[30] With a quarter-inch piece of skin, one could produce 1,000 genetic copies of Dr. Christian Barnard, or of anyone else! Cloning could, among other things, be used to resolve the ancient controversy of heredity versus environment. On the other hand, there are grave dangers and undreamed-of complications. What is to prevent the Adolf Hitlers from making copies of themselves? Will cloning fuel the population explosion? What legal rights will clones be accorded (inheritance for example)? Will religions recognize clones as having a "soul"? Who will decide who will be able to have clones made of themselves? Couples may face the choice of having children naturally or raising children who are copies of themselves.

Breaking the genetic code. Biochemical genetics is the discipline which studies the mechanisms whereby genes control the development and maintenance of the organism. Current research is focused on understanding more precisely the roles of DNA (deoxyribonucleic acid) and messenger RNA (ribonucleic acid) in affecting the growth and maintenance of humans. When genes, DNA, and RNA are more fully understood, it will be possible sometime in the future to keep people alive, young, and healthy indefinitely.[31] It is predicted that aging will be controlled, and any medical condition (for example, an allergy, obesity, cancer, arthritic pain) will be relatively easily treated and eradicated. Such possibilities stagger the imagination. Many legal and ethical questions will arise; perhaps two of the more crucial will be who shall live and who shall die, and who shall be permitted to have children. Such a fountain of youth may even occur within some of our lifetimes.

Such technological developments hopefully provide a perspective for some of the future influences on the American family and on the field of social welfare. The current moral and ethical issues resulting from technological advances with birth control and abortion may well look "pale" in comparison to issues that apparently will soon arise. If the predictions regarding human embryo implants, test-tube babies, and cloning are accurate, there will also be significant implications for the field of social welfare; for example, genetic counseling may become a very prominent social service.

At the present time the American family is experimenting with a number of new forms, some of which are apt to be found functional and satisfying and gradually become widely incorporated. These new forms will briefly be mentioned, with the future determining which ones will endure. The implications for the field of social welfare will also be indicated.

Childless couples accepted. In our society there is currently a myth (belief with no rational basis) that something is wrong with a couple if they decide not to have children. Having children is recognized legally and religiously as being one of the central components of a marriage. In some states deceiving one's spouse before marriage about the desire to remain childless is grounds for an annulment. Perhaps in the future the myth of having children will be destroyed: by the concern about overpopulation, by the high cost of raising children (the average cost now of raising a child from birth to age 18 is estimated to be over $55,000,[32] and by couples switching their interests from the domestic tasks related to raising children to other types of recreational, cultural, educational and leisure-time experiences. If this trend continues, recreational and leisure-time programs for adults may have an increasing emphasis in social welfare.

Postponing raising children until after retirement. Biological innovations, such as growing embryos in laboratory controlled apparatus, will in the future permit couples the freedom to decide at what age they wish to raise children. Young couples today are often torn between a time commitment to their children and to their careers. In our society most couples now have children at the busiest time of their lives. Deferring raising children until retirement will provide substantial activity and meaning to old age. A major question, of course, is whether such a family pattern will lead to a large increase in the number of parentless children due to death, and perhaps have implications for services involving adoptions and foster care. Another important question is whether such a pattern would lead to serious generation gaps in values between the elderly parents and their young children.

Professional parents. Toffler predicts our society will develop a system of professional parents, trained and licensed, to whom a number of natural parents will turn for raising their children.[33] The natural parents would of course be permitted frequent visits, telephone contacts, and allowed to care for the children when they desired. Toffler states, "Even now millions of parents, given the opportunity, would happily relinquish their parental responsibilities—and not necessarily through irresponsibility or lack of love. Harried, frenzied, up against the wall, they have come to see themselves as inadequate to the tasks."[34] The high rates of child abuse, child neglect, and teenage runaways seem to bear out the fact that in a large number of families the overall parent-child relationship is more dissatisfying than satisfying.[35] Already many parents are partially using professional parents to raise their children in day-care centers.

In our society there is currently a myth

that bio-parents should care for their children, even when they find such a responsibility to be dissatisfying. Only a tiny fraction of bio-parents currently terminate their parental rights. Why? Could it be that many parents who have an unsatisfying relationship with their children are reluctant to give up their parenting responsibilities because of the stigma that would be attached. Two hundred years ago divorces were also practically unheard of, mostly due to a similar stigma. Now, with an increased acceptance of divorces, more than one-out-of-three marriages are being terminated. If a high rate of marital unions become unsatisfying, is it not also reasonable to expect that a number of parents who have relatively little choice in the characteristics their children will possess, may also find the relationship with their children to be more dissatisfying than satisfying? The point is further made when it is remembered that a number of pregnancies are unplanned, and even unwanted.

Serial and contract marriages. Culturally, religiously, and legally, marriages are still expected to be permanent, for a lifetime. Such a view implies that the two partners made the right decision when they married, that their personalities and abilities supplement and complement each other, and that their personalities and interests will continue to develop in tandem for the rest of their lives. All of these suppositions along with the permanency concept of marriage are being called into question, partly by the high divorce rate.

With the high rate of divorce and also of remarriage, a number of sociologists have pointed out that our society is subtly entering into marriages being serial in nature; that is, a pattern of successive temporary marriages.[36] Serial marriages among movie celebrities have been widely publicized for a number of years. Viewing marriage as being temporary in nature may be a factor in reducing some of the embarrassment and pain that still is associated with divorce today, and perhaps result in an increase in the number of unhappily married people who will seek a divorce. Divorce per se is neither good nor bad; if both of the partners find their lives to be happier and more satisfying following legal termination, the end result may well be viewed as desirable.

The high and increasing divorce rate has resulted in the development of extensive services involving premarriage counseling, marriage counseling, divorce counseling, single parent services and programs, and remarriage counseling for spouses and the children involved. If marriage is increasingly viewed as temporary in nature, divorces may become even more frequent, and result in an expansion of related social services.

Several sociologists have proposed the temporary conception of marriage be legally institutionalized by a contract marriage, for example, where the couple would legally be married for a two-year period, and (only in those marriages where there are no children) the marriage would automatically be terminated unless the couple filed legal papers for a continuation.[37]

Another marital arrangement embodying the temporary marriage concept is "trial marriage" which is increasingly being tested out by young people. Living together without a ceremony usually means daily living together with sharing of expenses. Closely related, and perhaps more common, however, is where the man and woman maintain separate addresses and domiciles, but for several days a month actually live together. Perhaps this later form is more accurately described as being a "serial honeymoon" rather than a "trial marriage." Acceptance of trial marriages is currently even being advocated by some religious philosophers,[38] and may in the future be no longer recognized as "illegal" by statutes.

Although cohabitation is not legally recognized in most states, there are increasing instances where courts are ruling that cohabiting couples who decide to dissolve their nonmarital living arrangements have certain legal obligations to one another quite similar to the obligations of a married couple. For example, in a much publicized case in 1979 a California court judge ruled that actor Lee Marvin must pay $104,000 to a woman he cohabited with for six years.

Open marriages. O'Neill and O'Neill contrast traditional marriages with an emerging new type, "open marriage," which they are advocating.[39] A traditional or "closed marriage," the O'Neills assert, embodies such concepts as (a) possession or ownership of mate, (b) denial or stifling of self, (c) playing the couples game by the expectations of doing everything together during available leisure time, (d) the man being dominant and out in the world while the woman is domestic, passive, and stays at home with the children, and (e) absolute fidelity. An open marriage in contrast, offers freedom to pursue individual interests, flexible roles in which meeting financial responsibilities and domestic tasks are shared, expansion and growth through openness, and is based on open communication, trust, and respect. Individual growth and expansion are encouraged, and it is expected that one person's growth will facilitate the other partner's development. Marriage counselors are increasingly seeing couples where serious interaction difficulties occur because one spouse has the traditional orientation, while the other has an "open marriage" orientation. The emerging feminist movement and the changing roles of women in our society have

brought into public awareness the conflict between open and closed marriages. Marriage counselors are now seeing a large number of couples where the wife is seeking a career, her own identity, and a sharing of domestic responsibilities; while the husband with a traditional orientation wants his wife to stay at home and take care of the domestic tasks.

Group marriages. This form of marriage provides insurance against isolation. One variety, communes among young people, has received considerable publicity and there have been hundreds in existence.[40] The goals, as well as the structure, vary widely, involving diverse social, political, religious, or recreational objectives.[41] Perhaps surprisingly, geriatric communes (group marriages of elderly people) are also being advocated by a number of sociologists.[42] Such marriages may be a solution to a number of social problems of the aged. It may provide companionship, new meaning and interest to their lives, and also be an arrangement where the elderly with reduced functioning capacities may be of mutual assistance to each other. In such a living arrangement, the elderly can band together, pool resources, hire nursing or domestic help if needed, and have the feeling that "life begins at 60." In nursing homes a fair number of the elderly are presently developing relationships which have similarities to a group marriage.

Homosexual marriages and adoptions. Gay liberation groups have been formed in this country which seek to inform the public about the "naturalness" of this form of sexual expression, and which are attempting to change current legislation.[43] England has already rewritten its statutes; homosexual relations between consenting adults in that country are no longer considered a crime.

Several years ago a Roman Catholic priest in Holland married two homosexuals.[44] Since then, a number of marriages between homosexuals have taken place in churches in this country.

In the future, adoption agencies and the courts may face decisions whether placing children for adoption with married homosexuals is to be permitted. Such a decision may center around whether homosexual relationships are to be regarded as "natural" or "unnatural," with opponents perhaps being hardpressed to demonstrate that homosexual activities have undesirable consequences. Single people are already being permitted by some agencies and courts to adopt children; so the argument that a child needs both a male and female figure in the family is diluted.

Transracial adoptions. Oriental and American Indian children have been adopted by white parents for the past three decades, with the outcome being generally accepted as desirable.[45] About 20 years ago certain white couples began adopting black children. A number of questions have arisen about the desirability of this type of placement which brings together into a family unit the two polar races in our society. To answer some of these questions, Zastrow compared the satisfactions derived and problems encountered between transracial adoptive parents and inracial adoptive parents.[46] Three independent measures of overall outcome were used, and on all three the outcome of transracial adoptions was found to be as satisfying as inracial adoptions. In addition, transracial adoptive children were found to have been accepted by relatives, friends, neighbors, and the general community following placement. The transracial adoptive parents reported that substantially fewer problems have arisen due to the race of the child than even they anticipated prior to the adoption. They also indicated they had the parental feeling that the child was really their own following placement, and they reported becoming "color blind" following placement; for example, they came to see the child not as black, but as an individual who is a member of their family. Unfortunately none of the children in the study were older than six years. Some observers, a number of whom are black, have raised questions whether black children reared by white parents will experience serious identity problems as they grow older; for example, will they experience difficulty in deciding which race to identify with, difficulty in learning how to cope with racial discrimination due to being raised in a white home, and difficulty in interacting with both whites and blacks due to a speculated confused sense of who they are. On the other hand, advocates of transracial adoption respond to asserting that the parent-child relationship is more crucial to identity formation than the racial composition of the members of the family.

A transracial adoptive family

The question of course is critical, especially since there are a large number of homeless black children and a shortage of black adoptive parents.

Co-marital sex. The term *co-marital sex* refers to mate swapping, and other organized extramarital relations in which both spouses agree to participate. Co-marital sex is distinctly different from a traditional extramarital affair, which is usually clandestine as the spouse involved in the affair tries to hide its occurrence from the other spouse.

While some couples appear to be able to integrate co-marital agreements into their lives successfully, others find their marriages breaking up as a consequence.[47] According to marriage counselors, a major reason why couples drop out of such co-marital relationships, and sometimes end their marriage, is because of such emotional reactions as jealousy, competition, and possessiveness.[48]

The interest in co-marital sex and extramarital sex raises the age-old question of whether any one individual can satisfy all of the intimate sexual and intrapersonal needs of another.

Single parenthood. Although marriage and parenthood are in many people's minds viewed as going together, single parenthood is emerging as a prominent form in our society. There are several ways to become a single parent. In many states it is possible for unmarried people to adopt a child. Another way is for an unmarried, pregnant woman to refuse to marry and yet to keep her child after it is born. Some unmarried fathers have now been successful in obtaining custody of their child. Today the negative stigma attached to being single and pregnant is not as strong as it once was, but it is still seriously frowned on by some.

A form close to single parenthood is the one-parent family, in which a person divorces or legally separates and assumes custody of one or more children while choosing not to remarry. While it has traditionally been the mother who has been awarded custody of the children, today an increasing number of fathers are being granted custody of the children by the courts. Another arrangement that is emerging is shared custody where both the mother and father have their children part of the time.

Do single parents and one parent families pose a serious problem for society? Do children need two parents? No definitive answers are yet available. It is clear, however, that such arrangements are increasing. There are now approximately 3.5 million one-parent families, with a total of about 7 million children.[49]

The single life. In our society women, and to some extent men also, are brought up to believe that one of their most important goals is to marry. Women who remain unmarried are labeled "old maids." Elaborate rituals have been developed to romanticize engagement and marriage. Unfortunately, many couples discover after the honeymoon, that marriage is neither that romantic nor exciting, and may even become monotonous, dull, and constricting. A number of people are currently dealing with unfulfilled marriages by a series of divorces and remarriages. Perhaps in the future others may turn away from the responsibilities and restrictions of marriage by remaining single.[50] Temporary and sometimes long-term deep emotional relationships may be entered into without the duties and restrictions imposed by a legal arrangement. The bachelor life for males appears to be romanticized somewhat for men; it may increasingly become so, and the single life for women may also become romanticized and recognized as a desirable way to have quality experiences and to actualize one's capabilities.

Yet, if remaining single becomes more prominent it has significant implications for social welfare as statistics show higher rates of depression, loneliness, alcoholism, suicide, drug abuse, and alienation among those who are single.

To summarize, it appears the family of tomorrow will face a future shock. Technological developments (particularly in biology and medicine, for example, cloning and human embryo implants) may dramatically affect the family, raising a number of ethical, legal, social, and personal questions. In addition, the family is experimenting with a number of different forms which may dramatically alter the central characteristics of future families. Among the forms are: childless couples, postponement of raising children until retirement, professional parents, serial and contract marriages, one-parent families, co-marital sex, open marriages, group marriages for all age-groups, homosexual marriages and adoptions, transracial adoptions, and remaining single. Other changes may also be experimented with, for example, increases in interracial marriages and marriages involving partners of unequal ages. Because of technological advances and the experimentation with new family forms, the style of living for all families may be substantially changed. Some will probably find these changes exciting, personally satisfying and functional; others may be less adaptable and find such changes to be extremely difficult and perhaps even overwhelming, resulting in personal disintegration. In any case, changes that are made in the American family will have important implications for the field of social welfare.

SUMMARY

The goal of social welfare is to fulfill the social, financial, health and recreational needs of everyone in a society. The provision of social services has become one of the most important activities in our society in terms of the money spent, the human misery treated, and the number of people served.

Social welfare overlaps with sociology, psychology and other disciplines on a knowledge base level. When theories and research in other academic disciplines have direct applications to the social welfare goal of enhancing the social functioning of people, then this knowledge is also part of the knowledge base of social welfare.

Social welfare overlaps with social work at a practice (service) level. Almost all social workers are employed in the field of social welfare, but there are also many other professional and ocupational groups that are employed within this field. Social welfare is erroneously conceived at times as being synonomous with public assistance; yet public assistance is only one of over a hundred social welfare programs.

Social welfare institutions are composed of social service programs and social service organizations, the purposes of social welfare institutions are to prevent, alleviate, or contribute to the solution of recognized social problems so as to improve the well-being of individuals, groups, and communities directly.

Currently, there are two conflicting views of the role of social welfare in our society; the residual versus the institutional orientation. The residual approach characterized social welfare programs from early history to the Depression of the 1930s, at which time programs with an institutional orientation began to be implemented. Social welfare programs have in the past been influenced, and to some extent still are, by the protestant ethic, the laissez-faire economical view, Social Darwinism, individualism, the Industrial Revolution, and by humanitarian ideals.

There are apt to be important changes in the social welfare field in the future, perhaps largely due to anticipated technological advances. In summary form, technological advances largely determine changes in our lifestyles; lifestyle changes largely determine changes in our future social, financial, health, and recreational needs; and the latter changes largely determine changes in needed social service programs.

Dramatic changes are anticipated in the American family of the future, due to technological advances in biology and medicine, and to the current experimentation with new family forms. Some of these new forms are apt to be found dysfunctional and will be discarded, while others will be found satisfying and functional, and will probably be incorporated into the "typical" family of the future. The anticipated technological advances and the adoption of new family forms will result in the creation of new social service programs, and the expansion of certain existing programs. Unless such changes are carefully examined and planned, our society faces a future shock.

NOTES

1. Elizabeth A. Ferguson, *Social Work: An Introduction* (Philadelphia: Lippincott, 1963), pp. 2–11.

2. National Association of Social Workers, *Encyclopedia of Social Work,* vol. 2 (New York: NASW, 1971), p. 1446.

3. National Association of Social Workers, *Standards for Social Service Manpower* (New York: NASW, 1973), pp. 4–5.

4. Harold Wilensky and Charles Lebeaux, *Industrial Society & Social Welfare* (New York: Free Press, 1965).

5. Ibid., p. 14.

6. Ibid.

7. Lester F. Ward, *Dynamic Sociology,* reprint of 1883 ed. (New York: Johnson Reprint, 1968).

8. "Where Tax Dollars are Raised and How They're Spent," *U.S. News & World Report,* February 4, 1980, p. 80.

9. U.S. Department of Health, Education and Welfare, Welfare Myths and Facts, (Washington, D.C., U.S. Government Printing Office, 1972).

10. Bradley R. Schiller, *The Economics of Poverty and Discrimination,* 3d ed. (Englewood Cliffs, N.J.: Prentice-Hall, 1980), p. 24.

11. W. F. Ogburn and M. F. Nimkoff, *Technology and the Changing Family* (New York: Houghton Mifflin, 1955).

12. Alvin Toffler, *Future Shock* (New York: Bantam Books, 1970), p. 27.

13. Ibid.

14. U.S. Bureau of the Census, *Statistical Abstract of the United States, 1979* (Washington, D.C.: U.S. Government Printing Office, 1979).

15. "Working Women," *U.S. News & World Report,* January 15, 1979, p. 64.

16. Ogburn and Nimkoff, *Technology and the Changing Family.*

17. Ibid.

18. Ann Rundell, "It's Hard to Find White Babies to Adopt," *Wisconsin State Journal,* February 6, 1972, sec. 7, p. 4.

19. Philip Reilly, *Genetics, Law, and Social Policy* (Cambridge, Mass. Harvard University Press, 1977), p. 190.

20. "CBS Reports—The Baby Makers" (television program, October 1979).

21. L. Rifken, *Who Should Play God?* (New York: Dell Publishing Co., 1977).

22. Ibid.

23. Ibid.

24. "Exclusive Sperm Bank Rekindles Controversy" *Wisconsin State Journal,* March 1, 1980, sec. 1, p. 7.

25. "A Rush of Test-Tube Babies," *U.S. News & World Report,* August 7, 1978, p. 22.

26. Rifkin, *Who Should Play God?*

27. Reilly, *Genetics, Law, and Social Policy.*

28. G. Bylinsky, "What Science Can Do about Hereditary Disease," *Fortune,* September 1974, pp. 148–60.

29. David M. Rorvik, "Making Men and Women without Men and Women," *Esquire Magazine,* April 1969, pp. 110–15.

30. Kenneth Denlinger, "Science Could Reproduce a Namath," *Washington Post,* February 8, 1972.

31. Rorvik, "Making Men and Women."

32. John D. Moorhead, "Cost of Children Soars," *Wisconsin State Journal,* January 16, 1979, sec. 3, p. 1.

33. Toffler, *Future Shock.*

34. Ibid., pp. 243–44.

35. Alfred Kadushin, *Child Welfare Services,* 3d ed. (New York: Macmillan, 1980).

36. Ethel Alpenfels, "Progressive Monogamy: An Alternate Pattern?" in *The Family in Search of a Future,* ed. Herbert Otto (New York: Appleton-Century-Crofts, 1970), pp. 67–74.

37. Ibid.

38. "Trial by Marriage," *Time Magazine,* April 14, 1967, p. 112.

39. George O'Neill and Nena O'Neill, *Open Marriage* (New York: M. Evans, 1971).

40. John Haughey, "The Commune-Child of the 1970s," *America,* March 13, 1971.

41. Albert Ellis, "Group Marriage: A Possible Alternative?" in *The Family in Search of a Future,* pp. 85–98.

42. Victor Kassel, "Polygamy after Sixty," *Geriatrics* 21 (April 1966).

43. Carl Wittman, "A Gay Manifesto," *Liberation,* February 1970.

44. Toffler, *Future Shock.*

45. David Fanshel, *Far from the Reservation* (Metuchen, N.J.: Scarecrow Press, 1972).

46. Charles Zastrow, *Outcome of Black Children-White Parents Transracial Adoptions* (San Francisco: R&E Research Associates, 1977).

47. Brian Gilmartin and D. V. Kusisto, "Some Personal and Social Characteristics of Mate-Sharing Swingers," in R. Libby and R. Whitehurst, eds., *Renovating Marriage* (San Francisco: Consensus Publishers, 1973), pp. 146–66.

48. Duane Denfeld, "Dropouts from Swinging," *The Family Coordinator,* January 1974, pp. 45–49.

49. U.S. Bureau of the Census, *Current Population Reports,* series P–20, no. 323, April 1978, p. 26.

50. Rosalyn Moran, "The Singles in the Seventies," in *Intimate Life Styles,* ed. Joann and Jack Delora (Pacific Palisades, Calif.: Goodyear, 1972), pp. 338–44.

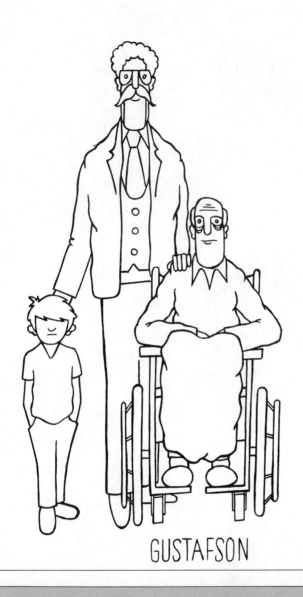

GUSTAFSON

chapter **2**

A MULTISKILLED PROFESSION

A social worker needs training and expertise in a wide range of areas to be able to effectively handle problems faced by individuals, groups, and the larger community. While most professions are increasingly becoming more specialized (for example, nearly all medical doctors now specialize in one or two areas), social work continues to emphasize a generic (broad based) approach. The practice of social work is analogous to the old, now fading general practice of medicine; a general practitioner in medicine had training to handle a wide range of common medical problems faced by people, while a social worker has training to handle a wide range of common social and personal problems faced by people. The case example on the following page highlights some of the skills needed by social workers.

This "success" case (in most cases the outcome is not as fully successful) documents a wide range of knowledge and skills displayed by Mr. Tounsend: interviewing skills, knowledge of how to effectively counsel people with sexual problems and feelings of depression, ability to work effectively with other agencies, premarital counseling skills, research and grant writing skills, program development and fund raising skills, and knowledge of how to handle ethical/legal issues that arise.

Perhaps the most basic skill that a social worker needs is to be able to effectively counsel clients. If one is not able to do this, one should probably not be in social work, certainly not in direct service. Probably the second most important ability is to be able to interact effectively with other groups and professionals in the area. A social worker, analogous to a general practitioner, should have a wide range of skills and intervention techniques that will enable him/her to intervene effectively with: (*a*) the common personal and emotional problems of clients, and (*b*) the common social problems faced by groups and the larger community. Social workers also need to have an accurate perception of their professional strengths and weaknesses. If a situation arises that a worker knows he/she does not have the

Social work as a profession and a career

A CASE INVOLVING SUICIDE AND SEX DEVIANCY

Dr. John Pritchard referred Dick Cherwenka to the Riverland Counseling Center (a mental health center). Mr. Cherwenka had briefly been hospitalized after slashing his wrists. This case was assigned to Tom Tounsend, a social worker, who in the recent past had counseled most of the agency's attempted suicide cases. At the first two sessions Mr. Cherwenka presented an unusual account of the events that led to his slashing his wrists.

His main problem centered around his desire to fondle the genitals of young girls (9 to 12 years old) whenever he felt depressed, tense, or at a "low tide." In the past four years he had been arrested on three occasions for this offense. The last time, 11 months ago, he was placed on probation for two years, and the judge warned he would be sentenced to prison for an indeterminate sentence as a "sex deviant" if there were a recurrence of the offense. The afternoon of the evening in which he slashed his wrists, he had felt quite depressed. While driving home from work he stopped at a playground, and began talking to a young girl. He offered her a ride home and she accepted. Instead he drove out into the country where he fondled her. The girl was terrified. Mr. Cherwenka then drove her back, dropped her off a few blocks from her home, and informed her that serious harm would come to her if she told anyone. Mr. Cherwenka, after thinking about what he had done, became even more depressed and slashed his wrists a few hours later.

The worker at this point informed Mr. Cherwenka that he (the worker) faced an ethical/legal question of whether the police should be informed, and would have to discuss his obligations with the director of the agency. Mr. Cherwenka indicated he understood, and proceeded to relate the following account of why he believed he developed the desire to fondle young girls.

He had normal childhood experiences until at age 8 his mother died. After his mother's death, his father continued to raise him and his sister who was 14 months older than he. However, his father changed; he became bitter toward life and began drinking heavily. In the evening he was at times in a drunken stupor. During these times he would be abusive, verbally and physically, to his children. Dick and his sister became very fearful of their father when he was drunk, and sought ways to hide from him. Gradually, they learned to hide together under a blanket. While fearful and tense under the blanket, they sought ways to occupy their time and reduce their fear; and thereby began fondling each other. Mr. Cherwenka indicated this activity of hiding and fondling under a blanket when their father was drunk lasted for nearly three years, until an aunt moved into their home and began raising them.

The social worker agreed with Mr. Cherwenka that his present desires to fondle young girls apparently resulted from his past learning experiences of coping with unwanted emotions. The problems that needed to be dealt with now were: (*a*) what ethical/legal obligations Mr. Tounsend and the mental health center had in regard to this admitted offense; (*b*) how to prevent Mr. Cherwenka from fondling young girls in the future; (*c*) closely related, how to help Mr. Cherwenka handle unwanted emotions; (*d*) how to prevent Mr. Cherwenka from desiring to take his life in the future; and (*e*) since Mr. Cherwenka was engaged and planning to marry in two months, an additional situation that needed to be handled was his future relationship with his fiancée.

After two more meetings, the following treatment plan was developed and then later implemented. Mr. Tounsend discussed the ethical/legal obligations of this case with the agency director. It was decided that the probation department needed to be informed. Mr. Tounsend discussed this decision with Mr. Cherwenka. Mr. Tounsend then arranged a meeting with Mr. Cherwenka and his probation officer. Following this meeting it was agreed that the offense would be noted, but proceedings to revoke Mr. Cherwenka's probation would not be initiated as long as Mr. Cherwenka remained in counseling and no other offenses occurred.

The problems of preventing Mr. Cherwenka from fondling young girls and from taking his life in the future were then dealt with. It was agreed that whenever Mr. Cherwenka had strong desires to again fondle young girls, or to take his life, he should call Mr. Tounsend (day or night) who would then meet with him, and stay with him until his desires subsided. In the year that followed Mr. Cherwenka called Mr. Tounsend on two occasions. In addition, once Mr. Tounsend was on vacation, and Mr. Cherwenka checked himself into the mental health center overnight as an inpatient.

Gradually, by using rational therapy (described in Chapter 5) Mr. Cherwenka gained better control of his feelings of depression and his other unwanted emotions. Several meetings with Mr. Cherwenka and his fiancée were also held. After the initial shock of learning about Mr. Cherwenka's interest in young girls, the two fully discussed their relationship and agreed to postpone their marriage for a year, while continuing the engagement.

As indicated earlier this case was only one of several potential suicide cases that Mr. Tounsend was handling. These cases led him to the conclusion that an emergency telephone number was needed that would be widely publicized and would be staffed 24 hours a day with professional counselors. He gathered data on the number of suicides in the area in the past year and obtained information from hospitals in the community about the number of attempted suicides. This data supported the need for an emergency counseling service. Mr. Tounsend then wrote a grant proposal and after ten months of searching for funding was funded by a joint grant from the United Way and the Easter Seals Society.

training or expertise to handle, then the worker needs to be a "broker" and link those affected with available services.

A BRIEF HISTORY OF SOCIAL WORK

Social work as a profession is of relatively recent origin. To attempt to meet the needs of people living in urban areas, the first social welfare agencies began to be developed in the early 1800s. These agencies, or services, were private agencies which were developed primarily at the initiation of the clergy and religious groups. Up until the early 1900s these services were provided exclusively by members of the clergy and well-to-do "do-gooders" who had no formal training and little understanding of human behavior or how to help people. The focus was on meeting such basic physical needs as food and shelter, and attempting to "cure" emotional and personal difficulties with religious admonitions.

An illustration of an early social welfare organization was the Society for the Prevention of Pauperism, founded by John Griscom in 1820.[1] This society aimed to investigate the habits and circumstances of the poor, to suggest plans by which the poor could help themselves, and to encourage the poor to save and economize. Among the remedies used were house-to-house visitation of the poor (a very elementary type of social work).

By the latter half of the 1800s there were a fairly large number of private relief agencies that had been established in large cities to help the unemployed, the poor, the ill, the physically and mentally handicapped, and orphans. Programs of these agencies were uncoordinated, and sometimes overlapping. Therefore an English invention—the Charity Organization Society (COS)—caught the interest of a number of American cities.[2] Starting in Buffalo, New York, in 1877, COS was rapidly adopted in many cities. In charity organization societies, private agencies joined together to: (1) provide direct services to individuals and families—in this respect they were forerunners of social casework and of family counseling approaches, and (2) plan and coordinate the efforts of private agencies to meet the pressing social problems of cities—in this respect they were precursors of community organization and social planning approaches. Charity organizations conducted a detailed investigation of each applicant for services and financial help, maintained a central system of registration of clients to avoid duplication, and used volunteer "friendly visitors" extensively to work with those in difficulty. The friendly visitors were primarily "doers of good works" as they generally gave sympathy rather than money and encouraged the poor to save and to seek employment. Poverty was looked upon as due to a personal shortcoming. Most of the friendly visitors were women.

Concurrent with the COS movement was the establishment of settlement houses in the late 1800s. Toynbee Hall was the first settlement house established in 1884 in London; many others were soon formed in larger U.S. cities. A large number of the early settlement house workers were daughters of ministers. The workers were from the middle and upper classes who would live in a poor neighborhood so they could experience the harsh realities of poverty. Simultaneously they sought to develop ways in cooperation with neighborhood residents to improve living conditions. In contrast to "friendly visitors" they lived in impoverished neighborhoods and used the missionary approach of teaching residents how to live moral lives and improve their circumstances. They sought to improve housing, health, and living conditions; find jobs; teach English, hygiene, and occupational skills; and sought to change environmental surroundings through cooperative efforts. Settlement houses used change techniques that are now called social group work, social action, and community organization.

On the one hand settlement houses placed their emphasis on "environmental reform," while at the same time "they continued to struggle to teach the poor the prevailing middle-class values of work, thrift, and abstinence as the keys to success."[3] In addition to dealing with local problems by local action, settlement houses played important roles in drafting legislation, and in organizing to influence social policy and legislation. The most noted leader in the settlement house movement was Jane Addams of Hull House in Chicago, who summarized what a settlement house was as follows:

> The Settlement, then, is an experimental effort to aid in the solution of the social and industrial problems which are engendered by the modern conditions of life in a great city.[4]

Settlement house leaders believed by changing neighborhoods, they would improve communities; and through altering communities, they would develop a better society.

It appears the first paid social workers were executive secretaries of charity organization societies in the late 1800s.[5] In the late 1800s charity organization societies received some contracts from the cities in which they were located to administer relief funds. In administering these programs, COS hired people as executive secretaries to organize and train the friendly visitors and to establish accounting procedures to show accountability for the funds received. To improve the services of friendly visitors, executive secretaries needed to establish standards and training courses. In 1898 a training course was first offered for charity workers by the New York Charity Organization Society. By 1904 a one-year program was offered by the New York School of Philanthropy. Soon after this time, colleges and universities began offering training programs in social work.

Richard Cabot introduced medical social work into Massachusetts General Hospital in 1905.[6] Gradually social workers were employed in schools, courts, child guidance clinics, and other settings.

Early training programs in social work focused on both environmental reform efforts, and on efforts to change individuals to better adjust to society.

In 1917 Mary Richmond published *Social Diagnosis,* a text which presented for the first time a theory and methodology for social work.[7] The book focused on how the worker should intervene with individuals. The process is still used today and involves study (collecting information), diagnosis (stating what is wrong), prognosis, and treatment planning (stating what should be done to help clients improve). This book was important as it formulated a common body of knowledge for casework.

In the 1920s, Sigmund Freud's theories of personality development and therapy became popular. The concepts and explanations of psychiatrists appeared particularly appropriate for social workers, who also worked in one-to-one relationships with clients. The psychiatric approach emphasized intrapsychic processes and focused on enabling clients to adapt and adjust to their social situations. Therefore, social workers switched their emphasis from "reform" to "therapy" for the next three decades. In the 1960s, however, there was a renewed interest in sociological approaches or reform by social workers. Several reasons account for this change. Questions arose about the relevance and appropriateness of "talking" approaches with low-income clients who tend to be nonverbal and who have urgent social and economic pressures. Furthermore, the effectiveness of many psychotherapeutic approaches has been questioned.[8] Other reasons for the renewed interest include the increase in status of sociology and the mood of the 1960s which raised questions about the relevancy of social institutions in meeting the needs of the population. Social work at the present time embraces both the reform and the therapy approaches.

Not until the end of World War I did social work begin to be recognized as a distinct profession. The Depression of the 1930s and the enactment of the Social Security Act in 1935 brought about an extensive expansion of public social services and job opportunities for social workers. Since 1900 there has been a growing awareness by social agency boards and the public that professionally trained social workers are needed to competently provide social services. In 1955 the National Association of Social Workers was formed which represents the social work profession in this country. The purpose of this association is to improve social conditions in society and promote high quality and effectiveness in social work practice. The association publishes (a) several professional journals with the most noted being *Social Work*, (b) *The Encyclopedia of Social Work*, and (c) a monthly newsletter entitled *NASW News*. The newsletter has current social work news information and also a list of position vacancies throughout the country.

Currently there is considerable interest in developing a system of registration or licensing of social workers. Professionals in medicine, law, teaching, and nursing are required to have an official license, or a certificate, or to be registered before they can provide a professional service. In Germany, Austria, France, and Sweden social workers need a license to practice. It is being argued that a system of registration or licensing in social work would assure the public that qualified personnel are providing social work services and would also advance the recognition of social work as a profession. As of September 1977 there were 22 states that had passed legislation to license or regulate the practice of social work.[9] Although a young profession, social work is growing and gaining increased respect and recognition.

PROFESSIONAL ACTIVITIES

Social work and social welfare activities constitute one of the most important functions in our society in terms of the number of people affected, the human misery treated, and the amount of money spent.[10] As indicated earlier, "Social work is the professional activity of helping individuals, groups, or communities to enhance or restore their capacity for social functioning and to create societal conditions favorable to their goals."[11] A social worker is a "change agent" who works with individuals, groups, families, and communities. The term *social worker* is generally applied to graduates (either with bachelor's or master's degrees) of schools of social work who are employed in the field of social welfare. There are several types of professional social work activities.

Social casework is aimed at helping individuals, on a one-to-one basis, to meet personal and social problems. Casework may be geared to helping clients adjust to their environment, or to changing certain social and economic pressures which are handicapping an individual. A few illustrations of the activities of a caseworker include helping individuals and families with a wide variety of personal difficulties; securing financial aid as well as needed social services; counseling the handicapped such as the mentally ill, the blind, and the disabled; counseling juveniles and adults in correctional settings; placing children in foster homes or arranging for their adoption; and working in medical and mental hospitals as a member of a rehabilita-

Brief counseling at a detention center

tion team. Casework is practiced in a wide variety of agencies, including hospitals, mental health clinics, courts, family counseling centers, adoption agencies, day-care centers, public welfare departments, child guidance clinics, nursing homes, maternity homes, schools, neighborhood centers, and institutions for the aged, for criminals and delinquents, for the mentally ill and retarded, and for dependent and handicapped children.

Group work is designed to further the intellectual, emotional, and social development of individuals through group activities. In contrast to casework or group therapy, it is not primarily therapeutic, except in a broad sense. Different groups have different objectives; for example, socialization, information exchange, curbing delinquency, recreation, changing socially unacceptable values, and helping to achieve better relations between cultural and racial groups. For example, a group worker at a neighborhood center may through group activities seek to curb delin-

quency patterns and change socially unacceptable values; or a worker at an adoption agency may meet with a group of applicants to explain adoption procedures and to help applicants prepare for becoming adoptive parents. Activities and focuses of groups vary: arts and crafts, dancing, games, dramatics, music, photography, sports, nature study, woodwork, first aid, home management, information exchange, and discussion of such topics as politics, sex, marriage, religion, and selection of a career. Group work is used in such settings as Boy Scouts and Girl Scouts, YMCAs and YWCAs, schools, churches, child welfare agencies, Red Cross agencies, community centers, playgrounds, camps, and in most institutions.

Group therapy is aimed at facilitating the social and emotional adjustment of individuals through the group process. Participants in this kind of group usually have adjustment difficulties. Group therapy has, within the past two decades, been used much more extensively. It has several advantages over one-to-one counseling, such as the operation of the "helper therapy" principle which maintains it is therapeutic for the helper (which can be any member of a group) to feel s/he has been helpful to others. In contrast to one-to-one counseling, group pressure is often more effective in changing maladaptive behavior of individuals, and group therapy is a time-saver as it enables the therapist to treat several people at the same time. A few examples in which group therapy might be used is for individuals who are severely depressed, or who have drinking problems, or who are victims of a rape, or who are psychologically addicted to drugs, or who have a relative who is terminally ill, or who are single and pregnant, or who are recently divorced. Group therapy is used in such settings as mental hospitals, mental health clinics, family counseling agencies, correc-

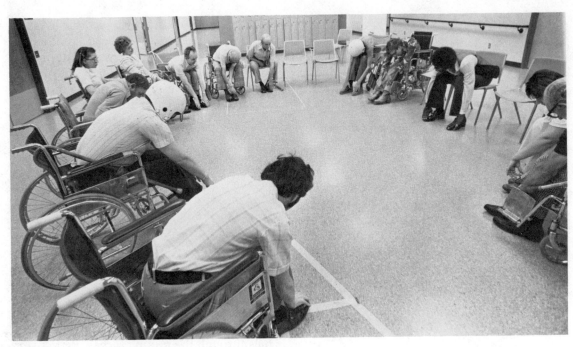

Group physical exercises for adults with handicaps at a rehabilitation center

tional institutions, maternity homes, hospitals, and residential facilities for youth.

Family therapy can be considered as one type of group therapy and is aimed at helping families with interactional, behavioral, and emotional problems that arise. Problems include parent-child interaction problems, marital conflicts, and conflicts with grandparents. A wide variety of problems are dealt with in family therapy or family counseling, such as disagreements between parents and youth on choice of friends, drinking and pot smoking, domestic tasks at home, curfew hours, communication problems, sexual values and behavior, study habits and grades received, and choice of dates. Family therapy is used in such settings as family counseling agencies, adoption and foster care agencies, mental hospitals, mental health clinics, school social work settings, and residential treatment centers.

Community organization is the process of stimulating and assisting the local community to evaluate, plan, and coordinate its efforts to provide for the community's health, welfare, and recreation needs. Perhaps it is not possible to define precisely the activities of a community organizer; but such activities are apt to include encouraging and fostering citizen participation, coordination of efforts between agencies or between groups, public relations and public education, research, planning, and being a resource person. A community organizer acts as a catalyst in stimulating and encouraging community action. Agency settings where such specialists are apt to be located include community welfare councils, social planning agencies, health planning councils, and community action agencies.

Administration involves directing the overall program of a social service agency. Administrative functions include setting agency and program objectives, analysis of social conditions in the community and making decisions relating to what services will be provided, employing and supervising staff members, setting up an organizational structure, administering financial affairs, and securing funds for the agency's operations. In a small-sized agency these functions may be carried out by one person, while in a larger agency several people may be involved in administrative affairs.

Other areas of professional activity in social work include research, consulting, planning, supervision, and teaching (primarily at the college level).

There used to be an erroneous conceptualization that a social worker was either a caseworker, a group worker, or a community organizer. Practicing social workers know such a conceptualization is faulty as every social worker is involved as a change agent in working with individuals, groups, families, and community groups. The amount of time spent at these various levels varies from worker to worker, but every worker will, at times, be assigned and expected to work at these four levels and therefore needs training at all these levels.

ROLE MODELS FOR SOCIAL WORK PRACTICE

In working with individuals, groups, families, and communities a social worker is also expected to be knowledgeable and skillful in using a variety of role models. The particular role model that is selected to be used (ideally) should be determined by what will be most effective given the circumstances.

Enabler. In this role a worker *helps* individuals or groups: to articulate their needs; to clarify and identify their problems; to explore resolution strategies; to select and ap-

ply a strategy; and to develop their capacities to deal with their own problems more effectively. This role model is perhaps the most frequently used approach in counseling individuals, groups, and families. The model is also used in community organization primarily when the objective is to "help people organize to help themselves."

Broker. A broker links individuals and groups who need help (and do not know where help is available) with community services. For example, a wife who is frequently physically abused by her husband might be referred to a shelter care program for battered women. Nowadays even moderate-sized communities have 200 or 300 social service agencies/organizations providing community services. Even human service professionals are often only partially aware of the total service network in their community. A recent trend for a fairly large number of agencies (such as neighborhood centers, mental health clinics, public welfare departments, agencies serving the elderly, and agencies providing family planning services) is to employ "community outreach workers" whose function is to inform residents about available services, identify individuals and families with problems, and link such families with available services.

Advocate. The role of an advocate has been borrowed from the law profession. It is an active directive role in which the social worker is an advocate for a client or for a citizen's group. When a client or a citizen's group is in need of help and existing institutions are uninterested (and sometimes openly negative and hostile) against providing services, then the advocate's role may be appropriate. In such a role, the advocate provides leadership for collecting information, for arguing the correctness of the client's need and request, and for challenging the institution's decision not to provide services. The object is not to ridicule or censure a particular institution but to modify or change one or more of their service policies. In this role the advocate is a partisan who is exclusively serving the interests of a client or of a citizen's group.

Activist. An activist seeks basic institutional change; often the objective involves a shift in power and resources to a disadvantaged group. An activist is concerned about social injustice, inequity, and deprivation. Tactics involve conflict, confrontation, and negotiation. Social action is concerned with changing the social environment in order to better meet the recognized needs of individuals. The methods used are assertive and action oriented (e.g., organizing welfare recipients to work toward improvements in services and increases in money payments). Activities of social action include factfinding, analysis of community needs, research, the dissemination and interpretation of information, organization, and other efforts to mobilize public understanding and support in behalf of some existing or proposed social program. Social action activity can be geared at a problem which is local, statewide, or national in scope.

In addition to these role models it is important for social workers to be skilled at public speaking and public education. Potential clients and service providers are often unaware of present services or gaps in services. Social workers occasionally talk to a variety of groups (e.g., high school classes, public service organizations such as Kiwanis, police officers, staff at other agencies) to inform them of available services or to advocate the need to develop new services for clients having unmet needs. In recent years a variety of new services has been identified as being needed (e.g., runaway centers, services for battered women, rape crisis centers, and group homes for youth).

SOCIAL WORK STEREOTYPES

The image of a social worker has undergone a more rapid change than perhaps any other profession. Forty years ago there was a stereotype of a social worker as being a moralistic upper middle-class, older lady, carrying a basket of food, who had little understanding of the people she tried to help. The image is much more positive today, reflecting the improved professional nature of the training and services provided. The image is also much more varied. Glasser listed several stereotypes of social workers held by different segments of the population.

1. The social worker is a kind, warm, generous, helpful person who makes it possible for people to live richer, more satisfying lives.
2. The social worker is a frustrated maiden lady who meddles in other people's business.
3. The social worker is a knowledgeable, dedicated crusader for the needs of all people, particularly the underprivileged.
4. The social worker is a radical whose real underlying motive is to bring about a change in the social order.
5. The social worker is a hardhearted, denying administrator of rules and regulations who checks on people to see that they don't cheat the agency.
6. The social worker is a professional whose training and experience enable him/her to help with a wide range of problems people have in everyday living.[12]

Dolgoff and Feldstein summarize some other social work stereotypes:

Depending upon who is doing the "name calling," social workers are referred to in many ways: do-gooders, bleeding hearts, radicals intent on changing our society, captives of and apologists for "the establishment," organizers of the poor, and servers of the middle class. All these are ways in which people stereotype social workers and the functions they perform in society.[13]

No doubt there are other stereotypes.

KNOWLEDGE, SKILLS, AND VALUES

If a social worker is to provide clients with competent service, the worker must have *knowledge, skills,* and *values* that are consistent with effective practice. (The reader is not expected to have a comprehensive understanding of the material covered in this section—instead this material is only presented to introduce the reader to the essential knowledge, skills, and values for social work practice.)

Knowledge base

Knowledge has been defined as the ". . . acquaintance with or theoretical or practical understanding of some branch of science, art, learning or other area involving study, research, or practice, and the acquisition of skills."[14] To describe the knowledge base a social worker should have, a summary of a conceptual formulation developed by Kadushin will be presented.[15]

A. General social work knowledge. This general knowledge can be categorized into three broad areas:

1. Social welfare policy and services—including content on social problems, social services designed to prevent and treat such problems, service gaps, contemporary social issues; content on how social policy is formulated, forces affecting policies, how to critically analyze and change social policy; and the role of the social worker in formulating policy.
2. Human behavior and the social environment, including content on human growth, personality development (both normal and abnormal); cultural values and norms; community processes; and other aspects influencing the social functioning of individuals and groups.
3. Methods of social work practice, including intervention strategies in casework, group work, and community organization, and content on research and administration.

B. Knowledge about a specific practice field. For example, a worker in the mental health field must have a knowledge of:

1. The various theories on why some people develop emotional problems.
2. What are the contributions of hereditary and social learning factors.
3. How to assess and diagnose emotional disorders.
4. The various treatment programs that are available in the community.
5. How to assess when a person should be institutionalized, and an awareness of the negative effects of labeling and long-term institutionalization upon a person.
6. How to critically analyze the merits and shortcomings of various treatment programs.
7. The effects of psychotropic drugs on people (for example, tranquilizers and antidepressant drugs).
8. How to treat clients with contemporary psychotherapy theories—such as psychoanalysis, reality therapy, rational therapy, transactional analysis, and behavior modification.

C. Knowledge about a specific agency. A social worker at a mental health center, for example, has to know information about the following:

1. What are the eligibility requirements for clients to receive services.
2. What are the procedures for admitting a client for inpatient services.
3. What are the required court procedures for admitting someone against their consent (involuntary commitment).
4. Who is to pay for the services which clients receive.
5. What records for accountability purposes are to be kept.
6. What are the processes for placing a client in foster care or in a group home.
7. What is the expected role of a social worker in working as a team member with psychiatrists, psychologists, nurses, occupational therapists, and other professionals.
8. What are the specific modes of treatment used by the agency in working directly with individuals, families, and groups.
9. What specific treatment programs are provided by the agency, and what is the expected role of the social worker in each of these programs.

D. Knowledge about each client. The worker needs to know in detail the following information:

1. What are the specific personal and/or social problems faced by each client.
2. Background information on each client, such as age, early childhood development, family relationships, school history, employment history, contact with other social agencies, and general health.
3. What are the contributing factors to the client's problems—such as financial, peer pressure, school or employement relationships, family pressures, racial or ethnic factors, friendship relationships, life goals, interests, and meaningful activities.
4. Client's perception and definition of his/her problems.
5. Client's set of values and morals that influence these problems.
6. Client's strengths, along with shortcomings, in being able to cope with the problems.
7. Client's motivation to want to improve his/her circumstances.
8. Knowledge about possible treatment strategies for each client's particular problems.

Skill base

Skill is the *ability* to use knowledge effectively and readily in execution or performance.[16] Baer and Federico have developed an elaborate list of skills needed for beginning level social work practice—some of which will be listed here.[17]

Observing activities and situations.
Collecting data.
Analyzing data.
Identifying social problems.
Listening.
Communicating effectively.
Interviewing.
Providing information.
Interacting with others.
Clarifying attitudes and feelings.
Clarifying implications of choices.
Supporting and and encouraging.
Motivating others.
Teaching others.
Identifying goals.
Selecting appropriate intervention strategies.

Monitoring service delivery.

Contracting.

Mediating.

Advocating.

Referring persons.

Relating to colleagues.

Case recording.

Assessing one's own intervention activities.

Federico has indirectly described social work skills by outlining roles and activities:

1. *Outreach worker:* Reaching out into the community to identify need and follow up referrals to service contexts.
2. *Broker:* Knowing services available and making sure those in need reach the appropriate services.
3. *Advocate:* Helping specific clients obtain services when they might otherwise by rejected, and helping to expand services to cover more needy persons.
4. *Evaluation:* Evaluating needs and resources, generating alternatives for meeting needs, and making decisions between alternatives.
5. *Teacher:* Teaching facts and skills.
6. *Mobilizer:* Helping to develop new services.
7. *Behavior changer:* Changing specific parts of a client's behavior.
8. *Consultant:* Working with other professionals to help them be more effective in providing services.
9. *Community planner:* Helping community groups plan effectively for the community's social welfare needs.
10. *Care giver:* Providing supportive services to those who cannot fully solve their problems and meet their own needs.
11. *Data manager:* Collecting and analyzing data for decision-making purposes.
12. *Administrator:* Performing the activities necessary to plan and implement a program of services.[18]

The acquisition of social work skills depend partly on innate abilities of people, and partly on past learning experiences. In addition, social work educational programs facilitate further learning of such skills by theoretical material (e.g., material on how to interview), by practicing such skills (e.g., videotaping students in simulated counseling situations), and by extensively supervising students in practicum courses.

Unlike many professionals, the social worker does not bring many tangible resources to a helping situation (a physician, for example, has a wide range of equipment to help diagnose problems, and a wide range of tangible treatment techniques such as medication). The social worker, on the other hand, brings a body of knowledge, a repertoire of skills, and a set of values—all of which are fairly abstract. Since there are literally hundreds of intervention strategies that can be used to improve the social functioning of clients, the skill of social work practice requires both the appropriate selection of techniques for a particular situation and the capacity to use the techniques effectively.

Value base

Should the primary objective of imprisonment be rehabilitation or punishment? Should a father committing incest be prosecuted with the likelihood of such publicity in the community leading to family breakup, or should an effort first be made, through counseling, to stop the incest and keep the family intact? Should a wife who is occasionally abused by her husband be encouraged to remain living with him? Should an abortion be suggested as one alternative for resolving the problems of someone who is single and pregnant? Should youth who are claimed to be uncontrollable by their parents be placed in correctional schools? If a client of a social worker threatened serious harm on some third person, what should the worker do? All of these questions involve making decisions based not on knowledge but on values. Much of social work practice is dependent upon making decisions based on values.

Pincus and Minahan concisely define *values,* and describe the differences between values and knowledge:

> Values are beliefs, preferences, or assumptions about what is desirable or good for man. An example is the belief that society has an obligation to help each individual realize his fullest potential. They are not assertions about how the world is and what we know about it, but how it *should* be. As such, value statements cannot be subjected to scientific investigation; they must be accepted on faith. Thus we can speak of a value as being right or wrong only in relation to the particular belief system or ethical code being used as a standard.
>
> What we will refer to as knowledge statements, on the other hand, are observations about the world and man which have been verified or are capable of verification. An example is that black people have a shorter life expectancy than white people in the United States. When we speak of a knowledge statement as being right or wrong, we are referring to the extent to which the assertion has been confirmed through objective empirical investigation.[19]

The National Association of Social Workers (NASW) has recently revised its Code of Ethics. This Code of Ethics summarizes important practice ethics for social workers. A summary of major principles of this code is presented here, with the complete code being presented in the appendix.

Values underlying social work practice will briefly be summarized here.

Respect for the dignity and uniqueness of the individual. This value or principle has also been called *individualization.* Individualization means viewing and treating a person as a unique, worthwhile person. The social work profession firmly believes each person has inherent dignity which is to be respected.

Every human being is unique in a variety of ways—value system, personality, goals in life, financial resources, emotional and physical strengths, personal concerns, past experiences, peer pressures, emotional reactions, self-identity, family relationships, and deviant behavioral patterns. In working with a client a social worker needs to perceive and respect the uniqueness of the client's situation.

Individualization is relatively easy for a social worker to achieve when that worker is assisting clients who have similar values, goals, behavioral patterns, and personal characteristics as the worker. Individualization is harder to achieve when a worker is assigned clients who have values or behavioral patterns that the worker views as disgusting. For example, a worker holding traditional middle-class values may have more difficulty in viewing a client with respect when that client has killed someone, or is a homosexual, or has raped someone, or is filthy and continually uses vulgar language. A general guideline in such situations is that the worker should seek to accept and respect the client, but not accept the deviant behavior that needs to be changed. If a worker is not able to convey that s/he accepts the client (but not the deviant behavior), a helping relationship will not be established. If such a relationship is not established then the worker will have practically no opportunity to help the client make constructive changes. A second guideline is that if a worker views a client as being disgusting and is unable to

NASW Code of Ethics*

Summary of Major Principles

I. THE SOCIAL WORKER'S CONDUCT AND COMPORTMENT AS A SOCIAL WORKER

    A. *Propriety.* The social worker should maintain high standards of personal conduct in the capacity or identity as social worker.

    B. *Competence and Professional Development.* The social worker should strive to become and remain proficient in professional practice and the performance of professional functions.

    C. *Service.* The social worker should regard as primary the service obligation of the social work profession.

    D. *Integrity.* The social worker should act in accordance with the highest standards of professional integrity.

    E. *Scholarship and Research.* The social worker engaged in study and research should be guided by the conventions of scholarly inquiry.

II. THE SOCIAL WORKER'S ETHICAL RESPONSIBILITY TO CLIENTS

    F. *Primacy of Clients' Interests.* The social worker's primary responsibility is to clients.

    G. *Rights and Prerogatives of Clients.* The social worker should make every effort to foster maximum self-determination on the part of clients.

    H. *Confidentiality and Privacy.* The social worker should respect the privacy of clients and hold in confidence all information obtained in the course of professional service.

    I. *Fees.* When setting fees, the social worker should ensure that they are fair, reasonable, considerate, and commensurate with the service performed and with due regard for the clients' ability to pay.

III. THE SOCIAL WORKER'S ETHICAL RESPONSIBILITY TO COLLEAGUES

    J. *Respect, Fairness, and Courtesy.* The social worker should treat colleagues with respect, courtesy, fairness, and good faith.

    K. *Dealing with Colleagues' Clients.* The social worker has the responsibility to relate to the clients of colleagues with full professional consideration.

IV. THE SOCIAL WORKER'S ETHICAL RESPONSIBILITY TO EMPLOYERS AND EMPLOYING ORGANIZATIONS

    L. *Commitments to Employing Organizations.* The social worker should adhere to commitments made to the employing organizations.

V. THE SOCIAL WORKER'S ETHICAL RESPONSIBILITY TO THE SOCIAL WORK PROFESSION

    M. *Maintaining the Integrity of the Profession.* The social worker should uphold and advance the values, ethics, knowledge, and mission of the profession.

    N. *Community Service.* The social worker should assist the profession in making social services available to the general public.

    O. *Development of Knowledge.* The social worker should take responsibility for identifying, developing, and fully utilizing knowledge for professional practice.

VI. THE SOCIAL WORKER'S ETHICAL RESPONSIBILITY TO SOCIETY

    P. *Promoting the General Welfare.* The social worker should promote the general welfare of society.

* Reprinted by permission of the National Association of Social Workers: "NASW Code of Ethics," as revised by the 1979 Delegate Assembly. National Association of Social Workers, Inc., Washington, D.C.

establish a working relationship, then that worker should transfer the case to another worker. There should be no disgrace or embarrassment in having to transfer a case for such reasons as it is irrational for a worker to expect to be able to like every client and that every client will like that worker.[20]

Social workers occasionally encounter "raw" situations. For a while I worked in a mental hospital for the "criminally insane" and had a variety of clients who had committed a wide range of asocial and bizarre acts: including incest, rape, murder, sodomy, sexual exhibitionism, and removing corpses from graves. I've worked in a variety of other settings and encountered other raw situations. Achieving an attitude of respect for people who commit bizarre actions is difficult at times to achieve, but rehabilitation will not occur unless it is achieved.

Social psychologists have firmly established the theoretical principle that people's image of themselves develops largely out of their interactions and communications with others. A long time ago Charles Cooley called this process the "looking glass self-concept."[21] The "looking glass" says people develop their self-concept in terms of how other people relate to them. Specifically if a person receives respect from others and is praised for his/her positive qualities, that person will feel good about him/herself, gradually will develop a positive sense of worth, will be happier, and will seek responsible and socially acceptable ways to continue to maintain the respect of others.

On the other hand, if a person commits a deviant act and *then* is shunned by others, viewed as different, and treated with disrespect, that person is apt to develop a negative self-concept, and it has been found that people with negative self-concepts will either withdraw from society, become emotionally disturbed, or express their discontent in delinquent and deviant actions.[22]

The principle of individualization also plays a key role in social work treatment. Various problems, needs, goals, and values of clients involve different patterns of relationships with clients and different methods of helping. For example, a teenage boy who is placed in a group home because his parents have found him to be "uncontrollable" may need an understanding but firm counselor who sets and enforces strict limits. At times the youth may need encouragement and guidance in how to perform better at school. If conflicts develop between the youth and other boys at the group home, the counselor may need to play a mediating role. If the youth is shy, counseling on how to be more assertive may be needed. If his parents are fairly ineffective in their parenting role, the counselor may seek to have the parents enroll in a Parent Effectiveness Training program.[23] If the youth is being treated unfairly at school or by the juvenile court, the counselor may play an advocate role for the youth and attempt to change the system. If the youth has behavior problems, the reasons need to be explored and an intervention program developed.

Client's right to self-determination. This principle asserts that clients have the right to hold and express their own opinions and to act upon them, as long as in so doing they do not infringe upon the rights of others. This principle is in sharp contrast to the layperson's view that a social worker seeks to "remold" clients into a pattern chosen by the worker. Instead, the efforts of social workers are geared to enhancing the capability of clients to help themselves. Client self-determination derives logically from the belief in the inherent dignity of each person. If people have dignity, then it follows that they should be permitted to determine their own lifestyles as far as possible.

Social work believes that making all decisions and doing everything for a client is self-defeating as it leads to increased dependency, rather than greater self-reliance and self-sufficiency. In order for people to grow, to mature, to become responsible, people need to make their own decisions and to take responsibility for the consequences. Mistakes and emotional pain will at times occur. But that is part of life. We learn by our mistakes, and by trial and error. The respect for the client's ability to make his/her own decisions is associated with the principle that social work is a cooperative endeavor between client and worker (client participation). Social work is done *with* a client, and not *to* a client. Plans imposed on people without their active involvement have a way of not turning out well.

Self-determination implies that clients should be made aware that there are alternatives for resolving the personal or social problems they face. Self-determination involves having clients make decisions; that is, making a choice selected from several courses of action. If there is only one course of action, there is no choice and therefore clients would not have the right of self-determination. As will be expanded upon in later chapters the role of a social worker in helping clients involves: (*a*) building a helping relationship, (*b*) exploring problems in depth with clients, and (*c*) exploring alternative solutions, with clients then choosing a course of action. This third step is the implementation of the principle of self-determination.

Self-determination means that the client, not the worker, is the chief problem solver. Workers need to recognize that it is the client who *owns* the problem, and therefore has the chief responsibility to resolve the problem. This is an area where social workers differ markedly from most other professions. Most other professionals, such as physicians and attorneys, advise clients as to what they believe clients ought to do. Doctors, lawyers, and dentists are viewed as being experts in advising clients. Clients' decision making after receiving the expert's advice in such situations is generally limited to the choice of whether or not to accept the professional's advice.

In sharp contrast, social workers should not seek to establish an expert-inferior relationship, but a relationship between equals. The expertise of the social worker does *not* lie in knowing or recommending what is best for the client. Rather, the expertise lies in assisting clients: to define their problems, to develop and examine the alternatives for resolving the problems, to maximize the client's capacities and opportunities to make decisions for themselves, and to help

clients to implement the decisions they make. Many students when they first enter social work, or some other helping profession, mistakenly see their role as being that of "savior" or "rescuer." Mathew Dumont is highly critical of the rescuer role:

> The most destructive thing in psychotherapy is a "rescue fantasy" in the therapist—a feeling that the therapist is the divinely sent agent to pull a tormented soul from the pit of suffering and adversity and put him back on the road to happiness and glory. A major reason this fantasy is so destructive is that it carries the conviction that the patient will be saved only through and by the therapist. When such a conviction is communicated to the patient, verbally or otherwise, he has no choice other than to rebel and leave or become more helpless, dependent, and sick.[24]

Confidentiality

Confidentiality is the implicit or explicit agreement between a professional and his/her client to maintain the private nature of information about the client. An "absolute" implementation of this principle means that disclosures made to the professional will not be shared with anyone else, except when authorized by the client in writing or required by law.

Because of the principle of confidentiality, professionals can be sued if they disclose information which the client is able to document has a damaging effect upon him/her.

One of the reasons confidentiality is important is because clients will not be apt to share their "hidden secrets," personal concerns, and asocial thoughts and actions with a professional if they believe that information will be revealed to others. A basic principle of counseling is that clients must feel comfortable in fully revealing themselves to the professional without fear that their secret revelations will be used against them.

Confidentiality is absolute when information revealed to a professional is *never* passed on to anyone or anything in any form. Such information would never be shared with other agency staff, fed into a computer, or written in a case record. A student or beginning practitioner tends to think in absolutes, and may even naïvely promise clients "absolute confidentiality."

Absolute confidentiality is seldom achieved. Social workers today generally function as part of a larger agency. In such an agency much of the communication is written into case records and shared orally with other staff in the system as part of the service-delivery process. Social workers share details with supervisors, and many work in teams where they are expected to share information with other team members. Therefore, instead of absolute confidentiality, it is more precise to indicate that a system of "relative confidentiality" is being used in social work practice.

Confidentiality is a legal matter, and at the present time there is a fair amount of uncertainty as to what is legally a violation and what is not. There have been few test cases in court to determine what is, and what is not a violation of confidentiality. Let me provide a brief summary of how agencies are now handling issues related to confidentiality.

At agencies now it is generally an accepted practice that it is permissible to discuss a client's circumstances with other professionals at that agency. At many agencies, such as a mental hospital, the input of many professionals at the agency (psychiatrist, psychologist, social workers, nurses, physical therapist, and so on) is used in assessing a client and developing a treatment plan.

Many agencies feel it is inappropriate to share or discuss a client's case with a secretary. (Yet, the secretary does the typing and usually knows as much about each client as the professional staff.)

Most agencies believe it is inappropriate to discuss a client's case with professionals at another agency, unless the client first signs a release of information form. (Yet, informally professionals employed by different agencies do at times share information about a client without the client's authorization.)

At the present time nearly all agencies share case information with social work interns. (Whether it is legally permissible to share information with student interns has not been legally determined.)

It is certainly permissible to discuss a case for educational purposes with others if no identifying information about the specific person is given. Yet, this is another "gray" area as the person talking about the case will not be able to precisely determine when identifying information is being given. Take the following example.

Some years ago I was employed at a maximum security hospital for the criminally insane and had on my caseload a young male who decapitated his 17-year-old girl friend. Such a criminal offense is indeed shocking and rare. People in the client's local area will never forget the offense. If I was to discuss this case in a class at a university (which I occasionally do), I would never be fully assured that no one would be able to identify the offender. There is always the chance that one of the students may have lived in the client's home community and recognize the offender.

Another problematic area is the thorny question of when should a professional violate confidence and inform others. Again, there are many "gray" areas surrounding this question.

Most state statutes permit or require the professional to inform the appropriate people when a client admits to a past or intended *serious* criminal act. Yet, the question of how serious a crime must be before there is an obligation to report it has not been resolved. On the extreme end of the "severity" continuum (for example, when a client threatens to kill someone) it has been established that a professional *must* inform the appropriate people—such as the police and the intended victims.

In regard to the question of how serious a crime must be before it is reported Wilson notes:

> How serious must a crime be in order for the professional to take protective measures? Obviously, crimes involving someone's life are sufficiently serious. But what about destruction of personal property, theft, and the hundreds of misdemeanors that are so minor that they are rather easily overlooked? Unfortunately, there seems to be no clear-cut definition of what constitutes a serious crime, and it appears that this will have to be determined by the courts in individual case rulings.[25]

Without guidelines, a professional has to use his/her own best judgment when a client's actions or communications warrant protective measures and what those measures should be. A student intern or beginning practitioner is advised to ask his/her supervisor when questions in this area arise.

For example, a few years ago I was the faculty supervisor for a student in a field placement at a public assistance agency. The student intern had an unmarried ADC mother on his caseload. A trusting, working relationship between the intern and the mother was developed. The mother then informed the student she was dating a person who was sometimes abusive to her when drunk. The mother further indicated there was a warrant for the boyfriend's arrest in another state for an armed robbery charge. The student intern contacted me inquiring whether it was his obligation to inform the

police, thereby violating confidentiality. My response was to discuss this with his agency supervisor to find out the agency's policy.

Wilson further concludes:

> In summary, a professional whose client confesses an intended or past crime can find himself in a very delicate position, both legally and ethically. There are enough conflicting beliefs on how this should be handled, so that clear guidelines are lacking. Social workers who recieve a communication about a serious criminal act by a client would be wise to consult an attorney for a detailed research of appropriate state statutes and a review of recent court rulings that might help determine the desired course of action.[26]

There are a number of other areas where a professional is permitted, expected, or required to violate confidentiality.* These areas include:

When a client formally (usually in writing) authorizes the professional to release information.

When a professional is called to testify in a criminal case (state statutes vary regarding guidelines on what information may be kept confidential in such criminal proceedings, and therefore practitioners must research their own particular state statutes in this area).

Most state statutes permit a professional to disclose confidential information if a client brings suit against him/her (e.g., for malpractice).

When a client threatens suicide, a professional may be forced to violate confidentiality to save the client's life. While the treating professional is encouraged to violate confidentiality in

---

* An extended discussion of these areas is contained in Suanna J. Wilson, *Confidentiality in Social Work: Issues and Principles* (New York: Free Press, 1978).

such circumstances, there is not necessarily a legal requirement to do so.

When a client threatens to harm his/her therapist.

Most states require legal authorities be informed when a professional becomes aware that a minor has committed a crime, when a minor is used by adults as an accessory in a crime, or when a minor is a victim of criminal actions. Again, the question arises of how serious the crime must be before it is reported.

Many states require that evidences of child abuse or neglect be reported by professionals to the designated child-protection agency.

When a client's emotional or physical condition makes his/her employment a clear danger to him/herself or others (for example, when a counselor discovers a client who is an airplane pilot has a serious drinking problem).

In all these areas professional judgment must be used in deciding when the circumstances justify violating confidentiality (for example, making a judgment as to when child abuse or neglect may be occurring).

Advocacy and social action for the powerless. Social work has recognized an obligation to be an advocate for those who have little power to ensure their rights and are therefore oppressed or dispossessed. Social work believes that society has a responsibility to all of its members to provide security, acceptance, and satisfaction of basic cultural, social, and biological needs. Only when an individual's basic needs are met is it thought possible for people to develop their maximum potentials. Since social work believes in the value of the individual, it has a special responsibility to protect and secure

the civil rights based upon democratic principles. Social workers have a moral responsibility to work toward eradicating discrimination for any reason. Civil rights of clients need to be protected in order to preserve human dignity and self-respect.

Focus on family. Often the focus of social work services is on the family. A family is seen as an interacting independent system. The problems faced by any person are usually influenced by the dynamics within a family, as illustrated in the following example.

A school teacher became concerned when one of her pupils was consistently failing and referred the child for psychological testing. Testing revealed a normal IQ, but failure was found to be due to a low self-concept (the girl was reluctant to do her academic work as she saw herself as being incapable of doing it). A school social worker met with the family and observed that the low self-concept was primarily a result of the parents' ridiculing and criticizing the child, and from seldom giving emotional support, encouragement, or compliments.

Since a family is an interacting system, change in one member affects others. For example, with some abusive families it has been noted that the abused child is at times a scapegoat for the parents to vent their anger and hostility. If the abused child is removed from a home, another child within the family is at times selected to be the scapegoat.[27]

Another reason for the focus on the family rather than on the individual is that the other family members are often needed in the treatment process. For example, other family members can put pressure on an alcoholic in order to have him/her acknowledge a problem exists. The family members may also need counseling to help them to cope with the person when drinking, and these family

Family counseling

members may play important roles in providing emotional support for the alcoholic's efforts to stop drinking.

Accountability. Increasingly federal and state governmental units, and private funding sources, are requiring that the effectiveness of service programs be measured. Gradually, programs found to be ineffective are being phased out. While some social workers view accountability with trepidation and claim the paperwork involved interferes with serving clients, social work has an obligation to funding sources to seek to provide the highest quality services. The value of accountability in recent years has been shown by program outcome studies which have demonstrated orphanages are not the best places to serve homeless children, that long-term hospitalization is not the best way to help those who are emotionally disturbed, that probation generally has higher rehabilitative value than long-term confinement in prison, that the Job Corps program of the 1960s was too expensive for the outcomes achieved, that mentally retarded children can be better served in their home communities through local programs than by confinement in an institution, and that runaways are better served by runaway centers than by placing them in detention or in jail.

Social workers need to become skilled at evaluating the extent to which they are being effective in providing services. At the agency level and program level a wide variety of evaluation techniques are now available to assess effectiveness of current services, and to identify unmet needs and service gaps. One of the most useful approaches is management by objectives (MBO). This technique involves identifying at program levels what are the objectives of the program, specifying in measurable terms how and when these objectives are to be met, and then periodically measuring the extent to which the objectives will be met.

Management by objectives is perhaps also the most useful approach that every social worker can use in order to assess his/her effectiveness. Many agencies are now requiring each of their workers, *with the involvement of their clients,* to: (*a*) identify and specify what will be the goals for each client—generally this is done together with clients during the initial interviews, (*b*) having the client and the worker then write down in detail what each will do in order to accomplish the goals—deadlines for accomplishing these tasks, are also set, and (*c*) when treatment is terminated (and perhaps periodically during the treatment process) the extent to which the goals have been achieved are then assessed.

If goals are generally not being achieved the worker needs to examine the underlying reasons. Perhaps unrealistic goals are being set. Perhaps the program or the treatment techniques are ineffective. Perhaps certain components of the treatment program are having an adverse effect. Perhaps other reasons account for the low success rate. Depending on the reason for the goals not being achieved, appropriate changes need to be made.

On the other hand, if the goals are generally being met the worker can use this information to document to funding sources and to his/her supervisors that high-quality services are being provided.

The institutional orientation. There are currently two conflicting views of the role of social welfare in our society: the residual orientation versus the institutional orientation. These two views have been described at length in Chapter 1. Social work believes in the institutional approach, and seeks to develop and provide programs with this orientation. Social work believes society must provide opportunities for growth and development that will allow each person to realize his/her fullest potential. Social work believes that society has a responsibility to all its members to provide security, acceptance, and satisfaction of basic cultural and biological needs. This belief rejects the views of rugged individualism and Social Darwinism.

SOCIAL WORK EDUCATION

Two-year associate programs

During the past decade a number of community colleges and technical schools have begun offering two-year associate programs related to social work education. These programs provide training for a wide range of associate degrees with such titles as:

Social Work Aide/Social Service Associate/ Social Service Technician

Probation and Parole Aide

Mental Health Associate/Mental Health Aide

Human Services Technician/Human Services Aide

Child Care Technician/Residential Child Care Aide

Community Service Assistant/Community Services Technician/Community Social Service Worker

All of these degrees are considered preprofessional degrees, and seek to achieve two simultaneous goals—training for employment, and to provide some base courses that *may* transfer to four-year educational programs.

As yet associate degrees are not accredited by the Council on Social-Work Education (CSWE). (This council presently reviews social work baccalaureate and masters programs throughout the United States to determine whether individual programs meet the standards to warrant accreditation.) Standardization of associate programs in social work probably will not be achieved unless CSWE decides to seek to review associate programs for accreditation.

Undergraduate education. Similar to graduate programs, undergraduate programs are accredited by the Council on Social Work Education. This council is a national organization whose purpose is to set standards for social work education, and to promote and improve the quality of education in social work programs. Students attending schools with accredited programs have assurance that the quality of education meets national standards, and generally have an advantage in securing employment following graduation as social welfare agencies give a hiring preference (ranging from a small to a large amount) to graduates from accredited programs.

Until the early 1970s, undergraduate social work education was generally recognized as an academic or preprofessional degree, with the master's degree being recognized as the professional degree in social work. However, since a majority of people employed in the social welfare field do not have a graduate degree, the need for professional training at the baccalaureate level was recognized. Effective July 1, 1974, accreditation requirements for undergraduate programs were substantially changed to emphasize professional preparation. In fact, the Council on Social Work Education required that an accredited baccalaureate program "shall have as its primary stated educational objective preparation for beginning professional social work practice."[28] Other objectives, secondary in importance, that baccalaureate programs are apt to have include: (a) preparation of students for graduate professional education in social work and (b) preparation for intelligent, informed citizenship which brings an understanding of a wide range of social problems, intervention techniques on resolving such problems, and an understanding of social welfare concepts.

Along with this change from an academic to a professional preparation focus, was an explicit statement of curriculum requirements that, according to the Council on Social Work Education:

1. Builds on, and is integrated with, a liberal arts base that includes knowledge in the humanities, social, behavioral, and biological sciences.
2. Provides content in the areas of (a) social work practice, (b) social welfare policy and services, (c) human behavior and social environment, and (d) social research.
3. Requires educationally directed field experiences with engagement in service activities for at least 300 clock hours, for which academic credit commensurate with the time invested is given.[29]

Video tape equipment used to help social work students develop their counseling capacities: Interviews are taped and then played back to students

The curriculum objectives of undergraduate programs are generic (broad based) as they seek to develop a variety of skills and knowledge bases, including:

Ability to effectively counsel individuals on a one-to-one basis, and in groups.

Knowledge of the wide range of available social welfare services.

Capacity to critically analyze social welfare programs, policies, and issues.

An understanding of human development and behavior, including biological, psychological, and sociocultural influences.

Capacity to understand and apply social research.

An understanding and an appreciation for ethnic, racial, and cultural diversity.

A working knowledge of a variety of intervention techniques that are used in casework, group work and community organization.

Graduate education. M.S.W. (Master of Social Work) programs as a rule require two academic years of study. However, a number of graduate programs are granting advanced standing to students holding an undergraduate major in social work. Advanced standing (up to one academic year of credit) is given on the basis of the number of "core" courses taken as an undergraduate. Core courses are those that are required in both undergraduate and graduate programs; and include courses in social welfare policy and services, in social work practice or methods courses, in human behavior and the social environment, in social research, and in field placement.*

Because of the professional preparation focus of graduate programs, field work is an

---

* Guidelines for granting advanced standing in M.S.W. programs differ between programs, and therefore interested students should consult with the graduate schools they desire attending.

important emphasis in all M.S.W. programs, with an average of two to three days per week being spent at an agency while receiving intensive supervision.

Although there is variation in format and structure of master's programs, almost all of the programs have the following two components: (a) Part of the program has a generic social work practice focus. Courses taken to meet this generic practice focus are similar (and at some schools identical) to the core courses of an undergraduate program. Some schools offer this generic focus during the first year, a few during the first semester, while others have course content in this area

for both years. (b) For the second part of the program the student selects a concentration area from several available options, and then takes courses in this study area. There is considerable variation between graduate schools in the concentration options that are offered. The Council on Social Work Education annually publishes *Summary Information on Master of Social Work Programs* which summarizes the concentration options at each school. Some of the concentration options are policy analysis, planning, research and administration, community organization, direct practice with individuals and small groups, direct practice with large

Role playing a counseling situation in class

groups, program development, community mental health, family functioning, health care, inner-city neighborhood services, social work in school systems, child welfare, consultation, aging, and crime and delinquency.[30]

Persons with M.S.W. degrees often, within a year or two following graduation, assume supervisory or administrative responsibilities.

At the advanced graduate level there are two additional programs that are offered by some schools: (a) a "third year" program with the aim of strengthening the professional skills of the student, and (b) a Doctor of Social Work degree (D.S.W.) or a Doctor of Philosophy degree. The doctoral program requires two or more years of postgraduate studies.

Employment settings and opportunities in social work

There are currently more employment opportunities available in social work than in many other fields, and the future looks encouraging. Social services and their delivery are becoming a more integral part of our fast-paced existence and the demand for qualified personnel is expected to expand. If you are looking for the challenge of working with people to improve social and personal difficulties, then you should seriously consider a career in social work.

From 1960 to 1979 the number of employed social service workers grew by 400 percent, from 95,000 to 385,00![31] Although personnel projections are at times filled with error, the Bureau of Labor Statistics considers the outlook for social work employment to be good, with additional annual openings estimated at 25,000.[32]

A wide variety of employment settings are available for social workers, including foster care, adoption, probation and parole, public assistance, counseling, services to single parents, day-care services, school social services, services to minority groups and to veterans, recreational services such as Boy Scouts and YWCA programs, social services in a medical or mental hospital, antipoverty programs, social services in a nursing home and other services to the elderly, marital counseling, drug and alcohol counseling, services to the emotionally disturbed or mentally handicapped, abortion counseling, family planning services, services to the blind and disabled, sexual counseling, equal rights services, protective services, services in sheltered workshops, research, social action, and fund raising. (These settings will be described in detail in the chapters that follow.) In addition to these direct services there are employment opportunities for those with experience and advanced professional training in social planning, community organization, consultation, supervision, teaching, and administration. There is a wide variation in pay, ranging approximately between $8,000 to $50,000 depending on type of job, geographic location, experience, training, and the skills possessed by the employee.

At our school we are convinced those who are most likely to secure employment in social work following graduation are those who are outgoing, dynamic, and able to "sell" themselves during an interview as having the competence, confidence, and skills to perform the job they are applying for. Involvement in groups and extracurricular activities while at college facilitates the development of these capacities, along with being a volunteer at one or more social service agencies. A high number of our students secure employment through the relationships they develop with staff during their field placement. If they do well at their field placement and a vacancy occurs, they have an inside track in being hired. Also, through developing acquaintances with staff at an agency, they hear about employment opportunities at other agencies, and frequently also receive a positive letter of reference from their field placement.

A frequent question asked by students who are considering majoring in social work is, "Is a graduate degree needed to get a job in social work?" Definitely not. The vast majority of employed social workers hold only a baccalaureate degree.[33] In addition, there are some agencies who prefer to hire a person with a baccalaureate degree, as it is less expensive. However, it should be noted that, as in most fields, a master's degree provides higher status, greater promotion opportunities, and perhaps more gratifying work.

YOUR FUTURE—SOCIAL WORK?

Test your interest:

1. Do you enjoy working closely and intensely with people?
2. Do you think you could cope with failure?
3. Do you think you would be willing to acquire the knowledge, skills and values necessary to make life more meaningful to individuals, groups, and communities?
4. Do you think you would like a profession dedicated to social change?

If you honestly are able to answer "yes" to each of these questions, you may well have the potential to become an effective social worker.

As said earlier, perhaps the key skill needed to be a competent social worker is the capacity to relate to, and counsel individuals.

Increasingly in training social work students educators are finding that students who are best able to counsel others are those who know themselves; that is, have a high

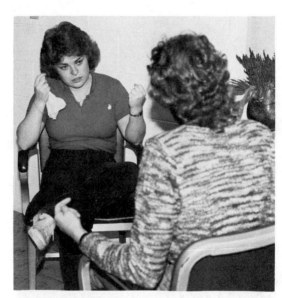

A student in field placement counseling a depressed client

level of self-awareness. A counselor has to be perceptive regarding what clients are thinking and feeling. To be perceptive the counselor has to be able to place him/herself in the client's situation and determine (with the client's values and pressures), "What is this person really feeling and thinking?" Unless the counselor has a high level of self-awareness, it is very unlikely he/she will be able to determine what others are thinking and feeling.

There are a variety of approaches that have been developed to increase personal awareness or self-awareness including: biofeedback, transcendental meditation, muscle relaxation, gestalt therapy, identity formation, sensitivity training, and encounter groups.* (Some programs in social work are now offering interpersonal skill courses

---

* A good review of the specific techniques used in these approaches is contained in Stewart L. Tubbs and John W. Baird, *The Open Person . . . Self-Disclosure and Personal Growth* (Columbus, Ohio: Charles E. Merrill, 1976).

Meditation: One way to learn more about self

which are designed to develop self-awareness and interpersonal awareness capacities.)

One of these approaches, identity formation, will be presented here.* Identity formation is the process of determining who you are and what you want out of life. Arriving at an identity you will be comfortable with is one of the most important tasks you will ever have to face. Whether or not you are interested in a social work career, the following information on identity could have considerable importance for your future. As noted,

_____

* This material on identity formation is adapted from an article written by this author entitled "Who Am I: Quest for Identity" in *The Personal Problem Solver*, ed. Charles Zastrow and Dae Chang (Englewood Cliffs, N.J.: Prentice-Hall, 1977) pp. 365–70.

it is especially significant for those considering a social work career, as knowing oneself enhances substantially one's ability to counsel others.

Identity development is a lifelong process, and there are gradual changes in one's identity throughout one's lifetime. During the early years our sense of who we are is largely determined by the reactions of others (the looking glass self-concept previously mentioned). For example, if a neighborhood, for whatever reason, perceives a young boy to be a "troublemaker," a "delinquent," they are then likely to accuse the youth of delinquent acts, treat him with suspicion, and label his semidelinquent activities as being "delinquent." Although frequently accused and criticized, the youth, to some extent, soon begins to realize enacting the delinquent role also brings certain rewards; it brings him a type of status and prestige, at least from other youth. In the absence of objective ways to determine whether he is a "delinquent," he relies on the subjective evaluations of others. Gradually a vicious cycle develops; the more he is related to as a delinquent, the more he is apt to view himself as a delinquent, and the more apt he is to enact the delinquent role.

Glasser indicates a useful perspective for viewing identity is in terms of a success versus failure orientation.[34] Those who develop a success identity (view themselves as generally being successful) have two characteristics: love and self-worth. They feel they are loved and viewed as being a worthy human being by at least one other person; and in turn they feel they love others and view themselves as being worthwhile. People with failure identities are those who feel they are not loved, or do not have a sense of self-worth. People with failure identities are apt to be depressed, lonely, anxious, reluctant to face everyday challenges, and indecisive. Escape through drugs or alcohol, withdrawal, criminal behavior, or the development of emotional problems are common.

However, since identity is a lifelong process, significant positive changes in one's identity can be achieved even by those with serious failure identities. An important principle is: *Although we cannot change the past, what we want out of the future, along with our motivation to achieve what we want, is more important (than our past experiences) in determining what our future will be.*

How to determine who you are: Some of the most important questions you will ever have to face are:

1. What kind of person are you?
2. What kind of person do you want to be?
3. What do you want out of life?
4. Who are you?

Without answers to such questions you will not be prepared to make such major decisions as selecting a career, deciding where to live and what type of lifestyle you want, deciding whether to marry, and deciding whether to have children. Unfortunately, many people muddle through life without ever arriving at answers to these questions. Answers are not easy to arrive at. They require considerable thought, and trial and error. During the time you are searching for a sense of who you are, also expect a great deal of anxiety to arise. However, if you are to lead a satisfying, fulfilling life, it is imperative that you seek answers to these questions in order to give direction to your life, and to know what will make your life meaningful. In order to assist you in arriving at a sense of who you are and what you want out of life, a series of more specific questions are listed in ",Questions for Arriving at a Sense of Identity." As you arrive at answers to these specific questions, you will simultaneously be arriving at an increased awareness of who you are.

Questions for arriving at a sense of identity

In order to determine who you are, you need to work on arriving at answers to the following more specific questions:

1. What do you find satisfying/enjoyable?
2. What are your religious beliefs?
3. What is your moral code? One possible code is to seek to fulfill your needs, and to seek to do what you find enjoyable, while doing so in a way that does not deprive others of the ability to fulfill their needs.
4. What are your sexual mores? All of us should develop a consistent code that we are comfortable with, and that helps us meet our needs without exploiting others. There is no one right code—what works for one, may not work for another, due to differences in lifestyles, life goals and personal values.
5. What kind of a career do you desire? Ideally, you should seek a career in which you find the work stimulating and satisfying, that you are skilled at, and that earns you enough money to support the lifestyle you desire.
6. What area of the country/world do you desire to live? Variables needing to be considered are climate, geography, type of dwelling, rural or urban setting, closeness to relatives or friends, and characteristics of the neighborhood.
7. Do you desire to marry? If yes, to what type of person, when, and how consistent are your answers here with your other life goals?
8. Do you desire to have children? If yes, how many, when, and how consistent are your answers here with your other life goals?
9. What kind of image do you want to project to others? Your image will be composed of your dressing style and grooming habits, your emotions, personality, degree of assertiveness, capacity to communicate, material possessions, moral code, physical features, and voice patterns. You need to honestly assess your strengths and shortcomings in this area, and seek to make improvements in the latter. Seeking counseling in problem areas may be desirable.
10. What do you enjoy doing with your leisure time?
11. Do you desire to improve the quality of your life, and that of others? If yes, in what ways, and how do you hope to achieve these goals?
12. What type of people do you enjoy being with, and why?
13. What type of relationships do you desire to have with your relatives, your friends, your neighbors, with people you meet for the first time?
14. What are your thoughts about death and dying?

15. What do you hope to be doing 5 years from now, 10 years, 20 years? What are your plans for achieving these goals in these time periods?
16. Do you view yourself as generally being a success, or as generally being a failure? If you have a failure identity, you desperately need to work on arriving at answers to the above questions. It may also be helpful to read "How to Cope with a Sense of Failure" by Merlin Manley.[35]

Having answers to most of these questions will provide a reference for developing your views to the remaining unanswered questions. To have a fairly well-developed sense of identity you need to have answers to most, but not all, of these questions. Very few persons are able to arrive at rational, fully consistent answers to all these questions. Be honest about your strengths and shortcomings. For practically any shortcomings there are specific intervention strategies to bring about improvement.

In addition, expect some changes in your life goals as time goes on, as you grow as a person, changes are apt to occur in your beliefs, attitudes, values, and in activities that you find enjoyable.

Your life is shaped by different events that are the results of decisions you make and decisions that are made for you. Without a sense of identity, you will not know what decisions are best for you, and your life will be unfulfilled. With a sense of identity, you will be able to direct your life toward goals you select and find personally meaningful.

SUMMARY

A social worker is a multiskilled professional; s/he needs training and expertise in a wide range of areas to be able to effectively handle problems faced by individuals, groups, and the larger community. Analogous to a general practitioner in medicine, a social worker should have a wide range of skills and intervention techniques.

Ability to effectively counsel clients is perhaps the most basic skill needed by a social worker. Second in importance is probably the ability to interact effectively with other groups and professionals in the community.

Social work as a profession is of relatively recent origin, with formalized training in social work first being offered at universities in the early 1900s, and people first being hired as social workers around 1900.

A social worker is a "change agent" who works with individuals, groups, families, and communities. There are several types of professional social work activities: casework, group work, group therapy, family therapy, community organization, administration, research, consulting, planning, supervision, and teaching. Role models for social work practice include: enabler, broker, advocate, and activist.

Forty years ago the stereotype of a social worker was that of a moralistic upper middle-class, older lady, carrying a basket of food, who had little understanding of the people she tried to help. With the rapid development of social work as a profession, there are now many stereotypes (generally more positive) of what a social worker is.

In order to provide clients with competent service, social workers must have knowledge, skills, and values that are consistent with effective practice. The value base of social work includes: respect for the dignity and uniqueness of each individual, client's right to self-determination, confidentiality, advocacy, and social action to ensure the rights of those with limited power, focus on family, accountability, and an institutional orientation.

The primary educational objective for undergraduate social work programs accredited by the Council on Social Work Education is preparation for beginning professional social work practice. A majority of people em-

ployed as social workers do not have a graduate degree. As in most fields, however,
persons with a master's degree in social work
generally have a higher status and greater
promotion opportunities.

The chapter concluded with a discussion
of the importance for social workers to have a
high level of self-awareness and to have a
sense of who they are and what they want
out of life.

Arriving at a sense of identity is one of the
most important and difficult quests in life,
for everyone. With a sense of identity you
will be able to direct your life toward goals
you select and find personally meaningful.

NOTES

1. Robert M. Bremner, "The Rediscovery of Pauper-
   ism," *Current Issues in Social Work Seen in Historical
   Perspective* (New York: Council on Social Work
   Education, 1962), p. 13.

2. Nathan E. Cohen, *Social Work in the American
   Tradition* (Hinsdale, Ill.: Dryden Press, 1958), p.
   66.

3. Dorothy G. Becker, "Social Welfare Leaders as
   Spokesman for the Poor," *Social Casework* vol. 49,
   no. 2 (February 1968), p. 85.

4. Jane Adams, *Twenty Years of Hull House* (New
   York: Macmillan, 1959), original publication 1910,
   pp. 125–26.

5. Ralph Dolgoff and Donald Feldstein, *Understanding
   Social Welfare* (New York: Harper & Row, 1980),
   pp. 233–34.

6. Ibid., p. 235.

7. Mary E. Richmond, *Social Diagnosis* (New York:
   Free Press, 1965).

8. H. J. Eysenck, "The Effects of Psychotherapy," in
   Handbook of Abnormal Psychology (New York: Basic
   Books, 1961), pp. 697–725.

9. "Oregon Passes Title Protection Law; 22 States
   Now Regulate Social Work," *NASW News* vol. 22
   (September 1977), p. 10.

10. Dolgoff and Feldstein, *Understanding Social Wel-
    fare.*

11. National Association of Social Workers, *Standards
    for Social Welfare Manpower* (New York: National
    Association of Social Workers, 1973), pp. 4–5.

12. Melvin A. Glasser, "Public Attitudes toward the
    Profession: What Shall They Be?" *NASW News* vol.
    3, no. 4 (August 1958), p. 7.

13. Dolgoff and Feldstein, *Understanding Social Wel-
    fare,* p. 223.

14. Alfred J. Kahn, "The Nature of Social Work Knowl-
    edge," in *New Directions in Social Work,* ed. Cora
    Kasius (New York: Harper, 1954), p. 196.

15. Alfred Kadushin, "The Knowledge Base of Social
    Work" in *Issues in American Social Work,* ed. Alfred
    J. Kahn (New York: Columbia University Press,
    1959), pp. 39–79.

16. Armando Morales and Bradford W. Sheafor, *Social
    Work: A Profession of Many Faces,* 2d ed. (Boston:
    Allyn and Bacon, 1980), p. 138.

17. Betty L. Baer and Ronald Federico, *Educating the
    Baccalaureate Social Worker* (Cambridge, Mass.:
    Ballinger, 1978), pp. 92–95.

18. Ronald Federico, *The Social Welfare Institution* (Lex-
    ington, Mass.: Heath, 1973), pp. 146–147.

19. Allen Pincus and Anne Minahan, *Social Work Prac-
    tice: Model and Method* (Itasca, Ill.: F. E. Peacock,
    1973), p. 38.

20. Albert Ellis and R. Harper, *A New Guide to Rational
    Living* (North Hollywood, Calif.: Wilshire Book,
    1975).

21. C. H. Cooley, *Human Nature and the Social Order*
    (New York: Scribner's 1902).

22. William Glasser, *The Identity Society* (New York:
    Harper & Row, 1972).

23. Thomas Gordon, *Parent Effectiveness Training* (New
    York: Wyden, 1973).

24. Mathew Dumont, *The Absurd Healer* (New York:
    Viking, 1968), p. 60.

25. Suanna J. Wilson, *Confidentiality in Social Work:
    Issues and Principles* (New York: Free Press, 1978),
    pp. 116–17.

26. Ibid., p. 121.

27. Alfred Kadushin, *Child Welfare Services,* 3d ed.
    (New York: Macmillan, 1980).

28. "Standards for the Accreditation of Baccalaureate
    Degree Programs in Social Work" (New York:
    Council on Social Work Education, 1974), p. 13.

29. Ibid., pp. 13–14.

30. *Summary Information on Master of Social Work Pro-
    grams: 1975* (New York: Council on Social Work
    Education, 1975).

31. "Where Jobs Will Be in 1980s," *U.S. News & World
    Report,* October 15, 1979, p. 76.

32. Ibid., p. 76.

33. Sheldon Siegel, *Social Service Manpower Needs: An
    Overview to 1980* (New York: Council on Social
    Work Education, 1975), p. 10.

34. Glasser, *Identity Society.*

35. Merlin Manley, "How to Cope with a Sense of
    Failure," in *Personal Problem Solver,* ed. Charles
    Zastrow and Dae Chang (Englewood Cliffs, N.J.:
    Prentice-Hall, 1977), pp. 35–45.

GUSTAFSON

chapter 3

A social worker employed in a correctional setting attends a 20-year high school class reunion. At this social event, the social worker introduces herself as a probation and parole agent and describes her job as supervision of legal offenders and providing counseling or casework services. During the course of the evening the social worker meets lawyers, members of the clergy, teachers, barbers, dentists, stewardesses, real estate agents, insurance agents, bartenders, business people, and so on.

General questions in this conversational setting arise such as:

If you work with people in solving problems, what is the difference between your job and that of a psychiatrist, a psychiatric nurse, or a sociologist?

If you discuss problems with people, what is the difference between your job and that of a minister or a teacher?

* This chapter was written for this text by Robert Scheurell, associate professor and coordinator of the undergraduate social work program, School of Social Welfare, University of Wisconsin—Milwaukee.

If you listen to other people complain, what is the difference between your job and that of a bartender or a friendly neighbor or a relative?

If you make decisions to arrest people and send them to prison, what is the difference between your job and that of a law enforcement official or a judge?

If you provide financial counseling and prepare budgets, what is the difference between your job and that of a financial counselor, a home economist, or a welfare worker?

The list of questions raised could easily be expanded. All of these questions however have two central themes:

1. Where does a specific service occupation fit into the network of a large number of service occupations?
2. What makes a specific service occupation unique from other service occupations?

The focus of this chapter is on exploration, elaboration, and explication of the above two central themes.

Human services and helping professions: A problem of identity*

A wide variety of human services at one location

SERVICE ECONOMY OF THE UNITED STATES

In 1965 Victor Fuchs stated:

> This country [United States] is pioneering in a new state of economic development. We are now in a "Service Economy," that is, we are the first nation in the history of the world in which more than half of the employed population is not involved in the production of food, clothing, housing, automobiles, and other tangible goods.[1]

The above quotation is both a definition of a service economy as well as a prophetic statement of the immediate economic trends with consequent reorganization of our social structure. It is a definition in the sense that a service economy means more than one half

of the employed population is in service industries, and prophetic in the sense that the statistics for employment in the service sector have rapidly increased since Fuchs made the statement in 1965. When Fuchs made the above statement, 54.8 percent of the work force were employed in service industries. By 1976 this percentage had increased to 67.8 percent, and it is projected at 71 percent for 1985.[2]

Recently the literature in the field of social welfare is beginning to reflect the terminology of a service society. The following terms are appearing in a number of texts: *human services*[3], *service economics*[4], *helping professions*[5], *and the relationship of social work to the human services*[6]. In essence there has been a book explosion on various aspects of the service economy. Yet, few of these books provide an overview of human services as they primarily focus either on the helping professions or on the concept of a service economy.

Service economy and social organization

All societies have a social structure, and this social structure is related to the structure of the economic system. *Social organization* has been defined by Olsen as "the process of merging social actors into ordered social relationships which become infused with cultural ideas."[7] As people continue to interact with others, social organization gradually develops through the process of establishing rules, norms, and values to guide behavior.

A brief example may be helpful in describing the process of social organization. A group of 10 children meeting for the first time elect to play a game. Only two of the children know the rules of the game. Consequently one can observe that half the time is spent in explaining the game by the two children who already know the game to the other children; one quarter of the time is spent in playing the game, and one quarter of the time is spent debating the rules of the game. If these 10 met only this one time, you could say they spent most of their time trying to get organized. If these same 10 children met

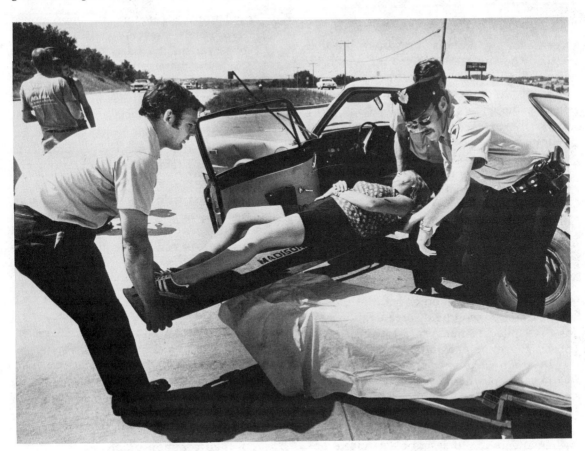

Emergency services following an accident

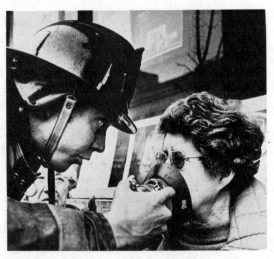

Fire fighter providing first aid during a fire

weekly for two months you would find that perhaps one quarter of their time would be spent debating the rules of the game, and three fourths of their time would be spent in playing the game. By the end of the third week they: (*a*) would have established definite boundaries or rules of the game, (*b*) would have developed a value system for the game, and (*c*) would have precedents to handle decision making. Through observing, you could predict which children are likely to rebel against the rules. In effect, at a microlevel (low order of abstraction) these 10 children would have developed some form of social organization.

Social organization can be viewed from a high order of abstraction or point of interest (for example, a worldwide organization such as the United Nations) to a lower order of abstraction or point of interest (for example, a small group such as a family). There are a variety of analytical constructs to describe social organization. The model used here is that of Olsen in *The Process of Social Organization*.[8] This model is particularly useful when attempting to describe a service econ-

omy, since the language and concepts used are compatible with those used by individuals who describe human services.[9]

Marvin Olsen in describing levels of social organization developed a classification of social organization from a low order of abstraction to a high order of abstraction, using characteristics such as definable boundaries, observable structure, stability over time, unique culture, size of grouping, complexity or subspecialization, and degree of formalness.[10]

The typology of social organization described by Olsen from a low order of abstraction to a high order of abstraction is as follows:[11]

> Population: a category of unorganized individuals that is identified by an observer on the basis of one or more common characteristics (this characteristic does not constitute a social organization in and of itself, but provides the potential for social organization).
>
> Aggregation (collectivity): a social organization that is relatively spontaneous in origin, temporary in duration, and minimally organized.
>
> Social class: a loosely ordered and unified social organization, based upon similarities of power, privilege and prestige; or conversely, the lack of these characteristics.
>
> Group: a social organization whose members know and identify with each other personality as individuals.
>
> Family: a social group further characterized by a kinship (blood or marriage) relationship among its members.
>
> Community: a social organization that is territorially localized and through which its members satisfy most of their daily needs and deal with most of their common problems.

Association: a social organization that is more or less purposefully created for the attainment of relatively specific and limited goals. The four major types of associations are: *business, mutual aid, service,* and *commonweal.*

Network: a functionally specialized social organization that links together numerous associations, groups, and other types of organizations throughout a society, all of which are interrelated through their concern with a common set of activities. Examples are: economic, political, religious, military, education, social welfare, family. (Note: the terms *network* and *social institution* are used interchangeably.)

Society: a broadly inclusive social organization that possesses both functional and cultural autonomy which dominates all other types of social organization.

Confederation: a loosely organized combination of relatively autonomous societies which cooperate in some joint activities without relinquishing their separate sovereignties.

Web of organizations: organizations that overlap and interlock with each other, forming a gigantic social web. The totality of this web is human experience. The concept of "web or organizations" as a social organization represents the observable fact that many types of social organizations are interrelated.

The classification system used by Olsen is not mutually exclusive, since an individual or group would belong to one or more levels of social organization simultaneously. For analytical purposes, however, one chooses specific levels of social organization for exploration of certain observable facts or explication of observable facts. The focus of our concern is those categories of social organization which relate to service economics and human services. Therefore, our primary concern is with those categories of social organizations called networks and associations. Figure 3–1 shows schematically the levels of

FIGURE 3–1 Schema of social organizations

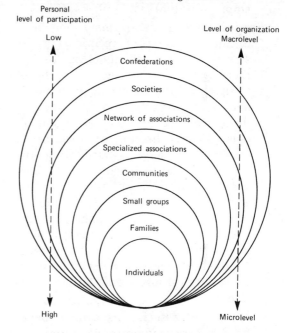

social organization beginning with "individuals" and ending with the macrolevel of "confederations."

Using the classification of Olsen in describing social organizations the two most useful categories in relationship to service economics are network and association.

The concept network as previously defined refers to a functionally specialized social organization that links together numerous associations which have a common set of activities. Therefore, one can refer to the economic network, religious network, political network, education network, and so on.

Networks in general consist of four major types of associations:[12]

Business associations: primary benefit is making money for the owners (for example, private industry).

Mutual benefit associations: primary benefit is to its own members (for example, a union).

Service associations: primary benefit is to the consumer or recipient of the service. These associations can be further classified into: tertiary (services focusing on the provision of domestic and quasi-domestic products such as those provided by a barber, cosmetologist, funeral director, or stewardess); quarternary (services facilitating the division of labor—such as those provided by airline, railroad, shipping, and trucking personnel); quinary (services focusing on changing or improving the recipient's lifestyle such as those of premarital and marital counseling vocational rehabilitation, sensitivity groups, and public welfare).

Commonweal associations: primary benefit is to serve the entire community or society (fire fighting, law enforcement and military).*

Service industries and human services

As indicated in an earlier section, service industries account for the majority of employed individuals in the United States. The

major categories of service industries according to the U.S. Department of Labor are:[13]

Transportation and public utility.

Trade.

Finance, insurance, and real estate.

Services (e.g., health care and auto maintenance).

Government, including military.

Obviously, not all of these categories have people problem solving as their primary goal.

The definitional problem is to differentiate human service industries and related occupations from the other part of service industries. Gersuney's classification of service association is a starting point for the differentiation of human services from other service areas.[14] Gersuney classified service associations into three types:

Tertiary: includes restaurants, hotels, barber and beauty shops, laundry and dry cleaning establishments, home repair and maintenance, handicrafts performed in the home, and other domestic or quasi-domestic services.

Quarternary: includes transportation, commerce, communication, finance and administration; services that facilitate the division of labor.

Quinary: includes health care, education and recreation; services designed to change and improve the recipient in some way.

The quinary sector of service associations closely approximates the goal of human services: "to change and/or improve the recipient in some way." Therefore those service industries which generally fall into the category of tertiary or quarternary services (domestic and quasi-domestic, trade, transportation, finance) are not part of human services. Gersuney fur-

---

* A specific group may belong to one or more associations since many groups have multiple goals. For example, consider the following activities of law enforcement: the social control function is a commonweal association; their crisis intervention programs constitute a service association; and police unions are mutual benefit associations. The categories of associations are not mutually exclusive, but do provide a conceptual mechanism to view society.

Police officer aiding an apparent heart attack victim

ther classifies the quinary sector of services into the following four types:[15]

Life-cycle services: services designed to facilitate passage from one stage to another; such as premarital counseling, death and dying institutes.

Occupational opportunity services: services designed to create new or expanded job opportunities; such as the educational system, affirmative action and vocational rehabilitation.

Alteration of self-services: services designed to enhance or create personal behavior change such as gestalt groups, psychiatric treatment.

Problem-oriented services: services designed to handle specific problems and hopefully enable the individual to resolve or overcome them; such as public welfare and corrections.

A common theme which pervades the classification of services used by Gersuney is that the quinary sector of services essentially focuses on people to people contact (counseling, therapy) versus people to things (TV repairer, mechanic) and people to data (finance, insurance). A beginning differentiation of human services from other service occupations is the concept people to people.

Human services. Human services can be defined as those systems of services and

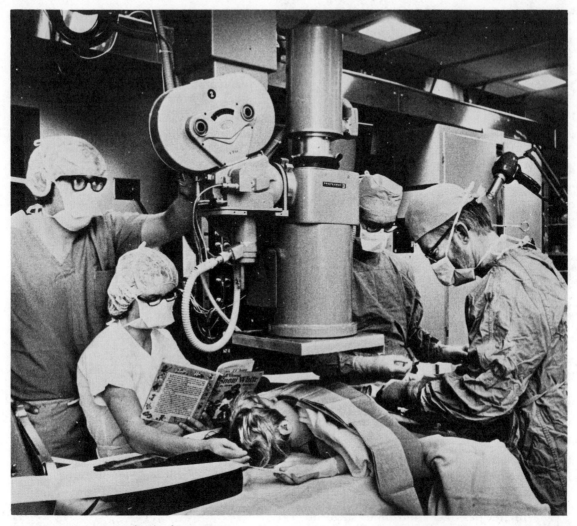

Physicians and a nurse performing heart surgery

allied occupations and professions which concentrate on improving or maintaining the physical, mental health, and the general well-being of individuals, groups or communities in our society. Human services would include those services which provide:

1. Protection (law enforcement, courts, corrections, public health, fire control, housing codes).

2. Personal services (counseling, therapy, rehabilitation, substitute care).
3. Information and advising (consulting, education, consumer affairs, librarian).
4. Maintenance services (public welfare, social security, child care).

Figure 3–2 presents a further listing of these four human service categories.

FIGURE 3–2   Sample network of human service systems which affect an individual*

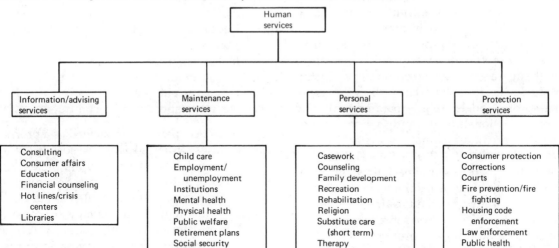

* This schema of a network of human services is useful for analytical purposes and assumes that a service system may provide more than one form of service. The correctional system which has a primary goal of protection also includes elements of: (*a*) personal services (casework, therapy); (*b*) information/advising services (consulting, crisis centers, education) as well as (*c*) maintenance services (institutions). For a more detailed listing of these four human service categories, see Alfred Kahn, *Social Policy and Social Services* (New York: Random House, 1973), pp. 12–34.

A bartender listening to a person's troubles

Alfred Kahn indicates there is a tendency to use the term *human services* for what in the past has been called *social welfare*.[16] Actually, *human services* is a broader term than *social welfare* as it includes services that are usually not considered social welfare services; such as library, law enforcement, housing code enforcement, consumer protection, and fire prevention and fire fighting. As indicated in Chapter 1, the term *social welfare* is more limited as it focuses on resolving social problems.

HUMAN SERVICES AND HELPING PROFESSIONS

The focus in the prior sections of this chapter has been on service industries and systems of service. The concern as one further discusses human services is: who does what in which service system? In some parts of the human service system there is little development of professionalism (for example, fire fighting) and in other areas a high development of professionalism (medicine). Where a profession exists, there is usually a high degree of specialization (eye doctor, nose doctor, foot doctor) as well as the use of paraprofessionals (e.g., paramedics) and nonprofessionals (e.g., candy striper; that is, a volunteer in a hospital who is a "friendly visitor" to patients). Professions and occupations today are highly specialized horizontally (by problem or task) and vertically (by degree of training and education). Table 3–1 shows examples of horizontal and vertical specialization for the professions of law, medicine, social work, and theology.

The term *profession* is usually assigned to an occupation which requires a high degree of mental activity with decision-making functions and usually requires academic and experiential training.* For example, a physician is expected to make a diagnosis and decide which treatment technique to use. A person becomes a physician after a period of academic training and a period of internship. In contrast, a volunteer in a hospital is not expected to make major decisions, has not had academic training, and has not had a period of internship.

A common method for looking at professions and professionalism is to describe the attributes of a profession and then look at a specific occupation to see whether it possesses a number of these attributes. In general, a profession has the following characteristics:

1. Has professional organization and culture.
2. Has a specialized body of knowledge.
3. Has an ethical code and a sense of altruism.
4. Requires intellectual (university) training.
5. Is service oriented.
6. Has autonomy.
7. Has a system of self-regulation.
8. Develops specialized techniques.

Which occupations are viewed as a profession varies from society to society, and within societies, depending upon the degree of sanction, autonomy, and prestige given to a specific occupation. Generally in our society, law, medicine, and theology are considered professions without question. These three occupational groups have a long history dating back to pre-Christian days. Most other groups considered to be professions are either specializations of the original three professions or have developed since 1900.*[17]

The *Encyclopedia of Careers and Vocational Guidance* (1975) lists 75 occupations as professions.[18] Of these 75 occupations, 39 can be considered by the prior definition of human services to be human service professions or have human service potential. These are: anthropologist, architect, chiropractor, clergyperson, college placement officer, dentist, dietician, economist, historian, home economist, guidance counselor, hospital administrator, lawyer, librarian, medical records technician, occupational therapist, optometrist, osteopath, personnel worker, physical therapist, pharmacist, physician, podiatrist, political scientist, psychologist, public relations agent, recreation leader, registered nurse, rehabilitation counselor, school counselor, social worker, sociologist, speech pathologist and audiologist, teacher (kindergarten/elementary), teacher (secondary),

---

* Note: For a nonsophisticated overview of occupations and professions, see William Hopke, *Encyclopedia of Careers and Vocational Guidance,* vol. 2 (Chicago: J. G. Ferguson and Company, 1975).

* Note: Everett Hughes in *Education for the Professions of Medicine, Law, Theology and Social Welfare* (New York: McGraw-Hill, 1973) compares and contrasts law, medicine, social work, and theology as professions.

TABLE 3–1   Some examples of horizontal and vertical specialization of occupational groupings

Vertical specialization by degree of professionalization or training	Horizontal specialization (speciality by problem or task) by occupational grouping			
	Law	Medicine	Social work	Theology
Professional Ph.D., M.S., or B.S. degrees, depending upon profession	Corporate law Criminal law International law Maritime law Tax law	Internist Neurological surgeon Obstetrics/ gynecology Orthopedics Psychiatry	Correctional social work Community planner Psychiatric social work School social work	Minister Priest Rabbi
Paraprofessional A.A. degrees, special training	Court stenographer Legal secretary Paralegal aide	Laboratory technician Paramedic Operating room assistant X-ray technician	Case aide Child care worker Correctional officer (guard) School aide	Lay deacon Lay Sunday school directors
Volunteer No special training except orientation sessions	Intake aide Research aide	Candy striper Friendly visitor Home visitor	Hot lines Housecoping Volunteers in probation	Advisory board members Sunday School teachers Youth activity leaders

teacher (university), urban planner, and vocational counselor.

Professions which represent academic social sciences such as anthropology, economics, political science, and sociology are included in the above list since they have applied aspects that relate to solving problems. Professions such as architect, librarian, medical records technician, and urban planner are included since there is potential for human services work as part of their tasks.

Although these professions have human service elements, not all of them are considered to be a helping profession. A *helping profession* is one which assists persons with a spectrum of problems through direct personal contact, according to a recent conference on social welfare education.[19] Using the above definition, this conference listed the following helping professions.[20]

Education.

Health.

Home economics.

Law.

Ministry.

Police science.

Social welfare/social work.

Combining the above definition of helping professions with the classification of professions as utilized in the *Encyclopedia of Careers and Vocational Guidance* and the characteristics of "explicitly relational and interpersonal," we can describe the following occupations as helping professions:

Anthropologist, chiropractor, clergyperson, college placement officer, dentist, economist, home economist, guidance counselor, law enforcement officer, lawyer, occupa-

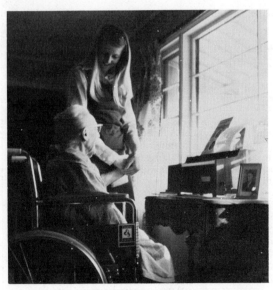

A homemaker helping an elderly person to live independently

tional therapist, osteopath, personnel worker, physical therapist, physician, podiatrist, political scientist, psychologist, recreation leader, registered nurse, rehabilitation counselor, school counselor, social worker, sociologist, speech pathologist and audiologist, teacher (kindergarten/elementary), teacher (secondary), teacher (college), and vocational counselor. Of the 39 professions which could be considered as human services, 29 could be considered helping professions or having helping profession potential, such as the academic areas of anthropology, economics, political science, and sociology.

Commonality of the helping professions

If the helping professions are unique from other professions, we should be able to delineate some unique or distinctive characteristics. The author's contention is that there are some unique characteristics to the helping professions (which provide a common

element for all of them) and these can be categorized as structural and interactional.*

Some common *structural characteristics* of organizations and systems which provide services in the helping professions are as follows:

1. A commitment to providing service. Both the professional organization and the operational organization will have written policies or statements which indicate that providing service is their reason to be. The Code of Ethics for the National Association of Social Workers contains a statement on "commitment to service" and the stated purpose of most correctional agencies is "protection of society and *rehabilitation of the offender*." Similar statements can be found in the Code of Ethics of the American Medical Association, American Bar Associations, in hospitals, and in courts.

2. A dependent clientele. Since individuals, groups or larger social units come to the expert (voluntarily or in some cases involuntarily) to have problems solved, they usually depend upon the expert to make recommendations or decisions. Therefore the relationship between the provider or purveyor of a service and person seeking service is one of dominance and submission. A person normally accepts with resignation and compliance the diagnosis and recommendation of a physician, and will submit to an arrest by a police officer. In the educational system, chil-

---

* Note: The distinction between structural and interactional attributes is based upon an earlier paper by Robert Scheurell entitled "Social Network: A Salient Approach for Social Work." *Wisconsin Sociologist*, Spring/Summer, 1972. Structural attributes refer to those which characterize the organization or system for the delivery of services, and interactional attributes refer to those which characterize the personnel who provide services.

dren will usually accept the teacher as "the authority."

3. Institutionalized referral system. Most helping professional organizations do not heavily advertise to seek clients. Instead clients come to them through other agencies, general knowledge, or informal resources. State prisons do not advertise their services or use public relations techniques to attract inmates and patients. Their clientele are sent to them by other agencies after having gone through a rather elaborate process, for example, arrest, court hearing, conviction.

4. Credentialing process. Most helping professions have a fairly rigid classification system of work activity based upon education and degrees ranging from Ph.D. through M.S., B.S., associate degrees and high school education. Table 3–1 provides examples of credentialism.

5. Specialization. The helping professions have a high degree of specialization (the vertical and horizontal specializations referred to earlier), partly as a consequence of: (a) the credentialing process, (b) the variety of different tasks to be performed and (c) the breadth of knowledge needed. For example, there are 32 medical specialties and at least 11 social work specialties.

6. Generally operate through large organizations. Many services are implemented through large-scale bureaucracies such as hospitals, mental institutions, and public welfare departments. Even when the service is provided through a smaller unit there is still a well-organized and at times a ritual-like atmosphere in obtaining services.

7. Parallelism of services. Many people are aware that a number of services are provided through a dual system (at times duplicative and competitive) of public and private services. Actually, there is a third competing system, which for a lack of a better term, I label the folk system. The folk system is an informal one such as friends, neighbors, relatives, and also includes nonsanctioned forms of service such as voodoo, and medicine men. An example of parallel systems in medicine and law enforcement follows:

	Medicine	Law enforcement
Public system.....	County hospital	City or state police
Private system....	Private hospital	Merchants' police
Folk systems......	Medicine men	Vigilante group

8. Role clusters. Helping professionals find themselves filling certain role clusters although the way they perform in these roles will vary from profession to profession. Some common role clusters are: enabler, supporter, detector, broker, advocater, mobilizer, instructor, behavior changer, restorative, information processor, administrator, care giver, consultant, rule maker, rule implementor.[21]

Some common interactional characteristics of the providers of services are as follows:

1. Adherence to a problem-solving process model. Depending upon different authors, the steps involved in the problem-solving process model vary from five to seven. The basic steps in the problem-solving process are:
   a. Defining the problem situation.
   b. Determining causes of or conditions associated with the specific problem.
   c. Determining the possible approaches or treatment plan to solving the specific problem.

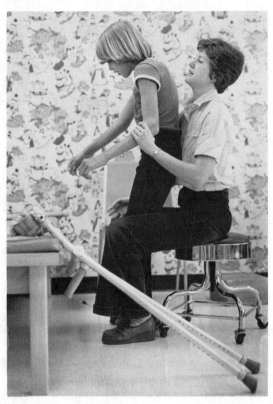

A physical therapist working with a young client who has cerebral palsy

Counseling by a clergyman in a prison

    d. Determining the most feasible approach or treatment plan to solve the specific problem.

    e. Applying the selected approach or treatment plan to the specific problem.

    f. Evaluating the effectiveness of the approach or treatment plan in solving the specific problem.

2. Communication skills, both verbal and nonverbal. These skills involve those of observation, recording, reporting, speaking, writing, and interviewing. The person should have an understanding of verbal and nonverbal communication as well as a sense of timing and affect in talking with people.

3. Development of a relationship. The helping professional relies on person to person interaction and relationship skills in helping a person with a problem.

    The helping process essentially has three parts:

    a. Establishment of a relationship between the person seeking help and the person offering or providing help.

    b. Use of the relationship as a medium of help which includes aspects of determination of reality, empathetic listening and talking, and provision for emotional support.

    In using a relationship as a medium of help some of the following characteristics are found in the process: mutual discussion, some unpleasantness, specific in purpose, offers something new, has an element of choice, is nonjudgmental, and occurs in the present (the interview situation).

4. Ethos and professional commitment. Professionals have a code of ethics guiding their behavior and their sense of com-

mitment in providing services to the clients.[22]

Table 3–2 compares the four professions of law, medicine, social work, and theology in some of the common interactional characteristics.

Differences among the helping professions

Although there are some common characteristics which delineate helping professions from other human service professions, it is obvious there are differences between them. If there were no differences there would be no need for the multiplicity and proliferation of the helping professions.

Undoubtedly there are many ways in which one can compare and contrast professions. The model presented here assumes five basic distinctions among professions; the knowledge base, value base, interventive

repertoire, historical precedent and problem focus.

Knowledge base. Depending upon the helping profession, the underlying knowledge base may be in social science, natural science, philosophy, or a combination. Within the knowledge base there again is a concentration on whether the material is in technique, understanding people, a specialized area, and so on.

For most professions only part of the knowledge base is learned in the university or academic training. The remainder of one's knowledge is learned through internship programs, field training, and later learning through experience.

Value base. Each helping profession has a code of ethics which articulates the values. Printed code of ethics for the helping professions sound remarkably the same, that is,

TABLE 3–2 Examples of common interactional characteristics of four professions

	Profession			
Common elements	Medicine	Law	Theology	Social work
Problem-solving process model	a. Information b. Diagnosis c. Treatment plan d. Treatment e. Follow-up	a. Information b. Case or legal precedent c. Debate case d. Decision e. Follow-up	a. Information b. Theological or moral precedent c. Suggest alternatives d. Follow-up	a. Define problem b. Find cause c. Treatment plan d. Treatment e. Evaluation
Communication skills	Information Action/reaction and some interaction	Information Action/reaction and some interaction	Information and behavior modification type Transaction and interaction	Information and behavior modification type Transaction and interaction
Development of a relationship	Specific, short-term, objective	Specific, short-term, objective	General, long-term, objective and specific, short-term, objective	Specific, long-term, objective and specific, short-term, objective
Ethos and professional commitment	See American Medical Association Code of Ethics	See American Bar Association Code of Ethics	See specific denominations' code of ethics	See National Association of Social Workers Code of Ethics

TABLE 3–3 Examples of differences among four professional groupings

Difference elements	Professional groupings			
	Medicine	*Law*	*Theology*	*Social work*
Knowledge base	Nature science Physiology Anatomy Pathology	Philosophy Social science/legal precedent Civil law Criminal law System of justice	Theology Philosophical principles Morality	Social science Human development Cultural variation Methods of interaction
Value base	Humans as a physical system contract diseases Concern is pathology and does not focus on the value of the individual	Humans as social animals have conflicts over rights Basic concern is justice and does not focus on the value of the person	Humans are good but commit errors Concern is the whole person	Humans are good Individuality and understand whole person
Interventive repertoire	Surgery Drugs Advice	Case analysis Advice Information	Counseling Advice Information Prayer	Casework, which may include psychotherapy Group work Community organization
Historical precedent	Pre-3000 B.C.	Pre-3000 B.C.	Since humankind existed	Since 1900
Problem focus	Physical problems	Legal problems	Moral problems	Social problems
Predominant role clustering	Restoration	Advocate	Supporter	Behavior changer

service oriented, client comes first, objectivity, and so on. However, as one investigates the code of ethics and value base in more detail one can detect differences in value assumptions regarding humans, the role of the professional, and area of concern (that is, whole person or specific problem).

Interventive repertoire. All helping professionals intervene in problems. Examples of interventive techniques range from legal precedent, chemotherapy and surgery, psychotherapy, to moral advising the admonition. The style and range of intervention activities will vary depending on the profession's knowledge and value base.

Historical precedent. Most individuals have a perception that the professions which exist have been in existence for a long time. The actual fact is that only three professions were recognized prior to 1900. These were law, medicine, and theology. Each of these professions have been in existence since about 3000 B.C. or earlier. However, university training for medicine and law is rather recent (since 1850). Theology as a profession has been at the university level since the Middle Ages.

A social worker counseling a couple

Problem focus. This attribute is an intuitive one in the sense that we can classify professions in terms of the specific concerns they concentrate on. For example; law-legal problems; medicine-health problems; social work-social problems; and theology-significance-of-self problems. There is some overlap of problem focus for the professions; however, the problem focus aspect clearly differentiates between certain helping professions.

Predominate role clustering. Roles for specific helping professions will vary depending upon the specialization within the profession. For example; in law a key role is that of advocate, in medicine a key role is that of restoration, in social work a key role is behavior changer, and in theology a key role is supporter. (These role differences among the four exemplary helping professions are only examples of role differences. The reader cannot assume these are the only role differences, or that the other helping professions do not engage in these roles).

Table 3–3 compares and contrasts the professions of medicine, law, theology, and social work on the characteristics above, which delineate differences among the helping professions.

SUMMARY

This chapter began with a concern about how to identify and classify service occupations and how to differentiate between human services and helping professions. The themes for the chapter are the location of service industries within our society's economic network, the location of human services within service industries, and finally the location of helping professions within the human services.

A brief analysis of the work force in 1976

showed 67.8 percent of those employed were working in service industries, which clearly shows our society has become a "service economy." The concepts of service economies and service industries were then related to a definitional process of differentiating human services from the general concept of service industries.

A definition of *human services* was developed: *those systems of services and allied occupations and professions which concentrate on maintaining the physical, mental health and the general well being of individuals, groups or communities in our societies.* It was noted that *human services* is a broader term than social welfare; human services encompasses all social welfare services, and also includes additional services such as fire fighting and library services.

The remaining definitional problem was to take the concept of human services and specify those professions which could be called helping professions. Characteristics of a profession were described and the following definition of a *helping profession* was developed: *a profession which assists persons with a spectrum of problems through direct personal contact.* Figure 3–3 is a schema of the analysis between service industries, human services, helping professions, and social work.

Having through a circuitous route finally defined helping professions, the next question was: What are the commonalities and differences between helping professions? Common characteristics of helping professions include structural and interactional attributes. *Structural characteristics* include commitment to service, dependent clientele, institutionalized referal system, credentialing process, specialization, large organizations, parallelism of services, and role clusters. *Interactional characteristics* include adherence to a problem-solving model, communication skills, development of relationships, a professional ethos.

Differences among the professions are a consequence of knowledge base, value base, interventive repertoire, historical precedent, problem focus, and predominate role clustering. Based upon the information contained in the chapter and using the charts on com-

FIGURE 3–3 Schema of the relationship between service industries and the helping professions

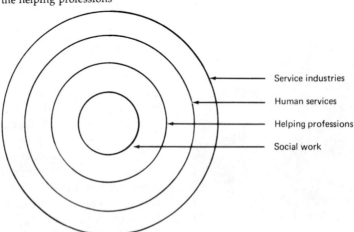

parison of professions you should be able to answer the two questions posed in the beginning:

1. Where does a specific service occupation or profession fit into the scheme of a service society?
2. What makes a specific occupation or profession differ from another?

NOTES

1. Victor Fuchs, "The Growing Importance of Service Industries," Occasional Paper no. 96 (New York: National Bureau of Economic Research, 1965), p. 1.

2. U.S. Department of Labor, *Occupational Outlook Handbook, 1978–79 ed.* (Washington, D.C.: Government Printing Office, 1978), p. 14.

3. See Joan Wright and William Burmeister, *Introduction to Human Services* (Columbus, Ohio: Grid Inc., 1973); Joan Chenault, *Human Services Education and Practice: An Organic Model* (New York: Human Services Press, 1975; Robert Vidaver, *Developments in Human Services Education and Manpower* (New York: Behavioral Publications, 1973; Evelyn Schulman, *Intervention in Human Services* (St. Louis: C. B. Mosely, 1974); Karin Eriksen, *Human Services Today* (Reston, Va.: Reston Publishing, 1977).

4. Victor Fuchs, "Productivity Differences within the Service Sector," Occasional Paper (New York: National Bureau of Economic Research, 1967); Victor Fuchs, *The Service Economy* (New York: National Bureau of Economic Research, 1968); Victor Fuchs, *Production and Productivity in the Service Industries* (New York: National Bureau of Economic Research, 1969); Alan Gartner and Frank Riesman, *Service Society and the Consumer Vanguard* (New York: Harper & Row, 1974); Carl Gersuney and William Rosengren, *The Service Society* (Cambridge, Mass.: Schenkman Publishing, 1973); Daniel Bell, *The Coming of the Post-Industrial Society* (New York: Basic Books, 1973).

5. Paul Halmoss, *Personal Service Society* (Scheoken Press, 1970; Murray Levine and Adeline Levine, *Social History of Helping Services: A Clinic, Court, School and Community* (Englewood Cliffs, N.J.: Prentice-Hall, 1970); Lawrence Brammer, *The Helping Relationship: Process and Skills* (New York: Columbia University Press, 1973); State University of New York at Buffalo, School of Social Welfare, *Proceedings, Conference on Education for Social Welfare* (New York: State University of New York at Buffalo, 1970).

6. Alfred Kahn, *Shaping the New Social Work* (New York: Columbia University Prss, 1973); Alfred Kahn, *Social Policy and Social Services* (New York: Random House, 1973); Elaine Cummings, *Systems of Regulation* (New York: Athenon Press, 1968); Naomi Brill, *Teamwork: Working Together in the Human Services* (New York: Lippincott, 1976); James Dugger, *The New Professional: Introduction for the Human Services/Mental Health Worker* (Monterey, Calif.: Brooks Co., 1975); Everett Hughes, *Education for the Profession of Medicine, Law, Theology, and Social Welfare* (New York: McGraw-Hill, 1973).

7. Marvin Olsen, *The Process of Social Organization* (New York: Holt, Rinehart & Winston, 1968), p. 1.

8. Ibid., pp. 10–103.

9. See, for example, Gersuney and Rosengren, *Service Society,* pp 5–6.

10. Olsen, *Process of Social Organization,* pp. 64–84.

11. Ibid., pp. 86–102.

12. Gersuney and Rosengren, *Service Society,* p. 6.

13. U.S. Department of Labor, *Occupational Outlook Handbook, 1976–1977 ed.,* p. 14.

14. Gersuney and Rosengren, *Service Society,* p. 5.

15. Ibid., p. 6.

16. Kahn, *Shaping the New Social Work,* p. 10.

17. See Hughes, *Education for the Professions,* for a detailed analysis of these four professions, including a brief history.

18. William Hopke, *Encyclopedia of Careers and Vocational Guidance, vol. 2, Careers and Occupations* (Chicago: J. G. Ferguson, 1975), pp. i–ii.

19. State University of New York at Buffalo, p. 42.

20. Ibid., pp. 44–45.

21. This conceptualization of the structural characteristics of helping professions and role clustering is a composite of characteristics from a variety of sources, such as Gersuney and Rosengren, *Service Society,* pp. 7–16. Alan Gartner and Riesman, *Service Society and Consumer Vanguard,* pp. 20–30, Olsen, *Process of Social Organization,* pp. 64–84 and Ronald Federico, *The Social Welfare Institution: An Introduction,* 2d ed. (Lexington, Mass.: D. C. Heath, 1976), pp. 87–97.

22. In conceptualizing the interactional characteristics, I have heavily used Federico, *Social Welfare,* pp. 236–44, and Evelyn Schulman *Intervention in Human Services* (St. Louis: C. B. Mosley, 1974), pp. 1–30.

GUSTAFSON

part two

Social problems and social services

chapter **4**

The hurt of being poor

"You mean you want to take a look at a hillbilly!"

Homer Burleigh, 33 [and] immobile with resentment, blocked the doorway of his flat. Like 20,000 other Southern whites living in . . . Chicago's Uptown, he had his pride, his problems, and an innate suspicion of the Eastern city slicker.

Homer Burleigh finds it hard to stay angry for long and he led the way inside. Four of his five children, ages two, three, five, and seven (a ten-year-old boy was still in school), ran about in bare feet, dressed only in underpants. Mrs. Burleigh, a wan, hard, very pregnant woman, also was barefooted. . . .

He walked into a small kitchen, sat down, . . . and sighed. He was in trouble and he knew it. . . . Homer Burleigh was penniless, about to be evicted, maybe even jailed. Much of this was his own fault, the panicked response to crises. . . . Homer Burleigh made mistakes when the margin of safety with which he had to live permitted no mistakes whatever. . . .

. . . the last of the final welfare payment had been spent and in four days he was to be evicted for nonpayment of rent.

"If the arm continues this way, and if they don't give me assistance, I'm going to have to put the kids in a home." His eyes filled. . . .

And so the lines of failure seemed to converge for Homer Burleigh: a motherless home full of contention, almost no formal education, an impoverished landscape to grow in with no hope for a young man, . . . a drifting of life without need for the consequences of more children. But he was not an evil man, or a lazy one. His was simply the fragile vessel of endemic poverty, never strong enough to withstand a prolonged storm. And his children seemed doomed to go forth in a similarly brittle craft.[1]

Poverty is relative to time and place

Poverty is still our number one social welfare problem, partly because of the number of people affected, and partly because it is interrelated with nearly every other social problem.

An encouraging trend is that the number of people below the poverty line is decreasing. For the first time in human history, the poor are a minority in this country; prior to

Poverty and public welfare

the 20th century the bulk of the population lived in poverty. In 1937 President Franklin D. Roosevelt stated, "I see one third of a nation ill-housed, ill-clad, ill-nourished."[2] In 1962, the President's Council of Economic Advisers estimated that 35 million people—or one fifth of the nation—were in poverty.[3] Now (1980) about 11 percent of the nation, 25 million people, are estimated to be below the poverty line.[4]

Poverty is relative to time and place. Those labeled poor today would certainly not be poor by the standards of 1850, nor would they be viewed as poor by the standards existing in India, or in other underdeveloped countries. In the 1890s no one felt particularly poor if they did not have electric lights, yet today a family without electricity is usually considered to be poor.

Defining poverty is a policy problem

In spite of all of the time spent on poverty research, we as yet have not agreed on how to define poverty. A family of four living on a farm who earns $6,000 per year may not view themselves as being "poverty stricken"; especially if they have no rent to pay, are able to grow much of their own food, and are frugal and creative in securing essential needs. On the other hand, a family of four that earns $7,000 per year in a city which has a high cost of living may be deeply in debt, especially if they have high rent and unexpected medical bills. The feeling of being impoverished is more apt to occur in cities because of the obvious displays of affluence. The real "hurt" of poverty occurs from the *feeling* that lack of financial resources is preventing one from having equal opportunities and from the *feeling*, then, that one is a second-class citizen. Poverty hurts most when it leads one to view oneself as inferior or second class. Psychological definitions of poverty, however, are seldom used because

of the difficulty in determining who are affected.

The usual definitions of poverty are based on a lack of money. Income per year is the measure most commonly used. There are two general approaches: the absolute and the relative.

The absolute approach deems a certain amount of goods and services are essential to an individual's or a family's welfare. Those who do not have this minimum amount are viewed as poor. The fundamental problem with this approach is that there is no agreement as to what constitutes "minimum" needs. In 1973, for example, the National Welfare Rights Organization, an advocate group for welfare recipients, calculated $7,200 a year was required to provide the basic economic needs of a family of four; the official federal government standard of poverty was $4,540; and the state of Mississippi set the level at $600 per year for a family of four.[5] Depending on the level selected, the number and the percent of the population who are poor are substantially changed, along with the characteristics of those defined as poor.

The relative approach, in essence, states a person is poor when his/her income is substantially less than the average income of the population. For example, anyone in the lowest fifth (or tenth, or fourth) of the population is regarded as poor. By defining poverty in these terms, we avoid having to define absolute needs, and we also put more emphasis on the inequality of incomes. With a relative approach poverty will persist as long as income inequality exists. The major weakness with a relative measure of poverty is that it tells us nothing about how deprived, or how well, the people at the bottom of the income distribution actually live. With poverty measures, ideally, we want to know not only how many people are poor, but also how desperate living conditions are.

The government has chosen to use the absolute approach to defining poverty. In 1979 the government set the minimum amount of money required to sustain a non-farm family of four (that is, the poverty line) at $7,160.[6]

Who are the poor?

Michael Harrington points out the poor are "invisible" in our society; that is, their clothes are not markedly different, our superhighways carry us quickly past dilapidated homes, and the poor are such a heterogeneous group that they are not politically organized to make their needs known.[7]

Although the poor are a heterogeneous group Marilyn Flynn has identified the following social characteristics that have a strong statistical association with poverty:

Female head of household: Nearly 40 percent are poor.

Sex: Seven out of every ten single poor people are women.

Race: One out of every three black persons is poor, compared to one out of ten white persons. Yet, because our nation's population is composed primarily of whites (over 85 percent) most poor people are white (about 66 percent).

Elderly: Forty percent of the elderly (those 65 and older) are poor. One fifth of the total poverty population is 65 or over.

Slums five blocks from the U.S. Capitol in Washington, D.C.

Family size: Larger size families are more apt to be poorer, partly because more income is needed as family size increases. Of the nation's 25 million poor, nearly 10 million are children.

Education: Achieving less than a ninth grade education is a good predictor of extreme poverty. Sixty-seven percent of the very poorest in our society live in families headed by persons who left school before the ninth grade. Completing high school, however, is not a guarantee for adequate wages and avoiding poverty. Achieving a university degree generally is a route to avoid poverty, as only 3 percent of those with a college degree live in poverty.

Employment: Not having a job is, of course, associated with poverty. However, contrary to popular opinion, 43 percent of low income female family heads are employed, and 61 percent of low income male family heads have a job. About a million family heads work 52 weeks a year, yet earn less than the poverty level.

Jobs alone cannot end poverty. About 90 percent of the married men who do not work are disabled, retired, or have an illness. Furthermore, nearly three quarters of unemployed female heads of households are unable to work because of home and family responsibilities.

Geography: A majority of poor people now live in the urban areas of the North and West, particularly in inner city areas. Yet the states in the Deep South still have the highest percent per state of people who are poor, most of whom live on farms or in rural areas. Poverty is also extensive on Indian reservations, in Appalachia, and among seasonal, migrant workers.[8]

What causes poverty?

There are a number of possible causes of being poor:

A high unemployment rate.
Poor physical health.
Physical disabilities.
Emotional problems.
Extensive medical bills.

Alcoholism.
Drug addiction.
Large-size families.
Job displacements due to automation.
Lack of an employable skill.
Low education level.
Female head of household with young children.
No cost of living increases for people on fixed incomes.
Racial discrimination.
Having an "ex-convict" label.
Living in a geographical area where jobs are unavailable.
Divorce, desertion, or death of a spouse.
Gambling.
Budgeting problems and mismanagement of resources.
Sex discrimination.
Being a crime victim.
Having antiwork ethic values.
Underemployment.
Low-paying jobs.
Mental retardation.
Being beyond the age of retirement.

The above list is not exhaustive. However, it serves to show there are: (a) a large number of causes of poverty, (b) eliminating the causes of poverty would require a wide range of social programs, and (c) poverty interacts with almost all other social problems—such as emotional problems, alcoholism, unemployment, racial and sex discrimination, medical problems, crime, gambling, and mental retardation. The interaction between poverty and these other social problems is complicated. As indicated, these other social problems are contributing causes of poverty. Yet, for some social problems, poverty is also a contributing cause of these problems (such as emotional problems, alco-

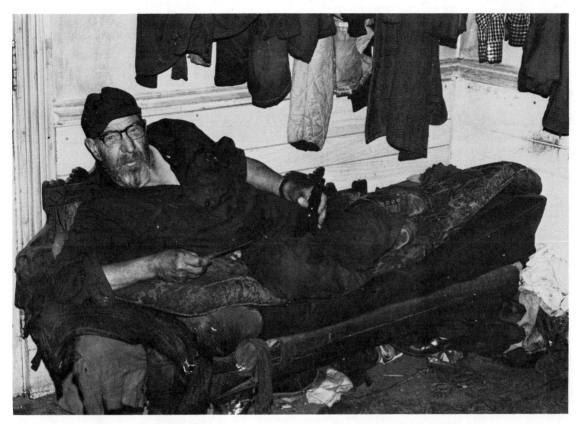

An elderly person living in poverty

holism, and unemployment). And, being poor intensifies the effects (the hurt) of all social problems.

To some extent poverty is passed on from generation to generation. This cycle of poverty is diagrammed in Figure 4–1.

Poverty is functional

This section is presented with tongue in cheek. Obviously, poverty has many dysfunctions, mainly to the poor themselves, but also to the affluent. However, by realizing poverty has some functions, it helps us to understand why some decision makers are not actively seeking to eradicate poverty.

A home in Appalachia

FIGURE 4–1 Cycle of poverty

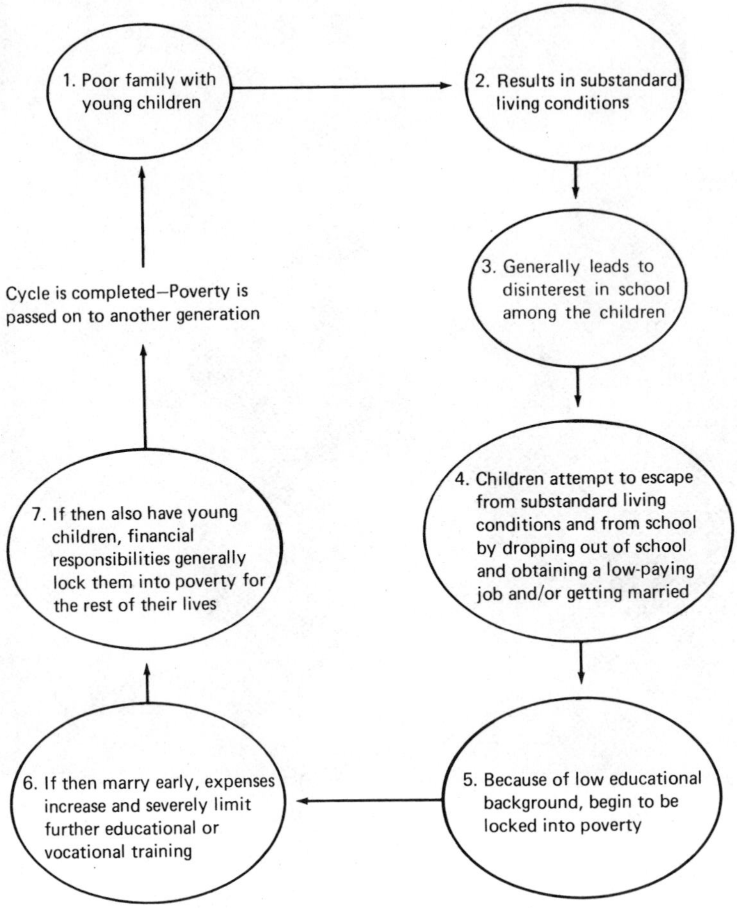

Eleven functions provided by the poor for affluent groups are summarized by Sullivan et al.:

1. They are available to do the unpleasant jobs that no one else wants to do.
2. By their activities, they subsidize the more affluent (an example of an activity is domestic service for low pay).
3. Jobs are established for those people, such as social workers, who provide services to the poor.
4. They purchase goods, such as those of poor quality, that otherwise could not be sold.
5. They serve as examples of deviance that are frowned on by the majority and that thereby support dominant norms.
6. They provide an opportunity for others to practice their "Christian duty" of helping the less fortunate.
7. They make mobility more likely for others because they are removed from the competition for a good education and good jobs.
8. They contribute to cultural activities by providing, for example, cheap labor for the construction of monuments and works of art.

9. They create cultural forms (e.g., jazz and the blues) that are often adopted by the affluent.
10. They serve as symbolic opponents for some political groups and as constituents for others.
11. They often absorb the costs of change (e.g., by being the victims of high levels of unemployment that result from technological advances).[9]

Also, denigrating the poor has the psychological function for some Americans of making them feel better about themselves.

Programs to combat poverty

Since poverty interacts with nearly every other social problem, almost every existing social service—to some extent—combats poverty (such as Alcoholics Anonymous, health care programs, vocational rehabilitation, parents without partners, foster care, adoption, day care, Headstart, housing programs, urban renewal, community action programs). Such programs indirectly reduce poverty by alleviating other social problems that happen to interact with poverty. Such programs are described in other sections of this text. This section will instead describe income maintenance programs which are directly designed to alleviate poverty.

(Although not politically viable, poverty could be totally eliminated in our society by further taxing the rich, and redistributing this tax money to the poor in such a way to raise everyone above the offical poverty line.)

INCOME MAINTENANCE PROGRAMS

Historical perspective. The way a society cares for its needy reflects its values. In primitive societies the needs of those who were not self-sufficient were met by family or other tribal members. During the medieval period in Europe, poor relief was a church responsibility.

The famous Elizabethan Poor Law of 1601 in England combined humanitarianism with the protestant ethic. This law was enacted as the general public viewed begging (not poverty) as a social problem. The law established three separate programs: (*a*) The able-bodied poor were offered work. If they refused they were whipped, imprisoned, or sent back to their birthplace. (*b*) The impotent poor (the elderly and disabled) were either given public relief or placed in almshouses. (*c*) Children whose parents could not provide for them were bound out as apprentices to other adults. This Poor Law established the principle of categorical relief by distinguishing between the ablebodied (undeserving) poor and the impotent (deserving) poor. Nearly all the principles contained within this Poor Law became incorporated into the "relief" programs of colonial America.

In the 19th century a controversy raged in both England and the United States between advocates of the workhouse and supporters of "outdoor relief," (assistance to persons in their own homes). "Outdoor relief" raised concerns about fraud, and citizens feared cash handouts might destroy moral fiber. On the other hand, workhouses (also called almshouses) were generally overcrowded and unsanitary, and contrary to their stated goal they offered no activity for the able bodied. Also in the 19th century the first social service organizations began to develop in urban areas to attempt to serve the needy. These organizations were private and church sponsored, and primarily offered food and shelter. They attempted to meet personal problems with religious admonitions.

Americans until the Great Depression believed in the myth of individualism; that is, the belief that each person is master of his/her own fate. Those in need were viewed as being lazy, unintelligent, or as justly being punished for their sinful ways.

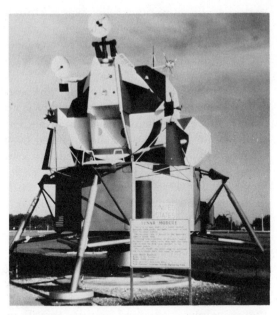

Lunar module used to land on the moon: We can travel to the moon, but have been unable to eradicate hunger in this country

The Great Depression of the 1930s called into question the individualism myth. Nearly a third of the work force was unemployed.[10] With large numbers of people unemployed, including the middle class, a new view of relief applicants developed: they were persons not essentially different from other people who were caught up in circumstances beyond their own control. Private relief agencies (including private agencies receiving funding support from local governing entities) were unable to meet the financial needs of the unemployed. There was a rapid breakdown in traditional local methods of giving aid to the poor.

Harry Hopkins, a social worker from Iowa, was appointed by President Franklin Roosevelt to oversee national employment programs and emergency assistance. Hopkins became one of Roosevelt's closest advisers and exerted considerable influence in designing and enacting the 1935 Social Security program. As indicated in Chapter 1 this program was of major significance as it initiated the federal government's role in three areas: (*a*) social insurance programs, (*b*) public assistance, and (*c*) social services.

In the early 1960s the large number of poor people (one fifth of our population) became a national concern.[11] President Johnson initiated the War on Poverty with the hope of eradicating poverty and creating the Great Society. Although poverty has been reduced, the optimism of the early 1960s was severely tempered by a number of factors. The Vietnam War drained resources that could otherwise have been spent on domestic programs and also led to violent protests and reassessments of our political and social institutions. In addition, many of the community action programs that were created (such as the Job Corps) proved to have high administrative expenses with the outcomes falling short of stated objectives. The rising crime rate and the turmoil in our inner cities also resulted in poverty receiving a reduced priority.

The Depression years have faded from national memory. Allegations of welfare fraud, high tax rates, and increasing relief roles have again in the 1970s and 80s become a national concern. Welfare has again become a political whipping boy. The 1970s saw a shift from a liberalized extension of the philosophy of public responsibility for the well-being of all citizens to the age-old distinction between the "undeserving" and the "deserving" poor. There have been renewed efforts (the Social Security Amendments of 1972 and the Talmadge Amendments of 1971) to force assistance recipients into the labor market. Fiscal conservatives, for example, are blaming the economic collapse of Great Britain and the financial problems of some of our large cities on "welfare state" programs. In the late 1970s and early 1980s there have been several taxpayers' revolts in some states (triggered by Howard Jarvis and Proposition 13 in California) which are focused on getting states to pass statewide referendums to cut taxes, and thereby reduce services—including social welfare services. As indicated in Chapter 1, the conflict between residual and institutional approaches to social programs continues to exist.

A.   Social insurance programs

Old Age, Survivors, Disability, and Health Insurance (OASDHI). This social insurance program was created by the 1935 Social Security Act. OASDHI generally is referred to as "social security" by the general public. It is the largest income insurance program, and is designed to partially replace income lost when a worker retires or becomes disabled. Cash benefits are also paid to survivors of "insured" workers.

Payments to beneficiaries are based on previous earnings. Since OASDHI is an insurance program there is no "means test" to establish eligiblity; rich as well as poor are eligible if insured. Benefits are provided to fully insured workers at age 65 or older (age 62 if somewhat smaller benefits are taken). Dependent husbands or wives over 62 and dependent children under 18 (no age limit on disabled children who become disabled before 18) are also covered under the retirement benefits.

Participation in this insurance program is compulsory for nearly all employees. The program is financed by a payroll tax assessed equally to employer and employee. The rate has gone up gradually. Eligibility for benefits is based upon the number of years in which social security taxes have been paid.

Although OASDHI has become a widely accepted program, there are two controversies that have been generated. One controversy has been the limitation on earnings for retired recipients. The original intent of the Social Security Act was to encourage older workers to retire from the labor force. Therefore, there was a strict limitation on the amount that could be earned by recipients. The usefulness of some elderly workers, the inadequacy of OASDHI benefits received, and the increasing recognition of the psychological advantages of some sort of continued employment after retirement have periodically raised concerns about income restrictions and have led to periodic liberalization of these restrictions.

A second concern in recent years has been the financial soundness of OASDHI. Since 1935 the social security tax has led to a buildup in the trust fund for OASDHI. But the liberalization of benefits in recent years along with spiraling costs has raised concerns that the system may soon be paying out more than it is taking in. In times of high unemployment and recession, the number of workers paying into OASDHI is decreased. The decline in the birthrate, with a steadily increasing retired population may also create problems for OASDHI as the number of recipients may increase faster than the number of the younger working population. If OASDHI is not to collapse, benefits may have to be scaled back, taxes increased, or both.

Medicare.   In 1965 Congress enacted Title XVIII (Medicare) to the Social Security Act. Medicare provides two coordinated programs of health insurance for those over 65. Plan A provides for hospitalization and extended care, and is financed on a self-supporting basis by an additional surcharge on the Social Security Act. All recipients of OASDHI retirement benefits are eligible. Plan B is a voluntary insurance plan for medical services, especially physician's charges. Medicare is a public health insurance program and is more fully described in Chapter 13.

Unemployment insurance. This program was also created by the 1935 Social Security Act, and provides benefits to workers who have been laid off or, in certain cases, fired. Unemployment insurance is financed by a tax on employers. In 1974 Congress approved an extension of benefit periods for the unemployed, and this aspect of the program is financed equally by federal and state funds. The weekly benefit amount for which unemployed are eligible, along with the number of weeks, varies from state to state. In many states the unemployed are eligible for benefits about a year in duration. To be eligible in most states a person must: (*a*) have worked a certain number of weeks in covered employment, (*b*) be ready, willing, and able to work, (*c*) file a claim for benefits and be registered in a public employment office, and (*d*) demonstrate that unemployment is due to a lack of work for which the employee is qualified.

Unemployment insurance benefits help individuals and families who become unemployed due to a lack of work. In our society, where employment is valued highly, being without work can be a demeaning experience.

In recent years the unemployment rate has ranged from 6 to 8 percent of able-bodied workers. Such a high rate clearly indicates a lack of available jobs.

On the other hand, the Unemployment Insurance Program has received sharp criticism in recent years as it has been claimed that some of the unemployed would rather collect insurance benefits (and spend the winter in a warmer climate) than making a concerted effort to obtain employment.[12]

Workers' compensation insurance. This program provides both income and assistance in meeting medical expenses for injuries sustained on a job. This program was enacted after a series of lawsuits by injured employees against employers—the only recourse employees had. The first workers' compensation program was the Federal Employees Compensation Act in 1908. Individual states gradually passed workers' compensation laws modeled after the program for federal employees. By 1920 all but six southern states had such laws, but it was not until 1948 that all states had adequate coverage.[13] Cash benefits are paid for total or temporary disability or death. Medical benefits cover hospital and doctors' fees. Rehabilitation benefits are also available for those needing aftercare and retraining in order to again become employable.

Workers' compensation is financed by a tax on employers.

B. Public assistance programs

Public assistance is sometimes viewed as being synonymous with "welfare" by the general public; yet there are hundreds of other social welfare programs. Public assistance has primarily residual aspects, and applicants must undergo a "means test" which reviews their assets and liabilities to determine eligibility for benefits.

Adherents to the residual view of public assistance generally hold the following opinions:

1. Assistance should be made as unpleasant as possible as a deterrent to its use. This is to be accomplished by giving relief in kind, rather than money, by threatening prosecution, by continuous re-evaluation of need, by making it only temporary, stopping it if illegitimacy is involved, and removing children from their own homes when these homes do not come up to standard.

2. Relief should be made unpleasant by requiring recipients to work for it regardless of the nature of the work, or how depressed the wage, or whether the requirement would be used as means for securing cheap labor, and not-withstanding income from this work is still labeled relief.

3. Assistance should be discouraged by making payments too low for anyone to really want it. It is argued by advocates of this approach that assistance in amounts greater than would be received by the lowest paid most menial worker, would encourage individuals to seek assistance in lieu of employment.

4. Outsiders should be prevented from seeking help by extending emergency aid for only short periods of time.

5. People should be forced to remain on their jobs or return to employment, by denying assistance to anyone who is guilty of a "voluntary quit."[14]

In contrast, the institutional view of public assistance (generally held by social workers) assumes or advocates:

1. Providing an income floor for all citizens and the elimination of hunger and destitution, or their threat as an instrument of social policy.

2. Extending relief to applicants who can qualify under eligibility requirements; that is, remove it from subjective, biased, and capricious considerations. Relief should be based on need as it is determined to exist by objective, rather than subjective, criteria, and as a legally determined right.

3. It is assumed that workers, generally, prefer income from employment to public welfare and that motivations to work are built into the economy in the form of

social, cultural, and economic advantages to the employed man or woman.

4. Psychological and social barriers sometimes stand in the way of rehabilitation and employment. Counseling and other services may be needed to restore certain individuals to economic and social self-sufficiency.

5. Preservation of the independence and self-respect of the applicant for assistance is a prime consideration in the administration of programs of relief.

6. A punitive approach defeats the purpose for which assistance is used, namely, the restoration of the individual to normal functioning; it deepens feelings of inadequacy and dependency, causes embarrassment and humiliation, and brings destructive psychological defenses into play.

7. There are many pulls in society that tend to make work more appealing than public welfare—a higher standard of living, the prestige and sense of importance one receives from work, tenure, the emoluments of society, and others.[15]

There are several distinguishing features of public assistance programs:

Programs have a means test. Individuals applying for assistance have their income and assets examined in order to determine whether their financial needs meet the eligibility requirements for assistance. The means test is designed to ensure that individuals receiving assistance do not already have sufficient resources for a minimum level of subsistence. Resources that are examined include both earned and unearned income. Earned income is money in the form of salary or wages. Unearned income includes benefits from other public and private financial programs, gifts, life insurance an-

Applying for employment and for unemployment compensation. Is unemployment compensation a disincentive to seeking work?

nuities, stock dividends, rental income, inheritances, support payments from relatives, and so on.

Case-by-case determination of eligibility and benefit levels. All applicants have their applications for assistance closely reviewed on a case-by-case basis. Although there are federal, state, and local guidelines on eligibility, and on how much is allowable as a benefit for eligible persons, the staff who administer public assistance have substantial discretion in deciding whether a client will receive special allowances in addition to basic benefits. Staff also have discretion in deciding which social services and other resources might be mobilized on behalf of the client. Eligibility determination, along with benefit level determination, is a cumbersome, lengthy process involving review of extensive documents.

Benefits are viewed as charity. In contrast to social insurance benefits which recipients are viewed as legally entitled to, public assistance benefits are viewed as charity. In this country poor persons are not viewed as having a constitutionally established right to a minimum income. (In comparison, some foreign countries, such as Great Britain, recognize the right of those in poverty to be maintained and protected by government.)

Program benefits are paid from general government revenues. Public assistance benefits at the federal, state, and local levels are financed through taxes on personal income and on property. In the federal budget expenditures for all public assistance programs represent about 10 percent of all allocations.[16]

Prominent public assistance programs will now be briefly described.

Supplemental Security Income (SSI). Under this program the federal government pays monthly checks to people in financial need 65 years of age and older, and to those in need at any age who are blind or disabled. In order to qualify for payments applicants must have no (or very little) regular cash income, own little property, and have little cash or few assets that can be turned into cash (such as stocks, bonds, jewelry and other valuables).

The SSI program became effective January 1, 1974, and replaces the following programs which were created by the 1935 Social Security Act: Old Age Assistance, Aid to the Blind, and Aid to the Permanently and Totally Disabled. SSI is the first federally administered assistance program (prior to this time, other public assistance programs were administered through state governments). The word *supplemental* in the term *supplemental security income* is appropriate as, in most cases, payments supplement whatever income may be available to the claimant. Even OASDHI benefits are supplemented by this program.

SSI provides a guaranteed income (a floor of income) for the aged, the blind, and the disabled.

Aged, blind, and disabled are defined as follows:

Aged—65 or over.

Blind—Vision no better than 20/200 (even with glasses) or tunnel vision (limited visual field of 20 degrees or less).

Disabled—A physical or mental impairment which prevents a person from doing any substantial gainful work and which is expected to last at least 12 months or result in death.

Administration of SSI has been assigned to the Social Security Administration. Fi-nancing of the program is through federal tax dollars, particularly income taxes.

General assistance. This program is supposed to serve those needing temporary rather than long-term financial support. It is designed to provide financial help to those in need who are ineligible for any other income maintenance program. No clearly stated eligibility requirements exist for general assistance. GA is the only public assistance program which receives no federal funds. It is usually funded by property taxes. In large cities, such as New York and Chicago the state contributes substantially toward meeting the costs of GA. In most localities, however, the program is financed and administered at the local level, either through the county, the township, or by a village or city. In many local governmental units, a political official has arbitrary jurisdiction over whether an applicant receives help. Most expenditures for GA are for medical care. In-kind payments are frequent. Whenever feasible, communities have attempted to move GA recipients into federally funded public aid programs, as this reduces local expenses.

Payments for GA tend to be minimal and grudgingly made to discourage people from applying and becoming dependent on welfare. With in-kind and voucher payments, GA conveys to recipients the suspicion that they are incapable of managing their own affairs. In some parts of the country GA has demoralizing effects and has much in common with poor relief in the Elizabethan period.

Since able-bodied unemployed men and women sometimes find it necessary to seek GA benefits, GA is sometimes viewed as a public assistance program for the "undeserving poor."

Medicaid. This program provides hospital and medical care to certain poverty-stricken people. Those eligible are persons who are recipients of Aid to Families with Dependent Children or SSI recipients. In addition, states have:

the option to include persons who are able to provide for their own daily living but whose income and resources are not sufficient to meet all of their medical costs. . . . Families with larger incomes may be eligible for help with their medical bills if their net income after deducting their medical expenses does not exceed the income limit set by the state for meeting daily maintenance expenses.[17]

Medicaid is administered by the states with financial participation by the federal government. Direct payments are made to providers of services. To qualify for Medicaid, recipients must undergo a means test (as is required for every public assistance program).

Food stamps. In the mid-1960s our nation was shocked to learn that millions of Americans were starving or malnourished. In the late 1960s CBS produced a documentary program "Hunger in America" visually showing the plights of 10 million Americans who are hungry in this country. Many of the people with inadequate diets are poor. Research also suggests severe nutritional deficits in expectant mothers may lead to irreversible brain deficits in the child.

The food stamp program is designed to combat hunger. Food stamps are available to public assistance recipients and to low-income families. These stamps are then traded in for groceries. Funding for the food stamp program has grown from 600 million in 1970 to an estimated 8.7 billion in 1980—an increase of nearly 15 times in magnitude in a 10-year period. The program in 1980 was feeding 1 of every 11 Americans.[18] The rapid rise in cost of the program is partly due to rising food costs, and partly due to a large increase in recipients—from 4.3 million in

1970 to 21.4 million in 1980.[19] The spiraling cost of the program has generated considerable controversy in Congress over the question of how to control the program's runaway costs. Defenders of the program assert that the costs are outweighed by its accomplishments—mainly the elimination of malnutrition in many parts of America.

Housing assistance. Similar to food stamps and Medicaid, housing assistance is an "in-kind" income program, rather than a cash income program. Poor families are eligible for housing assistance. Generally, such assistance is provided in the form of public housing, usually large housing projects that are owned and operated by the government. In a public housing project the tenants enjoy low-cost (subsidized) rents. Since they pay less than the market value of their apartments, they are effectively receiving an income transfer, which on the average is approximately $1,000 a year.

In addition to the public housing projects, there are also housing assistance programs for low-income people who are renting and even buying their homes and apartments in the private market. In these programs, the rent or mortgage payment is reduced with the Department of Housing and Urban Development (HUD) making up the difference.

Aid to families with dependent children (AFDC). This program is the most stigmatized public assistance program. The general public's conception of "welfare" is the AFDC program. Originally this program was called Aid to Dependent Children (ADC).

More money is spent on AFDC than on any other public assistance program. Yet, several times as much money is spent on social insurance programs than on AFDC.[20] The stigma attached to AFDC is partially shown by the fact that the average montly grant per recipient is lower than for general

TABLE 4–1 Cash assistance programs, 1979

Program	Number of current recipients	Average benefit per recipient (per month)	Total annual payments ($billions)
Supplemental Security Income (SSI)	4,200,000	$132	$ 6.7
Aid to Families with Dependent Children (AFDC)	10,300,000	87	10.7
General Assistance (GA)	750,000	131	1.2
Total	15,250,000		18.6

SOURCE: Bradley R. Schiller, *The Economics of Poverty and Discrimination,* 3d edition (Englewood Cliffs, N.J.: Prentice-Hall, 1980), p. 167.

assistance or for supplement security income[21] (see Table 4–1).

In 1980 about $11 billion was spent on the AFDC program.[22] The reason the AFDC program is so expensive is because a majority of all persons receiving public assistance are on AFDC rolls.[23]

The precise definition of eligibility for AFDC varies from state to state. Payments are made for both the parent and the children in eligible families. To be eligible, the children must be deprived of parental support or care because of a parents' death, continued absence from the home (desertion, divorce, separation), or because the father and mother were never married. States may, if they wish, provide aid to the children of unemployed parents who are living together. About half the states have this AFDC-UP program which provides payments to children of unemployed parents. With AFDC-UP the breadwinner must agree to actively seek work, register with the State Employment Service, and participate in work training programs.

About 80 percent of AFDC families are headed by a single parent, usually the mother and usually because of the father's absence from the home.[24]

The Aid to Dependent Children (ADC) program was enacted by the 1935 Social Security Law. One of its objectives, then, was to enable mothers with young children to remain at home. In 1962 the title was changed to Aid to Families with Dependent Children (AFDC). Since 1935 our values surrounding working mothers have changed, and there now is substantial effort, for psychological and financial reasons, to help AFDC mothers obtain gainful employment.

Financing and administering AFDC programs represent a sharing of federal and state control—and in many states counties participate in the financing and administration. The federal government, through the Department of Health and Human Services writes regulations to implement the Social Security Laws. States, and often counties, then write their own regulations, within federal guidelines, relating to eligibility criteria, benefit standards, and qualifications of public assistance staff. If a state fails to comply with federal guidelines, it may lose federal support.

Decisions about AFDC eligibility are made by the executive, legislative, and judicial branches of government; and at federal, state, and local levels. As a result, the program is cumbersome, slow to change to meet emerging needs, and is heavily involved in paperwork, "red tape," and bureaucratic processes.

> **WELFARE FRAUD MAKES HEADLINES**
>
> ### WOMEN ACCUSED OF WELFARE FRAUD
>
> CHICAGO (AP)—A woman and her two adult daughters were charged Wednesday with cheating welfare agencies out of $250,000 over the last 11 years, authorities said.
>
> One of the sisters, . . ., 32, used eight names for herself and dozens of names for fictitious children in collecting $150,000 in public aid checks, said James G. Piper, an assistant state's attorney. She was charged with 385 counts of theft.
>
> Her sister . . ., 26, was charged with 105 counts of theft and the mother . . ., 51, with 59 counts.
>
> SOURCE: *Wisconsin State Journal*, May 29, 1980, p. 3. (Welfare fraud is rare but makes the news, while the merits of AFDC do not.)

MYTHS ABOUT WELFARE

Because AFDC is such a controversial program, a number of current beliefs about AFDC families will be examined in order to determine the extent to which these views conform with available evidence.

Myth 1. *Most welfare children are illegitimate.* Fact—A sizable majority, over two thirds, of the children receiving AFDC benefits are "legitimate."*[25] To help AFDC families avoid unwanted pregnancies, the federal government in recent years has made family planning services available.

Myth 2. *Welfare makes it profitable for women to have illegitimate babies.* Fact—The size of families on AFDC has actually been declining, particularly since 1967, reflecting a general trend in the birthrate for the population as a whole. In 1977 the average size for the AFDC population was 3.6 persons—the same as the national average for all families.[26] A majority of AFDC families consist of

---

* NOTE: The author strongly objects to labeling any child "illegitimate."

a mother and one or two children.[27] In those small number of families in which another child is born after the family is receiving benefits, the main reason may well be the lack of appropriate family planning resources being available. Finally, it has been estimated in 1980 that on the average an AFDC family would experience a boost of $900 per year for each additional child.[28] Since it is estimated that it costs over $50,000 to raise a child from 0 to age 18, the amount of "profit" a mother might expect to realize from having an additional child is minuscule.

Myth 3. *Give them more money and they'll drink it up.* Fact—As of August 1979 the average monthly grant per recipient in the United States was $87.00,[29] hardly enough to meet basic essentials. How would you like to live on $87 per month? Furthermore, most AFDC families report that if they received extra funds it would go for essentials.[30]

Myth 4. *Most welfare recipients are cheaters and frauds.* Fact—If fraud is defined as a deliberate and knowing attempt by a client to deceive the agency, then fraud is low. A national survey in 1976 found that 1 out of every 20 AFDC recipients were getting checks they were ineligible for.[31] Since determining eligibility is a cumbersome, complex process, most of these errors were identified as honest mistakes by state and local public assistance agencies or by recipients. The greatest difficulty about money paid out for AFDC is not fraud but error—mistakes unintentionally made either by the agency or the recipient. A recent survey found one out of four AFDC recipients was being paid the wrong amount—either too little or too much.[32] There is a substantial need to streamline the management of AFDC and reduce mistakes.

Myth 5. *The welfare rolls are soaring out of control.* Fact—Most of the case load growth in the AFDC program occurred before 1973, with dramatic increases between 1970 and 1973. Since early in 1976, the number of people on AFDC in the United States has gradually fallen back from a high of 11.4 million in March 1976 to an average of 10.2 million in August 1979, a decrease of 10.5 percent.[33] There are many reasons for this recent stabilization including the declining birthrate and increased use of family planning resources.

Myth 6. *Welfare is just a money handout, a dole.* Fact—Most families on AFDC receive one or more social services designed to meet personal and social problems, and to hopefully make them self-supportive. Social services that are available vary widely from area to area, and may include health care, financial counseling, counseling on home management, employment counseling, day care, vocational rehabilitation, homemaker services, consumer education, assistance in child rearing, Headstart, job training, and marriage counseling. As indicated earlier, the provision of social services to low-income families was one of the three programs enacted by the 1935 Social Security Act.

Myth 7. *People on welfare are able-bodied loafers.* Fact—Contrary to public opinion, there are few able-bodied persons receiving assistance. The vast majority of AFDC recipients are children. The largest group of able-bodied adults are AFDC mothers, most of whom head families with no able-bodied male present. About 16 percent of these mothers already work, with an additional 13 percent actively seeking work, receiving work training, or waiting to be called back after a layoff.[34] Many of the remaining mothers have serious barriers to obtaining employment: having very young children to rear, needing to obtain a moderate paying job that would offset the costs of child care, needing skill training, and needing extensive medical or rehabilitative services before becoming employable. Contrary to the stereotype of the "welfare mother" as being shiftless, lazy, and unwilling to take a job, Goodwin has found that even long-term AFDC mothers continue to have a strong work ethic but lack skills and confidence to obtain a job.[35]

About half the states have AFDC-UP, the program for unemployed or partially unemployed fathers. The number of recipients in this program has always been small. Of the able-bodied males in this program, all are required by law to be actively looking for work or to be receiving work training to be eligible for benefits.

Myth 8. *Most welfare families are black.* Fact—The largest racial group among AFDC families is white (52.6 percent). Blacks represent 43.0 percent. The other 4.4 percent is composed of other racial minorities.[36] Since blacks comprise about 11 percent of the U.S. population, and over 40 percent of the AFDC recipients, the stigma attached to AFDC may be partly due to racial discrimination.

Myth 9. *Why work when you can live it up on welfare?* Fact—The average AFDC monthly payment per recipient in 1979 was $87, hardly enough to live it up.[37]

Myth 10. *Once on welfare, recipients will spend a lifetime on welfare.* Fact—Only 10 percent of the households receive AFDC benefits for 10 years or longer. Half of the recipients are off the rolls within two and a half years.[38]

Myth 11. *Welfare is eating up tremendous chunks of our tax money, causing inflation, and "bleeding the country dry."* Fact—At the federal level about 5.5 percent of the federal budget is allocated to AFDC, Medicaid, and food stamps.[39] At the state level even a smaller percent of the budget is allocated to public assistance programs.

The poverty cycle among AFDC families

A key question is whether our present punitive, residual approach to AFDC is influencing children born into AFDC families to grow up to be recipients themselves. Are we training whole generations for a life of dependency? If we stigmatize and are punitive to a mother who is not gainfully employed, are we not also damaging her children and thereby passing dependency on to another generation? Statistics show that many people on public assistance had parents who were also recipients.[40] Also, it has been found that the longer a family receives assistance, the higher the rate of social problems their children manifest in their teenage years—higher rates of illegitimacy, early marriage, emotional problems, truancy, delinquency and dropping-out of school.[41]

Shortcomings of AFDC program

There are a number of deficiencies in this program:

Most recipients are kept in poverty by inadequate assistance grants which average well below the poverty level.

The program stigmatizes recipients, makes them feel like second-class citizens, and may even create long-term dependency which is passed on to another generation. This stigma also keeps many eligible, needy people from applying.

In states not having AFDC-UP, unemployed husbands are sometimes forced to desert their families so that the families will be eligible for benefits. (As of 1980, only half the states had an AFDC-UP program).

Eligibility determination is very cumbersome and complicated. The administrative structure is also complicated, with decisions being made at federal, state, and local levels, and at the three branches of government (executive, legislative, and judicial). It has been estimated that half the money spent on AFDC is spent on administration and eligibility determination.

AFDC does not provide benefits to all people under 65 who are poor. Childless couples, healthy single individuals, and families with a breadwinner employed full time (though at below poverty level wages) are ineligible.

In recent years there has been a proliferation of new public assistance programs that are available to low-income families: such programs include Headstart, public housing, Work Incentive (WIN), Medicaid, and Energy Assistance (to pay for heat). The proliferation of these programs have led to some problems in informing eligible recipients and to problems (from a taxpayer's view) that assertive families are receiving more than their "fair share" of assistance. Flynn describes this latter problem:

> A relatively new problem in benefit standards has arisen over the past fifteen years as a result of the proliferation of means-tested programs sponsored by the government. A growing number of individuals and families now receive benefits from more than one source. For example, in a large metropolitan environment, an ambitious and assertive poor family might establish eligibility in the following programs: AFDC, food stamps, public housing, Medicaid, free school lunches, Headstart, and community day care. The total value of the benefits to one hypothetical AFDC family in New York City who participated in all these programs would equal the purchasing power of a worker with a gross income of $11,500 per year. On the other hand most American communities do not have all these resources nor are most assistance recipients knowledgeable and confident enough to pursue all the opportunities for public support.[42]

PROPOSED ALTERNATIVES

Family allowances. The United States is the only Western industrialized country without a family allowance program. Under a family allowance program the government pays each family a set amount based on the number of children. If payments were large enough, such a program would aid in eliminating poverty, particularly in large families. In 1969 Alvin Schorr estimated that if payments of $50 per month were made for each child, three fourths of the poor children would no longer be living in poverty.*[43]

---

* With the high rate of inflation that we have had, the monthly payment would now have to be substantially increased to eliminate poverty in most low-income families.

There are some strong criticisms of a family allowance plan. If payments are made to all children the program would be very expensive with much of the money going to nonpoor families. This problem could be solved, as Denmark has done, by varying the family allowance payments with income and terminating payments after a certain level of income is reached. (A criticism of such an approach, though, is that it would then involve a "means test" and continue to stigmatize recipients.) A second criticism of a family allowance program is that it would provide an incentive to increase the birthrate—at a time when overpopulation is a major concern. A final criticism of a family allowance program is that it would not provide payments to single individuals and childless couples who are poor.

Government as last resort employer. The unemployment rate of able-bodied workers in recent years has been between 6 and 8 percent. In addition, an estimated million family heads are working full time but earning wages below the poverty line.[44] Guaranteed work for able-bodied workers is favored by a large majority of the general public (78 percent in a Gallup Poll).[45] The government could establish a program in which all able-bodied poor could earn a certain minimum amount above the poverty line.

Yet, there is a question whether such a program is politically feasible. Public work projects are generally viewed by the general public as being expensive, unproductive and inefficient. Low-wage employers are also likely to object as such a program is apt to be competitive as workers may earn more by working for the government than for low-wage employers.

Another criticism is that such a program would better serve only a small fraction of AFDC recipients; as indicated earlier only a small minority of public assistance recipients are presently employable.

Negative income tax. Under such a plan the Internal Revenue Service would send checks to all families below a certain income, depending on family size. An early proponent of the negative income tax, Dr. Milton Friedman, suggested that such a plan could replace all other social insurance and public assistance programs. In his original proposal, he suggested a family of four could be gauranteed an annual income of $1,500.[46] To provide a work incentive, he suggested that the government payment would be reduced by a "negative tax" of $1 for each $2 increase in income from work. With such a plan, when work reached $3,000, there would be no further government payment. Above $3,000, the worker would begin paying the regular "positive" income tax. A sharp criticism of this plan is that the $1,500 guaranteed, base income for a family of four is far below the poverty line.

Many variations of the negative income tax are possible, and some are being tested by the federal government. The minimum income guarantee for a family of four, for example, could be set at the poverty line, while the incentive to work factor (negative income tax rate) could range widely. But such plans could be very expensive.

Using a hypothetical example, with a guaranteed base level of $4,000 for a family of four, and the negative income tax factor at 25 percent—allowing a family to keep $75 out of every $100 earned—the family would receive subsidies until the break-even point of $16,000:

Example:	$ 4,000	guaranteed base
	$12,000	negative income tax factor at 25 percent—allowing a family to keep 75 percent of, in this case, $16,000 in earnings
	$16,000	break-even point

Negative income tax plans have been widely debated by Congress, U.S. presidents, social workers, and many other groups and organizations. Such plans would shift the focus of income maintenance programs from "charity" to a "right" of entitlement to a guaranteed income. The stigma of being a recipient would sharply be reduced, and the program would be relatively simple to administer as eligibility would be based on income tax returns. Furthermore, the program would serve everyone who is poor, and if the base level is at the poverty line, poverty would be eradicated. Another advantage would be to reduce equity problems which have occurred under present programs where nonworking people are eligible for several types of benefits (e.g., food stamps and Medicaid) and may be able to achieve a higher standard of living than a low-income employed person who is eligible for few, if any, benefits.

A number of unanswered questions, however, have been raised by a negative income tax plan: (a) Such plans are based on the filing of income tax forms. If a family has little or no income (and no assets) must they wait nearly a year until their tax form is filed before being eligible for benefits? (b) Will a guaranteed income destroy the incentive to work? (c) The cost of living varies greatly between urban and rural areas and between different parts of the country—should financial adjustments be made for this? But perhaps the biggest problem with a negative income tax plan is what has been called the "unholy triangle"; that is, developing a plan that:

1. Has an adequate guaranteed base level.
2. Allows low-income workers to keep a sufficiently high percentage of their earnings so the incentive to work is not destroyed.

3. Is not exorbitantly expensive so that our national economy is not severely affected.

The federal government has shown considerable interest in negative income tax programs, as evidenced by the enactment in 1974 of the Supplemental Security Income program which has a guaranteed income base. There are also a number of federal negative income experiments in New Jersey, Iowa, Pennsylvania, North Carolina, Seattle, Denver, and Gary.[47] In 1977 President Carter proposed replacing the current welfare system with a program having negative income tax and guaranteed income concepts.

Congress failed to pass President Carter's welfare reform proposal, with liberals claiming it did not go far enough in helping poor people and with conservatives being appalled at the plan's $20 billion annual cost over and above existing expenditures.[48]

In 1980 many fiscal conservatives were elected to political leadership positions, including President Ronald Reagan. President Reagan ran on a platform that called for reduced federal expenditures for welfare and

that called for giving states and localities greater control over welfare programs. With this conservative position, chances for a negative income tax plan being enacted are sharply reduced. In the next few years the federal government will probably focus on trying to cut back expenditures for public welfare programs.

Social services: Title XX

Title XX of the Social Security Act was a major new piece of legislation which was signed into law by President Ford in January 1975. Title XX is called "Grants to States for Services" and pertains to the operation and administration of public social services; generally those services provided by the welfare department (in some states called the department of human resources, and in some others called social services department).

Title XX is significant because:

1. It recognized the provision of social services as a valid function of government, not simply an adjunct to the public assistance program.

2. It gives states the authority to determine, within broad parameters, what services will be provided, to whom, and where they will be provided. Under Title XX a state may offer services statewide, or it may provide different services in different geographic areas depending on local needs. Janet Harnett describes the flexibility states now have in making these decisions:

> it would be possible, for example, to offer one service in four out of a state's ten geographic areas; to offer another service statewide to all persons at 40 percent of the median income level and that same service to protective service cases at 60 percent of the median income level. A state could also offer, for example, day care statewide to all persons at 50 percent of the median income level and additionally offer day

A demonstration by a welfare rights organization

care in four geographic areas to persons with mentally retarded children at 80 percent of the median income level.[49]

3. It gives states the option to provide social services to a broad range of persons, not only to public assistance recipients. Under Title XX services may be provided to public assistance recipients and to others up to 115 percent of the state's median income depending on state choice in this area.

The program is a grant-in-aid program which means that states must put up 25 percent of the money expended in order to claim the 75 percent match from the federal government. (Family planning expenditures are matched at a 90 percent to 10 percent rate.)

There are five goals of Title XX to which all services must be directed, which are described as:

1. Achieving or maintaining economic self-support to prevent, reduce, or eliminate dependency.
2. Achieving or maintaining self-sufficiency, including reduction or prevention of dependency.
3. Preventing or remedying neglect, abuse, or exploitation of children and adults unable to protect their own interests, or preserving, rehabilitating, or reuniting families.
4. Preventing or reducing inappropriate institutional care by providing for community-based care, home-based care, or other forms of less intensive care.
5. Securing referral or admission for institutional care when other forms of care are not appropriate, or providing services to individuals in institutions.[50]

There are several other important features of Title XX:

1. Title XX has two "universal" services, which must be provided without regard to income eligibility. There services are information and referral services, and services directed at the goal of preventing or remedying abuse, neglect, or exploitation of children or adults.
2. Title XX requires that fees related to income must be charged for services provided to individuals who have income over 80 percent of the state's median income adjusted for family size. For persons whose income is less than 80 percent of the median income, states have the option of assessing a fee.
3. Although wide latitude is given to states regarding what services will be provided, Title XX also contains some specifics. For example, there are specific child-care standards and child-care ratios. Also, there are specific limitations on expenditures for medical and remedial care, on educational services, on room and board, and on services to persons in institutions.
4. Title XX outlines a specific process for the purpose of informing citizens of the state's social services programs and obtaining their participation in the planning and decision making concerning these programs. Janet Harnett describes this public review and comment process:[51]

> Previously, states developed a State Service Plan which was approved by HEW. Now, under Title XX, the governor of the state must publish and make available to all citizens of the state the Comprehensive Annual Services Plan (CASP), must receive comments from the public on this plan, and must utilize these comments in making a final plan for state social service delivery.
>
> Highlights of the public participation process include the publication of a detailed summary and of a proposed services plan, a 45-day comment period, and publi-

cation of an ad announcing the availability of the final services plan. Not only the full service plan but also the newspaper ads must contain a description of the services, the eligibility criteria, the geographic areas where these services are available, and other data.

5. Title XX is not new money, as a ceiling limit was placed on social services expenditures. Generally what this means is that if a state decides to increase its expenditures in one service area (or develop a new service), it has to reduce its expenditures on one or more existing services.

Social work and public welfare

Since the enactment of the 1935 Social Security Law, a wide variety of social services have been provided to public assistance recipients. The particular services provided vary widely from area to area (depending on state and county decisions), but include such services as counseling, day care, protective services, foster home care, services to the physically and mentally handicapped, information and referral, homemaker services, financial counseling, assistance in child rearing, family planning, health services, vocational training and employment counseling. A large number of social workers are employed to provide such services.

Until 1972 social services and financial assistance were combined, and social workers were involved in financial eligibility determination. The 1972 Amendments to the Social Security Act separated services and assistance. Now, public assistance recipients are informed of available social services, and of their right to request such services. Financial eligibility is now determined by clerical staff.

The late 1960s raised a number of questions about whether casework has any posi-

tive effects (similar questions were also being raised about the effectiveness of psychotherapy).[52] As a result, demonstrating accountability is receiving increased emphasis in the social services.

Social work does have its gratifications—as comes from helping someone with a personal or social problem. Yet, social work is at times frustrating. These frustrations occur quite frequently in public welfare and include:

Having extensive paperwork to fill out.

Trying to meet the needs of clients when their needs are not served by existing programs.

Trying to change the huge public welfare bureaucratic structure to better meet the needs of clients. The public welfare system is slow to change to meet emerging needs, and is filled with extensive "red tape."

Having a larger case load than one can optimally and effectively serve.

Trying to keep informed about the numerous changes (program, organizational, and eligibility determination) that occur on an ongoing basis.

Working with discouraged clients who lack the necessary motivation to work toward improving their circumstances. Social work "interns" in field placement and new social workers frequently report this as being their greatest frustration and a severe "reality shock." They anticipated that after carefully working out a "casework plan" with a client to resolve some problem, that the client would follow through. Unfortunately, in many cases this does not happen. Future appointments may be broken by the client, and even if the client responsibly keeps future appointments, he/she is apt to have excuses for not following through on the commitment. These excuses can usually be interpreted to represent a lack of motivation.

Working with discouraged people

The key variable in determining if clients will make positive changes in their lives is whether they have the motivation to make the efforts necessary to improve their circumstances. Failure in counseling, or casework, generally occurs when clients do not become motivated.

Many public assistance recipients are discouraged. Continued economic pressures, and generally a long series of past "failure" experiences when they have tried to improve their circumstances, have frequently sapped their motivation. Discouraged people tend to be traveling through life in an unhappy "rut" that is dull, stagnating, generally unfulfilling, but is also seen by them as safe, predictable, and providing some security. For them to make extensive efforts to improve their circumstances is viewed as risky, frightening, and having unpredictable and uncertain results. Many feel it is safer to remain in their present "rut," than to try something new which might further expose their weaknesses and result in psychological "hurt."

Seeking a job, finding transportation, and making day-care arrangements may be seen as "overwhelmingly" difficult for an unskilled AFDC mother with young children who has never previously been employed. For a wife with five children who periodically is physically beaten by her husband, seeking counseling or making separation arrangements may be seen as highly risky as the future would be uncertain and she may fear such actions would only make her husband more abusive. For a person with a drinking problem who has recently lost his last two jobs, giving up drinking may be seen as giving up his main support "crutch."

In order to motivate a discouraged person, the social worker has to be an "encouraging person." According to Lewis Losoncy an encouraging person does the following:[53]

Has complete acceptance for the discouraged person and conveys "I accept you exactly as you are, with no conditions attached." (The worker should not, however, convey acceptance of the deviant behavior that needs to be changed.)

Has a nonblaming attitude so that the discouraged person no longer feels a need to lie, pretend, or wear a mask.

Conveys empathy that the worker is aware and can to some extent feel what the discouraged person is feeling.

Conveys to the discouraged person that the counselor is genuinely interested in his or her progress and conveys that the counselee is an important, worthwhile person. In order for discouraged persons to believe in themselves, they generally need an encouraging person who conveys the idea that they are important, worthwhile persons.

Notices (rewards) every small instance of progress—for example, if the person is wearing something new, say "That's new, isn't it? It really looks good on you." This is particularly valuable during the beginning of the relationship.

Conveys to the discouraged person that the counselor has confidence in the capacity of the discouraged person to improve.

Conveys sincere enthusiasm about the discouraged person's interests, ideas, and risk-taking actions.

Has the capacity to be a nonjudgmental listener so that the discouraged person's real thoughts and feelings can be expressed freely, without fear of censure.

Has the time to spend listening and understanding the discouraged person as fully as possible. Motivating a discouraged person takes a long, long time. Discouraged people generally have a long history of failures.

Has a sincere belief in the discouraged person's ability to find a purpose in life.

Allows the person to take risks without judging them.

Reinforces *efforts* made by the discouraged person. The important thing is that one tries not necessarily succeeds. By making efforts to improve, there is hope.

Helps the discouraged person to see the falsehood and negative consequences of self-defeating statements (such as "I'm a failure"). Every person has skills and deficiencies, and every person should be encouraged to improve both their strengths and weaknesses.

Recognizes that all that can be done is to give one's best efforts in trying to motivate a discouraged person. Success in motivating a discouraged person is not guaranteed. To give up hope of motivating a discouraged person means the worker will no longer be effective in working with this discouraged person.

Is skilled at looking for uniquenesses and strengths in an individual. These uniquenesses are communicated to the discouraged person so that the person begins to realize he or she is special and worthwhile. This process leads to a sense of improved self-worth and strengthens the courage to take risks and change.

Helps the discouraged person to develop perceptual alternatives (other ways of looking at life). For example, for a woman who is periodically physically beaten by her husband it is appropriate to point out that other women in similar situations have separated from their husbands, which has led eventually to either an improved marital relationship or to a happier, independent life.

Is aware of the negative consequences of overdependency in a relationship. When the discouraged person is on the way to taking risks and making constructive changes, the worker should start to help the discouraged person to develop "self-encouragement," in which the counselee is encouraged to make and trust his or her own decisions and encouraged to take more risks.

SUMMARY

Poverty is our number one social problem, even though the number and percent of people below the poverty line have gradually decreased during this century. Poverty is relative to time and place. An agreed upon definition of poverty does not as yet exist.

The usual definitions of poverty are based on a lack of money, most commonly using annual income to gauge who is poor. Income definitions either use an absolute approach or a relative approach. The real "hurt" of poverty involves not only financial hardships, but also the psychological meaning that being "poverty stricken" has for a person.

Those most likely to be poor include female heads of households, single women, nonwhite persons, the elderly, large-size families, those with a low educational attainment, and the unemployed.

The causes of poverty are numerous. Poverty is interrelated with all other social problems. Since poverty interacts with nearly every other social problem, almost every social service, to some extent, combats poverty.

The major income maintenance programs to combat poverty were created by the 1935 Social Security Act. The federal government's role in providing social insurance programs and public assistance programs was initiated by this act.

Social insurance programs have primarily institutional aspects, and receive less criticism than public assistance programs, which have primarily residual aspects. There are many negative myths about public assistance programs, especially the AFDC program. A danger of punitive, stigmatized public assistance programs is that poverty and dependency may be passed on to another generation.

The AFDC program does have a number of shortcomings, which perhaps can best be met by replacing it with a negative income tax plan.

Although the profession of social work has gratifications, it also has frustrations, including paperwork, "red tape," working in a bureaucratic structure that is slow in changing to meet emerging needs, and working with discouraged people who do not follow through on "casework plans" to improve their circumstances.

NOTES

1. Ben H. Badikian, *In the Midst of Plenty: The Poor in America* (Boston: Beacon Press, 1964), pp. 29–40.

2. Second inaugural address of President Franklin D. Roosevelt (January 20, 1937).

3. President's Council of Economic Advisers, *Economic Report of the President*, (Washington, D.C.: U.S. Government Printing Office, 1964), pp. 56–57.

4. Marilyn Flynn "Public Assistance" in *Contemporary Social Work*, ed. Donald Brieland, Lela B. Costin, and Charles R. Atherton, 2d ed. (New York: McGraw-Hill, 1980), p. 162.

5. Bradley R. Schiller, *The Economics of Poverty and Discrimination*, 2d ed. (Englewood Cliffs, N.J.: Prentice-Hall, 1976), p. 7.

6. "Carter Takes Another Shot at Welfare Reform," *U.S. News & World Report*, June 4, 1979, p. 42.

7. Michael Harrington, *The Other America* (Baltimore: Penguin Books, 1962).

8. Marilyn Flynn, "Poverty and Income Security" in *Contemporary Social Work*, ed. Donald Brieland et al. (New York: McGraw-Hill, 1975), pp. 88–89.

9. Thomas Sullivan et al., *Social Problems* (New York: Wiley, 1980), p. 390.

10. Flynn "Public Assistance," p. 165.

11. See, for example, Harrington, *The Other America*.

12. Leila Pine, "Good Life on Unemployment," *Wisconsin State Journal*, August 29, 1976, pp. 1, 8.

13. Helen M. Crampton and Kenneth K. Keiser, *Social Welfare: Institution and Process* (New York: Random House, 1970), p. 73.

14. These conservative views are summarized by Samuel Mencher, "Newburgh: The Recurrent Crisis in Public Assistance," *Social Work 7* (January 1962): 3–4.

15. Rex A. Skidmore and Milton G. Thackeray, *Introduction to Social Work*, 2d ed. (Englewood Cliffs, N.J.: Prentice-Hall, 1976), pp. 111–12.

16. Flynn, "Public Assistance," p. 172.

17. Flynn, "Poverty and Income Security," p. 102.

18. "Still More Billions for Food Stamps," *U.S. News & World Report*, May 26, 1980, p. 7.

19. Ibid., p. 7.

20. U.S. Bureau of the Census, *Statistical Abstract of the United States: 1979* (Washington, D.C.: U.S. Government Printing Office, 1979).

21. Ibid.

22. Ibid.

23. Bradley R. Schiller, *The Economics of Poverty and Discrimination*, 3d ed. (Englewood Cliffs, N.J.: Prentice-Hall, 1980).

24. Department of Health, Education and Welfare, *Services to AFDC Families* (Washington, D.C.: U.S. Government Printing Office, October 1972), pp. 20–27.

25. *"Welfare Myths vs. Facts* (Washington, D.C.: U.S. Department of Health, Education and Welfare, 1972).

26. U.S. Senate, Committee on Finance, Subcommittee on Public Assistance, *Staff Data and Materials on Public Assistance* (Washington, D.C.: U.S. Government Printing Office, 1978), p. 11.

27. Ibid.

28. Flynn, "Public Assistance," p. 176.

29. Schiller, *Economics of Poverty and Discrimination*, p. 167.

30. "Wisconsin: Welfare Facts & Figures" (Madison, Wis.: Department of Health and Social Services, 1978).

31. U.S. Congress, Joint Economic Committee, Subcommittee on Fiscal Policy, *Issues in Welfare Administration: Welfare—An Administrative Nightmare*, Studies in Public Welfare, paper no. 5 (Washington, D.C.: U.S. Government Printing Office, 1972), p. 35.

32. Ibid., p. 35.

33. U.S. Bureau of the Census, *Statistical Abstract*.

34. Sar A. Levitan, *Work and Welfare in the 1970s*, Welfare Policy Project (Durham, N.C.: Duke University, Institute of Policy Science and Public Affairs, 1977).

35. Leonard Goodwin, *Do the Poor Want to Work?* (Washington, D.C.: Brookings Institution, 1972).

36. U.S. Bureau of the Census, *Statistical Abstract*.

37. Schiller, Economics of Poverty and Discrimination, p. 167.

38. U.S. Department of Health, Education and Welfare, *Findings of the 1973 AFDC Study: Part I* (Washington, D.C.: National Center for Social Statistics, 1974), p. 80.

39. "Wisconsin: Welfare Facts & Figures."

40. Perry Levinson, "The Next Generation: A Study of Children in AFDC Families," *Welfare in Review* 7 (March–April 1969): 4–12.

41. Ibid.

42. Flynn, "Public Assistance," p. 180.

43. Alvin L. Schorr, "A Family Allowance Program for Preschool Children," in *Poverty Policy*, ed. Theodore M. Marinor (Chicago: Aldine Atherton, 1969), p. 123.

44. Flynn, "Poverty and Income Security," p. 89.

45. Paul A. Brinker and Joseph J. Klos, *Poverty, Manpower, and Social Security* (Austin, Tex.: Austin Press, 1976), p. 538.

46. Ibid., p. 535.

47. Ibid., pp. 536–37.

48. "Carter Takes Another Shot at Welfare Reform," p. 42.

49. Janet S. Hartnett, "Title XX—An Overview and an Update," *Tri-Regional Workshop on Maternal and Child Health Services, 1976 Proceedings* (Austin, Tex.: University of Texas, School of Social Work, 1976), p. 64.

50. Ibid., p. 63.

51. Ibid., pp. 64–65.

52. For example, see Richard B. Stuart, *Trick or Treatment: How and When Psychotherapy Fails* (Champaign, Ill.: Research Press, 1970).

53. Lewis Losoncy, *Turning People On* (Englewood Cliffs, N.J.: Prentice-Hall, 1977).

chapter 5

A PERSPECTIVE

Several years ago I worked at a maximum security hospital for the "criminally insane." On my case load were a number of people who committed some bizarre crimes, due to emotional and interpersonal problems. Since professionals in the field of social welfare have to handle many "raw" human situations, a few of the more bizarre occurrences will be mentioned to give the reader a "flavor" of such situations that arise.

In one case a 22-year-old male decapitated his 17-year-old friend. In another a married male with four children was arrested for the fourth time for exposing himself. In still another a male dug up several graves and used the corpses to "redecorate" his home. Another married man was committed after it was discovered he was involved in an incestual relationship with his 11- and 13-year-old daughters. Another man was committed after several efforts to deliver sermons in local taverns, and after he kept maintaining clouds followed him around in whatever direction he was going. Another went AWOL from the service, and within a week proceeded to kidnap and rape five women. Another brutally killed his father with an axe. Bizarre? Yes, definitely! But if one took the time to examine these cases, and looked at what the offenders were thinking when they committed these crimes, one would be able to gain an understanding of: (a) why the bizarre actions occurred, (b) what would have prevented the bizarre actions from happening, and (c) what services are now needed to prevent the offenders from again getting into trouble upon their release.[1]

To illustrate, the grave digger's case will briefly be summarized. Jim Schmidt (name has been changed) was 46 years old when he began digging graves and redecorating his home. His mother had died three and a half years earlier. Unfortunately, his mother was the only person that provided meaning to his life. He was shy and had no other friends, and the two had lived together in this small, rural community for the past 22 years. After his mother's death he became even more isolated, with no friends, living by himself.

Emotional problems and counseling

Being very lonely, he wished his mother was still alive. As happens with many people who lose someone close, he began dreaming his mother was still alive. His dreams appeared so real, that upon awakening he found it difficult to believe his mother was definitely gone. With such thoughts he began thinking his mother could in fact be brought back to life. He concluded that by bringing corpses of females to his home, it would help bring his mother back (now, to us this idea certainly appears irrational, but being isolated he had no way of checking what was real and what was not). Feeling very deeply the loss of his mother, he decided to give the idea a try. He of course needed counseling services (then and now) that would help him adjust to his mother's death, that would help him find new interests in life, that would help him to become more involved with other people, and that would enable him to exchange thoughts with others to check out what is real and what is not.

EXTENT AND CAUSES

Emotional and interpersonal problems are two global labels covering an array of problems: depression, excessive anxiety, feelings of inferiority or isolation, being alienated, being sadistic or masochistic, marital problems, broken romances, parent-child relationship problems, being hyperactive, being overly critical, overly dependent, or overly aggressive, having a phobia, being compulsive or having an obsession, feeling guilty, being shy, showing violent displays of temper, being vindictive, having nightmares or insomnia, and so on. All of us, at one time or another, have emotional and interpersonal problems. Some problems we are able to handle ourselves, others we need help with from friends, relatives, or professional counselors.

For each problem there are unique, and in many cases a number of potential causes. Depression, for example, may be caused by loss of a loved one or loss of something else considered highly valuable, by feelings of guilt or shame, by knowledge of a future undesirable impending event (for example, discovery of a terminal illness), by aggression turned inward, by certain physical phases as menopause, by feelings of inadequacy or inferiority, and by feelings of being lonely or isolated. There have literally been hundreds of thousands of books published on the causes and ways to treat the wide array of emotional and interpersonal problems.

A presidential Commission on Mental Health appointed by President Jimmy Carter concluded that approximately 15 percent of the population, at any point in time, is in need of some type of mental health service, and that nearly 25 percent of the population suffers from depression, anxiety, and other symptoms of emotional disorder.[2] In addition, practically all of us encounter serious emotional difficulties at some time in our lives: for example, emotional problems surrounding a broken romance or marriage, addiction to alcohol or drugs, being a rape or other crime victim, failing at a goal we've set, and so on.

BRIEF HISTORY OF MENTAL ILLNESS CARE

A variety of emotional and behavioral problems have been labeled as being "mental illnesses" (whether mental illness in fact exists will be discussed in a later section).

The history of treatment for the emotionally disturbed is fascinating, but also filled with injustices and tragedies. George Rosen documents that most societies have developed unique ways of viewing mental illness and treating those so labeled.[3] In some societies deviants have been valued highly, even treated as prophets having supernatural powers. In others the emotionally disturbed have been viewed as evil threats and even feared as being possessed with demonological powers. For instance, during a brief period in our colonial history certain of the disturbed were viewed as being "witches" and burned at the stake. Prior to the 19th century the severely disturbed were confined in "almshouses" received only harsh, custodial care, and were often chained to the walls. [4]

In the 19th century a few mental institutions in France, England, and United States began to take a more humanitarian approach to treating the disturbed. Although the severely disturbed were still confined in institutions, they began to be viewed as either having an illness or as having an emotional problem. The physical surroundings were improved, and there were efforts to replace the harsh, custodial treatment with a caring approach recognizing each resident as being a person deserving respect and dignity. Unfortunately, these humanitarian efforts were not widely accepted, partly because they were considered too expensive. Most of the severely disturbed continued to be confined in overcrowded, unsanitary dwellings, with inadequate care and diet.

In 1908 Clifford Beer's book, *A Mind That Found Itself*, was published. [5] Beers had been confined as a patient, and the book recounted the atrocities occurring in his "madhouse." The book reached a wide audience and sensitized the public to the emotional trauma being experienced by those confined. Under Beer's leadership, mental health associations were formed which advocated the need for improved inpatient care and initiated the concept of outpatient treatment.

Sigmund Freud developed his psychoanalytic theories about the causes and ways to treat emotional problems between 1900 and 1920. Emotional problems were seen as being mental illnesses, resulting from early traumatic experiences, internal psychological conflicts, fixations at various stages of development, and from unconscious psychological processes. Most segments of the counseling professions (psychiatry, clinical psychology, social work) accepted from the 1920s to the 1950s Freud's and other psychoanalytic theorists' views in regards to diagnosing and treating the disturbed. Freud's influence was successful in having the public accept a more humanitarian approach in treating the disturbed.

However, in the 1950s questions began to arise about the effectiveness of the psychoanalytic approach. It was expensive, an analysis took four or five years, and research studies began appearing showing the rate of improvement for those undergoing analysis was less than for those receiving no treatment. [6] Since the 1950s a variety of counseling approaches have been developed which reject most or all of the concepts underlying psychoanalysis; these newer approaches include behavior modification, rational therapy, reality therapy, transactional analysis, radical therapy, gestalt therapy and client-centered therapy.*

It should be mentioned that certain segments of the medical profession have continued to maintain since the 19th century that mental illness is akin to other physical illnesses. They assert that infectious diseases, genetic endowment, and metabolic disorders were the causes of mental disorders. [7] However, only a few specific organic causes have been identified: general paresis, for instance,

---

* A good summary of these therapies is provided in: *Current Psychotherapies*, ed. Raymond Corsini (Itasca, Ill.: F. E. Peacock, 1979); *Social Work Treatment*, ed. Francis J. Turner (New York: Free Press, 1979); and Charles Zastrow, *The Practice of Social Work* (Homewood, Ill.: Dorsey Press, 1981).

which is a progressive emotional disorder, has been linked to syphilis; and pellagra, another disorder, has been found to result from dietary deficiency. The notion that mental disorders are physiological led to certain medical treatments that now appear to be tragedies. In the 18th century bloodletting was widely used. In the early 20th century electroconvulsive therapy (where the brain receives an electrical shock resulting in a brief coma) and prefrontal lobotomies (surgical slashing of the frontal section of the brain) were used to "remove" the mental illness. Such approaches have little therapeutic value and cause lasting brain damage, particularly lobotomies which leave the patient docile and retarded.

In the past 25 years there have been two major developments in the treatment of the severely disturbed. (*a*) The discovery and use of psychoactive drugs, both tranquilizers and stimulants—the initial hope was that such drugs would cure severe disturbances, but it was soon realized that such drugs provided primarily symptom relief and thereby enabled the disturbed person to more accessible to other therapy programs and approaches.[8] (*b*) The second development was deinstitutionalization. Mental health practitioners realized that mental hospitals, instead of "curing" the disturbed, were frequently perpetuating disturbed behavior via long-term hospitalization. The disturbed were labeled as mentally ill, and through long-term hospitalization would define themselves as being "different" and enact the insane role. Also they became adapted to the relaxed, safe life of a hospital, and the longer they stayed the more they perceived the outside world to be threatening. Mental health professionals now only use hospitalization for those whose emotional problems pose a serious threat to their own well-being or to that of others. In almost all cases such hospitaliza-

tion is brief and time limited. Included in the concept of deinstitutionalization has been a significant expansion of services designed to meet the needs of the disturbed in their home community: including community-based mental health centers, halfway houses, rehabilitation workshops, social therapeutic clubs, and foster care services for the disturbed. A criticism of the deinstitutionalization approach has been that some communities have returned long-term hospitalized patients to society *without* developing adequate community-based support services.

COMMUNITY MENTAL HEALTH CENTERS

Counseling services for emotional problems are provided by nearly every direct service, social welfare agency; including public welfare agencies, probation and parole agencies, penal institutions, school social services, family service agencies, adoption agencies, sheltered workshops, social service units in hospitals, and nursing homes. However, in many communities, mental health centers are a primary resource for serving those with emotional problems.

Community mental health centers were given their impetus with the passage by the federal government of the Community Mental Health Centers Act of 1963. This act provided for transferring the care and treatment of the majority of "mentally ill" persons from state hospitals to their home communities. The emphasis is on local care, with provision of comprehensive services (particularly to underprivileged areas and people).

Other emphases are: (*a*) early diagnosis, treatment and early return to community, (*b*) the physical location of the centers "near and accessible to" the populations they serve, (*c*) the establishment of centers on the basis of "catchment areas" containing between 75,000 and 200,000 people, and (*d*) the provision of comprehensive care having five basic components: (1) inpatient care; (2) outpatient care; (3) partial hospitalization (that is, day, night, and weekend care); (4) emergency care; and (5) consultation/education.

Services provided are expected to relate to a wide range of problem areas and population groups; such as the disturbed, the aged, minorities, and those with alcohol and other drug-related problems.

Professionals in a community mental health center come from all the helping professions: including psychiatrists, social workers, psychologists, psychiatric nurses, specialized consultants, occupational and recreational therapists, paraprofessionals, and volunteers.

Typical services include outpatient care, inpatient care, alcohol and chemical abuse treatment, work evaluation, occupational therapy, family and group therapy, transportation services, counseling of children and adults, crisis intervention (including 24-hour emergency care), community education, and field training of students in the helping professions.

Community mental health services have in recent years received increasing criticism. Studies have found some community mental health services are ineffective and inadequate.[9] Patients still have high readmission rates and inadequate levels of adjustment to the community.[10] Many centers have been ineffective in dealing with the personal and societal problems of large numbers of poor people, with many of these so-called comprehensive centers providing little more than traditional inpatient and outpatient care for middle-class patients.[11]

On the other hand proponents of community mental health centers argue that the results of such centers have been impressive. They point out that their programs have

Occupational therapy at a comprehensive mental health center

reduced the number of people in state mental hospitals from 555,000 in 1955 to 191,000 in 1975.[12]

DOES MENTAL ILLNESS EXIST?

Currently there is a substantial controversy in the mental health field regarding whether mental illness does in fact exist. The use of mental illness labels involves applying medical labels (that is, schizophrenia, paranoia, psychosis, neurosis, insanity) to emotional problems. Adherents of the medical approach believe the disturbed person's mind is affected by some generally unknown, internal condition. That unknown, internal condition, they assert, might be due to genetic endowment, metabolic disorders, infectious diseases, internal conflicts, unconscious use of defense mechanisms, and traumatic early experiences that cause emotional fixations and prevent future psychological growth.

Critics of the medical (mental illness) approach assert such medical labels have no diagnostic or treatment value, and frequently have an adverse labeling effect.

Thomas Szasz was one of the first authorities to assert that mental illness is a myth—does not exist.[13] Beginning with the assumption that the term *mental illness* implies a "disease of the mind," he categorizes all of the so-called mental illnesses into three types of emotional disorders and discusses the inappropriateness of calling such human difficulties "mental illnesses":

1. Personal disabilities, such as excessive anxiety, depression, fears, and feelings of inadequacy. Szasz says such so-called mental illnesses may appropriately be considered "mental" (in the sense in which thinking and feeling are considered "mental" activities), but he asserts they are not diseases.
2. Antisocial acts, such as bizarre homicides and other social deviations. Homosexuality used to be in this category, but was removed from the American Psychiatric Association's list of mental illnesses in 1974. Szasz says such antisocial acts are only social deviations and he asserts they are neither "mental" nor "diseases."
3. Deterioration of the brain with associated personality changes. This category includes the "mental illnesses" in which personality changes result following brain deterioration from such causes as arteriosclerosis, chronic alcoholism, general paresis, or serious brain damage following an accident. Common symptoms are loss of memory, listlessness, apathy, and deterioration of personal grooming habits.

Szasz says these disorders can appropriately be considered "diseases," but are diseases of the brain (i.e., brain deterioration which specifies the nature of the problem) rather than being a disease of the mind. Szasz states.

> The belief in mental illness as something other than man's trouble in getting along with his fellow man, is the proper heir to the belief in demonology and witchcraft. Mental illness exists or is "real" in exactly the same sense in which witches existed or were "real."[14]

In actuality, there are three steps to becoming labeled "mentally ill": (*a*) the person displays some strange deviant behavior, (*b*) the behavior is not tolerated by the family or local community, (*c*) the professional labeler, usually a psychiatrist, happens to believe in the medical model and assigns a mental illness label. Thomas Scheff and David Mechanic provide evidence that whether the family/community will tolerate the deviant behavior, and whether the professional labeler believes in the medical model, are more crucial in determining whether someone will be assigned a "mentally ill" label, than the strange behavior exhibited by the person.[15]

The point that Szasz and many other writers are striving to make is that people do have emotional problems, but they do not have a mystical, mental illness. Terms that describe behavior they believe are very useful: for example, *depression, anxiety,* an *obsession,* a *compulsion, excessive fear, feelings of being a failure.* Such terms describe personal problems that people have. But the medical terms, they assert (such as schizophrenia and psychosis), are not useful because there is no distinguishing symptom which would indicate whether a person has, or does not have, the "illness." In addition, Offer and Sabshin point out there is considerable variation between cultures regarding what is defined as a mental illness.[16] The usefulness of the medical model is also questioned because psychiatrists frequently disagree on the medical diagnosis to be assigned to those who are disturbed.[17]

In a dramatic study psychologist David Rosenhan demonstrated that professional staff in mental hospitals could not distinguish "insane" patients from "sane" patients.[18] Rosenhan and seven "normal" associates went to 12 mental hospitals in five different states claiming they were hearing voices. All eight were admitted to these hospitals. After admission these pseudopatients stated they stopped hearing voices and acted normally. The hospitals were unable to distinguish their "sane" status from the "insane" status of other patients. The hospitals kept these pseudopatients hospitalized for an average of 19 days, and all were then discharged with a diagnosis of "schizophrenia in remission."

The use of medical labels, it has been asserted, has several adverse labeling effects.[19] The person labeled mentally ill (and frequently the therapist) believes that s/he has a disease for which unfortunately there is no known "cure." The label gives the labeled person an excuse for not taking responsibility for his/her actions (for example, innocent by reason of insanity). Since there is no known "cure," the disturbed frequently idle away their time waiting for someone to discover a cure, rather than assuming responsibility for their behavior, examining the reasons why there are problems, and making efforts to improve. Other undesirable consequences of being labeled mentally ill are: the individual may lose some of his/her legal rights;[20] may be stigmatized in his/her social interactions as being dangerous, unpredictable, untrustworthy, or of "weak" character,[21] and may find it more difficult to secure employment or recieve a promotion.[22]

The question of whether mental illness exists is indeed a very important question. The assignment of mental illness labels to disturbed people has substantial implications for how the disturbed will be treated, for how others will view them, and for how they will view themselves. Cooley's "looking glass self-concept" crystalizes what is being said here. The "looking glass" says we develop our self-concept (our idea of who we are) in terms of how other people react to us. If someone is labeled mentally ill, other people are apt to reach to him/her as if he/she were mentally ill, and that person may well define him/herself as being different, "crazy," and begin playing that role.

OTHER ISSUES

Civil rights. State laws permit the involuntary hospitalization of people in mental health hospitals, which can be seen as an infringement of their civil rights to liberty. While state laws differ, in many jurisdictions people may be hospitalized without their consent and without due process.[23] In some jurisdictions a person may be sent to a mental hospital against his/her consent for treatment on the statement of a physician.[24]

When this author worked at a hospital for the "criminally insane" there was a patient who was originally arrested on a disorderly conduct charge for urinating on a fire hydrant. Some neighbors thought he might be "mentally ill," so the judge ordered that he be sent to a mental hospital for a 60-day observation period to determine his sanity. The hospital judged him to be "insane" and "incompetent to stand trial" on the charge. Now, he was neither considered to be a threat to harm himself nor to harm others. But, with the hospital's finding, the judge confined him to a maximum security hospital for the criminally insane, and when I worked there he had already been hospitalized for nine years—for committing an offense that if found guilty he probably would have been required to only pay a small fine. Involuntary confinement has been a controversial practice for years.

Another problem in some mental hospitals is that patients do not receive adequate treatment even after several years of confinement. Inadequate treatment is a civil rights violation because in 1964 Congress established a statutory right to treatment in the Hospitalization of the Mentally Ill Act.[25]

Decisions about providing treatments such as electroconvulsive therapy (which has questionable value and may cause brain damage) also raise civil rights questions. The severely disturbed are often unable to make rational choices for their own welfare. Permission of relatives is sometimes obtained, but this still denies patients their fundamental rights.

The above problems caused the President's Commission on Mental Health to recommend due process be followed in arriving at decisions involving enforced hospitalization and treatment.[26] Recent federal court decisions have also reflected these concerns; they have held that mental illness is not a sufficient basis for denying liberty, and that hospitalized mental patients have a right either to adequate treatment or to release.[27]

Plea of innocent by reason of insanity. In 1979 a jury found Dan White innocent by reason of insanity on charges of the premeditated murder of city Mayor George Moscone and city supervisor Harvey Milk. This verdict was rendered, even though testimony presented clearly showed these murders had been carefully planned and carried out by White.[28] The general public was as shocked by the jury's decision as it was by the crime. With this jury's decision, White will probably be confided in a mental hospital for a few years and then released.

In another recent case, Kenneth Bianchi (called the Hollywood "Hillside Strangler") was accused of murdering 13 women in the Los Angeles area and 2 more in Washington state. Six different psychiatrists examining Bianchi came to three different conclusions about his mental state: two judged him to be sane, two judged him to be insane, and two were undecided.[29]

Cases such as White and Bianchi have forced the courts and psychiatrists to begin to examine more carefully the plea of innocent by reason of insanity. As indicated earlier the terms *mental illness* and *mental health* are poorly defined. Mental illness (insanity) may not even exist. In a number of trials involving the insanity plea it has become "routine" for the prosecuting attorney to use as witnesses those psychiatrists who are apt to judge the defendant to be "sane," while the defendant's attorney uses as witnesses those psychiatrists who are apt to arrive at an "insane" decision.

Psychiatrist Lee Coleman urges the insanity defense be eliminated altogether in courts in order to resolve this dilemma. Eliminating the insanity defense would allow the courts to deal with the guilt or innocence of an individual without interference from psychiatrists. Coleman states, ". . . victims are no less injured by one who is mentally sound and violent."[30] Coleman further urges that if the individual convicted later wished helped for emotional or behavioral problems, s/he could then request it.

Use of psychotropic drugs. Psychotropic drugs include tranquilizers, antipsychotic drugs (such as thorazine), and antidepressant drugs. The use of psychotropic drugs, since their discovery in 1954, has been given substantial credit for the marked decrease in the number of patients in state hospitals, from 555,000 in 1955 to 191,000 in 1975.[31]

Psychotropic drugs do not "cure" emotional problems but are useful in reducing high levels of anxiety, depression, and tension.

Americans make extensive use of psychotropic drugs, particularly tranquilizers. Valium, Librium, Equanil, and other mild tranquilizers are widely used. Most general practitioners prescribe tranquilizers for the large number of patients who complain of tension and being emotionally upset. "Popping pills" (both legal and illegal) has become fashionable. The dangers of excessive drug use include physical and psychological dependence and unwanted side effects. There is also the danger that because drugs provide temporary symptom relief, users may focus their attention on taking pills rather than on making the necessary changes in their lives to resolve the problems causing the anxiety, depression, or tension. Physicians face a dilemma in balancing the benefits of psychotropic drugs against the dangers of abuse, particularly when such drugs are sought by patients for extended periods of time.

SOCIAL WORK AND MENTAL HEALTH

Social workers were first employed in the mental health field in 1906 to take social histories of newly admitted patients to Manhattan State Hospital in New York.[32] Since then they have been involved in providing a variety of preventive, diagnostic, and treatment services.

Over the years the treatment emphasis has moved from treating the individual to treating the family. Social workers, psychologists, and psychiatrists now function interchangeably as individuals, family, and group therapists. All three professional groups are also involved in designing and administering mental health programs. Other professionals involved in working as a team in mental health facilities include psychiatric nurses, occupational therapists, and recreational therapists.

It has been estimated that half the professionals who provide mental health services in the United States today are social workers.[33] Many social agencies, in addition to community mental health centers, provide counseling and psychotherapy to people having emotional problems. Such agencies include schools, family counseling agencies, public welfare departments, hospitals, adoption agencies, and probation and parole departments. An increasing number of clinical social workers are opening private practices to furnish individual, family, and group therapy for a variety of emotional problems. Increasingly, payments from public and private insurance programs reimburse social workers for providing therapy on a private basis.

The National Association of Social Workers (NASW) has been promoting state licensing (or registration) requirements to ensure the public that social work practitioners meet high standards of competence. With the expansion of private practices by clinical social workers, the need for licensing is increasing.

NASW has also established a national Registry of Clinical Social Workers. Requirements for membership are:

A master's or doctoral degree in social work from a graduate school of social work accredited or recognized by the Council on Social Work Education; two years or 3,000 hours of post-master's clinical social work practice under the supervision of a master's degree level social worker, or, if social work supervision could be shown to have been unavailable, supervision by another mental health professional with the added condition of giving evidence of continued participation and identification with the social work profession; at least two years or 3,000 hours of direct

A wide variety of professionals at a mental health center: Psychologist, recreational therapist, volunteer coordinator, psychiatrist, social worker, psychiatric nurse, drug counselor, occupational therapist, librarian

clinical practice within the last ten years; be a member of the Academy of Certified Social Workers (ACSW) or be licensed in a State at a level at least equivalent to ACSW standards. The clinical social worker has specialized knowledge of human growth and behavior and of internal, interpersonal and environmental stress on social functioning. This knowledge must be combined with practice skills in treatment modalities which alleviate such problems.[34]

Until a few years ago, social work in the mental health field was generally practiced in a subordinate role to psychiatry. But with an increasing recognition that emotional problems are primarily problems in living, rather than organic in nature, social workers are increasingly being employed in agencies to provide counseling and psychotherapy, without being supervised by a psychiatrist.

The primary therapy approach used to treat people with emotional or behavioral problems is psychotherapy or counseling (the author will use these two terms interchangeable as there do not appear to be clear-cut distinctions between the two).

Counseling is a broad term covering individual, family, and group therapy. A skilled counselor has knowledge of: (a) interviewing principles, and (b) global and specific treatment approaches. Material in these two areas will briefly be presented. This material is designed to give the reader a "flavor" of what counseling is composed of. Additional theoretical material covering these two areas is presented in social work methods and field placement courses. Through role playing of contrived counseling situations, and later working with clients, social work students gain skill and confidence in putting this material into practice. Sharpening and further developing one's counseling skills does not end with acquiring a degree in a counseling field; it is an ongoing, lifelong process.

COUNSELING

Counseling services are provided by practically every direct service social welfare agency. Some agencies, such as welfare departments and mental health centers, provide counseling services covering almost all emotional or interpersonal problems. Other more specialized agencies provide counseling designed for specific problems (for example, drug abuse counseling, abortion counseling, sexual counseling, genetic counseling, and parent effectiveness training); areas that require considerable background knowledge and training in using highly developed treatment techniques.

Capacity to effectively counsel is one of the key skills needed in social workers; in fact, it may be *the* most important skill. Acquiring in-depth skill at counseling in one area (for example, marriage or adoption counseling) prepares that person for counseling in other areas. The key learning variable is acquiring skill at in-depth counseling, as this skill is transferable. Because in-depth counseling is transferable to other areas, undergraduate and graduate social work programs are able to take a generic (broad-based) approach to social work training. The emphasis is placed on in-depth training in counseling, rather than on training students for specialized counseling areas.

How to counsel*

Counseling someone with personal problems is neither magical nor mystical. Although training and experience in counseling is beneficial, everyone has the potential of helping another by listening and talking through difficulties. Counseling with a successful outcome can be done by a friend, neighbor, relative, yourself, the local barber, hairdresser, banker, and bartender, as well as by social workers, psychiatrists, psychologists, guidance counselors, and the clergy. This is not to say that everyone will be successful at counseling. Professional people, because of their training and experience, have a higher probability of being successful. But competence and concern, rather than degrees or certificates, are the keys to desirable outcomes.

There are three phases to counseling: (1) building a relationship, (2) exploring problems in depth, and (3) exploring alternative solutions. Successful counseling gradually proceeds from one phase to the next, with some overlapping of these stages. For example, in many cases while exploring problems, the relationship between the counselor and the counselee continues to develop; and while exploring alternative solutions, the problems are generally being examined in greater depth.

* This section on "How to Counsel" is reprinted from an article written by this author with the same title in *The Personal Problem Solver,* ed. Charles Zastrow and Dae Chang (Englewood Cliffs, N.J.: Spectrum Books, 1977). Reprinted by permission of Prentice-Hall, Inc., Englewood Cliffs, New Jersey.

Counseling a young client at a runaway center

Building a relationship

1. The counselor should seek to establish a nonthreatening atmosphere where the counselee feels safe to communicate fully his or her troubles while feeling accepted as a person.

2. In initial contacts with the counselee, the counselor needs to "sell" him/herself, not arrogantly, but as a knowledgeable, understanding person who may be able to help and who wants to try.

3. Be calm, do not express shock or laughter when the counselee begins to open up about his or her problems. Emotional outbursts, even if subtle, will lead the counselee to believe that you are not going to understand his or her difficulties, and he or she will usually stop discussing them.

4. Generally be nonjudgmental, not moralistic. Show respect for the counselee's values and do not try to sell your values. The values that work for you may not be best for someone else in a different situation. For example, if the counselee is premaritally pregnant, do not attempt to force your values toward adoption or abortion, but let the counselee decide on the course of action after a full examination of the problem and an exploration of alternative solutions.

5. View the counselee as an equal. "Rookie" counselors sometimes make the mistake of thinking that because someone is sharing their intimate secrets, the counselor must be very important, and they end up arranging a superior-inferior relationship. If the counselee feels that he or she is being treated as an inferior, he or she will be less motivated to reveal and discuss personal difficulties.

6. Use "shared vocabulary." This does not mean that the counselor should use the same slang words and the same accent as the counselee. If the counselee sees the counselor as artificial in use of slang or accent, it may seriously offend him or her. The counselor should use words that the counselee understands and that are not offensive.

7. The tone of the counselor's voice should convey the message that the counselor empathetically understands and cares about the counselee's feelings.

8. Keep confidential what the counselee has said. People unfortunately have nearly irresistible urges to share "juicy secrets" with someone else. If the counselee discovers that confidentially has been violated, a working relationship may be quickly destroyed.

9. If you are counseling a relative or a friend, there is a danger that, because you are emotionally involved, you may get upset or into an argument with the other person. If that happens it is almost always best to drop the subject immediately, as tactfully as possible. Perhaps after tempers cool the subject can be brought up again, or perhaps it may be best to refer the counselee to someone else. When counseling a friend or relative, you should be aware that when you find yourself becoming upset, further discussion will not be productive. Many professional counselors refuse to counsel friends or relatives because they are aware that they are emotionally involved. Emotional involvement interferes with the calm, detached per-

spective that is needed to help clients explore problems and alternative solutions.

Exploring problems in depth

1. Many "rookie" counselors make the mistake of suggesting solutions as soon as a problem is identified, without exploring the problem area in depth. For example, an advocate of abortions may advise this solution as soon as a single female reveals that she is pregnant, without taking the time to discover whether this person is strongly opposed to abortions, really wants a baby, or intends to marry soon.

2. In exploring problems in depth, the counselor and counselee need to examine such areas as the extent of the problem, how long the problem has existed, what the causes are, how the counselee feels about the problem, and what physical and mental capacities and strengths the counselee has to cope with the problem, prior to exploring alternative solutions. To illustrate, if a single female is pregnant, the counselor and counselee need to explore the following questions: How does the person feel about being pregnant? Has she seen a doctor? About how long has she been pregnant? Do her parents know? What are their feelings and concerns if they know? Has the girl informed the father? What are his feelings and concerns if he knows? What does she feel is the most urgent situation to deal with first? Answers to such questions will determine the future direction of counseling. The most pressing, immediate problem might be to inform her parents, who may react critically, or it might be to secure medical services.

3. When a problem area is identified, there are usually a number of smaller problems that may occur. Explore all these. For example, how to tell the father, obtaining medical care, obtaining funds for medical expenses, deciding where to live, deciding

whether to leave school or work during the pregnancy, deciding whether to keep the child, making plans for what to do after the child is delivered or the pregnancy terminated.

4. In a multiproblem situation, the best way to decide which problem to handle first is to ask the counselee which problem he or she perceives as most pressing. If the problem can be solved, start with exploring that subproblem in depth and developing together a strategy for the solution. Success in solving a subproblem will increase the counselee's confidence in the counselor, and thereby further solidify the relationship.

5. Convey empathy, not sympathy. Empathy is the capacity to show that you are aware of and can to some extent feel what the counselee is saying. Sympathy is also a sharing of feelings, but it has the connotation of offering pity. The difference is subtle, but empathy is problem-solving oriented and sympathy is usually problem-prolonging. Giving sympathy usually causes the counselee to dwell on his or her emotions without taking action to improve the situation. For example, if one gives sympathy to a depressed person, that person will keep telling you his or her sad story over and over, each time having an emotional outpouring supported by your sympathy, without taking any action to improve the situation. Telling the story over and over only reopens old wounds and prolongs the depression.

6. "Trust your guts." The most important tool that a counselor has is him/herself (his or her feelings and perceptions). A counselor should continually strive to place him/herself in the client's situation (with the client's values and pressures). To use the earlier example, if the client is 17 years old, single, pregnant, and has parents who are very critical of the situation and who want her to have an abortion, a competent counselor would continually strive to feel what

she is feeling and to perceive the world from her perspective, with her goals, difficulties, pressures, and values. It probably never happens that a counselor is 100 percent accurate in placing him/herself in the counselee's situation, but 70 to 80 percent is usually sufficient to gain an awareness of the counselee's pressures, problems, and perspectives. This information is very useful in assisting the counselor in determining what additional areas need to be explored, what he or she should say, and in figuring out what might be possible solutions. Stated in a somewhat different way, a counselor should ask him- or herself, "What is this person trying to tell me and how can I make it clear that I understand not only intellectually but empathically?"

7. When you believe that the client has touched upon an important area of concern, further communication can be encouraged by:

a. Nonverbally showing interest.
b. Pauses. "Rookie" counselors usually become anxious when there is a pause, and they hasten to say something, anything, to have conversation continue. This is usually a mistake, especially when it leads to a change in the topic. A pause will also make the counselee anxious, give him or her time to think about the important area of concern, and then usually motivate him or her to continue conversation in that area.
c. Neutral probes; for example, "Could you tell me more about it?" "Why do you feel that way?" "I'm not sure I understand what you have in mind."
d. Summarizing what the client is saying; for example, "During this past hour you made a number of critical comments about your spouse; it sounds like some things about your marriage are making you unhappy."

e. Reflecting feelings; for example, "you seem angry" or "You appear to be depressed about that."

8. Approach socially unacceptable topics tactfully. Tact is an essential quality of a competent counselor. Try not to ask a question in such a way that the answer will put the respondent in an embarrassing position. Suppose, for instance, that you are an adult who has a good relationship with a teenager and have reason to suspect that person has "hangups" about masturbation. How would you tactfully bring up the subject to discuss? One possible approach is, "When I was your age, I had a number of hangups about masturbating. That was unfortunate. Most teenagers masturbate, but many have strong feelings of guilt or shame about it. Although masturbation has been stigmatized, it is in reality a natural outlet for sexual feelings and is not harmful. In fact, Masters and Johnson recommend frequent masturbation, either alone or with a partner. If you have some worries about this, perhaps we could talk about them." Informing the youth that you also had hangups about this subject personalizes it and tells the teenager that you have experienced some of the concerns he or she is currently facing. Communication and relationship building are fostered.

9. When pointing out a limitation that a counselee has, mention and compliment him or her on any assets. When a limitation is being mentioned, the counselee will literally feel that something is being laid bare or taken away. Therefore, compliment him or her in another area to give something back.

10. Watch for nonverbal cues. A competent counselor will generally use such cues to identify when a sensitive subject is being touched upon, as the client will generally become anxious and show anxiety by a changing tone of voice, fidgeting, yawning, stiff posture, and a flushed face. Some coun-

Marriage counseling

selors even claim that they can tell when a client becomes anxious by observing when the pupils of the eyes are dilating.

11. Be honest. An untruth always runs the risk of being discovered. If that happens, the counselee's confidence in the counselor will be seriously damaged, and perhaps the relationship seriously jeopardized. But being honest goes beyond not telling lies. The counselor should always point out those shortcomings that are in the counselee's best interest to give attention to. For example, if someone is being fired from jobs because of poor grooming habits, this needs to be brought to that person's attention. Or if a trainee's relationship skills and personality are not suited for the helping profession, that trainee needs to be "counseled out" in the interest of clients and in the trainee's own best interests.

12. Listen attentively to what the counselee is saying. Try to view his or her words, not from your perspective but from the counselee's. Unfortunately, many people are caught up in their own interests and concerns, and they do not "tune out" those thoughts while the counselee is speaking. This guideline seems very simple, but it is indeed difficult for many to follow.

Exploring alternative solutions

1. After (or sometimes as part of) a subproblem is explored in depth, the next step is for the counselor and the counselee to consider alternative solutions. The counselor's role is generally to indicate the possible alternatives and then to explore with the counselee their merits, shortcomings, and consequences. For example, with the case of the premaritally pregnant girl, if she decides to continue the pregnancy to full term, possible alternatives for the subproblem of making plans for living arrangements include keeping the child, a possible marriage, seeking public assistance, foster care after delivery, a possible paternity suit, placing the child for adoption, obtaining the assistance of a close relative to help care for the child.

2. The counselee usually has the right to self-determination, that is, to choose the course of action among possible alternatives. The counselor's role is to help the counselee clarify and understand the likely consequences of each available alternative, but generally not to give advice or choose the alternative for the counselee. If the counselor were to select the alternative, there are two possible outcomes: (1) the alternative may prove to be undesirable for the counselee, in which case the counselee will probably blame the counselor for the advice and the future relationship will be seriously hampered, and (2) the alternative may prove to be desirable for the counselee. This immediate outcome is advantageous, but the danger is that the counselee will then become overly dependent on the counselor, seeking the counselor's advice for nearly every decision in the future, and generally being reluctant to make decisions on his or her own. In actual practice, most courses of action have desirable and undesirable consequences. For example, if the unmarried mother is advised to keep her child, she may receive considera-

ble gratification from being with and raising the child, but at the same time she may blame the counselor for such possible negative consequences as long-term financial hardships and an isolated social life.

3. Counseling is done *with* the counselee, not *to* or *for* the counselee. The counselee should have the responsibility of doing many of the tasks necessary to improve the situation. A good rule to follow is that the counselee should take responsibility for those tasks that he or she has the capacity to carry out, while the counselor should only attempt to do those that are beyond the capacities of the counselee. Doing things *for* counselees, similar to giving advice, runs the risk of creating a dependency relationship. Furthermore, successful accomplishment of tasks by counselees leads to personal growth and better prepares them for taking on future responsibilities.

4. The counselee's right to self-determination should be taken away only if the selected course of action has a high probability of seriously hurting others or the counselee. For example, if it is highly probable that a parent will continue to abuse a child, or if the counselee attempts to take his or her own life, intervention by the counselor is suggested. For most situations, however, the counselee should have the right to select his or her alternative, even when the counselor believes that another alternative is a better course of action. Frequently, the counselee is in a better position to know what is best for him or her, and if the alternative is not the best, the counselee will probably learn from the mistake.

5. The counselor should attempt to form explicit, realistic "contracts" with counselees. When the counselee does select an alternative, the counselee should clearly understand what the goals will be, what tasks need to be carried out, how to do the tasks, and who will carry out each of them. Frequently, it is desirable to write the "con-

tract" for future reference, with a time limit set for the accomplishment of each task. For example, if the unmarried mother decides to keep her child and now needs to make long-range financial plans, this goal should be understood and specific courses of action decided upon—seeking public assistance, seeking support from the alleged father, securing an apartment within her budget, and so on. Furthermore, who will do what task within a set time limit should be specified.

6. If the counselee fails to meet the terms of the "contract," do not punish, but do not accept excuses. Excuses let people off the hook; they provide temporary relief, but they eventually lead to more failure and to a failure identity. Simply ask, "Do you still wish to try to fulfill your commitment?" If the counselee answers affirmatively, another time deadline acceptable to the counselee should be set.

7. Perhaps the biggest single factor in determining whether the counselee's situation will improve is the counselee's motivation to carry out essential tasks. A counselor should seek to motivate apathetic counselees. One of the biggest reality shocks of new trainees entering into the helping professions is that many clients, even after making commitments to improve their situation, do not have the motivation to carry out the steps outlined.

8. One way to increase motivation is to clarify what will be gained by meeting the commitment. When counselees meet commitments, reward them verbally or in other ways. Seldom punish if commitments are not met. Punishment usually increases hostility, without positive lasting changes. Also, punishment only serves as a temporary means of obtaining different behavior; when a person no longer believes that he or she is under surveillance, he or she will usually return to the "deviant" behavior.

9. For a number of tasks where the counselee lacks confidence or experience in carry-

ing out, it is helpful to "role play" the task. For example, if a pregnant single girl wants help in knowing how to tell her boyfriend about the pregnancy, role playing the situation will assist the girl in selecting words and developing a strategy for informing him. The counselor can first play the girl's role and model an approach, with the girl playing the boy's role. Then the roles should be reversed so that the girl practices telling her boyfriend.

Other helpful hints to counseling could be given here, but the basic format is to develop a relationship, explore problems in depth, and then to explore alternative solutions. These guidelines are not to be followed dogmatically; they will probably work 70 to 80 percent of the time. The most important tool that a counselor has is him/herself (feelings, perceptions, relationship capacities, and interviewing skills).

One final important guideline—the counselor should refer the counselee to someone else, or at least seek a professional counselor to discuss the case with, for any of the following situations: if the counselor feels that he or she is unable to empathize with the counselee; if the counselor feels that the counselee is choosing unethical alternatives (such as seeking an abortion) that conflict with the counselor's basic value system; if the counselor feels that the problem is of such a nature that he or she will not be able to help; and if a working relationship is not established. A competent counselor knows that he or she can work with and help some people but not all, and that it is in the counselee's and the counselor's best interests to refer the person to someone else who can.

Global and specialized-counseling approaches

In addition to having a working knowledge of interviewing principles, an effective counselor needs to have a knowledge of

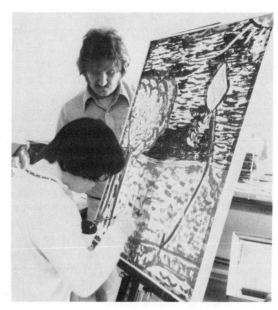

Art therapy: One of many specialized treatment techniques

global counseling theories and of specialized treatment techniques to be able to diagnose precisely what problems exist, and how to intervene effectively. There are a number of contemporary global counseling approaches: psychoanalysis, Adlerian psychotherapy, client-centered therapy, rational therapy, behavior modification, gestalt therapy, reality therapy, transactional analysis, radical therapy, and encounter approaches.* These therapy approaches generally present theoretical material on: (*a*) personality theory, or how normal psycho-social development occurs, (*b*) behavior pathology, or how emotional problems arise, and (*c*) therapy, or how to change disturbed behavior.

---

* As indicated earlier a good summary of contemporary, global counseling approaches is provided in *Current Psychotherapies*, ed. Raymond Corsini, (Itasca, Ill.: F. E. Peacock, 1979); *Social Work Treatment*, ed. Francis J. Turner (New York: Free Press, 1979); and Charles Zastrow, *The Practice of Social Work* (Homewood, Ill.: Dorsey Press, 1981).

An effective counselor generally has a knowledge of several treatment approaches, and then depending on the unique set of problems being presented by the client, is able to "pick and choose from his/her bag of tricks" which intervention strategy is apt to have the highest probability of success. In addition to global counseling approaches, there are a number of specialized treatment techniques for specific problems; for example, assertive training for people who are shy or overly aggressive, specific sexual counseling techniques for such difficulties as premature ejaculation or organismic dysfunction, parent effectiveness training for parent-child relationship difficulties.* An effective counselor strives to gain a working knowledge of a wide variety of treatment techniques in order to increase the likelihood of being able to help clients.

For illustrative purposes, one global therapy approach, rational therapy, will be summarized.

RATIONAL THERAPY

The two main developers of this approach are Albert Ellis and Maxie Maultsby.[35] The approach has the potential to enable those who became skillful in rationally analyzing their self-talk, to control or get rid of any undesirable emotion they encounter.

It is erroneously believed by most people that our emotions and our actions are primarily determined by our experiences (that is, by events that happen to us). On the contrary, rational therapy has demonstrated that the primary cause of all our emotions and actions is what we tell ourselves about events that happen to us.

All feelings and actions occur according to the following format:

Events: (or experiences)

Self-talk: (Self-talk is the set of evaluating thoughts you give yourself about facts and events that happen to you)

Emotions: (may include remaining calm)

Actions:

An example will illustrate the above process:

Event: Cheryl, the five-year-old daughter of Mr. and Mrs. Shaw, is playing with her brother and knocks over and breaks a lamp.

Mr. Shaw's self-talk: "That lamp was our favorite, we bought it on our honeymoon—it's irreplaceable. This is awful."

"Spare the rod and spoil the child—some stiff discipline will make her shape up"

"As head of this household it's my duty to make her shape up. I'll teach her a lesson she'll never forget, with the spanking of her life"

"She's always breaking things, I think this might have been intentional—I'll teach her to have respect for me and for our valuable items"

---

* A good summary of a number of specialized treatment techniques is contained in *The Personal Problem Solver*, ed. Charles Zastrow and Dae Chang. (Englewood Cliffs, N.J.: Spectrum Books, 1977).

Emotions: Anger, disappointment, frus-
   ↓   tration
Actions: Spanking and yelling at Cheryl,
            with the severity of the spank-
            ing bordering on abuse

If on the other hand Mr. Shaw gives himself a different set of self-talk, his emotions and actions will be quite different:

Event: Cheryl, the five-year-old daughter
   | of Mr. and Mrs. Shaw is playing
   | with her brother and knocks over
   ↓   and breaks a lamp
Mr. Shaw's self-talk: "This was a lamp we
                        cherished, but I
                        know she didn't
                        break it intention-
                        ally. It was an acci-
                        dent. My getting an-
                        gry at this point
                        won't help."

                        "I might have pre-
                        vented this accident
                        by informing Cheryl
                        and our son that
                        they can only
                        "horse" around in
                        this house in the rec
                        room and in their
                        bedrooms."

                        "With young chil-
                        dren some accidents
                        are bound to hap-
                        pen."

                        "The most construc-
                        tive thing I can do at
                        this point is to say
                        that I understand that
                        it was an accident,
                        that all of us are dis-
                        appointed that the
                        lamp broke, and tell
                        them in the future
                        their   "horsing"

                        around should be
                        limited to the rec
                        room and the bed-
                        rooms.
   ↓
Emotions: Some disappointment, but gen-
   ↓   erally remaining calm
Actions: In an understanding fashion
            talking to the children and ex-
            pressing his thoughts in line
            with his self-talk.

The most important point about the above processes is that our self-talk determines how we feel and act; and, by changing our self-talk we can change how we feel and act. Generally we cannot control events that happen to us, but we have the power to think rationally*[36] and thereby change *all* of our unwanted emotions and ineffective actions.

The rehabilitative aspect of this conceptualization of self-talk is that any unwanted emotion and any ineffective behavior can be changed by identifying and then changing the underlying self-talk.

The self-talk we give ourselves about specific events that happen to us is often based upon a variety of factors, including: our beliefs, attitudes, values, wants, motives, goals, and desires.[37] For example, the self-talk a married woman might give herself upon being informed by her husband that he wants a divorce would be influenced by her desires (or lack of desires) to remain married, by her values and beliefs about being a divorcee, by her attitudes toward her husband and how she believes getting a divorce would be consistent or inconsistent with her present goals, and by her beliefs about the

---

* According to Maultsby rational thinking and rational behavior: (*a*) is based on objective reality, (*b*) helps you protect your life, (*c*) helps you achieve your short- and long-term goals more quickly, (*d*) helps you get out and stay out of significant trouble with other people, (*e*) helps you prevent significant unwanted emotions.

reasons why her husband says he wants a divorce.

Another important point about "self-talk" is that with repeated occurrences of an event, a person's emotional reaction becomes nearly automatic, because the person rapidly gives him/herself a large set of self-talk gradually acquired through past experiences. For example, a few years ago I counseled a woman who became intensely upset and depressed every time her husband came home intoxicated. In examining her emotional reactions it became clear that due to repeated occurrences she would rapidly tell herself the following upon seeing him inebriated:

> "He's making a fool of himself and myself."
>
> "He's foolishly spending money we desperately need."
>
> "For the next few hours I'm going to have to put up with his drunken talk and behavior—this is awful."
>
> "He loves drinking more than he loves me as he knows I do not want him to get drunk."
>
> "Woe is me."

The use of rational therapy will be demonstrated in the following two cases.

A depression. Judy Johnson, a 22-year-old college student became depressed. Her circumstances were analyzed with a college counselor according to the following ABCD format of rational therapy for changing unwanted emotions:

A = Event

Hal Navarre informed Judy, after a two-year engagement, that he thought it was best that they did not marry.

B = Self-talk by Judy

B_1 = That scoundrel has ruined my future happiness.

B_2 = I will never be able to find anyone who truly loves me.

B_3 = I did everything for him—how can he hurt me in this way!

B_4 = I will never be able to face my friends and family again after this!

C = Emotion

Depression

The reasons why such self-talk are irrational were then discussed between the counselor and Judy. For example, B_1 does not achieve short- and long-term goals, nor does it prevent significant unwanted emotions.

The next step was "D" to develop rational self-talk challenges to each irrational self-talk. Step D is the therapy part of the ABCD format. A few examples arrived at by Judy following counseling were:

D_1 (challenges to B_1) = "My future happiness does not depend on marrying Hal."

"Marriage is certainly no guarantee of future happiness."

"If Hal does not want a permanent relationship with me, it is better we split now than after a ring ceremony."

D_2 (challenges to B_2) = "I have had a number of dates in the past with other guys, many of whom seemed attracted to me."

"My parents and close girl friends are very close to me."

"There are a number of guys I know that I would be interested in dating."

D_3 (challenges to B_3) = "Hal is a good person; he apparently is not ready for marriage at this time."

"Hal is not the primary source of my feeling hurt—the hurt is mainly due to my self-talk."

D_4 (challenges to B_4) = "My family and friends are close to me; they will help me in any way that they can."

"I've got to start making plans for a different future—informing my family and friends is the first step."

By Judy's continuously thinking the rational ideas described above, her self-talk about her broken engagement began changing. Her depression faded, and she soon was making constructive plans for her future graduation from college.

A second, somewhat more involved case using the principles of rational therapy is as follows.

The Don Juan wife.* After four and a half years of marriage, a husband discovered that his wife had had affairs with several other men, and the couple were wondering whether to continue the marriage. The husband was angry and possessive with his wife, having such self-talk as, "She has cheated on me," "she is disgracing me," "she is threatening the future of our mar-

riage, and also my current way of living." On the other hand, he still had strong feelings of affection toward her and wanted to continue the marriage on the condition that she would promise not to have another extramarital affair.

The wife felt some guilt about hurting and deceiving her husband and stated that she was still "in love" with him. However, she stated that she could not abide by the condition of having to discontinue extramarital affairs. Her self-talk about her desire to have extramarital affairs was, "I not only love my husband but also other men," "I need to have sex with more than one man to provide variety and meaning to my life," "I do not believe people were born to be monogamous." This set of self-talk prompted the counselor to probe further, to examine her self-talk regarding what she found enjoyable about extramarital sex. Her self-talk revealed, "I enjoy the feeling of being able to seduce someone who I am attracted to," "The people I seduce then feel somewhat obligated to me," and "The conquest of someone who is very attractive is three quarters of the thrill."

Several approaches to resolve this situation were possible, including a divorce or continuing the marriage with the husband attempting to psychologically become accommodated to his wife's extramarital affairs. A third strategy was, however, chosen. Through counseling, the wife discovered that what she was primarily seeking from extramarital affairs was not sex per se but the thrill of a conquest and making others feel obligated to her. With this insight, she came to realize that the "thrill of a conquest" was less important than maintaining her marriage. In addition, her "need for a conquest" was partially met by taking a part-time job as a commercial artist. She also realized that her desire to make people feel obligated to her was inconsistent with her ideas about not exploiting others and also inconsistent

---

* This case, recorded by Warren Shibles and the author is excerpted from "Romantic Love vs. Rational Love," in *The Personal Problem Solver*, ed. Charles Zastrow and Dae Chang (Englewood Cliffs, N.J.: Spectrum Books, 1977). Reprinted by permission of Prentice-Hall, Inc., Englewood Cliffs, New Jersey.

with her self-concept and her life goals. Therefore, she switched to attempting to form more equalitarian, constructive relationship with others. This couple was also referred to a professional sexual counseling center in the area to explore ways to make their sex life more exciting.

SUMMARY

Emotional and interpersonal problems are two global labels covering an array of problems. All of us, at times, experience emotional and interpersonal problems. Serious or severe emotional problems are sometimes labeled "mental illnesses."

The history of treatment for the emotionally disturbed is fascinating, but also filled with injustices and tragedies; ranging from viewing the disturbed as prophets to fearing they are possessed with demonological powers. Recent major developments are the discovery and use of psychoactive drugs and the trend toward deinstitutionalization.

A major controversy is whether mental illness exists. Adherents of the medical approach believe the disturbed person's mind is affected by some generally unknown, internal condition. Critics of the medical model assert that disturbed people display a social deviation or have an emotional problem but do not have a disease of the mind. Further, they assert mental illness labels have no diagnostic or treatment value and frequently have an adverse labeling effect.

Another major issue in the mental health field is civil rights concerns over: (*a*) involuntary confinement, (*b*) inadequate treatment, and (*c*) enforced use of treatment approaches that have adverse side effects. Other issues include the usefulness of the plea of innocent by reason of insanity and the extent to which psychotropic drugs should be used.

It has been estimated that half the professionals who provide mental health services are social workers. Many social agencies provide services to people having emotional and behavioral problems, even though a primary responsibility for such services has been assigned to comprehensive mental health centers.

The main therapy approach used to treat people with emotional and behavioral problems is psychotherapy or counseling. Counseling services are provided by practically every direct service social welfare agency. Capacity to effectively counsel others is perhaps the most important skill needed by social workers. In being a competent counselor it is essential to have a working knowledge of interviewing principles and of a wide range of treatment approaches. There are three distinct phases to counseling: building a relationship, exploring problems in-depth, and exploring alternative solutions.

NOTES

1. Charles Zastrow, *Talk to Yourself* (Englewood Cliffs, N.J.: Prentice-Hall, 1979).

2. *The President's Commission on Mental Health*, vol. 1 (Washington, D.C.: U.S. Government Printing Office, 1978), p. 8.

3. George Rosen, *Madness in Society, Chapters in the Historical Sociology of Mental Illness* (New York: Harper & Row, 1969).

4. Ibid., pp. 172–95.

5. Clifford W. Beers, *A Mind That Found Itself* (New York: Longmans, Green, 1908).

6. H. J. Eysenck, "The Effects of Psychotherapy: An Evaluation," *Journal of Consulting Psychology* 11 (1955): 319–24.

7. Walter A. Friedlander and Robert Z. Apte, *Introduction to Social Welfare*, 4th ed. (Englewood Cliffs, N.J.: Prentice-Hall, 1974), p. 436.

8. Ibid., p. 439.

9. Anthony J. Vattano "Mental Health" in *Contemporary Social Work*, ed. Donald Brieland, Lela B. Costin, and Charles R. Atherton, 2d ed. (New York: McGraw-Hill, 1980), p. 283.

10. "Special Report: Schizophrenia, 1976," *Schizophrenia Bulletin* 2, no. 4 (1976), pp. 44–45.

11. Franklin D. Chu and Sharland Trotter, *The Madness Establishment* (New York: Grossman, 1974.

12. Alcohol, Drug Abuse and Mental Health Administration, *Mental Health Statistical Note No. 146,* HEW Publication No. (ADM) 78–158 (Washington, D.C.: U.S. Government Printing Office, March 1978).

13. Thomas S. Szasz, *The Myth of Mental Illness* (New York: Hoeber-Harper, 1961).

14. Thomas S. Szasz, "The Myth of Mental Illness," in *Clinical Psychology in Transition,* comp. John R. Braun (Cleveland: Howard Allen, 1961).

15. Thomas Scheff, *Being Mentally Ill* (Chicago: Aldine, 1966); and David Mechanic, "Some Factors in Identifying and Defining Mental Illness," *Mental Hygiene* 46 (1962): 66–74.

16. Daniel Offer and Melvin Sabshin, *Normality: Theoretical and Clinical Concepts in Mental Health* (New York: Basic Books, 1966), p. 253.

17. Lawrence C. Koll, Viola Bernard, and Bruce P. Dohrenwend, "The Problem of Validity in Field Studies of Psychological Disorder," in *Urban Challenges to Psychiatry,* ed. Bruce P. Dohrenwend and Barbara Snell Dohrenwend (New York: Wiley, 1969), pp. 429–60.

18. D. L. Rosenhan, "On Being Sane in Insane Places," *Science* 179 (1973): 250–57.

19. Scheff, *Being Mentally Ill.*

20. Szasz, *Law, Liberty and Psychiatry* (New York: Macmillan, 1963).

21. D. L. Phillips, "Rejection: A Possible Consequence of Seeking Help for Mental Disorder," *American Sociological Review* 28, (1963) 963–73.

22. Edwin M. Lemert, *Social Pathology* (New York: McGraw-Hill, 1951).

23. Vattano, "Mental Health," p. 292.

24. Ibid., p. 292.

25. Ibid., p. 292.

26. The President's Commission on Mental Health, pp. 69–72.

27. Chu and Trotter, *Madness Establishment,* p. 40.

28. "Psychiatric Testimony Clouds Justice in the Courtroom," *Freedom,* February 1980, p. 1.

29. Ibid., p. 4.

30. Ibid., p. 4.

31. Vattano, "Mental Health," p. 287.

32. Ibid., p. 293.

33. Ibid., p. 294.

34. *NASW Register of Clinical Social Workers, Supplement to the First Edition* (Washington, D.C.: National Association of Social Workers, 1977), p. x.

35. Albert Ellis, *Reason and Emotion in Psychotherapy* (New York: Lyle Stuart, 1962); and Maxie Maultsby, *Help Yourself to Happiness* (Boston: Maultsby, Marborough/Herman, 1975).

36. Maultsby, *Help Yourself to Happiness.*

37. Zastrow, *Talk to Yourself,* pp. 59–80.

chapter **6**

A BACKGROUND PERSPECTIVE: VIOLENCE IN FAMILIES

We tend to view the family as a social institution in which love and gentleness abound. Sadly, the opposite is often true, with violence being pervasive in American families.

Child abuse, spouse abuse, and other physical violence occur in more than half of all U.S. households.[1] An estimated 50 million people fall victim annually to physical harm at the hands of another family member.[2] Studies show that in 20 percent of child abuse cases, a spouse is also abused.[3] It's not just wives who are harmed—husbands are slapped or shoved with about the same frequency as are wives.[4]

When considering spouse abuse, however, it should be noted the greatest physical harm is to women. Studies show men cause more serious injuries, partly because they are more prone to use weapons.[5] Nearly 11 percent of all murder victims are killed by their spouses.[6] It should be noted women also tend to endure cruelty and abuse much longer, at times because they feel trapped because of unemployment and financial insecurity. Spouse abuse is often victim-precipitated—that is, the recipient of the abuse is frequently the first to use verbal or physical violence in the incident.[7]

Violence in families is not limited to child and spouse abuse. Statistics from a study funded by the National Institute of Mental Health found that more children assault their parents, than the number of children who are abused by their parents.[8] Violence between children is also common—a recent study found 138,000 children ages 3 to 17 used a weapon on a brother or sister during a one-year period.[9]

Parent abuse is a new term that is increasingly receiving attention. This term primarily refers to elderly parents who are abused by their children whom they live with, or depend upon. The public is virtually unaware of the battered aged, but an estimate is there may be a million or more who are abused by their adult children.[10] Koch and Koch provide one case example:

In Chicago, a 19-year-old woman confessed to torturing her 81-year-old father and chaining

Child abuse/neglect and protective services

him to a toilet for seven days. She also hit him with a hammer when he was asleep: "I worked him over real good with it. Then after I made him weak enough, I chained his legs together. After that I left him and rested. I watched TV for a while."[11]

In one of the few parent-abuse studies available Lau and Kosberg found in a Cleveland study that the following four types of abuse to be most prevalent:

Physical abuse, which included direct beating and the withholding of personal care, food, medicine, and necessary supervision.

Psychological abuse—verbal assaults and threats provoking fear.

Material abuse or theft of money or personal property.

Violation of rights—forcing a parent out of his or her own dwelling usually into a nursing home.

Three-fourths of the cases in the Cleveland study involved physical abuse; almost half included psychological abuse; and in almost every case, there was a violation of rights.[12]

The victims of family violence—battered children, battered parents, and battered wives—have common disadvantages. They are generally smaller in size, have less physical strength, and generally feel helpless in relation to the aggressors. Often they feel helpless because they depend on their aggressors for physical, financial, and emotional support.

Prior to the 1960s there was little attention given to violence in families, partly because the family was viewed as a sacred institution and a private domain—what goes on within families was viewed as a personal concern and the responsibility of family members alone, not outsiders. Over the past two decades there has been an increasing awareness that violence in families is a major social problem.

Along with this recognition has been the development of new services for the victims. An example of new services has been the establishment of shelter homes for battered women. These shelters give abused women an opportunity to flee from the abusive situation, with shelter being provided for the women and their children. Such women also generally receive counseling, assistance in finding a job, and legal help. In some areas programs are also being established for the husbands, with efforts being made to provide marriage counseling to both spouses and 24-hour hot lines being established that encourage potential spouse abusers to call when they are angry.

The passage of Title XX Amendment to the Social Security Act in 1975 made protective services (directed at preventing or remedying abuse, neglect, and exploitation) mandatory services that states must provide for children and for adults.

Child abuse has, by far, received the most attention, and programs in this area have been in existence for over 100 years. Because children are most vulnerable to abuse and because most social workers dealing with family abuse are involved in protective services to children, the focus of this chapter is on child abuse and neglect.

THE PROBLEM

Although definitions of child abuse and neglect vary somewhat from state to state, Alfred Kadushin summarizes the kinds of situations as including:

1. Physical abuse.
2. Malnourishment; poor clothing; lack of proper shelter, sleeping arrangements, attendance, or supervision. Includes "failure to thrive" syndrome, which de-

scribes infants who fail to grow and develop at a normal rate.

3. Denial of essential medical care.
4. Failure to attend school regularly.
5. Exploitation, overwork.
6. Exposure to unwholesome or demoralizing circumstances.
7. Sexual abuse.
8. Somewhat less frequently the definitions include emotional abuse and neglect involving denial of the normal experiences that permit a child to feel loved, wanted, secure, and worthy.[13]

Physical abuse. In the past 25 years there has been considerable national concern about the "battered-child syndrome." The Children's Division of the American Humane Society conducted a nationwide survey of newspaper reports on child abuse and concluded:

> The forms or types of abuse inflicted on these children is a negative testimony to the ingenuity and the inventiveness of man. By far the greater number of injuries resulted from beatings with various kinds of implements and instruments. The hairbrush was a common implement used to beat children. However, the same purpose was accomplished with deadlier impact by the use of bare fists, straps, electric cords, TV aerials, ropes, rubber hose, fan belts, sticks, wooden shoes, pool cues, bottles, broom handles, baseball bats, chair legs and in one case, a sculling oar. Less imaginative, but equally effective, was plain kicking with street shoes or with heavy work shoes.
>
> Children had their extremities—hands, arms, and feet—burned in open flames as from gas burners or cigarette lighters. Others bore burn wounds inflicted on their bodies with lighted cigarettes, electric irons or hot pokers. Still others were scalded by hot liquids thrown over them or from being dipped into containers of hot liquids.
>
> Some children were strangled or suffocated by pillows held over their mouths or plastic bags thrown over their heads. A number were drowned in bathtubs and one child was buried alive.
>
> To complete the list—children were stabbed, bitten, shot, subjected to electric shock, were thrown violently to the floor or against a wall, were stamped on, and one child had pepper forced down his throat.[14]

This survey went on to report these abused children incurred the following kinds of injuries:

> The majority had various shapes, sizes, and forms of bruises and contusions. There was a collection of welts, swollen limbs, split lips, black eyes, and lost teeth. One child lost an eye.
>
> Broken bones were common. Some were simple fractures; others compound. There were many broken arms, broken legs, and fractured ribs. Many children had more than one fracture. One five-month-old child was found to have 30 broken bones in his little body.
>
> The grimest recital of all is the listing of internal injuries and of head injuries. The head injuries particularly were a sizeable group. Both the internal injuries and the head injuries were responsible for a great many of the fatalities. In this group we find damage to internal organs such as ruptured livers, ruptured spleens and ruptured lungs. Injuries to the head were concussions or skull fractures, with brain hemorrhage and brain damage a frequent diagnosis.
>
> This is indeed a grim, sad, sordid and horror-filled recital of what happens to children in communities in almost every state of the Union.[15]

Physical abuse involves beating a child to the point where s/he sustains some physical damage. The line between physical abuse and harsh parental discipline is difficult to define. Silver et al. note:

> . . . if a parent punishes a child with a belt, is it after the fourth slash with the belt that parental rights end and child abuse begins; is it

AN ACTUAL CASE   The *Wisconsin State Journal* on September 2, 1972, reported:*

CHICAGO (UPI)—Johnny L., 7, never got back to the small Wisconsin farm and the lake where he first caught a fish.

The battered child died Thursday in a hospital here.

He had been unconscious since July 28 from a beating he received after he was taken from the foster home in Wisconsin and returned to his natural parents.

His father, William, 31, was charged with murder.

Johnny, who had spent most of his life in foster homes, had been living with Mr. and Mrs. Robert K. for almost four years when a court order forced him to return to his natural parents in Chicago.

"When his parents wanted him back, I knew he had to go. I tried to make it easy. I told him 'John, you have to go back, your father loves you.' But he ran to the top of the stairs and cried," Mrs. K. said.

"He said, 'I'm never going back,' At night he'd pray: 'Please God, don't let them take me back.' "

But in late March the K.s drove Johnny back into the city. "We never saw him again until after the beating. He looked so small in the hospital. All bruises and so thin. But I still had hope. I thought it would work out and he'd come back home to the farm. I was going to fatten him up," she said softly.

Johnny was beaten July 28 after he said he wanted to go home to the K.s, police said. He was taken to a hospital in a coma. Doctors performed emergency surgery for severe brain damage.

After he was admitted, Johnny's two brothers and two sisters were placed in foster homes. The move was ordered after one of his sisters, Julie, 2, was injured when she fell from a window in the L. apartment. Her mother was not home.[16]

* Identifying names have been deleted from this newspaper report.

after the belt raises a welt over two millimeters that it becomes abuse versus parental rights.[17]

Definitions of abuse also vary. Definitions narrow in scope restrict abuse to actual se-rious injury sustained by the child, while broader definitions include intent to harm the child and verbal abuse.

In the late 1960s, in response to a growing national concern about child abuse, all states adopted child abuse and neglect reporting laws. Such laws are essentially a case-finding device. The laws require that professionals (such as physicians, social workers, hospital administrators, school administrators, nurses, and dentists) must report suspected cases of child abuse to certain specified agencies, such as the local police department and the county welfare department.

The true national incidence of child abuse is unknown. Accurate data is difficult to get for two reasons: the failure of citizens and professionals to report suspected cases and the reluctance of abused children to talk. Many battered children, believing their punishment is deserved, keep mute when interviewed by those who might help.

Estimates of the number of abused children each year range widely from 60,000 to 6.5 million children in America.[18] Jerome E. Leavitt notes, "More children under five years of age die from mistreatment by parents than from tuberculosis, whooping cough, polio, measles, diabetes, rheumatic fever, and appendicitis combined."[19]

Another danger of child abuse is that violence breeds violence. George C. Curtis reports there is evidence that abused children may "become tomorrow's murderers and perpetrators of other crimes of violence."[20] When they become parents, there is also a higher probability they will become abusive parents.[21] Theoretically, abuse generates an unusually high degree of hostility, which in future years may well be channeled into violence.

Although in rare cases abuse is non recurrent, generally it is repeated. Nonrecurrent abuse is usually difficult to document as the abuser can contrive a plausible explanation for the injuries received.

Statistics on abused children compiled from state reports by the National Center on Child Abuse and Neglect in 1976 found the following:[22] Over two thirds of the abused children required no medical treatment, with the most frequent injury being welts and bruises. The fatality rate was 0.5 percent, and only 6 percent of the children required hospitalization. In looking at age, 65 percent were six years of age or older. Boys were more frequently abused than girls, particularly for children under age 10. Teenage girls, however, were more frequently abused than teenage boys—a finding that was attributed to the inclusion of sexual abuse in the statistic; and due to sexual abuse being much more frequently reported among teenage girls.

The National Center on Child Abuse and Neglect also compiled data on the parents involved in the abuse, and found the following:[23] Abuse was more apt to occur among mother-headed, single-parent families, among parents with limited education and employment skills, and among nonwhite families. Fathers were somewhat more often the abusers than the mothers (55 to 45 percent, respectively). There was evidence of "family discord" and stress due to limited

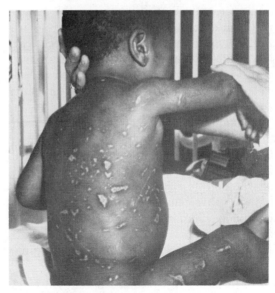

An abused child

financial resources in many of the families. (It is possible that the higher incidence of abuse in lower classes may partly result from the fact that middle and upper class parents are in a better position to conceal the abuse.[24])

Contrary to public opinion most abused children (over two thirds) are permitted to remain in their homes by protective services even after abuse is determined.[25] The primary service offered by protective services is "casework counseling," with foster care, day care, and homemaker services being provided in a small proportion of cases.[26]

Physical neglect. In contrast to child abuse, child neglect is more apt to be a problem of omission rather than commission. Specific types of physical neglect include: (a) child abandonment, (b) letting a child live in filth, without proper clothing, unattended, unsupervised, and without proper nourishment, (c) educational neglect in which a child is allowed to be absent from school, and (d) medical neglect in which no effort is made to secure needed medical care for the child.

Although neglect has received less national attention than child abuse, the majority of situations in which protective service agencies must intervene is for neglect. The National Clearinghouse on Child Abuse and Neglect has found neglect to be occurring in twice as many families as child abuse.[27]

In rare cases, such as child abandonment, the parent rejects his/her parental role. In most child neglect cases, however, the parent inadequately performs the role. Alfred Kadushin defines a typical neglectful mother as being, "physically exhausted, mentally impoverished, emotionally deprived, and socially isolated."[28] Generally neglectful parents are poverty stricken or live on marginal incomes.

Vincent De Francis provides the following description of what a social worker encountered in investigating a neglect complaint:

What I saw as I entered the room was utter, stark, disorganization. The room was a combined kitchen-dining room. At the other end of the room two scrawny, owl-eyed frightened children—a girl of about four and a boy of three—stared silently at me. Except for thin cotton undershirts, they were stark naked. They had sore crusts on their legs and arms. They were indescribably dirty, hair matted, body and hands stained and covered with spilled food particles. Sitting on a urine-soaked and soiled mattress in a baby carriage behind them was a younger child—a boy about two.

The floor was ankle-deep in torn newspapers. There were feces in about a half-dozen spots on the floor and the air was fetid and saturated with urine odor.

There were flies everywhere. What seemed like giant roaches were crawling over the paper-strewn floor. The kitchen sink and gas stove were piled high with greasy and unwashed dishes, pots and pans.[29]

Sexual abuse. Increased attention is now being given to sexual abuse of children. Sexual abuse not only includes sexual intercourse (genital or anal) but also masturbation, oral-genital contact, fondling, and exposure. Here again an unambiguous definition of abuse is not available. Sexual intercourse is definitely abuse. But other forms of contact are harder to judge as being abuse. At some point hugging, kissing, and fondling become inappropriate.

The abusers may include parents, older siblings, or extended relatives. A few years ago I was the faculty supervisor for a student in field placement at a public welfare department who had a 15-year-old girl on her case load who was pregnant by her father for the third time!

In the past families generally attempted to "hide" the abuse, and it usually was not reported. Now, with an increasing openness about human sexuality there is an increasing trend for family members to seek professional help.

A home in which the parents were charged with child neglect

In the largest proportion of cases with which protective services become involved, the sexual abuse is between father and daughter. Less common is abuse by a stepfather or the mother's boyfriend. Rarely is there a reported case of mother-son sexual abuse or of sibling abuse.[30]

Most often sexual abuse occurs in the child's home. The child is usually pressured, rather than physically forced, to participate. The age range of the abused child is from several months to adulthood, although most reports involve teenagers.[31]

Children are unlikely to report sexual abuse as they often have loyalties toward the abuser and fear the consequences for themselves, for the abuser, and for the family.

Sexual abuse is increasingly being conceptualized as being different than physical abuse or physical neglect. A clear understanding of the motivations for the abuse is not yet known. Available studies will briefly be summarized.

Walters sees resentment and hostility toward the wife as the father's motivation for incest. When father-daughter incest occurs, the woman is made to feel she has failed as both a mother and a wife.[32]

Rosenfeld, however, turns the dynamics around and views incest as a result of the female child's efforts to obtain affection from the father and as an act of hostility by the child toward the mother.[33]

Tormes sees the wife as being a willing, passive, ineffectual "participant" in the incest drama.[34]

After reviewing a number of studies, Kadushin concluded that mothers of sexually abused girls were often fearful of their husbands, often uninterested in sexual relations with their husbands, and often assigned extensive child care and homemaking responsibilities on the abused daughter.[35] The daughters were frequently treated as "little mothers." Death, illness, or frequent absence of the wife increased the chances of incest occurring. The mother in some instances was found to subtly encourage the incest; more often the mother failed to be responsible for adequately protecting the daughter by denying what was occurring and by attempting to keep peace at any cost.

Unwholesome or demoralizing conditions. Children who are exposed to the following situations are also considered in need of protective services: parents who are involved in continued prostitution, criminal activity, drug addiction, and severe alcoholism. Such exposure is considered injurious to the moral development of children.

Exploitation. This category involves forcing a child to work for unreasonably long hours, and encouraging a child to beg, steal, or engage in prostitution.

Emotional neglect. Meeting a child's affectional needs is as important to normal growth and development as meeting the child's physical needs. Yet, emotional neglect is difficult to define and document in the precise terms required by law. Take the following example:

Gary, age 9, was the only child of Mr. and Mrs. Jim N. The N. family lived in a suburb of a metropolitan area, and Gary's physical needs were adequately met. Yet Gary was not doing well in school. He repeated the first grade and now is repeating the third grade. Gary was referred for psychological testing and was found to have a very low self-concept. His self-concept was so negative he refused to study math for fear of failing and would not participate in any competitive games with peers. He instead preferred to play by himself, with toys appropriate to children of an age level of five. A home study found that Mr. N. was a stoic, unaffectional person who was seldom at home as he spent long hours in operating a service station he owned. Mrs. N. had such a distasteful personality and disposition that she was unable to hold a job and had no close friends. Below average in intellectual functioning, she only completed the ninth grade. In her interactions with Gary she was observed to have a short tolerance level, would frequently berate and criticize him, and call him "stupid" and "an idiot." Gary appeared somewhat fearful of her and tried to avoid interacting with her. Both parents refused to take parent effectiveness training or to receive counseling.

This case example raises a number of yet unanswered questions surrounding emotional neglect. Are Gary's personal problems (low self-image) a result of his interactions with his parents or due to some other factors (for example, school environment, or a past traumatic experience, or to an inherited disposition)? Even if it is assumed his problems are due to his parental interactions, how can this be proven in court? And, will his personal problems be reduced or intensified if he were to be removed from home and placed in a foster home?

The National Clearinghouse on Child Neglect and Abuse defines emotional neglect:

as failure to provide the child the emotional nurturing or emotional support necessary for the development of a sound personality, as for example, subjecting the child to rejection or to a home climate charged with tension, hostility and anxiety-producing occurrences which result in perceivable problems in children.[36]

Interpreted liberally (broadly) the problem with this definition of emotional neglect is that practically every parent at times is guilty of such neglect. Other definitions of emotional neglect encounter the same problem.

Although there is general agreement that writing an acceptable definition of emotional neglect is difficult, there is also solid agreement that some children do suffer from emotional neglect—even when they are adequately cared for physically.

Emotional neglect is very difficult to document in court. When emotional neglect is accompanied by physical neglect, protective service agencies make a case based on physical neglect.

Abusive and neglectful parents

Why do some parents abuse or neglect their children? Abuse and neglect cover a wide variety of behaviors that have diverse effects on children. No single cause can fully explain why parents abuse or neglect their children. Available research indicates these two groups of parents may have little in common. Abuse appears to be more of a response to psychological stress, while neglect appears to be more of a response to social stress.

The following factors have been found to be associated with parents who abuse their children:

1. Some abusive parents were themselves abused as children. If not abused, they generally had a lack of stable love relationships in their childhood, and an in-

adequate gratification of early emotional needs.

2. Although abuse, like neglect, is more heavily concentrated among lower classes, it is more randomly distributed than neglect throughout the population.

3. Frequently, one child is singled out to be the target of the abuse. A variety of reasons appear to account for this. The child may be viewed as mentally slow or a potential delinquent. Where there is marital conflict, one child may be chosen as the victim because he/she resembles the disliked spouse. One child may cry more, be more hyperactive, or be more demanding of parental care. The child may be punished because he/she was conceived prior to marriage, or because he/she is illegitimate, or because he/she is the result of an unwanted pregnancy.

4. In some cases the abused child contributes to the selection process by making greater than normal burdens on parental patience: by having severe temper tantrums; feeding, speech or toilet-training problems; being restless, negative, unresponsive, listless, whiny, or fussy.

5. The child who is the victim may in disturbed families be essential for the psychic stability of the family. It appears some disturbed families need a "whipping boy" or "scapegoat" to maintain an equilibrium within the family. Sometimes when an abused child is removed, another is selected to be the victim, and thereby fulfill this "stability" role.

6. Abusive parents often show an absence of guilt, have a tendency toward social isolation, have a high level of overall aggressiveness, are prone to impulsivity, tend to have emotional problems, have feelings of inadequacy, and have a high vulnerability to criticism.

7. Environmental stress factors (e.g., marital problems), economic pressures,

and social isolation sometimes help trigger abuse.

8. Abusive parents tend to believe in strict discipline, and tend to view misbehavior by their children as being willfull, deliberate disobedience. Also, they are characterized by a high demand for the child to perform so as to gratify the parent.

9. Alcohol/drug abuse plays an important contributing role in some cases.[37]

The following factors have been identified to be associated with child neglect:

1. The preponderance of families come from the lower socioeconomic classes.

Financial deprivation is a major contributing factor. Many also have inadequate housing.

2. A high percentage (60 percent in some studies) are one-parent families, generally headed by a female.

3. Neglectful parents have also been found to frequently have an atypically large number of children.

4. A fair number of neglectful mothers are below normal in intellectual capacity.

5. Neglectful parents (particularly the mothers who have most contact with children) are physically and emotionally exhausted, have health problems, are

Physical neglect

socially withdrawn or isolated, frustrated, are apathetic, and lack hope. Such factors lead them to be "indifferent" toward their children.

6. Neglectful parents tend to have had emotionally deprived early childhood experiences. Similar to abusive parents, they failed to have stable affectional relationships when they were young. Such early childhood experiences appear to lead to current "emotional inadequacies," and then when combined with severe financial and environmental stress results in physical and emotional exhaustion.

7. Neglectful families are not without intrapsychic distress, but are generally less emotionally disturbed than abusive parents. Similar to abusive parents they tend to be socially isolated.[38]

PROTECTIVE SERVICES

Brief history. Under the concept of *parens patriae,* the state is ultimately a parent to all children. When the natural parents neglect, abuse, or exploit a child, the state has the legal right and responsibility to intervene. Protective service has been defined as "a specialized casework service to neglected, abused, exploited, or rejected children. The focus of the service is preventive and nonpunitive and is geared toward rehabilitation through identification and treatment of the motivating factors which underlie" the problem.[39]

In earlier history the child was regarded as chattel (an item of personal property). In its fullest expression, this gave parents the right to sell the child, exploit his/her labor, offer the child as a sacrifice, and even to kill the child at birth. Although most communities regulated and restricted such rights, it was not until the era of industrialization that children were considered to have certain rights. These rights have gradually been expanded. Until the early 20th century when

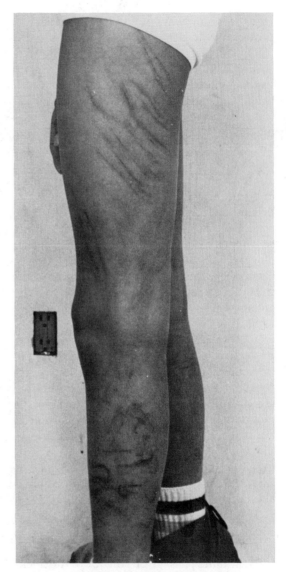

A 12-year-old boy abused with an extension cord

child labor laws were finally enacted, parents were allowed to exploit the labor of their children.

Agencies providing protective services in America trace their origin to the case of Mary Ellen in 1875. Mary Ellen was severely beaten and neglected by a couple who had raised her since infancy. Concerned community citizens were unaware of any legal approach to protect her. In desperation, they appealed to the Society of the Prevention of Cruelty to Animals. (It's interesting to note that organizations existed to protect animals at this time, but not children.) Mary Ellen was brought to the court's attention by this Society as an "animal" who was being abused. The court accepted the complaint, partly because laws existed protecting animals from abuse. Protection was given to Mary Ellen, and the abusive couple was sentenced to prison. Following this dramatic case, a Society for the Prevention of Cruelty to Children was formed in New York. Gradually other similar societies throughout the United States were formed, laws protecting children from abuse and neglect were enacted, and agencies providing protective services were established.

Almost from the start, two focuses for protective services were initiated: a law enforcement approach and a rehabilitative approach. The law enforcement focus emphasized punishment for the abusive or neglecting parents, while the rehabilitative approach emphasized the importance of helping the parents, and keeping the family together, rather than disrupting it. Since the early 1900s, protective services have generally taken the rehabilitative approach.

The late 1960s and the 1970s showed an explosive growth of interest in services to prevent and treat child abuse. With this interest came passage of Title XX to the Social Security Act in 1975 making protective services mandatory for each state and providing federal reimbursement for most costs. A federal Child Abuse Prevention and Treatment Act was passed in January 1974 which provides direct assistance to states to help them develop child abuse and neglect programs.

Processes in protective services. Extensive efforts have been made to encourage parents who have maltreated their children (or feel they may maltreat them) to request agency services voluntarily. Radio and TV announcements, along with posters, announce the availability of parental-stress hot-line services that parents may call in many communities.

Parents who maltreat their children, however, do not generally apply for help. Currently, initiation of services frequently results from the legal requirement of mandatory reporting by professionals of suspected abuse, physical neglect, sexual abuse, and emotional injury. The list of professionals required to report includes, among others, social workers, school personnel, doctors, day-care center personnel, legal personnel, nurses, and dentists. The agencies to which reports are to be made are generally the local police department, the county welfare department, or the county sheriff. These laws grant civil and criminal immunity to the professionals required to make such reports, and also specify penalties for failure to report.

Each state has the legal right and responsibility to intervene when a child is being abused, neglected, or exploited. This right and responsibility are delegated to protective services (in many states protective services are located within public welfare departments).

Case finding is almost always through a complaint referral. Complaints generally are filed by neighbors, relatives, public health nurses, physicians, school authorities, police, or another social agency. A complaint is a report of a possible neglect or abuse situation that needs exploration. The complainant may remain anonymous (not provide his/her own name). Occasionally unfounded complaints are made to "harass" a parent.

Some complainants feel guilty about having made a report, and they are given reassurance that they are performing a very useful function that is necessary to protect and safeguard children. They are also informed their identity (name) will not be revealed to the family against which the report has been made.

All complaints are then investigated by the protective service agency. Many agencies make the initial contact by letter. This letter identifies the agency, gives a general explanation of the service and indicates a concern has been expressed which needs to be looked into. Such a letter gives parents a chance to privately react and prepare for a meeting with a social worker.

Other agencies prefer an unannounced visit. This approach has the advantage of allowing the social worker to view the home environment in its day-to-day appearance. Whether or not a letter is used, the initial approach is direct and frank. The social worker conveys that a situation of potential danger to a child has been expressed, and

---

LETTER TO PARENTS IN WHICH A COMPLAINT OF CHILD ABUSE OR NEGLECT HAS BEEN FILED*

July 26, 1977

Mr. & Mrs. ———————
Racine, WI

Dear Mr. & Mrs. ———————

Information which raises question about the care your child is receiving has come to our attention. When such reports reach our agency, it is our legal responsibility to explore them. We realize there are always two sides to any such report, and therefore, we would like to talk with you in person about this information. If there is any need for help, this contact with you should assist us in determining in what way we could be most helpful to you.

I have been assigned as your social worker in this matter. I would appreciate it if you would contact me within forty-eight (48) hours after you receive this letter about an appointment to discuss this situation. My office hours are from 7:30 A.M. to 4:00 P.M. Monday through Friday, and my telephone number is 636-3348. If I am not in when you call, please leave your name and number, and I will return your call.

Thank you for your anticipated cooperation.

Sincerely,

Protective Service Intake Worker
RACINE COUNTY DEPARTMENT OF SOCIAL SERVICES

* Reprinted with permission of Racine County Department of Social Services (Wisconsin).

needs to be explored; if a potential danger does exist, the worker's responsibility and interest are to be helpful to both the parents and their children.

The social worker attempts to obtain an objective and accurate description of the situation. Specific information relevant to the complaint is sought. For example, if the complaint is that a child appears malnourished and is frequently absent from school, specific questions are asked about the daily diet of the child, what illnesses he/she has had and when, and the specific dates and reasons why the child has been absent from school. Such details are necessary to determine if the child is in fact in danger and what help (if any) is needed. Such detailed information is also essential as evidence if a petition is made to the court for removal of the child from the home. Obtaining this information has to be done tactfully as it is also important that the social worker seeks to develop a working relationship with the parents.

During this evaluation process the social worker almost always seeks to see the child who has been alleged to be in an endangered situation.

If abuse or neglect exists, the objective is to convey to the parents that the focus of protective services is to prevent further neglect or abuse and to alleviate the factors that are now a danger to the child. Because many families charged with abuse or neglect have multiproblems, services may be far ranging (for example, health, educational, financial, housing, counseling, employment, parent effectiveness training, homemakers, day care, and so on).

If there is no evidence of neglect or abuse, the case may be closed after the initial interview. For families with serious problems, continued services may be provided for years.

If the child is clearly in danger (for example, repeated severe abuse) or if the parents are unable or unwilling to make changes essential for the long-term well-being of the child, the child may have to be removed from the home. Protective service agencies view court action as "a means of protecting the child rather than prosecuting the parents."[40]

If the social worker decides it is necessary to remove the child from the home, the parents' voluntary consent is first sought. If this is not received, a petition is made to the court that the child needs protection (court action is atypical in protective services as studies suggest roughly 90 percent of cases are closed without it).[41]

After a petition is filed, a preliminary hearing is held within a few weeks. Parents are permitted to be represented by an attorney, and the normal adversary court procedures are followed. The social worker has to support the petition with documented facts. The judge has the responsibility of protecting the rights not only of the child but also of the parents. At the preliminary hearing the parents are asked if they will consent to or contest the petition. If they decide to contest and if evidence of abuse and neglect is substantiated, a trial is held.

In making a disposition a number of avenues are open to the judge. He/she may decide there is not sufficient evidence of neglect or abuse to warrant any action. Or, the judge can place the child under supervision of the court, while permitting the child to remain at home. Such supervision puts pressure on the family to make needed changes, with the threat of the child being removed if the changes are not made. The judge also has the option of placing the child under protective legal custody. Under this arrangement legal custody of the child is assigned to a social agency who then has the authority to remove the child if essential changes are not made. The judge can also terminate the parents' legal rights and place the child under guardianship of the agency. Under this disposition, the child is automatically removed from the home.

For children who are in imminent danger, many jurisdictions have provisions which allow either the protective service agency or the family court to immediately remove the child. Such children are then usually placed in a foster home for a temporary period of time.

Involuntary services. Protective services cannot withdraw from the situation if it finds the parents are uncooperative or resistant. For most social services, clients are voluntary recipients; generally they are interested in receiving services. Protective services is one of the few services where participation is involuntary (probation and parole is another).

Since protective services are involuntary and since provision of services is based on an "outside" complaint, the recipients are apt to view the services as an invasion of privacy. The initial contact by the social worker is therefore likely to arouse hostility, be viewed as a threat to their family autonomy, and perhaps raise some guilt about incidents where they have mistreated their children in the past. Having ones functioning as a parent questioned and explored arouses substantial emotional feelings.

Although the focus of protective services is rehabilitative and nonpunitive, Varon found in a study that former protective service clients generally viewed the service as being punitive and investigatory.[42]

Some recipients of protective services remain hostile and resistant throughout the time period in which services are provided. Others are brought to form a productive, working relationship with the agency, with positive changes being much more apt to occur. A few are cooperative from the beginning, perhaps because they recognize their family needs help.

In working with parents who neglect or abuse their children, the social worker has to show respect for the parents as people, while in no way conveying acceptance of their mistreatment. The worker needs to convey empathy with their situation, be warm, and yet be firm about .the need for positive changes. This approach is illustrated in the following interview:

> The C. family was referred to the child welfare agency by a hospital which treated the six-year-old boy, Wade, for a broken arm suffered in a beating by his mother. . . .
>
> Both parents said they whipped the children because they believed in firm discipline, and they challenged the worker's right to question this. Mr. C. again attempted to avoid the subject of Wade's beating by describing at length how strict his parents had been with him. . . .
>
> Again the worker brought the conversation back to the C's own disciplinary practices by saying that children had to be dealt with firmly, but the injury of a child was a serious matter. He added, "I can understand that one may be so upset he has trouble controlling himself." Mrs. C. hesitatingly said, "I was so upset and too angry," and broke into tears. The worker replied that, if together they could try to understand why Mrs. C. gets so upset, perhaps the behavior would not continue. Mr. C., who had been silent for a while, said he realized it was serious and that he did not approve of Mrs. C. beating the children but did not know what to do. He had told her that this was bad for the youngsters, but she continued. Mrs. C. remarked that looking back on Wade's beating was a terrible experience. She did not realize she had injured him until his arm became swollen. She supposed it was her anger and her temper that did it. She would like to talk to someone and she does need help.[43]

In working with families who maltreat their children the protective service worker has to be ready to perform a variety of roles: teacher, enabler, adviser, coordinator of treatment, intervener, supporter, confidante, and expediter. The focus has to be on constantly identifying concrete needs, selecting intervention approaches, and providing concrete services. Workers must also be ready to work with other professional groups: the doctors treating the child, school teachers, lawyers, and judges.

A wide variety of treatment resources have been utilized in attempting to make the needed changes. Crisis nurseries, extended day-care centers, and emergency foster homes provide short-term shelter to relieve a potentially damaging crisis situation. Parent effectiveness training programs, group therapy, and family-life education programs sometimes are useful in curbing the abuse or neglect. Homemakers relieve the frustrated, overburdened mother of some of the daily load of child care. Emergency relief funds are sometimes provided to meet immediate rent, heat, food, and electricity needs. Behavior modification programs have been used, such as modeling and role playing, to change the behaviors of parents toward their children. "Emergency parents" have been used in some communities to go into a home and stay with a child who has been left unsupervised and unprotected. Psychotherapy and counseling have also been provided by protective service workers and other professionals. A self-help group, Parents Anonymous, will be discussed at a greater length at the end of this chapter. (It should be noted very few communities have the resources to provide most of the above listed services. In many communities the primary intervention resource available to protective service workers is their own counseling capacities.)

Sexual abuse cases have been especially difficult. In the past when incest was reported, the victim (usually a teenage girl) was generally placed in a foster home. Such action usually resulted in informing the local community of the sexual abuse. Often, neighbors, relatives, and friends expressed shock and began shunning all members of the family. Such disruption usually intensified the marital conflict between husband and wife, and generally led to permanent break up of the family. In some communities the husband was also prosecuted, which further intensified the conflicts within a family. In recent years a number of protective service agencies have been seeking to keep the family intact, particularly when all three of the members involved (husband, wife, and victim) express a desire to keep the family intact. One intervention approach first involves separate meetings with each family member to determine if they want to make an effort to keep the family intact. If they do, the father must acknowledge to his wife and daughter that he is at fault (as often the child feels guilt). The father must also state that he will cease the abuse. Other members are informed of their rights and also urged to contact the worker if the father makes inappropriate suggestions. The father is also informed that further abuse will result in prosecution. Following this beginning, the concerns of each individual, and the interpersonal conflicts between the members, are then worked on.

Kadushin has reviewed studies on the effectiveness of protective services and concludes:

> In summary, the evaluation studies suggest that the agencies have achieved some modest measure of success. The amount of change one might reasonably expect the agencies to effect must be assessed against the great social and personal deprivation characteristic of the client families. Even the modest success achieved may have been more than could have been expected initially.

The resources available to treat these families are limited. The technology available to the worker in trying to effect change in such families is blunt and imprecise. . . .

Scarce resources backed by a weak technology applied to a group of involuntary, disturbed clients resistive to change and living in seriously deprived circumstances would seem to guarantee the likelihood of limited success.[44]

Social workers have found protective services to be demanding. "Burnout" occurs at a higher rate among protective service workers than in other child welfare areas.

RIGHTS OF CHILDREN VERSUS RIGHTS OF PARENTS

The rights of parents have had a long history. Earlier in American history the law guarded the rights of parents, while giving little attention to the rights of children. In recent years defining and protecting the rights of children has received national attention, as indicated by a variety of child advocacy efforts and the specification of various "bill of rights for children" proclamations. Protective services, particularly in contested court cases, encounters the problem of defining the respective rights of parents and children. Maas and Engler found the balance of rights between parents and children varies from community to community.[45]

Some of the situations where this balance becomes an issue are the following. If parents for religious reasons are opposed to their child receiving medication for a serious health problem, should the state intervene? Should the state intervene where an unmarried parent is sexually promiscuous, but yet is meeting his/her children's basic physical and emotional needs? Should the state intervene where a child is being raised in a homosexual environment, or in a commune where lifestyles and mores are substantially different? Should the state intervene in families where a child has serious emotional problems and the parents refuse to seek professional help? Should the state intervene in certain ethnic or minority settings where educational needs are not being met? Should intervention occur when a father uses harsh discipline by whipping a child two or three times a week? Should the state intervene in families where there is long-term alcoholism and serious marital discord? Should the state intervene where a child is living in filth, has ragged clothing, and seldom bathes, but where the child's emotional and social needs are being met?

Different workers, different judges, and different communities would probably disagree on what should be done. The reluctance to intervene may have tragic consequences, as indicated in the following case:

In 1953, a boy of 13 was referred to a children's court because of chronic truancy. A psychiatric examination established the fact that the boy was "drawn to violence" and represented "a serious danger to himself and to others." Psychiatric treatment was recommended by the psychiatrist and social workers concerned with the boy's situation. The mother refused to accept the recommendation and refused to bring the boy back for treatment. Should the mother have been forced to accept treatment for the boy? This is the question of limits of protective intervention. Nothing was done. Ten years later the boy, Lee Harvey Oswald, assassinated President Kennedy.[46]

Parents Anonymous

Parents Anonymous is a national self-help organization for parents who have abused or neglected their children. Because self-help organizations (such as Parents Anonymous, Alcoholics Anonymous, Parents of Gays and Lesbians, Overeaters Anonymous, and Weight Watchers) have had considerable rehabilitative success, PA will be described in this section. It is one of several approaches that can be used in helping parents who abuse their children.

PA was originally established in 1970 by Jolly K. in California, who was desperate to find help to meet her needs. For four years prior to this time she struggled with an uncontrollable urge to severely punish her daughter. One afternoon she attempted to strangle her daughter. Desperate, she sought help from the local child-guidance clinic. She was placed in therapy. When asked by her therapist what she could do about this situation, she developed an idea as she explained, ". . . if alcoholics could stop drinking by getting together, and gamblers could stop gambling, maybe the same principle would work for abusers, too."[47] At her therapist's encouragement she therefore formed "Mothers Anonymous" in 1970, and started a few local chapters in California. By 1979 the organization had grown to over 900 chapters in the United States and Canada, and the name has been changed to Parents Anonymous (since fathers who abuse their children are also eligible to join).[48]

PA uses some of the basic therapeutic concepts of Alcoholics Anonyous. PA is a crisis intervention program that offers two main forms of help: (1) a weekly group meeting in which members share experiences and feelings and learn to better control their emotions, and (2) personal and telephone contact among members during periods of crisis, particularly when a member feels a nearly uncontrollable desire to take their anger or frustration out on a child.

Parents may be referred to PA by a social agency (including protective services), or be self-referrals of parents who are aware they need help.

Cassie Starkweather and S. Michael Turner describe why some parents who abuse their children would rather participate in a self-help group than receive professional counseling:

> It has been our experience that most (abusive) parents judge themselves more harshly than other more objective people tend to judge them. The fear of losing their children frequently diminishes with reassurance from other members that they are not the monsters they think they are.
>
> Generally speaking, PA members are so afraid they are going to be judged by others as harshly as they judge themselves that they are afraid to go out and seek help. Frequently our members express fears of dealing with a professional person, seeing differences in education, sex, or social status as basic differences that would prevent easy communication or mutual understanding.
>
> Members express feelings of gratification at finding that other parents are "in the same boat." They contrast this with their feelings about professionals who, they often assume, have not taken out the time from their training and current job responsibilities to raise families of their own.[49]

PA emphasizes honesty and directness. In the outside world, parents who are prone to abuse their children learn to hide this problem as society finds it difficult to stomach. In contrast, the goal in PA is to help parents admit and accept the fact that they are abusive. The term *abuse* is used liberally at meetings. PA has found that this insistence on frankness has a healthy effect. Parents are relieved, as finally they have found a group of people who are able to accept abusive parents for what they really are. Furthermore, once they are able to admit they are abusive, only then can they begin to find ways to cope with this problem.

During PA meetings parents are expected to actually say why they are beating their child, and the members challenge each other to find ways to curb the abuse. Members also share constructive approaches that each has found useful, and efforts are made to help each other develop specific plans for dealing with situations that have in the past resulted in abusive episodes. Members learn to recognize danger signs and to then take the necessary action to curb the potential abuse.

PA stresses protecting members' anonymity and confidentiality. This protection permits group members to discuss their experiences and asocial thoughts without risk of public disclosure. The fact that they are sharing their experiences with other parents who have abused children assures their being able to "confess" without danger of humiliation, recrimination, or rejection.

Group members develop a sense of "oneness," and often the group becomes a "surrogate family." Each group member is given the phone numbers of all others in the group and are urged to "reach for the phone instead of the child" when feeling distressed. Members are gradually transformed into "lay professionals" who are able to help other abusers and who perceive themselves skillful at this because they have, at one time, been child abusers.

The group leader or chapter chairperson is always a parent who at one time abused a child. Members can identify more readily with such a person than they can with a professional therapist. Among the reasons PA is successful are that it diminishes the social isolation of abusive parents and provides them with social supports.

SUMMARY

Child abuse, spouse abuse, and parent abuse occur in more than half of all U.S. households. Family violence in the past 20 years has become recognized as one of our major social problems. Because children are most vulnerable to abuse, and because most social workers dealing with family abuse are

involved in protective services to children, the focus in this chapter is on child abuse and neglect.

Protective services is an involuntary service for families in which children are being abused or neglected. Neglect covers a variety of situations: not meeting basic physical needs, lack of supervision, denial of essential medical care, failure to attend school, exploitation of the child, exposure to unwholesome conditions, and emotional neglect.

Physical abuse is. dramatic, and has received considerable national attention. Recently, increased attention is being given to sexual abuse of children. Child neglect has received less national attention as the damage is not as overt, even though it occurs more frequently than physical abuse. Physical abuse, physical neglect, sexual abuse, and particularly emotional neglect are terms that are somewhat ambiguous and difficult to precisely define. Estimates of the incidence of neglect and abuse vary widely.

In considering causative factors, abuse appears to be more of a response to psychological stress, while neglect appears to be more of a response to social stress.

The focus of protective services is preventive, nonpunitive, and rehabilitative. Extensive efforts are made to maintain the mistreated children in the home of their parents. Most children who are serviced by protective services are not removed from their home. However, if children are obviously endangered, there are legal procedures to remove the child.

Protective services are involuntary, and are also seen by some families as being an invasion of their privacy. As a result, professionals providing protective services are more apt to encounter greater hostility and resistance from the families being served than in other social service areas.

Arriving at an acceptable balance between

rights of parents and rights of children is an unresolved issue in protective services.

One of the more recent approaches to helping parents who abuse their children is Parents Anonymous. PA is a self-help group, and appears to have considerable promise in helping parents develop more effective interaction patterns with their children.

NOTES

1. "Battered Families: A Growing Nightmare," *U.S. News & World Report*, January 15, 1979, p. 60.
2. Ibid., p. 60.
3. Ibid., p. 62.
4. Ibid., p. 62.
5. Ibid., p. 62.
6. Ibid., p. 62.
7. Thomas Sullivan et al., *Social Problems* (New York: Wiley, 1980), p. 551.
8. "Battered Families," p. 60.
9. Ibid., p. 62.
10. Lewis Koch and Joanne Koch, "Parent Abuse—A New Plague," *Parade*, January 27, 1980, p. 14.
11. Ibid., p. 14.
12. Ibid., p. 14.
13. Alfred Kadushin, *Child Welfare Services*, 3d ed. (New York: Macmillan, 1980), p. 158.
14. Vincent De Francis, *Child Abuse—Preview of a Nationwide Survey* (Denver: American Humane Association, Children's Division, 1963), pp. 5–6.
15. Ibid., p. 6.
16. "Johnny L., 7, Dies of Beating," *Wisconsin State Journal*, September 2, 1972, sec. 2, p. 16.
17. Larry Silver et al., "Does Violence Breed Violence? Contribution from a Study of the Child-Abuse Syndrome," *American Journal of Psychiatry*, September 1969, pp. 404–7.
18. See Kadushin, *Child Welfare Services*, 3d ed., pp. 169–71; and "Battered Families," p. 60.
19. Jerome E. Leavitt, *The Battered Child* (Morristown, N.J.: General Learning Press, 1974), p. 3.
20. George C. Curtis, "Violence Breeds Violence—Perhaps?" in Leavitt, *The Battered Child*, p. 74.
21. Leavitt, *The Battered Child*, p. 183.
22. Kadushin, *Child Welfare Services*, 3d ed., p. 160.
23. Ibid., p. 161.
24. LeRoy Pelton "Child Abuse and Neglect—The Myth of Classlessness," *American Journal of Orthopsychiatry* 48, no. 4 (October 1978): 608–616.
25. Kadushin, *Child Welfare Services*, 3d ed., p. 199.
26. Ibid., pp. 199–212.
27. American Humane Society, *National Analysis of Official Child Neglect and Abuse Reporting* (Denver: American Humane Association, 1978).
28. Alfred Kadushin, *Child Welfare Services*, 2d ed. (New York: Macmillan, 1974), p. 249.
29. Vincent De Francis, *Special Skills in Child Protective Services* (Denver: American Humane Association, 1958), p. 11.
30. Edward Sarafino, "An Estimate of Nationwide Incidence of Sexual Offenses against Children," *Child Welfare* 58, no. 2 (February 1979): 127–33.
31. Ibid.
32. David R. Walters, *Physical and Sexual Abuse of Children—Causes and Treatment* (Bloomington; Indiana University Press, 1975).
33. Alvin A. Rosenfeld, "Incest and the Sexual Abuse of Children," *Journal of the American Academy of Child Psychiatry* 16 (1977): 334–36.
34. Yvonne M. Tormes, *Child Victims of Incest* (Denver: American Humane Association, 1963).
35. Kadushin, *Child Welfare Services*, 3d ed., p. 188.
36. American Human Society, *National Analysis*.
37. Leavitt, *The Battered Child*; Kadushin, *Child Welfare Services*, 3d ed., and C. Henry Kempe and Ray E. Helfer, *Helping the Battered Child and His Family* (Philadelphia: Lippincott, 1972).
38. Leavitt, *The Battered Child*; and Kadushin, *Child Welfare Services*. 3d ed.
39. Vincent De Francis, *The Fundamentals of Child Protection* (Denver: American Humane Association, 1955), p. 2.
40. Ellen Thomson, *Child Abuse—A Community Challenge* (Buffalo, N.Y.: Henry Stewart, 1971), p. 44.
41. Kadushin, *Child Welfare Services*, 2d ed., p. 264.
42. Edith Varon, "Communication: Client, Community and Agency," *Social Work*, April 1964.
43. Anna Mae Sandusky, "Services to Neglected Children," *Children*, January–February 1960, p. 24.
44. Kadushin, *Child Welfare Services*, 3d ed., p. 212.
45. Henry Maas and Richard Engler, *Children in Need of Parents* (New York: Columbia University Press, 1959).
46. Kadushin, *Child Welfare Services*, 2d ed., p. 274.
47. Phyllis Zauner, "Mothers Anonymous: The Last Resort," in Leavitt, *The Battered Child*, p. 247.
48. "Battered Families, p. 60.
49. Cassie L. Starkweather and S. Michael Turner, "Parents Anonymous: Reflections on the Development of a Self-Help Group," in *Child Abuse: Intervention and Treatment*, ed. Nancy C. Ebeling and Deborah A. Hill (Acton, Mass.: Publishing Sciences Group, 1975), p. 151.

chapter 7

A classic cartoon pops up with regularity in magazines and the press. Father is at the door, arm raised and finger pointing out into the cold, cruel, and stormy world. The person leaving home is a young girl, usually with a shawl covering her head, shoulders, and the "wee bundle" in her arms. The caption under the cartoon tries to be witty, because that is what cartoons are all about. But what is so witty or funny about this cartoon? Not much. It happens every day, and to the people involved it isn't a laugh a minute.

Centuries ago there were deposit boxes at the roadside and in front of the churches in which one could place unwanted babies. Some of them were found alive. Today newborn babies are often found in churches, cars, and in boxes along the curb. Some of them are found alive.

* This chapter was written for this text by Ursula Sennewald Myers, ACSW, formerly a social work supervisor of a single-parent unit and now director at a social services agency. Ms. Myers uses the term *illegitimacy* reluctantly inasmuch as there is some question as to its validity and appropriateness. Her concerns are elaborated further on in this chapter.

Certain primitive peoples protected their tribal social structure by requiring infanticide of those mothers who had no official "husband." In this way, they protected the tribe from excess dependent members. In today's world, it is common to read of newborn babies found dead in plastic bags, garbage cans, and refuse piles—victims, mother and child alike, of contemporary tribal mores.

Are we kinder, wiser, and more tolerant and civilized in our attitudes toward and relationships with these social victims today? We shall attempt an answer to this question in this chapter on the single parent.

We will also look at a major sociological phenomenon of the 1970s and early 1980s, the increase in the rate of pregnancies to single adolescents (women 19 and under). At the same time the rates in all other age-groups are decreasing. Why this paradox? Is it indeed an uncontrollable fact of life for future generations of teenagers? Can the trend be reversed? What are the influences pervading the world of the teenager which glamorize early sexual experiences? Out-of-

"Illegitimacy" and services to single parents*

wedlock pregnancies are generally unwanted pregnancies, in spite of the infrequent but well-publicized births of "love children" to single persons in the public eye, who are also, and not incidentally, rather comfortably located in the upper socioeconomic class. Why are so many more teenagers having babies? How do social workers involve themselves with this target system?

Someone once said that experience was the best teacher. Perhaps. It is not necessary, however, to have had a child as a single person to learn about what social work services the single parents want and need and how to go about delivering these services. Much of the material in this chapter derives from the experiences gained in a single-parent unit of a public social services agency located in what politicians are fond of calling "Middle America," and where the many who migrated here have found a broad spectrum of political, philosophical, cultural, and sociological persuasions. We will therefore look at the single parent from the perspective of one public social service agency—and the

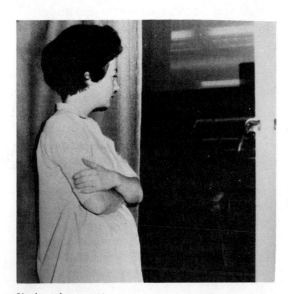

Single and pregnant

view from the window is a concrete block wall, literally, and sometimes in practice, figuratively.

AN OVERVIEW

Society tends to view pregnancy and parenting outside of marriage as pathological. Single parenthood threatens the traditional social structure of the two-parent family. It generally lacks the support system provided motherhood in marriage. Most cultures have, historically, also attempted to control adolescent sexual activity.[1] There has been, however, a gradual moderation in recent years in our societal attitude toward the single parent. While out-of-wedlockism is still considered deviance, we are beginning to recognize our social and practical responsibilities toward the young mothers and their children. We now have legislation designed to allow pregnant women to complete their education, and also federal and state assistance programs such as Aid to Families with Dependent Children, child care payments, maternity aid programs. The current high rate of divorce with the resultant increase in one-parent families permits the unmarried parent to fade into the social environment much more readily than in the past.

But these developments are quite recent. The early attitude toward out-of-wedlock pregnancies and births was one of "ignore them and they will go away"—and they did. The young women went away from school by dropping out, either voluntarily or forcibly leaving their educational programs. The out-of-wedlock mothers went away into dependency, either on public assistance or their parents, and remained out of the productive job market indefinitely. They often went away from their families by running, to ultimately join transitory subcultures or to become prostitutes. The children born to these children went away into a world of risk—risk of neglect, abuse, inept parenting, poor health, poor housing, and poverty.

Some children born of single parents went as far away as death, the final separation. We are still, in the late 20th century, experiencing newborn infants found dead in plastic garbage bags, coal bins, trash cans, and under dormitory rubbish.

What, then, are the causative factors? The *Encyclopedia of Social Work* (1965 edition) cited as answers poor environment, heredity, low intelligence, immature judgment, being "oversexed," mental defectiveness, lack of education, and finally, exploitation of women.[2] There was not much of a negative nature left to cite. There seemed to be prevalent an old-fashioned concept that bad social conditions (poverty, lack of education) produced "bad" (pregnant) girls and conversely, a "good" environment would produce "good" girls. (This argument soon lost its relevancy as the good girls, pregnant in spite of their environments, began to come out of the closet.)

In the introduction to Klerman and Jekel's study *School-Age Mothers*, Charles Gershenson proposes that "this social problem . . . was a consequence of the interaction of some of the most powerful social issues of the country's historical and cultural heritage: poverty, discrimination, and sexuality of youth . . . [and] its linkage to the welfare system"[3] and hence dependency.

Clark Vincent, in his early classic, *Unmarried Mothers*, traces the historical perspective of social attitudes from the pre-1930s to the late 1950s.[4] Prior to the 1930s, *bad*ness was equal to "bad" behavior, which in turn caused out-of-wedlock children to be born. Immorality and low intelligence were symptomatic of this badness. Then in the 30s, society (or rather, sociologists) came to the conclusion that a "bad" environment (that is, poverty, broken homes) caused "bad"

behavior, and hence caused out-of-wedlock births. The late 30s brought the cultural, or anthropological, way-of-life rationale and to "witness" it, the black culture was frequently cited, and not always rationally, from my point of view. The stereotypes of the black male as "stud" and the black woman as indifferent to the number of children she bore were unscientific, unfair, and unfounded.

By the time the 40s arrived, culture as the causative factor had become unfashionable. We were now psychoanalyzing the single, pregnant woman. Emotional disturbance was the precipitating factor in becoming pregnant out-of-wedlock. Since the illegitimacy rate was steadily increasing during these years, we apparently had quite an increase in crazy ladies as well. Nothing much was said about the mental health of the male partner.

Single pregnancies were thought to be manifestations of subconscious desires, of a dysfunctional relationship with one's mother, or the resolution of subliminal problems. Those of us in social work practice in the 1980s find this belief still prevalent, even though there are no studies to prove the efficacy of the emotional disturbance premise as the exclusive precipitating factor. Social workers very comfortably respond positively to those who say the woman's psychological needs are being met by the pregnancy as being valid in *some* cases. She may have become emotionally distraught, however, after the fact of pregnancy became confirmed. In as many cases, however, there may have existed cultural phenomena which encouraged the single pregnancy. Ignorance was then, and continues to be, a major factor contributing to the birth of children of single parents.

What of the 1950s? The "good life" fiction of the early 50s gave way to the reality of poverty, political unrest, the early civil rights movement, poor housing, unemployment, and the "fun" morality. "Do your own thing" was the theme of a bumper-sticker culture. Society became the identified patient in the late 1950s, and births to single parents became symptomatic of a larger social illness. The social illness of illegitimacy tended to be "cured" up to the late 50s by early marriages, maternity home placements (particularly among white families), and termination of parental rights (with the child placed for adoption), or informal transfer of the parenting responsibilities to relatives, most likely the maternal grandmother. Middle-class pregnancies of any race were not looked at as socioeconomic problems to taxpayers or society, for they provided society with adoptable infants while at the same time not imposing a financial burden on the country.

No one really knew what to do about the 1960s. In dismaying numbers, young people disengaged themselves from previous social norms and entered worlds of counterculture, cynicism, and perhaps justified disillusion. Drugs and alcohol became their security blanket.

The blanket was full of holes. The rate of out-of-wedlock births increased among teenagers.

Did this increase simply reflect prevailing social influences beyond the teenager's immediate culture? It would seem so. Vincent described these influences as early as 1961: (a) the "fun" morality, wherein there is little critical evaluation of precipitating factors or attitude changes and needs gave way to wants which became needs (and feeling good was essential); (b) the "other-directed" search for approval, wherein others determine your self-esteem; (c) "self-fulfillment" (a phrase into which we can all pour our own substance); (d) "victim," or "everything happens to me, I can't control my own behavior, life does."[5] Retrospectively, it seems

strange that we expected young persons, particularly sexually active ones, to do, individually, what society as a whole had, and has, not done—to rise above those very influences that pervaded the entire social structure of our country.

In the 1970s the influences continued and so did the inconsistencies. Existing attitudes toward the cause and effect of "illegitimacy" were nothing other than paradoxical and hypocritical. We covertly (and by the late 70s, overtly) encouraged sensual behavior and sexual intercourse; the media bombarded us with sexual titillation as it sold automobiles and shaving cream along with the virtues of a simultaneous, multi-multi-ORGASM!

But don't get caught even today. If you get caught doing all those titillating things and get pregnant, you are a social problem. You are premaritally (who said anything about getting married?) pregnant, illicitly (what is licit?) pregnant, illegitimately (only if you live in 38 states and the District of Columbia—so move) pregnant, and pregnant out of wedlock. (Who ever said in wedlock was a guarantee of bliss didn't check out today's staggering divorce rates. *Nine* out of every ten teen marriages end that way.)

Consistency in our attitudes and behavior toward single pregnancies has not been one of our national virtues. At least the Puritans in Massachusetts were consistent: between 1620 and 1839 they openly tried 1,244 cases of fornication before their parish congregations.[6] We have still, in many states, laws on the books against fornication, while at the same time disc jocks are playing records that move it in and move it out.

If anyone, then, is consistent in belief and behavior today, it is probably the teenager and young adult. It appears that they are generally thumbing their noses at the hypocrisy and inconsistency of present sexual mores and making their own rules and their own babies in ever-increasing number as single parents. One does not necessarily *have* to follow the other, however, and young men and, in particular, women are still ignoring the control they are now free to exert over conception, no matter what their age. The focus of the 80s might well be the encouragement of assertive behavior and assertive mentality in women, particularly among teenagers. Call it assertive femaleness. Equate it with responsible sexuality.

When a young client was asked why she became pregnant, she gave a very simple answer, "I like to screw!" She, at least, was finally able to make the connection between what she had been doing and what she had become—pregnant. If society in the 1980s still does not seem to want to make the connection between sex and the single person and single-person pregnancies, how can we expect the people that are part and parcel of that society to do so? As we will see in the data that follows, a very important part of our population—the American teenager—has not been making the connection.

FACTS, FIGURES, AND TRENDS

Statistics can be confusing or clarifying, boring or exciting. We may not like what they have to say, but they usually help to understand the dimensions of a problem. The data that follows is pared down in quantity but hopefully will provide clarifying information and some sense of perspective on the facts and figures of single parenting.

Historical data from 16th- and 17th-century "very merrie olde" England indicates that the number of brides pregnant at the altar ran as high as 46 percent in some villages. We were not collecting data in the United States at that time, but more recent Bureau of Census figures show an understated 7.4 percent for the years 1900–1910.[7] More current related figures indicate that

between 1938 and 1958, the annual number of reported out-of-wedlock births in the United States increased from 87,900 to 208,700. The annual rate, or number of these births per 1,000 females between the childbearing ages of 15–44, increased from 7 to 21 percent. During this 20-year period, the *rate* increased least in the 15 to 19 age-group and most in the 25 to 29 age-group. The actual *number* of teenage parents increased considerably, however, because of the increase in the number of girls born between 1945 and 1958, compared to 1938 to 1944. Between 1940–58, the total percentage increase in the rate of illegitimate births to women of childbearing age was 250 percent![8] And between 1962 to 1970, during a steady increase in the rate of out-of-wedlock births, the overall registered live birthrate was in contrast decreasing.

By the early 70s, a noticeable change was taking place in the pattern; the rate for out-of-wedlock births began to follow the downward trend of the total birthrate. Both were increasing in number but at a slower rate of speed. In 1974, the number of registered live births increased over 1973 by only 0.7 percent; during the first 10 months of 1975, the increase over the previous year was but 0.5 percent. The national birthrate in the United States decreased from 120 per thousand women (15–44) in 1960 to 68 per thousand in 1974.[9]

A crucial factor hidden among these statistics was that the downward trend in the increase in the illegitimacy rate *applied* to all age-groups except for 15- to 19-year-old white women. Between 1971 and 1972 there was an increase in this group of 4 percent, between 1972–73, 10 percent, and 4 percent again between 1973 and 1974.[10]

Data presented early in 1980 by Wendy Baldwin and substantiated in a later report by the Center for Disease Control in Atlanta indicated once again a decrease in the rate per thousand, while at the same time the actual number of teenage pregnancies increased. Even though the actual number of women 19 and under has decreased, a larger proportion of them are sexually active and at an increasingly earlier age. An encouraging note to those who see premature pregnancies among the very young as a critical matter is that in spite of the overall increase, national family planning efforts may have had some effect on the 14 and under age-group, whose birthrate declined and abortion rate stablized.[11]

Percentage trends, or that portion of the total number of live births which were born to single parents, might be easier to relate to. Hartley indicates that in Europe the percentage of live births born to single parents, or illegitimate, peaked in 1945 and has gradually lessened since then. In the United States, however, the percentage trend is upward. In 1916, 2.2 percent of live births were out of wedlock; in 1940, 4 percent; and in 1945, 5 percent. The annual percentage figure remained at 5 percent until 1950, at which point it began to climb to 10 percent in 1969.[12]

By 1975, 14.2 percent of all births in the United States were to single parents according to the National Center for Health Statistics.[13] One needs to remember that this data on illegitimacy is compiled from reports from 38 states and the District of Columbia. The 38 states reporting do not include two of our major population areas, New York and California. If these states would indicate birth status on their birth certificates, which they do not, one can reasonably assume that the percentages for 1975 would certainly be higher!

In data made public December 31, 1976, the Center estimated 447,900 "illegitimate" births among the total 3,144,198 registered live births in the United States in 1975, an increase of 7 percent over 1974. "This increase resulted mainly from a sharp increase of 11 percent among white women"—for the third consecutive year. Illegitimate births among black women increased by only 5 percent.[14] According to Sol Gordon, in 1975 there were also an estimated 1 million teenage pregnancies, of which 280,000 delivered as single parents, 340,000 were resolved by precipitous marriages, and the balance by either abortion or spontaneous miscarriage.[15]

By 1976 there were 1 million single-parent families in the United States, 500,000 headed by teenagers.[16]

As the 80s began, it was estimated there were nearly a million births a year to teenagers and a total of 1.3 million single-parent families in the U.S.[17] These estimates appear to be rather liberal but may well be realized when the effects of June 30, 1980 Supreme Court ruling restricting the use of Medicaid funds for abortions are felt among pregnant teenagers from poor families.[18]

The issue of abortion will be discussed later in this chapter, but what of the teenager?

It is with this vulnerable and challenging target system, the teenager, that most of our social work practice takes place. The physical and emotional developmental tasks of the adolescent years are all-consuming; the additional demands of pregnancy on this already task-saturated system makes the description of teenage pregnancies as "high risk" all too valid.

Just what is single-parent social work? How do counselors work with our pregnant teenagers and their counterparts, the alleged fathers? What social services are provided, and why? What are the mandates under which social workers practice their profession?

CURRENT SINGLE-PARENT
SERVICE UNDER TITLE XX

The Social Security Amendments of 1975 (Public Law 93–647, commonly known in the profession as Title XX) provided the umbrella under which all public social services agencies must function. Title XX's general regulations and broad perspective has been discussed in Chapter 4; there are certain specific areas under this umbrella which have direct impact on the provision of social services to single parents. In addition to Title XX, there are also statutory regulations which further specify the powers and duties of state departments of health and social services in relation to unwed parents and out-of-wedlock children.

Wisconsin's Comprehensive Social Services Plan for Title XX and the Wisconsin statutes relating to health and social services may well be typical of the 50 state programs and laws now in effect in the United States, and will be used as examples. Wisconsin Statutes, Chapter 46, Social Services, Section 46.03 (7) (a) "Children and Youth" spells out the department's powers and duties regarding single parents as follows:

> (a) Promote the enforcement of laws for the protection of . . . children born out of wedlock; . . . and take the initiative in all matters involving the interests of such children where adequate provision therefore has not already been made. (b) When notified of the birth or expected birth of a child born or likely to be born out of wedlock, see to it (through advise and assistance to the mother or independently) that the interests of the child are safeguarded, that steps are taken to establish its paternity and that there is secured for the child (as near as possible) the care, support and education that would be given if legitimate.[19]

These stipulations are repeated in Wisconsin's recently revised Children's Code.

Apparently the legislators wanted to spell out their message clearly and emphatically, and thus placed virtually identical mandates in two separate statutes.

One of the Title XX goals (the long-range focus of any given service case) as established by federal regulation is Goal III, a combination of: (*a*) *protection* (Goal 111a—preventing or remedying neglect, abuse or exploitation of children and adults unable to protect their own interests), and (*b*) *strengthening families* (Goal 111b—preserving, rehabilitating, or reuniting families). This goal, on occasion in combination with Goal II (*self-sufficiency*—achieving or maintaining self-sufficiency including reduction or prevention of dependency) is most frequently the focus of the delivery of social services to single parents. The objectives, or primary conditions that the client and the social services worker plan to achieve or maintain, are primarily the following: mentally healthy individual or family, satisfactory interpersonal relationships, resolution of problem of family planning, and resolution of problems regarding present or recent pregnancy. In some client-counselor agreements, the objectives would also include resolution of drug abuse or alcohol problems, adequate education, resolution of abuse, neglect or exploitation, adequate living arrangements, and satisfactory home and family management.[20] The social services worker may perform in the role of advocate, coordinator, counselor, and evaluator in his/her working relationship.

In Chapter VI of the *Wisconsin Comprehensive Social Services Plan*, which became effective July 1, 1976, and superseded all previous social service manuals for the delivery of such services within the state of Wisconsin relating to accountability, there are substantive sections devoted to confidentiality, child abuse, children born out of wedlock, and family planning. The requirements of the service delivery system are specified, as is the manner in which these requirements are to be implemented; for example, living arrangements during pregnancy are described (remain in own home, maternity home, boarding home or work wage home, foster home or group home placements), financial planning and assistance are specified (its purpose and sources), educational needs of school age parents, paternity action, planning for the child, termination of parental rights, legitimation of the child, and other elements are carefully spelled out.[21]

As one can see, in the provision of services to single parents there is problem universality and problem exclusivity. The universal problems are housing, money matters, education, and parenting and child care, among others. The problems rather exclusive to the pregnant single parent are high-risk pregnancy (especially among the teenage population), educational dropoutism, decision making in regard to lifelong role, and the interpersonal and legal relationships between both single parents.

What does a single-parent social services unit within a public agency strive to provide in the way of universal and exclusive services to this vulnerable client group? A purpose statement developed some time ago by me for presentation to a social services board met with some consternation—it was considered "professional gibberish," and perhaps to a layperson it would be just that. It is hoped that aspiring students in the social services field might comprehend its meaning without much difficulty.

> Our unit is the provider of intensive psychosocial counseling for two interrelated target systems; unmarried parent units and dysfunctional family constellations. Services offered, and/or mandated, range from *preventive* programs such as family planning, pre-marital counseling, child development and child care counseling, and parent training to *remedial* programs, i.e., marriage and sexual counseling, adolescent trauma counseling, family therapy, and abortion counseling, to *interventive* and *crisis-oriented services* involving child neglect investigations, termination of parental rights, foster placement of children, parent rehabilitation, and child advocacy. In providing these services, our goal is to maximize each system's potential for self-actualization, self-realization, and self-esteem.[22]

What all this means in regard to the individual social worker is that they seek to help the single parent achieve enhanced self-realization and self-actualization, and see this as a primary professional role. Their function is to intervene in, and to help the single parent cope with, both sociological stress factors as well as psychological tasks. The focus of this single-parent unit is generally in line with that recommended by school-age parent authority Marion Howard.[23]

Let us look, then, at the actual business of service delivery within this Single-Parent Unit. The social service areas inherent in the practice of social work within the unit are as follows, but not necessarily in the order listed:

Alternative counseling—Abortion counseling, keeping the child, terminating parental rights, foster placement of the baby, separation counseling, adoption counseling.

Family planning counseling—Birth control information for both sexes, referral to family planning clinics, decision-making factors in birth control.

Educational needs—Remaining in educational programs, alternative programs.

Preparation for delivery of child, both physically and mentally—VD information, drug and alcohol abuse information and referral, pre- and postnatal counseling, preparation for childbirth, general maternal mental and physical health counseling.

Self-awareness and identity problem counseling (particularly among the teenage population)—May include sexual counseling, adolescent identity and crisis counseling, rape counseling.

Interpersonal relationships—With alleged father and with the couple, family counseling with families of both partners, relationships with own parents and siblings.

Legal matters—Paternity action, termination of parental rights procedures, legitimation and/or adoption procedures, education rights.

Child development—Physical and emotional needs.

Alleged-father counseling—Rights and responsibilities, legal procedures, birth control counseling, premarital counseling, among others.

Alternate living arrangements—Foster care and foster placement, maternity home care, housing problems, foster home relicensing.

Child welfare counseling—Abuse and neglect investigations, parent education and rehabilitation, foster placement.

Financial and money management counseling.[24]

These are, then, the actual services provided. Why, aside from recent obvious public notoriety about teenage pregnancies, did such a unit come into being? The primary reasons were twofold: in response to a specific need in the community and to fulfill the social work profession's mandate to be a helping agent for community, group, and individual target systems. Not incidental, of course, were the statutory mandates, both federal and state to protect the well-being of the child and to provide family planning information and referral. To assist single parents to become more effective in their roles was certainly a basic goal. Inherent in all of the services, goals, objectives and social work roles was one major focus—that of preventive programming, the reduction of the incidence of pregnancy among single persons. With the coming of more permissive contraceptive and medical care legislation and with higher court decisions validating freedom of choice, we may well see a change in the pattern of births to single parents. As of now, however, the impact is yet to be felt.

Now, how do the social service workers go about providing these counseling components? First, by a participatory planning, or joint agreement, process between the worker and the client. Second, a variety of social work methods are utilized. Basic to counseling the single parent is the one-to-one therapeutic relationship; other methods used are co-counseling, group work, family therapy, community organization, public information programs, school system resource providers, and professional involvement in organizations such as the National (and Wisconsin) Alliance Concerned with School-Age Parents and Community Single Parent Counselor organizations.

The ongoing case load in the single-parent unit out of which this specialist operates consists, on an average, of 46 primary persons (pregnant women clients). This number does not include the important others on the case periphery—the alleged father, the immediate families of both single parents, their extended families, and all the many other involved professional persons such as school personnel, health care personnel, juvenile court and probation personnel, and the clergy. The reality of social work practice at an intensive level with large case loads (certainly well above the ideal 25 client standard recommended by the Child Welfare League) is, then, that of crisis intervention for the most part, and the 40-hour workweek for the social worker is sciencefiction, at the very least.

(Chapter 20 of this text presents several case examples of the problems faced by young pregnant women who are single, and the types of services that are provided. The interested reader is advised to turn to this chapter.)

There are a number of continuing concerns which invade the real world of counseling the unmarried parent. These concerns appear and reappear in the daily contacts with clients, and remove this target system from any semblance of *average*ness . . . What of the role of parental authority? (Parents of minor unmarried mothers often make the decisions for the young woman, and exercise strong bonds of control which are difficult for a teenager to resist.) What is the impact of the cultural group? The peer group? What impact do economic factors have on the availability of alternatives to pregnancy? How does a community perceive early sex education versus contraception after one pregnancy? Who will speak for the alleged father? What prompts the plan for disposition of the baby? Has it been carefully worked through? How prepared is the mother to care for the child? What is the predisposition for capable mothering—for child neglect or abuse? If the young pregnant woman is a teenager, is she being covertly discouraged from continuing her education? And finally, the core concern of all single-parent specialists—what precipitated the pregnancy—is it a problem for the client or was it a planned occurrence? And what can be done to effect a meaningful and feasible family planning program for the individual client and thus avoid further unplanned pregnancies.

(There appears to be confusion, even among experts in the counseling sector, as to the current role of social workers in the provision of family planning counseling. Some sociologists believe that social workers do not give any birth control information but deal only with the psychological aspects of sexual behavior, while others believe that social workers deal only with the practical aspects of contraceptive counseling and ignore the psychological aspects of pregnancy and premature parenting. We can only speak from the experiential vantage point. Unless our experiences and observations are myopic and unusual, however, we consider the misconceptions unfounded and disagree with them emphatically. Perhaps Title XX, with its mandatory offering of family planning services to all Aid to Families with Dependent Children clients, and its required provision of such services to all social services clients requesting such counseling, will of necessity require family planning in-service training for involved social workers, and will lay to rest blanket criticisms of the effectiveness of social workers in their roles as contraceptive counselors. It is hoped so.)

Consider, then, some of the aspects of current service delivery. If there is a focal point to single-parent services, it is to ensure the emotional and physical well-being of the infant by intervening in the life of the young mother in a positive way. Most of the pregnant women seeking counseling wish to talk to someone who is not emotionally involved in their problem and who can help them in an objective manner. As a part of focusing on the child's well-being (and in most of the current service cases, the client is also a minor) the counselor helps the young woman decide on her future societal role: shall she continue to be a mother and keep her unborn or terminate her parental rights so that the infant may be adopted? If the decision is to keep the child, the counselor focuses on helping the client become a nurturing, responsible parent. (If she keeps the

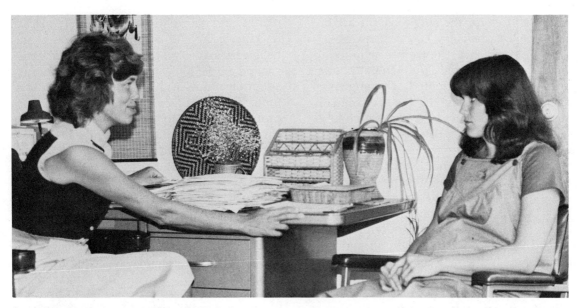

Counseling a young, pregnant client who is single

child, she will be in keeping with a trend in which, in Wisconsin at least, 80 percent of white unmarried mothers and 92 percent of nonwhite unmarried mothers in 1977 kept their babies.[25] The comparable figures for 1971 were 64 percent and 88 percent, respectively.[26] If the decision is to terminate, the focus of services is to help her and the alleged father (who may or may not be terminating *his* rights) work through the physical and emotional trauma of the reality of the decision. It cannot be stressed sufficiently that participatory decision making is on a continuum throughout the entire lifetime of the counseling relationship.

In a chapter written on premarital pregnancies for *The Personal Problem Solver,* I listed the stages in planning that are generally useful to follow in making decisions regarding life goals:

1. Define your problem.
2. Define the alternatives.
3. Make out a pro/con list on each alternative.
4. Evaluate.
5. Decide: What is the most viable alternative for you in your present situation and in terms of your long-range goals?[27]

Some of the aspects of keeping versus terminating rights that are pertinent to the decision-making task relate directly to contemporary mores. The social stigma of single parenthood has lessened to some extent, as we now have both single adoptive and single foster parents and certainly a multitude of one-parent families by virtue of divorce. Unmarried single parents are thus not as visible as they have been in the past. There are support systems available to help ensure successful parenting to these young people: financial aid is available through government welfare programs and support payments from the alleged father, continuing education is supported by laws against discrimination against pregnant teens and school-age parents, child care monies are available to those parents in school or in training programs, and psychological counseling services for the single parent are becoming more prevalent.

In our experience, the woman who terminates her parental rights is generally long-range goal, reality oriented. The stigma of single parenthood is for her perceptually more marked. She sees the coming child as an encumbrance or as totally out of place in her present and future world, her immediate culture, and her internal mental health system. She is usually aware that her pregnancy is untimely and that she cannot cope with the vital needs of an infant at this point in her life. The separation process can result in a broad spectrum of responses, all perfectly normal and human. Both or either parent may feel a sense of loss, grief, emptiness, and unreality. There may be a sense of relief and even pleasure at terminating for some, while others may become depressed and withdrawn. Some work through the grief process to a point of rational and emotional acceptance, while others may completely sever themselves from the pregnancy by "cutting out" that part of their lives and/or totally denying its reality. Even though the decision-making process is ultimately a rational exercise, the service provider must understand and accept the often conflicted emotions of the single parent engaged in this process. The social worker will obviously provide support to the woman at this time, but can also be the facilitator in moving through the emotional and rational processes.

Should the young woman ultimately decide to terminate her parental rights, the social worker will engage her in preparation for the physical and emotional separation from the child and will assist in getting through the maze of forms, hearings, paternity statements, and other legal requirements inherent in this procedure.

Foster care and adoption. As almost all of the infants on whom the parents are termi-

nating parental rights are temporarily placed in foster care, and as some of the pregnant teenagers may need this (or maternity home) shelter, a brief look at foster care services and adoption processes might be in order at this time. The basic goals of foster care are to protect the child, to rehabilitate the parents, and to return the child to its family as soon as it is feasible to do so. It is a temporary provision of substitute care for a child whose parents are unwilling or unable to meet the needs of the child in its own home, and, except for extremely short-term emergency placement, involves transfer of the child's legal custody to the agency responsible for foster placement. Removal of a child from the parent's legal custody is not engaged in lightly and requires court action to become binding on both parties (the agency and the parent).

Foster placement for the infants whose parental rights are to be voluntarily terminated are in placement *by choice* of the mother. As such, it may or may not involve visitation to the foster home, for the mother may opt to disengage completely from the baby once she has delivered. There is great flexibility in planning for separation during this period, and each team of mother, alleged father, and social worker will arrive at the plan best suited to meet at least some of everyone's needs. The length of time the infant remains in foster placement depends for the most part on the availability of time on court calendars for the termination of parental rights hearing, and rarely on the availability of adoptive homes.

By the time parental rights to the infant have been terminated, a number of other vital activities have also been completed. The search for the best possible adoptive family for that child has resulted in the study and selection of an adoptive couple, although the couple may not be fully aware of that fact until the actual termination has been effected in court. (The natural parents have the right,

An unwed mother holds her baby for the first time and must decide whether or not to keep him

until the judge officially terminates their rights, to change their minds, and therefore it is prudent to in turn wait to notify the adoptive parents.) The medical histories of both parents, if at all possible, have been compiled to provide genetic and physical health information to the placing agency as well as the adoptive parents. Efforts are made to meet the wishes of the terminating parents as to religious affiliation, racial, and physical characteristics and geographic location of the adoptive parents. Indeed, the process of becoming an adoptive parent through a licensed agency is much more rigorous than that entailed in becoming a natural parent!

Adoption, according to Friedlander, is a legal, social, and psychological process which ensures a dependent child a permanent family.[28] Wee see it as all that, and more. It begins with a legal process, the legal

termination of parental rights by the natural mother and the legal termination of the rights of *all* of alleged fathers (natural, adjudicated, alleged, and unknown) through the court. (The issue of the unmarried father will be discussed later in this chapter.) At the time of the final hearing on termination, the custody of the child is transferred either to a licensed adoption agency (private or public) or to a relative. Or, in some cases, a "consent to adoption" process is used whereby the natural mother will, áfter the natural father has terminated, place the child for adoption with and by a specific party, but still through *legal court procedure.*

If the child's custody is remanded to a licensed agency, the agency will either place it temporarily in a foster home while the health status of the child is determined, or if this has been previously established, then the child may go directly to the adoptive parents for placement. States vary on the length of time they require for that interim between placement and final adoption adjudication. The purpose of this period is to ascertain as thoroughly as possible that the "match" is a good one for all concerned. If the agency has been doing its homework, the adoption will invariably work out well and be successfully finalized. If the placement is of questionable quality, then it is in everyone's best interest to either wait for a specific period for reevaluation or to admit that the match-up has not been an appropriate one. In that case, the child will either be placed with new adoptive parents, or will temporarily be foster placed pending placement with another adoptive parent(s).

Most adoptive agencies have historically discouraged procedures other than nonrelative adoptions and have favored nondisclosure proceedings and sealed records. Recent trends such as "open adoptions" (whereby natural *and* adoptive parents are officially "known" to each other), the *Gruccio* decision

An adoption hearing

(New Jersey) in early 1977 (which determined that adults who were adopted might under certain circumstances see their official birth documents)[29] and the adoption of foster children by their foster parents have "softened" the hard-line, nondisclosure stances of many adoption agencies.

Public social services agencies do not, and *will* not, participate in any termination of parental rights—adoptive placement procedures which violate the legal rights of any of the parties affected (the child, the natural parents or the adoptive parents) and hence are never a party to the still prevalent "black market baby" business. Although professionally frowned upon, some attorneys and physicians act as go-betweens for single, pregnant women and couples seeking an adoptive child. The price in these negotiated adoptions is high for both the child and the adoptive parents.*

---

* For in-depth information regarding adoptions, see the list of suggested readings at end of chapter.

The above is but a cursory look at a complex services area. As was indicated earlier, few single parents make the choice to go this route. For those that do, it is a difficult journey. For those that do not, the road may be equally as bumpy, but the support system is there to act as shock-absorber, so to speak.

Community health professionals comprise a vital part of this support system. Because single pregnancies are considered medically at risk, and because infants born of single parents are considered high-risk infants, efforts are made to involve the pregnant woman in a preventive and protective medical program, both physical and mental, early in the pregnancy. Unplanned pregnancies are a primary interventive factor in the formal educational process, and service providers must advocate for the single parent and adequate conventional, or alternate, classroom educational programs for each individual student.

There is, of course, no typical single pregnant woman, just as there is no typical illegitimate child. Each person, woman and child, father and grandparent, is unique. What does exist is the common denominator of singleness and pregnancy for the woman, and single-parentness for the child.

Out of the academic and field experiences in social work practice rise a number of issues which must be addressed by society and by social services counselors. Among the most urgent are teenage pregnancies and their prevention, the status of the teenage and alleged father, and the whole issue of responsible sexuality, particularly as adolescents conceptualize it.

SOME ISSUES TO CONSIDER . . .

Society still seems to be fixated on, and wants to attack, the *effects* of premature, premarital, or extramarital sexual activity and pregnancies rather than its *causes*. Perhaps that is because one of the effects is at least physically obvious, while the causes are not quite as visible.

THE SINGLE FATHER

Let us first discuss the dilemma of one of the least visible, the natural father. The courts call him alleged, putative, unknown, adjudicated; in 1970, Reuben Pannor called him the forgotten man,[30] but in 1975 promoted him to the unmarried father.[31] In an article written for an area newspaper in 1975, I viewed him as an average person, Anyman; a shadow person at best.

In the past this shadow person has been ignored or considered of fleeting importance in the lives of the single mother and the child. Times have changed, however, and a new set of game rules, via court decisions in favor of the single father, is creating mayhem among some involved counselors, lawyers, and fathers, causing

concern to others (adoption agencies in particular), and pleasure to a few.

The first indication that the father of a child born out of wedlock was to be considered more than a shadow person in the child's life came with a 1972 U.S. Supreme Court decision in *Stanley* v. *Illinois*, April 3, 1972. This ruling held the State of Illinois statute regarding the custody rights (or lack of them) of the unwed father unconstitutional. Stanley had, the court deemed, been denied equal protection of the law. The decision determined that a hearing must be held to establish the fitness or lack of fitness before said unwed fathers' custodial rights could be removed. The *Rothstein* and *Lewis* cases (Wisconsin) resulted in the Supreme Court requirement that both parents must receive notice of the termination of parental rights' hearings and must have *both* their rights terminated before any adoption proceedings could take place in regard to the child of issue. A final Wisconsin decision provided for a "paternal interest" declaration by the natural father.[32]

The latter was included in the law under which Wisconsin residents now operate, and which is typical of most legislation pertaining to the alleged father, and in which are stated the rights of the natural father of children born out of wedlock. A "parent" of a child born out of wedlock is the natural mother and the person adjudged in a court to be the natural father. The rights of the putative father include the filing of a "Declaration of Paternal Interest in Matters Affecting the Child." Termination of the natural parents' rights can be finalized only under specific sections of the law regulating hearings, the mother's stipulation of the natural father, and the inability to identify the putative father. In substance, then, existing revised legislation protects the natural father's rights to his child by requiring termination of both parents' rights.[33] This is in contrast to previous practice where only the mother's rights were terminated prior to the adoption of an infant.

All of the above does not mean, however, that the alledged father automatically is given custody of the child of issue if the natural mother terminates her rights. He must first be adjudged the father of this child by a court of law, and to be so judged requires a clear and convincing preponderance of evidence. Custody is not automatically transferred to the alleged father at this point, either, as he must also convince the court of his fitness and ability to care for the child.[34] Although we have come a long way since the days when the alleged father had no voice in the welfare of his child, we still place the burden of proof on the father should he wish to keep his child; proof of paternity, proof of fitness and proof of parenting ability. Should not the mother of the child require the same "certification"? Is this not still discrimination under the law and a distortion of equal rights? If one were an advocate of the child only, would it not (particularly in cases where the fitness of the mother is highly questionable, but not overtly neglectful nor abusive), even prior to the birth of the child, be more equitable under the law to appoint a guardian ad litem for all the minors involved, especially the unborn (or delivered) child?

It is obvious that, under our present court system, this practice would of necessity be limited to contested paternity or custody cases only. We are not suggesting that it be applied universally for all paternity cases coming before the court in matters of adjudication and support. It is, however, essential that social services counselors spell out very clearly to both single parents their rights and responsibilities early in the counseling relationship.

One cannot only look at the single father as a depersonalized legal entity. He is, after all, human enough to have fathered a child, to have sexual identity, and to have involvement, be it negative or positive, with the single mother. Now that we have looked at the law, let's look at the person. Not too much is known about him because he is much like all other male human beings. He does not grow an extra inch on his nose a la Pinocchio for every child he has fathered out of wedlock. He doesn't wear a tee shirt emblazoned with the letters AF and surrounded by fancy embroidery. He does have more than economic responsibility for the child to contend with, however, to set him apart from his counterpart, the married father. He has to face his own family and that of the pregnant girl. If he is a minor, this can be very traumatic, as most social workers know. He may also face social stigma or the possibility of an ill-advised early marriage. This last possibility is a reality in our society, for one third of all brides are pregnant at the time of marriage, and one third to one half of all teenage (19 and under) marriages are precipitated by pregnancy. Marrying at this young age usually also means moving in with one or the other set of parents and/or having financial help. "Maturity" is forced on the youngsters situationally rather than developing through normal psychological and physical development. Nine out of 10 of these marriages end in divorce within five years.[35]

Furstenberg, in his 1966–72 Baltimore study, found that "the most important link in the chain between an unplanned pregnancy and later marital failure is the weak economic position of the male who fathers the child out of wedlock and marries a single mother.[36] Premature department from school and entry into the job market ill-prepared for skilled jobs results in fixating them at low-income levels and adding the stress of economic worries to an already shaky marriage.

It is essential that social workers involve themselves with these young men as persons, not just as alleged fathers, even though that must be a primary focal point of the professional relationship. What motivates the AF's behavior? Does he consciously relate the act of sexual intercourse to the consequences? Is he acting out of machismo? (Sorenson indicates that first intercourse is significant to boys because of anticipated enhancement of status, self-esteem, and elevation to adulthood.[37] Is sexual intercourse and lack of contraception a retaliatory gesture against females? (What female? Why mother, of course!) Does he simply enjoy the physical and emotional pleasure of the act? Is he involved in a pleasurable relationship with a female and likes the idea of being a father but is not sure he will like the reality? Do both the idea and the reality appeal to him? Does he have strong ego involvement in producing a child? And most importantly, will he be a responsible sexual partner in the future and practice birth control?

Reaching the alleged father to engage him in counseling has traditionally been difficult. Times are changing and our experience has been that the fathers are becoming more involved, voluntarily, than in the past. Sauber and Rubenstein's study showed that well over half of the study group fathers contributed some financial support to the mother of their child, voluntarily— whether they were living together or not. Four fifths of the mothers studied had contact with the alleged fathers of their babies.[38] The single mothers are of course the primary vehicle through which contact with the alleged father is made. There have been instances where the alleged father has taken the initiative, but there are still many reluctant travelers! While some

fathers perceive any contact from a social agency as harassment, it is hoped that the social worker can help most of them to see the involvement as a part of the growth process toward maturity.

A checklist of points to be stressed by the social worker in their counseling with the alleged father was presented in a 1970 article by Ruben Pannor and might well be used as guidelines for the initial counseling phase:

1. The call is not from a legal agency of arm of the law, but from a *social agency.*
2. The agency worker does not have preconceived ideas regarding solutions but will assist in exploring all alternatives.
3. The father's predicament requires help the agency with its body of knowledge and experience can provide.
4. An out-of-wedlock pregnancy is serious and carries with it long-range implications for the father, the mother, and the baby.
5. The importance of the father's role in the solution of the problem, by supporting the mother who is already coming to the agency for help, is stressed.
6. Legal implications, such as statutory rape, may have to be explained, at the worker's discretion, to impress upon the father the importance of making an appointment with the agency.
7. Although admittedly a last resort, it may be advisable to discuss local statutes concerning single fathers and actions that could be taken to bring about involvement in legal context.[39]

More and more young men are exercising their rights as natural fathers and single parents. Even though each paternity situation must be judged on its own merits, and even though the burden of proof of fitness is on the natural father, it is certainly apparent to single-parent counselors in the field that social work as a profession must assume a more assertive and positive stance toward that person who is coming out of the shadows, the single father.

CONTRACEPTION, PREGNANCY, AND THE AMERICAN TEENAGER

Don't boogie on the Hill if you're not on the pill. *

Teens are doing a lot of boogieing these days, and it's not always at a dance. What is also apparent, judging from available data, is that they aren't on the pill or any other means of contraception.

An overview of teenage pregnancy by Green and Lowe of Zero Population Growth, Inc., gave the following perspective on the issue:

Births to teenagers.
  Nearly one in five births in the United States is to a teenager.
  Between 70–85 percent of these births are unplanned.
  One fourth of all women aged 20 had had at least one child.
Contraception
  Teenage pregnancy is largely the result of nonuse or sporadic use of contraception.
  Only 1 in 5 sexually active teenage women uses contraception consistently; among those who do not, 7 in 10 think they cannot become pregnant.
  The condom, withdrawal, and the pill account for almost three fourths of all contraceptive use.
Pregnancy
  Nearly 3 in 10 teens who have early intercourse become pregnant.
  One third of all births to teens are out of wedlock, and teenagers account for half of all out-of-wedlock births.

Contraceptive services
  Over 2 million unmarried women aged 15–19 are in need of contraceptive counseling; only one fifth to one third of them are reached by organized family planning clinics.[40]

Around the world, unmarried adolescents, with only a few exceptions are excluded from official family planning programs and find it difficult to obtain safe and effective contraception or abortion services. In 1963 there were 100,000 births to females aged 18 and under. In 1975 there were 1 million pregnancies to women 19 and under, 280,000 of which were out-of-wedlock births and 340,000 to married teenagers.[41] (The remainder were terminated by abortions.) Thus, in 12 years, the number of teenage pregnancies increased almost sixfold, or 600 percent. Out of the 1 million families headed by single parents in 1976, 500,000 were teenagers. Between 1974 and 1977 American teenagers registered increasing numbers and proportions of out-of-wedlock births.[42] By the end of the 70s, we seemed to be going nowhere but up.

What does all this mean? It means, as Sol Gordon has so succinctly put it, that "adolescents will have sex whether we like it or not, whether there are restrictive laws or not, whether there is sex education in the schools or not."[43] To me it means that some teenagers want to have fun and will therefore have sexual intercourse; some them want to have love and will therefore have sexual intercourse; some will submit to peer pressure and will therefore have sexual intercourse; some will want to share friendship and will thus have sexual intercourse. A few will be victims and will thus have intercourse. Few will equate sexual intercourse with pregnancy or as a means to that state. Indeed, "the psychological explanation that teenage girls have a conscious or subconscious desire to become pregnant is a theory

---

* Comedienne Joan Rivers on the "Tonight" show, November 25, 1976, after reading that more babies were born to unmarried women than to married women in the District of Columbia in 1976.

that seriously interferes with efforts to organize constructive birth control programs for adolescents."[44] Agreed. And one must also include in some phase of any such program, education for responsible parenthood. However, as Kristin Luker has indicated in her book *Taking Chances*, education does not necessarily mean taking responsible action.[45] I believe that education must go hand in hand with a heavy program of provocative reality therapy (in the general sense of the word *therapy*) to facilitate connecting cause to effect (sexual intercourse to pregnancy) and to bring the adolescent into the *real* world. And what indeed *is* the real world to teenagers today? It is a matter of their perception of situation, time, and place. It is their sense of self and the recognition of an eventual goal of self-determination, both vital developmental tasks of adolescence.

An unwanted and/or premature pregnancy impinges on these developmental tasks of the adolescent and literally overloads the system, both internally and externally.

> According to available data, menarche is attained 2½ to 3½ years earlier today than a century ago. In the United States, the average age at menarche is 12.5 years, while the average age of physical maturity is 17 years of age. If pregnancy occurs before attainment of physical maturity, the girl is more likely to have complications of pregnancy. Studies show adolescent mothers with higher rates of premature delivery, toxemia, prolonged labor, feto-pelvic disproportion and cesarean section. . . . Because of the diverse biosocial problems of young mothers, fragmented delivery modes which do not consider the whole person leave much to be desired.[46]

The young body must meet the physiological demands of both adolescence and pregnancy, while the psyche must attend to the normal developmental tasks of determining identity and developing a value system, as well as effecting the role of mother and coping with the biochemical and emotional trauma of pregnancy. No wonder the teenage pregnant girl seems to live within an overloaded system. (And if the single father does not feel the physiological effects, he is not entirely free of the psychological tasks.) The young couple has one foot in adolescence and the other in the adult role of parenthood.

In his 1972 book, *The Pregnant Teenager*, Osofsky commented that, what with 40 percent of the out-of-wedlock births occurring among teenagers, it might well be considered an epidemic condition.[47] By 1976, 50 percent of the out-of-wedlock births were occurring among the teenage population.[48] A 2 percent decline in this proportion in 1977 was only because the rates of women between the ages of 20 and 24 increased.[49] Why this premature parenthood? What would appear to be the rationale for venturing into a world at risk—risk of health, education, economic, social, and psychological well-being, peer relationships, and family?

A father of teenage sons held the view that teenagers perceived their sexual behavior as a step to emancipation and adulthood, that this was one area in the lives of young persons that was beyond the control of adults. He also felt that implicit in their actions was seemingly a lack of a sense of doom or fallibility. (The "Who me? Not me!" syndrome of disengagement of cause to effect is thus simply described in different language.)

What answers do the teenagers give? The Sorenson survey published in 1973 indicated the following reasons for nonuse of birth control among the female teenagers canvassed:

1. A certain degree of ignorance—lack of information, inaccurate information, or out-and-out misinformation.

184

2. Lack of access to, or availability of, contraceptives.
3. Opposition to birth control.
4. Not motivated to use because:
   Careless.
   Too much trouble.
   Parents would find out.
   Partner would be disappointed.
   Spoils spontaneity of the act.
   It is the boy's responsibility.
   You can always get an abortion as an insurance policy.
   A pregnancy is not possible or is not a reality.
   Not *really* having sex at all![50]

The Shah, Zelnik, and Kantner study of 1975, "Unprotected Intercourse among Unwed Teenagers," tends to support Sorenson.[51] Gordon maintains that "the only trait pregnant teenagers share, besides sexual experience, is a lack of knowledge about the reproductive process and birth control.[52]

How can social workers and family planning clinics work to combine educational programs with cause-effect, logical consequences, or reality therapy (or whatever else works) counseling? Some practical suggestions are:

1. Provide co-counseling sex education sessions to mixed male/female couples or groups.
2. Describe the techniques of sexual satisfaction and gratification that do *not* involve sexual intercourse.
3. Provide birth control information and have devices available; work to motivate their use.
4. Reduces the emphasis of not having a husband when pregnant and emphasize the deprivations of pregnancy per se—the lack of personal freedom and mobility.
5. Emphasize the ineffectiveness of some contraceptive methods.
6. Glamorize contraception.
7. Suggest abortion be looked at as a last resort not as a general contraceptive method.[53]
8. Glamorize contraception and long-range goals.
9. Glamorize contraception and short-term benefits.
10. Glamorize contraception for both sexes.
11. Glamorize ownership of one's own body, particularly the young woman's.

What effect, however, can social services agencies and family planning clinics providing these programs have on the rise in teenage pregnancies if the consumers do not have access to them and if they are unavailable or insufficient in number? Very little, obviously. The World Health Organization reported in mid-1976 that teenage pregnancy and abortions were on the rise around the world and faulted not the young people but government and society for their regressive stances on sex education.[54] It is assumed by some that with the liberalized legal picture (starting in January 1973 with the Supreme Court ruling on abortion)[55] in terms of contraception, abortion, and minors' rights to these services without parental consent, young women will have access to these services, will use them, and hence the rate of births to single parents will drop markedly.

This is a precipitous assumption. While the courts of our land have forced liberalization, many teenagers simply do not have family planning clinics or medically approved abortion clinics available to them, particularly if they live in rural areas. And some public social services agencies, in spite of Title XX mandates, comply only marginally, if at all, to the family planning program service delivery requirements. Many public agencies have no counseling program of *any* kind for the sexually active or pregnant teenager.

Young persons who are oriented to long-range goals will practice responsible sex by either abstinence from sexual intercourse or the use of birth control methods.[56] The less mature, short-term goal-oriented teenager will most likely, however, still function under the "Who me? Not me!" syndrome, and will eventually become pregnant, as did those 500,000 in 1976. They seem to exist in a state of anomie and be indifferent to the consequences of premature pregnancy. Do they really disengage their overt sexual behavior from its logical consequences?

In the mid-60s, Mary Calderone of SIECUS voiced the belief that people rarely behave reproductively . . . they behave sexually primarily and reproduce secondarily.[57] The Sorenson report substantiated this in 1973 and Sol Gordon has been verifying it in his writings and lectures for several years. Last but not least, the line social worker engaged in counseling teenage single parents *knows* it is true.

How do adolescents perceive their sexuality? They appear to perceive it as a positive response to what might be considered the negative aspects of the real world. They seek intimate, personal relationships to counter the current anonymity, the alienation of society, the rigidity of the protestant ethic given lip service by adults, and the antihumanist drift of our society. According to Sorenson.

> Young people enjoy sex for physical effects, but their sexuality is filled with human values. . . . they do not view sex as a social problem and are not very interested in what society has to say about it. . . . Personal autonomy and the situation ethic are the order of the day; young people prefer to decide for themselves what is right and wrong sexually. . . . This is the key difference young people see between themselves and adult society with respect to evaluating adolescent sexual behavior.[58]

As to the utility of sex, young people generally agree on the following: physical pleasure is not the most important thing in a sexual relationship, sexual intercourse is a good communications tool, sexual inter-

course meets the needs for new experiences, sexual activity among the young is perceived as forbidden fruit and hence a challenge, sexual relations are an index of maturity, peer group pressure is to some extent a motivating factor, sex is an escape from loneliness and other pressures, and finally, sex is seen as a challenge to society.[59] Would that they would consciously equate sexual behavior with pregnancy.

We found that in 1976 less than 10 percent of all sexually active women were using contraceptives of any kind, including strawberry douche! While the majority of teenagers tend to agree that more of them are having intercourse because of the availability of the pill, the *fact* of the increase in pregnancies in this age-group belies the use of available birth control methods, even more available after the court decisions of 1976. Perhaps the casual attitude toward out-of-wedlock pregnancies prevails because abortion is available as a viable alternative. Luker's study tends to support this premise.[60]

The Sorenson survey tends to show that adolescents consider their sexuality as natural and *not* immoral, and that it has nothing to do with badness or goodness—except if it is used for immoral purposes or ends (coercion, brutality, exploitation). Thus, basic to their perspective is what is the *purpose* of sexual behavior. The situational ethic (people do what is best to meet the requirements of the given situation) prevails, and personal values and physical desires predominate. Sorenson concludes that individuals primarily use their conscience rather than the dictates of society to guide their sexual actions and behavior.[61] Hass in his 1979 report, *Teenage Sexuality,* reflects a continuance of this search for personal and sexual values.[62]

Unfortunately, *how* one does this is rarely discussed, nor are the prerequisites or internal controls.

It is apparent to those of us in practice that social controls over out-of-wedlock pregnancies are lessening. Laws, customs, and traditions are changing, and *being* changed by the very population that we are relating to—the single parent. Family controls are softening, perhaps because of the chronic lack of communication that plagues the American family in particular, as well as the natural conflict (between children and parents) of dependence versus independence. Traditional religion is still, to some teenagers, a vital force—but to others religion is a *personal* search for meaning and self. Marriage is perceived by the adolescent as a sharing, one-to-one relationship involving intimacy and commitment. It is not, however, necessarily patterned after the traditional father at work, mother in the kitchen roles (which sadly remind this writer of the Hitlerian model of the ideal woman who spent her time in the kitchen, in church, or *mit ehre Kinder*). What with over half the families in the United States containing working mothers, it is certainly hoped that young people will model their marriages in terms of more contemporary needs and desires.

ABORTION

With marriage perceived as a long-term, delayed goal by more and more young people and with unprotected intercourse the norm for teenagers who are sexually active, is then abortion the most viable alternative to pregnancy? It would seem so, but is it? We will briefly look at the issue of abortion in relation to out-of-wedlock pregnancies, but will purposely avoid discussion of the morality or immorality of the matter. There are ample resources which thoroughly discuss both sides of the issue. (Chapter 18 in this text provides a detailed account of the morality issue.) Our premise is that social work as a profession must view abortion as a legal

right of every client, should she make this choice, and must therefore sublimate personal beliefs to that end. It is the practitioner's responsibility to facilitate intelligent, rational, and autonomous decision making on the part of the individual client, and to support that decision, whatever it may be. Abortion counseling, both in terms of information and referral and in terms of ongoing counseling is in most states overtly recognized as a part of family planning services as provided by public social services agencies.

The 1973 Supreme Court decisions (*Roe* v. *Wade; Doe* v. *Bolton*) left the choice of abortion to the woman and her doctor.[63] In the July 1976 Supreme Court *Missouri* decisions, state laws requiring a married woman to obtain her husband's consent or a minor to have parental permission to obtain an abortion were declared unconstitutional.[64] Subsequent to the 1973 decision, there were approximately 745,000 legal abortions performed in that year; 900,000 in 1974, and an estimated 1 million in 1975. The proportion of legal abortions performed on women 19 and under has remained constant at one third of all abortions, but the actual number has increased annually from 191,000 in 1972 to 325,000 in 1975,[65] and 367,000 by 1977.[66]

Should not the liberalized laws regarding the availability of contraceptive information and devices, coupled with the laws relating to minor's rights, have significant impact on the incidence of pregnancies and births to adolescent single parents? One would hope so. Recent studies do not provide a great many reasons for optimism, however. The Sklar and Berkov study indicated that legal abortion has made a more marked contribution to the reduction of illegitimate birthrates among states with liberalized laws than in those states with restrictive laws.[67] At the same time, however, the number of families headed by single teenagers has been steadily increasing (see previous data in this chapter). Will the liberalized access to contraceptives effected in 1976 increase their use among teenagers, and in turn reduce the use of abortion as a contraceptive method? It is too early as of this date to obtain data or to make conjectures. The Luker study (*Taking Chances: Abortion and the Decision Not to Contracept*) theorizes that abortion will continue to be a contraceptive method as long as *motivation* to use contraceptive devices is inconsistent, even though the means are readily available.[68]

Nor does the liberalization of the law necessarily equate with accessibility. A recent study by the National Center for Disease Control in Atlanta, Georgia, indicated that distance from major metropolitan areas was a definite factor in the more limited use of abortion as an alternative to pregnancy by rural women than by urban dwellers. It was suggested that the federal government funnel more family planning funds into rural areas to facilitate accessibility to these services.[69]

And while the law itself was liberalized, one cannot discuss "access" to services without looking at: (*a*) the Hyde Amendment of 1976 (effected in 1977), (*b*) the political drift of the late 70s, and (*c*) the potential impact of the June 30, 1980 Supreme Court decision which in effect approved of the restrictions on federally funded abortions as established under the Hyde Amendment. It must be remembered that the Supreme Court did not invalidate the freedom of choice premise set forth under the *Roe* and *Doe* decisions but did indeed essentially limit that freedom of choice to women who are able to pay for such abortions. And so "poor women do not have a constitutional right to publicly funded abortions. . . . In perhaps its most controversial action of the current term, the court voted 5–4 to uphold a six-year ban by Congress, known as the Hyde Amendment, that

prohibits federal funding of abortions (*Harris* v. *McRae*)." The decision is permissive in that states may continue funding abortions, and nine states and the District of Columbia have done so voluntarily, with nine states continuing under court orders.[70] Medicaid-funded abortions are expected to fall from over 300,000 to about 2,000. One third of all abortions in the United States in 1977–78 were to women under age 19. According to Baldwin's research, abortion is a major form of fertility control among adolescent women.[71]

One of the Republican platform positions in 1980 was to support a constitutional amendment to ban all abortions, except those needed to save a woman's life. With the election of a number of conservatives in 1980, there are apt to be renewed efforts to restrict (or ban) access to legal abortions.

Medical authorities tend to agree that pregnancy is a life-endangering condition for children under the age of 14, and perhaps even 16 in terms of the total maturational process. What of these children? Are we limiting access to medical options for these youngsters if they are poor? What manner of poverty web are we spinning for children of the poor?

The young people requesting abortion counseling from social service agencies come from the poor and from the financially able. They come from all areas, urban, rural, suburban, and "no known address." And whatever their financial condition, they should not be turned away. Although they are all unique individuals, they have in common a difficult decision; the more difficult the anticipated burden of the out-of wedlock child, the less inclined the woman is to have the child. These women range from the young, pretty, nonwhite college student from whom an illegitimate child is not in the tradition of her family and would seriously hamper her college education; to the 16-year-old girl and her 17-year-old boyfriend who wish to see a social worker to discuss alternatives to her seven-week pregnancy; to the distraught mother of a 15-year-old severely retarded girl who has long been sexually exploited and is now pregnant; to the 17-year-old who has had three previous abortions, one stillborn child, and is pregnant again by the same man; to the 15-year-old emotionally disturbed girl whose physician has recommended an abortion but who refuses to have one; to the 12-year-old rape/incest victim; to the 41-year-old American Indian mother of two (youngest child age 16) who has experienced birth control failure; to the fragile 18-year-old Roman Catholic woman who is being pressured by her fiancé into marriage and wants to talk to a counselor. Some reach the decision to have an abortion; some do not and make alternative plans. They defy statistical categorization.

However, recent social work experience with the sexually active adolescent seeking abortion counseling indicates that they are making use of their newfound right to privacy and not involving their parents in their decision-making processes, nor are they greatly influenced by their parents' attitudes on abortion. (It would be well to note here that part of the counseling process is to gently encourage the adolescent to share the "problem pregnancy" with parents, for the pregnancy does not exist in a vacuum, nor does the adolescent. However, the ultimate decision is up to the young person, and many have very valid reasons for keeping their decision a private affair.) Perhaps the liberalizing court decision will facilitate more rational decision making on the part of young persons, as it will eliminate for many the enormous fear of parental reaction to an out-of-wedlock pregnancy and/or planned-for abortion. Of course, this fear is frequently a factor for many of the young women who are denying their pregnancy, or who are carrying the child to term and have found it impossible to tell their parents. (One of the most frequently requested services of social workers in the initial phase of counseling is "Help me tell my parents I'm pregnant, please!")

Who are the typical teenagers who are choosing abortion as the most viable alternative to their unwanted pregnancies? A recent report in *Family Planning Perspectives* gives this profile: they are older teens, parents are "better" educated, families are intact and smaller than most, they are more apt to be white and the father more apt to be a professional person. (Would this be the group that formerly would have terminated their parental rights? I think so.) The full-term teenagers' families profile somewhat differently: parents are usually divorced and families were larger to begin with, father was an unskilled or semiskilled person, more tended to drop out of school—and often marry.[72]

Those of us in practice know there is no such thing as a "typical" teenager. The eyes of each young person we see carry universal messages of fear, uncertainty, pain, defiance, and sometimes, but all too rarely, joy.

What can be done by those in the helping professions, particularly social workers, to bring less of the former and more of the latter into the eyes of our young people?

RESPONSIBLE SEXUALITY

Accidents Cause People—Park with Care

Bumper Sticker, 1980 vintage

It doesn't take long for most adults, and social workers in particular, to realize there are no guarantees of happiness in this world. Great joy, when it arrives, is rare, infrequently spontaneous, and usually involves knowledge, planning, and work. And that certainly applies to a mutually satisfying sexual relationship of any kind. Unfortunately, most adults equate sexuality, joy, and responsibility with adulthood, as though these were all adult provinces and prerogatives. These are not their exclusive provinces, however. Young adults and teenagers, given accurate and substantive information, nonjudgmental counseling and an adequate support system can and do, if given the opportunity, practice intelligent decision making at least as often as adults do and may also have their share of joyful experiences as well. (Given the track record of adults in terms of current divorce rates and requests for sexual counseling, it wouldn't take much for teenagers to move well ahead of said adults!) Intelligent decision making is not necessarily a factor of age.

The ability to practice responsible, and happy, sexuality is predicated on several basics. The primary "basic," or essential element, is a comprehensive, factual, and accurate educational program. And we are not talking about vocational education, or "learning by doing"!

This comprehensive educational program would include at minimum:

1. Basic biological information (plumbing, if you will) and facts of reproduction, pregnancy, childbirth, contraception (birth control), venereal disease, abortion, and other health areas, including the medical risks of premature pregnancy and parenthood.
2. A look at some other consequences of irresponsible sexuality, or the sociological risks of premature parenthood:
   a. Economic dependency (unless you are independently wealthy).
   b. Interruption and/or dropping out of educational programs.
   c. Lack of housing or inadequate housing.
   d. Uneven availability of child care programs and facilities.
   e. Inability to consistently meet the role requirements of motherhood while also meeting those of being a teenager.
3. Information on alternatives to sexual intercourse, such as psychologist Robert Sorensen's premise that petting should be encouraged as a substitute for intercourse.[73]
4. Legal status of minors, male and female rights, and education responsibilities.
5. Parenting skills training:
   a. Legal and sociological expectations, rights and responsibilities.
   b. Child development, physical and emotional.
   c. "How to do what" child care training by health care professionals.
   d. Parent effectiveness training.
6. Family living training in interpersonal relationships, role expectations, decision making, conflict resolution, financial counseling, human sexuality, alternate lifestyles, friendship and commitment, and that favorite of social workers, family dynamics.

Another basic would be a viable support system to facilitate and encourage the decisions made via the education process: Family planning clinics and teen clinics; comprehensive and coordinated service systems involving health care, education, and counseling; and hotlines and crisis centers (for anyone!). In only a few communities do these "facilities" exist, however, much to the detriment of young and old.

The final two big basics are motivation (to use all that information) and accessibility. The first is entirely internal to the individual, the second external but not necessarily beyond one's control. With strong motivation, responsible people can often move mountains, find resources, and do something positive about their sexual situation as a part of initiating responsible behavior and controlling their own destinies.

AND TO CONFRONT . . .

How, then, can the social work profession confront the deficits in our social services system which hinder the delivery of these basics to the consumer most wanting and needing them—the single parent, potential or actual?

Public social services agencies, under the benediction of Title XX and child welfare statutes, must become leaders, originators, and coordinators of comprehensive service programs for the sexually active and/or pregnant teenager and young adult. Departments of social services are available not only to the economically deprived, but to all young persons designated in need of protection under the child welfare and social services statutes (as previously discussed in this chapter). Their natural function of information and referral as well as direct services providers places them in an ideal position to guarantee that all the needs of the consumer are met, or at least available. This applies particularly to the pregnant teenager, whose unique health, educational, economic, housing and counseling needs can rarely if ever be met by one human services agency.

The single-parent unit which I supervised is an imperfect example of such a service delivery system. It is imperfect because, even with the blessing of its administration, it remains understaffed, and not for lack of creative programs and creative, dedicated counselors. Even so, the recidivism rate (for second pregnancies while still single) of previous clients is normally at 8 percent or lower. If the avoidance of a second single pregnancy by 92 percent of former clients can be considered "success," then the current services delivered by these social workers certainly has merit and utility, both for the young women clients, their children, and for the community (not to mention the taxpayer, who is "us").

Prevention programs must be made available and accessible to all who need them and who desire their services. Prevention programs include: (a) family planning and health clinics for women and for men, (b) mobile counseling, health, and contraceptive clinics (certainly a more constructive use of the van by teens than its present mobile bedroom status), (c) human sexuality education programs for parents so that they can comfortably, at least relatively, communicate this information to their children, (d) sex education in the classroom K through 12 for all intelligence levels, (e) telephone information and referral resource systems, and (f) readily available multimedia information such as the Ed-U Press comic book series on VD and contraception to name but two.[74] Last but not least, courses designed to free up young women for self-determination of role, choice-making, and ownership of their own bodies are essential to preventive programming. (A local junior high school teacher has been offering a course called "I Am Woman" for several years. It is very popular; its focus is on enlarging the perceived role of women and on assertive consciousness-raising. By itself, it does not seem earthshaking, but its acceptance in the curriculum of a conservative midwestern city school system is a major marvel indeed.)[75]

Social workers in both public and private sectors can encourage their agency administrators to mount an assertive public relations program spelling out not only the hard and soft single-parent services available to the community, but also the short- and long-term disadvantages of premature single parenthood.

They can also act positively to assure community compliance with laws that prohibit discrimination against the pregnant girl or woman, the alleged father, or the single parent, male or female. Most organizations and individuals are unaware of the current legal status of minors in regard to rights and responsibilities. The social worker and the social services agency can become viable public information resources in these areas as well as those previously mentioned.

Although there are undoubtedly many other vehicles to encourage responsible behavior, sexual and otherwise, the last one offered here is the comprehensive services community center concept. If social work is indeed to respond to the best interests of the consumer, then it is beholden to bring the many human service agencies utilized by the client system into one central location—one with public transportation readily available. It seems incredible that those persons most needing services, and frequently with limited funds, are thoughtlessly shuttled from place to place. Not only would the "center" concept be advantageous to the consumer, it would encourage the establishment and utilization of the comprehensive coordinated service program suggested earlier.

The center would have available to single parents all those services so vitally needed and so frequently requested: health care services, child care facilities, parenting courses, contraceptive counseling, child development information, housing services, financial aid services, homemaking training, vocational guidance, and of course, single-parent counseling services.

One phase of the center's programming should be an active outreach system whereby teams of social workers, health care and contraceptive providers, child care trainers, financial aid workers, and vocational counselors would go where the target population tends to be—in the schools, teen centers, community action centers, vocational rehabilitation centers, and so forth—to

"sell" their services with a positive advertising campaign.

Also supplementing the community services center would be a system of outposts located in or near consumer areas utilizing old homes, vacant stores, or existing neighborhood center facilities. Those teams assigned outreach responsibilities would also staff these outposts and provide both soft (contraceptive counseling, sex education, and housing locators, for example) and hard (contraceptive devices, pregnancy and venereal disease tests, and financial aid) services to teens and young adults on site.

Is the social climate becoming more receptive to the wants and needs of the single parent, potential and actual, and thus more inclined to support these programs designed to correct service deficits? We think so, for times are indeed achangin'.

AND TO PONDER . . .

Single parenthood may still be defined as a social problem by many, but it is no longer an aberration, nor is it as visible as it once was. Our rising divorce rate has produced many single parent families. Thus the unmarried parent in our culture becomes less physically and socially obvious as he/she melts into the common whole. The integration process promises to be slow, but there are accepted supports given to the young parent which in the past were either unavailable or led to stigmatization. Legislative, financial aid, educational, child care, and counseling programs and the simple fact of peer acceptance have all been instrumental in lessening this social stigma.

And the concept of "illegitimacy" is being questioned; are these questions legitimate? If the concept is essential merely to collate national birth data, then one must assume the accuracy of that data is somewhat suspect. New York, California, and Massachusetts do not register nor report illegitimate births,[76] and most certainly contain a good portion of our national population, as anyone who has watched national elections on television knows. The definition of illegitimacy is not even consistent and varies among states; some states recognize common-law marriages as legitimate and some do not. Thus some parents are illegitimate, some not; it all depends on their residence status! Reporting the birth status of the child, in reality, only stigmatizes the child (in spite of confidentiality efforts). The innocent child thus becomes the innocent victim, whether we admit it or not.

According to Klerman, and certainly supported by social work experience, most professionals and even some legislators agree that the stigma of illegitimacy should be removed from out-of-wedlock infants and birth certificates.[77] (For a further discussion of stigmatization, see Erving Goffman, *Stigma*.)[78]

Basic to the concept of illegitimacy is the legitimacy of marriage. But what of marriage? Why relate so much of our behavioral reality as sexual human beings to marriage? (Social and sexual researchers seem to engage in study after study of "premarital" sexual this and "premarital" sexual that.) As is apparent in Vincent, Hartley,[79] and other literature, unmarried parents are still studied from the point of view that any behavior threatening the social institutions of marriage and the family is a social problem; ergo—premarital pregnancies are overt threats, premarital sexual relations are covert and hence less threatening. Marriage is thus the reference point.

However, the term may well be losing its validity as a time frame determinant or descriptive phrase because many young people do not relate to marriage as the only framework in which to satisfy or legalize their sexual needs and wants, nor are a considera-ble number considering marriage as an early event in their life plan. More and more women are comfortably looking at marriage as a redundant concept, particularly as the ultimate goal of intimacy. If a pregnancy occurs out of sexual intimacy, abortion is an alternative they accept as viable, just as is having the child and raising it as a single parent or unmarried couple. And in the eyes of the adolescent in particular, marriage is not related to as a sexual institution, at least not in the same way adults perceive it.[80] That this drift leads to concern on the part of social scientists is no surprise, for the child, the family (and marriage) have long been considered the perpetuators of social and cultural patterns.

The concern is based on hard facts; *it* is legitimate. In a report summarized in *Family Planning Perspectives* in late 1975, Paul Glick indicated that singles living together was the fastest growing lifestyle among young adults, and that between 1970 and 1974, the number of young men "sharing their residence with an unrelated person of either sex increased twice as much as it had in the entire previous decade." (Note: we can assume that some of those either sex persons were markedly female.) He also indicated that the percent of households headed by a married adult under 25 decreased from 81 percent in 1960 to 72 percent in 1970 to 60 percent by 1974.[81]

It is certainly obvious that most of these shared living arrangements among young adults are not resulting in shared pregnancies. Data previously cited on the decreasing incidence of pregnancy among young adults, and the increased use of abortion facilities for this age-group support this assumption. Perhaps, as Betty Rollin suggested several years ago in her article on the motherhood myth that we as a society should support planned unparenthood and the joys of not having any children at all.[82]

It is apparent to single-parent social workers that the children of unplanned pregnancies would most often echo Ms. Rollin's suggestions, for they are the children most likely to be physically and emotionally neglected, abused, have maturational and developmental lags,[83] be psychologically dependent, have lower intelligence levels, and be behind in grade levels at school.[84] They are indeed at risk. Kadushin cites an American Humane Society report which indicates that half of the abused children studied were conceived out of wedlock,[85] and presumably, given previous data, unplanned. In a lecture given at a symposium in late 1976 at the University of Wisconsin's Madison campus, Ashley Montagu described a study of children deprived of parental nurture and affection; X rays made of the bones of unloved, unwanted children showed growth stoppages, while X rays of a control group of loved children showed an absence of such markings on long bone tissue. The unloved children's long bones indicated arrested growth periods not present in the control groups.[86] Hartley provides a comprehensive list of negative consequences to the child born of a single parent. She cites the "battered child syndrome" as having three and one half times the likelihood for the child of single parents than for the child born of married parents.[87] Single, school-age parents are found to have a combination of very low tolerance for crying and unrealistic expectations of the child's development (they expect too much too soon) which leads to harsh abusive behavior, such as spanking tiny infants[88] for alleged "misbehavior." Thus the high-risk aspect of precipitous pregnancies continues long after delivery indeed.

Much has been written, too, on the economic effects of early parenthood. In a succinct report written in the summer of 1978, Kristin Moore wrote of teenage childbirth and welfare dependency, having found a direct correlation between teenage motherhood and low incomes and/or dependency on aid to Families with Dependent Children in later life. For example, the 1976 bill for women whose first children were born while they were teenagers was conservatively estimated at $4.65 billion . . . "whereas it has been estimated that it would cost just about $112 million to provide modern birth control services to every sexually active teenager at risk of an unintended pregnancy who is not currently receiving them"[89] The cost effectiveness of such a program in both money and the *quality* of life is all too apparent!

If we correlate these facts with our earlier input on adolescent disengagement of cause (sexual intercourse) to effect (unplanned pregnancy), and the subsequent increase in premature, unplanned pregnancies among teenagers, it would seem to child advocates (and who among us is not a child advocate) that our social system is headed for a catastrophe at worst and major confrontation at best.

Social work as a profession, and the single-parent child welfare social worker in particular, is mandated to engage itself in positive, supportive, and forceful advocacy for the single parent, the child in this family, and the sexually active adolescent (and yes, even the adolescent who does *not* want to be sexually active!). Social work, particularly the public sector, needs to put its money where its mouth is, to put it succinctly.

SUMMARY

We have looked at social work and the single parent from many, but certainly not all, perspectives: a brief historical view has been presented, some social attitudes have been reviewed, data have been collated, and the realities (and the deficits) of the current social services delivery system have been carefully spelled out. Some proposals for alleviating those deficits have been offered, along with a discussion of pertinent issues which must indeed be addressed by social work as a profession. Above all, we have tried to emphasize the human element, the most significant and vital factor for both the provider of services (the social workers) and the consumer—the pregnant adolescent, the school-age parent of either sex, the child in the family, the extended families themselves, and the community.

Social work must address itself fully to the issue of the single parent in our society, and there is no room for simplistic solutions. We are deeply involved in a human, societal phenomenon of great magnitude where children are begetting children, and know not why.

Teenage mothers have a suicide attempt rate *10* times that of the general population. Pregnancy is the number one reason teenage girls permanently drop out of school.[90] Crisis intervention and ongoing participatory counseling with this vulnerable group are essential to provide them with the needs they overtly express—housing, financial, child care, personal and social adjustment, employment and job training, medical care, and legal aid—and those covert needs they express in other ways—independence and respect, to be considered with dignity and worth, and a longing for friendship.[91] Even when the adolescent mother seeks fulfillment of these needs in early marriage, she is likely in 90 percent of these marriages to become a single parent through divorce. "Therefore, it might be said that once an unplanned pregnancy occurs in adolescence, it hardly matters whether the young mother marries. In time, she may be almost as likely as the unwed mother to bear the major, if not the sole, responsibility for . . . her child."[92]

Those 1 million single-parent families "created" each year, over 500,000 headed by teenagers, do not appear out of a test tube or a vacuum. People do not behave in a vacuum; they soak up their global and immediate environments and either act, or react, to them, *if* they perceive themselves as having the choice of action or reaction. (Studies prove that young females are not enamoured of being pregnant or by the role of mother, least of all an unmarried one.)[93] Social work counselors must see themselves as enablers to these young people: they must stress the positive factors in developing the ability to make viable decisions and cope constructively with the consequences; to learn to recognize and respect themselves and others as unique and worthy. And above all, the single-parent worker can help the young parents become a part of society, not apart from it.

NOTES

1. William Burr Hunt, "Adolescent Fertility—Risks and Consequences," *Population Reports,* Series J, no. 10 (Washington, D.C.: George Washington University Medical Center, 1976).

2. Harry L. Lurie, ed., "Unmarried Parents," *Encyclopedia of Social Work*, 15th issue (New York: National Association of Social Workers, 1965).

3. Lorraine Klerman and James Jekel, *School-Age Mothers* (Hamden, Conn.: Shoe String, 1973).

4. Clark E. Vincent, *Unmarried Mothers* (New York: Free Press, 1961).

5. Ibid.

6. Ibid.

7. Shirley Foster Hartley, *Illegitimacy* (Berkeley and Los Angeles: University of California Press, 1975).

8. Sol Gordon, *The Sexual Adolescent* (New York: Duxbury Press, 1973).

9. U.S. Department of Health, Education and Welfare, National Center for Health Statistics, "Advance Report—Final Natality Statistics, 1974," *Monthly Vital Statistics Report* (Maryland: Health Resources Administration, 1976).

10. Ibid.

11. Wendy Baldwin, "Adolescent Pregnancy and Childbearing—Growing Concerns for Americans," *Population Bulletin*, vol. 32, no. 2 (January 1980) (Washington, D.C.: Population Reference Bureau, 1980).

12. Hartley, *Illegitimacy*.

13. "One of Seven Births in 1975 Illegitimate," *Milwaukee Sentinel*, January 1, 1977.

14. Ibid.

15. Sol Gordon, "Teenage Sexuality," address given at a Family Planning Symposium, Madison, Wis., May 6, 1976.

16. Ibid.

17. Thomas Cocknell, "Review of Population Change and Parenthood," *Rand Checklist* (Santa Monica, Calif.: The Rand Corporation, 1979).

18. "Abortion Ruling," *Milwaukee Journal*, July 1, 1980.

19. *Wisconsin Statutes* 1973, Chapter 46, Social Services, Section 46.

20. Wisconsin Department of Health and Social Services, State of Wisconsin, *Wisconsin Comprehensive Social Services Plan* (Madison: Department of Health and Social Services, Division of Family Services, 1976).

21. Ibid.

22. Ursula Myers, "Purpose Statement for Single Parent and Family Services Unit," presentation at Rock County Department of Social Services Board meeting, March 1974.

23. Marion Howard, "A Discussion of State Laws and State and Local Policies as They Relate to Education of Pregnant School-Age Girls," consortium on Early Childbearing and Childrearing, Washington, D.C. 1972.

24. Myers, "Purpose Statement for Single Parent Unit."

25. Wisconsin Department of Health and Social Services, Division of Community Services (prepared by Mary Lou Palm), *Unmarried Parents in Wisconsin* (Madison, Wis., 1978).

26. Wisconsin Department of Health and Social Services, Division of Family Services (prepared by Nancy Ahrens and Mary Lou Adler) *Unmarried Mothers in Wisconsin* (Madison, Wis., 1972).

27. Ursula S. Myers, "When Premaritally Pregnant," *The Personal Problem Solver*, ed. Charles Zastrow and Dae Chang (Englewood Cliffs, N.J.: Prentice-Hall, 1977).

28. Walter A. Friedlander, *Introduction to Social Welfare* (Englewood Cliffs, N.J.: Prentice-Hall, 1968).

29. "Adoptees Win Right to Know," *Milwaukee Journal*, February 2, 1977.

30. Reuben Pannor, "The Forgotten Man," *Nursing Outlook* 18, no. 11 (November 1970).

31. Reuben Pannor and Byron Evans, "The Unmarried Father Revisited," *Journal of School Health* 45, no. 5 (May 1975).

32. Laura Daniel, "Chapter 263, Laws of 1973, Rights of Natural Fathers of Children Born Out of Wedlock: An Initial Summary" (Wisconsin: Division of Family Services, Madison Regional Office, 1975).

33. Ursula Myers, "He Will Be Heard" Series, *Beloit Daily News*, July 24, 25, 30, 1975.

34. Ibid.

35. "Teen Pregnancy Is U.S. Problem," *Wisconsin State Journal*, June 26, 1978.

36. Frank Furstenberg, "The Social Consequences of Teenage Parenthood," *Family Planning Perspectives* 8, no. 4 (July/August 1976), pp. 148–64.

37. Robert Sorenson, *Adolescent Sexuality in Contemporary America* (New York: World Publishing, 1973).

38. Mignon Sauber and Elaine Rubenstein, *Experiences of the Unwed Mother as a Parent* (New York: Community Council of Greater New York, 1965).

39. Pannor, "The Forgotten Man."

40. Cynthia P. Green and Susan J. Lowe, compilers, *Teenage Pregnancy: A Major Problem for Minors* (Washington, D.C.: Zero Population Growth, 1976).

41. Klerman and Jekel, *School-Age Mothers.*

42. Baldwin, "Adolescent Pregnancy and Childbearing."

43. Gordon, *Sexual Adolescent.*

44. Ibid.

45. Kristin Luker, *Taking Chances: Abortion and the Decision Not to Contracept* (Berkeley, Calif.: University of California Press, 1975).

46. Maternal and Child Health Information, "Adolescent Profile," Maternal and Child Health Services—Health Services and Mental Health Administration, no. 26, November 1972.

47. Howard Osofsky, *The Pregnant Teenager*, rev. ed. (Springfield, Ill.: Charles C Thomas, 1972).

48. Gordon, *Sexual Adolescent.*

49. Baldwin, "Adolescent Pregnancy and Childbearing."

50. Sorenson, *Adolescent Sexuality.*

51. Farida Shah, Melvin Zelnik, and John Kantner, "Unprotected Intercourse among Teenagers," *Family Planning Perspectives* 7, no. 1 (January/February 1975).

52. Gordon, *Sexual Adolescent.*

53. Sorenson, *Adolescent Sexuality.*

54. "Teenage Pregnancy on Rise," *Milwaukee Journal*, August 22, 1976.

55. "Law Week Report on the Supreme Court Abortion Decisions," *The United States Law Week*, January 23, 1973.

56. Shah, Zelnik, and Kantner, "Unprotected Intercourse."

57. Mary Calderone, "Sex and the Adolescent," *Clinical Pediatrics* 5, no. 3 (March 1966).

58. Sorenson, *Adolescent Sexuality.*

59. Ibid.

60. Ibid.

61. Ibid.

62. Aaron Hass, *Teenage Sexuality* (New York: Macmillan, 1979).

63. "Law Week Report on the Supreme Court Abortion Decisions."

64. Digest, "High Court Forbids Parental Spouse Veto over Abortions," *Family Planning Perspectives* 8, no. 4 (July/August 1976).

65. Frederick Jaffe and Joy Dryfoos, "Fertility Control Services for Adolescents: Access and Utilization," *Family Planning Perspectives* 8, no. 4 (July/August 1976).

66. Baldwin, "Adolescent Pregnancy and Childbearing."

67. Digest, "Legal Abortion Reduces Out-of-Wedlock Births," *Family Planning Perspectives* 7, no. 1 (January/February 1975).

68. Luker, *Taking Chances.*

69. "Rural Women Have No Easy Access to Abortion," *Milwaukee Journal,* January 23, 1977.

70. "Abortion: Who Pays?" *Congressional Quarterly,* July 5, 1980.

71. Baldwin, "Adolescent Pregnancy and Childbearing."

72. Jerome Evans, Georgianna Selstad, and Wayne Welcher, "Teenagers: Fertility Control and Attitudes before and after Abortion, Childbearing or Negative Pregnancy Test," *Family Planning Perspectives* 8, no. 4 (July/August 1976).

73. Mary Beth Murphy, "All the Way Called Too Far Too Soon," *Milwaukee Sentinel,* May 1, 1976.

74. Sol Gordon and Roger Conant, "VD Clap-trap," "Protect Yourself from Becoming an Unwanted Parent" (Syracuse: Ed-U Press, 1972).

75. Sally Cullen, "I Am Woman Mini-course," Marshall Junior High.

76. U.S. Department of Health, Education and Welfare, *Trends in Illegitimacy*—United States 1940–1965, National Vital Statistics System, Series 21, No. 15 (Washington, D.C.: The Department, December 1974).

77. Klerman and Jekel, *School-Age Mothers.*

78. Erving Goffman, *Stigma* (Englewood Cliffs, N.J.: Prentice-Hall, 1963).

79. Vincent, *Unmarried Mothers;* Hartley, *Illegitimacy.*

80. Sorenson, *Adolescent Sexuality.*

81. Paul Glick, "Singles Living with Unrelated Member of Opposite Sex Found Fastest Growing Life-Style among Young Adults," *Family Planning Perspectives* 7, no. 5 (September/October 1975).

82. Betty Rollin, "Motherhood: Who Needs It?" *Look* 34, no. 19 (September 22, 1970).

83. Letters from readers, "June Sklar and Beth Berkov Reply," *Family Planning Perspectives* 6, no. 4 (1974).

84. Gordon, *Sexual Adolescent.*

85. Alfred Kadushin, *Child Welfare Services* (New York: Macmillan, 1967).

86. Ashley Montagu, Lecture (symposium) Madison, Wis.: October 28–29, 1976.

87. Hartley, *Illegitimacy.*

88. F. Ivan Nye, *School-Age Parenthood,* Extension Bulletin 667 (Pullman, Wash.: Washington State University Cooperative Extension Service, 1976).

89. Kristin Moore, "Teenage Childbirth and Welfare Dependency," *Family Planning Perspectives* 10, no. 4 (July/August 1978).

90. Klerman and Jekel, *School-Age Mothers.*

91. Sauber and Rubenstein, *Experiences of the Unwed Mother.*

92. Furstenberg, "Social Consequences," p. 159.

93. Gordon, *Sexual Adolescent.*

SUGGESTED READING

Baran, Annette; Pannor, Reuben; and Sorosky, Arthur. "Open Adoption" *Social Work* 21, no. 2 (March 1976).

Bernstein, Rose. *Helping Unmarried Mothers.* New York: Association Press, 1971.

Edinger, Lucy, and Forbush, Janet. *School-Age Pregnancy and Parenthood in the United States.* Washington, D.C.: National Alliance Concerned with School-Age Parents, 1977.

Gaylor, Anne Nicols. *Abortion Is a Blessing.* New York: Psychological Dimensions, Inc., 1975.

The Alan Guttmacher Institute. *11 Million Teenagers.* New York: Planned Parenthood Federation of America, Inc., 1976.

Hass, Aaron. *Teenage Sexuality.* New York: Macmillan, 1979.

Rains, Prudence Mors. *Becoming an Unwed Mother.* Chicago: Aldine Atherton, 1971.

Zackler, Jack, and Braustadt, Wayne. *The Teenage Pregnant Girl.* Springfield, Ill.: Charles C Thomas 1975.

chapter 8

Our society has always been racist

I will say, then, that I am not, nor ever have been in favor of bringing about in any way the social and political equality of the white and black races; that I am not, nor ever have been, in favor of making voters or jurors of Negroes, nor of qualifying them to hold office, nor to inter-marry with White people . . . and inasmuch as they cannot so live, while they do remain together there must be the position of superior and inferior, and I as much as any other man am in favor of having the superior position assigned to the White race.

Abraham Lincoln[1]

PREJUDICE AND DISCRIMINATION

Prejudice means to prejudge, to make a judgment in advance of due examination. The judgment may be unduly favorable or negative. In terms of race relations, however, prejudice refers to negative prejudgments. Allport defines prejudice as thinking negatively of others without sufficient justification.[2] His definition has two elements: an unfounded judgment and a feeling tone of scorn, dislike, fear, and aversion. In regard to race, a prejudiced person applies racial stereotypes to all members of the group according to preconceived notions of what he/she believes them to be like and how he/she thinks they will behave. Racial prejudice results from the belief that skin color and other physical characteristics cause differences in behaviors, values, intellectual functioning, and attitudes.

The word *discriminating* has two very different meanings. It may refer positively to the ability of someone to be discerning and perceptive. However, in minority group relations, it refers to an act, or practice, of making categoric differentiations based on a social category ranked as inferior, rather than judging an individual on his/her own merits. Racial discrimination is based on racial prejudices. Prejudices are converted into actions to deny members of minority groups equal access to opportunities and privileges. Individuals who are targets of discrimination are excluded from certain types of employment, educational and recreational opportunities, certain residential housing areas, membership in certain religious and social organiza-

Racial discrimination and strategies for achieving equal rights

tions, certain political activities, access to community services, and so on.

Racial stereotypes result from making discriminations in terms of color or other physical characteristics. In our history, for example, there was the erroneous stereotype that Indians could not use alcohol rationally. This belief was then translated into laws that existed for a number of years which prohibited Indians from buying and consuming alcohol. A more recent stereotype is that blacks have "natural rhythm" and therefore have greater natural ability to play basketball and certain other sports. While such a stereotype at first glance appears complimentary to blacks, it has broader, negative implications. The danger with this stereotype is that if people believe the stereotype, it may well suggest to them that other abilities and capacities (such as intelligence, morals, and work productivity) are also determined by race. In other words, believing this positive stereotype increases the probability that people will also believe negative stereotypes.

Racial discrimination is the problem of whites

Myrdal points out that minority problems are actually majority problems.[3] The white majority determines the "place" of non-whites in our society. The status of different racial groups varies in our society because whites apply different racial stereotypes to different racial groups; e.g., blacks are viewed and treated differently than Japanese. Elmer Johnson notes: "Minority relationships become recognized by the majority as a social problem when the members of the majority disagree as to whether the subjugation of the minority is socially desirable or in the ultimate interest of the majority."[4]

Concern about discrimination and segregation has also received increasing national attention because of a rising level of aspiration among racial groups who demand (sometimes militantly) equal opportunities and equal rights.

Causes of racial discrimination

No single theory provides a complete picture of why racial discrimination occurs. By presenting a variety of theories, the reader should at least be better sensitized to the nature and sources of discrimination.

The sources of discrimination are both internal and external to those who are prejudiced. Psychologists note prejudice may satisfy certain psychic needs of those prejudiced. A few examples will be presented. A minority group may be blamed for one's own failures, thereby providing a prejudiced person with an excuse for his/her failures. For example, a person who has difficulty in obtaining a job may blame affirmative action programs.

A minority group may also serve as a projection of a prejudiced person's fears and lusts. Projection is a psychological defense mechanism in which one attributes to others characteristics that one is unwilling to recognize in oneself. For example, people who view blacks as preoccupied with sex and as lazy may be projecting their own internal concerns about their sexual fantasies and about their industriousness onto another group.

Another psychic need satisfied by discrimination is the release of tension and frustration. A prejudiced person who is frustrated in achieving a goal may seek a "scapegoat" on whom to vent anger and frustration. Similar to a person who takes job frustrations out at home on the spouse or on family pets, some prejudiced people vent their frustrations on minority groups.

Still another psychic need that may be satisfied by discrimination is the desire to counter feelings of insecurity or inferiority. Insecure people may feel better about themselves by putting down another group as they then can tell themselves that they "are better than some people."

There are also historical explanations for prejudice. Charles F. Marden and Gladys Meyer note that the racial groups now viewed by white prejudiced persons as being second class were viewed since early American history as being groups that have been either conquered, enslaved, or admitted into our society on a subordinate basis.[5] For example, blacks were imported as slaves during our colonial period and stripped of human dignity. The native Americans (Indians) were conquered, and their culture was viewed as inferior. Mexican-Americans were allowed to enter this country primarily to do seasonal, low-paid farm work.

Prejudice is also a learned phenomenon and is transmitted from generation to generation through socialization processes. Our culture has stereotypes of what different racial group members "ought to be" and the ways racial group members "ought to behave" in relationships with members of certain outgroups. These stereotypes provide norms against which a child learns to judge persons, things, and ideas he/she encounters. Prejudice, to some extent, is thus developed through the same processes by which we learn to be religious and patriotic, or to appreciate and to enjoy art, or to develop our value system. Racial prejudice, at least in certain segments in our society, is thus a facet of the normative system of our culture.

Race is a social concept

Montague considers "race" to be one of the most dangerous and tragic myths in our society.[6] Race is erroneously believed by many to be a biological classification of people. Yet, there are no clearly delineating characteristics of any "race." Throughout history, the genes of different societies and "racial" groups have occasionally been intermingled. No "racial" group has any unique or distinctive genes. In addition, biological differentiations of racial groups have gradually been diluted through such sociocultural factors as changes in preferences of desirable characteristics in mates, effects of different diets on those who reproduce, and such variables as wars and diseases in selecting those who will live and reproduce.[7]

In spite of definitional problems, it is necessary to use racial categories in the social sciences as race has important (though not necessarily consistent) social meanings for people. In order to have a basis for racial classifications, a number of social scientists have used a social rather than a biological definition. A social definition is based on the way in which members of a society classify each other by physical characteristics. For example, a frequently used social definition of a black person in America is anyone who either displays overt black physical characteristics or is known to have a black ancestor.[8] The sociological classification of races is indicated by different definitions of a race among various societies; for example, in the United States anyone who is not "pure white" and is known to have a black ancestor is considered to be black; while in Brazil anyone who is not "pure black" is classified as white.[9]

Race, according to Montague, becomes a very dangerous myth when it is assumed that physical traits are linked with mental traits and cultural achievements.[10] Every few years, it seems, some noted scientist stirs the country by making this erroneous assumption. For example, Arthur Jensen recently asserted whites are more intelligent, as IQ tests show whites average 10 to 15 point higher scores than blacks.[11] Jensen's findings have been sharply criticized by other authorities as falsely assuming that IQ is largely genetically determined.[12] These authorities contend that IQ is substantially influenced by environmental factors, and it is likely that the average achievement of blacks, if given similar opportunities to realize their potentialities, would be about the same as whites. These authorities also assert that if blacks were assumed to be biologically inferior in intelligence, it would be disastrous as it would serve to rationalize oppression and rigidly assign black people to a second-class, low-income status.

Elmer Johnson summarizes the need for an impartial, objective view of the capacity of different racial groups to achieve:

> Race bigots contend that, the cultural achievements of different races being so obviously unlike, it follows that their genetic capacities for achievement must be just as different. Nobody can discover the cultural capacities of any population or race . . . until there is equality of opportunities to demonstrate the capacities.[13]

Most scientists, both physical and social, now believe that in biological inheritance, all races are alike in everything that really makes any difference. With the exception of several very small, inbred, isolated primitive tribes, all racial groups appear to show the same distribution of every kind of ability. All important race differences that have been noted in personality, behavior, and achievement (e.g., that blacks have natural rhythm) appear to be due to environmental factors.

The effects and costs of discrimination

Grace Halsell is a white woman who through chemical treatments changed the color of her skin to look like a black person for a brief period of time in order to determine what it means to "live black" in a white world. She reports on her experiences in working one day as a maid for a white woman in the South:

Long before I have one job completed there are new orders: "Now sweep off the front porch, the side porch, the back porch, and mop the back porch." The tone is unmistakably that of the mistress-slave relationship—

I feel sorry for her. We are two women in a house all day long, and I sense that she desperately wants to talk to me, but it can never be as an equal. She looks on me as less than a wholly dignified and developed person. . . .

My eight hours are up. She asks if I know where to catch the bus. No, I say, should I turn left or right "when I go out the front door?" The *front door* comes out inadvertently, because I am only trying to get an idea of directions. She hands me five dollars and ushers me to the back door, quite pointedly.

Two bus transfers and an hour later, I am back in "nigger-town." Near the Summers Hotel, young, bright-eyed Negro children I've come to know wave, smile, and say "hi!"

I want to tell each one of them because I feel so degraded, so morally and spiritually depressed, "Don't do what I did! Don't ever sell yourself that cheap! Don't let it happen to you."

And I want to add, "Even if you have to rob, sell your body in another way, whatever you do, don't do what I did." The assault upon an individual's dignity and self-respect has intolerable limits, and I believe at this moment my limits have been reached.[14]

Racial discrimination is an extra handicap. Everyone in our competitive society seeks to obtain the necessary resources to lead a life he/she can be contented and comfortable with. Being a victim of discrimination is another obstacle which has to be overcome. Being discriminated due to race makes it more difficult to obtain adequate housing, financial resources, a quality education, employment, adequate health care and other services, equal justice in civil and criminal cases, and so on.

Discrimination also has heavy psychological costs. All of us have to develop a sense of identity—who we are and how we fit into a complex, swiftly changing world. Ideally, it is important that we develop a positive self-concept, and strive to obtain worthy goals. Yet, according to Cooley's "Looking Glass Self" our idea of who we are and what we are is largely determined by the way others relate to us.[15] When members of a minority group are treated by the majority group as if they were inferior, second-class citizens, then it is substantially more difficult for such members to develop a positive identity. Thus, people who are the objects of discrimination encounter barriers to developing their full potentials as human beings.

Discrimination is also economically detrimental to most members of the majority group. It impairs intergroup cooperation and communication. It has resulted in race riots particularly in our inner cities which have caused a number of deaths and cost billions of dollars. Discrimination also is a factor in contributing to social problems among minorities—for example, higher rates of crime, emotional problems, alcoholism, drug abuse—all of which have cost billions in social programs. Szymanski also argues that

A low-income black family in the South

discrimination is a barrier to collective action (e.g., unionization) between whites and nonwhites (particularly people in the lower income classes) and therefore is a factor in perpetuating low-paying jobs and poverty.[16]

Finally, discrimination in the United States undermines some of our nation's political goals. Many other nations view us as hypocritical when we advocate human rights and equality. In order to make an effective argument for human rights on a worldwide scale, we must first put our own house in order by eliminating racial and ethnic discrimination.

INSTITUTIONAL RACISM

Racism is the belief in the racial inferiority of minority groups. People holding racist stereotypes often think, speak, and act in terms of those stereotypes.

In the last two decades institutional racism has become an increasing concern. Institutional racism occurs when an organization has policies that provide less than equal treatment to minority groups. Sometimes the discrimination is obvious, but many times is is subtle. Because of civil rights laws, very few social agencies directly and officially deny access to minorities, but yet discrimination still occurs by informal and formal policies.

The following examples reflect institutional racism. An agency with branch offices may assign less skilled staff and provide lower quality services in an office located in a minority neighborhood. A public welfare department may encourage white applicants to request funds for special needs (e.g., clothing) or to use certain services (for example, day care and homemaker services with the costs charged to the agency), while nonwhite clients are not informed or less enthusiastically informed of such services. Agencies may take longer to process the requests of nonwhites for funds and services. Agencies may discriminate against nonwhite staff in terms of work assignments, hiring practices, promotion practices, and pay increases. Probation and parole agencies may tend to ignore minor violations of the rules for parole of white clients, but seek to return to prison nonwhite parolees having minor violations of parole rules. Mental health agencies may tend to assign "psychotic" labels to nonwhite clients, while assigning labels indicating a less serious disorder to white clients. White staff may be encouraged to provide intensive services to clients they have a good relationship with (often white clients) and told to give less attention to those clients "they aren't hitting it off well with" (and they may be disproportionately nonwhite).

BACKGROUND ON RACIAL GROUPS

The largest racial group in America is the majority white race (over 80 percent).[17] Blacks compose about 11 percent.[18] There are about 12 million Hispanic Americans living in the United States, constituting about 5.5 percent of the population—and there may be as many as 8 million additional Hispanics who are living and working illegally in the United States.[19] The other nonwhite groups compose about 2 percent of our population, and primarily include American Indian, Japanese, Chinese, and Filipino. There are also small numbers of the following nonwhite groups: Aleuts, Asian Indians, Eskimos, Hawaiians, Indonesians, Koreans, and Polynesians. In educational attainment, occupational status, and average income most of these nonwhite groups are clearly at a disadvantage to the white groups. (The two major nonwhite groups that now approach whites in terms of socioeconomic status are the Japanese and Chinese.)

Blacks. The United States has always been a racist country. Although our forefathers talked about freedom, dignity, equality, and human rights, our economy prior to the Civil War depended heavily on slavery.

Many slaves came from cultures that had well-developed art forms, political systems, family patterns, religious beliefs, and economic systems. However, their home culture was not European, and therefore slave owners viewed it as being of "no consequence" and prohibited slaves from practicing and developing their art, their language, their religion, and their family life. For want of practice, their former culture soon died in America.

The life of a slave was harsh. Slaves were not viewed as human beings but as chattel to be bought and sold. Long, hard days were spent working in the field, with the profits of their labor primarily going to their white owners. Whippings, mutilations, and hangings were commonly accepted white control practices. The impetus to enslave blacks was not simply racism. Many whites believed that it was to their economic advantage to have a cheap supply of labor. Cotton growing, in particular, required a large labor force that should also ideally be cheap and docile. Marriages among slaves were not recognized by the law, and slaves were often sold with little regard to the effects on marital and family ties. Throughout the slavery period and even after it, blacks were discouraged from demonstrating intelligence, initiative, or ambition. For a period of time it was even illegal to teach blacks to read or write. Acting lazy and stupid were means of survival for most blacks under slavery.

Some authorities have noted the opposition to the spread of slavery preceding the Civil War was primarily due to the northern fears of competition from slave labor and the rapidly increasing migration of blacks in the

North and West rather than moral concern for human rights and equality.[20] Few whites at that time accepted the principle of racial equality, not even Abraham Lincoln, who viewed blacks as inferior to whites.

Following the Civil War, the federal government failed to develop a comprehensive program of economic and educational aid to blacks. As a result most blacks returned to being economically dependent on the same planters in the South who had held them in bondage. Within a few years laws were passed in the South prohibiting interracial marriages and requiring racial segregation in schools and public places.

A rigid caste system in the South hardened into a system of oppression known as "Jim Crow." The system prescribed how blacks were supposed to act in the presence of whites, asserted white supremacy, embraced racial segregation, and denied political and legal rights to blacks. Blacks who opposed Jim Crow were subjected to burnings, beatings, and lynchings. Jim Crow was used to "teach" blacks to view themselves as inferior and to be servile and passive in interactions with whites.

World War II opened up new employment opportunities for blacks. A large migration of blacks from the South began. Greater mobility afforded by wartime conditions led to upheavals in the traditional caste system. Awareness of disparity between ideal and reality led many people to try to improve race relations, not only for domestic peace and justice but to answer criticism from abroad. With each gain in race relations, more blacks were encouraged to press for their rights.

A major turning point in black history was the U.S. Supreme Court decision in Brown v. Board of Education in 1954 which ruled that racial segregation in public schools was unconstitutional.

Since 1954 there have been a number of organized efforts by both blacks and certain segments of the white population to secure equal rights and opportunities for blacks. Changing deeply entrenched racist attitudes and practices has been filled with turmoil: for example, the burning of our inner cities, the assassination of Martin Luther King, Jr., and clashes involving black militant groups. There has been significant advances. Wide ranging civil rights legislation has been passed, protecting rights in areas such as housing, voting, employment, and use of public transportation and facilities. Charles Henderson and Bok-Lim Kim summarize the current situation:

> Blacks are on the move, physically, economically and socially. In the 1960s and early 1970s Blacks migrated from the rural South into the cities of the nation's North and West. There, with greater choices, many have been progressing from unskilled low-paid jobs into white-collar and skilled occupations. In search of better housing and better jobs, many have been moving from the city to the surrounding suburbs. A migrant population has been giving way to settled, urban dwellers as increasing numbers are moving economically and socially from extreme poverty into middle-class status.
>
> Many Blacks, however, are left behind both in the rural backwaters of the South and in urban ghettos. In many instances White progress has been so much greater that it overshadows Black gains.[21]

Four out of five blacks now live in metropolitan areas, over half of them in our central cities.[22] American cities are still largely segregated, with blacks primarily living in black neighborhoods. In recent years the main thrust of the civil rights movement among blacks has been economic equality. The economic gap between blacks and whites continues to be immense. Black families are three times as likely as white families to fall below the poverty line.[23] Since the early

1950s the black unemployment rate has been about twice that for whites. Unemployment is an especially severe problem for black teenagers, whose rate of unemployment is about 35 percent, as compared with about 15 percent for white youth.[24]

Occupational status in our society is crucially related to self-esteem and lifestyle, as demonstrated in the following statement by a 39-year-old black male living in a state which does not have an AFDC-UP program (the AFDC-UP program is described in Chapter 4):

> How can you have any pride? I'm a part-time worker—a part-time husband. I guess I'm really a part-time man. I can't find enough to do to keep food on the table. Guess some people would think that I'm the sorriest man that ever wore out shoe leather. It ain't that I don't have no get-up, it's just that I can't find nothing to do. I had to leave home so the children could eat. While I'm sitting here with you, they're out looking for me. That ain't so bad—what really hurts is that my wife is going to tell them people down at the welfare that some other man is the baby's daddy or else she thinks she can't get no aid. If they take her off the welfare she'll starve. So every time she has another baby she gives a different guy's name—excuse me for bawling, man, I just can't help it—but it sure ain't no justice when a man's got to make his own children bastards in order to feed them.[25]

We, as a nation, have come a long way since the Supreme Court's decision in 1954. But, we still have a long way to go before we eliminate black poverty and respond to the deep frustrations of the black masses in our ghettos. Living conditions in black ghettos remain as bleak as they were when our inner cities erupted in the late 1960s.

Hispanic Americans

Hispanic Americans are Americans of Spanish origin. Hispanics are a diverse group bound together by their language, culture, and ties to Roman Catholicism. This broad categorization includes Mexican-Americans (Chicanos), Puerto Ricans, Cubans, people from Central and South America, the West Indies, and others of Spanish origin. We can touch on only some of their varied history and current status here.

FIGURE 8–1 Percentage distribution of Hispanic Americans by type of Spanish origin, 1976

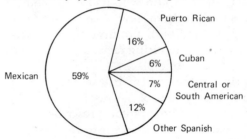

SOURCE: U.S. Bureau of the Census, "Persons of Spanish Origin in the United States: March 1976," *Current Population Reports* (Washington, D.C.: U.S. Government Printing Office, 1977.)

Mexican-Americans. The largest Hispanic group in the United States is Mexican-Americans. Unknown to many Americans, Mexican-Americans have had a long history of settlement and land ownership in America. In the 1700s and 1800s there were a number of small Spanish communities in the American Southwest—in areas that have since gained statehood in Texas, Arizona, New Mexico, and California. These early Mexican-Americans were generally small landholders. In the 1800s Anglos moved into these regions, and competition for good land became fierce. Many Mexican-Americans had their land taken away by large Anglo-owned cattle and agricultural interests. Texas was once part of Mexico. In 1836 the settlers (including many of Spanish descent) staged a successful insurrection against the Mexican government, and in 1845 Texas was annexed to the United States. As a consequence many of the Spanish settlers became American citizens.

Since the 1850s there has been a steady migration of Mexicans to America, with a number of the immigrants entering this country illegally. A high percentage of Mexicans live in poverty in Mexico, so the quest for higher wages and a better life have lured many Mexicans to this country.

Relations between Anglos and Mexican-Americans have on occasion become vicious and ugly. Similar to black-white confrontations, there have been many riots between whites and Mexican-Americans.

Many Mexican-Americans now live in urban barrios (Spanish-speaking sections of U.S. cities that have become ghettos) in such cities as Los Angeles, Denver, and Chicago. Although a few are moving up in socioeconomic status, most are employed in low-paid occupations.

A number of Mexican-Americans are employed in temporary, seasonal work, largely on farms. Some migrate North in the summer to be farm laborers, and return to the Southwest in the fall. In rate of acculturation and assimilation, they are among the least "Americanized" of all ethnic groups.[26] They are reluctant to seek help from social agencies, partly because of their pride and partly because of language and cultural barriers.

An increasingly large segment of this ethnic group is becoming involved in the "Chicano" movement. A Chicano is "not Mexican, not Spanish, but a product of a Spanish-Mexican heritage and an Anglo-Saxon influence."[27] The Chicano resents the stereotypes that demean Mexican-Americans—particularly the image of laziness, as they are employed to do some of the hardest physical labor in our society. The Chicano movement asserts institutional change is needed to be more responsive to the needs of Chicanos. There now is a Chicano-oriented school in San Jose, California, and there is a thrust to

develop Chicano studies programs at many other universities. Similar to blacks, Chicanos prefer that social welfare services for Chicanos be planned by, and controlled by, Chicanos.

The civil rights activities of blacks have provided encouragement for the Chicano's more militant stance. In addition, second- and third-generation Mexican-Americans have fewer ties to Mexico than did their elders, and they are oriented more toward the majority American culture in terms of aspirations and goals. Yet, economically Mexican-Americans, similar to blacks, generally have low-paying jobs, high rates of unemployment, high rates of being below the poverty line, high rates of infant mortality, low levels of educational attainment, and high levels of substandard housing. Their standard of living is no better, and possibly slightly worse, than that faced by blacks.

Puerto Ricans. After World War II large numbers of Puerto Ricans migrated to the United States, largely because of population pressure and insufficient job opportunities on the island. Although found in all the states, they have settled mainly in New York City where they are heavily employed in the garment industry and as service workers. Those migrating from Puerto Rico were from the higher socioeconomic classes in Puerto Rico. Although their earnings in the United States are higher than in Puerto Rico, they have experienced lower job status than other whites in New York and are housed primarily in slum ghettos.

For the Puerto Rican, the Spanish culture has been dominant, but also influenced by Taino Indian, American, African, and European. In Puerto Rico, status is based on culture or class, not on skin color. Interracial marriages have been extensive in Puerto Rico. Upon entering the United States most appear "white," but some are perceived as "black." Newcomers, understandably, become puzzled by the higher priority given to skin color in this country. In New York City Puerto Ricans have the lowest level of education, the lowest salaries, the highest rate of unemployment, and the highest rate of public assistance recipiency.[28]

Rivera summarizes the unique factors facing Puerto Rican migrants to New York City:

> As United States citizens, Puerto Ricans can move freely between the island and the continent. The migration tends to follow economic trends in both the United States and Puerto Rico. The heaviest migrant waves from Puerto Rico came in the early 1950s, encouraged by faster and cheaper air transportation as well as by the demand for semiskilled and unskilled labor.
>
> The average Puerto Rican migrant is young, has little formal education, and comes from the rural areas, in some cases an urban slum. His move to the United States is not seen as permanent; he intends to go back to the island after making some money. Consequently, he does not see the need to become assimilated and grow roots in this land, nor to give up his language and his culture. In many cases, this fact constitutes a problem in his adjustment to this society, particularly in the establishment of community and political organizations. Some Puerto Ricans are able to save some money and fulfill their dream of returning to Puerto Rico to start a small business or buy a house and retire. Many others return, poor and frustrated, only to find that there is no place for them in Puerto Rico either. Some families are caught in a pattern of traveling between the United States and Puerto Rico without making a satisfactory adjustment in either place. Ironically, many never make it back to the island and their children prefer to stay here.[29]

Cubans. Cuban-Americans are generally recent migrants to the United States. Most are political refugees, having fled Cuba following the takeover of the government by Fidel Castro in 1959. In 1976 there were an estimated 750,000 Cubans living in the United States.[30] In 1980 Castro again opened the doors to his socialist island, and over 100,000 more Cubans fled to this country. Cuban-Americans tend to differ from other Hispanics in that they are generally well educated, and often have a managerial or professional background. Large numbers have settled in southern Florida, particularly the Miami area.

Hispanos. After the Mexican-American War in 1848, Mexico ceded a large territory to the United States, thus making U.S. citizens of a number of Spanish-speaking people. Many of their descendants call themselves "Hispano" to distinguish themselves from the Mexican-Americans who migrated later from Mexico. Still residing primarily in the Southwest, Hispanos are predominately a rural people, and have had limited contact with the outside world. Their standards of living are low and by white standards, still primitive. They are living in a 17-century culture, and are using agricultural techniques from that period. About 40 percent of New Mexico's population is composed of Hispanos.[31]

American Indians. When Columbus first came to America in 1492 there were about a million Indians in this country who were fragmented into more than 600 distinct societies.[32] Tribal wars between Indians were common, and there were wide variations between tribes in customs, culture, lifestyles, language, religious ceremonies, and so on. The whites gradually expanded settlements, moving westward and slowly taking the land from the Indians. Unable to mobilize a common defense, all Indian tribes were defeated by 1892.

In 1887 Congress passed the General Al-

Homes of Hispanos in New Mexico

lotment Act which empowered Congress to unilaterally revise treaties made by Indians. This action opened the way for land-hungry whites to take the productive land held by Indians. From 1887 to 1928 the number of acres of land held by Indians decreased from 137 million acres to 50 million acres, with most of the remaining land being some of the least productive land in the country.[33]

The whites have made the Indians' former living patterns nonfunctional. "The buffalo are gone," meaning Indians can no longer sustain themselves through hunting and fishing. Segregation on reservations has further served to damage their pride and sense of self-worth. Government programs now attempt to meet subsistence needs, but also have served to pauperize them. Being disillusioned, Indians on Reservations have high rates of suicide, alcoholism, illiteracy, poverty, homicide, child neglect, and mortality.

Earlier in this century the plight of Indians was largely ignored because of their isolation on remote reservations. They received the most paternalistic treatment of all minorities through the Bureau of Indian Affairs. For many years the BIA had programs designed to destroy their culture, religion, and language. Today the BIA has become the symbol of Indian frustration and despair.[34] In the 1960s and 70s the plight of the Indians received national concern, and many whites, particularly the young, have become actively involved in the problems facing Indians. Films depicting the "glorious" victories of the whites over "savages" have been replaced by the realization that our forefathers exploited the Indians by taking away their land and destroying their way of life.

During most of the 20th century Indians have been passive. However, confrontations at such sites as Alcatraz and Wounded Knee in recent years show increased organized efforts by Native Americans to make changes. The term *Native Americans* emphasizes the Indians' heritage and their claim to America.

For much of this century American In-

White-Native American confrontation

dians were the most impoverished minority in our society. Recently there has been a surprising, dramatic increase in the economic status of Indians. There have been enormous strides in tribal education, with an increasing number attending college. Also, Indians are now establishing commercial ventures on reservations in such fields as oil, coal, timber, vacation resorts, factories, and farming. These enterprises have been so successful that the median household income has surpassed that of blacks, Puerto Ricans, and Mexican-Americans.[35] The economic situation of Indians has improved much faster than was generally expected. It should be noted, however, that most tribespeople are still much poorer than whites. Most Indians describe their recent economic advances as the most encouraging resurgence since white settlers took their ancestral lands.[36]

Asian-Americans

Japanese. Until 1900, few Japanese migrants came to America, partly because of legal restrictions against their migration and partly because of the unfriendly reception they received in this country. Japanese-Americans refused to accept discrimination, which aroused the antagonism of white Americans.

After the turn of the century migration increased. They settled primarily on the West Coast. By 1941 (when Pearl Harbor was atacked), there were few distinctive settlements outside the West Coast, only in New York and Chicago. During World War II the loyalty of Japanese-Americans was viewed with intense suspicion, and they severely felt the impact of prejudice, war hysteria, and the denial of certain civil rights. On March 2, 1942 the commander of the Western Theater of Operations established relocation centers (concentration camps) to which Japanese-Americans who lived on the West Coast were sent. The confused policies of our nation during this war is indicated by the fact that 33,000 Japanese-Americans served in the armed forces for the United States, while 110,000 Japanese-Americans were confined in concentration camps.[37] Not only were their civil rights violated, they also were forced to sell their property. Following the war, their return to the West Coast met with some initial opposition, but a counterreaction soon developed among whites emphasizing fair play and acceptance. Since 1946, Japanese-Americans have settled in other parts of the country, and their socioeconomic status is now approaching that of whites.

Chinese. In the 1800s Chinese were encouraged to immigrate for jobs in U.S. mines, on railroad construction, and for farm work. These immigrants soon encountered hostility from some whites, particularly in western states, because of their willingness to work for low wages. Their racial and cultural distinctiveness also made them targets for scapegoating, particularly during periods of high unemployment. Charles Henderson et al. comment on the extent to which Chinese were subjected to racism during this time period:

> Racism against Asians is shown in the 1854 decision of the California Supreme Court in *The People* v. *Hall.* The appellant, a white Anglo-American, had been convicted of murder upon the testimony of Chinese witnesses. Was such evidence admissible? The judge ruled that Asians should be ineligible to testify for or against a white man. This ruling opened the floodgate for anti-Chinese abuse, violence, and exploitation. Group murders, lynchings, property damage, and robbery of the Chinese were reported up and down the West Coast. Because of the harsh treatment of the Chinese, any luckless person was described as not having a "Chinaman's chance."[38]

The struggles of China against Japan before and during World War II brought about a more favorable image of Chinese-Americans.

In the early 1900s Chinese-Americans were concentrated largely on the West Coast, but since the 1920s have tended to disperse throughout the nation. They tend to settle in large cities, and many live in Chinatowns (a section of a city where primarily Chinese-Americans reside) in such cities as Los Angeles, San Francisco, New York, Boston, and Chicago.

The Chinese have been subjected to less racial discrimination in Hawaii than on the mainland. They continue to be subjected to some racial discrimination, as indicated by the infrequency of intermarriage, and limited contact with the dominant culture. Chinese-Americans continue to have a large lower class, although they have experienced recent social and economic progress.

Other Asians. Other Asian-Americans in the United States include the Filipinos, Koreans, Burmese, Indonesians, Guamanians, Samoans, South Vietnamese, and Thais. A large number of South Vietnamese immigrated to this country in the early 1970s following the end of the Vietnam War. Contrary to a popular stereotype, Asian groups are not homogeneous. Each ethnic group has its own history, religion, language, and culture. These Asian-American groups also differ in terms of group cohesion, levels of education, and socioeconomic status. Comparable to the mistake of viewing all Europeans as a single entity, it is a mistake to view all Asians as a single entity.

Like other disenfranchised groups, Asian-Americans are victimized by discrimination. Immediate problems include housing, education, income maintenance, unemployment and underemployment, health care, vocational training and retraining. Because of language and cultural barriers many needy Asians (particularly new immigrants and the aged) do not seek out services to which they are entitled.

STRATEGIES AGAINST DISCRIMINATION

Mass media appeals. Newspapers, radio, and television at times present programs that are designed to explain the nature and harmful effects of prejudice, and promote the "harmony" of humanity. Mass media is able to reach large numbers of people simultaneously. By expanding public awareness of the existence of discrimination and its consequences, the media may strengthen control over racial extremists. But, the media has limitations in changing prejudiced attitudes and behaviors; it is primarily a provider of information, and seldom has a lasting effect in changing deep-seated prejudices. Highly prejudiced persons are generally unaware of their own prejudices. If they are aware of their prejudices, they generally ignore mass media appeals as irrelevant to them or dismiss the appeals as propaganda.

Greater interaction among the races. Increased contact among races is not in itself sufficient to alleviate racial prejudice. In fact, increased contact may, in some instances, highlight the differences between groups, and increase suspicions and fear. Simpson and Yinger reviewed a number of studies, and concluded that prejudice is likely to be increased when contacts are tension-laden or involuntary.[39] Prejudice is apt to subside when individuals are placed in situations where they share characteristics in nonracial matters; for example, as coworkers, fellow soldiers, or classmates. Equal status contacts, rather than inferior-superior status contacts, are also more apt to reduce prejudices.[40]

Civil rights law. In the past 25 years equal rights have been legislated in areas of employment, voting, housing, public accommodation, and education. A key question is "How effective are laws in changing prejudice?"

Proponents of civil rights legislation make certain assumptions. The first is that new laws will reduce discriminatory behavioral patterns. The laws define what was once "normal" behavior (discrimination) as now being "deviant" behavior. Through time, it is expected that attitudes will change and become more consistent with the forced nondiscriminatory behavioral patterns.

A second assumption is that the laws will be used. Civil rights laws were enacted after the Civil War, but were not widely implemented and gradually were eroded. It is also unfortunately true that some officials will find ways of evading the intent of the law by eliminating only the extreme, overt symbols of discrimination, without changing other practices. Thus the enactment of a law is only the first step in the process of changing prejudiced attitudes and practices.

Activism. The strategy of "activism" attempts to change the structure of race relations through direct confrontations of discrimination and segregation policies. Activism has three types of politics.[41]

The "politics of creative disorder" operates on the edge of the dominant social system, and includes boycotts, rent strikes, job blockades, sit-ins at segregated restaurants, public marches, and product boycotts. This type of activism is based on the concept of nonviolent resistance.

A second type, "politics of disorder," reflects alienation from the dominant culture and disillusionment with the political system. In this type those being discriminated against resort to mob uprising, riots, and other forms of violence. In 1969 the National Commission on Causes and Prevention of Violence reported that 200 riots had occurred in the previous five years when our inner cities erupted.[42] In the early 1980s we are again seeing some riots in our inner cities. The focus of most of these riots has been minority group aggression against white-owned property.

A third type of activism has been called the "politics of escape." Those using this strategy engage in passionate rhetoric about how they are being victimized. But since the focus is not on arriving at solutions, the rhetoric is not productive, except perhaps for providing an emotional release.

The principal value of activism or social protest seems to be the stimulation of public awareness of certain problems. Continued protest past a certain (although indetermi-

nate) point appears to have little additional value.[43]

School busing. Housing patterns in many large metropolitan centers have led to "de facto" segregation; that is, blacks and certain other nonwhite groups live in one area, while whites live in another. (De facto segregation is segregation which is not prohibited by law.) This segregation has affected educational opportunities for nonwhites. Nonwhite areas have fewer financial resources, and as a result the educational quality is often substantially lower than in white areas. In recent years courts in a number of metropolitan areas have ordered that a certain proportion of nonwhites must be bused to schools in white areas and that a certain proportion of whites must be bused to schools in nonwhite areas. The objectives are twofold, provide equal educational opportunities and reduce racial prejudice through interaction. In some areas school busing has become accepted and appears to be meeting the stated objectives. In other areas, however, the approach is highly controversial and has exacerbated racial tensions. Busing in these areas is claimed: (a) to be highly expensive; (b) to destroy the concept of the "neighborhood school" in which the facility serves as a recreational, social, and educational center of the community; and (c) to result in lower quality education. A number of parents in these areas feel so strongly about busing that they are sending their children to private schools. In addition, some have argued that busing increases "white flight" from neighborhoods where busing has been ordered.[44] Whether busing increases or decreases residential segregation is still very controversial. Busing remains a hotly contested issue, and it is still uncertain whether its long-term effects will be beneficial or detrimental.

Affirmative action. Affirmative action programs provide for preferential hiring and admission requirements for minority applicants. Affirmative action programs cover minority groups and women. These programs also require that employers must: (*a*) make active efforts to locate and recruit qualified minority applicants, and (*b*) in certain circumstances have hard quotas under which specific numbers of minority members, regardless of their qualifications, must be accepted to fill vacant positions (e.g., a university with a high proportion of white, male faculty may be required to fill half of its faculty vacancies with women and with members of minority groups). Affirmative action programs require that employers must demonstrate, according to a checklist of positive measures, that they are not guilty of discrimination.

A major dilemma with affirmative action programs is that preferential hiring and quota programs involve reverse discrimination, where qualified majority-group members are sometimes arbitrarily excluded. There have been several successful lawsuits claiming reverse discrimination. The best known case to date has been that of Alan Bakke who was initially denied admission to the medical school at the University of California at Davis. He alleged reverse discrimination as he had higher grades and higher scores on the Medical College Admissions Test than several minority applicants who were admitted under the university's minorities quota policy. In 1978 his claim was upheld by the U.S. Supreme Court in a precedent setting decision.[45] The Court ruled that strict racial quotas were unconstitutional, but the Court did not rule out that race might be used as one among many criteria in making admissions decisions. There will undoubtably be more court cases before a coherent policy emerges in this area.

Charles Henderson et al. summarizes some of the views of whites and minority groups about affirmative action:

> The minority worker in white agencies often asks himself: "Why have I been hired?" . . . The worker may meet resistance from white colleagues if he or she is a product of "affirmative action," seen by some white people as simply "reverse discrimination." Whites may be quick to say that competence is what counts. Blacks perceive this as saying that they are not competent. Considering the many ways in which whites have acquired jobs, blacks wonder why competence is now suggested as the only criterion for employment. For every white professional who may dislike affirmative action to compensate for past exclusions and injustices, there is a black professional who feels that it is tragic that organizations have had to be forced to hire minorities.[46]

Human relations programs. A number of school systems are developing human relation programs, which are designed to alleviate prejudice and discrimination. The program developed by the Madison, Wisconsin Public School System will be briefly described for illustrative purposes.[47]

The goal is "to help the children gain a better understanding of themselves as individuals and a recognition, understanding and respect for individual differences in others."[48]

The program has several steps, along with some suggested activities, books and other helpful hints for parents and teachers to use with their children. Some of the key concepts are:

1. Each person is unique, with all people having common needs.

2. Each person has things they can do well and those they cannot do so well. It is a serious mistake to use yourself as a yardstick to measure other's abilities, or to use others as a yardstick to measure yours. Words such

Human relations program at school

as "stupid" or "dumb" hurt deeply, especially when one is doing the best he/she can in a given area.

3. Each person has different attitudes, ideas, beliefs and values. Although the beliefs of others may differ from ones own, they are no less important.

4. Prejudice differs from a dislike. Prejudice is defined broadly as "when you are against someone you do not know because of some/one of their differences."[49] This school system has found that first graders are more prejudiced against "fat" children than against children of a nonwhite race.

5. The program assists children in learning some of the differences found in people, and how a lack of understanding about these differences can be related to prejudice. The program explains that melanin is the black pigment responsible for light and dark skin color differences. The more melanin you have, the darker you are; but melanin of course in no way governs the personality or behavior of a person. Suntanning occurs because the skin produces more melanin to protect it from the hot sun; yet tanning does not change the inner "self," only the outside wrapping. Besides skin color differences, students are given an understanding of other individual differences (such as retardation, religious differences, epilepsy, hearing impairments, and so on) so they can be more respectful of such differences.

6. The program also assists students in learning about and appreciating cultural and ethnic differences.

Such human relation programs offer considerable promise of being a highly effective strategy in alleviating discrimination in the following areas: race, sex, ethnic or cultural differences, religious or political differences, physical or mental handicaps.

HOW TO HANDLE INCIDENTS OF RACIAL DISCRIMINATION*

There goes that old feeling again, that dehumanizing, empty and deep-down inside helpless reaction to an assault on my dignity . . . a judgment made and acted upon without the content of my character . . . discrimination. This time I'm going to do something about it, but what? Where do I go and what rights do I have? Could I be wrong, am I really the victim of discrimination or am I simply overreacting? A voice from within, heard by millions of America's people of color . . . the visible minorities.

Discrimination: Remnants from the past

On December 1, 1955, Rosa Parks of Montgomery, Alabama, refused to obey the longstanding Jim Crow ordinance that required blacks in Alabama and elsewhere to occupy seats in the rear of the bus. Her feet hurt so she refused to give up her seat to a white and would not move back. Mrs. Parks was arrested; unknowingly, she had begun what became the famous Montgomery Bus Boycott. The result of that year-long bus boycott, which kept 17,000 blacks from riding the buses in Montgomery, was a ruling from the U.S. Supreme Court that laws requiring segregated seating on public conveyances were unconstitutional. In addition to the legal results of that action, the boycott had a very important psychological impact upon all people in this country. It proved that minor-

ity citizens need not accept discriminatory laws but could, in fact, command equal rights when united behind a common cause.[50]

Racial discrimination in the late 1970s, more than two decades after the Montgomery Bus Boycott, is stripped of most of its legal power. The passage of strong civil rights legislation during the past years has moved the United States into what might be considered a "second reconstruction era." The overseers of the first reconstruction were the military. The overseers of the laws today, aside from the courts, are the Equal Employment Opportunity Commission (EEOC), National Association for the Advancement of Colored People (NAACP), Office of Federal Contract Compliance/Employment Standards Administration, Office for Civil Rights, Department of Health, Education, and Welfare (HEW),* various state departments of industry, labor, and human relations/divisions of equal rights, and others, including the most important—we the people.

The laws providing equal rights are now a fact, but they must be understood, guarded, and implemented. The legal separation of people based on color, class, or sex no longer exists, but what does remain are attitudes. If it were not for such things are prejudiced mentalities and discriminatory institutions, we might be able to point with pride to our laws, as Congressman Joseph Rainey of South Carolina did about the justice of the South Carolina constitution during the reconstruction period. He said:

> Our convention, which met in 1868 and in which Negroes were in a large majority . . . adopted a liberal constitution, securing alike equal rights to all citizens, white and black, male and female, as far as possible. Mark you, we did not discriminate, although we had a

---

* This section is excerpted from an article written by Marlene A. Cummings in *The Personal Problem Solver,* ed. Charles Zastrow and Dae Chang (Englewood Cliffs, N.J.: Spectrum Books, 1977). Reprinted by permission of Prentice-Hall, Inc., Englewood Cliffs, New Jersey.

---

* In 1980 HEW was renamed Department of Health and Human Services.

majority. Our constitution towers up in its majesty with provisions for equal protection of all classes of citizens.[51]

Congressman Rainey had no experience with a previous reconstruction to anticipate the suppression or crippling of the equal rights laws that had been enacted. We do have today a history of what became of such outstanding pieces of legislation as The Freedman's Bureau (1865); Thirteenth Amendment (1865); Civil Rights Bill of 1867; and the Fourteenth Amendment (1866), after the First Reconstruction Act of 1867 was abolished. After the military rule provided by the Reconstruction Act had been lifted in the South, equal rights took a beating from the Ku Klux Klan, politicians who sought government power for personal gain, corrupt northern carpetbaggers and southern scalawags, and these rights seemingly died a violent death. The laws remained on the books and were left to gather dust on the shelves. We remained for too long a period, a country big on laws and small on commitment to them. It has been said in many ways that a person or country ignorant of its history is doomed to repeat it—it is up to us, the most important overseers of our rights, to guard, contest, protest, and challenge any threat to them. It is imperative that we handle incidents of discrimination or we might move into a time very similar to the postreconstruction era.

"Could I be wrong, am I really the victim of discrimination, or am I simply overreacting?" In a society where racial justice and equality have suffered setback after setback and blatant neglect, it is not surprising to find that people who are struggling to attain equal rights question whether they are actually being discriminated against or are simply overreacting. A vital part of handling racial discrimination then becomes the attainment of knowledge about the nature of the prob-lem. Prejudice usually is the prime motivating force behind discrimination. It is important to have a clear understanding of what prejudice and discrimination are. The definition of ethnic prejudice, which serves as a base for this discussion, is the one given by Gordon Allport, a psychologist and researcher noted for his work in social psychology.

> Ethnic prejudice is an antipathy based upon a faulty and inflexible generalization. It may be felt or expressed. It may be directed toward a group as a whole, or toward an individual because he or she is a member of that group.[52]

Discrimination as defined by Dr. Allport is the understanding underlying the substance of this discussion.

> Discrimination. Here the prejudiced person makes detrimental distinctions of an active sort. He undertakes to exclude all members of the group in question from certain types of employment, from residential housing, political rights, educational opportunities, churches, hospitals, or from some social privileges. Segregation is an institutionalized form of discrimination, enforced legally or by common custom.[53]

To understand prejudice and discrimination is to help the persons questioning their own reactions to an incident gain a greater level of confidence in their judgment. Persons being discriminated against may question the necessity of definitions when they have indeed felt the rejection. However, feelings cannot effectively file complaints. Many employers who intentionally discriminate against people are well aware of the actions that can be used against them and have developed many sophisticated ways to hide their real intent. It takes an alert and equally aware person to assess the situation adequately and later to follow up with a complaint.

The fear of discrimination is a very real threat to minority group members (blacks,

Native Americans, Chicanos, Americans of Puerto Rican and Asian ancestry, and others) because so much of it has been personally experienced. A recognition of this fear and how it might become so ingrained as to create undue anxiety are important to consider. Anxiety can interfere with a person's perception of a situation and weaken his or her ability to handle discriminatory situations properly. Chronic anxiety tends to put people on the alert and to predispose them to see any stimuli as threatening or menacing.[54] This could represent the indecision over whether an incident is discriminatory or not. An awareness of historical discrimination-related anxiety and a recognition of it in oneself can give an individual a sounder base from which decisions can be made about discriminatory incidents. One of the most frustrating situations for a person assigned to investigate charges of discrimination must surely be the complainant who fails to furnish adequate information because of a basic lack of understanding about the factors described earlier.

"What is there for one to do something about . . . just what is discrimination?" Just knowing the definition of a word is not enough to determine adequately when an act of injustice has occurred; that requires some action. Discrimination appears in many forms; to facilitate ways of dealing with discriminatory incidents, I have grouped them into two categories.

The first type of discrimination is that which is not controlled by law but is discrimination nonetheless, "de facto." This kind of discrimination is the result of habits that have been formed by social attitudes of the past and the kind that must be constantly challenged if there are ever to be meaningful changes. Following is an example.

Scene: department store. Incident: Several people are waiting their turn at a counter. The person next to be served is a black woman; however, the clerk waits on several white customers who arrived later. The black woman finally demands service, after several polite gestures to call the clerk's attention to her. The clerk proceeds to wait on her after stating, "I did not see you." The clerk is very discourteous to the black customer, and the lack of courtesy is apparent because the black customer had the opportunity to observe treatment of the other customers. De facto discrimination is most frustrating—there was no law broken, the customer was served. Most people would rather just forget the whole incident, but it is important to challenge the practice even though it will possibly put you through more agony. One of the best ways to deal with this type of discrimination is to report it to the manager of the business. If it is at all possible, it is important to involve the clerk in the discussion. The discussion should include:

An inquiry about the store's policy on serving minorities.

What expectations the store has for clerk/customer relations.

An explanation from the clerk concerning the incident. This approach requires an unemotional, assertive approach, which can be difficult when one is feeling upset about a dehumanizing incident. It is important, however, because all customers should be treated fairly.

You may expect a good deal of defensiveness from both the clerk and the manager, but your confrontation will certainly be a learning situation for both of them. Sometimes it may be necessary to write a letter to the manager, especially if the situation is not conducive for you to discuss the situation in person.

Other examples of de facto discrimination include:

Harassment from store detectives.

Failure to accept checks from members of minority groups with a statement, "We don't accept checks here," after it has been observed that the policy has not been applied to white customers.

Minimal service in restaurants.

The same procedure should be followed as for the example given earlier.

Frederick Douglass, noted abolitionist, lecturer, and author said, "Power concedes nothing without a demand—it never did and it never will. Find out just what people will submit to, and you've found out the exact amount of injustice and wrong which will be imposed upon them. This will continue until they resist, either with words, blows or both. The limits of tyrants are prescribed by the endurance of those whom they oppress." Frederick Douglass has been dead since 1895, and we are still resisting injustice.

"What Rights Do I Have?"—"de jure" discrimination. Many acts of injustice fit into the category of "de jure" discrimination. This means that a law clearly has been broken and that there are measures that can be taken to correct the injustice. Antidiscrimination laws received a great boost by the passage of the Civil Rights Act of 1964. Every member of a visible minority group should be aware of what rights are protected by this act. The Voting Rights Act of 1965 and the Civil Rights Act of 1968, provision for open housing, are other antidiscrimination bills essentially geared to implement the Bill of Rights.

President Lyndon B. Johnson, during a television address in July 1964 to announce the signing of the Civil Rights Act of 1964, stated the purpose of the bill:

Its purpose is not to punish. Its purpose is not to divide but to end divisions which have lasted all too long.

Its purpose is national not regional. Its purpose is to promote a more abiding commitment to freedom, a more constant pursuit of justice and a deeper respect for human dignity.[55]

On the question of how to achieve the goals of the Civil Rights Act, President Johnson added:

We shall achieve these goals because most Americans are low-abiding citizens who want to do what is right. This is why the Civil Rights Act relies first on voluntary compliance, then on the efforts of local communities and states to secure the rights of citizens.

It provides for the national authority to step in only when others cannot or will not do the job.[56]

"What does all this mean?" One of the greatest obstacles in the way of dealing with incidents of discrimination are the antidiscrimatory laws themselves. There seems to be no end to the acts, bills, and titles. One person, after spending hours trying to acquaint herself with her rights, threw up her arms in desperation, termed them all "title twitties," and said she was back where she started.

The federal law basically says that all citizens have equal rights in all areas by law. Compliance with the laws are left up to local and state governments, with the individual having rights to challenge the decisions of these bodies through the federal government. There are, however, provisions under Title VI of the Civil Rights Act, which guarantees that no person shall be subject to any form of discrimination in any program receiving federal aid. It also empowers federal agencies to take appropriate steps to counteract any such discrimination, particularly by denying federal funds to any state or local agencies that practice discrimination.[57]

Let's take a look at the rights that are protected. There are 11 titles under the Civil Rights Act of 1964 and 3 titles under the Civil Rights Act of 1968. They all basically address themselves to antidiscrimination legislation and can be grouped into four major categories: education, employment, housing, and public accommodations. The voting rights act guarantees all citizens the right to vote. To summarize, it can be said that all people now have equal rights by law and that in many cases these laws will have to be challenged when there is no compliance.

"What is there to do about de jure discrimination?" It is necessary to have all the background information discussed previously to have a good case for filing complaints or suits and to know that you do have a case. Unfortunately, much of the burden of responsibility for correcting injustices lies with the victim. It is bad enough to be discriminated against; however, to go through further trouble can be worth it. A right given is certainly worth enforcing and keeping.

Antidiscrimination legislation has sought changes in education and attitudes rather than judicial enforcement for implementation of the laws. Conciliation and persuasion are key techniques that agencies use prior to initiating legal investigations and hearings. Taking all this into consideration, the question still remains as to what to do when you have been discriminated against.

1. *Find out who enforces the particular antidiscrimination legislation pertinent to your complaint.* Does the agency you are concerned with have a compliance officer (one who enforces the antidiscrimination legislation)? If your particular agency does not have a compliance officer, what agency in your area does? This information may be obtained by contacting your local Equal Opportunity Commission, Human Rights Commission, or Equal Rights Agency, if they are available in your community. Otherwise, information can be obtained about filing general discrimination charges by writing to U.S. Equal Employment Opportunity Commission,

Washington, D.C. 20506 or U.S. Commission on Civil Rights, Washington, D.C. 20445. (Agencies equipped to answer inquiries about specific complaints are listed at the end of this chapter.)

2. *Determine how a complaint should be made.* Usually the compliance agency or officer will assist you with this determination. Whether a letter or a complaint form is required will depend upon the nature of the complaint and with whom it is to be filed. A telephone call to the agency in your community that handles antidiscrimination complaints is often all that is necessary to take care of this step.

3. *File your complaint using the method designated by the compliance agency.* Your complaint should specify why you feel you have been discriminated against, giving as much specific information as possible. It is well to assess your case to place it in the proper perspective. It is acceptable to file a complaint where there has been a pattern of discrimination affecting others as well as yourself. Individuals as well as agencies can usually file complaints on behalf of an individual who has been discriminated against. Some types of antidiscrimination legislation require that you file a complaint within 180 days and others give no time limit. You should ask the compliance officer about this stipulation. There is always an advantage in filing a complaint soon after the incident has taken place. The information retained is usually more accurate, and in some places results from your complaint are slow in coming.

4. *Can you expect harassment from the agency discriminating against you?* Establishments or agencies are prohibited from discharging or discriminating against any employee or applicant for employment because a complaint has been made against them. This also holds true in institutions of educa-

tion where a student may wish to file a complaint.

5. *Other things to do about discrimination.* Inquire at your local bar association about attorneys who specialize in civil rights cases. Hire one and leave most of the work up to the attorney. This route, provided you have the finances, will usually end up in court. If you cannot afford to hire an attorney, contact your local legal aid services. Fees for legal aid services are usually based on the client's ability to pay. If a suit is filed where there is a settlement expected, some lawyers may agree to take your case on consignment. This means they will expect a percentage of what you win in the decision.

Consult your local NAACP. They will usually be able to offer you advice about where to go. They may agree to have one of their attorneys work on your case, depending upon whether the decision can affect large numbers of people or result in amendments to put more "teeth" into existing laws. The effectiveness and types of services that can be rendered by the NAACP depend to a large extent upon the community and the support it receives, because it is a voluntary agency. Also consult your local Urban League. The League's major function in personal discrimination matters is informational. This agency could save you the trouble of writing for information because they are usually well stocked with all the recent information on antidiscrimination laws and compliance agencies.

6. *What can you expect to happen to your complaint when filed through a government compliance agency?* You can expect some compliance with the law or the compliance agency will take the next step, which would involve federal enforcement such as revoking federal funds, delaying new awards of federal funds, and barring the agency from receiving any future funds. The Depart-

ment of Justice or Attorney General may also file a suit against the agency. In employment complaints, back pay can be obtained, but this usually occurs as a result of a lawsuit. In these instances, attorney's fees are paid as well as the court cost when the agency has been found in violation of a civil rights law.

Government agencies

Government agencies to be contacted about specific discrimination complaints are:

1. Office of Federal Contract Compliance/ Employment Standards Administration, U.S. Department of Labor, Washington, D.C. 20210

   Discrimination in employment (including hiring, upgrading, salaries, fringe benefits, training and other conditions of employment) on the basis of race, color, religion, national origin or sex. Covers all establishments with federal contracts over $10,000 or grants.

2. Office of Civil Rights
   Department of Health and Human Services, Washington, D.C. 20425

   Employment discrimination as above, specifically where federal funds are used to provide employment. Covers all establishments with federal grants, loans, and contracts (except contracts of insurance or guaranty).

3. U.S. Equal Employment Opportunity Commission
   Office of the General Consul
   1800 G. Street N.W., Washington, D.C. 20506

   All employment-related discrimination. Referrals may be given for local agencies.

State Departments of Industry, Labor, and Human Relations/Equal Rights Division (check directory in your area)

All discrimination covered by law, housing, education, employment. Referrals may be given for local agencies.

4. Mayor's office

For all types of discrimination, it is wise to see if there is a local Equal Opportunities Commission or Human Relations Agency.

Review of the legal status of minorities

Employment rights have been covered in this chapter, but a brief review of the legal status of minorities in the areas of voting, housing, public accommodation, and education is important.[58]

Voting. Double standards for minorities are prohibited in all voting procedures. Specifically, the law has abolished literacy, knowledge, and character lists as qualifications for voting.

Housing. There is a federal open housing ordinance; however, many states have not adopted an ordinance. Some states may require a Supreme Court decision on a complaint that has been filed.

Public accommodations. Discrimination in the use of public accommodations—hotels, motels, restaurants, gasoline stations, and places of amusement—whose operations involve interstate commerce, is prohibited.

Public facilities. Exclusion from and unequal treatment in all public-owned and operated facilities, including parks, stadiums, and swimming pools is prohibited.

Education, public schools. Technical and financial aid is provided to all school districts engaged in the process of desegregation. The attorney general is empowered to sue for desegregation, provided private citizens are not in a position to do so.

Institutions of higher education and professional schools. Where any federal funding is granted, discrimination for admission is prohibited.

Summary

The United States has traveled a long way on the path toward achieving equal rights for all citizens. The laws have been passed that are necessary for the attainment of these rights. In fact, they have been in existence since the Bill of Rights was passed, but we have needed additional ammunition in the form of acts, titles, and amendments. You, the overseer of your rights, must remember what happened in the past reconstruction era and not allow it to happen again.

DISCRIMINATION AND SOCIAL WORK

Social work has an obligation to vigorously work toward ending racial discrimination. Charles Henderson and Bok-Lim Kim summarize seven recommendations that are consistently advocated in the literature of each racial group:

1. Clients are entitled to a general understanding of their culture so they are not served inappropriately out of ignorance.
2. All clients should be served without discrimination or prejudice.
3. Minority clients should have a voice in planning and managing services provided for them.

Youths in row-boat

4. Minority staff members are generally best qualified to serve members of their own group and should be hired to do so.
5. Opportunities for promotion and advancement should be available to minority employees on an equitable basis.
6. Minorities should be accorded special opportunities for professional training. This may mean modifications in educational programs.
7. Minority faculty members are essential. Credentials of experience and skill are more important than academic degrees.[59]

Ione Dugger Vargus reports the following problems arose when minority graduate social work students worked in white-dominated social agencies:

1. Some were given all-black case loads.
2. Students were expected to be authorities on blacks and were frequently consulted by other workers.

3. Some white workers considered themselves the experts on black people and accepted no suggestions or ideas.
4. When black workers were permitted to develop their own ways of making contact and channeling services, white workers were upset by the departure from the rules.[60]

Most students remarked that while they would prefer to work with blacks, an all-black case load implied that both the clients and the worker were inferior.

The students did not like to be perceived as authorities on blacks because they recognized that individual differences made pat answers impossible. They felt some conflicts in giving advice to white practitioners, unless the practitioner had already tried several approaches before seeking advice. They felt that practitioners should work on their own cases. If they had tried several ideas already, the request was just like any other consultation.

The social work professional needs to recognize the reality of practice in a culturally diverse environment. Social workers do have many of the prejudices and misperceptions of the general society. The tendency to use one's own prejudices and stereotypes poses danger for the well-meaning practitioner. For example, a social worker assigned to a Native American client might assume that the quietness of the client suggests either an uncooperative client, or that the client is fully agreeing with the worker. Unfortunately, it is possible neither assumption is accurate. As a general rule a Native American will not challenge or correct a worker who is off the track because to do so would violate "noninterference." Noninterference is a basic value of Native American culture which asserts that Native Americans should handle unwanted attempts at intervention with withdrawal: emotional, physical, or both.[61]

Another response pattern of white social workers that is counterproductive with Native Americans is the attempt to maintain direct eye contact. Such face-to-face eye contact is considered rude and intimidating by many Native Americans.[62]

A bilingual practitioner working in a Chicano community may not possess the needed knowledge to understand all aspects of the language. For example, the special language of the barrio often contains words that have a variety of connotations that differ from formal Spanish.[63] As a consequence the worker who does speak Spanish must be acutely alert to the possibility that the words may have very different meanings for clients living in a barrio.

A worker, then, working with diverse cultural groups must:

1. Acquire a knowledge of self, including one's stereotypes, values, feelings, attitudes and beliefs.
2. Acquire a knowledge of the culture and characteristics with whom one is working.
3. Acquire an understanding of the unique effects that standard counseling and intervention approaches will have on the client group.
4. Learn to challenge and change the stereotypic perceptions that s/he has of the client group.

The reader should not get the impression that working effectively with a different cultural group presents insurmountable barriers and obstacles. In actuality, the similarities between worker and clients almost always outweight the dissimilarities.[64]

SUMMARY

Our country has always been racist, but there has been considerable progress in recent years in alleviating racial prejudice and discrimination. Yet, we cannot relax. Racial discrimination continues to have tragic consequences for many members of nonwhite racial groups. Individuals who are targets of discrimination are excluded from certain types of employment, educational and recreational opportunities, certain residential housing areas, membership in certain religious and social organizations, certain political activities, access to some community services, and so on. Racial discrimination is also a serious obstacle to developing a positive self-concept and has heavy psychological and financial costs.

Racial discrimination is a problem of whites, as whites in our society are the primary discriminators. The sources of racial prejudice are psychological, historical, and also based on socialization processes in our racist society.

Race is primarily a social concept, rather than a biological concept.

There are numerous nonwhite racial groups in our nation, each with a unique culture, language, history, and special needs. This uniqueness needs to be understood and appreciated if we are to achieve progress toward racial equality.

Strategies against discrimination include mass media appeals, increased interaction among races, civil rights legislation, protests and activism, specific programs such as school busing, affirmative action, and human relation programs in school systems. It is also very important that people be aware of their civil rights and if victimized by discrimination, be able to effectively handle incidents of racial discrimination.

As a profession, social work has an obligation to vigorously work toward ending racial discrimination.

NOTES

1. Excerpted from a speech by Abraham Lincoln in Charleston, Illinois, in 1858, as reported in Richard Hofstader, *The American Political Tradition* (New York: Knopf, 1948), p. 116.
2. Gordon, W. Allport, *The Nature of Prejudice* (Reading, Mass.: Addison-Wesley, 1954), p. 7.
3. Gunner Myrdal, *An American Dilemma* (New York: Harper & Brothers, 1944).
4. Elmer H. Johnson, *Social Problems of Urban Man* (Homewood, Ill.: Dorsey Press, 1973), p. 344.
5. Charles F. Marden and Gladys Meyer, *Minorities in American Society* (New York: American Book, 1962).
6. Ashley Montague, *Man's Most Dangerous Myth: The Fallacy of Race*, 4th ed. (Cleveland: World Publishing, 1964).
7. Johnson, *Social Problems*, p. 350.
8. Arnold Rose, *The Negro in America* (New York: Harper & Row, 1964).
9. Paul Ehrlich and Richard Holm, "A Biological View of Race," in *The Concept of Race*, ed. Ashley Montague (New York: Free Press, 1964).
10. Montague, *Man's Most Dangerous Myth*.
11. Arthur Jensen, "How Much Can We Boost I.Q. and Scholastic Achievement?" *Harvard Educational Review* 39 (1969): 1–123.
12. Ashley Montague, ed., *Race & I.Q.* (London: Oxford University Press, 1975).
13. Johnson, *Social Problems*, p. 50.
14. Grace Halsell, *Soul Sister* (New York: Fawcett Crest, 1969), pp. 156–57.
15. C. H. Cooley, *Human Nature and the Social Order* (New York: Scribner, 1902).
16. Albert Szymanski, "Racial Discrimination and White Gain," *American Sociological Review* 41 (June 1976): 403–14.
17. Thomas Sullivan, et al., *Social Problems* (New York: Wiley, 1980), pp. 410–45.
18. U.S. Bureau of the Census, *1970 General Population Characteristics* (Washington, D.C.: U.S. Government Printing Office, 1970).
19. "It's Your Turn in the Sun," *Time,* October 16, 1978, p. 48.
20. Charles H. Henderson and Bok-Lim Kim, "Racism," in *Contemporary Social Work,* ed. Donald Brieland, Lela Costin, and Charles Atherton (New York: McGraw-Hill, 1975), p. 180.
21. Ibid., p. 185.
22. Sullivan, et al., *Social Problems*, p. 422.
23. Ibid., p. 423.
24. U.S. Department of Commerce, *Social Indicators, 1976* (Washington, D.C.: U.S Government Printing Office, 1977).
25. William Moore, Jr., *The Vertical Ghetto* (New York: Random House, 1969), p. 71.
26. Helen M. Crampton and Kenneth K. Keiser, *Social Welfare: Institution and Process* (New York: Random House, 1970), p. 111.
27. Lydia R. Aguirre, "The Meaning of the Chicano Movement," *Social Casework* 52 (1971): 259.
28. J. Julian Rivera, "Growth of a Puerto Rican Awareness," *Social Casework* 55 (February 1974): p. 86.
29. Ibid., p. 84.
30. Sullivan, et al., *Social Problems*, p. 417.
31. Crampton and Keiser, *Social Welfare*, p. 109.
32. Johnson, *Social Problems*, p. 349.
33. Crampton and Keiser, *Social Welfare*, p. 104.
34. Henderson and Bok-Lim Kim, "Racism," p. 191.
35. "Business Breakout for America's Indians," *U.S. News & World Report*, May 28, 1979, p. 68.
36. Ibid., p. 70.
37. Johnson, *Social Problems*, p. 349.
38. Charles Henderson, Bok-Lim Kim, and Ione D. Vargus, "Racism," in *Contemporary Social Work,* ed. Donald Brieland, Lela Costin, and Charles Atherton, 2d ed. (New York: McGraw-Hill, 1980), p. 403.
39. George E. Simpson and J. Milton Yinger, *Racial and Cultural Minorities*, 3d ed. (New York: Harper & Row, 1965), p. 510.
40. Sullivan, et al., *Social Problems*, p. 437.
41. Johnson, *Social Problems*, pp. 374–379.

42. Ibid., p. 376.

43. Sullivan, et al., *Social Problems,* p. 438.

44. Ibid., p. 439.

45. Allan P. Sindler, *Bakke, DeFunis and Minority Admissions: The Quest for Equal Opportunity* (New York: Longman, 1978).

46. Henderson, et al., "Racism," 2d ed., p. 414.

47. Roland L. Buchanan, Jr. and Marlene A. Cummings, *Individual Differences: An Experience in Human Relations for Children* (Madison, Wis.: Madison Public Schools, 1975).

48. Ibid., p. 1.

49. Ibid., p. 13.

50. Harry Ploski and Roscoe C. Brown, *The Negro Almanac* (New York: Bellwether Co., 1967), pp. 27–28.

51. William Katz, *Eyewitness: The Negro in American History* (New York: Toronto, London: Pitman Publishing Corp., 1967), p. 262.

52. Gordon W. Allport, *The Nature of Prejudice* (Garden City, N.Y.: Doubleday Anchor Books, 1954), p. 10.

53. Ibid., p. 15.

54. Ibid., pp. 146–47.

55. Harry Ploski and Ernest Kaiser, *The Negro Almanac: The Black Experience in America* (New York: Bellwether, 1971), pp. 147–48.

56. Ibid., pp. 147–48.

57. Ibid., p. 147.

58. Ploski and Kaiser, *Negro Almanac,* pp. 243–73.

59. Henderson et al., "Racism," p. 193.

60. Ione Dugger Vargus "The Minority Practitioner," in *Contemporary Social Work,* ed. Donald Brieland, Lela Costin, and Charles Atherton (New York: McGraw-Hill, 1975), p. 421.

61. Jimm G. Good Tracks, "Native American Noninterference," *Social Work* 18 (November 1973): 30–34.

62. Ronald G. Lewis and Man Keung Ho, "Social Work with Native Americans, *Social Work* 20 (September 1975): 378–82.

63. Dolores, G. Norton, "Incorporating Content on Minority Groups into Social Work Practice Courses," in Council on Social Work Education, *The Dual Perspective* (New York, 1978).

64. Grafton, H. Hull, Jr., "Social Work Practice with Diverse Groups," *The Practice of Social Work,* ed. Charles Zastrow (Homewood, Ill.: Dorsey Press, 1981).

GUSTAFSON

chapter *9*

Women who work full time are paid 59 percent of what men are paid who work full time.[1] The average woman college graduate is paid less than the average male high school dropout.[2]

Examples of erroneous sexist stereotypes

HOW TO TELL A BUSINESS MAN FROM A BUSINESS WOMAN. . .

He's aggressive; she's pushy.

He's good at details; she's picky.

He loses his temper because he's so involved in his job; she's bitchy.

When he's depressed (or hung over) everyone tiptoes past his office; she's moody so it must be her time of the month.

He follows through; she doesn't know when to quit.

He's confident; she's conceited.

He stands firm; she's hard.

He has judgments; she's prejudiced.

He's a man of the world; she's been around.

He drinks because of excessive job pressure; she's a lush.

He isn't afraid to say what he thinks; she's mouthy.

He exercises authority diligently; she's power-mad.

He's close-mouthed; she's secretive.

He's a stern taskmaster; she's hard to work for.

He climbed the ladder to success; she slept her way to the top!

SOURCE: Author unknown

HISTORY OF SEXISM

In almost every known society women have had a lower status (although not always willingly) than men. Women have been bound by more social restrictions, and have consistently received less recognition for their work than men. Women have been regarded differently than men, not only biologically, but also emotionally, intellectually, and psychologically. Double standards have often existed for dating, marriage, social, and sexual conduct.

Most religions (including Judio-Christian, Hindu, and Islam) in their traditional doctrines ascribe an inferior status to women. This tradition continues to exist today in most countries, even though women attend church more often, hold firmer religious beliefs, pray more often, and are more active in church programs.[3] In many Christian religions, women cannot become ministers or priests. Some orthodox Jewish men offer a daily prayer of thanks to God for not making them a woman.[4]

In primitive societies men were generally hunters, a prestigious activity. Women, on the other hand, were expected to bear as many children as possible. Because of the

Sexism and efforts for achieving equality

high death rate in nonliterate societies, children were highly valued. Women spent much of their adult lives being pregnant, nursing infants, and raising the older children. Women, since they were forced to remain around the home, were also assigned the less prestigious "domestic tasks" of cooking, sewing, and washing. Once these sex roles became part of tradition, these distinctions not only were recognized as practical means of doing the necessary work but also came to be seen as "natural" ways for men and women to behave.

Gradually more behavior patterns were added to these sex role distinctions. Because men were trained at hunting, these skills led them to be recognized as the defenders of their tribe in case of attack from other tribes. Child-rearing patterns were developed to teach boys to be aggressive and to be leaders. Women, on the other hand, were assigned supportive roles to men, and were taught to be more passive, dependent, and to provide emotional support to their men.

Prior to the Industrial Revolution, practically all societies had come to assign distinct roles to men and to women. Women were generally involved in domestic and child-rearing activities, while men were involved in what were then considered to be the productive* (such as hunting and economic support) and protective functions for the family. It should be noted women in preindustrial societies were also often involved in food producing and economic support, such as making clothes, growing and harvesting garden crops, and helping on the farm. But their specific responsibilities were often viewed as being inferior and requiring fewer skills.

---

* The use of the term *productive* indicates the higher status that was assigned to the role of men. In actuality, the roles of women were often as productive, or more productive, in meeting the essential tasks needing to be performed.

The Industrial Revolution during the 19th century brought about dramatic changes in sex roles. Men, instead of working on a small farm, went outside of the home to work in a factory or other setting to provide economic support. As a result the economic role of women declined as they had fewer farming tasks. The roles of women became increasingly defined as child rearing and housework. Yet, the amount of time required to perform these roles declined for several reasons. Families had fewer children. With mass education, older children went to school. Gradually laborsaving devices reduced the domestic tasks (e.g., baking bread, canning vegetables, and washing). As the traditional roles of women began to change, some women began to pursue activities (e.g., outside employment) that had traditionally been limited to men. With these changes sex roles began to blur, becoming less clear cut.

During the early 1900s modern birth control procedures became available. Through this advance women gained greater freedom from the traditional roles of child rearing and housework.

During World War II large numbers of women were employed outside the home for the first time to take the places of men who had been drafted into the military. During the war years, over 38 percent of all women 16-years-of-age and over were employed, causing a further blurring of traditional sex roles.[5]

The struggle for women's rights in America has been going on for over a century. In 1848 two feminists, Susan B. Anthony and Elizabeth Stanton, organized the first women's rights caucus in the state of New York.[6] These early leaders demanded suffrage (the vote for women) and the reform of many laws that were openly discriminatory toward women. It took over 70 years, until 1920 to pass the Nineteenth Amendment to the Constitution which gave the vote to women. Unfortunately, the huge struggles and number of years in passing this amendment led many women leaders to believe that the right to vote went hand in hand with sexual equality. After the 1920 passage, the "women's movement" was nearly dormant for the next 40 years.

In the 1960s there was a resurgence of interest in sex role inequality for a variety of reasons. The civil rights movement had a consciousness raising effect in that people became more aware of inequalities. More women were attending college and thereby became more informed about inequalities. As women moved into new occupational positions, they became more aware of discriminatory practices. Finally, there was an explosion of research demonstrating that sex role differences were not generally biological differences, but were in fact due to socialization patterns; and that the effects of such sex roles were often discriminatory toward women.

A few such studies will be mentioned.

Money, Hampson, and Hampson conducted a study in 1955 on hermaphrodites.[7] A hermaphrodite is a person born with both male and female sexual characteristics, but nonetheless is called either a male or female at birth, and then is related to as being of that labeled sex. These researchers did *not* find a significant correlation between physical characteristics and the hermaphrodite's own feelings about their sexual identities. These people were fulfilling sex role expectations of their labeled gender, although their observable sex characteristics often would tend to place them in the other category. This research raised questions about the biological determination of sex roles.

Other studies have found dramatic differences in socialization patterns between males and females. Boys are given more sports equipment and task-oriented toys (like construction sets) to play with, while girls are given more dolls and toys relating to marriage and parenthood.[8] During the first few months of life, girls receive more distal stimulation (like looking and talking) from their parents, while boys receive more proximal stimulation (like rocking and handling).[9] Fathers tend to play more aggressively with sons than with daughters.[10] In some Middle East societies, males are reared and turn out to be more emotional and sensitive than females, while females tend to be more impassive and practical.[11] In Sweden, most heavy-machinery operators are women.[12] In the Soviet Union most physicians are women.[13]

Betty Friedan in her 1963 book *The Feminine Mystique* provided the ideological base for the resurgence of the women's movement.[14] By the term *feminine mystique,* Friedan referred to the negative self-concept, lack of direction, and the lack of self-worth among women. The book served as a rallying point for women and led Friedan to form the National Organization for Women (NOW) in 1966. Today NOW has over 60,000 members, making it the largest women's rights group in the country, and an influential political force.[15] NOW and other women's groups have been working to end sexual discrimination, to work toward sexual equality, to end double standards, and to improve the self-identity of women.

The Civil Rights Act of 1964, primarily intended to end racial discrimination, also prohibited discrimination on the basis of sex. Yet, a number of state laws have persisted that involve social differentiation between men and women, and local businesses in some states are as yet not covered by sex discrimination laws.[16]

In 1972 the Equal Rights Amendment (ERA) received congressional approval, but it requires ratification by three fourths (38) of the states to become the Twenty-Seventh Amendment to the Constitution. ERA states, "Equality of rights under the law shall not be denied or abridged by the United States or any state on account of sex."

The progress toward ratification of ERA has been slowed, and filled with controversy. Emotions have run high on both sides. If ratified, proponents assert ERA would eliminate numerous state laws that are discriminatory toward women.[17] Opponents of ERA argue the passage of ERA would mean women could be drafted into the armed forces. They further argue that women would lose preferential treatment in divorce actions and it would make parents equally liable for alimony, child support, and spouse support. They assert certain labor laws that give preferential treatment to women would have to be revised, such as the amount of weight women may lift on the job. They also assert that "maternity leaves" would have to be made available to husbands who want to stay home with a newborn child.[18]

Even though ERA is presently stalled, there have been a variety of statues that have been passed designed to prevent sex discrimination.

The federal Equal Pay Act of 1963, along with similar state laws, requires equal pay for equal work. As mentioned, the Civil Rights Act of 1964 outlaws discrimination on the basis of race, color, sex, or religion. Executive Order 11246, amended by Executive Order 11375 on October 13, 1967, forbids sex discrimination by federal suppliers and contractors and provides procedures for enforcement. In addition, numerous court decisions have set precedents establishing the illegality of sex discrimination in hiring, promotions, and rates of pay.[19] Several landmark decisions have required employers to pay female employees millions of dollars to compensate for past wage discriminations.[20]

The Equal Credit Act of 1974 bars discrimination on the basis of marital status or sex in credit operations. A number of states have passed laws prohibiting discrimination against pregnant women in hiring, training, and promotion.[21]

Affirmative action programs (described in Chapter 8) also apply to women. The following employers are required to have affirmative action programs—government contractors and suppliers, recipients of government funds, and businesses engaged in interstate commerce. Affirmative action primarily applies to job vacancies. Employers must demonstrate active efforts to locate and recruit minority applicants (defined to include women); must demonstrate positive efforts to increase the pool of qualified applicants (for example, special training programs for minorities); give preference to hiring minority applicants; and in some cases set hard quotas which specify numbers of minority members that must be accepted (re-

Growing number of women are now occupying traditional male roles: A female fire fighter

gardless of qualifications) to fill vacant positions. The clout of affirmative action programs is the threat of loss of government funds if employers do not have effective affirmative action programs.

The women's movement has made remarkable advances in the past 20 years. Yet, substantial sex discrimination and restrictive sex role stereotyping still remains.

THE PROBLEM

Sexism is prejudice or discrimination against women. While women are a numerical majority in our society, they are considered to be a minority group because they are victims of discrimination on many fronts and have unequal access to valued resources.

Occupation and income. The jobs held by women tend to be concentrated at the bottom of the occupational status hierarchy, as indicated in Table 9–1.

Women tend to be concentrated in the lower paying, lower status positions of secretaries, child care workers, receptionists, typists, nurses, hairdressers, bank tellers, cashiers, and file clerks. Men tend to be concentrated in higher paying positions: lawyers, judges, engineers, accountants, college teachers, physicians, dentists, and sales managers.

As noted earlier, full-time working women are paid only 59 percent of what full-time working men are paid.[22]

Even with a number of sex discrimination laws being passed, job discrimination has been found in a number of studies.[23] For example, female graduate students in the social sciences have superior academic records, yet female Ph.D.s are less likely to receive tenure and to attain the rank of full professor.[24]

In 1980 women held fewer than 10 percent of the nation's elective offices. Of 100 U.S.

senators, only 1 was a woman. Of 435 members in the House of Representatives, only 16 were women. Of 50 governors, only 2 were women.[25]

Women hold fewer than 1 percent of the top-management positions in American corporations, fewer than 2 percent of the directorships of top corporations, and about 5 or 6 percent of all middle-management positions in this country.[26]

Overall, women earn less income than men in practically every job category, according to the Census Bureau.[27] Even in the armed forces where pay levels are standardized, it is less likely that women will receive additional income for "flight pay," "combat pay," or "hazardous duty" pay.[28] It is true that differences in income between men and women by job category are partly due to seniority pay from men having worked longer, but studies taking seniority into account have found women tend to receive less pay for doing the same job.[29]

There are probably many reasons for these occupational and income differences between men and women. Female children are socialized to seek lower paying occupations and careers; boys, for example, are more apt to be encouraged to be lawyers and doctors, while girls are encouraged to be teachers and secretaries. Men and women are also "sex typed" for various jobs. For example, males looking for employment are encouraged by prospective employers to apply for higher status positions, while women are encouraged to apply for lower level positions.[30] Then there is the tendency for our society to assign lower pay to job categories where women are concentrated: for example, receptionists, secretaries, and typists. Lower pay for women holding the same jobs as men suggests there are also discriminatory practices occurring even after women are hired.

Paul Horton and Gerald Leslie provide additional reasons for this disparity be-

TABLE 9–1 Employment positions held by women

	Total number of workers employed	Proportion held by women
Secretaries	3,421,000	99%
Child care workers	443,000	98
Receptionists	531,000	97
Typists	1,006,000	96
Registered nurses	879,000	96
Hairdressers, cosmetologists	526,000	88
Bank tellers	408,000	90
Bookkeepers	1,726,000	90
Cashiers	1,326,000	87
Health service workers	1,747,000	89
File clerks	274,000	85
Librarians	208,000	80
Counter clerks (nonfood)	343,000	78
Office machine operators	759,000	74
School teachers	3,024,000	71
Food-service workers	4,095,000	69
Retail clerks	2,316,000	70
Social workers	444,000	60
Office managers	343,000	58
Real estate agents	502,000	44
Cleaning-service workers	680,000	34
Writers, artists, entertainers	1,141,000	36
College teachers	562,000	32
Accountants	868,000	27
Bank, financial officers	543,000	27
Sales managers	666,000	21
Physicians and dentists	724,000	11
Electrical and electronic engineering technicians	194,000	10
Protective service workers (police, etc.)	1,324,000	8
Lawyers, and judges	462,000	9
Engineers	1,267,000	3
Construction craftsworkers	2,404,000	1

SOURCE: U.S. Bureau of the Census, *Statistical Abstract of the United States, 1978* (Washington D.C.: U.S. Government Printing Office, 1978), pp. 418–21.

tween men and women which stem from sex role socialization:

> Motivation for career advancement is difficult to measure, and rash generalization is dangerous. Yet there are good reasons to suspect that intense career ambitions have been less common among women than among men. Beginning in early socialization, most girls are trained to please and to charm others; most boys are trained to impress and outdistance

others. Boys are trained to dominate and lead, girls to submit and follow. Boys are taught to make demands upon others; girls learn to serve others' needs. Boys are praised for their strength, girls for their prettiness and graciousness. As adults, men in our society are evaluated primarily according to their career success ("meet my son, the doctor"), while women have been evaluated primarily according to their skill in human relationships ("she has a handsome husband and three darling children"). Husbands who knowingly neglected their families to pursue career advancement (moonlighting, night school, weekends working at the office) were praised for their ambition, while wives who allowed their careers to interfere with family life were scolded and scorned. A women's spectacular success might alienate men, and much has been written about the avoidance-of-success syndrome in women.[31] In sum, it is reasonable to believe that some part of the different career successes of men and women is caused by women's lesser feeling of need for career achievement and a lesser willingness to sacrifice other values to its attainment.[32]

Human interactions

In spite of the attention the women's rights movement has received, sex role stereotyping is still having an immense effect on interactions and causing numerous problems.

Young girls in many families are still raised by their parents to be mothers and homemakers—and/or encouraged to seek employment of a lower status and of lower pay.

Boys are encouraged to play more competitive games than girls. Boys are urged to be outgoing and aggressive, while young girls are encouraged to be passive and reserved.[33]

Surveys of textbooks in preschool, elementary, junior high, and high school portray female characters as being more passive and dependent and less creative than males.[34]

A significant part of the socialization process occurs in school. Nearly 90 percent of grade school teachers are female, while close to 90 pecent of principals are male.[35] Thus, children see men in superior, decision-making positions and see women in subordinate positions. One study found grade school teachers generally hold traditional sex role stereotypes; that teachers erroneously believe that males are innately more aggressive and more capable of abstract reasoning than females.[36]

Young children are at an impressionable age. Such sex role stereotyping often becomes self-fulling prophecies. According to Cooley's "looking glass self-concept," people will come to view themselves as others relate to them.[37] Boys are discouraged from showing overt affection, are taught to seek material rewards, to be dominant in dating and marital relationships, to seek respect, power, and prestige. Boys are socialized not to cry, to keep their concerns within themselves, to be "macho."

In contrast, girls are taught to be more passive, nurturing, maternal. Research shows some females are taught to actually fear success and achievement, and to "play dumb" in order to "boost the male ego."[38] To be feminine, females are expected to display softness, helplessness, tenderness, "sugar and spice and everything nice."

Even contemporary theories in psychology describe women as being more passive, emotional, having a lack of abstract interests, and having an instinctive tenderness for babies.[39] Even though masculinity and feminity are largely learned roles, contemporary psychological theories subtly imply, erroneously, that sex role differences are largely genetically determined.[40] Freud's theory of the development of the female personality is probably the most sexist and outrageous. Freud theorized that young girls discover their genitals differ from boys, which leads them to have "penis envy." Because they differ, they conclude they are biologically inferior to males and then develop a passive, submissive personality as a way to adjust to interactions with males who are viewed as superior.[41]

There are many sexist implications built into the English language. Until a few years ago the male-related expressions (like he) were employed when speaking of human beings. Additional commonly used words and phrases which subtly (and erroneously) imply the superiority of males include man-made, mankind, manned, manpower, chairman, congressman, businessman, mailman, salesman, foreman, policeman, the best man for the job, and man and wife.

It is customary for women upon marriage to take their husbands' last name, again subtly suggesting the dominance of males. Sexism is indeed pervasive in our society.

The effects of sexism on human interactions are immense. Some examples will be briefly described. Parents place more social restrictions on teenage daughters than on teenage sons. Daughters cannot stay out as late, their friends are more closely monitored, they are less likely to obtain the family car for going out, and they are discouraged from getting involved in athletic activity.

There are a lot of pressures on women to have the "Miss America" look; to have well-developed busts, shapely figures, and attractive features. Practically all women find it difficult to maintain (even if they once had) such features. Unfortunately, less attractive women receive less attention from males, find it more difficult to obtain dates, and may find it more difficult to obtain higher status employment.

There are many double standards for male and female social interactions. If teenage males are sexually active, they are viewed as being "Don Juans," while sexually active teenage females are called "whores" and other derogatory names. Males are allowed to a greater extent to be aggressive and to use vulgar language. There are social restrictions on females from entering certain nightclubs and other entertainment places. Married women who have an affair are usually subjected to more disapproval than married men.

In interactions between males and females there is a tendency for the male to seek to be dominant and for the female to either seek and equalitarian relationship or to be submissive. A few examples will be presented. In dating, the male usually is expected to ask the female for a date and to select what they will do on a date. Often, males try to be "macho," while some females play along by being "submissive," "passive," or "feminine." There is a tendency when both husband and wife are working for the wife to follow her husband to a new geographic area when the location of the husband's job changes.[42]

Often there are power struggles between males and females related to sex role expectations. Males may seek to dominate, while females seek equalitarian relationships. Marriage counselors are now seeing many couples where the husband wants his wife to play the traditional role—to stay at home, raise the children, and do the household work. If the wife does work, the husband often demands that the job not interfere with the wife doing the domestic tasks and wants the job to be viewed as a "second income" in contrast to a "career." Wives who want equalitarian relationships, and who are becoming increasingly aware of the negative effects of sex role stereotyping, are apt to have power struggles with husbands who seek to have them fulfill the traditional wife role.

Jessie Bernard has noted that women experience more depression and greater dissatisfaction in marriage than men.[43] Women are expected to make most of the adjustments necessary to keep the marriage intact. Middle-aged women frequently suffer severe depression when many of their tasks as mothers and homemakers are phased out—especially if they do not have outside jobs.[44] Research demonstrates that employed wives are happier than full-time homemakers.[45] The situation of women who are battered by their husbands yet continue to live in these circumstances sadly documents the extent to which some women will follow a course of being passive, submissive, and dependent.

Sex role stereotypes probably also play a role in women being treated as sex objects by some men and in women being sexually harassed at work, at school, and in other interactions.

It is not only female stereotypes that cause human interaction difficulties. Males also experience problems in living up to the image of a "model man." A male is expected to be strong, to be a sturdy oak, to never be depressed, vulnerable, or anxious. He is not supposed to be "sissy," or feminine. He is expected not to cry or openly display feminine emotions. He is expected to be the provider, the breadwinner, to be competent in all situations. He is supposed to be physically strong, self-reliant, athletic, to have a manly air of confidence and toughness, to be daring and aggressive, to be brave and forceful, to always be in a position to dominate any situation, to be a Clint Eastwood.[46]

It is impossible for any male to live up to these stereotypes. Yet, there are considerable pressures on males to try, or to suffer consequences. Take the example of Senator Edmund Muskie in the Democratic presidential primary campaign in 1968. Senator Muskie was the leading candidate for the nomination. Then a newspaper in New England made some derogatory accusations about his wife, and Muskie reacted by "breaking down and crying" in public. Very quickly the American public concluded that Muskie did not have the emotional stability to be president, and his popularity plummeted in the polls. David and Brannon describe another example,

> A friend explained to me that he broke down and cried in front of a colleague at the office after some personal tragedies and office frustrations. He explained, "The news of my crying was all over the office in an hour. At first no one said anything. They just sort of looked. They couldn't handle the situation by talking about it. Before this only girls had cried. One of the guys did joke, 'Hear you and Sally been crying lately, eh?' I guess that was a jibe at my masculinity, but the 'knowing silence' of the others indicated the same doubts. What really hurt was that two years later, when I was doing very well and being considered for a promotion, it was brought up again. My manager was looking over my evaluations, read a paragraph to himself, and said, 'What do you think about that crying incident?' You can bet that was the last time I let myself cry."[47]

Because of male stereotypes, many men view themselves as failures when they cannot meet the financial needs of their families. Some men get badly beaten from getting into fights. Many women find it frustrating to interact with men who are unable to be honest and open about their feelings. Not being able to live up to the "model man" image makes many men unhappy, depressed, and unfulfilled. Trying to live up to such stereotypes often causes considerable psychological stress and may result in a wide range of psychosomatic illnesses—headaches, ulcers, colitis, constipation, alcoholism, hypertension, insomnia, rashes, and so on.

RECENT DEVELOPMENTS AND THE FUTURE

There is currently a sex role revolution occurring in our society. Women as well as men are increasingly becoming aware of the negative effects of sex role distinctions. Increasingly there are courses on this topic in high schools, vocational schools, and colleges.

Women are becoming more involved in athletics than they were in the past, and entering certain types of competition previously confined to males. Women are now to a greater extent playing basketball, football, softball, and volleyball. There are increasing numbers of women in track and field events, swimming, boxing, wrestling, weightlifting, golf, tennis, and stock car racing.

Women are also pursuing a number of professions and careers that previously were nearly all male: the military, armed forces officers, engineers, lawyers, judges, fire fighters, physicians, dentists, accountants, administrators, police officers, and managers. Entering such new careers often has obstacles. Glassman, for example, reports that women who have become police officers receive stares from other citizens and are often viewed with suspicion by male partners.[48] Male partners fear women may break under pressure, that women may not be able to subdue and handcuff a resisting offender, and that women may not be able to handle disorderly males and several other types of violent situations. Male officers tend to feel both hostile and protective about patrolwomen, and one woman's failing is often held up as an indictment against all the rest.

There are also changes in human interactions, with more women being assertive and seeking out equalitarian relationships with males. To some extent, men are also (more

Army officer cadets

slowly) beginning to realize the negative effects of sex role distinctions. Men are gradually realizing that the stereotyped model man role limits the opportunities open to them in terms of emotional expression, interpersonal relationships, occupations, and domestic activities. Sawyer has noted:

> If men cannot play freely, neither can they freely cry, be gentle, nor show weakness—because these are "feminine," not "masculine." But a fuller concept of humanity recognizes that all men and women are potentially both strong and weak, both active and passive, and that these and other human characteristics are not the province of one sex.
>
> The acceptance of sex role stereotypes not only limits the individual but also has bad effects on society generally.[49]

Not only are women taking on new roles and entering new careers, but so are men. It is increasingly becoming more common for men to accept equal responsibility for domestic tasks and many child-rearing tasks. There are now more male nurses, secretaries,

Men are also taking on new roles: a male secretary

child care workers, nursery school teachers, telephone operators, and flight attendants.[50]

What will the future be like in terms of sex roles? Sex role stereotypes are now undergoing change. Predicting the precise direction that sex role stereotypes will take is difficult. Sullivan et al. note,

> . . . it seems likely that any meaningful change in our sex role structure will involve some degree of redefinition of both masculinity and femininity. In the years to come, it is likely that we will see significant shifts in the way children are socialized and revisions of our legal system that affect both men and women. The extent of the change that will occur is something that cannot yet be determined. . . . We are in the midst of a very exciting era of experimentation. We have an opportunity to shape our destiny in this area. If people decide that sexual differences are important, this need not entail a return to the inequality, discrimination, and oppression that were common in the past and still linger today.[51]

Some feminists and social scientists have urged men and women to be socialized to be flexible in their role playing and to seek to express themselves as human beings rather than in traditional feminine or masculine ways.[52] This new idea is called "androgyny," from andro (male) and gyne (female). The notion is to have people explore a broad range of role playing possibilities, and to choose to express emotions and behaviors without regard to sex role stereotypes. People, thus, are encouraged to pursue tasks and careers they are most competent and comfortable with and to express attitudes and emotions they really feel. If a male wants to be a cook or an elementary school teacher and a female wants to be a soldier or an athlete and they're good at it, then it is functional for society if both develop their talents and are allowed to achieve all of which they are capable of.

SEXISM AND SOCIAL WORK

Since 60 percent of social workers are female,[53] there is the notion that social work is a female-dominated profession.

Some other statistics suggest otherwise. Fanshel in a study of NASW members found the proportion of men in leadership positions (i.e., in administration) was twice that of women—37 percent versus 18 percent.[54] The Council on Social Work Education in 1978–79 found that of social work faculty members in the United States, 52.2 percent were men.[55] In addition 71 percent of full-time professors were men, indicating a higher concentration of males at this more prestigious rank.

In 1976 Szakacs compiled statistics on leadership positions by sex in federally funded private nonprofit organizations throughout the United States—of 868 agencies, only 141 (16 percent) were headed by women.[56]

Fanshel did a study of salary differences between men and women of NASW members. At most levels (administration, casework, and academia) salaries were higher for men than for women.[57]

Ursula S. Myers: one of the few female executive directors of a county public welfare department

Taken together these statistics suggest males tend to occupy leadership positions in social work, and there is some evidence that male social workers are paid more than female social workers.

But there is evidence that the profession is responding to women's issues, and there are efforts to increase female representation in leadership positions.

In 1978 the number of women enrolled in social work doctoral programs exceeded the number of men—55 percent to 45 percent.[58]

In 1973 the elected and appointed national leadership of the National Association of Social Workers was 74.7 percent male. In 1976, due to affirmative action efforts, the leadership was evenly divided between males and females.[59] The ratio of board members in 1970 for the Council on Social Work Education was four males to every female; in 1977 the representation of women was 42.1 percent.[60]

In 1973 the Delegate Assembly of NASW responded to the women's movement by adding the elimination of sexism to poverty and racism as basic concerns and priorities for the profession. The Council on Social Work Education has required in accreditation standards for baccalaureate and masters programs that content on women's issues must be included throughout the curriculum. CSWE also has an accreditation standard which prohibits sexual discrimination in social work educational programs, and mandates affirmative action programs for women administrators, faculty, students, and staff in social work educational programs.

NASW Legal Defense Fund has provided financial support in sex discrimination cases. In addition, NASW is supporting the Equal Rights Amendment, has

Karen Reibetanz, Ph.D.: one of the few executive directors of a sheltered workshop who is female

voiced opposition to the Hyde Amendment (which prohibits the use of federal funds for abortions), and is working on other issues related to sexism.

On a practice level it is important for social workers to understand that the traditional socialization process and the sex role stereotypes in our society account for many of the problems which confront female, as well as male clients. Workers should be skilled in helping clients to actualize themselves, and to stop being negatively influenced by rigid sex role sterotypes. As noted earlier, many interactions problems between males and females in our society are consequences of sex role stereotyping. One therapy approach that is widely being used to help both men and women more effectively express themselves and gain skills in countering sex role stereotypes is assertive

training (described in Chapter 21). Consciousness-raising groups are being held, largely with women, to help them become more aware of sex role stereotypes, help them establish a better self-concept, and to foster contact with others who are also working to end sexism.

The growing awareness of sexism and women's issues has led to the provision of improved services to groups that were largely ignored—victims of rape, battered wives, women seeking abortions, husbands and wives with marital concerns, people with sexual dysfunctions, single-parent households headed by women, and displaced homemakers.[61]

SUMMARY

In almost every known society women have had a lower status than men. Women have traditionally been assigned housework and child-rearing responsibilities, and socialized to the passive, submissive, and feminine. The socialization process and sex role stereotyping have led to a number of problems. There is sex discrimination in employment, with men who work full time being paid nearly twice as much as women who work full time. There are double standards of conduct between males and females. There are power struggles between males and females because men are socialized to be dominant in interactions with women, while women often seek equalitarian relationships. Sex role stereotyping and the traditional female role has led women to be unhappier in marriages and to be more depressed.

Sex role stereotyping is pervasive in our society, with aspects being found in child-rearing practices, the educational system, religion, contemporary psychological theories, our language, mass media, the business world, marriage and family patterns, and our political system.

It is almost impossible for a woman to fully fill the traditional model women role—to have the "Miss America" look, to be feminine, passive, submissive, expressive, and to be "sugar and spice and everything nice." To try to fill such stereotypes has led to considerable unhappiness and distress.

The women's movement that had a resurgence in the 1960s is revolutionalizing sex role stereotypes and the socialization process. A number of laws forbidding sex discrimination have been enacted. Women as well as men are pursuing new careers and are taking on roles and tasks that run counter to traditional sex stereotypes. The androgyny notion is gaining strength and involves people exploring a broad range of role playing possibilities and choosing to express emotions and behaviors without regard to sex role stereotypes.

Interestingly, the women's movement probably has as many payoffs for males as it does for females. Males also find it extremely difficult and encounter many problems in trying to fulfill the stereotypes of the model man role—to always be dominant, strong, never depressed or anxious, to hide emotions, to be the provider, to be self-reliant, aggressive, brave, and to never cry. Men are gradually realizing that the stereotyped model man role limits the opportunities open to them in terms of interpersonal relationships, occupations, emotional expression, and domestic activities.

The profession of social work has made commitments to eliminate sexism within the profession and in the broader society. Although 60 percent of practicing social workers are female, more males are concentrated in administrative and other leadership positions in social work. Social workers need to become skilled in helping clients to actualize themselves, and to stop being negatively influenced by sex role stereotypes.

NOTES

1. U.S. Bureau of the Census, "Money Income and Poverty Status of Families and Persons in the United States: 1977," in *Current Population Reports*, advanced report, Series P–60, no. 116 (Washington, D.C.: U.S. Government Printing Office, 1978).

2. Clarice Stasz (Stoll), *Female and Male: Socialization, Social Roles, and Social Structure*, 2d ed. (Dubuque, Iowa: William C. Brown, 1978).

3. Joseph H. Fichter and Virginia K. Mills, "The Status of Women in American Churches," *Church and Society*, September–October 1972.

4. Thomas Sullivan et al., *Social Problems* (New York: Wiley, 1980), p. 464.

5. Francine D. Blair, "Women in the Labor Force: An Overview," in *Women: A Feminist Perspective*, ed. Jo Freeman (Palo Alto, Calif.: Mayfield Publishing, 1979), p. 272.

6. Sullivan et al., *Social Problems*, p. 452.

7. John Money, J. G. Hampson, and J. L. Hampson, "An Examination of Some Basic Sexual Concepts: The Evidence of Human Hermaphroditism," *Bulletin of the John Hopkins Hospital*, 1955, pp. 301–9.

8. H. L. Rheingold and K. V. Cook, "The Contents of Boys' and Girls' Rooms as an Index of Parents' Behavior," *Child Development* 46 (June 1975): 461.

9. Eleanor Maccoby and Carol Jacklin, *The Psychology of Sex Differences* (Stanford, Calif.: Stanford University Press, 1974).

10. Ibid.

11. Clarice Stasz Stoll, ed., *Sexism: Scientific Debates* (Reading, Mass.: Addison-Wesley, 1973).

12. Warren Farrell, *The Liberated Man* (New York: Random House, 1975).

13. Sullivan et al., *Social Problems*, p. 455.

14. Betty Friedan, *The Feminine Mystique* (New York: Dell Books, 1963).

15. Sullivan et al., *Social Problems*, p. 475.

16. Paul B. Horton and Gerald R. Leslie, *The Sociology of Social Problems*, 6th ed. (Englewood Cliffs, N.J.: Prentice-Hall, 1978), p. 424.

17. Ibid., p. 24.

18. Sullivan et al., *Social Problems*, pp. 475–76.

19. Horton and Leslie, *Sociology of Social Problems*, p. 423.

20. "$2 Million Settlement Is Reported in Women's Bias Suit against NBC," *New York Times* February 13, 1977.

21. "ERA Stalled, But Women Make Piecemeal Gains," *U.S. News & World Report*, August 20, 1979, p. 56.

22. U.S. Bureau of the Census, "Money Income and Poverty Status."

23. Sullivan et al., *Social Problems*, p. 466.

24. Alice Rossi, "Status of Women in Graduate Departments of Sociology, 1968–1969," *American Sociologist* 5 (1970): 1–12; Rita James Simon et al., "The Woman Ph.D.: A Recent Profile," *Social Problems* 15 (Autumn 1967): 221–36.

25. Lloyd Shearer, "Missing Half," *Parade*, July 27, 1980, p. 7.

26. "Women and Power—A Status Report," *New York Times*, May 1, 1977, sec. 3, pp. 1, 4.

27. U.S. Bureau of the Census, "Money Income in 1976 of Families and Persons in the United States," in *Current Population Reports*, Series P-60, no. 114 (Washington, D.C.: U.S. Government Printing Office, July 1978).

28. Sullivan et al., *Social Problems*, p. 468.

29. Ibid., p. 468.

30. Richard M. Levinson, "Sex Discrimination and Employment Practices: An Experiment with Unconventional Job Enquiries," *Social Problems* 22 (April 1975): 533–43.

31. Peter J. Weston and Martha T. Shuch Mednick, "Race, Social Class, and the Motive to Avoid Success in Women," *Journal of Cross-Cultural Psychology* 1 (September 1970): 283–91; Matina S. Horner, "Toward an Understanding of Achievement-Related Conflicts in Women," *Journal of Social Issues* 28, no. 2 (1972): 157–75; Lois Wladis Hoffman, "Fear of Success in Males and Females," *Journal of Consulting and Clinical Psychology* 42 (April 1974): 353–58.

32. Horton and Leslie, *Sociology of Social Problems*, p. 424.

33. Sullivan et al., *Social Problems*, pp. 460–65.

34. Lenore Weitzman, et al., "Sex Role Socialization in Picture Books for Preschool Children," *American Journal of Sociology* 72 (May 1972): 1125–50; Sullivan et al., *Social Problems*, p. 463.

35. Marcia Guttentag and Helen Bray, "Teachers as Mediators of Sex Role Standards," in *Beyond Sex Roles*, ed. Alice Sargent (St. Paul, Minn.: West Publishing, 1977), pp. 395–411.

36. Pam Maye and Sara McMillan, "Student Project," in *Masculine, Feminine or Human?* ed. Janet Saltzman Chafetz (Itasca, Ill.: F. E. Peacock, 1974).

37. Charles H. Cooley, *Social Organization* (New York: Scribner, 1909).

38. Matina Horner, "Fail: Bright Women," *Psychology Today*, November 1969, pp. 36–38; Vivian Gornick, "Why Women Fear Success," *MS*, Spring 1972, pp. 50–53.

39. Viola Klein, *The Feminine Character: History of an Ideaology* (Urbana, Ill.: University of Illinois Press, 1975.

40. Sullivan et al., *Social Problems*, p. 463.

41. See Judd Marmor, "Changing Patterns of Femininity," in *Family in Transition*, ed. Arlene S. Skolnick and Jerome H. Skolnick (Boston: Little Brown, 1971), pp. 210–21.

42. Horton and Leslie, *Sociology of Social Problems*, p. 420.

43. Jessie Bernard, "The Paradox of the Happy Marriage," in *Women in Sexist Society*, ed. Vivian Gornick and Barbara K. Moran (New York: Basic Books, 1971), pp. 145–62.

44. Pauline B. Bart, "Depression in Middle-Aged Women," in *Women in Sexist Society*, ed. Vivian Gornick and Barbara K. Moran (New York: Basic Books, 1971), pp. 163–86.

45. Carol Tarvis and Carole Offir, *The Longest War: Sex Differences in Perspective* (New York: Harcourt Brace Jovanovich, 1976), p. 223.

46. Deborah S. David and Robert Brannon, eds., *The Forty-Nine Percent Majority: The Male Sex Role* (Reading, Mass.: Addison-Wesley, 1976).

47. Ibid., pp. 53–54.

48. Carl Glassman, "How Lady Cops Are Doing," *Parade*, July 27, 1980, pp. 4–5.

49. Jack Sawyer, "On Male Liberation," in *Men and Masculinity*, ed. Joseph H. Pleck and Jack Sawyer (Englewood Cliffs, N.J.: Prentice-Hall, 1974), p. 172.

50. "Now, Men Are Going for 'Women's Jobs,'" *U.S. News & World Report*, October 16, 1978, pp. 97–98.

51. Sullivan et al., *Social Problems*, p. 474.

52. Horton and Leslie, *Sociology of Social Problems*, pp. 425–26.

53. U.S. Bureau of the Census, *Statistical Abstract of the United States, 1978* (Washington, D.C.: U.S. Government Printing Office, 1978), pp. 418–21.

54. David Fanshel, "Status Differentials: Men and Women in Social Work," *Social Work* vol. 21 (November 1976): 450–51.

55. Allen Rubin and G. Robert Whitcomb, eds., *Statistics on Social Work Education in the United States, 1978* (New York: Council on Social Work Education, 1979), p. 10.

56. Juliana Szakacs, "Is Social Work a Woman's Profession?" *Womanpower: A Quarterly Newsletter of the Committee on Women in Social Welfare*, February 1977, p. 3.

57. Fanshel, "Status Differentials," p. 452.

58. Rubin and Whitcomb, eds., *Statistics on Social Work Education*, p. 37.

59. Mary Ann Mahaffey, "Sexism and Social Work," *Social Work* 21 (November 1976): p. 419.

60. Ketayun H. Gould, "Sexism" in *Contemporary Social Work*, ed. Donald Brieland, Lela Costin and Charles Atherton, 2d ed. (New York: McGraw-Hill, 1980), p. 429.

61. Ibid., pp. 427–28.

GUSTAFSON

chapter **10**

HUMAN TIME BOMB FACTORY

AUTOBIOGRAPHY OF A BITTER INMATE REVIEWING HIS CRIMES AND PRESENTING HIS VIEW OF LIVING CONDITIONS IN PRISON*

It is a scientific principle that any "body" put under enough pressure will explode. We as people are no exception to this rule.

Upon entering prison one is told that if he breaks an institutional rule, he will be given a ticket or a report by an officer and if one has too many tickets he will not make parole. The institutional rules are so broad that they encompass everything from not wearing socks (no show for two weeks) to masturbation (10 days in the hole). The prison officials are using the inmates' desire for freedom to force conformity. By this they are putting the inmates under pressure. This is not the only source of pressure.

Upon entering prison, the "fish" (new inmate) is put under pressure by the older "cons" to conform to the convicts' code of ethics, which consists of rules such as no telling on other inmates, no talking to the officers unless he speaks first, etc.

If the "fish" is young (I first entered this place at the age of 17. Since then I have been on the "streets" twice, the times I was out. Both times does not amount to 7 months. I am now 25 years old), white, and good looking, pressure (The pressure is both physical and mental. One inmate from a gang will jump on a new inmate and take him to the hole. Pressure will be put on this inmate by the officers to tell why the fight started. Once this inmate is let out of the hole another inmate will jump on him and take him to the hole) will be applied by the older "cons" to make him a "queen." If a new inmate shows any sign of fear, pressure will be applied for his commissary.

Crime and correctional services

The institutional rules and the convicts' code of ethics are in direct conflict with each other. The inmate is in the middle with both sides trying to claim him. Each day I hear officials ask why? Why did this model inmate suddenly explode? The answer is simple—pressure or tension. The prison are nothing more than bomb factories. Through pressure, they are creating "human time bombs" which will either explode in prison or on the streets once an inmate is released. . . .

As I sit alone in this cage with nothing to do but time, I try to figure out how I arrived at this diabolical place, prison. As I gaze through the thin shadow that separates the past from the present, I can begin to grasp some of the influences and factors that I allowed to chart my course down this one way, dead-end street that only leads to prison, or even worse, the death house.

I was born in 1944 in Chicago, the youngest of five children, four boys and one girl. I experienced a normal childhood until at the young and tender age of six "God" took my mother to Heaven. I couldn't quite understand God's reasoning. All I was told was that my mother was now happier than she was on earth. Yet, this did not alter or lessen my feelings of loneliness and emptiness. "God" is happy. My mother is happy. My father is drunk, and I am alone and scared for the first time in my life.

In my grief I turned to my brother Bill, the second youngest of us "kids," and to my sister Cindy, but they were too heart sick to be bothered with my problems. I wanted love, attention, recognition, understanding—in other words I wanted my mother. People offered empty words and told me that they knew how I felt, but how could they (I thought)?

I got my love, attention, and recognition (but not understanding) in my own way. By the time I reached the age of (reason?) seven I had already taken my first steps down the cold, lonely and vicious street that brought me to my present station in life. Blindly I followed this street, never questioning where it would lead me. I had a police record for petty theft (shoplifting) and vandalism. At the age of nine I was arrested with another youth for breaking into his grandmother's house. As a result of this arrest I was confined for the first time in a cage like some wild animal. In this man made hell, I first came to know and live with fear. I can clearly remember how I tried to hide the tears in my eyes and the fear in my heart. I feared not only the other "kids" from age eight to eighteen, blacks and Mexicans and whites—but also the "men" in charge.

These "men" would ask who needed to use the washroom. If you raised your hand, the "men" would have you form a line in the hall—and then make you do five hundred knee-bends or one hundred, depending on how you had to use the washroom. A piss was only a hundred knee-bends, but to take a shit was worth five hundred. It was common to be slapped or kicked around by these "men."

During later confinements in the delinquency I found that they also had "women nurses." These women "nurses" would have the male patients strip and shower in front of them. I know! I will never forget the embarassment of stripping down in front of these "nurses" with their eyes bulbing. I was sent to the dispensary to have my lip stitched up (from a fight I was involved in) and before I could get any medical attention I had to take a shower.

At the age of eleven I was committed to the Illinois Home for Boys. I was committed manifestly as a truant, but actually it was for burglary and auto-theft. The conditions there were bad but they seemed bearable compared to other institutions. Today as I write this, June 1, 1969, orphans and unwanted children are still confined with the hard core delinquents of the streets. But thank God (if there is a God) money has finally been appropriated for a new detention home where orphans will be separated from the delinquents.

I was shocked to find out that this new institution was not like the rumors and tales I had been told. In the two and one half months I was there, on my first visit, I completed my fifth and sixth years of grade school. The detention was in my somewhat subjective views, a place where rehabilitation is possible. Rehabilitation may be taught there, but it seldom lasts when a person returns to his own mileux. The speed limit increases on this road as one gets closer to the end. After three trips I was quickly promoted to two "camps." Both of these camps have great merit as far as helping youth goes. They taught me the meaning of trust, how to work and earn money (one dollar a day.). There are limits however, in that they take a child out of his home environment where his problems exist and cure him in a new environment. Then they place him back where his problems began.

I reached the end of my road, as a delinquent, when I arrived at Kampell. This is the state's institution for the hardest juvenile offenders. The conditions there were the worst I have encountered in a state run institution. If you broke the rules of this institution you were put in the hole. The hole consists of two doors, one of bars and the other of plate steel, and walls and floors and ceiling of concrete. There were no lights. You were stripped naked and given one blanket. The guards would throw water on you if you acted wrong, or if they just happened to feel like throwing water. The Officers were mostly middle-aged and weak. To compensate for their weakness they gave special privileges to big and strong inmates (a goon squad). These inmates would beat the hell out of other inmates in the hole. The officers also had keys of metal approximately six inches long. Many former inmate has scars on his face and head to testify that those keys had more than one use.

In 1961 a scandal finally reached society about the place. The warden and many officers were fired, and I often wonder why so many of these officers are now working here.

From my many transfers to different institutions, I was ready to enter the adult phase of this dead-end road. I turned seventeen and began a series of visits to various jails. I am sure that you are aware, due to recent expose's by the mass media, of conditions in these jails.

To state that this penitentiary is mismanaged would be the classic understatement. It is not managed at all. From the Warden right down to the newest officer, with very few exceptions along the way, it is run by heartless, poorly educated (in the professional sense,) insensitive bums, men who could not hold other jobs. Drunks on this Prison's security and custodial staff far outnumber drunks in a proportionate number of members in society. Old, decrepit, and vicious in their petty ways, the officers and Warden do indeed compliment each other—they, instead of the inmates, should be confined in cages—for they are in truth the animals.

The conditions and institutional rules of this prison are beyond belief. Sexual assault is so common it is to be observed by anyone who wishes to observe it. The filthy condition of the dining room where inmates eat, the poor quality of food, combine to make meal-times a dreaded occurence—and inmates who cannot suppliment their diets through the commissary, or through stealing, are indeed in trouble. While meat is sent here for the inmates it is never given to them. They literally receive the scraps from the officer's tables and the Warden's tables. Visitors see the Officers' Dining room and kitchen, and eat there. And no visitor comes here without receiving the full treatment: he is conducted by an officer, usually a Lt. or captain, on a tour of all the best spots in the institution. He sees the TV College, but he doesn't see the lack of academic freedom or the inefficiency of the College Director. He sees the New Administration Building, but he doesn't see the filthy conditions of the West or North Cell Houses, and never is a visitor allowed to try out one of the beds, or just stand in a cell and be locked in. It is a feeling the authorities, namely the Warden don't want the visitors to feel—the feeling of pity or disgust. Also, no visitor is allowed to walk alone among the inmates and speak with them freely. There is always a guard or two with a visitor, not to protect the visitor, that isn't necessary at all, but to prevent the visitor from walking among the men and learning for himself what conditions are like. It is indeed strange that a man is expected to live in a tiny cell, while the officers are housed, the single ones, in large comfortable (by comparison) rooms in the officers quarters, and not become bitter. It is indeed even stranger that a man is expected to become rehabilitated, while observing such conduct by the officers and the warden—conduct that shows how retarded society is—how ill informed. What man is rehabilitated by a surrounding of political corruption, signs of criminal activity on the part of the Warden and many officers. What man can be helped to a state of resocialization by officers who can see views only through contempt-filled eyes, and a warden who cares nothing at all about their problems. As long as the Warden makes a good impression on the visitors, representatives of society, he doesn't give a damn about us. But let us embarrass him and look out! Memos fly from his desk at a torrid rate.

Every aspect of this prison and this warden is a hindrance to rehabilitation. Corruption walks hand-in-hand with inefficiency, callousness strides forward with progressive stupidity, and the road the inmates follow to get here—that well worn road to dead-end—leads them back again, and again, and again. Or it leads them to suicide, violent death, or moral degenerate behavior.

This is how I view this prison, the man and his merry band of accomplices. Can I be rehabilitated here, never in a million years. I can realize a personal need for rehabilitation, but the most I can do here is hang on, and pray that I will be strong enough to rehabilitate myself after my release from here.

* This autobiography is excerpted from *The Prison: Voices from the Inside,* ed. Dae H. Chang and Warren B. Armstrong (Cambridge, Mass.: Schenkman Publishing Co., 1972), pp. 157–64. Permission to reprint has gratefully been received from the copyright owners. This autobiography is reprinted using the inmate's own words and grammar.

It should be noted the specific charges made by this inmate have not been verified. However, without a doubt, living conditions within prison are not that "nice." One reason is that society is trying to punish those confined for having committed one or more crimes that are not "nice" either. In the following excerpt from an autobiography and inmate describes the crimes he and a friend committed.

DESCRIPTION BY AN INMATE OF THE EVENTS LEADING TO HIS INCARCERATION*

I was arrested in Chicago for "Aggravated Kidnapping, Rape, Aggravated Battery, etc." I was at this time 17 years old. I will not claim my innocence or guilt in this paper, since I am telling only one side of the story (my own), but I will relate the facts of my arrest and subsequent imprisonment.

I left work at the warehouse at approximately 5:00 P.M. on the evening of my arrest and returned home. At home I changed clothes, picked up a friend a couple of blocks from my home, and together we went to a tavern on 31st Street. We arrived at the tavern shortly after six o'clock, and began drinking. We drank, and played the juke box, until midnight. Both of us were very drunk by this time, but I felt well enough to drive. My new car was parked outside the tavern. It was raining quite hard, and had been for several hours.

We jumped into my car, with the intention of going somewhere to eat. My friend was only 18 years old, and looked it, so I ran into another tavern and bought more beer, then we drove to a popular drive-in restaurant. At the restaurant we ordered hamburgers, and ate them in the car with our beer. It was 1:15 when we left the restaurant, I remember the time because I was listening to the car radio as we pulled out of the parking lot. Only one block from the restaurant my friend asked me to pull into an alley so he could urinate. I pulled into an A&P parking lot, and left the car parked under a flood light so no one would accidentally run into it. From the parking lot I ran down an alley to an over-hanging garage roof, to get out of the rain while I urinated, and I didn't see which way my friend Bob ran.

As I stood under the garage overhang I heard two screams, and pulling my pistol I ran back toward the car. When I arrived at the car, Bob and a girl were in the back seat, so I jumped into the car. I recognized the girl immediately, she was the girl-friend of the leader of a rival gang. She didn't know Bob but she knew me, so she ceased her struggling with Bob. Bob shouted for me to start the car and "Let's go!" Knowing the screams, at that time of the morning, would bring people, I started the car and drove away. I was also shocked at the way the girl was dressed. All she had on was a pair of "baby-doll pajamas" and I figured Bob had taken her out of her home. Bob was telling her to take off her clothes, which she did, but she was asking me to make Bob let her alone. I pulled into another alley, about six blocks from where we had picked her up, and stopped to talk to her and Bob. Bob in the time I was driving had attempted to rape her, but hadn't succeeded. I told him to cool it while I talked to her. She wasn't frightened while I talked, but Bob was getting mad. She told me that her boyfriend and her Grandmother would "pay lots of money" if we didn't kill her. Bob really hated her boyfriend, and that remark set him off. He punched the girl in the face.

At that moment a police car entered the alley, and swept my car with a spotlight. I immediately fired a shot thru the windshield of the police car, and pushed the gas pedal to the floor. The police car gave chase. The alley was a long one, and I was traveling at approximately 60 miles per hour before leaving it. Near the mouth of the alley Bob cut the girl's throat and threw her out of the car in front of the police car. Naturally the police stopped. But other police cars were already attempting to block the area. Bob left the car about 15 minutes later, jumping out to run on foot, but I remained with the car until I wrecked it against a telephone post. Then I ran for approximately a mile, before becoming exhausted and taking shelter in the passageway between two homes. This is where the police arrested me. Needless to say, my treatment by the police was somewhat rough (an understatement).

The girl, who had somehow survived serious injury, was treated at the hospital and released.

* This description first appeared in *The Prison: Voices from the Inside*, ed. Dae H. Chang and Warren B. Armstrong (Cambridge, Mass.: Schenkman Publishing Co., 1972), pp. 40–42. Permission to reprint has gratefully been received from the copyright owners.

Crime is one of the most serious problems facing our nation. Former President Nixon remarked on several occasions that crime is our "number one enemy" and that "we must declare war against it." (Ironically, President Nixon and many of his top administrative officials later faced criminal charges—with some being imprisoned—in connection with the Watergate affair.)

TABLE 10–1 Number of reported major crimes—1978

Crime	Number
Murder	19,560
Forcible rape	67,130
Robbery	417,040
Aggravated assault	558,100
Burglary	3,104,500
Larceny-theft	5,983,400
Motor vehicle theft	991,600

SOURCE: Federal Bureau of Investigation, *Crime in the United States, 1978: Uniform Crime Reports* (Washington, D.C.: U.S. Government Printing Office, 1979), p. 35.

There are over 11 million major Crime Index Offenses reported to law enforcement agencies in the United States.[1] Major Crime Index Offenses are listed in Table 10–1.

TABLE 10–2 Crime clock

The occurrence of reported crimes according to time in the United States
1. Murder—1 every 27 minutes
2. Forcible rape—1 every 8 minutes
3. Robbery—1 every 76 seconds
4. Aggravated assault—1 every 57 seconds
5. Violent crime—1 every 30 seconds
6. Motor vehicle theft—1 every 32 seconds
7. Burglary—1 every 10 seconds
8. Larceny-theft—1 every 5 seconds
9. Property crime—1 every 3 seconds

SOURCE: Federal Bureau of Investigation, *Crime in the United States, 1978: Uniform Crime Reports* (Washington, D.C.: U.S. Government Printing Office, 1979), p. 6.

Undoubtedly all of us have committed one or more crimes in the past and have been a crime victim. In addition to the major crimes which have previously been listed, there are the following crimes which are classified by the FBI as being "somewhat less serious": arson, forgery, counterfeiting, fraud, embezzlement, buying and receiving stolen property, vandalism, carrying weapons, prostitution, drug abuse violations, gambling, child and spouse abuse, liquor law violations, drunkenness, disorderly conduct, vagrancy, juvenile runaways, and curfew and loitering law violations.[2]

It should be noted that most crimes are not "solved." One report found that for every 100 offenses known to police, there were only 21 offenses for which someone was arrested and 5 offenses for which there were convictions.[3]

GLOBAL THEORIES OF CRIME[4]

A large number of global theories (theories that attempt to explain the causes of all crimes) have been developed. To give the reader a "flavor" of such theories a few will be summarized.

Demonology was popular in primitive societies. The theory asserted that those who engaged in criminal activity were possessed by the devil. The only way to cure the person, it was believed, was to remove the evil spirit through prayer, a ritual, or by torture. Sometimes the entire body would be destroyed to remove the evil.

The *Classical School* was popular during the 18th and 19th centuries, and was based on hedonistic psychology. Classical theory asserted that a person makes a decision regarding whether to engage in criminal activity based on the anticipated balance of pleasure minus pain. Each person was assumed to have a free will, and acted solely on the

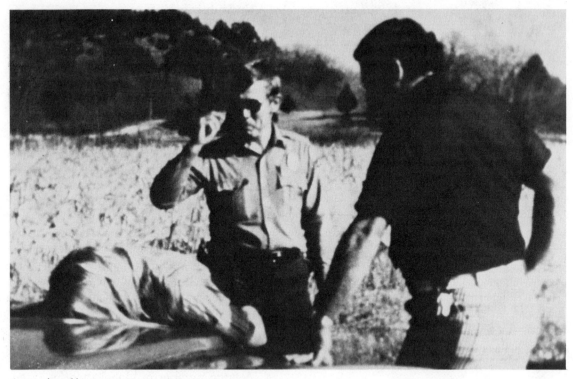

Arrest of a robbery suspect

basis of the anticipated hedonistic calculations. Advocates of this school assumed this explanation was a full and exhaustive explanation of causality. Applied to corrections, this approach urged that definite amounts of punishments be assigned to each offense in order that the prospective offender could calculate anticipated pleasures and pains. Also the penalties assigned should be slightly more severe than anticipated pleasures in order to discourage criminal activity. This approach has waned in popularity since the 19th century as it has been severely criticized for not allowing for other causes of crime, and because the punitive approach which it advocates has not been very successful in curbing further criminal activity.

Phrenology was popular until the turn of this century. Phrenologists maintained that crime was related to the size and shape of the human skull. The grooves, ridges, and number of bumps of a skull were closely scrutinized. The shape of the brain which was influenced by the exterior of the skull was thought to be sufficient to predict criminal behavior. Although there were isolated incidents where offenders whose skulls fit the guidelines of being "criminal-prone" were more harshly treated, this approach was not widely incorporated into correctional systems.

Marxist-Leninist theory assumes that all crime results from the exploitation of workers and from severe competition among people. Crime disappears, according to neo-Marxists, when society achieves a "classless" status. The basic tenet of communism is "from each according to their ability, to each

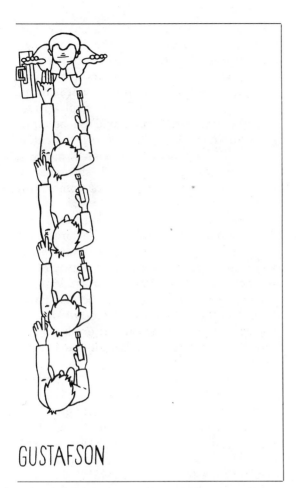

GUSTAFSON

according to their need." Communist countries continue to base their crime control and corrections policies on basic Marxist principles. Although Communist countries assert that crime will not occur in a classless, socialist society, criminal activity is occurring in these countries.

The *mental deficiency theory,* which was popular until the 1930s, asserted that criminal behavior resulted from "feeble-mindedness" which was alleged to impair the capacity to acquire morality and self control, or to appreciate the meaning of laws. As mental tests became standardized and widely used, it was discovered that many criminals achieved average or above average intelligence scores, and the theory waned in popularity.

Psychoanalytical theory is not a single coherent theory but a variety of hypotheses developed by psychoanalysts from the pioneering work of Sigmund Freud since the turn of the century. Generally these theories postulated that delinquent behavior results when the restraining forces of the superego (one's conscience and self-ideal) and the ego are too weak to curb the instinctual, antisocial pressures from the id. Psychoanalytic theory asserted that man's nature was basically determined by id instincts, many of which were antisocial and immoral in character. This theory postulated current behavior was largely controlled by early learning experiences. Deviant behavior was viewed as stemming from unconscious conflicts, fixations, and repressed traumatic experiences. The psychiatric school, of which psychoanalysis is a large component, has had a significant influence on corrections. Psychiatry has promoted the medical model approach to emotional problems. Criminal justice systems have given credence to this approach, and frequently request psychiatrists to determine the "sanity" of accused offenders. If an offender is judged by the court to be "innocent by reason of insanity," the offender is sent to a mental hospital, instead of a jail, to recuperate. Psychiatry has also categorized individuals into numerous categories in terms of their "mental" functioning. One category, "sociopath," has had considerable relevance for corrections. A sociopath was thought to be a person who had no moral constraints against engaging in criminal activity, and would do so whenever it was personally advantageous, even though others would be hurt. Since 1950 Thomas Szasz and others have seriously questioned the medical model approach to emotional problems, and have asserted that mental

Shoot-out after a bank robbery

illness is a myth.[5] Szasz asserts that people have emotional problems but not a "disease of the mind" as implied by the medical model. Courts, however, continue to use the mental illness model.

There is a wide variety of *sociopsychological theories,* only two of the more prominent will be mentioned here.

Psychodynamic problem-solving theories view deviant behavior as being contrived by the personality as a way of dealing with some adjustment problem. The problem is generally viewed as a conflict among various ingredients of the personality: wishes, drives, fears, strivings, loyalties, code of ethics. Situational factors are generally deemphasized as the problem is commonly thought of as a conflict within the personality.

Edwin H. Sutherland, who is perhaps the best known criminologist in contemporary sociology, advanced his famous theory of *Differential Association* in 1939.[6] In essence the theory asserted that criminality is a learned consequence of an excess of intimate associations with criminal behavior patterns; that is, whether a person decides to commit a crime is based on past and present learning experiences in intimate personal groups which define whether it will be advantageous to violate laws. This learning includes the specific content and direction of motives, drives, rationalizations, and attitudes; as well as learning techniques of committing crime.

There are many other sociological, as well as psychological, theories. The preceding summary, of course, is not exhaustive nor does it attempt to evaluate the validity of the theories presented. These theories identify a few of the reasons why crime occurs. However, all of these theories fall short of answering many crucial questions. There is no current theory which explains all the various types of criminal behavior.

Theories that attempt to explain all types of crime have a built-in limitation. Crime is a global label covering a wide range of offenses: purse snatching, auto theft, check forgery, prostitution, drunkenness, possession of narcotics, and sexual exhibition. Obviously, since the behavior exhibited by perpetrators of these crimes varies widely, the motives or causes underlying each must vary widely. Therefore, a theory that attempts to explain why crime occurs must give attention to explaining the wide range of motives for committing crimes. The theories reviewed above are not very useful in describing *why* one individual may commit a forgery, while another may commit rape, while yet another may burglarize someone, or why others do not commit such crimes. Without knowing why a crime occurs, it is extremely difficult (and unlikely) that an effective rehabilitation approach can be developed.

This author has developed a theory focusing on how to identify the underlying motives for committing a crime. In essence the theory asserts: *the reasons for any criminal act can be determined by examining what the offender was telling him/herself prior to and during the time when the crime was being committed.*[7] This theory is derived from rational therapy, which was described in Chapter 5. The *Charles Manson* case will be used to illustrate that identifying what a person was thinking prior to and during the time of the criminal act will explain why the crime occurred.

On August 9, 1969 actress Sharon Tate was slain in her home, along with four other people. The next night Leno LaBianca (a wealthy president of a grocery chain company) and his wife were brutally stabbed to death. In the weeks that followed Charles Manson and several of his followers were arrested and later convicted for these murders. Charles Manson was head of a commune, "The Family," that lived in Death Valley, California. Why did Manson and his followers commit these bizarre murders? Vincent Bugliosi, prosecuting attorney for the state of California, was able to document that the following thinking processes led Manson to order these killings.[8]

Manson hoped that brutal murders of the prominent and wealthy would create fear and panic among whites. Manson thought whites, unable to determine who actually killed these people, would conclude these murders were committed by blacks. Manson theorized that whites, out of fear, would go into the ghettos and start killing black people, thus causing a race war. Such a war, he thought, would also lead to a split between liberals and conservatives who would then begin killing each other. During this time Manson thought the "true black race" (at various times identified by Manson as the "Black Panthers" or the "Black Muslims") would go into hiding and would be unaffected. After almost all whites had perished,

the "true black race" would come out and kill the remaining whites, except for Manson and his followers who would be in hiding in Death Valley. Manson further thought that the remaining blacks would not have the capacities to govern the nation and that after failing to govern would then turn to him to be the leader of the nation (Manson was found to be "sane," and was convicted of first-degree murder.)

A BRIEF HISTORY OF CORRECTIONS

Punitive versus treatment approach. Current correctional systems in America and throughout the world contain conflicting objectives, some components are punishment oriented while others are treatment oriented. Manifestations of this confusions are the existence, side by side, of correctional programs intended primarily for deterrence and retribution, and others designed to reform offenders. Only rarely do punitive and treatment components complement each other. Generally the two components, when combined, result in a system that is ineffective and inefficient in curbing criminal activity. The only explanation for correctional systems having these conflicting objectives is "history." Current correctional systems cannot be understood without a knowledge of their development. This section will trace their development, beginning with primitive, nonliterate societies and follow their growth to the present.

The origins of the punitive approach began in primitive societies, who, as might well be expected, informally punished tribal members when they committed certain acts regarded as "wrong." Primitive societies' illegal acts were not always precisely defined, but were informally understood. The reaction to wrongdoing was varied, with the punitive reaction being only one of many reactions (others included acceptance, and excusing the lawbreaking). With the rise of the feudal system, elementary court systems were established. Wrongs were viewed as crimes; that is, as offenses against the group as well as against the victim. As a result the society felt they had a right and an obligation to react to lawbreaking. The usual reaction to crime became the punitive reaction, and severe corporal (bodily) punishments were sometimes administered. However, the philosophy that punishment by the group had some intrinsic value was not as yet clearly established. W. L. Lee supports this assertion by describing the objectives of punishment during the early feudal period in England:

> A detected criminal was either fined, mutilated, or killed, but punishment, as we now understand the term, was seldom inflicted; that is to say, the dominant idea was neither to reform the culprit nor to deter others from following in his footsteps. If a man was killed it was either to satisfy the bloodfeud or to remove him out of the way as a wild beast would be destroyed; if a man was mutilated by having his fore-finger cut off or branded with a red-hot iron on the brow, it was done not so much to give him pain as to make him less expert in his trade of thieving and to put upon him an indelible mark by which all men should know that he was no longer a man to be trusted; if a fine were levied, it was more with a view to the satisfaction of the recipients of the money or cattle or what not, than with the intention of causing discomfort or loss to the offender.[9]

It was only a few centuries ago, beginning with the 18th century, that it was widely advocated that inflicting pain on the offender had intrinsic value. Debates that arose around the wisdom and effectiveness of the punitive approach to lawbreakers gave rise to three schools of criminology in the 18th century: the classical, the neoclassical, and the positive.

The classical school was based on the doctrine of psychological hedonism, which maintained that people calculate the pleasures and pains of anticipated actions, and govern their behavior by choosing the action which will bring them the greatest balance of pleasure minus the pain. Applied to criminology, the classical school therefore advocated a measured, fixed amount of pain be applied to each criminal act. The amount of the pain needed to be definite so that the prospective lawbreaker could calculate the amount of pain, and the amount of pain needed to be slightly greater than the amount of anticipated pleasure. Also, it was asserted that the amount of punishment must be the same for all if it is to be calculated, regardless of social status, financial situation, mental capacities, age or other conditions.

The neoclassical school arose shortly after the classical. This school asserted the classical doctrine was generally valid, but needed to be modified in certain areas. Children and "lunatics" were not thought capable of calculating pleasures and pains, and it was therefore urged they not be treated as criminals or punished. Also, this approach advocated consideration of certain "mitigating circumstances," that is, crimes committed for self-protection. The neoclassical approach became in the 19th century the primary philosophy for designing Western criminal justice systems. The reaction to crime should not, according to this approach, be purely punitive. Some lawbreakers were recognized as accountable and deserving of being punished, while others were not viewed as being responsible, for a variety of reasons, and were therefore handled in some other manner than using the punitive approach. Individual responsibility was a key concept in this school.

In conflict with the classical and neoclassical schools was the positive or Italian school which held lawbreakers were not responsible for their acts and therefore should not be punished. This school maintained that a crime was a natural phenomenon, similar to an attack by a bear, the sting of a bee, a killing frost, or a hurricane. Lawbreakers who could be rehabilitated, should be. For society's self-protection (and not for punishment) society had the right to segregate (incarcerate) or put to death those who could not be reformed. Since individual responsibility was denied, the judicial system which assesses guilt was viewed as inappropriate.

Some of the seeds of the present treatment approach to criminals are to be found in the positive school. The trend during the last century has been a decrease in utilizing the punitive approach with a corresponding increase in using the treatment approach. Both approaches are now in vogue; at times they are used together in direct conflict. With the treatment approach, the social situation and the personality of the lawbreaker are studied. Needs of the individual are assessed, and reasons for his/her criminal behavior are gauged. Based on this study a treatment plan is then developed, which might include services covering a variety of areas: vocational, educational, housing, individual counseling, family or group counseling, medical services, job finding. If the criminal is a threat to society or continues to be involved in criminal activities, society should protect itself by segregating that person.

The late development of the treatment approach in corrections is understandable because its base, social services, is also of recent origin. Professional training in counseling and other social services was first offered at universities in the early 1900s.

The punitive approach to corrections

Varieties of punishment. Throughout history there have been various approaches utilized to punish offenders. These methods can be summarized as physical torture, social humiliation, financial loss, exile, the death penalty, and imprisonment.

Physical torture. Most societies have at one time or another used this method. Specific examples of corporal (bodily) punishment have included stocks, whipping, flogging, branding, hard labor, confinement in irons and cages, arm twisting, and mutilation of bodily parts. Corporal punishment was particularly popular during the medieval periods. Practically all types of corporal punishment are no longer assigned by European or U.S. courts.

Social humiliation. Actions to reduce the social status of an offender is another method of punishment. This approach flourished in the 16th and 17th centuries, and remnants remain today. Specific techniques included some that also had corporal punishment facets: the stocks, the pillory, the ducking stool, branding, and the brank. The brank was a small cage that was placed over the offender's head, which had a bar that was inserted into the mouth of the offender to prevent him/her from talking; occasionally this bar had spikes in it. Some of these methods were temporary, for example, the stocks, while others had a permanent effect on the offender, for example, branding. Although one of the objectives of the permanent methods was to curb future crime, they frequently had the opposite effect as they overtly labeled the offender, thereby making it difficult to secure employment and earn a living in a law-abiding manner.

Deprivation of civil rights is another approach to socially humiliate the convicted offender. In the Roman Empire anyone convicted of a serious crime would lose the right to hold office, the right to vote, the right to be a court witness, the right to represent another in the courts, and the right to marry in the future. The practice of taking away certain civil rights following the conviction of a serious crime has continued from the era of the Roman Empire to the present time. The principal rights that are taken away from convicted felons by most states in this country are: (*a*) the right to vote, while on probation or parole, (*b*) the right to hold public office, (*c*) the right to practice certain professions, for example, the right to practice law, and (*d*) the right to own or possess any firearms.[10]

Financial penalties. The practice of confiscating some of the offender's property imposing a fine) originated in early literate societies. Literate societies have, however, varied widely in their utilization of this reaction to a convicted offender. Originally, in early feudal literate societies, a victim could claim damages depending on the amount of the injury. At that time the king claimed either a part of this payment or an additional payment from the offender to offset the state's trial cost and the state's loss due to the disruption of the peace.

The use of fines in criminal law became widely used in this country about a century ago and is now by far the most frequent court approach to reacting to offenders. Sutherland and Cressey estimate that more than 75 percent of all penalties imposed at the present time are fines.[11] The advantages of a fine are: (*a*) it provides revenue to the state, (*b*) it costs the state almost nothing to administer, especially in comparison to the cost of imprisonment, (*c*) the amount of the fine can easily be adjusted to the enormity of the offense, to the reaction of the public, and to the wealth and character of the offender, (*d*) it does inflict a material type of suffering, and (*e*) it can easily be paid back if the alleged offender is later found to be innocent. A serious disadvantage is that it is highly discriminatory toward the poor as they have less ability to pay.

Courts are also increasingly requiring in their sentencing decisions that the offender make restitution payments to the victim, in line with the amount of injury. This kind of

Criminal court proceedings

reaction to crime is more treatment oriented, as it attempts to give the offender an opportunity to "make good." Restitution is, of course, also advantageous to the victim. Restitution and reparation are used most frequently for minor offenses. Generally, the offender is placed on probation, with restitution being a condition of probation. Much of the work of probation departments is now centered around being a collection agency to obtain restitution payments from probationers.

Exile. Almost all societies have exiled some offenders, but deportation on a large scale has only been used since about the 16th century. Most societies have, at times, exiled political criminals. The Roman Empire prohibited some people from entering certain areas (for example, the city of Rome) and also prohibited others from leaving a specified area (for example, an island to which they had been exiled). From 1600 to the time of the American Revolution, England passed laws which allowed courts to exile large proportions of their criminal population to America. This practice was strongly opposed by most colonies and ended following the American Revolutionary War.

Exile has also been used by many other countries. In the 16th century, Portugal sent offenders and prostitutes to Brazil and later sent criminals to Angola. Napoleon was of course exiled to a small island. Russia, since 1823, has been transporting certain offenders to a penal colony in Siberia. Italy transports some offenders to islands near its mainland. The United States continues to deport alien criminals. Many counties and municipalities in the United States give persons accused or convicted of a crime a set number of hours to "get out and stay out" of their jurisdiction.

Death penalty. The extent to which the death penalty has been used has varied con-

siderably in different societies. The methods used to execute offenders have also varied widely. The methods used to execute have included hanging, electrocution, shooting, burning, gas, drowning, boiling in oil, breaking at the wheel, the guillotine, stoning, the iron coffin, piercing with a sharp stake, the sword, and poison. In essence, almost every lethal method has at one time or another been used by some society.

The use of the death penalty in America has had an unusual history. In America "witches" were burned at the stake in colonial days. When the West was being developed, those who stole a horse or committed certain other crimes were sometimes shot or hanged (sometimes by a lynch mob or a "kangaroo" court). From the time of the Civil War until the recent past, blacks in the south who were thought to have committed a serious crime against whites (for example, rape) were sometimes lynched. Gas chambers, firing squads, and electric chairs have also been used in the recent past.

From 1967 to 1977 the death penalty was not used in this country, partly due to U.S. Supreme Court decisions that the penalty was unconstitutional. In October 1976 the Supreme Court changed its position on this issue and ruled that states may execute murderers under certain guidelines. On January 17, 1977, Gary Gilmore was the first person in a decade to be executed. The sensational case attracted national attention. The continued use of the death penalty is still a national issue.

The primary argument for using the death penalty for certain crimes is that it is assumed it will have a deterrence effect. This assumption is questionable as statistics show no clear-cut evidence that when a country adopts a death penalty there is a corresponding decrease in serious crime rates.[12] Also, there is not clear evidence that when a country discontinues use of the death penalty there will be an increase in serious crimes.[13] Additional arguments against use of the death penalty are: (*a*) it constitutes cruel and unusual punishment as it is the ultimate punishment, (*b*) if the convicted person is later found innocent, the penalty is irreparable, (*c*) the "eye for an eye" approach is inconsistent with civilized, humanitarian ideals, (*d*) the "right to life" is a basic right that should not be infringed upon.

In the past century there has been a distinct trend among nations to either decrease the use of the death penalty or to abolish it entirely.

Imprisonment. The penal system currently has enormous importance for our society. A large number of people are incarcerated each year. Nationally, the recidivism rate (return to prison sometime after release) is estimated to be over 50 percent, which raises questions about its effectiveness in curbing future criminal activity.[14] In the past two decades there have been several large-scale prison revolts (for example, Attica Prison, New York, in 1971 and New Mexico State Penitentiary in 1980) that have raised the concern of the general public.

Extensive use of imprisonment as a penalty did not occur until the 13th century in England, and shortly thereafter in other European countries. Conditions within prisons prior to this century were deplorable. Frequently the young were confined with hardened criminals, and women were not separated from men. Only custodial care was

Police officers entering a maximum security prison to quell a riot

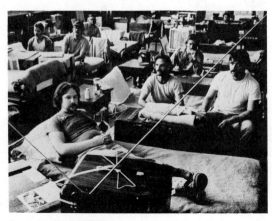

Overcrowding may lead to a prison riot

provided, frequently with "hard labor" work projects. There were a number of prison reform reports from 1700 to 1850 which criticized within prisons the use of intoxicating liquors, sexual orgies, gambling, and the personal lewdness of security officers. Some prisons confined inmates in solitary confinement for months at a time, and corporal punishment was also frequently used.

Since 1800, prisons have become more specialized. Jails are used for the shorter sentences, and for those awaiting trial. Separate institutions have been built for confining the young, for women, and for those labeled as criminally insane. Prisons also have varying degrees of security: maximum, moderate, and minimum. Special programs have also been developed to meet individual needs of inmates; for example, alcohol and drug abuse programs, educational and vocational training, medical and dental programs, recreational programs.

Prisons are still distasteful, and sometimes physically dangerous institutions to be confined in, but the horrors of prison life have been reduced. In addition to rehabilitative programs, improvements have been made in safeguarding civil rights of inmates, in diet, in abandoning long-term solitary confinement, in ventilation, in cleanliness, in physical facilities, in methods of discipline, in promoting contact between inmates and the outside world, in providing libraries, and in reducing the monotony of prison life. Gone are such humiliation approaches as shaving the head, chaining inmates, striped clothing, and the ball and chain. Also, corporal punishment methods, such as whipping, are no longer officially approved.

The first American institution built specifically for housing juvenile offenders was opened in New York City in 1825. There are now over 300 state and local training schools. From the outset it was contended that such institutions were not prisons, but schools to educate and reform the young. However, until the recent past most could be best described as prisons in terms of functions, methods of discipline, and daily routine. Even today a few are still prison oriented. One of the most significant developments in juvenile institutions has been the cottage-type architecture which

Prison cell block

provides a more homelike setting. The first were established in Massachusetts and Ohio in 1858. Such settings facilitate, but do not necessarily assure a treatment orientation.

Objectives of incarceration

The conflict between the punitive and the treatment approach to corrections is strikingly clear in our penal system. Until a few centuries ago the purpose of incarceration was to punish an offender. The recent history of imprisonment in Europe and America reveals an increased emphasis on treatment and a shift away from punishment. There are several reasons for this shift. Practically all prisoners return to society, and it is becoming increasingly recognized that punitive approaches alone do not produce the desired reformation. When an individual's behavior cannot be tolerated in a community, it is indeed a mistake to expect that locking a person in an artificial environment, without providing rehabilitative programs, will sufficiently prepare that person to be a productive citizen upon his/her return. In addition, in this era of accountability the high recidivism rate, an estimated 50 percent, is an unacceptable rate, especially since the annual cost of incarceration per inmate is several thousand dollars.

The more specific objectives for imprisonment are: (a) to reform offenders so they will no longer commit crimes, (b) to incapacitate criminals so they cannot commit crimes for a period of time, thereby protecting society, (c) to achieve retribution for the victim, and to some extent for the state, and (d) to serve as a warning to the general public, thereby having a deterrence effect.

A major problem with these objectives is that some components conflict. The infliction of pain and suffering is aimed at meeting the retribution and deterrence objectives, but most punitive approaches are counterproductive in having reformative value.

There are also some dangers with using imprisonment. Association with other offenders may result in prisons serving as "schools for crime" in which inmates learn additional lawbreaking techniques from other inmates. A second danger is that incarceration may label the offender as being a "lawbreaker." One variant of labeling theory is Cooley's "looking-glass self" concepts.[15] Cooley postulated that persons develop their self-concept (who and what they are) in terms of how others relate to that person. In the case of convicts and exconvicts, if they are related to as if they are "dangerous, second-class citizens who are law-violators," they may begin to perceive themselves as

Damage to a cell resulting from a fire set by an inmate

being "law-violating." If this labeling effect is in fact operating, it has critical implications for the rehabilitation process because if people incarcerated come to perceive themselves as being "law-violators" they are likely to play such a role upon their release. Sutherland and Cressey, in the same vein, state, "Hatred of the criminal by society results in hatred of society by the criminal."[16] Relating to criminals as being dangerous, and segregating and making them keep their distance (both while they are incarcerated and following their release) may force them into a career of criminal activity.

A third danger of long-term imprisonment is "institutionalization." Some prisoners, especially those who have had problems in adjusting to outside society, may become adapted to the prison routine. After several years they may actually feel more comfortable being confined (with their basic needs being met) than having to return to the world outside, which has undergone substantial change since their entry into prison. They also will have established a circle of friends, within the prison, from whom they receive respect. If they encounter problems upon their return to society (for example, securing employment), they may yearn, at some level, to return to prison.

The treatment approach

There are literally hundreds of treatment programs available in the corrections system. Space limitations prevent an exhaustive coverage of these programs, but a brief summary of major programs will be covered in this section. It is necessary, however, to remember that the punitive reaction has the continuous effect of decreasing the efficiency and effectiveness of treatment programs.

The policy of individualized treatment of offenders has been increasingly popular since the 19th century. Individualized treatment developed as a reaction to the classical school which advocated uniform penalties on criminals. Throughout history, however, there has been a dual standard of justice, with the rich and politically influential being: (a) much less likely to be charged with a crime, (b) much less likely to be found guilty when accused—because of their "character," their position in society, and because of better legal representation, and (c) much less likely to receive a severe sentence if found guilty. The handling of white-collar crimes is an example of this practice at the present time.

Counseling. Both one-to-one counseling and group counseling have increasingly been used in prisons, and by probation and parole officers in this century. The aim is to identify the specific problems of each offender (including the reasons that motivated him/her to become involved in criminal activity), and then to develop specific programs for meeting these needs. The needs may cover a wide array of areas, including: medical, psychological, financial, family and peer relationships, housing, educational, vocational training and employment. Attention is also given to the criminal's attitudes, motives, group and peer relationships, and rationalizations regarding criminality. The effectiveness of counselors (social workers, probation and parole officers, psychologists, vocational rehabilitation counselors) is somewhat mitigated by their "dual" role perception by offenders. Some offenders view them as someone who will be able to assist them with a wide variety of needs, while others view them as being members of a supervision/discipline system who are authority figures in control of rewards and punishments. With the second conception, offenders are reluctant to discuss socially unacceptable needs and motives, and reluctant to establish a close relationship for fear that information divulged will be used against them.

Prison education. Education in prisons has two objectives: (*a*) acquiring formal academic training comparable to schools, and (*b*) the broader objective of resocializing inmates' attitudes and behaviors. To accomplish these objectives prisons use TV programs, movies, libraries, lectures, classroom instruction in academic subjects (covering elementary, secondary, and sometimes even college level material), religious programs, group discussions and recreational programs. It should be noted, however, that the bitter attitude that inmates have toward prison and to the prison administration is an attitude that continues, even today, to interfere with accomplishing educational objectives.

Vocational training. The objective of these programs is to train inmates in a job skill, suitable to their capacities, that will prepare them for employment upon release. The quality of such programs in institutions throughout the country varies greatly. In many institutions vocational training is defined as the maintenance work of the institution: laundry, cooking, custodial work, minor repairs, dishwashing. For a period of time vocational training was considered to be the key to rehabilitation, but now rehabilitation is seen as covering many other areas.

Prison labor. Throughout the history of prisons the idea that prisoners should be provided work has existed. Unfortunately, idleness and monotony are generally prevalent. When labor was first introduced in prisons, it was seen as a method of punishment. England, for example, for a long pe-

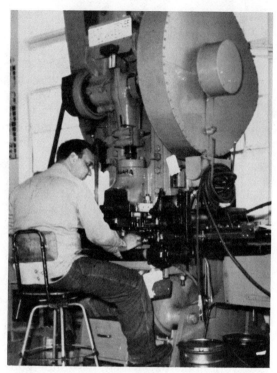

Making license plates in a prison

riod of time had inmates carry a cannonball on treadmills which had a meter to measure the number of units of work produced. For each meal inmates had to produce a certain number of units. Additional units were assigned for misconduct.

Currently there are two conflicting conceptions of work: (*a*) it must be productive and train inmates for employment upon release, and (*b*) it should be hard, unpleasant, or monotonous for retributive purposes. The latter view is still rationalized by some authorities as also having a reformative function as it is said to teach discipline, obedience, and conformity and to develop an appreciation for avoiding criminal activity.

Convict labor has been used to build roads, run agricultural farms, for fire fighting, for insect control programs, lumber camp labor, for doing laundry, making state license plates, and for a wide variety of other tasks. Huber Law programs in jails and work release programs in some prisons now allow inmates to work in employment settings during the daytime in the outside world, while being locked up in the evening.

Good time. Good-time legislation permits a prison review board to release a prisoner earlier if the prisoner has maintained good conduct. Most good-time laws specify that for every month of acceptable behavior, a certain number of days will be deducted from the sentence. New York state passed the first good-time law in 1817. Since then

most other states have passed good-time legislation. Good-time laws are designed to make inmates responsible for their conduct, to provide an incentive for good conduct and rehabilitation efforts, and to reduce problems with prison discipline.

Indeterminate sentences, which were first established in the 1800s, have similar objectives. Many sentences are now indeterminate in length, with a minimum and a maximum limit assigned to the amount of time an inmate can be incarcerated.

Parole and probation. Parole is a conditional release of a prisoner serving an indeterminate or unexpired sentence. Parole is

Auto body shop in a reformatory

granted by an administrative board (parole board) or an executive. While on parole, parolees are considered "in custody" and are required to maintain acceptable conduct and avoid criminal activity. Parole is designed to both punish (certain behavior is restricted and there is the threat of return to prison) and to treat the offender (a parole officer is generally assigned to counsel and help the parolee meet his/her needs). A primitive parole system was first developed in Australia in the early 1800s although there was little supervision or guidance after release. The concept of a parole system was first enacted in America by an 1869 New York state law.

Probation is granted by the courts and involves the suspension of a prison sentence of a convicted offender and giving him/her freedom during good behavior under the supervision of a probation officer. Probationers are viewed as undergoing treatment. There is, however, the threat of punishment; that is, being sent to prison should the conditions of their probation be violated. Similar to parole, probation contains reformation and retribution components. A Massachusetts law in 1878 was the first legislation authorizing a court to place offenders on probation under the supervision of a paid probation agent. Other states gradually adopted this alternative to incarceration.

Probation and parole officers have a "dual" responsibility, which has the potential of interfering with the rehabilitative process. One of the primary functions of a probation and parole officer is the "police" or authority role of monitoring closely the activities of probationers and parolees to observe whether they are violating laws, or violating the conditions of their parole/probation. Those being supervised continually are aware that the probation/parole officer has the authority to initiate procedures to revoke their probation/parole, which will send them to prison. Many probationers and parolees are distrustful of the criminal justice system and therefore wary of anyone (including probation and parole officers) who is associated with this system. This "police" role conflicts at times with the second primary function of probation and parole officers: the rehabilitative role. In order for rehabilitation to be most effective, the counselee must trust the counselor, must feel free to reveal socially unacceptable attitudes and activities to the counselor, and form a close working relationship with the counselor. Obviously, those probationers and parolees who view their supervising officer as primarily having a "police" role are apt to avoid forming a counseling relationship with their supervising officer.

Juvenile courts. The first juvenile court was established in Cook County, Illinois, in 1899. The philosophy of the juvenile court is that it should act in the best interests of the child. In essence, juvenile courts have a treatment orientation. In adult criminal proceedings the focus is on charging the defendant with a specific crime, on holding a public trial to

A young artist in a reformatory

determine if the defendant is guilty as charged, and if found guilty, to then punish the wrongdoer via a sentence.

In contrast, the focus in juvenile courts is on the future psychological, physical, emotional, and educational needs of children, as opposed to punishment for their past misdeeds. Reform or treatment of the child is the goal, even though the child or his/her family may not necessarily agree that the court's decision is in the child's best interests.

Of course, not all juvenile court judges live up to these principles, and there is a danger that court appearances by children can have adverse labeling effects. A Supreme Court decision in the famous *Gault* case of May 15, 1967 restored to juveniles procedural safeguards that had been ignored; including notification of charges, protection against self-incrimination, confrontation, and cross-examination.[17] Because of the adverse labeling effects of court appearances, especially with the increased formality of court procedures, there is currently a considerable effort to refer youth who are involved in "minor" violations to alternative, nonjudicial agencies, such as youth service bureaus.

SOCIAL WORK AND CORRECTIONS

The primary role played by social work in the criminal justice system has been confined almost exclusively to the correctional component of the system: as a social worker in a prison, as a probation and parole officer, or as a social worker in a correctional halfway house. There are only a few police departments that employ social workers to provide social services to individuals and families that police come in contact with.

In treatment programs it should be noted that individual and group counseling is only one of a variety of rehabilitation programs that may be provided. Others include religious programs, vocational training, study release, work release, and educational programs.

Many probation and parole officers are trained in social work. One of the important responsibilities of a probation and parole officer is to prepare a presentence report. A presentence report is a social history on the offender that is prepared to help guide the judge in sentencing. A presentence report is presented as follows:

PRESENTENCE REPORT

Walworth County Court
June 23, 1980

Name: James LaMartina

Address: 408 Walnut St.
           Delavan, WI 54987

Legal Residence: Same

Age: 34

Date of Birth: 5-8-46

Sex: Male

Race: Caucasian

Offense: Second Degree Sexual Assault

Penalty: Imprisoned not more than 10 years and/or fined not more than $10,000

Plea: Guilty on 6-10-80

Verdict:

Custody: Posted bail of $5,000

Citizenship: U.S.A.

Education: 11th grade

Marital Status: Married

Dependents: Two
(wife and a 4-year-old son)

Soc. Sec. No.: 393-42-9067

FBI No.: 287 1237

Detainers of Charges Pending: None

Prosecuting
Attorney: Richard Jorgenson, Asst. District Attorney

Defense Counsel: Donald Hauser

**OFFENSE:
OFFICIAL
VERSION**

Officers Karen Davenport and David Erdmier stated they arrested Mr. LaMartina in Lakeland County Park at 12:30 P.M. on June 5, 1980, while the offender was having sexual intercourse with a 17-year-old minor. Mr. LaMartina and the minor were in the backseat of the offender's car and were reported to be unclothed.

Mr. LaMartina stated he had met the woman in Don's Hillside Tavern earlier in the day. He stated this was the first time he had met her, and did not know her age—he assumed she was an adult. A check with Donald Leesburg, owner of the tavern, indicated that Mr. LaMartina was a frequent patron of the tavern, but that the woman was not a regular patron. The owner further stated the night of June 5, 1980 was busy. He noted Mr. LaMartina was there earlier that evening, but he was unaware whether Mr. LaMartina had met this woman at the tavern.

The minor appeared intoxicated at the time of the arrest. Identification the night of the arrest revealed her age to be 17 years and two months. She was returned home by the police to her parents who were very angry, and her father had to be restrained by officers Davenport and Erdmier from physically hitting her.

**DEFENDANT'S
VERSION OF
OFFENSE**

Mr. LaMartina stated he frequently stopped at Don's Hillside Tavern after work with fellow workers of the construction company he has worked with for the past six years. Mr. LaMartina stated this evening was the first time he had met this woman. He mentioned he began buying drinks for her and for the two other women friends she was with. He stated she drank considerably more than he had. He emphasized that he assumed she was at least 18 years of age.

Around midnight he asked her if she wanted a ride home, which she accepted. He drove instead to Lakeland County Park, where he emphasized she willingly agreed to go to the backseat with him and willingly became sexually involved.

When asked whether he had become sexually involved with other women, Mr. LaMartina became defensive and refused to answer.

PRIOR RECORD

Date	Offense	Disposition
9-7-72	Disorderly conduct	$80 fine
10-11-76	Driving motor vehicle while under the influence	$210 fine and group dynamics course

PERSONAL HISTORY

The defendant was born in Fort Atkinson, Wisconsin, on 5-8-46, the oldest of two children. His parents were dairy farmers. He attended public schools and completed 11th grade. He received mainly Cs and Ds in school and left school to help on the farm. He had a number of friends in school and was active in several sports, including the high school varsity basketball and baseball teams.

The defendant's father, Leonard, died following a stroke when the defendant was 22 years of age. His mother, Loretta, is still living on the family farm in rural Jefferson County. The defendant ran the farm for six years after his father's death and then sold the cattle in order to work for Johnstone's Road Construction Company. The farm only appeared to be marginally successful when the defendant had dairy cattle. The defendant still plants and harvests crops on the farm.

The defendant's sister, Janine, is 28 years of age and has been married for the past six years to Dennis Richter, a dairy farmer in Dane County.

Mr. LaMartina has been married for the past eight years to Sue Heinz (maiden name). Sue is 32 years of age and graduated from Milton College 10 years ago. She taught elementary school for the first four years of their marriage but has not taught school for the past four years—since the time when their son, Tim, was born. She and James LaMartina have lived in the LaMartina's farmhouse since their marriage.

Sue LaMartina separated from her husband shortly after she heard he was arrested. She and her son are now staying with her parents. She has ambivalent feelings about her husband. She stated he can be a good father and husband, but she is intensely irritated about his drinking and about his staying out late at night with his "cronies." She stated she suspected he may occasionally have been having affairs with other women but this incident is "the last straw." She stated she is seeing a counselor at the mental health center and has contacted an attorney and is contemplating a divorce.

Mr. LaMartina stated he does not want a divorce and appears sincerely remorseful about the family problems he has created. He stated if he and his wife can reconcile, he will change his ways—will not stay out late or become involved with other women. Mr. LaMartina has asked his wife to jointly attend marriage counseling with him, but she indicated she is still too emotionally hurt and embarrassed to be able to discuss the incident and their future with him.

There is some evidence that Mr. LaMartina has been drinking to excess for several years. Mr. LaMartina denies this, but his frequent stops after work at a tavern and his past arrest record suggest otherwise. The future of his marriage, however, appears to be a more immediate problem needing attention.

EVALUATIVE SUMMARY

The defendant is a 34-year-old male who entered a plea of guilty to second-degree sexual assault. The defendant was arrested while having sexual intercourse with a 17-year-old woman whom he met, apparently for the first time, earlier that evening at a tavern. The defendant apparently did not know the woman was a minor. The defendant's wife has separated from him following this arrest and is contemplating a divorce. The defendant expressed considerable remorse about the embarrassment and domestic strife he has caused.

Mr. LaMartina has a four-year-old son and has no prior serious arrest record. He may at times drink to excess. He completed 11 years of schooling, and has run a dairy farm. For the past six years he has been a road construction worker. His employer reports he is dependable and has been a good worker.

RECOMMEN-DATION

It is recommended that the defendant be fined and placed on probation. If placed on probation the defendant expresses willingness to seek counseling for his domestic problems. This counseling should also at some future time explore whether he has a drinking problem. The future of his marriage, however, needs first attention.

Respectfully submitted,

Ralph Franzene
Probation and Parole Officer
State of Wisconsin

In the field of corrections there are certain factors influencing treatment that social workers need to understand.

Custody-treatment conflict. In prison settings prison administrators primarily emphasize custody. Over 90 percent of the money spent in such institutions goes for custody.[18] When custody policies clash with treatment programs, treatment almost always comes in second. Prison administrators are primarily concerned with preventing escapes, curbing riots, and calming internal disruptions. New social workers in prison settings soon realize rehabilitation is not the primary focus.

Social workers in prisons, just like probation and parole officers, are often viewed by offenders as part of the larger authoritarian bureaucracy that caught and convicted them. Many offenders are distrustful of social workers as they feel they are still "monitoring" or "policing" them.

Offenders' "con game." Since the 1930s the criminal justice system has promoted both individual and group therapy. Prison administrators and directors of probation and parole programs have required offenders to participate in treatment programs. Social work practice realizes compelling clients to submit to treatment interventions interferes with establishing the necessary rapport with offenders. Yet, enforced treatment is commonplace in corrections.

Offenders are highly skilled at "conning" professional staff through persuasion and manipulation. Perhaps the majority of convicted offenders disdain corrections. This disdain is strengthened when they see therapy being forced upon them. Offenders quickly realize they must participate in such activities as individual and group counseling in order to have a good record. If imprisoned on an indeterminate sentence (as is common in most states) a good record will get them released on parole sooner. If on probation or parole, participation in "treatment" programs, offenders believe, may help in getting the probation and parole officer to do things for them or help in getting the officer to overlook minor violations of the rules for probation and parole.

The social worker should be aware that many offenders who request professional assistance are seeking to manipulate the worker rather than having a genuine interest in self-improvement.

HOW TO REDUCE CRIME

In the past decade there has been a national effort, with millions of dollars being spent, on new ways to reduce the crime rate. Yet, the crime rate keeps rising.[19] Many new proposals continue to be advanced: such as, (*a*) improved training for police officers, (*b*) expanding rehabilitative programs in prisons, (*c*) sentencing offenders to halfway houses or community-based treatment centers instead of to a distant prison, (*d*) increased use of probation and parole instead of imprisonment, (*e*) expansion of social services to multiproblem families to curb the development of criminal activity, and (*f*) decriminalizing certain victimless offenses such as prostitution and possession of marijuana. Space limitations prevent an exhaustive presentation of proposed new approaches to curbing crime.

One proposal, however, that has "promise" of reducing the number of crimes will be presented; it involves reducing the opportunity for crime to occur. This approach is being highlighted because it is an approach that *everyone* should be aware of and participate in.

Dae Chang describes this approach which developed from victomology, a new area of study in criminology:

Research shows that much crime—and by far the greatest portion of street crime and burglary—is the result of opportunity and luck rather than of careful and professional planning.

Someone sees an "opportunity"—in an open window, an empty house, a person alone in a dark alley—and acts on it. Muggers look for likely victims, not specific individuals; burglars, for a house they can enter, not a particular address. Preselected targets frequently are chosen precisely because they are seen as "easy marks."

Who is the victim of a crime? What causes crime? Who causes crime? There are some startling answers to these questions. In the majority of cases, the victim contributes, and in some cases is a major cause of a criminal act. All of us are potential victims. We frequently present the criminal or an individual with an invitation to commit a crime. We entice him, advertise to him, coax him, give him the opportunity and even implant the idea into his head. Through our carelessness, open disregard for our personal possessions, forgetfulness, attitudes, vanity, etc., we frequently invite someone to commit a criminal act either directly at ourselves or to our possessions. We also invite bodily harm upon ourselves by our actions in public and private. Our habits, attitudes, dress, etc., all are signals to the people who would be enticed into crime.[20]

In using this approach effectively one must keep asking oneself, "Is what I'm doing, or failing to do, making me vulnerable to becoming a victim of a crime?"

Precautions to prevent becoming a crime victim

1. Bolt lock doors and windows at home, and use exterior lighting to frustrate burglary techniques.
2. Engrave identification numbers on possessions to curb fencing of stolen property, which reduces the incentives for this type of crime.
3. If you are away from home for part of an evening, it is important to make the place look like somebody is home. Leave some lights on and some music as well. Or leave the television on, keeping it low so that it sounds like muffled voices. To someone outside it will sound as if either people are inside talking or the family is home listening to TV.
4. Double-secure sliding glass doors by placing lengths of metal rod or wooden dowels in the lower tracks to prevent the doors from being opened.
5. Put in exterior lighting over front and back doors of your home. Also, cut back close-in shrubbery around the house where it might be used to provide hiding for burglars.
6. If you hear someone breaking in at night, let the person know that you know s/he's there, but don't try to confront the burglar. If the burglar knows that someone is home, chances are the burglar will leave as fast as possible. If you confront the burglar unexpectedly, a fight may occur and someone could get hurt. Instead yell, "get the shotgun!" even when you are alone, or yell to the neighbors, or get on the phone to the police. One of the best places to have a strong, dead-bolt lock is on the inside of your bedroom door.
7. A small dog that barks a lot is a good deterrent to discourage a burglar from stealing things when you're away for the evening. The yapping of the dog will make the burglar wary that someone else will hear the barking, so the burglar will probably exit in a hurry.
8. Do not leave the key to your home under the door mat, in the mailbox, or on top of the door ledge.
9. Be cautious about inviting door-to-door salespeople into your home. Many communities now require salespeople to carry an identification card.
10. Do not leave possessions on lawns or in your driveway at night. If left, bicycles, barbeque grills, power tools, lawn mowers, and so on are easily removed.
11. Do not leave important papers, expensive jewelry, or large sums of money at home. Rent a bank security deposit box for security purposes. Security deposit boxes not only protect valuables from burglars but also from fires and natural disasters.
12. When going on an extended vacation make arrangements to have a friend check your home every few days. Do not let newspapers or mail pile up. The post office will hold your mail at no cost while you are away. Inexpensive light timers can be purchased to light a room or two during the evening hours to give the impression you are home.
13. When you are expecting someone to visit and you are unable to be home, do not leave a note on the outside: "Welcome—will be back at 8 P.M. Walk in and make yourself at home. Door is unlocked." Burglars readily accept such invitations.
14. Do not carry a large sum of money. If forced to carry a large sum, take along a second wallet, containing three or four bills and some expired credit cards, that you can give a thief if confronted.
15. When in a crowd, place your wallet in a safe place—for example, front pocket or a buttoned back pocket to frustrate pick-pocketing efforts.
16. Women should never leave their purses unattended.
17. Do not hitchhike or pick up hitchhikers. Hitchhik-

ing has led to a fair number of robberies and assaults. If you cannot avoid hitchhiking, be very selective who you accept a ride from.

18. Flashy equipment on autos will invite theft or auto break-ins. If you buy mag wheels, a stereo tape deck, a CB radio, fancy wheel covers, and other expensive gadgets you will draw attention to your car. The place where you park your car can be an invitation for it to be stolen or broken into. Be sure to always lock your car, put valuables in the trunk of the car, and never leave the key in the ignition.

19. If you are leaving your car someplace for a few days (e.g., at an airport) it is nearly theftproof if you pull the center wire out of the distributor—in addition to locking the car and taking the keys.

20. Leave identification off key chains so that if your keys are lost or stolen, no one knows what they open.

21. Women are advised to list only their last name and initials on mailboxes and in phone directories.

22. Avoid going alone to a dark parking lot. It may be cheaper to call a taxi than risk being mugged late at night.

23. There are a variety of approaches to avoid becoming a victim of rape, including physical techniques of self-defense (for example, the martial arts) and distasteful approaches (for example, informing the potential rapist you have cancer of the cervix or vomiting or urinating on the rapist). Cathryn M. Palesse has a review of such approaches.[21] Women should become familiar with such approaches and select a few that they would be comfortable with and prepared to use should an attack occur.

24. If you are confronted by an assailant, do not provoke the person. Most criminals are nervous during the commission of a crime. So try to remain calm, while trying to plan an escape without being harmed. If the assailant is a robber with a gun, try to make the transaction go as quickly and smoothly as possible. All it takes is a quarter inch of pressure, and off goes the gun. Only physically fight back if the assailant physically begins fighting with you. When fighting, two of the most vulnerable areas are the groin and the eyes. (Poking your thumbs assertively in the attacker's eyes will end the fight in your favor—it's a choice between you hurting the assailant or you're being hurt by the assailant.)

* These are only a few precautions. An expanded list is contained in Dae H. Chang, "How to Avoid Becoming a Victim of Crime," in *The Personal Problem Solver,* ed. Charles Zastrow and Dae H. Chang (Englewood Cliffs, N.J.: Prentice-Hall, 1976).

MAKING CORRECTIONS CORRECTIVE

Perhaps the first step in improving the correctional system is to clarify conflicting objectives. The present correctional system contains conflicting objectives, some are punitive in nature while others are treatment oriented. Manifestation of this confusion is the existence, side by side, of correctional programs intended primarily for deterrence and retribution, and others designed to reform offenders. Making life miserable for prison inmates is aimed at meeting the retribution and deterrence objectives, but most punitive approaches are counterproductive in having reformative value. A precondition for rehabilitative changes is an atmosphere in which recipients of services feel accepted, understood, and feel that others around them value them and are interested in working with them for their betterment. Such an atmosphere does not exist in prison.[22]

When the general public and public officials are confused regarding what should be the primary objective for incarceration, it is obvious prison administration officials and inmates will also become confused, and rehabilitative changes are unlikely to occur. With these conflicting objectives it is understandable that prisons are not very successful in reforming inmates, as shown by the high recidivism rate.

If our society decides retribution, deterrence, and vengence should be the primary goal, then we can expect a continued high rate of recidivism and continued high crime rates. However, from a society-benefit viewpoint it would seem the primary objective of a correctional system should be to curb future criminal activity of incarcerated offenders, in the least expensive way. Sutherland and Cressey document that almost all persons who are imprisoned are at some later date released.[23]

The current prison system is not only ineffectual in preventing recidivism, it is also expensive. The national average per capita cost for institutionalization of adult felons is about 14 times greater than the cost of probation services to adults.[24] It costs over $10,000 per year to keep a person in prison.[25]

If the correctional system had rehabilitation as its primary objective there would be a number of changes in the system. For example, sentencing wrongdoers is now primarily based on the nature of their past deeds. If a person committed several serious felonies, incarceration for a number of years is the likely sentence. But a reformative approach would, instead, similar to juvenile courts, primarily focus the supervision plan (that is, sentence) on the needs of the supervisee.[26] Needed services would be specified, and the responsibilities of the supervisee would be identified and may include a variety of requirements; such as maintaining or securing employment, enrollment in an educational or vocational program, receiving counseling or family therapy, undergoing medical or dental treatment, payment of debts, restitution. Removal from society would generally be used only after the supervisee failed to meet requirements of the supervision plan (for example, restitution) or when the supervisee was a definite threat to society.

I, however, am not advocating a "soft" correctional system that would excuse offenders from being accountable for their wrongdoing and relieve them of accepting future responsibilities. Rather a system is being advocated in which offenders, with professional assistance, assess their needs and goals and are treated as responsible individuals (with having to accept the consequences of their behavior and irresponsible actions). A system is urged in which supervisees would become acutely aware that they have the choice and the responsibility to decide which of two avenues they desire to pursue: (a) continuation of criminal activity following their release which will result in continued conflict with the law and probable return to a prison in the future, or (b) a more law-abiding, productive and respectful fu-

ture. If they choose the latter, they would be informed there are services (educational, vocational training) available to assist, but they would also be made aware that improving their situation requires being a responsible person and putting forth considerable effort. (This sketchily outlined approach in relating to and working with convicted offenders is based upon reality therapy.)[27]

The choice facing our society appears to be between a punitive system which enacts retribution but does not deter future crimes and a system that seeks to assist offenders in becoming productive citizens. The latter approach is not painless. It may include restitution to the victim, receiving counseling for personal or family difficulties, securing and maintaining employment, and enrollment in an educational or vocational program. All such activities require considerable work and effort, with the "pain" that is experienced being necessary as a means toward a goal. With a punitive approach, pain itself is the goal and usually does not have a result that is beneficial to the individual or to society.

SUMMARY

Crime is one of the most serious problems facing our nation. It is likely all of us have committed one or more crimes and have been the victim of a crime. Violent and serious crimes are of national concern.

A large number of global (comprehensive) theories have been developed to explain the causes of crime. Some of these theories were presented. One theory based on rational therapy asserts the reasons for any criminal act can be determined by examining what the offender was telling him/herself prior to and during the time when the crime was being committed.

One approach to reducing the high rates of crime results from recent research showing that victims generally provide opportunities for crime to occur. Everyone should be aware of precautions that should be taken to avoid becoming a victim of crime.

The history of corrections has moved from a punitive orientation to the present system which has both retribution and reformation components. The methods of punishment have also softened. Up until modern times, the death penalty and corporal punishment were frequently used. Courts have now turned to assigning financial penalties and using imprisonment. The objectives for incarceration have also undergone a change, from the punitive reaction to the present confusing orientation having both treatment and punishment objectives. The 50 percent recidivism rate of return to prison after release is currently unacceptable. In developing any program the first task is to precisely define and clarify objectives. The primary objectives of imprisonment are still confused.

The ways in which societies have punished convicted offenders are as atrocious as the atrocities offenders have inflicted on victims. Do we want the "eye for an eye" retributive approach which is ineffective in curbing future crime, or do we want something else?

NOTES

1. Federal Bureau of Investigation, *Crime in the United States, 1978: Uniform Crime Report* (Washington, D.C.: U.S. Government Printing Office, 1979).

2. Ibid.

3. Federal Bureau of Investigation, *Crime in the United States, 1974: Uniform Crime Report* (Washington, D.C.: U.S. Government Printing Office, 1975), pp. 37–42.

4. The following sections "Global Theories of Crime," "A Brief History of Corrections," and the subsections "The Punitive Approach to Corrections," "Objectives of Incarceration," "The Treatment Approach" are adapted from my article, "The History of Corrections," chap. 9, in *Introduction to Adminis-*

tration of Justice: A Syllabus and Workbook, ed. Dae H. Chang (Cambridge, Mass.: Schenkman, 1976). Permission to adapt this material has been received from the copyright owner, Dae H. Chang.

5. Thomas Szasz, *The Myth of Mental Illness* (New York: Hoeber-Harper, 1961).

6. Edwin H. Sutherland and Donald R. Cressey, *Criminology,* 8th ed. (Philadelphia: Lippincott, 1970).

7. Charles Zastrow, *Talk to Yourself* (Englewood Cliffs, N.J.: Prentice-Hall, 1979).

8. Vincent Bugliosi and Curt Gentry, *Helter Skelter* (New York: W. W. Norton, 1974).

9. W. L. M. Lee, *History of Police in England* (London: Methuen, 1901), p. 10.

10. Walter A. Friedlander and Robert Z. Apte, *Introduction to Social Welfare,* 4th ed. (Englewood Cliffs, N.J.: Prentice-Hall, 1974).

11. Sutherland and Cressey, *Criminology,* p. 317.

12. Ibid., pp. 331–36.

13. Ibid., pp. 333–34.

14. Ibid.

15. C. H. Cooley, *Human Nature and the Social Order* (New York: Scribner, 1902).

16. Sutherland and Cressey, *Criminology,* p. 354.

17. Alan Neigher, "The Gault Decision: Due Process and the Juvenile Court," *Federal Probation* 31, no. 4 (December 1967): 8–18.

18. Sutherland and Cressey, *Criminology.*

19. Federal Bureau of Investigation, *Crime in the United States, 1978.*

20. Dae H. Chang, "How to Avoid Becoming a Victim of Crime," in *The Personal Problem Solver,* ed. Charles Zastrow and Dae H. Chang (Englewood Cliffs, N.J.: Prentice-Hall, 1976).

21. Cathryn M. Palesse, "How to Avoid Becoming a Rape Victim: What to Do If You Are Raped," in *Personal Problem Solver.*

22. Dae H. Chang, Charles Zastrow, and Donald Blazicek, "Inmates' Perception of Significant Others, and the Implications for the Rehabilitation Process," *International Journal of Criminology and Penology* 3 (1975): 85.

23. Sutherland and Cressey, *Criminology.*

24. President's Commission on Law Enforcement and the Administration of Justice, *Task Force: Corrections* (Washington, D.C.: U.S. Government Printing Office, 1967), p. 28.

25. Ibid.

26. Nathaniel Canter, "A Dispositions Tribunal," *Journal of Criminal Law and Criminology,* May–June 1931, pp. 51–61.

27. William Glasser, *Reality Therapy* (New York: Harper & Row, 1965); and William Glasser, *The Identity Society* (New York: Harper & Row, 1972).

chapter 11

Call the phenomenon what you will, society has seemingly been ever perplexed and vexed by the strange, inexplicable symptoms of the malady, "youth." Six thousand years ago an Egyptian priest bemoaned the degeneracy of the times, as children no longer obeyed their parents. Socrates, in an often quoted paragraph, chastised the children of his day for their errant ways. Charles Dickens' account of organized juvenile crime and exploited children in *Oliver Twist* and Mark Twain's delightful tale of runaway Huck Finn made for good, if pointed, reading in the 19th and 20th centuries. Lively descriptions of outhouse tippings were sure to appear in the weekly papers around Halloween-time back in the early 1900s, merely examples of youthful exuberance.

Today we have the brutality of Hubert Selby, Jr.'s *Last Exit to Brooklyn* and the almost daily assault of news releases relating wanton criminal acts by children and youths, rich and poor alike. And, conversely, we

have children of all ages brutalized by jail confinement coexistent with adult criminals—confined for running away, for "being unmanageable," or "beyond parental control"—in violation of their legal rights under state Children's Codes, not to mention their human rights.

These runners have names. They are called Emily, Mark, Eric, Joseph, Willie, Jean, and Angela. They run against the tide—away from school, from boredom, from abusing parents, and from troubled selves; from troubled homes, indifferent homes, and happy homes; from troubled lives, from trouble—and into trouble. We label them juvenile delinquents. Their behavior ranges from passive aggression (tuning out in the classroom) to mischievousness (there are still outhouses in some rural areas) to uncontrollable behavior (defying family disciplinary measures and running away) to petty theft (shoplifting) to active aggression and crime (wanton vandalism, arson, and physical assault). They are age 17 and under. They come from all economic levels—affluence, middle-income, working poor,

* This chapter was written for this text by Ursula Sennewald Myers, ACSW.

Juvenile delinquency and current services*

A LOOK AT JOEY (OR PERHAPS A "JOSIE")

Joey: My Social Worker said I could write my Life History down for you guys because you are always getting the story from someone else's side. Peggy, my Social Worker, called it perspective, so here's my perspective on me at the present.

I am definitely not a rotten kid even though that is what my old lady usually calls me. She says "Hey come here you rotten kid." I don't answer until she calls me by my real name. Which is Joey. I am smarter than my brothers and sisters even though I can't read so good. (Do the people know that I am talking this into a machine? Huh? S..t. If they don't, you *tell* them!) My brothers and sisters are older than I am. Some of them are a lot older but they are still hanging around the house. They are a pain in the _____.

I look like myself, even though some people think I look like my old man. He works hard. I don't see him too much. My old lady works hard too and looks tired all the time. Their favorite stuff to drink is brandy. I've had some. It tastes okay. I like a hit off a joint better. You don't throw up from that.

My old lady is always behind in wash and stuff like that so I do my own laundry. I feel good when I see the clean clothes come out of the washer. It's a good thing I know how to do that stuff because that is part of my work project here at the cottage. Why they call this place a cottage beats me. There's no lake around anywhere.

The reason I'm at the Center is because I borrowed some soap and dog food from the super. My clothes were dirty and there wasn't any soap and my mother was sleeping and so I went to the store and took the soap. The dog food was right there and my dog was hungry so I took that too. So what's a little soap and dog food to a big super. It seemed a good thing to do because the dog was hungry and my clothes were dirty. You would think the man at the store would think it was a good idea to share—that's what they always tell us at school, you know—share the cookies and all that crap.

That's why I'm here at the center. I hope someone is feeding my dog.

COUNTY SOCIAL SERVICES,
CHILD WELFARE DIVISION

Social History–Joey J ——— Date of Birth: <u>11-2-68</u>

Early events

Our agency history predates the birth of Joey.

We were anonymously advised of probable abuse/neglect on the part of the J. family on 9-7-68 at which time our Child Welfare Intake Worker investigated and found no evidence of physical abuse, but a potential for emotional and physical neglect. Six children were found in the home, age eight and under, and all in various stages of undress. The parents were also there but had apparently been drinking and had neglected to feed the children. Our referral was made at 10:45 P.M. and the children indicated they had not eaten anything since breakfast. We were able to obtain the name of a close relative who was summoned and immediately took charge of the children as there was food available in the house, even though it had not been prepared. Mrs. J. began feeling very ill and it was found advisable to escort her to the Emergency room at a nearby hospital.

To summarize our continuing services, we subsequently provided intensive family therapy, Marriage counseling, referred to AA and the Alcoholic Treatment Center, provided homemaker and respite day-care services, financial counseling, referred to the health department for ongoing visits, and also referred to the county home economist for short-term follow-up. All these services were negotiated on a client contract basis. Schools were also contacted for co-counseling purposes.

Joey was born in the High Risk Center at _____ Hospital. He had a normal early childhood following a difficult birth. Involvement with the family was consistent and intensive for several years. Interpersonal skills improved. Mrs. J. appeared to be managing her responsibilities as home-maker and mother and to the best of our knowledge neither parent was drinking to excess after Joey's birth. Mr. J. continued to work at YY Company's main plant and provided an adequate income for this large family. On 2-6-75, Social Services was advised by the J.s that they no longer wished to be involved with our agency, and inasmuch as our contract was of a voluntary nature, and there had been visible improvement in meeting the children's needs, we agreed to discontinue services except at the client's initiative. After a wrap-up interview, the case was closed per above stipulation (of services at their request only).

SUMMARY

Current History

On 12-3-80 _____ County Juvenile Probation advised us of the referral to their department of one Joey J. by the _____ Police Department on charges of shoplifting. Prior behavior had included three counts of truancy, running away from home 6-11-80, shoplifting 8-4-80, and theft and property damage 9-16-80 (Joey "borrowed" a neighbor's bike because he would otherwise have been late for school). On all these instances, Joey was lectured and released by the police, except that the last incidence had involved informal contact with the Juvenile Probation Department. Joey's parents were advised before Judge _____ that their child had been arrested on December 3 by the _____ Police, and had been placed in their custody on that date, that subsequently a petition to find him delinquent had been presented to the court on December 8. The child was remanded to the Youth Shelter at the parents' request pending a hearing scheduled December 10. A guardian ad litem had been appointed by the court prior to the hearing. At the December 10 hearing, Joey was returned

Current information; status report

to the custody of his parents, with supervision to be provided by the Juvenile Probation Department. Procedures were in accordance with the *Gault* and *Winship* decisions.[1] Juvenile Probation was ordered to investigate and report the child's circumstances and recommend within 90 days.

On February 6 Joey was found wandering the streets with the family dog at 4:30 A.M.; on February 10 and February 27 similar instances occurred. Each time he was returned to his home with a lecture; Juvenile Probation was notified and would visit the home the next morning. They were advised that Joey was a "restless kid," wouldn't mind, and only cared about the dog. On 3-15-81 Joey was once again picked up for shoplifting (this time soap and dog food) and, after proper notification of parents and advising Joey of his rights, an emergency hearing was scheduled before Judge _____ to determine the best interests of the child. Attorney _____ continued as guardian ad litem. Both parents appeared at the hearing. At the informal hearing on that date, it was agreed by the parents, Attorney _____, and the Juvenile Probation Counselor that Joey be placed at the Mooring Clinic for a 90-day period of evaluation (psychological, educational, and physical). The family will be observed during Joey's weekend home visits. During the same period it is expected the Probation Department's home study will also be completed. The Agency's Assessment Panel will meet on June 1 and will then report to the court their findings at a hearing scheduled for 10 A.M., June 7, _____ County Juvenile Court. Recommendations regarding the disposition of this case are pending per that date.

Joey's dog was foster-placed with Police Officer _____ on 3-16-81. Mother and the three puppies are doing well.

and acute poverty. Their population cuts across all racial groupings. We will look at one of them, one who is not a real person nor an actual case but who is "real" nonetheless, and who is called Joey (or perhaps Josie).

What would the reader advise for Joey? How would the "problem" be approached? Should the family be perceived as the "identified patient"?[2] Is it within Joey, the child, that the causative factors lie? Is Joey engaging in acts we label delinquent out of perversity, or should these acts as in an earlier day, be simply called "mischief"? Is this child a symptom of our failed schools, churches, economic and social systems? Do we *really* want to save our children, or do we still mouth pious platitudes while building better bombs?

AN OVERVIEW

How do the social scientists view this dilemma? Their outlook is not encouraging.

First, the cause of crime has not been agreed upon by the academicians and practitioners. Some charge that social conditions such as the slum areas in the larger cities, are the breeding grounds for crime and delinquency. Others say that racism, discrimination, and unequal opportunity are the basic causes of crime and delinquency. Still others allege that our present public education system simply does not prepare the youth with a sense of security and responsibility which can promote delinquency and eventually criminality. Liberal critics say that unemployment, poverty, and self-degradation are the basic cause of crime and delinquency. Television, mass media, comic books and movies are blamed for the cause of crime and delinquency. As long as this diversity of opinion on the cause of crime exists, solutions will not materialize.

Second, almost all Americans, rich or poor, educated or uneducated, have engaged in some form of criminal activities. The rich rather than the poor, the educated rather than the uneducated, are the ones who escape this legal formality. . . . In this case, solutions are as simple as ridding society (of) the artificial criterion of criminality.

Third, society needs criminals in order to identify the non-criminals and in order to maintain social solidarity.[3]

Although theorists tend to vary° in their emphasis as to the nature and causes of youthful delinquency, they tend to agree that a basic problem is the conceptualization of delinquency. Conceptualizing the behavior as deviance merely means that the behavior is different from some other kind of behavior; that is, it either turns away from or is the direct opposite of a certain concept, action, or thought. What might be acceptable behavior in one culture or situation might well be considered wholly unacceptable in another. The norms of one society, culture, clan, or neighborhood are not necessarily the norms of another. Deviant behavior, then, quite possibly becomes situationally determined. Convenience, pragmatism and custom (sometimes called "common law") have thus merged to define certain behaviors on the part of young people as deviant (or turning away) and delinquent (or failing in duty).

The legal system has effectively determined who will be labeled deviant, or delinquent. (A discussion of juvenile justice and social work follows in a later section of this chapter). Gibbons describes the laws governing juveniles as "omnibus" and lists the offenses as,

> engaging in immoral or indecent behavior, exhibit immoral conduct around schools, engage in illegal occupations, knowingly associate with vicious or immoral persons, grow up in idleness or crime, patronize or visit policy shops or gaming homes, wander in the streets at night, habitually wander about railroad yards or tracks, are incorrigible, or deport themselves so as to injure themselves or others.[4]

He also provides a list of conditions under U.S. laws which are included in the statutory description of delinquency. There are 34, and the 5 most frequently found are as follows:

1. Violates a law or ordinance.
2. Habitually truant.
3. Associates with thieves, vicious or immoral persons.
4. Incorrigible.
5. Beyond the control of parent or guardian.[5]

Those of us in social work practice recognize the convenience of this last category as a catchall "out" for reluctant, exasperated, or incompetent parents.

Reed and Baali in their book, *Faces of Delinquency*, also briefly compared several state statutes, some of which vary as to age limit but few as to content.[6] Wisconsin's former Children's Code, like New York's, differentiated between a child (person under 18) who is delinquent,

> because he has violated any federal criminal law, criminal law of any state, or any county town or municipal ordinance that conforms in substance to the criminal law

and one who is allegedly in need of supervision, because:

> (a) he is habitually truant from school or homes, (b) he is uncontrolled by parent, guardian or legal custodian, or (c) he habitually so deports himself as to injure or endanger the morals or health of himself or others[7]

In most states, this latter group is labeled "status offender." But, in more progressive states, in an effort to avoid stigmatizing nonoffenders, such juveniles are now called CHIPS; that is, children in need of protection.

However, given our present juvenile justice system, and in spite of the efforts of a few enlightened legislators such as Senator Bayh, the parameters of the term *delinquent* can still be extended to include almost any behavior.

The key to being *labeled* a delinquent or not obviously lies in whether you are caught "acting out," to put it simply. Janeksela calls it the difference between being an "unofficial" delinquent (and estimates that over 90 percent of all people could be placed in this category) or one who has not been arrested, and an "official" delinquent, or one who has.[8] And once arrested, the frequency of the delinquency behavior, and arrests, increases. Thus, the true determinant of delinquent behavior is whether one gets caught engaging in illegal behavior or doesn't get caught. (Being adjudicated delinquent or not doesn't really seem to matter in the real world; even if the minor is cleared of all charges, the label follows the child in the community, particularly if it is a smaller city or town.)

Sociologists tend to perceive the term *delinquency* within a framework of social disorganization,

> including conflicts in basic values, a variety of social stratification influences including differentials in availability of legitimate means to attainment of cultural goals, widespread disrespect for law and order, the growing bureaucratization and impersonality of "mass society," and the racial and ethnic cleavages of a nominally democrat society.[9]

These factors present a sensible cause and effect framework for the concept of juvenile delinquency. Included in this framework are the theories of Durkheim, Merton, Cloward, and Ohlin[10] relating to anomie, differentials in access to success goals by illegitimate means, delinquent gangs, and social disorganization.

Poverty as a causative factor was brought into perspective as early as 1916 by William Bonger[11] and has since been incorporated into most theories, rather than viewed as the exclusive causative element. Differential association (or learning-by-doing in criminal groups) was first offered by Trade and later refined by Sutherland and Cressy.[12]

Vandalism at a school playground

The more contemporary sociogenic theories are equally as thought provoking and perplexing, as different and yet as unified. They essentially break down into two main themes, the classical theme of free will and self-determination of behavior, and that of determinism[13] (or what this writer calls external and internal "fate") and over which the person has no control. Matza, in his book *Delinquency and Drift* perceives the delinquent as "drifting" into this condition and attempts a combination of the two themes.[14] Cohen has proposed the delinquent subculture as cause,[15] with its rejection of middle-class standards and its own norm-set. Haskell has described the reference group theory (such as the family), and others the "gang" syndrome of adolescence as it relates to antisocial behavior. Cloward and Ohlin's now classic analysis of the development of delinquent norms, and the determinants of the varied norms within each system, *Delinquency and Opportunity*, discusses the delinquent gang in depth. They look at the development of delinquent subcultures, their unique, "extra-legal" lifestyles, and their life-patterns. The delinquent subcultures receiving their attention are

> what we call the "criminal subculture"—a type of gang which is devoted to theft, extortion, and other illegal means of securing income. . . . the "conflict subculture"—a type of gang in which the manipulation of violence predominates as a way of winning status. . . . the "retreatist subculture" a type of gang in which the consumption of drugs is stressed.[16]

Out of this arises the theory of differential opportunity systems.

How would Joey's situation be perceived by these theorists? Would the reference group analysts look at his family as the causative factor? Did Joey just slowly drift into lawbreaking habits? Was he influenced by peers?

Psychogenic theories go back to the days of demons, evil spirits, and ancient Egypt. The devil has been making people do bad things since time incarnate, and certainly has been a subject of intrigue in the late 20th century. The themes of free will versus determinism run through the psychogenic approach also. Is not the current "cost/benefit" approach to behavior and decision making really an offshoot of the old-fashioned pro/con list in reverse? Does not the Rational Behavior School (Albert Ellis and Maxie Maultsby) derive essentially out of the "free will" concept? And lastly, one of the chief molders of psychoanalytical theory is, of course, Freud, whose followers see antisocial, lawbreaking activity as deriving from inner conflicts, lability, and other subconscious emotional constructs.

Shall we send Joey to a group home or institution for the emotionally disturbed? Or shall we help him to look at his self-talk, particularly those "conversations" which take place at the time he is actually committing a deliquent act?

What of the biochemical causative factors? Little has been written regarding this matter, other than studies relating to the relationship of specific learning disabilities to school dropouts to juvenile crime. (We will discuss this area in a later section.) Might not an imbalance in brain chemistry or in the body's hormonal system lead to hyperactive, aggressive behavior? Fortunately, studies relating body and brain chemistry to mental illness and antisocial behavior are in process. In the meantime, it would appear that a conservative attitude toward mind-altering drugs seems prudent.

And in conjunction with biochemistry, what about the hormonal changes of adolescence. Could not the acting-out teenager be a "victim" of growing up, of maturation processes?

In a recent book aptly entitled *Juvenile Delinquency*, William Sanders develops the interactionist theory, one which seems to make sense.

> We can account for patterns of delinquency in terms of the likelihood of interacting with others who engage in delinquency, explain the various forms of delinquent activity in terms of the resources available to juveniles for establishing character, and account for an individual's involvement in delinquency by examining his association patterns and the value he places on establishing himself in terms of his peers. Finally, the sociolegal process is simply one form of the labeling process, in which situations and people are socially defined as delinquent or nondelinquent.[17]

(The above crime-causation theories are more fully described in Chapter 10.)

Just as definition, cause-effect analysis, and legal aspects are intertwined in a global concept of juvenile delinquency, so is history. And carrying this through logically, so is present reality. Young people were "acting out" long before a juvenile justice system was established in Cook County back in 1899, or the even earlier establishment of a Court of Chancery under English Constitutional law.[18] The concerns of Socrates and Charles Dickens were not figments of their imagination, but rather creative translations of their worlds. And gangs of rapacious youths were terrorizing the citizenry in the Elizabethan era, during the Industrial Revolution, and are even now, in midtown Manhattan, where an incident of gang-mugging of a middle-aged broker in broad daylight was recently related to this writer. The "gang" consisted of children eight and under. Their behavior was akin to Golding's *Lord of the Flies.* The broker no longer walks alone.

How extensive is bona fide crime among the young? (We have obviously moved from the status offender delinquent to the criminal delinquent, although this does not imply diminished concern for the former, who unfortunately may promote him/herself into the latter group.) Juvenile delinquency is one of our most serious social problems. Slightly over 40 percent of the people arrested for serious crimes in the United States are juveniles.[19] Most of the vandalism, many of the burglaries and auto thefts, and a sizable proportion of the muggings are committed by persons under age 18.[20] In 1978 four out of every five persons arrested under age 18 were male.[21] Yet, the arrest rate for juvenile females is increasing much more rapidly than for males. In the 10-year period from 1969 to 1978 the rate of arrests for males under 18 charged with committing serious crimes increased 19 percent, while the same rate for females under 18 increased 61 percent.[22]

Respondents in a survey of *Social Issues and Health Concerns* conducted in a midwestern state in 1979 consistently ranked juvenile delinquency among the top four community problems in their area.[23] The other three were crime, alcoholism, and drug abuse, certainly an interrelated group of social problems to even the most casual observer, particularly where juveniles are concerned. The proportion of adult to juvenile arrests in that same state and in that same year was 60 percent to 40 percent. It is interesting to note that 71 percent of all motor thefts, 65 percent of all vandalism, 67 percent of all arson, and 67 percent of all liquor law arrests were by juveniles. Of course, the classic juvenile "crimes" of curfew, loitering, and runaway arrests batted "1,000"—100 percent of these arrests were juveniles.[24]

Early in the summer of 1977 a group of Road America buffs gathered to camp in a midwestern state on the weekend of the first race of the season. A group of young people and a young man and woman engaged in an altercation during some part of that week-

Youth gang on street corner in South Bronx, New York

hopeless, helpless place and they either confront aggressively or drop out passively. Either way, they are likely to run afoul of the law.

"I'm Not typical, I'm ME!"

The thread running through most descriptions of the typical adolescent labeled delinquent is that of being a male, from a large broken family living in a large city, culturally deprived and extremely poor. He is usually black and he has dropped out of school. He feels trapped socially and economically. He finds identity in his gang. His chances for moving into a career of crime as an adult are good. Ignored he is not, for he is studied, interpreted and analyzed ad infinitum.

But wait! He may also be a white male, and he may be a she, if the statistics cited earlier are accurate, and we expect they are. And this typical delinquent may also be from a middle-class or financially well-to-do family. There is a strong body of evidence which shows that most of the incidents of delinquent behavior among middle-class adolescents rarely reach the juvenile probation agencies, or the juvenile courts. Most of them are dealt with informally. As Hahn states in his discussion on affluent and suburban delinquency

> 1. There is much more delinquency in suburbia than official statistics indicate, including a large number of offenses of types formerly considered part of the behavior pattern of lower class areas. 2. Much suburban delinquency does not become officially recorded because families cooperate in resolving problems by paying for damage, arranging private psychiatric care, etc., for an offending child.[27]

Previously cited literature by Sanders, Reed, and Gibbons, as well as Hahn, extensively address the issue of the broadening base of

end. The "altercation" ended in the immolation of the young woman, the flames allegedly lit by a juvenile male. The said juvenile was remanded to adult court to stand trial.

In a blistering issue, during an equally blistering summer of 1977, *Time* magazine, in an article entitled "The Youth Crime Plague" spelled out to their readers a horrendous tale of murder, rape, assault, and mayhem inflicted on innocent victims by children, equally innocent victims in their own way. Amoral teeny-bopper criminals, some as young as five and six, ply their trade.[25]

The violent acts described by *Time* were all real, and involved real people. People who suffered real agonies, bled real blood, and often died out of what is called sadism, sheer evil, and mindless rage[26] —all at the hands of our children. The violation of the old maxim "my rights end where your rights begin" is, among some of our youth, bordering on nihilism. For many of them, the world is a the "typical" delinquent. We can no longer confine the delinquent to the urban ghetto.

THE JUVENILE AND THE JUSTICE SYSTEM

Since much of the business of social services to the juvenile offender relate to the juvenile justice system, a brief look at this labyrinth is necessary. In addition, we have included Janeksela's diagram of the juvenile justice system (see Model 1)[28] and a model of the Wisconsin Juvenile Court process (Model 2)[29] as visual aids.

What of this juvenile justice system, which by 1980 was costing the American taxpayer $16 billion per year for detention facilities, correctional institutions, and a broad range of court and administrative services.[30] What is its history?

The juvenile court in America was conceived in Chicago in 1899 via the Juvenile Court Act of Illinois, which established a statewide system of courts having jurisdiction over all dependent, neglected and delinquent children.

> The two significant points about this court were: First, the age below which a child could not be a criminal was advanced from (common law) seven to sixteen years . . . [and made] provision for dealing with them under the softer name delinquents. Second, the work of the court was placed under chancery, or equity, jurisdiction.[31]

Thus, the principle of guardianship by the court was applied to children in need of protection and guardianship, including delinquents. The primary focus of the juvenile court was and is to look at the minor's behavior as a symptom, subject to diagnosis and amenable to treatment. The *Kent, Gault,* and *Winship* decisions came out of efforts to protect the rights of the juvenile, and established due process procedures for juvenile offenders. Briefly, *Kent* provided safe-

guards in the transfer of cases from juvenile court to adult court. *In Re Gault* clarified the rights of the juvenile to due process and fair treatment, and *In Re Winship* established that a juvenile charged with an "adult" crime can only be adjudicated delinquent if there is proof beyond a reasonable doubt.[32]

In most states, the intent of the juvenile justice system is (to varying degrees) to promote the best interests of the child. It is a system which, under the 1974 Juvenile Justice and Prevention Act, as previously indicated, cost more than $16 billion in 1980.[33]

Crow and McCarthy in their recent publication *Teenage Women in the Juvenile Justice System: Changing Values,* contend that the juvenile justice court system has had less interest in rehabilitating juveniles than in forcing them to conform to adult standards of behavior and shoring up family authority, especially regarding status offenders.[34] There may well be substance to these contentions, for the recent revision of the "new" Wisconsin Children's Code of 1978, for example, states that "the best interests of the child shall always be of paramount consideration, but the court shall also consider the interest of the parents or guardian of the child and the interests of the public."[35]

How does the child gain entry to the system? Obviously, most children do not, because even though they may be among the 90 percent who have committed offenses, they were not caught. Of those that are apprehended, most have a little chat with the police, technically called a "lecture" in juvenile court jargon, and are released on site. Some, even though they may have committed shoplifting, are referred to the Juvenile Probation Department, lectured, and dismissed. Others, who may have been caught in an act of violence, may be read their rights and placed directly in a juvenile detention center, or jail, by the arresting officer, pending a hearing in juvenile court.

MODEL 1   Operations of the juvenile justice system

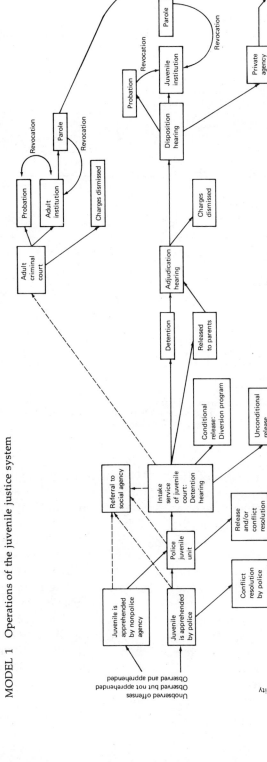

SOURCE: Galan M. Janeksela, "Youth, Delinquency, and the Juvenile Justice System," Dae H. Chang, ed., *Fundamentals of Criminal Justice*, 2d ed. (Geneva, Ill.: Paladin House, 1977), pp. 269–95. Permission to reprint has gratefully been received from Dae Chang and Galan Janeksela.

MODEL 2   Simplified, composite model of Wisconsin Juvenile Court process

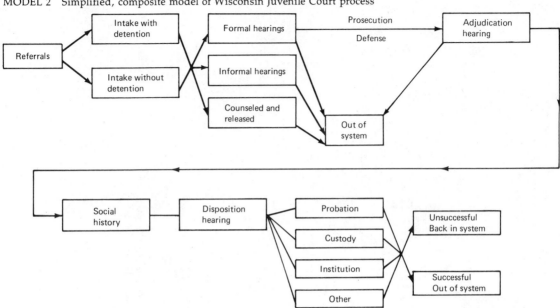

1. Detention may be brief or last until after disposition hearing.
2. Adjudication and disposition hearings may or may not involve prosecuting and defense attorneys.
3. Adjudication and disposition hearings may be held together or separated.
4. Social histories are completed in some cases that do not have disposition hearings, and all cases having disposition hearings do not have social studies.

SOURCE: John Howard Association, *Juvenile Court Services: Master Plan, Study, and Report-Wisconsin* (Chicago: John Howard Assn., 1977), p. 214. Permission to reprint has gratefully been received from John Howard Association, from Wisconsin Council on Criminal Justice, and from Wisconsin State Dept. of Health and Social Services.

The disposition in the best interests of the child depends on a series of variables. Has the minor committed a legal adult crime or a "status" offense—those acts uniquely juvenile (truancy, incorrigibility, being out of parental control)? How chronic is the behavior, or is this the first offense? Is the juvenile a part of a group or gang? Does the offense occur in a small community or a large city? How well, and for what, is the youth's family known to the community? Not only do these questions have immediate influence on the child, but they also have impact on the social services available to and utilized by the minor, the family, and the community.

(In a recent *Time* article is a section called "Games in Kiddie Court," a rather depressing but realistic look at the proceedings in a major metropolitan juvenile court.[36])

If, at the point of intake as described above, the young offender is not released, or remanded to parents or to a social services agency, the juvenile is then as indicated held for either a detention, adjudicatory, or dispositional hearing, or all three in turn. If the youth is found to have committed the alleged act at the adjudicatory hearing, the judge will then set a dispositional hearing date at which time the child may be placed on probation, placed in a center for diagnosis and evaluation, placed in the custody of the county social services department and possi-

A juvenile detention center

bly in a foster home, or placed in a youth shelter pending placement in a treatment institution or therapeutic group home.

Much of the reading in the area of juvenile offenses recommends removal of the status offense from the arena of the juvenile court,[37] and into the organizations and influence of social service agencies, community service programs, and alternate change-agent vehicles. It would be far better for the overworked judges and probation departments to divest themselves of the status offender (indeed, to divest the very status acts of the minor as "offenses"—who are they offend-

GAMES IN KIDDIE COURT	*Young toughs call it "kiddie court" because of its leniency; so do policemen and prosecutors. New York City Family Court, governed by strict laws designed to protect children and served by slack bureaucracies, primarily handles domestic disputes, but it is also where the kid criminals between 7 and 15 are sent.* **Time** *Bureau Chief Laurence I. Barrett watched delinquency proceedings in the Manhattan branch. His report:*

Opened only last year, the $28 million black granite building in Lower Manhattan resembles a modern free-form museum or college library. Inside, the light, airy waiting area could be mistaken for an airport lounge. There are no juries or casual spectators at the confidential proceedings, so the small courtrooms look like corporate conference chambers. Only the black robe and elevated bench maintain tradition.

The vocabulary would baffle courtroom buffs. There are "contacts" rather than arrests, "fact findings" instead of trials, "findings" in place of convictions. If guilt is established, the judge may order a "placement," not a sentence.

Few cases get that far. The city probation department screens out petty cases and releases most first offenders immediately after "contact." But tracing the child's arrest record is often difficult. Neither the court nor probation maintains a citywide data bank, though probation hopes to have a computerized system working by winter. Says Administrative Judge Joseph Williams: "You could have a youngster taken in here today who was picked up yesterday in Queens and last week in Brooklyn. We wouldn't necessarily know about the previous cases."

Unlike the regular district attorneys who handle suspects aged 16 and over, prosecutors in Family Court have no investigative staff to follow through in collecting evidence. Getting witnesses to cooperate is a major problem. One of the ugliest open cases at the moment involves a 12-year-old boy accused of stabbing an adult. The child is a "chicken," or male prostitute, and his victim was a "chicken hawk," his homosexual customer. After being wounded in his own bathtub, the man called police and signed a complaint. Stitched up and calmed down, he now wants to forget the whole thing. The boy remains free.

So do hundreds of other youngsters, even after the court has ordered otherwise. In an "intake part"—a court that, among other things, determines whether a kid should be held or paroled pending a hearing—Judge Phillip Thurston calls for the next docket number. It involves a 15-year-old, already being held on a narcotics charge, who had been remanded to a privately run shelter. Now he is to have a new hearing on a car theft. There is an awkward silence after the judge asks, "Well, where is he?" Papers are shuffled, and probation officer announces: "Judge, he wasn't sent down. He disappeared a few days ago. He's a chronic absconder."

A boy comes in with his sister, mother and Legal Aid Society lawyer. Most of the kids hustled through intake are black or Hispanic and poorly dressed; this one is Chinese and wears expensive boots. The boy, just 14, was picked up carrying a loaded .38 revolver. The judge explains that a formal hearing will be held in three weeks. He does not even ask the boy what he was doing with a gun. Probation recommends parole in the custody of the mother and the judge routinely grants it. The kid is now free to buy another gun.

In Judge Louis Otten's courtroom, a full hearing is to begin. The charge is sexual abuse of a 13-year-old girl by three boys aged 12, 13, and 15. The older two have had previous "contacts." A petition, or formal accusation, has been drawn. Many hours of work—and taxpayers' dollars—already have gone into the proceeding. But Otten dismisses the case. He has no choice; the victim's mother decided that her daughter should not appear. The boys grin as they leave.

In the next case, a 14-year-old suspect is up for brandishing a loaded pistol in school. The main witness, a teacher, is present. But a police department ballistics specialist—whose testimony is essential under the rules to establish whether the pistol was operable—has failed to appear. The judge riffles through the dossier and says: "He didn't show up in May, either." Otten reschedules the case for July, but the teacher will be on vacation. They settle on Sept. 19, and Otten warns that the case will be dropped if there is one more delay. The boy goes home.

Occasionally a youngster is found guilty. Judge Aileen Haas Schwartz presides over one such rarity. A black 14-year-old with a record was one of two kids accused of forcible theft of bicycles from two younger white children. The suspect has previously been accused of mugging an 85-year-old woman, but that incident was "A.C.D.'d"—adjourned in contemplation of dismissal. The accomplice in the bike case, having no previous "contacts," has been let off. The case is clearcut; both victims are in court ready to testify. One claims to have been struck and knocked down, but there was no injury. The suspect and his lawyer agree to an "admission"—the euphemism for a guilty plea—but only to third-degree grand larceny, a lesser offense than robbery and assault.

Schwartz then explains—slowly and carefully—the suspect's rights and makes sure he understands the admission and its implications. Looking bored, he nods silently. Sentencing, or "disposition," required still another hearing at a future date. Before that can occur, a full probation report must be made on the child's background. That can take months. "This one should be done on an urgent basis," Schwartz says. The boy goes home.

Larry Schwartzstein, chief prosecutor in Manhattan Family Court, speaks with studied bitterness. "I have kids tell me to my face that we can't do anything to them. They think it's a game. Witnesses are deathly afraid of reprisals. They feel that the court is more interested in the criminal than the victim." Last November Schwartzstein won a finding against a 15-year-old who had slashed an actor to death. Schwartzstein hopes to get a disposition hearing within two weeks—eight months after the manslaughter finding—if the probation department is finished with its investigation. Meanwhile, the small killer is free on parole.

Time, July 11, 1977, p. 27. Reprinted by permission from *Time,* The Weekly Newsmagazine; copyright Time Inc., 1977.

ing anyway, except their parents by running away, and this behavior is between parent and child to resolve, or the schools by truancy, and this is a problem of educators, not the justice department).

In trying to answer the question of why juveniles engage in various juvenile-status offenses, we have seen that running away, sexual experiences, and experimentation with assorted vices are peer-supported adventures among the young and that they are supported by the larger culture as adult activities. "Acting like an adult" often involves delinquent behavior. Yet the juvenile courts judge these activities, which are not considered bad by the population at large, to be evidence of delinquency. To explain why juvenile-status offenders make up a good part of the delinquent population, then we must point to the juvenile justice process. Without the strenuous efforts of the juvenile justice system to declare runaways, youthful drinkers, and girls (Girls!— why not BOYS?) who experiment with sex to be delinquent, there would be far less delinquency. Finally since the detention facilities provided by the juvenile justice system throw together burglars, rapists, and robbers and thereby provide the association and opportunities for learning some of the skills and attitudes necessary for more serious delinquency, the juvenile justice structure encourages and makes possible the very alternatives it is designed to prevent.[38]

The 1967 Report of the President's Commission on Law Enforcement and the Administration of Justice gave impetus to a growing concern about the rights of children, delinquency, and our "saving" processes,[39] as did the *Kent, Gault,* and *Winship* decisions. The Harvard Educational Review's 1974 publication *The Rights of Children* spelled out many of the continuing inequities.

A major milestone, the Juvenile Justice and Delinquency Prevention Act of 1974, authored by Senator Birch Bayh (D-Ind.), had as its goal the reduction of the instance of violent crimes committed by juveniles, as well as addressing in particular the issue of the "status" offender.[40] In 1980 Senator Bayh introduced a five-year extension of this program, one which had been passed virtually unanimously in its original form in 1974. The amended act proposes program and service development and implementation geared toward prevention, diversion, and diversity in the area of juvenile justice.

A 1977 report prepared for the state of Wisconsin by the John Howard Association had as one of its major recommendations (among many) the revision of the state Children's Code—a task recently completed.[41] A grass-roots study prepared for the Rock County Juvenile Court Advisory Committee by a select group of Wisconsin judicial system experts included in its major recommendations the following:

A. At least 50 percent of the juveniles apprehended by the three largest law enforcement agencies . . . should be handled within those local agencies rather than be referred to the juvenile probation department.

B. The three primary law enforcement offices should have at least one full-time juvenile officer.

C. Prohibit placing status offenders and probation violators who have not committed a criminal act in the county jail. (Note: this practice is *clearly*

against Wisconsin's *present* Children's Code.)

D. Provide 24-hours-a-day, seven-days-a-week detention intake screening.[42]

An example of a diversionary program is the Wisconsin Juvenile Restitution Project (funded in the late 70s by the U.S. Office of Juvenile Justice and Delinquency Prevention) which places young lawbreakers in jobs which in turn provide the restitution funds for the victims of their crimes.

Since the 1974 Juvenile Justice Act called for communities to develop "advanced techniques" in the prevention of delinquency, funds were also made available for rural diversionary programs, such as allocating funds to the Mountain Plains Youth Service Coalition, which provides a network of runaway services tying together rural communities in Colorado, Montana, South Dakota, and Wyoming.[43]

Efforts such as these are a step on the road to keep the acting-out child out of the juvenile justice system in the first place, and if entry is unavoidable, to limit the chances of moving from juvenile delinquency to juvenile crime.

SOCIAL WORKERS AS THE "CHILD SAVERS"[44]

How does social work fit into this vast, complex, and quite apparently imperfect system? Is it part of the problem? Are social workers in the role of juvenile probation workers so intertwined in the system that they become as imperfect as the system? Social workers like to think of themselves as a kind of *parens patriae* acting in lieu of the legal parent in the best interests of the child. Not an easy task at best, it becomes even harder when one must consider not only the rights of the child, but also those of the parent(s) and of society as a whole. The harsh realities of violent crimes committed by children (in 1976, one third of all the murders in Chicago were committed by youths aged 20 or younger, an increase of almost 30 percent over the previous year),[45] recidivism rates among the institutionalized delinquent, and increased delinquent behavior once the child becomes engaged in the juvenile justice system all make for a dismal outlook to the social worker who looks to some psychic payoff, no matter how small, from her/his career investment.

What are some of the service areas directly related to the juvenile justice system wherein social workers are presented with challenges and opportunities to practice their professional skills? We will look at the current service areas from the aspect of both the program and the functioning social worker.

Early diversionary programs are perhaps the most effective in preventing inappropriate entry into the juvenile justice system, and are aimed particularly at the status offender. (The delinquency "prevention" abilities of these programs, however, have not been effectively tested.) Social work staff located in police departments as juvenile officers may act as direct crisis intervention personnel, consultants to the police staff, rehabilitative staff, and as referral resources. Janeksela discusses diversionary agencies as independent units, citing their purposes to be: to prevent problems which otherwise would enter the juvenile justice system, to solve problems and resolve conflicts, and to provide services germane to the nature of the deviance and the necessity of official action. One such agency is the Youth Services Bureau, designed to coordinate services, as well as to provide actual social and rehabilitative services to juveniles. "The main concern of such a coordination agency should be changing juveniles' attitudes toward society and changing the community's attitudes toward juveniles."[46] Social work staff in these agen-

cies coordinate, counsel, refer, may fosterplace, and promote youth involvement in their programs. (This last is of particular importance.)

Sanders also sees the diversionary agency as the most hopeful social services provider, but not without its problems. Problems with definition of "diversion," with the use of probation personnel and structure, and the problem of interagency rivalry were apparent in agencies he observed.[47]

Some of the more traditional settings for delivery of social services are in the court-attached worker who provides the juvenile court staff with home studies, and who might represent the court both before and after adjudicatory hearings. The well-known PO, or juvenile probation worker (who in some states or counties functions directly as a court-attached worker, while in others is accountable to the Corrections Division's Juvenile Probation or Social Services Department) is an important element in the efforts to keep services to children humane, positive, and rehabilitative. Juvenile probation workers must be skilled in combining these child-centered responsibilities with those authoritative ones required of them by the law and society. Add to these mandates the constantly increasing case loads, and one might think the job too demanding. It is indeed demanding, but one can nonetheless find caring, dedication, and a wry sense of humor and perspective among most juvenile probation officers. Their work is generally one-to-one with the young client, but reality requires involvement with the family and frequently co-counseling with staff from other social service agencies engaged in providing services to the child and its family.

Children who have been remanded to adult criminal court because of commission of a criminal act, or who have been directly sentenced to a correctional institution for juveniles—usually called training schools or reformatories—are the object of concern and consternation among social work professionals. The validity of having such institutions has been questioned, for many of them are merely warehouses for kids and are without social work counselors, rehabilitative programs, follow-up programs or halfway houses. Yet the juvenile sociopath continues to be "sent up," rather than be housed and "treated" at the community level. Given a comprehensive internal community services program, the juvenile would still be more effectively served within the community, and less expensively in terms of money and personal disruption.

Assessment of the treatment needs of the juvenile who has been determined delinquent involves participation by several social service providers. To avoid inappropriate planning and placement, particularly of sociogenic cases, some communities have developed placement panels empowered to screen and approve or disapprove institutional placement referrals. An obvious objective and function of this panel is to maximize cost-benefits and cost-effectiveness of referrals and placements, since costs of institutional care continue to soar. Panel representatives might consist of court-attached staff or probation workers, social services agency staff, diagnostic center staff, youth shelter staff, and the like. They might not only have the responsibility of approval or disapproval of placement, but also of advice and referral.

If a child is institutionalized, it is imperative that the institution meet the unique needs of the child to begin with and that there be follow-up contacts and ongoing evaluation of the child in that institutional program.(!) All too often, children are removed from the community into treatment and, except for mandatory reviews prompted only by financial program requirements, are forgotten for another 12 months. Services to these children from home base must continue not only from the institutional program accountability point of view but from the perspective of continuity and caring for the child.

Social service and therapy programs that are community based are being encouraged by both the federal and state governments as

A cottage at a school for delinquent boys

well as the professional social work organizations, and certainly the line social worker. Included in these services are (*a*) respite foster homes for sociopathic juveniles, (*b*) therapeutic foster homes for mildly distressed youngsters, (*c*) intensive treatment teams geared to prevent institutionalization, via high-intensity individual and family therapy, (*d*) group therapy sessions modeled after the Provo Experiment, which was essentially an intensive peer counseling program for juvenile offenders led by a social worker and involving parents, and which proved quite successful as a self-help project.[48] and (*e*) community-based group homes which are staffed and "parented" by qualified personnel and licensed by the state Departments of Health and Social Services. These homes provide a therapeutic group milieu, involve the juvenile's family in their counseling processes, and maintain the juvenile in or near the home community.

The truly psychopathic child must also be given the opportunity to be treated in the community, although it is obvious that each of these children must be evaluated individually and be provided with programs to meet their unique needs. Since a certain percentage of all our child population, and certainly that of the juvenile delinquent, is suffering from emotional problems, professionals and parents responsible for their care must determine and *monitor* the best possible treatment program available. Unfortunately, for the severely disturbed child, the "best possible" available to them may be just passable in terms of current mental health treatment programs.

There appears to be a tendency among many professionals involved with juveniles to look at all acting out children as mentally ill, or psychopathic, and in need of treatment. Some, perhaps, but certainly not all. Most studies support the general "normalcy" of the juvenile and adult offender.[49]

Dr. Maxie Maultsby separates

1. Adolescent who act up—(normal adolescents) from
2. Adolescents who act-out—(neurotic adolescents) from
3. Adolescents who act bad—(antisocial adolescents) from
4. Adolescents who act for real—(psychotic adolescents) from
5. Adolescents who act their best—(mentally defective adolescents.)[50]

Follow-along and follow-up programs to support remediative changes made while in institutional placement help reinforce posi-

A room in a school for boys

tive social behaviors and facilitate entry into a strange and sometimes perceptibly hostile world. The well-known "halfway house" concept so frequently used for alcoholics and mental health center patients is also a viable program for juveniles who have been released from or going to institutional placement programs.

The Youth Home, functioning as an alternative to detention and jail, offers shelter and "time out," providing the opportunity for intensive short-term counseling before returning home. The counseling would of course include family, one-to-one, and peer group sessions. Unfortunately, some of these are turned into another kind of "warehouse" by the courts and other professionals, and in spite of conscientious and creative administrators and staff, develop into 30- to 60-day observation periods, with little contact from the placing social worker prior to group home or institutional placement. They become way stations going in the wrong direction!

A class in a school for delinquent girls

It is imperative that children and families not be permitted to flounder in a sea of disinterested and detached agencies unless they themselves are ready to separate and declare their independence.

SOME ISSUES AND ALTERNATIVES

Everyone is an expert when it comes to solving the problems surrounding juvenile delinquency and crime. Throw them in jail, some say (they mean get them out of here and away from me and mine). Get them out of the ghetto, and they'll act like "normal kids" (and so they burn down the camp). Get them involved in intensive family therapy (mom and pop are always to blame, aren't they?). Get them a job, and they'll learn what it is to work for a living ("I make more as a hooker than I can working for the Neighborhood Youth Corps; if you think I'm gonna quit, you're crazy"). Give them "decent" housing ("I'm a landlord, and you know what they did, huh? They ripped out the john and pulled the sinks offa the walls!"). It takes stubborn certainly to combat these responses and their causes, and who is that certain anymore?

Somewhere at sometime Saul Alinsky said don't give them bats and balls, given them bread and butter. And jobs. And security. And family. Most of all, family. Not just bodies but responsible, caring, consistent, tough, and gentle and fair families. Not crowded into two rooms but with *some* elbowroom. Not rich but not wracked with poverty either. Not abusive or cruel but not uncaringly permissive. Not perfect but merely slightly flawed and human. The characteristics of a "good" family life for growing children don't seem too much to ask adults to provide, but most of these characteristics are lacking in the lives of many of our juvenile delinquents. Some of these flawed interactions are to be found in the peer contacts of adolescents, with the juvenile courts, and the facilities available to the miscreants.

It should be evident by now that we cannot continue to view juvenile delinquency in terms of "lumpen theory," where everyone is thrown into the same pot and stirred with the same spoon until everything and everyone melts together. Status offenders (or preferably *non*offenders) can be helped through early discovery analyses in the schools, in the homes, and in the ghetto. Food, clothing, education, jobs, programs, housing, and hope can be purchased with the dollars we spend on neutron bombs, cigarettes, liquor, and pornography. (The real pornography lies in the ghettos of our big cities, where living is often dirty, rotten, and cheap, and people are afraid. Even the rats are freer than the humans with whom they share space.)

But juvenile criminals most certainly need to be confronted with the age-old theory of logical consequences. They are, in the final analysis, responsible for their own behavior. If a law is broken, there is a penalty. If the crime is of a serious, violent nature, the person committing the crime must most certainly expect to be held responsible for his/her actions. Communities are developing programs similar to the National Center on Institutions and Alternatives' "client-specific" punishment plans program where the punishment is designed to fit the crime.[51] Communities are also enacting tougher laws for juvenile criminals, enforcing them, and finding juvenile crime rates dropping. For most kids, jail is not a swell place to be. And for the young person who self-talks him/herself into a crime, there is not much payoff. Jail is a boring place in which to spend any part of one's life.

Community-based programs for prevention and protection seem to have the best chance of success in lowering the delinquency and juvenile crime rates. The Youth Service Bureau has the latent capacity to divert juveniles into positive programs. The Youth Community Coordination project, a pilot *prevention* program, has as its premises,

(1) Community institutions must permit you to experience rewarding and legitimate social roles if they are to grow up with a commitment to socially acceptable behavior and standards. (2) Some youth are denied access to legitimate social roles due to premature or otherwise inappropriate negative labeling by the community's primary institutions. (3) Youth who are denied access to desirable roles for whatever reason, lose their commitment to behave in socially acceptable ways—become alienated from society—and find substitute, antisocial behavior patterns, for example, commitment of status offenses or delinquent acts.[52]

Juvenile restitution programs, such as the Wisconsin project mentioned earlier in this chapter, are later stage diversionary efforts as they are designed for those teenagers who have already committed a serious offense but who, in the opinion of the juvenile court (or probation) worker and the juvenile judge, would benefit from the logical consequences/restitution philosophy of the program rather than from placement in a correctional facility.

Early evaluation reports on the Wisconsin program indicate a recidivism rate of less than 3 percent.[53]

Resources at the community level must have flexibility capabilities if they are to intervene on a broad-base level. An old, well-worn social work phrase, individualize the client, is appropo to diversionary efforts. Community-based treatment foster homes and group homes, specialized family therapy teams, and early intervention programs located in the schools and also utilizing the team approach should be available to the teenager in trouble. Multiresource capability is an expensive goal. However, compared to the cost of placement in a correctional facility (some $20,000 per child per year) community-based programs are highly cost effective.

Many involved systems—community, family, judicial, and economic—have received more, or less, of our attention. Certainly all are deserving of more examination. One we have not confronted is our educational system.

School is where almost all of us spend at least 10 to 12 years of our life, right? Wrong. About 60 percent of our school-age population spends that much time, the rest (between 30 to 40 percent by the time 12th grade is reached) have dropped out. And among these, the incidence of delinquency is 10 times greater than among those who have remained in school.[54] Much has been written on the system's failure to counsel and expedite individual educational goals. On the other hand, it would appear rather difficult to inspire students who are hungry, or into dope, or who are threatening teachers with switchblades. All these do something to the educational milieu. Schools do not exist in a vacuum any more than does the family or the child.

However, the educational system has indeed, although out of ignorance (*our* educational system—ignorant?), perhaps itself fostered juvenile delinquency. It is time to take a look at what some call minimal brain dysfunction, or specific learning disabilities, or dyslexia, or visual-perceptual handicap, or just L.D.

> We must admit that the problem of staying in school and always failing can be very frustrating. It cannot be a coincidence that in New Jersey three state training schools report an average reading grade level of 4.6. In Texas,

children between the ages of 10 and 16 and in penal institutions are reading at an average grade level of 3.2. In South Carolina the average grade level in reading for confined adolescents is 3.4. In Missouri the average reading level for all incarcerated adolescents is mid-fourth grade. As one collects data on the relationship between reading failure and delinquency, one becomes depressingly aware that the relationship is neither minimal nor regional in prevalence.[55]

This, from an educator.

And another statement from medical authorities:

> We all know what happens to children who do not receive effective help (for specific learning disabilities). The high incidence of school drop-outs, delinquency, and serious emotional disorders has been well documented by many research experts. These children often end up being alienated from society and often from their families. They lead unfulfilled lives of futility and frustration. Suicide sometimes results, especially in their teens.[56]

And the brief academic history of Peter X.:

> Peter's academic career began in nursery school, where he charmed the teachers, played heartily with the children, and smashed all the windows in the caretaker's car one afternoon when his mother was late in picking him up. When asked why, he said he felt like it. He apologized to the caretaker and paid his father back for replacing the windows bit by bit out of his small monthly allowance. He continued to please the teacher in first grade and was particularly good at finger-painting and group sports. He could pitch both south-paw and right-handed. He particularly enjoyed being read to but had to get up and walk around the room a lot while stories were in process.
>
> In second grade, he began to disturb the class by his restlessness and was often sent out into the hall to "settle down." He was still a charmer, and the teacher forgave him for most of his disruptive antics. His early abilities in

arithmetic had stabilized, and he was one of the few children in the room who had "homework." Peter X. still smiled and loved all the girls and they loved him, too.

Peter was eight in the third grade. He had his IQ tested, and when the teacher saw what it was, she frowned and tapped him on the head and said, "Pete, I think you are just a little bit lazy. I know you can do better if you try." Old Peter had thought he was trying pretty hard, but not much came out right, particularly his arithmetic. And those words! He was sure he was spelling them right on the weekly tests, but if he got two *right* it was a good day. Peter's father came to see the teacher and frowned also. That afternoon Peter came home, ate all the cookies his sister had made for her party, and put his fist through the dining room glass door. Dr. S. carefully stitched him up. Peter told him that if he could ever get past spelling he would like to be a doctor too.

Peter's fourth grade teacher was a jolly, kind lady who watched him a lot and played catch with him at recess. Sometimes she would go back into school with him, and they would try to read the preprimers the kindergartners used. It was hard for Peter to figure out words like "the god barked ta the shillren." Why would a god bark? And if he spelled a word right on Tuesday, why did he spell it wrong on Wednesday? He was no longer smiling as much.

One day Peter asked to go to the boy's room, went down to the school kitchen and turned on all the gas burners, and waited for the room to blow up the way his head was blowing up. The jolly lady took him home that afternoon and spent a long time in the kitchen talking to his mother and father. Peter took 64 cents out of his piggybank, put on his sweater, and walked out of the house.

Peter is not hard to find. He may be very young or be a teenager. He lives on everyone's block and is in everyone's classroom. He reverses letters, cannot copy figures or words accurately, is ambidextrous, is hyperactive and easily frustrated, says "pasghetti" instead of spaghetti (oh, isn't he cute!), often has poor motor coordination, can't read, can't spell, can't pay attention . . . and has a normal to above average IQ. He is also in everybody's reformatory, training school, and jail; he has dropped out of school and out of life.

The shocking part of this human waste is that it is not necessary; learning disabilities can be remediated. (A young man comes to mind, one who is now in medical school. At the end of his fifth-grade year, he was reading at a second-grade level at best, yet he had the ability to "cloak" his problem because of his high intelligence. A perceptive, concerned teacher who herself was grasping for straws suggested an out-of-state reading clinic for evaluation and remediation. At the conclusion of three semesters of a two-hour session per week, the young man was reading at an 11th-grade level with comparable comprehension skills. He is not a unique example of remediation. But he is unique, for he was one of the lucky ones—someone found him out!)

The California studies cited by Tarnapol found some 60 percent of the delinquent school dropout population as having a significant degree of specific learning disability.[57] Hogenson's studies indicated that "reading failure is the single most significant factor in those forms of delinquency which can be described as antisocially aggressive . . . assault, arson, sadistic acts, major vandalism.[58] These children need not end up as the Lee Harvey Oswalds of our world. He was indeed learning-disabled, but then so were Einstein, Edison, Leonardo da Vinci, and Nelson Rockefeller.

Social workers have a responsibility and a mandate to advocate for these young people and their families—*prior* to the child's arrival before the screening committee for institutional placements, not after.

SUMMARY

It once was that juvenile delinquency was a stigma ascribed to adolescents. The label, however, is now reaching back into the early years and early grades. Whether one should define this behavior as juvenile, or criminal, or impulsive infantile irrationality is a matter of continuing conjecture and debate. The *fact* is that juveniles with behavior patterns like Joey's have been socially and legally designated as problems and labeled delinquent. Some, whose acts are of a more violent nature, are being called youthful criminals.

But are juvenile delinquents necessarily the "bad guys" and the rest of humanity, except for adjudicated criminals, the "good guys"? Does this not depend on the frame of reference, such as individual, cultural, economic, and social values; and of course on federal, state, and local laws and their judicial interpretations which define and set the parameters of delinquency? In the end, we suspect, the latter reflect the former, and although laws may lag behind social inequities, their interpretation (the appropriateness of which depends on one's orientation) by the police, juvenile probation counselors, and the juvenile courts determines the reality of the current status of these young people as a group and as individuals.

Thus, the problem of juvenile delinquency is so complex as to confound the casual reader, provoke and frustrate the serious student, and depress the experts. In the end, the only "solution" appears to be a restructuring of all of society: to reprogram our social, economic, legal, and educational institutions; to examine and redetermine our social values; and to redefine our goals as a human race. This will require a global analysis of systems interaction, both generic, gross, and overt as well as specific, fragile and covert. The groundwork has been laid by many—society, social scientist, scholar, and subject alike.

Right here and right now, however, we seem no further along the road to resolution of our juvenile delinquency dilemma than in the days of Socrates.

NOTES

1. Don C. Gibbons, *Delinquent Behavior,* 2d ed. (Englewood Cliffs, N.J.: Prentice-Hall, 1976), p. 96.
2. Virginia Satir, *Conjoint Family Therapy* (Palo Alto, Calif.: Science and Behavior Books, 1967), p. 2.
3. Dae H. Chang, ed., *The Fundamentals of Criminal Justice* (Geneva, Ill.: Paladin House, 1976), p. vii.
4. Gibbons, *Delinquent Behavior,* p. 12.
5. Ibid.
6. John P. Reed and Fuad Baali, *Faces of Delinquency* (Englewood Cliffs, N.J.: Prentice-Hall, 1972).
7. Laws of Wisconsin, Chapter 48, *Children's Code:* 48.12, "Jurisdiction of Court over Children," pp. 985–86.
8. Galan M. Janeksela, "Youth, Delinquency and the Juvenile Justice System," in *Fundamentals,* ed. Dae H. Chang, p. 240.
9. Don C. Gibbons, *Society, Crime, and Criminal Careers,* 2d ed. (Englewood Cliffs, N.J.: Prentice-Hall, 1973), p. 198.
10. Richard A. Cloward and Lloyd E. Ohlin, *Delinquency and Opportunity* (New York: Free Press, 1960).
11. Martin Haskell and Lewis Yablonsky, *Crime and Delinquency* (Chicago: Rand McNally, 1971), p. 354.
12. Ibid., p. 359.
13. Ibid., p. 368.
14. D. Matza, *Delinquency and Drift* (New York: Wiley, 1964) p. 368.
15. Albert Cohen, *Delinquent Boys: The Culture of the Gang* (Glencoe, Ill.: Free Press, 1955).
16. Cloward and Ohlin, *Delinquency,* p. 1.
17. William Sanders, *Juvenile Delinquency* (New York: Praeger, 1976), p. 142.
18. Chang, *Fundamentals,* p. 249.
19. Federal Bureau of Investigation, *Crime in the United States, 1978: Uniform Crime Report* (Washington, D.C.: U.S. Government Printing Office, 1979), p. 194.
20. Ibid., p. 194.
21. Ibid., p. 189.
22. Ibid., p. 189.

23. Wisconsin Department of Health and Social Services, *Social Issues and Health Concerns* (Madison, Wis.: WDHSS, Division of Policy and Budget, 1979), p. 7.

24. Crime Information Bureau, *Wisconsin Criminal Justice Information: Crime and Arrests* (Madison, Wis.: Wisconsin Department of Justice, 1980), p. 61.

25. "The Youth Crime Plague," *Time,* July 11, 1977, pp. 18–19.

26. Ibid., p. 25.

27. Paul H. Hahn, *The Juvenile Offender and the Law* (Cincinnati: W. H. Anderson, 1971), p. 119.

28. Janeksela, "Youth and the Juvenile Justice System," p. 249.

29. John Howard Association, *Juvenile Court Services: Master Plan, Study, and Report-Wisconsin* (Chicago: John Howard Assn., 1977), p. 214.

30. "Bayh Cites Cost of Juvenile Justice System," *Crime Control Digest,* March 31, 1980, p. 4.

31. Edwin H. Sutherland and Donald H. Cressey, *Criminology,* 8th ed. (New York: Lippincott, 1970), p. 441.

32. Robert G. Caldwell and James A. Black, *Juvenile Delinquency* (New York: Ronald Press, 1971), p. 224.

33. "Bayh Cites Cost."

34. Meda Chesney-Lind, "Young Women in the Arms of the Law," in *Teenage Women in the Juvenile Justice System: Changing Values,* ed. Ruth Crow and Ginny McCarthy (Tucson, Ariz.: New Directions for Young Women, Inc., 1979), p. 103.

35. Wisconsin Statutes, Chapter 48 "Children's Code," rev. (Madison, Wis.: Wisconsin Department of Health and Social Services, 1978), p. 1059.

36. "Games in Kiddie Court," *Time,* July 11, 1977, p. 27.

37. Sanders, *Juvenile Delinquency;* Chang, *Fundamentals;* Hahn, *Juvenile Offender.*

38. Sanders, *Juvenile Delinquency,* p. 83.

39. President's Commission on Law Enforcement and the Administration of Justice, *Juvenile Delinquency and Youth Crime* (Washington, D.C.: U.S. Government Printing Office, 1967), pp. 4, 45.

40. "Bayh Cites Cost."

41. John Howard Assn., *Juvenile Court Services,* p. ix.

42. Technical Assistance Report, "Recommendations—Juvenile Justice Services, Rock County," May 1977 (unpublished report).

43. Office of Juvenile Justice and Delinquency Prevention, *Rural Programs* (Washington, D.C.: U.S. Department of Justice, 1979) pp. 2, 3.

44. Anthony Platt, *The Child Savers* (Chicago: University of Chicago Press, 1961).

45. "The Youth Crime Plague," p. 18.

46. Chang, *Fundamentals,* p. 252.

47. Sanders, *Juvenile Delinquency,* p. 214.

48. Stephen Schafer and Richard Knudten, *Juvenile Delinquency: An Introduction* (New York: Random House, 1970), p. 364.

49. Gibbons, *Society,* p. 504.

50. Maxie Maultsby, M.D., "Rational Behavior Therapy for Acting-out Adolescents," Monograph (Lexington, Ky.: University of Kentucky, 1973).

51. "Punishments That Fit the Crime," *Newsweek,* August 4, 1980, p. 60.

52. American Public Welfare Association, *Youth Community Coordination Project* (Washington, D.C., 1977).

53. "Young Lawbreakers Need This Chance," *The Milwaukee Journal,* March 12, 1980, p. 1.

54. Sutherland and Cressey, *Criminology,* p. 238.

55. Dennis Hogenson, "Reading Failure and Juvenile Delinquency," *Bulletin of the Orton Society* 24 (1974): 168.

56. Carl Kline and Carolyn Kline, "Severe Reading Disabilities: The Family's Dilemma," *Bulletin of the Orton Society* 23 (1973): 146.

57. Lester Tarnopol, *Learning Disabilities* (Springfield, Ill.: Charles C Thomas, 1969), p. 329.

58. Hogenson, "Reading Failure," p. 167.

GUSTAFSON

chapter **12**

INTRODUCTION

Education is one of the basic institutions in our society. Total estimated expenditures of public school systems are in excess of $60 billion annually. Although some of us have not had experience with social agencies, all of us have spent a number of years in school. In the past decade a number of issues confronting schools have emerged as schools attempt to meet the needs of all children. Some of these issues are:

Adjusting to declining enrollments resulting from a decreasing birthrate.

Concern over decreasing achievement scores received by students on standardized math and reading tests, and controversy over the meaning of these results.

Unionism and teachers' strikes.

Accountability to taxpayers.

Integration and busing.

The mainstreaming of children with special educational needs into the regular classroom.

The importance and focus of special educational programs.

The necessity of teacher preparation programs to emphasize individual differences in the behavior and development of children.

Sex and drug education.

Programs for alienated youth (students who drop out).

Obtaining the necessary funds to finance and provide quality education, given inflation and increasing property taxes.

Violence against teachers and students.

Vandalism in schools.

Censorship of reading materials.

The role of the school in taking on functions that were in the past provided by parents.

Competency-based education.

---

* This chapter was especially written for this text by Don Nolan, M.S.S.W., School Social Worker.

The problems of children and school social work*

Busing to achieve school integration

It is beyond the scope of this text to examine these issues in depth. Instead, this chapter will focus on some of the problems children have in school systems and how social work intervention techniques can help alleviate these.

PROBLEMS OF CHILDREN

In 1973, the U.S. Congress passed the Education for all Handicapped Children Act, now known as PL 94–142. That law speaks to the numerous physical, developmental, learning, and social-emotional problems which have hampered the education of children. In sweeping legislation, it also mandated that all individual school districts identify these problems within their populations and then develop specialized programs to meet the needs of these children. This has necessarily been a very large and difficult task. This chapter will not attempt to present an all-encompassing or historical view of this legislation but will instead focus on the types of problems that have been encountered by what could be termed *school support personnel:* social workers, psychologists, and counselors. Typical problems have been: (*a*) those

Teachers' strike

associated with learning disabilities, difficulty in learning to read, in retaining information, in comprehending it; (*b*) problems associated with poor attention span or distractability; (*c*) behavioral concerns, from passive withdrawal to noncompliant, physically aggressive behaviors; (*d*) problems associated with some degree of emotional disturbance, for example, the guilt-ridden child or the child with serious pathology associated with an inability to sort out the real world from the fantasized one; and (*e*) the problems of the developmentally delayed child; that is, the child who has some significant delay in intellectual, social, emotional, and/or physical development. A social worker, psychologist, or counselor could encounter some or all of these problems. For example, a school social worker in an elementary school or a secondary school may function in a variety of situations. S/he may be a member of a team working with either educable or trainable mentally retarded children, or with emotionally disturbed children and their families. S/he may be involved with a program for children under five years old that concentrates on early educational

intervention. Or in larger school systems, s/he may be a consultant to the administrative staff working on problems of program development, organizational analysis, and/or educational research. In each situation s/he would encounter different children and varying severity of problems. Therefore, it is necessary to understand that the demands of role, the environment, and one's own personal style will influence how problems are perceived and prioritized and ultimately what types of intervention techniques will be used.

Using an approach, particularly emphasizing role and method, we can look at the changing demands of the job of a school social worker (roles that have included caseworker, truant officer, group worker, counselor, advocate, consultant). Case examples will be used to demonstrate typical methods of interaction. Basically, school social work is a relatively new role. Prior to 1960 there were few school social workers and these were primarily employed by large urban school systems; for example, New York, Chicago. In fact, one of the earliest publications on school social workers was first published in 1955.[1] School social work, then, must be discussed within the context of its evolving role. Before doing this, however, it will be necessary to have a method of analyzing behavior, so that we have an initial base for understanding the nature of children's problems in schools. It is a practical necessity for any school social worker to have a knowledge of the dynamics of behavior, as social workers have been and will continue to be closely involved with problematic behavior in children. In fact, much of the definition of social work services offered in PL 94–142 regulations specifies: (*a*) defining the nature of social or behavioral problems, (*b*) utilizing individual or family counseling skills, and (*c*) utilizing other resources to impact on behavioral and social problems.

The nature of behavior

We will begin with the premise that behavior is purposeful, that we do things for a reason. We may not always know exactly why we are doing things, in that we do not analyze each of our behaviors. But we are always responding to a given situation with a set of beliefs, with a history of past attempts to solve a problem, and within the context of our present environment.[2] Albert Ellis, founder of rational emotive therapy, looks at behavior within the context of what he calls the ABCs of behavior. In essence, he says that B—a belief system composed of attitudes, interpretations, and emotions—is always juxtaposed between an activating situation (A) and a consequence (C).[3] This belief system for the person, child, or adult, is based on opinions the person has about him/herself and others in relation to his/her perceptions about his/her place in the larger world. The person, then, can decide on a course of action given certain circumstances. Children, just as adults, do not act in a random fashion. They act in relation to a decision they have made about the consistency and stability of their relationships with adults and other children.

There are antecedents of behavior which often depend on decisions they have made about their abilities, and not on their actual abilities. Thus, while it may seem that some children are misbehaving when they approach new situations, in reality they may have decided from past experience that they will have little success in the task and are thus misbehaving because they do not want to face the fear of failure again. The children have made a decision, although it may be based on what can be termed a mistaken belief system.[4] They wrongly assume that failure means they are worthless and that trying is not important. In order to understand how to alter that self-perception, one must look closer at some primary goals of behavior.

Rudolf Dreikurs et al. postulated that the force behind every human action is a goal. Everyone knows some of what they want, although often we do not act on those goals, but on unanalyzed means to reach these goals. It is possible to understand the psychological motivation of the child if one develops diagnostic skills to analyze four goals of misbehavior: attention getting, power seeking, revenge seeking, and assuming a disability.[5] Some children try to get attention, to always be the focal point for others, since they believe that otherwise they would be worthless. Other children attempt to prove their power in the belief that only if they can do what they want and defy adult pressure can they be somebody. Still others may seek revenge, the only means by which they feel significant is to hurt others as they feel hurt by them. Others may display actual or imaginary disabilities in order to be left alone, so that nothing is demanded of them. The crucial point is that whatever deviant behaviors children display, there are always reasons why children display deviance.

Anyone who has worked extensively with children, in any situation, can readily remember children who were acting out these goals. For example, Ted, who is constantly in front of the teacher, interrupting and always calling attention to himself by "forcing" the teacher to repeatedly reprimand him, is clearly seeking attention. John, who is usually confrontational, who is noncompliant to reasonable requests from the teacher, and who rejects praise and social reinforcers from the teacher, is in a power struggle. Carol, who physically injures others and who usually puts others and herself down, is probably seeking revenge for some perceived wrong. Phil, who is withdrawn, who sinks

Shy about freckles

down in his desk, who is shy with class-mates, and who fears new situations, is probably displaying a disability.

One must, or course, be careful not to overgeneralize or analyze too quickly. Be-havior is complicated and can be deceptive at times. However, if one uses the con-struct of goals of behavior, given the phi-losophy of purposeful behavior and actions, one has a starting point from which one may respond to these behav-iors. Thus, given a general philosophy of behavior as it applies to the educational system, one can talk about specific ways of intervening to solve problems.

SCHOOL SOCIAL WORKERS: A RESPONSE TO CRISIS

A number of different role models

Casework. Intervention has always been the essence of social work. Social workers have responded to the complexity of society and to the problems this complexity has caused with a variety of methods. Casework, traditionally, has been one of the first methods employed in any given area. This has made sense for the practitioner, in that casework encompasses the more clinical and best known aspects of social work. Basically, social workers have had to prove their worth, have had to prove that they do something different than what is already being done. Because social workers have substantial training in family dynamics, they can ana-lyze and diagnose common problems in the dysfunctional family. This is a skill that others in the typical school system do not have, and thus it is viewed as an area of particular expertise for the school social worker.

An example is the case of Michael. Mike, age 10, had a number of problems. He was physically aggressive toward other children and was prone to act with outbursts of emo-tion and anger when put in new or different situations. He had virtually no coping skills and came to school after weekends or vaca-tions in an angry violent mood. The family consisted of five children and his mother. The father was no longer living at home but visited on occasions. Mike's emotional prob-lems, and particularly his violent attitudes, were accentuated after these visits. In addi-tion, Mike had dirty, poorly kept clothing, which always seemed to be either too small or much too big. One of the problems, of course, was Mike's behavior in class. His goals of misbehavior were a combination of attention getting and power seeking. In an attempt to change this pattern of behavior, the social worker using a casework strategy: (*a*) made a referral to the County Department of Social Services to make sure that the family was getting all services that were available, for example, homemaking, medical, counseling; (*b*) modified Mike's behavior at school by devising a system of reinforcers that were important to him; (*c*) made sure that Mike found success in academic areas in school by helping the teacher individualize for Mike's needs; (*d*) tried to help the mother understand that Mike should not be put in situations in which he had to adopt a negative attitude toward adults; and (*e*) contacted the father about his relationship to his son. All of this takes considerable time and energy, the main point being that a consistent, organized, step-by-step approach is used by the social worker. Casework thus becomes a one-to-one involvement with a family in an attempt to solve a problem. Another example may help to further clarify this approach.

Phyllis, age six, was deaf. She was in a special education program for four days a week. There were a number of problems: noncompliant behaviors when Phyllis knew what was wanted of her, a difficulty in communicating in any way, and a number of medical problems. The social worker decided that a home intervention program was needed. Consistency was needed in the sign language program between home and school. Consistency and behavior management were needed in the home, for Phyllis was not expected to do anything there as the only demands were bathroom skills. The parents needed help to develop reasonable goals and expectations for Phyllis and then follow through on a program. Medically, Phyllis needed extensive diagnostic work done at a nearby hospital. The social worker made contact with the hospital, arranged for

a meeting, and then made sure follow-up came from the hospital. Again, the social worker set specific goals and followed these in an attempt to solve a multitude of problems.

Group work. As casework came to be considered outmoded in some areas of social work practice,[6] school social workers found another method of offering services. Group work became another means of intervening in school problems. Essentially the rationale was that the social worker could influence the lives and educational success of too few people when utilizing the casework approach. It was also presumed that few cases needed such intensive involvement from a social worker, that there was a point of diminishing returns after a given amount of time and involvement were expended. (Recent studies would say that this assumption may be in error, however.[7] In effect, another somewhat more hidden premise was that one should be involved with the less severe cases, in that one could have more successes and ultimately more extensively affect the lives of children. A number of examples will demonstrate these points.

The fifth grade of Ms. Tanner was being a problem for her. Specifically, four boys would not listen regularly, clowned around, and were not getting much done in class. In fact, some of the boys were doing less well academically than the past year, and were starting to go around as a group often getting into trouble on the playground. An intervention strategy was designed to create groups as a means of solving these problems. Two groups of five boys were created with two of the "problem" boys in each group. The groups worked in specific high-interest areas; for example, one group worked on a science project involving creating a metric unit for third grade, while the other studied the principles of flight and aerodynamics, making kites, paper airplanes, and finally, wooden models. There were a number of planned goals for each group. First, the social worker wanted to create new friendships and show the disruptive children models of more appropriate behavior, behavior which could be as rewarding as attention getting behavior. Second, cooperation was fostered in conjunction with the principles of peer pressure; all children worked toward step-by-step cooperative goals, for unless all helped, none could reach their goal. Finally, the social worker wanted everyone, the children in the group, their peers in the class, and their teacher, to realize that the boys could be productive and successful, so that in as far as possible, individual programming could be designed to meet these boys' needs.

In another case, group experience involved high school freshmen who were failing in their initial coursework. Study habits and poor motivation and attitude were the main concerns. In this case, the social worker organized a group of students who took a special course organized around ways of studying. The course was named "Ten Ways to Beat the System" and was structured in a way which allowed the student to learn a new mechanism of studying while not seeming to become part of the high school system. At the same time, a number of upper class students were organized to informally meet with the younger students in order to discuss some positive aspects of high school which the younger students could look forward to in future years. In addition, they offered guidance as to which teachers to avoid and from which teachers they could expect a fair deal. Thus, a number of groups were combined to offer an alternative to failure in the school system.

Truant officer. The social worker in the school has also performed a number of other roles. Truant officer was a fairly prevalent role, especially in large school systems. This is rarely the case now, although knowing the truancy laws and acting as an advocate for the child may be necessary at times. There are times when acting as an agent of social control (the law, the system) need not be looked at adversely. A case in point is a multiproblem family who had three boys in high school. Although none of the boys had reached the statutory age after which school was no longer compulsory, the parents decided to keep the boys at home so they could help the father in his job as a farmhand. The boys had mentioned to different teachers that they feared that this was about to happen, but they were afraid to tell their father that they wanted to attend school. The social worker was able to intervene in this case using the truancy laws to demonstrate to the parents that they had no choice but to send their children to school. In such a way the undesirable role of truant officer could be transformed into one that was advantageous for the children involved.

Counselor and parent liaison. The social worker as a counselor and/or parent liaison or parent trainer is also a fairly common role in school social work. Often those in the teaching profession who know little about the potential of social work services will expect the school social worker to be the person who will provide liaison between parent and teacher. Unfortunately, frequently there is also the assumption that the social worker will defend and justify the actions or educational planning of the teacher. This can cause somewhat strained relations between the social worker and the rest of the teaching staff, especially when a worker agrees with a parent that the school system ought to make changes in its educational programs to better serve the parent's child, and perhaps also better serve other children. This role requires a lot of tact and prior planning, as well as a relatively assertive view toward expanding social work services.

Since many school systems have never had social workers on their staff, it remains with the new school social worker to describe to them the many roles of social work, and the potential values these may have for the school system. This will be a long, and at times, frustrating process, for any fundamental change in basic system services will affect the balance and direction of all services. Consequently, the social worker must be in a position to prove that the changes s/he brings will ultimately benefit the system and thus will be worth the uneasiness that the other staff will feel in adjusting to a new person in a different and challenging role. Thus, persistence and what Albert Ellis terms *self-awareness*[8] (a nonrating acceptance of one's strengths and limitations) will be needed initially.

In the role of counselor, the social worker also brings to the situation a number of skills. However, other professionals have traditionally held the role of counselor in schools. Thus, there has been marginal role development in this area, although there has been some changes in recent years. As school social work services have developed, there has been a trend to look at the social worker as a therapist rather than a counselor. This distinction has been more than semantic, as advanced professional (master's degree) training has greatly increased the diagnostic and psychological skills of school social workers relative to other school professionals.

In essence, role development and expansion is a critical area of concern for school social workers. When joining a school system, there will be a number of expectations and specific job-related demands on them. New workers will necessarily meet these demands with a set of assumptions about their role in a system; that is, the specific, individual, unique things that they do as part of their profession. There are bound to be conflicts, for the older roles encompassing casework, group work, or parent liaison, may not provide enough flexibility to meet the demands of the change effort; that is, school social workers assume they are becoming a part of a system because needs of the system are not being met and aspects of the system need to be changed. To help ascertain how school social workers have attempted to solve this problem, we can discuss four distinct and somewhat newer approaches to their role.

Newer roles

Advocate. Recently one of the most provocative roles for the social worker has become that of advocate.[9] The assumption made for the adoption of this role is that when facing an educational bureaucracy as a complex system, or when attempting to use other systems for the benefit of the family or child, one needs to employ a person who understands, and is not intimidated by large, complicated systems. This can be a particularly useful role when working with families who are newly becoming acquainted with the educational system. For instance, in an early education program which is geared to help prekindergarten children who appear to display some evidence of developmental delay, the social worker can employ this role to help the parents understand their rights under the law including their rights to appeal program decisions if they feel the programs do not fit the needs of their child. S/he can explain who is teaching what materials and why this should help the child progress. S/he can be an initial contact person and the person who follows the child in the program, so that the parents can have a familiar person to contact who they can feel comfortable with and ask questions which they might otherwise consider silly or irrelevant. The social worker can also be the person who makes them aware of applicable medical or social service agencies which would be available to give them a better knowledge or their child or offer supportive services, when these are needed. finally, the social worker can be a person to talk to about the complexities, difficulties, fears, or guilt associated with raising a child who in some way is different from other children. A combination of all the above roles expands the role of home liaison and changes the emphasis to create an assertive role within the school system designed to meet needs which have not previously been met within the school context.

Behavioral specialist. There has also been a trend at some major universities to train school social workers in one discrete, highly recognizable skill. Within this context, an emphasis is often put on the social worker

becoming a behavioral specialist, a person who understands and can systematically apply principles of behavior, specifically behavioral modification. Within the schools, a knowledge of how to alter behavior has immediate and long-term applicability. Using behavioral skills the social worker can provide guidance on general learning principles as applied to overall teaching, and develop specific programs for children who are having difficulty adjusting to normal classroom routine. The examples illustrating this are numerous.

Phillip, age nine, was having difficulty attending to tasks and was usually noncompliant to directions. His teacher was having trouble understanding his behavior and motivating him toward usual classroom activities, for example, independent work in math and reading, participating in small group activities, and cooperating in play arrangements. A social worker with behavioral training was asked to intervene in the situation. After observing the ante-

Storytelling

cedents of the noncompliant behavior and taking base line data of on-task or attending behaviors in nonacademic situations,[10] the social worker was able to put together a program. The program included: (a) the planned use of social reinforcers (praise from the teacher), (b) a reward system built around the student's interest in science, in which other work had to be done before the work in science could begin, and (c) a system which included ignoring verbal noncompliance while reinforcing compliance from other students with praise and tangible rewards, such as helping with a special project and taking notes to the office. In this way his behaviors were changed in a relatively short time while a new program was developed to help the student continue to achieve academic success.

Balloon launch at a school

Mental health consultant.   The school social worker can also function as a mental health consultant to the other staff. Curriculum, today, if it ever was, is no longer as simple as reading, writing and arithmetic. Although there is currently substantial concern about teaching the "basics" in education, teachers must still seek to improve old curriculum and develop new materials. In this pursuit, it is not only the materials which can be questioned but the style in which they are taught. Since social workers have training in the social psychology of individual behavior, they can serve as consultants to the human relations aspects of curriculum and to teaching style. In this sense, one can look at the social worker in a preventive role, seeking to help teachers motivate students with stimulating materials. S/he can help create an approach which is not threatening but intriguing, questioning, and supportive of the process of learning. Naturally, one would also be involved in helping teachers decide that they should try to individualize education; that is, that they should devise materials and teaching styles that meet the needs of all children, no matter what their current academic level.

The social worker can help create a systematized approach to monitor progress and then create new approaches to facilitate remediation when necessary. In order to accomplish these goals it may be necessary to organize "brainstorming" sessions with all the teachers or begin an investigation of the materials available on a number of topics.

In this way social workers can help provide guidance in curriculum development with an overall emphasis on human relations. The inclusion of specific human relations goals in teaching has often been overlooked, even though many of the problems in the schools, trouble on the playground, problems with special education and regular education classes, can be seen as directly attributable to a lack of human relations materials. Children need to learn that "different is all right," that cultural or racial differences need not be feared but enjoyed, that all people deserve respect as human beings, and that values are learned concepts that can be changed.[11] School social workers, because of their training and unique place in the school, can provide the perspective needed to devise such a curriculum and help create systems for implementation.

Team member. Another role which is gaining increasing popularity is that of the social worker using his/her skills in conjunction with other members on a team. Within this role, the school social worker might be on a team with other professionals (psychologist, speech therapist, special education teacher, physical therapist, regular education teacher) who help to determine the special needs and particular programming needed for certain children. This is an area of implementation of PL–142, with the group of professionals commonly called an M-team (multidisciplinary team). In this case, the social worker might be: (a) involved with an initial assessment of the child and the family, with special emphasis on family functioning and the child's adaptive skills, (b) involved with the parents clinically, either through family therapy and role analysis or through training in special techniques, such as behavior modification or crisis intervention; or (c) involved in teacher observation, training, and evaluation.

The point here is that the social worker acts as part of a team, a member with certain discrete skills and knowledge, and in conjunction with the team seeks to alleviate problems. Although this may appear to be a somewhat more constricting role, as other methods may appear to offer more independence, it can be a very useful way to find the gaps in services and to decrease overlap between individual skills. It has its advantages, especially if one is responsible for a school (or a school system) with a large population.

As such, then, we have been generally looking at the school social worker as a person who responds to problems, as a person who employs whatever methods are at his/her disposal to correct situations. We can also look at the role somewhat differently, and although what the school social worker does may not change substantially, his/her perspective will.

SCHOOL SOCIAL WORK: AN ASSERTIVE ROLE

Allen Pincus and Anne Minahan in *Social Work Practice: Model and Method* postulate that the focus of social work practice should be between people and systems in the social environment.[12] If we then look at schools as a natural access point for families (most families must deal with schools at some point in their existence) social workers should be able to perform a truly unique role in the schools. Given the complex nature of society today, most people need to enhance their problem-solving abilities. Social workers can help in their regard, while they link people to systems, and improve existing service and delivery mechanisms. The schools are a critical link in the total societal resource system. Indeed, the neighborhood school is often the system with which the average citizen feels most comfortable. We then must examine the school and look for the inadequacies in its educational structure. The questions we need to answer are: what do we really need in order to determine success for the student, and how can be use the materials and personnel in the most efficient way? Through a

A CASE EXAMPLE OF THE ASSERTIVE ROLE

John is a 10-year-old boy in a special education class. He is in that class because he is considerably behind the rest of his age-group in reading and math. He also demonstrates some behavioral problems, particularly in stressful situations. He has not been termed an EMR (educable mentally retarded) child as of yet, but as he gets older and does less well academically, he may ultimately be tested to have an IQ in the educable range. He is involved in a specialized program called mainstreaming, in which he is placed in a regular education class for physical education, music, art, and social studies. In the beginning of the year there was hope for further mainstreaming into remedial reading and math, but behavioral problems have gotten in the way. A referral has been sent to the school social worker asking that a behavioral program be started and contending that mainstreaming should be stopped until further reassessment can be done. If one wishes to only put a "band-aid" on the problem, it would be relatively easy to start a behavioral program and withdraw the child from the situation. Seemingly all could accept this "solution," but what would it do for John's learning?

Another way of approaching the problem, in a more assertive role, is to form a group composed of the teacher, support personnel, and the principal to discuss mainstreaming as a general educational goal and to form flexible school policies regarding it. At the same time the social worker must provide a support system for the regular education teacher involved with John. This could include: (*a*) giving the teacher some general suggestions regarding behavioral management that are applicable to many children, (*b*) helping find curriculum and materials which are interesting to John and applicable to the rest of the group, (*c*) forming a group of students around John who would display good modeling behaviors, (*d*) writing a contract with John in which he could agree to certain limited goals for himself within the classroom, and (*e*) making sure through discussion in human relations that John has the potential for friendships in the regular education class. One could also support the special education teacher and continue to give reinforcement for mainstreaming students. Finally, one could make John's parents aware of the situation, so that they could talk about it at home and generally tell John how desirable they thought it was.

As such, then, one is designing a planned change effect, recognizing motivations for change and problems resulting from change. John is the focus for a much larger problem and is not *the* problem. He is the *access point* for the interconnection between a number of systems: regular education teachers, special education teachers, children with behavioral problems, and children with learning disabilities. As far as the school social worker is concerned, John is a catalyst for the creation of a system which will better serve many children.

system of assessing present data, determining goals, and forming active systems for the purpose of exercising influence, one can answer the above questions and ultimately build a better, more accessible, more demand-based school program.

The social worker has a very large role to play in this process for s/he can become an organizer, a leader, a catalyst toward change, a liaison with the needs and wishes of the community, and a specialist in devising systems to meet change-oriented goals. Typical problems that might occur are discovering: the particular deficiencies in the school and the community, the under- or unserved population, and the programs that are needed to get children back in school and to curb juvenile delinquency. Another might be to analyze the interaction between system components in the schools or between the schools and the county departments of social services; for example, to see if these components are really working together and if they have underlying assumptions which work at cross-purposes.

Whatever one does, one is working as an institutional change agent, a person analyzing ongoing programs and proposed new programs. The system-oriented approach seeks to change the goals of the traditional school social worker. While these goals formerly were to help the child adapt to the school, to use the learning opportunities available, and to modify pupil behavior to parent-child relationships so as to alleviate problems in the school, these goals are now changed to analyze which parts of the system are activating stress in a given situation, and then to alter that system so that the equilibrium of the system is again in balance. One must find and prioritize targets for change, acknowledging that one must use different approaches to solve different problems.

This approach should be clearer if we analyze a typical problem which could be referred to a school social worker. By reevaluating and refocusing on the problem, the goals of the assertive school social worker should become clearer and more meaningful.

SUMMARY

One of the key issues emerging in the educational process is that of accountability, demonstrating that one does something which is necessary to the system and which significantly and positively alters the lives of children within the schools. In essence, all must answer the questions: why do we exist, and what do we do that makes a difference? For school social workers that question is changing from a role relating skills focused on improving family functioning and behavior, to a role determining key issues in education and organizing programs to meet these needs. Within the new perspective one can employ skills utilizing casework, group work, understanding of families, behavior modification, a variety of counseling approaches, parent liaison, and curriculum development.

The important thing to understand is that an assertive view of social work can be related to virtually all aspects of school social work, although the implementation of change effects may differ significantly with the emphasis on different skills. School social work can become a very challenging, assertive profession. Many things are changing in the educational establishment, and it is likely that the new cabinet level Department of Education in the federal government will require school systems to make more changes and become more accountable. In many instances in the future, the lacking variable for the success of a program will be the ability to critically analyze the system and gain a renewed perspective from understanding the dynamics involved in a system. Basically, the school social worker is the person in the educational system who has the training and knowledge to do just this. Ultimately the leadership and program development the social worker provides can significantly affect children. Social workers, along with other professionals in the schools, can help achieve a real school without failure; that is, not a school system where failure is nonexistent, but a system in which failure is not critical, but only part of the learning process. In this way, the dynamic context of the social work role can achieve its fullest potential, for the social worker is able to use combinations of numerous skills or methods to examine and creatively deal with problems. One of the most satisfying aspects of the role is to watch others change from a static way of viewing problems to an approach that sees a multiplicity of ways to change systems. It is all too easy to forget that the most important factors affecting children in schools are the motivations, philosophies, and instructional methods of teachers. If one can help others to reanalyze how they see problems, while at the same time gain credibility for a new approach to analyzing problems, the time and energy needed to implement this approach will be worthwhile.

NOTES

1. See Mildred Sikkema, "The School Social Worker Serves as a Consultant," *Casework Papers* (New York: Family Service Association of America, 1955), pp. 75–82.

2. Alan Guskin and Samuel Guskin, *A Social Psychology of Education* (Reading, Mass.: Addison-Wesley, 1970), pp. 1–3.

3. Albert Ellis, *Humanistic Psychotherapy* (New York: McGraw-Hill, 1973), pp. 55–69.

4. Edward Jones and Harold Gerard, *Foundations of Social Psychology* (New York: Wiley, 1967), pp. 83–92.

5. Rudolf Dreikurs, Bernice Grunwald, and Floyd Pepper, *Maintaining Sanity in the Classroom* (New York: Harper & Row, 1971), pp. 17–21.

6. Joel Fisher, "Is Casework Effective?" *Social Work* 18 (January 1973): 5–21.

7. Arthur Michaels, David Cournoyer, and Elizabeth Pinner, "School Social Work and Educational Goals" *Social Work* 24 (March 1979): 138–41.

8. Ellis, *Humanistic Psychotherapy*, pp. 129–33.

9. See Mary J. McCormick, "Social Advocacy: A New Dimension in Social Work," *Social Casework* 51 (January 1970): 3–11.

10. For more detailed discussion of behavior modification, see Beth Sulzer and G. Roy Mayer, *Behavior Modification Procedures for School Personnel* (New York: Holt, Rinehart & Winston, 1972).

11. Sidney Simon, *Values Clarification* (New York: Hart Publishing, 1972), pp. 10–21.

12. Allen Pincus and Anne Minahan, *Social Work Practice: Model and Method* (Itasca, Ill.: F. E. Peacock, 1973), pp. 3–9.

chapter **13**

MEDICAL PROBLEMS AND THE
MEDICAL CARE SYSTEM

There are hundreds of thousands of different medical conditions, ranging in severity from a minor scratch to a terminal illness. The causes are also nearly infinite: accidents, infections, birth defects, viruses, bacteria, the aging process, stress, diet inadequacies, and so on.

Medical services in this country are organized into four basic components: physicians in solo practice, group outpatient settings, hospital settings, and public health services.

Physicians in individual or solo practice are more often found in rural areas. Such a physician is usually a general practitioner who is trained to provide treatment for the more common medical ailments. Supervision of general practitioners is minimal or nil; they are primarily accountable only to the patient. Except through referrals for consultation and occasional use of laboratories and hospitals, a physician in solo practice works in relative isolation from colleagues.

Group outpatient settings can be organized in several ways. A group of general practitioners may share facilities, such as a waiting room, examining room, and a laboratory. Or, each physician within a group may have a different specialty, and complement the skills of each other. Since medical knowledge and treatment techniques have become so vast and diverse, it is now impossible for a physician to have in-depth knowledge in all areas. A third type is where a third party (a university, union, business, or factory) employs a group of physicians to provide medical care for its constituency. A fourth type is where a group of doctors with the same specialty (for example, neurological surgery) provide services in the same facility.

A third subsystem of health care is the hospital setting which has a wide range of laboratory facilities, specialized treatment equipment, inpatient care facilities, and highly skilled technicians. Hospitals employ a wide range of medical personnel, including medical social workers. A hospital is generally the center of the medical care system in

Medical problems and medical social services

A CASE ILLUSTRATION

Janet Ely was hospitalized to have a hysterectomy because she had a tumor in her uterus. Janet was an attractive, single woman who was only 22 years old.

Prior to the surgery, the nursing staff noted she was apprehensive, depressed, and anxious. Following the surgery Janet became even more agitated and withdrawn. Her physician, Dr. Connors, again fully answered her questions related to her hysterectomy. Janet, however, appeared very concerned and confused about her future, making statements such as, "No one will ever marry me now," "Life isn't worth living," "My family doesn't care about me; no one does," "Oh well, I'm going to die soon anyway." At this point, Dr. Connors asked Janet if she would be willing to discuss such concerns with the social worker at the hospital, Miss Vicki Vogel, and she indicated she would.

Miss Vogel met with Janet five of the remaining seven days that she was hospitalized. Janet had a number of problems, primarily involving planning for her future. She had alienated nearly all her relatives when at age 17 she quit school in her senior year and began living with her 20-year-old boyfriend. A year and one half later her boyfriend discovered she was having an affair with another man, and angrily requested that she leave. She went to live with the other man, and became rather heavily involved in drinking and experimenting with drugs. A year ago Janet left this man, and moved to this area, and is now living with a divorcee.

Janet continued to have a number of questions related to her hysterectomy— "Would her sex life be changed?"; "Might the cancer reoccur?"; "Would the hysterectomy affect her future as a woman?"; "Can a person be orgasmic following a hysterectomy?" Miss Vogel attempted to provide some answers, and also arranged for Debra Nass (a 32-year-old woman who had had a hysterectomy three and one half years ago) to talk with Janet. Although some uncertainty remained (for example, the possible reoccurrence of a malignancy), Janet became more comfortable about having undergone a hysterectomy after talking to Mrs. Nass.

Janet, however, had a number of questions that she felt she needed to look at. She wondered why when people were nice to her, she sometimes was "rotten" to them. For instance, she mentioned she had lived with two different men, and each time she continued to have sexual relationships with other men. She also wondered what the future held for her. She was not skilled at a trade or a profession, and did not know what kind of a career, if any, she desired. She was very confused about what she wanted out of life, and also admitted that she had occasional blackouts from heavy drinking.

These problems were briefly discussed with Miss Vogel. The focus of social services at this hospital, however, was limited to short-term, "crisis" counseling. Because these complicated problems indicated longer term counseling was needed, Miss Vogel suggested, and Janet Ely agreed to, a referral to the mental health center in the area.

Several months later Miss Vogel heard from a friend of hers that Miss Ely had gotten engaged but had recently "on the spur of the moment" moved with another man to live on the West Coast.

In summary, the immediate psychological "crisis" situations surrounding the hysterectomy appear to have been resolved. However, problems still appear to remain in Janet's relationships with others.

communities. Due to the spiraling cost of hospital care and the lack of sufficient beds, many communities are now building nursing homes and convalescent homes for those needing fairly extensive medical care, but not inpatient hospital attention.

Public health services are organized on five levels: local (city or county), regional, state, national, and international. The majority of public health services to a community are provided through local health programs. The priorities in public health keep changing; as success is achieved in dealing with

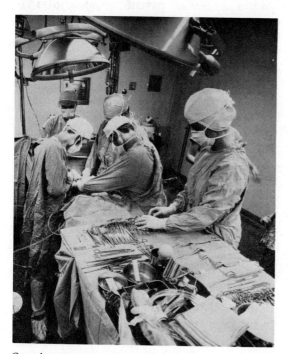

Open-heart surgery

one problem, other problems emerge demanding attention. Public health services have virtually eliminated a number of communicable diseases in this country, such as tuberculosis, polio, and smallpox. The focus of public health services is primarily preventive in nature. Illustrations of services provided through local health departments include:

a. Health counseling to families regarding family planning, prenatal and postpartum care, child growth and development, nutrition, and medical care.
b. Skilled nursing care and treatment to acute and chronically ill.
c. Physical rehabilitation to patients with strokes, arthritis, and similar medical conditions.
d. School health services to public and parochial schools and liaison between home, school, and community.
e. Disease prevention and control.
f. Immunization services.
g. Referral of families and individuals in order to make maximum use of available community resources.
h. Environmental sanitation which involves developing and enforcing codes, rules, and regulations designed to maintain and/or improve conditions in the environment which affect health—this activity covers a broad area from air and water pollution, food protection, waste material disposal, and sanitation of recreation facilities.

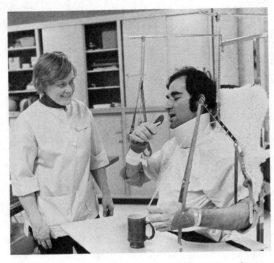

An occupational therapist teaching a quadriplegic how to self-feed

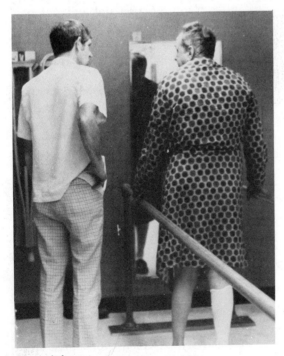

Physical therapy

i. Maintenance of an index of all area births, deaths, marriages, and current communicable diseases.

j. Health education and information services to stimulate the public to recognize existing health problems.

(Public health departments employ numerous public health nurses who at times provide counseling services similar to services provided by social workers.)

PROBLEMS IN HEALTH CARE

Preventive medicine. The major causes of death today are chronic diseases: cancer, heart disease, cerebrovascular disease (such as strokes), cirrhosis of the liver, diabetes, bronchitis, and the like.[1] Chronic diseases progress and persist over a considerable part of a person's life. Chronic diseases frequently exist long before we are aware of them because there are often no symptoms in the early stages, and because we ignore early symptoms. Social, psychological, and environmental factors are important influences in the progression of these diseases. Coronary heart disease, for example, is known to be associated with a diet of highly saturated animal fats (beef, butter, and cheese), and lack of consistent and vigorous exercise, heavy smoking, and stress.

A major problem is that modern medicine is oriented toward crisis medicine which is geared to treating people *after they become ill.* The crisis approach is effective in coping with some types of medical conditions, such as acute problems (for example, accident victims and patients having influenza or pneumonia). Unfortunately, with chronic diseases, once the symptoms manifest themselves, much of the damage has already been done, and it is often too late to effect a complete recovery. In order to more effectively curb the incapacitating effects of chronic diseases, the health care delivery system needs to emphasize the prevention of illness before extensive damage occurs. To date, preventive medicine has had a lower priority than crisis-oriented medicine—in terms of research funding, the allocation of health care personnel, and the construction of medical facilities.

Physicians often treat the symptoms of chronic illnesses, rather than the underlying causes. Patients who are tense or anxious are prescribed tranquilizers, rather than receiving therapy to reduce the psychological stress that is causing the tenseness. Patients who are depressed are prescribed antidepressant medication, rather than being counseled on the underlying reasons for the depression. Patients with psychosomatic disorders (for example, ulcers, migrane headaches, insomnia, diarrhea, digestive problems, hypertension) are often prescribed medication, rather than receiving therapy for changing certain aspects of their lifestyles that would reduce the underlying psychological stress that is a major factor in producing the psychosomatic problems.

In recent years a wide variety of holistic programs, which are preventive in nature, are beginning to be established in industry, in hospitals, in school settings, in medical clinics, and in other settings. Holistic medicine recognizes that our thinking processes function together with our body as an integrated unit, and gives attention to both the physical and psychological function of a person. Pelletier documents that the major determinants of most illnesses are our lifestyles (including exercise, diet, sleep patterns, and particularly stress reaction patterns).[2] Holistic medicine emphasizes teaching people proper exercises, diets, and how to reduce psychological stress in order to maintain health and curb the development of chronic disorders.

The high cost of health care. The cost of health care has risen astronomically in the past few decades. In 1925 it cost $3 per day for a hospital bed. By 1964 the average daily cost was $38. By 1977 the figure had reached $225.[3] Health care costs rose from 5.9 percent of total U.S. output in 1965 to 8.9 percent in 1978—and are expected to reach 10.2 percent by 1984.[4] Medical spending is expected to double between 1978 and 1984.[5]

The health care industry is now the third largest U.S. industry, with an estimated $229 billion being spent on health care in 1980.[6]

These rising costs have particularly been a problem for low-income groups and for the elderly who must survive on fixed incomes. In spite of various social welfare programs designed to ease the burden of health financing, the poor pay a substantially larger proportion of their income on health care than do the more affluent.[7]

Why have these costs risen so dramatically? A significant amount of this cost is due to dramatic technological advances in developing a wide range of lifesaving treatment interventions. This equipment, along with the cost of highly skilled personnel to operate the equipment, is expensive. Fifteen years ago we did not have such expensive medical equipment as cobalt machines, heart pacemakers, artificial heart valves, and microsurgical instruments to perform surgery under a microscope.

A second reason is the increased life span of Americans. Now, a larger proportion of our population is old, and the elderly require more health care than younger people. A third reason is because many technically and professionally trained groups (such as nurses and physical therapists) are demanding salaries consistent with their training and responsibilities.

Another reason is because third-party financing is increasingly paying medical

UNDERSTANDING AND REDUCING STRESS

Pelletier in *Mind as Healer, Mind as Slayer* documents that rational and positive thinking has a major impact in promoting healing and maintaining health, and that irrational and negative thinking is a major determinant of psychosomatic illnesses.[8] (Thinking is irrational if it does one or more of the following: (*a*) is not based on objective reality, (*b*) hampers you in protecting your life, (*c*) hampers you in achieving your short- and long-term goals, (*d*) causes significant trouble with other people, and (*e*) leads you to feel unwanted emotions.) Stress-related physiological and psychological disorders have now become our number one health problem.[9]

A simplified description of the effects of our thinking processes in determining psychosomatic illnesses is outlined as follows:

Stressor
- Events or experiences
  ↓
- Certain kind of self-talk: (e.g., "This is a very dangerous situation.")

↓

Stress
- Emotions: (such as tenseness, anxiety, worry, alarm)
  ↓
- Physiological reactions: (A general stress reaction will occur. The physiological changes of a general stress reaction have been described by Selye.[10] The symptoms include an accelerated heart and pulse rate, shallow respiration, perspiring hands, tenseness of the neck and upper back, a rise in red blood count for fighting infection, increased metabolism, and secretion of pro-inflammatory hormones. The physiological reactions that most students experience prior to giving a speech before a group are aspects of the general stress reaction.)

↓

If the emotional and physiological reactions are intensive and long term, a psychosomatic disease is apt to develop, such as an ulcer, migraine headache, diarrhea, heart problems, digestive problems, cancer, hypertension, bronchial asthma, hay fever, arthritis, enuresis, certain skin problems, constipation.

According to the above formula, there are two components of a "stressor": the event and the self-talk that we give ourselves about that event. "Stress" is the emotional and physiological reactions to a "stressor." Self-talk plays a key role in producing stress. The self-talk approach enables us to understand how positive events (as well as negative events) can lead to a stress reaction:

Event: Receiving a promotion.

Self-talk: "I now will have additional responsibilities that I may not be able to handle."

"If I fail at these new responsibilities, I will be fired and will be a failure. My career plans will never be realized."

"This promotion will make others in the office jealous."

"I'm in big trouble."

Emotion: Worry, tension, anxiety.

Physiological reaction: The general stress reaction will occur. If intensive and prolonged, conditions exist for a psychosomatic illness to develop.

Stress can be reduced in three primary ways. One way is to identify the irrational and negative self-talk, and then give yourself rational self-challenges (see Chapter 5 for examples of this approach). A second way is to become involved in activities that you enjoy, which will lead you to stop your irrational thinking and instead have you focus your thinking on events you view more positively. For example, if you enjoy golf, playing golf will lead you to stop thinking about your day-to-day problems, and instead lead you to think about the enjoyable experiences associated with golfing. Activities that are apt to stop your irrational thinking include hobbies, attending entertainment events, jogging and other exercise programs, biofeedback programs, muscle relaxation exercises, and meditation.[11] A third way to reduce stress is to change the event that is involved in producing stress; for example, taking a job that you view as having less pressure.

bills. Historically medical bills were primarily charged and paid by consumers. Now, most bills are charged to and paid by third parties—including private insurance companies and the public programs of Medicare and Medicaid. Physicians are more likely to recommend expensive diagnostic and treatment procedures if they feel it will not be a financial burden to the patient. In addition, the rise in the rate of malpractice suits encourages physicians to "play it safe" by using extensive diagnostic procedures. Third-party payments also tempt some physicians to perform surgeries that may be unnecessary. Klaw has concluded "at least one out of every five or six operations in the

United States is medically unjustified."[12] Appendectomies, tonsillectomies, and hysterectomies are particularly vulnerable to this alleged abuse.[13]

The spiraling costs of health care services has become an issue of national concern. Friedlander and Apte (along with many other authorities) partially blame the high cost on inadequate planning:

Our health system is a hodge-podge that has grown out of a variety of historical trends rather than out of conscious planning. Care is often fragmented, and is oriented toward treating episodic illnesses rather than toward maintaining the health of the whole person or family. Over time or simultaneously, one person might receive services from any or all of the four subsystems, but few individuals, rich or poor, can be said to receive really comprehensive continuous services from the care available to them. Some of the current high cost of care, in fact, can be attributed to the inefficiency, overlap of effort, and gaps in the system. Consumer groups are beginning to press for a better-organized comprehensive health system which would give quality care at lower cost. As yet, however, their voice is not strong enough to ovecome the opposition of the medical profession and other forces resisting change in the medical care system.[14]

FINANCING MEDICAL CARE

Medical expenses are paid for by private insurance, through governmental programs, and by direct payments from the individual to the health provider. In a recent year private insurance paid 26 percent of the total cost for health care, the consumer paid 34, and the government 40 percent.[15]

Most of the 40 percent of the federal government's health care bill is paid through Medicaid and Medicare. (The government also participates in the health insurance of

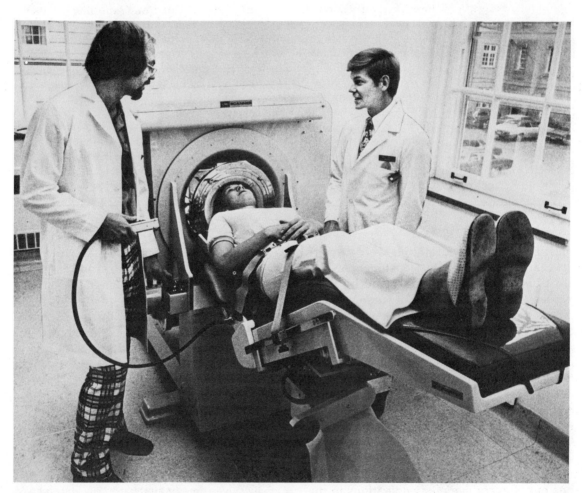

Brain scanner

federal employees, provides medical programs for families of members of the armed forces, and provides payments for those who have had military service through Veterans Administration hospitals.)

Medicaid. This program was established in 1965 by an amendment (Title XIX) to the Social Security Act. Medicaid primarily provides medical care for recipients of public assistance. It enables states to pay directly to hospitals, doctors, medical societies, and insurance agencies for services provided to recipients of public assistance. The federal government shares the expense with states, on a 55–45 basis to recipients of aid to families with dependent children and supplemental security income (formerly recipients of old-age assistance, blind aid, and disabled aid). Medical expenses that are covered include diagnosis and therapy performed by a surgeon, physician, and dentist; nursing services in the home or elsewhere; medical supplies, drugs, and laboratory fees.

Under the Medicaid program benefits vary from state to state. The original legislation encouraged states to include coverage of all self-supporting persons whose marginal incomes made them unable to pay for medical care. However, this inclusion was not mandatory, and the definition of "medical indigence" has generally been defined by states to primarily provide insurance coverage to recipients of public assistance.

While the stated purpose of Medicaid had been to assure adequate health care to the nation's poor and near poor, one study found that only half of the people living below the poverty line benefited.[16] The poor who are not covered receive either no medical care, or less than adequate care. Medical services are less accessible, and impersonal "charity" service discourages their use of the health services that do exist. Furthermore, since they are unable to pay their

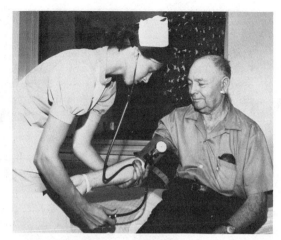
Checking a patient's blood pressure

medical bills, few doctors are willing to form a continuing doctor-patient relationship with them.

Medicare. The elderly are more afflicted with illnesses, yet have less income to pay for medical care. People over 65 now make up 11 percent of the population, and the percentage is increasing each year. Three times more is spent per capita for health of aged persons than for younger persons, mostly for hospital or nursing care.[17] Therefore in 1965 Congress enacted the Medicare program (Title XVIII of the Social Security Act). Medicare helps the elderly pay the high cost of health care. It has two parts—hospital insurance (Part A) and medical insurance (Part B). Everyone 65 or older who is entitled to monthly benefits under the Old Age, Survivors, and Disability Insurance program gets Part A automatically, without paying a monthly premium. Practically everyone in the United States 65 or older is eligible for Part B. Part B is voluntary and beneficiaries are charged a monthly premium. Disabled people under age 65 who have been getting social security benefits for 24 consecutive

$10.80 PREVENTS CANCER VICTIM FROM RECEIVING FEDERAL AID

FINANCIAL DISASTER FOR A FAMILY WHO EARNED TOO MUCH

Mrs. G. is dying of cancer. Her medical bills could reach $60,000, but she is ineligible for Medicaid. She once worked in a textile mill in Georgia, and is now receiving $239 a month in disability benefits. This amount is $10.80 more per month than a person can collect in unearned income and remain eligible for Medicaid. Had she not worked, Medicaid would be paying her medical bills.

Both Mrs. G. and her husband are described as hard working, honest people. A social security office staff member in the community commented:

> We see more of these cases than we would like to. We have had cases that are $1 over the limit. But Congress sets the budget and draws the line, and right now the cut-off for Medicaid is $228.20 a month.

SOURCE: *Wisconsin State Journal*, June 23, 1980, Section 1, p. 11.

months or more are also eligible for both Part A and Part B, effective with the 25th month of disability.

Part A—hospital insurance helps pay for time limited care in a hospital, in a skilled nursing facility (home), and for home health visits (such as visiting nurses). Coverage is limited to 90 days in a hospital, and to 100 days in a nursing facility. If patients are able to be out of a hospital or nursing facility for 60 consecutive days following confinement, they are again eligible for coverage. Covered services in a hospital or skilled nursing facility include the cost of room and meals in a semiprivate room, regular nursing services, cost of drugs, supplies, and appliances.

Part B—supplementary medical services helps pay for physicians services, outpatient hospital services in an emergency room, outpatient physical and speech therapy, and a number of other medical and health services prescribed by a doctor such as diagnostic services, X-ray or other radiation treatments, and some ambulance services. Each calendar year, as soon as covered medical expenses go over the annual $60 deductible, Part B will

usually pay 80 percent of the reasonable charges.

NATIONAL HEALTH INSURANCE

This country does not as yet have a national health insurance program. Great Britain and many other European countries have such a plan, in which public tax dollars are used to pay for medical care for all citizens. In the past two decades a number of elected officials and organizations have pressed for a public health insurance program. Now, many families receive partial coverage of costs through subscribing to private insurance plans, which are primarily available to employed persons and their families.

Those who are either marginally employed or unemployed are generally not covered by health insurance. As with many other social problems, illness is strongly associated with poverty.

Those who are poor tend to be more prone to illness due to an inadequate diet and to substandard living and working conditions. Since they do not have financial resources, they tend to avoid seeking medical help at the onset of an illness. As a result they have higher rates of chronic illnesses, and are confined for longer periods of time when hospitalized. Because of their poorer health, medical complications also arise more frequently when ill.

There are multiple reasons why a national health insurance plan is needed. The rapid rise in health costs makes it impossible for the poor, those of marginal income, and even middle-class families to pay for extensive medical bills. The poor who are not covered by Medicaid are unable to pay for even moderate medical expenses, thereby they often forego early treatment and develop more serious medical conditions. Medicare covers short-term hospitalization expenses for the elderly, but not long-term expenses. An extensive medical condition can wipe out substantial savings and force a family deep into debt; thereby changing dramatically their standard of living and lifestyles. Hospitals cannot survive without assured income when services are provided. Physicians as well need to be paid for their services. Even though public and private insurance coverage is increasing, 18 million Americans still have no health-insurance coverage.[18] In addition, 19 million Americans have insurance that does not cover ordinary hospital and physician services, and 46 million Americans have inadequate insurance against large medical bills.[19]

Since Franklin Roosevelt, all presidents (except Ronald Reagan) have been proposing national health insurance programs without any being passed—with the result that the U.S. is the only industrialized nation lacking a comprehensive national medical insurance system.[20] A variety of national health insurance programs have been advanced by Democratic and Republican legislators, administration officials, organized labor, representatives of private insurance companies, and the American Medical Association.

Approaches. The proposals for national health insurance involve four major types. In the public approach, governmental agencies would collect funds (for example, from employers and employees) and pay the claims. In the mixed public-private approach, health insurance funds would be collected by the federal government and disbursed by private insurance companies. A third approach involves giving tax credits to individuals for the purchase of private health insurance. A fourth approach involves a catastrophic emphasis in which the government pays for medical expenses only when a certain amount is exceeded.

To illustrate how a national health insurance plan might be set up, one proposal—former President Carter's plan—will briefly be described. The Carter 1979 plan emphasized the catastrophic approach as it would pay all of a family's hospital and medical expenses above $2,500 a year. Employers would pay at least 75 percent and employees no more than 25 percent of premium costs. For the unemployed, and poor and low-income families, benefits would be financed by federal and state revenues. The health insurance funds would be collected by the federal government, and disbursed by private insurance companies. With President Carter's defeat in 1980, the Carter proposal is probably *dead*.

Expectations vary as to the direction national health insurance will take in the United States. It is doubtful a national health insurance plan will be passed in the near future, partly because President Reagan and the 1980 Republican Party platform opposes national health insurance. The main objection to passage of a national health insurance program has been the cost to taxpayers, and

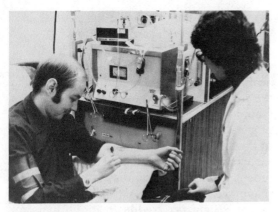

Patient learning to use a kidney dialysis machine

the effect such an expensive new program would have on the economy.

Health maintenance organizations

The present health care system is primarily curative in focus as it concentrates on illness and injury rather than on prevention. Most private health insurance policies do not at the present time cover periodic screening examinations, but only provide coverage when a person is actually sick or injured. Such a model puts a premium on rewarding providers of health services for treating illnesses, but not on preventing illnesses.

An alternative approach emphasizing preventive medicine is some form of a Health Maintenance Organization (HMO) plan. The federal government describes HMOs as follows:

> HMOs are organized *systems* of health care, providing comprehensive services for enrolled members, for a fixed, prepaid annual fee. No matter how each HMO may choose to organize itself (and there are various models), from the consumer's viewpoint they all provide a mix of outpatient and hospital services through a single organization and a single payment mechanism.

Because HMO revenues are fixed, their in-centives are to keep patients well, for they benefit from patient well-days, not sickness. Their entire cost structure is geared to preventing illness and, failing that, to promoting prompt recovery through the least costly services consistent with maintaining quality. In contrast with prevailing cost-plus insurance plans, the HMO's financial incentives tend to encourage the least utilization of high cost forms of care, and also tend to limit unnecessary procedures. . . .

In contrast with more traditional and alternative modes of care, HMOs show lower utilization rates for the most expensive types of care (measured by hospital days in particular); they tend to reduce the consumer's total health-care outlay; and—the ultimate test—they appear to deliver services of high quality. Available research studies show that HMO members are more likely than other population groups to receive such preventive measures as general checkups and prenatal care, and to seek care within one day of the onset of symptoms of illness or injuries.[21]

A number of HMO plans are already in operation, serving several million subscribers. Among the plans are the Health Insurance Plan of New York, the Kaiser-Permanente Plan, and the Group Health Association of Washington, D.C.[22]

With this initial success, preventive medicine plans are apt to be a future focus in health care.

MEDICAL SOCIAL WORK

Many public and private social welfare agencies (such as public welfare departments, adoption agencies, Family Service Agencies, neighborhood centers, probation and parole departments) are perceived as the specialty of social workers. Because such agencies are often managed by social workers, and social work is the primary service, such agencies are considered *primary* settings. Hospitals, medical clinics, and schools are, on the other hand, *secondary* settings, as the primary service is not social work. But this secondary focus does not reduce their importance for social work as health care and education serve a vital function and spend a substantial proportion of our national resources. Since social workers are not administratively in charge of secondary settings, problems related to status and influence sometimes arise. In such settings it is important for social workers to learn to work with those in control. The American doctor is the highest paid professional in our society, earning an average of over $50,000 per year, and physicians tend to expect a status consistent with their salary.[23] Some allied health professionals who work with physicians state that most doctors expect "godlike" respect.

The main setting for medical social work is the hospital. Dr. Richard C. Cabot first introduced social services into the Massa-

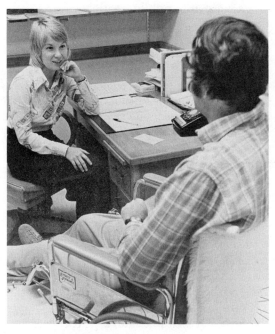

A medical social worker counseling a patient

chusetts General Hospital in 1905 in Boston. Now, almost every hospital has a social service department. Having a social services department is required by the American Hospital Association as a condition for accreditation.[24] Social workers not only provide direct casework with patients and their families, but also group work with certain patients, consultation, training of other professionals, and are involved in planning and policy development within the hospital and with various health agencies. At times medical social workers teach medical school courses in which they convey their professional knowledge of the sociopsychological components of illnesses and of the treatment process.

Increasingly it is becoming recognized that psychological processes are causative factors in nearly every illness; for example, in psychosomatic illnesses, alcoholism, depression, drug addiction, heart conditions, hypertension, susceptibility to viruses, bacteria and infections. The patient's emotions and motivation for recovery also substantially affect the treatment process. Venereal disease and cirrhosis of the liver, for instance, may evoke feelings of shame and guilt due to the stigma attached to these illnesses. People with heart conditions need to learn how to relax, avoid continued stressful conditions, and have the motivation to follow a prescribed diet. A miscarriage may result in a wide variety of emotional reactions that need to be dealt with. Adjusting to a chronic or permanent disability also evokes a variety of negative psychological reactions. A medical treatment team is increasingly dependent on social workers to attend to social and psychological factors that are either contributing causes of medical ailments or are side effects of a medical condition that must be dealt with to facilitate recovery and prevent the occurrence of nonfunctional dependency.

Physicians consider social work an allied

medical discipline, and in medical settings social workers become an integral part of the medical team. Along with doctors, nurses, and other therapists, social workers take part in the study, diagnosis, and treatment-planning processes for patients. A medical social worker frequently obtains important diagnostic information on the living conditions, environment, habits, personality, and income of patients. Since physicians are no longer as well acquainted with patients, such information is often vital in arriving at a diagnosis and a treatment plan. Through interviews with the patient and members of his family, the worker gains a perspective on the social and emotional components of the illness and how such components may affect treatment.

In medical social work (now often referred to as social work in the health field) a wide variety of problems and situations are encountered, examples of which are:

Helping terminally ill patients and their families adjust.

Counseling women who have had a mastectomy.

Helping a low-income wife from a distant area find lodging in the community while her husband undergoes heart surgery.

Counseling people who are so depressed they are contemplating suicide. Helping an unwed mother plan for the future.

Genetic counseling for a young couple who gave birth to a mentally retarded child.

Helping an executive of a large company to make plans for the future following a severe heart attack.

Counseling a woman about her emotional reactions following a miscarriage or a stillbirth.

Finding living arrangements that will provide some medical attention for people who no longer need to be hospitalized.

Counseling alcoholics and drug addicts or making appropriate referrals to other agencies.

Counseling patients about their apprehensions of undergoing surgery.

Helping someone suddenly struck with a permanent disability adjust and make plans for the future.

Meeting with relatives and friends of patients to help interpret the nature of the medical condition and perhaps solicit their help in a treatment plan to facilitate recovery.

Counseling someone with emphysema on how to stop smoking.

Counseling a rape victim on her psychological reactions.

Informing relatives about the medical condition of someone who has just had a severe automobile accident.

While dealing with such problems and situations, a social worker is almost always a member of a medical team that is headed by a physician.

The job of a social worker in the health field is a dynamic one which requires continued study and knowledge expansion. With the dramatic expansion of new therapy approaches for medical conditions (for example, organ transplants, new prescription drugs, extensive new surgery techniques, and so on), it is essential that medical social workers keep informed about new technological approaches.

Social work in hospitals tends to be short term, crisis oriented as there is generally a fairly rapid turnover of patients. Social workers are often involved in discharge planning (for example, making arrangements for patients to return to their families or to a convalescent home). Sometimes the social worker must act as an advocate to assure that the patient's rights are secured and that his/her needs are best served.

Although social workers in medical settings are primarily involved in direct services to patients and their families, there are occasions when they are involved in planning activities, administration of programs (for example, directing a hospice program for terminal patients to live their final months in dignity), research, and education of other professionals.

The development of specialized clinics and programs for genetics counseling, for abortion counseling, for treating alcoholics, for family planning, for treating drug abusers, and for serving the terminally ill, have created new opportunities for social workers in the health field. Often these programs are located away from hospitals. Nursing homes for the elderly and for the physically impaired are also increasingly employing social workers.

There is also a trend for group medical clinics, individual practitioners, family practice clinics, and prepaid health clinics to employ social workers to be part of a team in diagnosing and treating patients. Increasingly, social workers in such settings are working with high-risk groups playing a preventive as well as a therapeutic role. High-risk groups include teenage mothers, women requesting abortions, drug and alcohol abusers, persons undergoing organ transplants, severely depressed or highly anxious persons, persons under stress, persons attempting suicide, and amputees.

COUNSELING THE TERMINALLY ILL

One of the most difficult tasks of doctors, nurses, social workers, and other allied professionals in the health field is to help a terminally ill patient deal with dying. Death is often a frightening event, and the fear of death is a fear felt universally in all cultures. Material on counseling the terminally ill will briefly be presented to give the reader an experimental "feeling" of one of the most difficult counseling areas for health professionals.

Most people in our society die in a hospital. This setting, in itself, is one of the primary reasons that dying is so hard. Health professionals are committed to recovery, to healing. When someone is found to have a terminal illness, health professionals experience a sense of failure; in some cases even guilt that they cannot do more, or that they might have made a mistake that contributed to the terminal illness. A fair number of health professionals are not comfortable in counseling the terminally ill. They feel insecure, and do not know what to say or do. Oftentimes they have not come to terms with their own eventual death; that is, to see death as an integral part of their lives. If a professional person views death as a frightening, horrible taboo topic, he/she will never be able to face it calmly and helpfully with a patient.

Dr. Elisabeth Kübler-Ross (perhaps the foremost authority on death and dying in our era) has identified five stages that terminally ill patients may go through.[25] These stages are not absolute; not everyone goes through every stage according to the sequence described in the following figure. (Some patients never advance beyond the first or second stage).

The one thing that usually persists through all five stages is hope—hope for the discovery of an immediate "miracle" cure. Terminally ill patients all seem to have a little bit of it and are supported and nourished by it, especially during the most difficult times.

FIVE STAGES OF DYING THAT TERMINALLY ILL PEOPLE TYPICALLY PROCEED THROUGH

The following stages have been found to be a valuable paradigm in understanding why a terminally ill person may be behaving as s/he does:

Stage one: Denial—"It can't be." "No, not me." "There must be a mistake." This is generally the first reaction when a person learns he/she has a terminal illness. Doctor Ross believes such a reaction is functional as it helps cushion the impact that death will soon be inevitable.

Stage two: Rage and anger—"Why me?" "Look at the good things I've done, and still need to do for the members of my family." "This just isn't fair!" Patients resent the fact that they will soon die, while others remain healthy and alive. God is frequently a special target of the anger during this stage, as He is viewed as unfairly imposing a death sentence. Doctor Ross believes such anger is permissible and inevitable, and she adds, "God can take it."[26]

During this stage, family and hospital staff frequently experience difficulty in coping with the anger that is displaced in many directions and onto the surroundings. The patient may charge that the doctor is incompetent, that the hospital surroundings are inhumane, that the nurses are unconcerned about people, that there is too much noise, and so on. The underlying reasons generating the patient's anger need to be remembered during this stage. Reacting personally or angrily to the patient's anger will only feed into the patient's hostile behavior. During this stage conveying to the patient that he/she is an important person who is worthy of respect, time and understanding, will usually lead to a reduction of the angry demands.

Stage three: Bargaining—"I realize my death is inevitable, but if I could just live six months more I could. . . ." During this stage patients come to accept their terminal illness, but try to strike bargains (frequently with God) for more time. They promise to do something worthwhile or to be good in exchange for another month or year of life. Doctor Ross indicates even agnostics and atheists sometimes attempt to bargain with God during this stage.

Psychologically such promises may be associated with some underlying guilt. Frequently when such guilt exists it involves guilt for not attending church more regularly. It is helpful to have an interdisciplinary approach to counseling the terminally ill; in this stage it is often helpful to have a chaplain discuss such religious guilt with the patient.

Stage four: Depression—"Yes, it will soon be over.' "It's really sad, but true." The first phase of this stage is where the patient mourns things not done, past losses, and wrongs committed. This type of depression is frequently exacerbated by guilt or shame about acts of omission or commission. Counseling during this phase generally focuses on helping the patient to resolve feelings of guilt and shame; in some cases this may involve helping family members to make realistic plans for their future and to help the patient realize that other vital unfinished situations are being taken care of.

The second phase of this stage is where the patient enters a state of "preparatory grief" in which he/she is getting ready for the inevitable losses. During this stage the patient should not be encouraged to look at the sunny side of things, as this would interfere with the necessity for the patient to contemplate his (her) impending death. During this phase the patient generally becomes quiet and does not want to see visitors. S/he is in the process of losing everything and everybody s/he loves. If allowed to express this sorrow, s/he will find final acceptance of death much easier, and will be grateful to those who are able to sit quietly with him (her), without telling him (her) not to be sad. According to Doctor Ross, when a dying patient no longer continues to request to see someone to discuss his (her) situation, it is a sign s/he has finished his (her) unfinished business, and has reached the final stage.

Stage five: Acceptance—"I will soon pass on, and it's all right." Doctor Ross describes this final stage as "not a happy stage, but neither is it unhappy. It's devoid of feelings, but it's not resignation, it's really a victory."[27] During this stage visitors are often not desired as the patient no longer is in a talkative mood. Communications with a counselor may become more nonverbal than verbal. Patients may just want to hold the counselor's hand, while sitting together in silence with someone who is comfortable in the presence of a dying person.

SOURCE: Elisabeth Kübler-Ross, *On Death and Dying* (New York: Macmillan, 1969).

In regard to hope, the desired direction in counseling is to be honest with the patient about the probable outcome, while allowing the patient to hope for the million-to-one chance of a miracle recovery.

To work with the terminally ill requires maturity which only comes from experience. The most important communication is the "door-opening interview" in which the counselor lets the dying patient know that the counselor is ready and willing to share the dying person's concerns without fear and anxiety. A prerequisite is that the counselor has an attitude towards his/her own death which s/he is comfortable with.

Mwalimu Imara views dying as having the potential for being the final stage of

growth, and gives a number of suggestions on how to come to terms with one's own dying.[28] Having a well-developed sense of identity (that is, sense of who you are) is an important step. (Chapter 2 in his text elaborates on how to develop a positive identity.) Involved in developing a sense of identity is arriving at realistic life goals that one will have pride in achieving. Without a blueprint of what will give meaning and direction to our lives, we will experience our lives as fragmented and aimless.

Imara indicates the fifth stage of acceptance for a dying patient corresponds to a person with a healthy identity. A person who comes to accept a terminal illness has also arrived at a fairly well-thought-out, unified sense of him/herself. Death is the final stage of growth for a terminally ill person when the patient finally develops a unified sense of self, and becomes accepting of dying in the near future. Hopefully people will develop a healthy identity long before the final crisis, and thus be fairly prepared before the final crisis arises.

Imara adds that all of us experience separations and pains throughout life that lead to personal growth; for example, leaving family to attend kindergarten, leaving high school to seek work or attend college, leaving work and friends to seek a better position at a different geographic area, romantic and perhaps marital separations that hopefully lead to personal growth. Imara indicates

> abandoning old ways and breaking old patterns is like dying, at least dying to old ways of life for an unknown new life of meaning and relationships. But living without change is not living at all, not growing at all.[29]

Imara adds that making changes in our lives are filled with fears and anxieties. If such changes lead to personal growth, we will be prepared to face new challenges and changes in our lives. Through a willingness to risk the unknown, we are undertaking the search of ourselves. Such separations and new challenges raise fears and anxieties that are analogous to those that will arise when we become aware our death is near. Overcoming fears and anxieties that arise from current challenges (and learning more about ourself through these experiences) prepares us for the fears and anxieties that will arise when we are informed our death is near.

SUMMARY

Medical services in this country are organized into four subsystems: Physicians in solo practice, group outpatient settings, hospital settings, and public health services.

The cost of health care has risen astronomically in the past few decades. The health care industry is now the third-largest U.S. industry. The federal government provides the Medicaid program to cover the medical costs of public assistance recipients, and the Medicare program which provides partial health insurance coverage for the elderly. A national health insurance program is needed to cover catastrophic expenses which are not covered by most private insurance plans, and to meet the medical needs of those who are currently uninsured, or insufficiently insured. A variety of national health insurance programs have been proposed, with the main objection to such a program being the cost to taxpayers and the effect such an expensive program would have on the economy.

A major problem is that modern medicine is oriented toward crisis medicine which is geared to treating people after they become ill. In order to more effectively curb the incapacitating effects of chronic diseases, the health care delivery system needs to give greater emphasis to the prevention of illness before extensive damage occurs.

Health care is a secondary setting for social work. In such a setting social workers are generally a member of a team, and need to learn to work with those in charge. A medical treatment team is increasingly dependent on social workers to attend to sociopsychological factors that are either contributing causes of illnesses or are side effects of a medical condition that must be dealt with to facilitate recovery. As a member of a medical team, social workers have an important role in diagnosing and treating medical conditions.

A social worker in the health field needs skills and knowledge on how to counsel people with a wide variety of medical conditions. Some, such as counseling the terminally ill, require a high level of emotional maturity, a well-thought-out identity and a high level of competence in counseling.

NOTES

1. Thomas Sullivan et al., "Health Care," *Social Problems* (New York: Wiley, 1980), pp. 262–63.

2. K. R. Pelletier, *Mind as Healer, Mind as Slayer* (New York: Delta, 1977).

3. Sullivan et al., *Social Problems,* p. 281.

4. "Battle Begins over National Health Insurance," *U.S. News & World Report,* June 25, 1979, p. 63.

5. Ibid., 63.

6. Ibid., pp. 62–63.

7. Sullivan et al., *Social Problems,* p. 281.

8. Pelletier, *Mind as Healer, Mind as Slayer.*

9. Ibid.

10. Hans Selye, *The Stress of Life* (New York: McGraw-Hill, 1956).

11. These stress-reducing techniques are described in Charles Zastrow, *Talk to Yourself* (Englewood Cliffs, N.J.: Prentice-Hall, 1979).

12. Spencer Klaw, *The Great American Medicine Show* (New York: Viking Press, 1975).

13. Duane F. Stroman, *The Quick Knife: Unnecessary Surgery U.S.A.* (Port Washington, N.Y.: Kennikat Press, 1978).

14. Walter A. Friedlander and Robert Z. Apte, *Introduction to Social Welfare,* 4th ed. (Englewood Cliffs, N.J.: Prentice-Hall, 1974), p. 414.

15. *The Presidents Commission on Mental Health,* 1

(Washington, D.C.: U.S. Government Printing Office, 1978).

16. *Report of the Task Force on Medicaid and Related Programs* (Washington, D.C.: U.S. Department of Health, Education and Welfare, 1970).

17. Donald Brieland, Lela B. Costin, and Charles R. Atherton, *Contemporary Social Work* (New York: McGraw-Hill, 1975), p. 120.

18. "Battle Begins," p. 62.

19. Ibid., p. 62.

20. "The Battle Starts Over National Health Insurance," *U.S. News & World Report,* August 7, 1978, p. 54.

21. *Towards a Comprehensive Health Policy for the 1970's: A White Paper* (Washington, D.C.: U.S. Department of Health, Education and Welfare, May 1971), pp. 31–32.

22. W. Palmer Dearing, M.D., "Health Care System: Group Medical Practice," *Encyclopedia of Social Work* (New York: NASW, 1971), pp. 538–51.

23. U.S. Bureau of the Census, *Statistical Abstract of the United States, 1980* (Washington, D.C.: U.S. Government Printing Office, 1980).

24. Elisabeth Kübler-Ross, *On Death and Dying* (New York: Macmillan, 1969).

25. Elisabeth Kübler-Ross, *Death: The Final Stage of Growth* (Englewood Cliffs, N.J.: Prentice-Hall, 1975), p. 10.

26. Kübler-Ross, *On Death and Dying.*

27. Ibid.

28. Mwalimu Imara, "Dying as the Last Stage of Growth" in Kübler-Ross, *Death: The Final Stage of Growth,* pp. 147–63.

29. Ibid., p. 148.

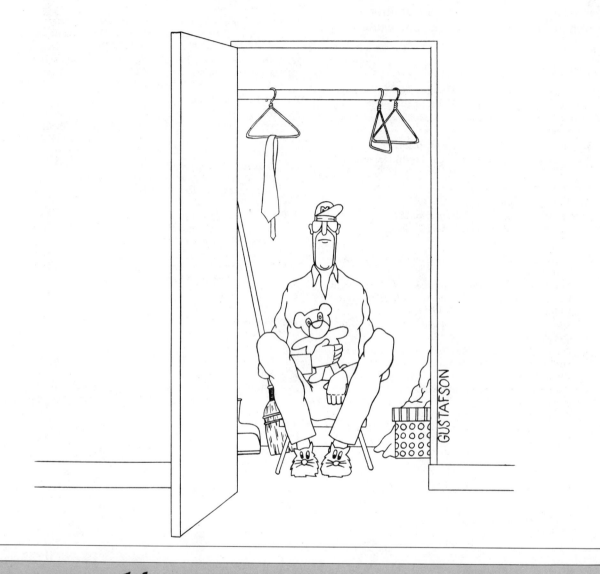

chapter 14

Soon after I was asked to submit a chapter for this text, I had the good fortune of meeting a couple by the name of Fred and Bev Jacobson. The Jacobsons had just been through a six-months experience that would take most of us a lifetime to assimilate. Their first child, a beautiful baby girl named Eve, was born in August 1976 after an uncomplicated pregnancy and delivery. She was diagnosed as being retarded soon after birth, and just as these parents were beginning to adjust to having a retarded child, Eve died unexpectedly at a residential facility on Christmas Day 1976 as the parents were on their way to visit her. They had her at the center only two days before so they could take a vacation out of state.

The rest of the Jacobson's story I will let them tell you by interjecting parts of a transcript of a discussion I had with them less than two months after Eve died. This family has been generous enough to share their

experiences with us. Through this chapter, Eve and her parents have given us a legacy for which I am personally grateful. Since Bev Jacobson is a practicing social worker, she was able to look at her experience from a dual perspective.

I have inserted portions of the transcript where I felt it would be helpful without analyzing it or drawing conclusions. The statements speak for themselves and to analyze them would be to diminish their impact.

The format for the chapter will be as follows:

1. Overview of mental retardation
   a. Definitions of terms.
   b. Nature and etiology of retardation.
   c. Prenatal diagnosis and prevention.
2. Parental reactions to mental retardation
   a. Reactions to having a retarded child.
   b. The grief process over time.
3. Social work intervention with parents of retarded children
   a. Casework intervention.
   b. Group work as an intervention technique.

* This chapter was written for this text by Maureen O'Gorman Foster with the collaboration of Fred and Beverly Jacobson. Foster was Coordinator of Family Services at a residential facility for the retarded and is currently executive director of a Hospice home health care program.

Mental retardation and current services*

OVERVIEW OF MENTAL RETARDATION

Definition of terms

There is no single area of human services and human service delivery systems that has taken such giant steps during the past 20 years as the area of mental retardation. Within the memory of many of us in the field, words like *imbecile, moron,* and *idiot* were used to describe those individuals who were generally classified as "feebleminded." These terms perpetuated elements of fear and mystique among the general public because of the connotation of the terms.

For the past century, the American Association on Mental Deficiency (AAMD) has been active in diminishing public ignorance, and establishing a system of classification of the retarded for use by professionals. Terms have been adopted to describe the approximate level of intellectual and adaptive behavior. AAMD defines *mental retardation* as referring to "significantly subaverage general intellectual functioning existing concurrently with deficits in adaptive behavior and manifested during the developmental period."[1] Roughly, the terms now used give an idea as to the intellectual and adaptive functioning of the individuals as determined by use of the standardized IQ tests and an assessment of the appropriateness of behavior according to age level. The terms and the scores used to make this determination on the basis of the Stanford-Binet and Cattell IQ tests are as follows:

Mild 68–52   Severe 35–20
Moderate 51–36   Profound 19 and below

Prior to 1973, the term *borderline retarded* was used to describe those individuals whose IQ was 1–2 standard deviations (IQ from 70 to 80) from the normal. This group has been dropped from the definition of mental retardation by including the words "substantially subaverage." The current thinking is that these individuals should be referred to as persons with "borderline intelligence."

The determination of the intellectual functioning of the retarded is made by a professional person trained in the administration of tests necessary to determine intellectual and adaptive functioning. These determinations are limiting insofar as they say nothing about the etiology or prognosis of the individual tested, and yet they do serve as a general guideline to social workers and other professionals in programming and planning.

Another term recently adapted for use is *developmental disability*. This term is more inclusive than mental retardation because it includes disabilities attributable to cerebral palsy, epilepsy, or other neurological conditions closely related to mental retardation or requiring treatment similar to mental retardation. As in the definition of mental retardation, these disabilities are limited to those that occur in the developmental period (below age 18) and which can be expected to continue to constitute a substantial handicap to the individual. The use of this broader term in recent legislation has made it possible to have this group considered eligible for services provided for in legislation for the retarded.[2]

Nature and etiology of retardation

An entire volume would be needed to adequately describe the various causes of retardation. Time and place necessitate a brief summary of the causes under the general categories suggested by AAMD. Examples will be given to assist the reader in placing those disorders like Down's syndrome (mongolism) and Phenylketonuria (PKU) with which most of the general public are familiar. The discussion will include new services and tests that have reduced the risks of mental retardation and that all social workers should be aware of in dealing with clients in every area of social service.

Mental retardation and gestational disorders. Many infants born prematurely (before 37 weeks gestation) or during what is considered the postmaturity period (generally more than seven days after the normal pregnancy period), are considered to be at increased risk for being mentally retarded. Specialized clinics for mothers who are known to be at increased risk for premature or postmature delivery are now available in many large metropolitan areas and are complemented by neonatal intensive care units for the infant. These reduce the risk of neurological damage as a result of gestational problems by providing teams of highly trained specialists and advanced equipment and testing devices.

Trauma or physical agent. Injury to the brain can occur at any time in the prenatal, perinatal, or postnatal development. If the brain is deprived of oxygen (anoxia) or receives an amount of oxygen insufficient to maintain functioning of the brain tissue (hypoxia), then brain cells will be destroyed and mental retardation may result. In the prenatal and perinatal period, this can occur for a number of reasons, including premature separation of the placenta, knotted umbilical cord, or difficult birth as a result of breech position to name a few. Causes of postnatal damage from trauma can occur from so many causes that to dwell on them would make most parents tremble with fear. In my experience along, I have seen children severely damaged as a result of battering by a parent or caretaker; child victims of near drowning in everything from a pail to a pond, and children who suffer trauma from football accidents, car and bicycle accidents, and accidents involving sleds, go-carts, horses, and motor bikes.

Infections and intoxications. Mental retardation following prenatal infection and intoxication is the result of such diseases and conditions as:

Rubella. Pregnant women who have a clinical or subclinical case of German measles (Rubella) during their first trimester of pregnancy have a substantially increased risk of having a child who is retarded and who has other congenital abnormalities such as blindness, deafness, microcephaly, and heart anomalies. Mass immunization programs during the last five years protect the generation of childbearing women of the future and provide some protection of women now in their childbearing years by reducing the source of infection. Blood tests are available to determine the level of protection a woman has against the virus so that she can become immunized before pregnancy. Public awareness and immunization may possibly make this cause a matter for historical consideration in the next 20 years.

Syphilis. This condition occurs from the infection of the fetus through the placenta. The results can be devastating and include many physical and behavioral problems in addition to mental retardation. To the extent that the services and treatment for venereal diseases are used, this cause of mental retardation might also be eradicated.

Other viral infections are known to be contributory; the above are examples of the more well known.

Toxemia. Although strides have been made in determining the conditions under which an unborn child might be affected by the mother's general health, there are far too many unanswered questions about the cause-effect relationship.

In addition to posing a risk for the pregnant woman, toxemia can pose a risk for the unborn infant if prolonged and untreated. Any woman getting early, regular, and specialized care during pregnancy can avoid the effects of toxic poisoning; screening for toxemia is a regular part of all prenatal care. Toxemia is a condition associated with the presence of toxic (that is, poisonous) substances in the blood.

Drug intoxication. Use of drugs during pregnancy should be limited to those prescribed by a physician. Many of the medications used in medical practice are harmful to the fetus.

Alcohol. The most serious risk to the developing fetus is the Fetal Alcohol Syndrome (FAS). This syndrome is associated with heavy drinking, generally considered to be five or six drinks on occasion. FAS is characterized by cranial and facial abnormalities, joint and limb anomalies, possible cardiac defects, and delayed physical and mental development. Binge drinking and regular social drinking have been associated with decreased weight of the fetus, increased risk of stillbirth, increased risk of anomalies, and behavioral deficits in the newborn.[3]

Maternal conditions other than above. Generally any mother who is a diabetic or has other metabolic conditions has an increased risk of having a retarded child.

Postnatal cerebral infection. Bacterial and viral infections such as meningitis and encephalitis can cause severe and irreversible brain damage, especially if not treated in the early stages of illness.

Disorders related to metabolism or nutrition. Included in this category are disorders of amino acid metabolism, like Phenylketonuria, and many disorders of lipids and carbohydrates. Retardation due to Phenylketonuria has been greatly reduced because of mandatory infant screening through blood tests in the neonatal period. Careful dietary programs have prevented or diminished the severe effects of this condition. The lipid storage disorders are less well known but include Tay-Sachs disease, and

Hunters and Hurlers syndrome. These involve a progressive degenerative process because of the accumulation of fatty substances in the cells, that is, "storage," eventually leading to the death of the affected individual. These conditions are inherited and while little is known about effective treatment, the incidence can be greatly reduced through genetic counseling programs and prenatal diagnosis. Also included in this general category are the disorders of endocrine function such as cretinism and the carbohydrate disorders.

Disorders of unknown prenatal influence. Conditions such as hydrocephalus and microcephalus fall under this category. Microcephalus refers to the reduced circumference of the head. As a primary condition, this disorder might be inherited as a recessive characteristic or might be secondary to fetal or neonatal brain damage. Hydrocephalus refers to a condition in which there is an increased amount of cerebrospinal fluid within the skull, usually causing an enlargement of the skull. Great strides have been made in diminishing the retardation resulting from hydrocephalus through neurosurgical techniques which prevent brain damage by decreasing the pressure that causes brain damage. Spina bifida means an incomplete formation of the spinal column. This condition may or may not be accompanied by hydrocephalus; if nervous tissue herniates through the defect it is called meningomyelocele and can cause paralysis in varying degrees.

Mental retardation association with chromosome abnormalities. Down's syndrome is the most common and best known of the disorders in this category. This condition, in which there exists an extra chromosome in the pair of number 21 chromosome, occurs in

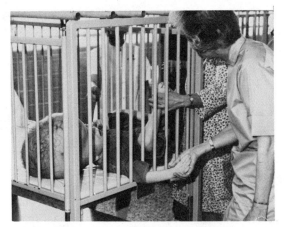

A hydrocephalic child: Neurosurgical techniques are now quite successful in decreasing the pressure that causes brain damage

children born to mothers of all ages. The incidence, however, in mothers over age 35 is substantially higher than in the general population (1 in 150 births for mothers over 35). Ordinarily diagnosis is made in the immediate neonatal period. These children bear a striking resemblance to one another. Intelligence range is from moderate to severe. Other chromosomal abnormalities can occur either in structure or number of many other chromosomes.

Environmental influences. There are a number of individuals whose function is impaired by adverse environmental factors and a lack of sufficient stimuli. In the past, these cases were referred to as the cultural-familial type and are likely to occur in economically deprived families or families where either or both parents are themselves impaired in their intellectual and adaptive development. The cause probably is multiple; a combination of genetic, inherited factors compounded by environmental influences like poor prenatal care, malnutrition, frequent accidents, infections, lack of discipline, good health habits, and stimulation.

After reading the survey of causes above, the temptation is to think that with all possibilities of having a retarded child, it is impossible to believe that one could have a baby who is normal and healthy and stays that way through the entire developmental period. The risk of having a retarded child is low and every prospective parent should approach parenthood with optimism. In fact, each parent does just that. Each person reading this chapter is assuming either consciously or subconsciously that the percentage of retarded children born in this generation will be born to someone other than themselves. Most likely each of the parents of retarded children I have dealt with thought the same thing. Other than retardation of the cultural-familial origin, the problems we have discussed have no respect for educational level, social status, or good intentions of the parents. While precautions can be taken to decrease the chances of retardation it can and does occur everyday in families where early and excellent prenatal care was sought, and the mother stayed away from all agents which are known or suspected to be toxic, and where no illness occurred during the gestational period and the birth was uncomplicated.

Social learning

Prenatal diagnosis and prevention

Impressive gains are being made in the field that have implications for prevention. Amniocentesis is a procedure where amniotic fluid is taken from the uterus of a pregnant woman at risk for the purpose of chromosome and biochemical analysis. Although some small risk of miscarriage is involved, amniocentesis is a fairly simple procedure. A needle is inserted through the uterus, and amniotic fluid is extracted for study. In early pregnancy this procedure can be used to detect Down's syndrome and other conditions associated with chromosomal abnormalities. Sex of the fetus can be determined for those conditions that are sex-linked. The parents may then be offered a therapeutic abortion if the fetus is known to be affected or is at risk of being affected. Amniocentesis may be used later in pregnancy, usually the last trimester, to determined maturation of the fetus. This is indicated if the mother has a complicated medical or gestational history.

Alpha-fetaprotein, a constituent of the amniotic fluid, is one substance used in prenatal diagnosis. There is evidence that elevated levels of this protein can also be found in blood of women who are carrying children with conditions associated with leakage of cerebrospinal fluid (anencephaly, meningomyelocele). Ultrasound is another technological advance used primarily to determine gestational age, to test for multiple births, and in some cases to confirm microcephaly and other gross abnormalities.

It is imperative to a social worker in the area of mental retardation to understand the reaction of parents to having a child who is mentally retarded. Whether we are working in a situation where the parent rather than the child is seen as our client or whether we're working with retarded children or adults, we will have to deal with parents who are continually trying to cope with having a retarded child.

PARENTAL REACTIONS TO MENTAL RETARDATION

Reactions to having a retarded child

Following is a brief survey of the emotional reactions of parents to having a child who is retarded. These reactions may occur one at a time or simultaneously and are in no way to be interpreted as "stages." They are in fact grief reactions, grief over the loss of the "perfect child" that each parent expects to have. It is also imperative to point out that these reactions are emotional reactions, reactions of the gut, and as such are not necessarily rational.

Denial. While it is not difficult to imagine the denial aspects of a parent's reaction as manifested by statements like "They must be wrong. I can't believe that this has happened to our baby (child)," social workers quite often do not recognize the manifestations of this reaction over time. The "doctor shopping" that sometimes occurs as well as the anger at professionals manifested at a school, workshop or clinical setting can also be a form of denial. Any situation in which professionals confirm, reaffirm, or expand upon information about the child or adult retarded's limitations can elicit a denial reaction.

Anger. The targets for anger relative to a child's retardation must be considered separately. These targets are: the child, professionals, friends, relatives, God, self, and spouse. Each of the areas in which a child fails to develop normally presents the parent with a burden that in and of itself can make the child a target for anger. A parent's expectation when having a child is that the child will initially be dependent and that this dependency will gradually diminish in each developmental area over time. Recognition that with a retarded child this is not neces-

INTERVIEW SHOWING SOME OF THE PARENTAL REACTIONS TO HAVING A MENTALLY RETARDED CHILD

M:* Bev, I wonder if you could tell me a little bit about Eve and her problems, when you found out about them, and how you reacted at the time you found out about her problems.

B: Well, I found out about Eve's problem a few minutes after she was born. I had a perfectly normal, uneventful pregnancy and I had not been aware of any difficulties until the obstetrician brought her to me and told me that things were not well with her. At that point it was obvious that she had serious deformities in the arms and legs, but it wasn't until a couple of days later that we became aware that there were problems with her central nervous system as well.

M: All of this was pretty much known to you then before you left the hospital?

B: Yes, the doctors and the nursing staff were very good about sharing all the information they had with us, so I think that we probably knew as much as they did at every step along the way while I was in the hospital.

M: Were there very early signs other than the obvious deformities in the extremities that problems existed; a seizure disorder or anything of that nature?

B: Well, she was very nonresponsive. She didn't open her eyes for several days. She had almost no voluntary movement. She ate very poorly. She seemed to be completely out of touch with the world around her.

M: Do you remember what your initial reaction was to finding out that Eve had problems?

B: My initial reaction was to faint and then the second time that the obstetrician told me that there were problems, I managed to hear him. My reaction after that was to be numb for a couple of days. I didn't feel much besides the certainty that I didn't want to spend the rest of my entire life caring for a severely handicapped kid.

F: It was clear to us after Eve was born that . . . it was like, you know, we wanted to return her—defective merchandise.

B: I used to have the most incredible fantasies—just that kind of thing and then I would have to like stop myself and say no, you can't exchange her for a better model. One of the first things I thought about was institutionalization. It took a couple of days before we could decide on a name for her and it took a couple of weeks before we could decide to bring her home with us. I think around the second or third day after she was born I started to feel very sad. I remember spending a day or two in the hospital just crying. I felt also that I didn't want to go home and face the rest of my life cause I had all I could deal with just being in the hospital, having somebody else taking care of all my needs. I wasn't sure I could do it myself.

M: You didn't take Eve home with you then right away?

B: No. That was partly out of her needs and partly out of Fred's and mine. She was eating very poorly and was not gaining weight and the doctors wanted to be able to monitor her condition fairly closely for a while. Also, I didn't feel ready to care for her at that point and I didn't know if

I wanted to make the kind of commitment to her that taking her home would entail.

M: Did you feel guilty at that time about considering institutional care or considering just not taking her home from the hospital?

B: Not very guilty, and looking back on it now, I'm kind of surprised about that. I think in some ways I've always been a very selfish person, or I'm comfortable with my selfishness. So, the fact that I thought about myself first wasn't that surprising, or that unacceptable to me. Also, both Fred's parents and mine were very supportive of our needs and didn't place on us any expectations that we should take care of this child no matter what. In fact, if anything, they were probably encouraging us in the other direction—to think of our own needs first.

M: You didn't find very judgmental attitudes then as you began making decisions that were important for you as a couple and for Eve?

B: In most cases, no. When we were first deciding whether or not to bring Eve home our pediatrician urged us quite strongly to do so feeling that it would be best in terms of her needs and also ultimately in terms of our feelings about her and about ourselves. I can recall feeling somewhat pushed by him at the time but realizing intellectually that he was right. Looking back on it I think that it was a very wise thing for him to do and I'm very glad he did it.

F: He encouraged us to bring her home without making any explicit, implied commitment that this was forever. He wanted us to give it a shot, see what we could do, then we would learn what effect it had on us and how well we could do it and what we could do and what we couldn't do, and that's exactly the way it turned out. We learned how to do it. We learned how to keep our lives, how to do it without sacrificing everything for this baby, this poor baby.

M: How successful were you in meeting all of these demands and not yet altering your lives?

F: Today I said to a friend of mine, who is going to have his first child in a month, things are never the same. That is just the way it is. It's a good thing. That is one of the most important things about having children is that things are not the same. If they were you would not have that extra thing that you get. But I thought we were on the whole successful. We didn't hide; she was well. It was a blessing that she was an easy baby to get along with. I think that if she had been a baby that cried all the time and raised hell and wouldn't travel and stuff like that, it would have been horrible in comparison, but she was extra mellow. She was very well, especially when she was very young, she was. . . .

B: She was almost totally not demanding.

F: She slept almost all the time, never cried. The only really tough thing was getting her to eat and that was a five-hour-a-day job. But outside of that, which is a time consuming thing, that is most of it. We could take her places. We only had been home a few days and we could take her to the movies and we alternated holding her on our laps and she didn't cause any trouble and we could take her to parties and things like that. Later on when she was more in touch with the outer world, one of the last things that we did with her was we took her to a Christmas party and she was wonderful. People held her and she was relaxed and warm and everybody enjoyed her and she behaved very nicely. At one point I thought she's tired and I put her in the bedroom and she started to fuss because she wanted to be with people, or apparently so.

M: During this period of time you had no idea that Eve was not going to survive her first year. Had you begun looking at the time consuming feedings stretched out over the next year to come or the next two years or four years? Had that been something you started dealing with yet?

B: Let me backtrack here a little bit. I think we had considered all along that she was a very fragile little child and that she might not live very long. We didn't really place any kind of time frame around that, though I assumed some place in the back of my head that she probably wouldn't live to adulthood. We had pretty much decided a couple of weeks before her death that we would place her in foster care, and the reasons for that were partly the time demand that her care necessitated and partially the fact that we were thinking about having another child. She was our first child and we still wanted a normal baby, and I really didn't feel that I could be pregnant and care for her at the same time because of my own emotional, physical constraints . . . from a pregnancy. And I also felt pretty sure that I couldn't care for two very dependent babies at the same time. It was clear to me that she would need to be cared for as an infant for many years. At the same time I wanted to be very involved in her life and her care—no matter where she was, and I was hoping to find foster parents that would accept the idea of shared parenthood.

M: What was the reaction of your extended family to your decision to place Eve in foster care?

B: They knew about it and had a hard time understanding. They could accept much more easily the idea of her being in an institution.

F: We also felt that a lot.

B: Right.

F: Just by that you're saying, well, she can't be cared for in a home; therefore . . . .

B: Right, and I think also our parents had a hard time seeing her as a person. She was a cluster of handicaps to them so I'm not sure they ever understood the reason that we decided to place her in foster care, and they also had a very hard time understanding that she was not in bad enough shape to be institutionalized. At the same time they really did trust us to do the right thing, I think, and didn't give us much pressure to make one decision or another nor offer much resistance. I think particularly considering that our parents live around a 1,000 miles away they were as supportive as they could have been and were certainly willing to do anything that we might have asked of them.

M: How did your friends react?

B: I think in terms of people at work, since I work in a helping agency the idea of placing a child in foster care is not quite as alien as in Fred's part of the world so I had a more accepting environment in terms of those decisions. I think also because Fred was uneasy about placing Eve I didn't have to experience my own uneasiness. If he had been more assured I think I would have gotten a little more uncomfortable.

F: Let me characterize the way I felt cause I can remember very clearly that I realized that. The point at which I realized I was going to have to work on this, and pick a person to tell and tell them was when I imagined the situation when she was no longer at home, and they asked me how she was and then I would have to essentially lie or conceal information. I absolutely didn't want to be in that situation under any circumstances. So I realized at that point that I had to set up a program for myself to get over this hurdle, and I was about to do it and I was kind of steeling myself for that task when she died. I guess I got off without having to do that difficult thing.

B: The extended family can certainly make things more easy or more difficult for you as parents of handicapped children, and though what I think Fred and I discovered is our own level of comfort with whatever action we had decided on greatly determined how other people were going to react, and if we were comfortable and very assured about our decision people didn't try very hard to shake us.

F: One of the things that I came to realize is that people have very, very strong feelings of what it is to be a parent. I think that this is one of the things that one's own parents expect you to have learned. They expect you to have the same expectations that they have. They think that one of the signs that they've brought you up correctly is. . . .

B: That you think the same way they do.

F: —You think the same way they do about parenting which is a sense of survival, of some kind of tradition. That seems to be the most direct thing because that's going to affect your children and in turn down the generations. Everyone has a strong sense; anyone who has children has a strong sense of what the responsibilities of a parent are, and I didn't have children and didn't have a very strong sense and I was very unsure of the decision to place Eve and very uncomfortable with the decision.

B: I think both of us were.

F: I told my parents that and I figured that they could accept that. I told them that it was a difficult decision but that we were doing as well as we could in making the decision. This was how it had come out and I think by then they could see that we were doing what we could and that we were doing okay. I think they respected the fact that the decisions were ours to make. But one of the things that was bothering me at the time that Eve died was that I hadn't told anyone at work that we were going to place her because I wasn't comfortable with confronting people's concepts of the responsibilities of parenting, especially the traditional idea that one sacrifices everything for one's children. I had trouble giving up that traditional idea even though I saw that it just doesn't work that way. It certainly wouldn't work that way with me. I felt if I were sacrificing for my child something that was very important to me, in the end it wouldn't come out straight. It would come out all twisted. I think I've seen a little of that in a lot of families, including my own, and I didn't want to fall into that trap, that easy rule that you always sacrifice everything for your children—your children are always more important than you. And yet I think it was something that was taught to me.

* The initial "M" refers to Maureen (author of this chapter), "B" to Bev, and "F" to Fred. This is a transcript of a taped conversation between the Jacobsons and myself shortly after we were introduced by a mutual friend.

sarily the case and that in any event the development will be painfully slow can be burdensome, even early in the life of the child. Potty training that is ordinarily accomplished in four to six months may take four to six years, and total independence may never be achieved. A parent may become angry with the child because of what they may perceive as obstinance on the part of the child. Again, it is important to remember that grief reactions need not be and often are not rational.

Professionals who deal with parents of developmentally disabled children are also likely targets for a parent's anger, at times because they deserve to be, and often just because they happen to be there. Several years ago a parent shared an experience she had had with a pediatrician at the time her child was diagnosed; Kelly was 18 months of age when her mother took her in for a physical. After asking a number of pertinent questions about the child's development and finding by the answers to those questions that the child was obviously delayed, he said, "Do you know why Kelly isn't doing these things?" When

the mother responded that she did not, the physician said, "Because she's mentally retarded." He had not even made a physical examination of the child at this point and did not take the time at any point to deal with the mother's shock.

It is easy to see in the example related above why a parent may be outraged. Even the most sensitive and skilled professional, however, may find him/herself the target of anger. The fact that a parent has had disappointing experiences with professionals in the past, the fact that the professional is relating information that the parent does not want to hear or accept, or just because the professional is present at a time when the parent needs to dissipate anger may account for this.

Anger at God is another common reaction of parents. The "why me" questions enter a parent's mind and parents may feel cheated or betrayed by God.

Anger at self and spouse that occurs hardly be separated from discussion of the guilt factors that will follow. Anger at spouse can be for a number of things, real or imagined, that a parent feels the spouse did or did not do to prevent the retardation. One mother with whom I worked refused to co-operate in giving information necessary to determine the etiology of her childrens' problems (four out of six were retarded) because she wished to continue blaming her husband and her in-laws for the retardation. The father in this case had a distant relative who was deaf and the mother feared genetic counseling that might reveal that the cause was different than what she suspected.

Guilt. Guilt is the feeling of having committed a breach of conduct. The breach of conduct involves actions, real or imagined, done or omitted. The tendency of parents, at least initially, is to be introspective. Before physicians or social workers are even dealing with the possible causes of the problems, parents are beginning to ask themselves questions like, "Why didn't I take him/her to a doctor sooner?" "Could this have been caused by my smoking during pregnancy?" This tendency to look to one's self for the cause is reinforced by nearly every professional with whom the parent deals. The questions asked over and over again are, "Did *you* smoke?" "Did *you* drink, take pills, become ill during pregnancy?" While I am not suggesting for a moment that these questions need not be asked or not be repeated once asked, I am suggesting that the professional be aware of the possible effects on parents of asking these questions. Once questions have been asked and documented they should be repeated only if necessary, and certainly not as a "warm-up" exercise in an interview situation.

Planning for the future of a retarded child poses many questions that again and again trigger a guilt reaction. Parents are often faced with the question of whether or not they can care for their retarded child, especially if the child is severely handicapped.

Frustration. Closely related to the previous discussion of anger is the discussion of frustration. Since all parents expect a near perfect child, all parents experience frustration even with normally developing children; children tend not to live up to parents' expectations. This frustration is magnified, however, at every stage of expected development with a child who is retarded, and continues as long as the retarded child lives. As mentioned earlier the parent may experience frustration over the length of time needed to achieve each skill. Once a school placement has occurred the parent may find that the expected developmental potential is much lower than previously thought.

Fear. The elements of fear common in accepting the developmental delays of a child are varied. Initially they may involve fear of shame from family and friends, or fear that normal siblings may suffer from having a brother or sister who is retarded. They may also fear the burdens caused by having a retarded child. Most parents realize that their own lifestyle will be altered more with the birth of a retarded child than with a normal child. Over time the fears only change in scope. Parents may fear that their child will be the target of ridicule when he/she begins school, or will be a social burden to their normal siblings. Adolescence brings the fear of providing for the social needs of a retarded child and providing a framework within which the adolescent retarded person can find sexual expression without exploitation. Overriding all the fears mentioned above is the fear that the parents will die before the retarded child or adult, thus perhaps leaving little protection of the rights of the retarded.

It is important to emphasize several points before examining the reactions of parents over time.

1. This list is not exhaustive. The reactions of a parent will depend on many factors including the severity of the retardation, the point in life at which the birth occurs, parental expectations for normal development, to name a few.

2. These reactions cannot in any way be described as "stages." These reactions will come and go, as seen in the section to follow, in varying degrees throughout the life of the developmentally disabled child.

3. None can be considered mutually exclusive. A parent may feel guilty and angry at the same time and hardly be able to recognize where one reaction begins and another ends.

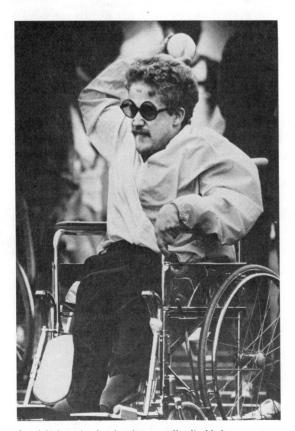

Special olympics for developmentally disabled

4. These reactions again are feelings that may, and often will, spontaneously occur, independent of rational thought processes that the parent will go through in coming to an acceptance of their child and that child's problems.

The grief process over time

The immediate grieving period. Experts on grief are inclined to say that a "normal" grief process lasts approximately six months, give or take a little time. Certainly, if the experts are correct, periods of "relapse" into an intense grieving can be both guilt producing and frightening. Parents who suffer an intense period of overwhelming grief a year or two after discovering their child is retarded may withdraw and remain silent for fear of appearing abnormal. The isolation thus imposed can be compounded by fear for one's own sanity. The conclusion easily drawn is, "If normal grief reactions are limited to a certain time span and I am suffering beyond that time span, I must not be normal." Needless to say, the result of setting any time limits on grief can produce devastating effects on the person grieving.

It is my contention that a "normal" grieving process is the life span of the griever. In order to examine this process, we will temporarily overlook the elements of shock that complicate the grieving process.

It is imperative that we begin by pointing out that any one or all of the emotional reactions referred to earlier can be present at any point in time when a person is grieving. The onset of grief usually begins at the point at which a parent knows or suspects his/her child is retarded. There will occur, subsequent to that moment, a series of intense grieving periods. At these times, the parent is acutely aware of and reacting to the loss of the perfect child. These intense grieving periods can be of varying lengths of time, but ordinarily will be of relatively short duration; this is particularly so if the parent has many demands on his/her time and energy, or many decisions to make about the child's medical care and future. Intense grieving periods may be very apparent to an onlooker because of emotional expression through crying, screaming, or mumbling aloud. On the other hand, they may be nearly impossible to detect other than by an occasional silence or staring. A parent to whom control is extremely important might even withdraw or retreat to experience these intense periods in private.

Alternating with intense periods of grief are periods, again of varying duration, when the parent may appear to be, and in fact to some extent is, almost completely unaware of the reality at hand. While these periods might be the result of consciously imposed control, there are times when there is no control exerted and no conscious awareness of the loss. This would appear to be a defense that the mind has to protect itself against the full impact of the loss.

Graphically, these periods might be illustrated as cyclical phenomena. The hills of the graph illustrate the intense grieving periods (IGPs) and the valleys the periods of defense.

Shock. Before examining grief over time it is imperative that some attention be given to the phenomenon of shock. In the case of any sudden severe crisis, the mind and body react in such a way as to protect the griever from the full impact of the trauma or insult that has occurred. Not unlike the process of defense described above, the parent may enter a state of mind where he/she reacts as if he/she is less than fully aware of the crisis that has occurred. The overall effect is one of psychological anesthesia. Characteristic of shock are certain somatic and psychological reactions that, while they may vary from

person to person, are seen frequently enough to be recognized as symptomatic of the shock reaction.

Somatic symptomatology. Somatic symptomatology includes:

1. Decrease in the need for and interest in nourishment and rest: We have all undoubtedly witnessed or experienced firsthand the ability of a grieving person to go for prolonged periods without the rest and nourishment that we would think needed in the time of stress. While I am not suggesting a deliberate abstinence or encouragement of abstinence from either food or rest, I am suggesting that the body has an apparent ability to get by with much less than would ordinarily be required. Persons in shock should be encouraged but *not coerced or forced* to eat or rest if they feel that it is impossible to do so. For the first 24 to 72 hours it may be more therapeutic for a parent to talk about his/her fears and disappointments. Eventually the body will automatically begin making demands on the griever to have its needs fulfilled.

2. Manifestations of illness not formerly present: A number of symptoms of illness may come and go during the initial grieving period. Nausea, shortness of breath, pain, hyperventilation, and choking are some of the more common manifestations. In some ways, these appear to be almost a reaction of the body to the neglect caused by shock. Often a griever who has ignored the pressure of others to eat or sleep will attend to themselves if frightened enough by these symptoms.

3. Insomnia and nightmares: When a person in shock does manage to get rest, it is not unusual to have those periods be fitful and traumatic. Regardless of the

fatigue, or perhaps as a result of it, the griever might find it virtually impossible to fall asleep; then once asleep, find that either nightmares or the "tossing and turning" feeling makes waking a relief by comparison.

Psychological elements of shock. Although some of the psychological elements of shock described may appear to be contradictory, it is important to remember that persons do not remain static in their reactions to stress or their environment.

Coping patterns that seem contradictory may cause those close to be concerned for the mental health of the parent who is in shock. In fact, these ordinarily reflect the symptomatology of shock and nothing more serious. I was once called to a general hospital to consult with staff about a parent who was just told her newborn son was a Down's syndrome child. The mother was not eating well and had no desire to see or hold her child. The staff physician decided she should terminate parental rights. I suggested the mother be given more time to adjust and come out of shock. Two weeks later the mother and father tearfully decided to try to take their child home. The child is now three years old and the pride of the family. Over a relatively short period of time, usually several days, the griever will return to more normal thought patterns and will follow the pattern described before in the section on the initial grieving period.

Some of the more common psychological reactions associated with shock include:

1. Emotional anesthetic effect: Persons in shock often do not react emotionally in a way that we consider to be appropriate given the nature of the crisis. Initially there may be a great outburst of emotion and verbal denials of the reality. "You must be wrong, it could not be my baby. You must be mistaken." After the reality has been substantiated beyond a doubt, a spontaneous and visible show of emotion may not occur again for days. Eventually, the face of the parent may take on such a "plastic" or "mask" quality that whatever changes in expression occur do not appear to reflect any emotion whatsoever.

2. Acute awareness of and need to attend to details: While many persons dealing with a parent would see themselves being helpful by assuming responsibilities of the parent, it might be unwise to do so. A person in shock often has a compulsive drive to be personally involved in all the decision making that occurs. Friends, relatives, physicians, and other medical professionals often are only too willing to make decisions for the parent based on what *they* feel is best for the individual rather than taking their cues from the parent. These decisions range from whether or not the child should be institutionalized to what (if any) medical or surgical intervention should occur.

3. Loss of ability to attend to details: Although it appears to contradict the above, the loss of ability to attend to details is also a characteristic of shock. While the parents may at one point wish to be involved personally with the decision making, they may later be eager to delegate this responsibility to another. It is also possible, and in fact common, for the parents to attend carefully and coherently to one set of problems or decisions and find it impossible to comprehend even a simple question raised on a different subject.

4. Fragmented thought and speech patterns: Often frightening to the parent, as well as the listener, is the tendency for thought and speech patterns to be-

come fragmented. Loosely connected or unconnected thoughts (many not rational or consistent with the reality at hand) surge forth. Opportunities for the parent to verbalize these thoughts should be made available; never should they be told, "You shouldn't think about it," or "Try to put it out of your mind now." A listener need not even point out to parents the ways in which their thought or speech patterns are inconsistent with reality. Ordinarily, no person knows the inconsistencies better than the parent. Part of their verbalizations often include such statements as, "I know this doesn't make sense," "I know he's retarded but. . . ."

Ordinarily, there is an acceptance on the part of the parents of the myriad of feelings and reactions that they may have during the first several days after learning their child is retarded. While the parents may not understand the fluctuating nature of the initial grief or the anesthetic effect of shock, they ordinarily will allow themselves a rather broad range of experiences which they will acknowledge as "normal" given the crises with which they are faced. In our society, however, the pace at which we live and the demands of daily living soon make demands. It is at this point (and beyond) that the parents may become frightened and impatient with their inability to respond in a "things-as-usual" manner. The parent may, and often does, begin to fear the emotional reactions they experience and the recurrence of initial grief.

Grief over time.   Today there exist sociological factors that have drastically affected the pressures of dealing with grief over time. Several of these factors bear mentioning at this time because of the impact on the parent.

In our rapidly paced and transient society, support systems in the form of church, family, and friends are scarce after the first several days or weeks following a loss. Even in small communities where these support systems may be available, the parent will find it necessary to deal with many different people very soon after a loss who may not be aware of it, or of its immediacy. There are many immediate and unfamiliar demands made on the parent that require dealing with banks, lawyers, insurance agencies, probate court, and the Social Security Administration, to name a few. The more mundane and familiar tasks of grocery shopping or taking the car to the garage can become very taxing because of the continual need to respond to a barrage of questions related to the loss.

While this loss of privacy and depersonalization of service contracts are inevitable, their toll on the parent can be profound. A parent meets all of these challenges but comes away from each one very alone and fatigued. Reactions to these intrusions compound, at times, leaving the parent confused and unsure as to whether his/her life will ever again return to normal.

During the first few days following a loss, the grief feelings occur only intermittently and the parent is permitted time to escape daily demands. Relatives and friends may be happy to help if the parents need time alone to think and plan. Soon, demands for attention are relentlessly made by family and often the retarded child. In order to meet these demands the parent is forced to exert control over his or her urge to think about the implications of having a retarded child. In moments of privacy, however, the parent will usually be overwhelmingly preoccupied with thoughts about what has happened. Concentration on other matters might seem impossible. The parent, partly out of necessity and partly as a result of concerted effort, will concentrate less and less on the loss. Several days may pass when they have little

Zoo outing for developmentally disabled

opportunity to think and perhaps no opportunity to react emotionally.

Eventually, however, repression or suppression of these feelings will take its toll. Defenses weaken and efforts to exert control dissipate. The parent may be struck with a sense of "panic" and intense grieving. As the intense feelings recur the parents may panic because they feel that they are incapable of adjusting to having a child who is retarded. They see other parents who appear adjusted and fail to realize that this adjustment does not occur spontaneously.

Eventually the demands of daily life, as well as the natural defenses of the mind

alluded to earlier, will quickly set up a pattern of grief over time similar to the initial pattern of grief. Intense grieving periods (IGPs) will alternate rhythmically with periods when the parent is almost totally unaware of the loss. There is, however, one very important difference. The time periods separating the IGPs over time become greater and greater. Initially, we have seen that they are separated by minutes or hours. Over time, they will occur hours or days apart, then weeks, then months, and eventually years. Healthily experienced, these IGPs will be separated by a progressively more normal lifestyle.

Patterns of grief. While IGPs may and often do recur without any rhyme or reason, there are times when they are more likely to occur. Parents may grieve intensely when they see their retarded child among peers the same age who are developing normally, or at a time when significant events occur in the lives of peers that remind the parents of the child's limitations; that is, graduations, weddings. Other situations that may trigger these responses are visits with professionals involved in a child's special program or visits to an institution or foster home where a child is placed.

Conclusion. While not exhaustive, there follows a list of factors which influence the grief patterns and process over time:

1. Coping mechanisms of the individual parent.
2. The cultural milieu in which the parent was reared.
3. The availability of familial or cultural support systems.
4. The manner in which the parent is dealt with by friends and relatives.
5. Opportunities for emotional expression.
6. Freedom of the parent to express emotions.

SOCIAL WORK INTERVENTION WITH PARENTS OF RETARDED CHILDREN*

Casework intervention

As the time periods between intense grieving periods lengthen, parents of a child who is retarded will begin forming an attachment to the child they have, rather than

---

* Specific services for the retarded (such as special education programs, day care, sheltered workshops, group homes, and work training) are described in Chapter 15.

continuing to mourn for the perfect child of their dreams. This reintegration can be a painful and prolonged process and one that can place irreparable strains on the marriage if the parents do not continue to talk to one another about their feelings of fear, frustration, denial, and so on. On the other hand, this period can be a period of personal growth and growth of the relationship.

Group work as an intervention technique

Parents of mentally retarded children who are facing changes that will affect their child and/or their family are likely to enter into a period of intense and perhaps prolonged grieving. Placement of a child in or out of an institution, school placement, or changes in educational or workshop settings are examples of these changes.

Over many years of group work practice with parents of severely retarded children who will in the future be placed in a residential setting, we developed a format for parent groups that can be adapted for use in many settings. The contract made with the parents is for a closed short-term group that will meet weekly for a maximum of four to six weeks. The groups should be held evenings or weekends so that both parents can attend. Whether the goal of the group is to teach parents behavior management techniques or to assist them in adjusting to change, the primary goal should be postponed until the third session. The purpose of the first two sessions is to provide a safe environment for the parents to dissipate feelings that they have about having a retarded child or adult.

Session 1—There is no topic with which parents are more familiar than the problems of their child. Each parent is asked to introduce themselves and tell the group about their retarded child and that child's problems. This provides the parent with the opportunity to hear their voice in the group

AN EVALUATION INTERVIEW WITH PARENTS OF A MENTALLY RETARDED CHILD

The Jacobsons share their ups and downs of the six months with Eve (their retarded child):

M: I wonder if you'd comment on what was happening between the two of you during the six months. In assessing families of children with problems one of my primary concerns is whether or not the parents are talking to one another about their feelings about having a retarded child.

B: I think we were pretty open with each other from the start and were pretty good about allowing the other person to feel whatever he or she happened to be feeling. Our levels of concern or involvement with Eve weren't always the same. The times that I got irritated with Fred were when I felt that he was more distant to himself than I was comfortable with; and then I would try and let him know about that although usually not at the precise moment that I became aware of it.

F: After I went back to work full-time I think that I escaped into my work. It was easy to do because work was very demanding and I think that I was in a sort of fantasy land. This is a very old pattern with me. It's something that I've done for years, but it never got so extreme that I was beyond being called back.

B: It's always been my job to call you back.

M: You were talking to one another?

F: Yeah, I think that we were. I'm not sure. I think that there were times when I wasn't really there. There were times when I went back to that stage where I just didn't want to know about it and I didn't for a while. I wasn't involved with doing things for Eve. I think that it's so valuable to be involved in caretaking, and especially in the specialty things that are needed for kids with disabilities because it gets you involved and being involved is being involved. If you're doing something then that gives you something to have feelings about, something to talk about, it allows you to observe change.

B: They also give you an investment in what's going on.

F: I would be afraid for families where one parent takes all the responsibility cause I don't think that the other parent could possibly know the situation. I suppose that's true of any child and I suppose that's one of the things that I learned. There were a couple of accidents that turned out to be very handy. We had an appointment (to take Eve to a clinic) on about a monthly basis but some of the time Bev just could not do it so I became familiar with this particular clinic. That was one area where I was the expert and that was good. It gave me one thing that I could pay attention to. There were certain things that had to be done for her that I could do very well and that was good. But I think that there were a lot of things especially in the middle few months of her life that I could have been more involved in than I was. But it's possible that I needed to draw back a little bit to become more comfortable. Well, that's always been my way so I suppose there will always be that component in my behavior, and it's hardly surprising I did it then. But, I feel very lucky that before she died I had gotten to the point where I felt I was involved, and I knew what was going on, and I was doing things and then it sort of made it complete.

M: Did you feel comfortable with what you were feeling and what each other were feeling?

F: I learned not to judge my feelings.

B: Yeah, I think that's the key to it . . .

F: And, also that certain feelings are appropriate at certain times and certain feelings are appropriate at other times.

B: God forbid that they should ever mix!

F: I think that people will think it's improper for you to feel certain things, but I wouldn't let that stand in my way. Propriety is not that important. I wanted to grin at Eve's funeral, and I did grin a couple of times, because there were certain things that made me grin. There were kids sledding down the hill you know in the idyllic scene through the trees, really very lovely and I just hope that I didn't hurt anyone's feelings but I come first. My feelings come first. Their feelings are their business. Nobody ever in Eve's whole life had to tell us that our feelings were wrong. First of all, I don't know what it means to say that a feeling is wrong. Feelings are not right or wrong. They are there or they're not there. . . .

Well, one of the things that came to me for the first time when Eve was born was that I saw the advantage of feeling bad—the good of feeling bad. I always used to think, "what good is it to cry" you just feel bad and what good is that so forget it—keep a stiff upper lip and don't show your feelings. But I found when Eve was born that when you feel bad and you show it and you think about it . . . I'll give you the thing that really blew my mind was the day she was born I was very upset. I cried and of course Bev was incapacitated. We had a close friend living with us and I called him and he came over and we cried together, and then I came home and it happened that Bev's mother called. I knew right away that I'd wanted to call her but I knew I couldn't keep anything from her. After that was over I went to bed cause I'd been up an awful lot. I fell asleep and for the next week I had no trouble falling asleep. My stomach was never upset, I didn't have indigestion. I ate, I slept, and I did what I had to do, and that just hadn't been my experience in the past. When I had trouble and bound it up and you know it came out in other ways.

M: So you really think there was a relationship between getting feelings out and your ability to go on.

F: You know I'm not so sure that it's a lesson for life. I still have trouble facing up to difficulties—you know emotions. But at least I have this experience to look back upon, to remember, and I can see, at least now I know the reason why we should express emotions. No one ever convinced me before.

M: Sometimes it's not until we get ulcers or a spastic colon, or migraine headaches, or all of the above that we learn that lesson. It's unfortunate that we have to have physiological side effects before we can remember.

F: I'm in a position now where I supervise people at work for the first time and now I know that when I'm mad at them I have to get mad at them. I've got to do something, you know, not throw something at them. But it's good for them. But that's not the important thing. The important thing is for me. If I'm going to do my job I've got to do it. I've got to find a release for me.

M: How did you respond to Eve over the six months she was with you, and what changes were there in that response?

F: After Eve's death we received a note from a relative about how it was better that the ordeal was over. I found that laughable. Not only was it not an ordeal, but it was the most valuable experience that I've ever had. Certainly the most valuable six months, the most growth-producing six months in my life.

B: I think what we were able to do, and I'm not sure how we got to that point, was to make this a positive experience. You know, we were always aware that it was tragic that she had all the disabilities that she did, but that didn't mean that we needed to focus on what a tragedy it was. And, instead, we were just much more interested in what we could do for her, and how to make her life and our lives as joyful and as productive as possible.

F: One of the good things I think that you have to do is think how can I enjoy my child? You know, you can be very blatant about it—How can I use my child for enjoyment? What is it about this kid that I like? Do I enjoy holding her? Do I enjoy bathing her? Do I enjoy the way she smells or looking at her or carrying her around or do I enjoy showing her off or dressing her up? One of the things that amazes me is that people think that changing diapers is a chore. I think that changing diapers is great because it's so easy to do. How can you mess it up?

B: On a squirming baby you can.

F: That's right. Eve didn't move around much so that made it much easier. The idea that fathers are afraid to change diapers I think is ludicrous. I understand of course that this has to do with the fact that women deal with dirt and men don't. I mean there's so many things about taking care of a baby that are so much harder and here's a really basic thing anybody can do.

M: The positive interaction opportunities during such a simple task as changing a diaper are just great.

F: That's right. I enjoyed holding her and just looking at her and dressing her. There were things about her that were a chore for me, like feeding her was a chore for the longest time. Then there were times when I had to take her to an appointment and get back to an appointment of my own and the doctor was often late. And then I had to run across the street with her and get a parking ticket, or whatever happened. You know that wasn't any fun. But that doesn't mean that everything about her, even though she had serious problems, and even though she was in a sense a tragic child, that doesn't mean that I couldn't have fun with her, and I couldn't enjoy her. I think that the idea that you should be somber and serious and unhappy all the time because your child has problems is something you have to get away from.

B: In fact, even after she died one of our early coping reactions was that we spent a lot of time running around making arrangements for the funeral. And after that was done, we just got very punchy and silly around that time. Somebody called us long-distance, I think expecting two very tearful, grief-stricken people, and we were in a very silly mood at that point.

F: I had to stop and explain to the person that I was a little punchy and would they please excuse me. You know, cause you could sort of hear these silences on the phone.

B: And, I can recall feeling embarrassed about my reactions because they didn't seem quite appropriate. But, this is where we were at that point.

F: I think that it's important for people to know that's okay. It's just like, it's the same story all over again—don't deny what you feel and I mean it's just a reaction. It's just something that happens.

M: That's the beautiful part of this whole discussion though, because my whole professional and personal life has been dedicated to be honest with what you feel.

F: The extremely frustrating thing was trying to feed Eve. It wasn't until about a month before she died that I got it together, and then I could do it without feeling it was a chore.

B: I think a large part of that was somehow you finally realized that the way that you fed her reflected your attitude. And the mechanics of what you were doing had an effect on how she was eating as well. It was an interactive process.

F: Yeah, I know I always used to suffer. I was much too rough with her. But I couldn't let down that anger and frustration and tune into the little things that she was doing that let me know that I was pushing on her mouth or pushing on her tongue or making her gag. Until I could sort of do that and pay attention to her very closely as I fed her, I wasn't able to do it effectively.

It was a real bugaboo with me, real tough thing for me, the feeding. I mean for a while I just said I can't do it, I'm sorry.

B: I was just furious.

F: Yeah, because Bev essentially had to work five hours a day to feed her.

B: It was clear to me what the trouble was. But I couldn't find a way of getting you to understand, and then you finally figured it out yourself. Since she was such a passive child it was easy to kind of overlook her personhood.

But she was a person and she did have preferences, and you really needed to tune into those rather than into your frustration at how long it took to feed her if you were going to get any success at all.

M: Would you comment a little bit on what things that you might see as falling into the realm of social worker practice either in a general hospital setting or in any setting where they might come in contact with parents of children with developmental problems?

B: I think being probably a listener and a clarifier are two of the most important functions that a social worker would provide. I don't think that it's necessary to have all the answers; in fact, in most cases it's impossible to. And to place that expectation on yourself is to guarantee a lot of feelings of failure. But I think that you can hear what someone else is saying, and help them make sense of what might be a very confusing and chaotic experience. I think that it's important also not to place any judgments on what their experiences are or what their solutions to their predicament are. One of the things that became very clear to me was the importance of our decision being tailored to our needs; for example, we both came to a decision quite early on that we would not drastically alter our lives or curtail activities and pleasures that were important to us to care for this child or any child. That meant facing the responsibility of placing her in an institution or a foster home at some point. If we had had a worker who felt very strongly that all children should live at home, that person would have made our decision and our feelings about caring for Eve much more difficult for us. Another very important thing a social worker can do is to help the parents focus on what can be done to help the child—and themselves—*now*. As Fred has mentioned before, focusing on the present is an excellent way to avoid trapping yourself in a cycle of self-pity and hopelessness. And being able to take some positive action to improve your child's life does wonderful things for your own sense of worth and your feelings about your child. This means both hooking the family up with resources, and helping them find ways of building in opportunities for learning and growth into the child's everyday care.

F: I's like to say that professionals are people who think they know better than the clients what's good for them. I think that it's true in every profession. That's a thing that characterizes professions that's very sad. The goal of the professional shouldn't be to make the decisions for the client, but to educate the client so he can make the decisions himself.

B: I found that, by and large, most of the nonphysicians whom we dealt with treated us as human beings who were capable of reading the situation as well as they could and of making decisions. I think occasionally people were a little intimidated by our ability to do that, but also most of them were pretty open about their feelings of intimidation so we were able to work through that rather nicely.

F: The dealings that I remember with social workers were held very much on the basis of equals and very open about the effect that Eve had on us and the constraints of their jobs and their positions. At times they were co-conspirators against the rest of the systems which I think is appropriate. And, if we took Eve to another doctor we would let on right away that we knew this and this and this about her, and what we wanted to learn by coming to this particular clinic, and it was clear to them what we thought their position should be. Most of them were willing to go along. I think that we were lucky, but our pediatrician was also very good about steering us towards specialists who he thought would go along with our way of operating.

Well, I think that anyone who we became involved with could tell that we weren't going to change. We were getting lots of rewards from acting that way because we felt that we knew what was going on and we were involved.

B: It occurs to me listening to this that we might seem terribly obnoxious. I wanted to say that I think that we made it clear all along that our interest in all of this was in helping our child, not in throwing our weight around. So, people were willing to work with us and allow us to work with them.

setting while they talk about a familiar topic where they are truly the expert. A secondary advantage is that parents have the chance to find out that their child and their problems with that child are less unique than what they thought.

After the introductions parents are asked to talk about how and when they found out about their child's retardation, who told them, and how they felt about the professionals that dealt with them at that time. This provides the parents with the opportunity to talk about all the reactions discussed earlier. Ordinarily this will be a time when much anger is dissipated. One of the most frightening things about grieving is the feeling that you are losing your mind because of the intensity of your feelings. Parents in the group most often recognize spontaneously that they are not crazy. If they were, others would not be expressing feelings similar to their own or reinforcing their expression of feeling through verbal and nonverbal cues.

Session 2—The reactions of siblings and extended family to the retarded child may pose a real problem for parents over time and be a source of guilt, fear, frustration, and often confusion. A sibling, for example, may go through periods of mourning about a sister or brother placed in a residential facility years after the placement occurs even though their initial adjustment was excellent. Another may go through a phase when they are ashamed to be seen in public with their retarded sibling. One mother I talked to had two normal daughters, one of whom ignored the retarded baby and was embarrassed by the child. The other daughter approached anyone and everyone and said, "This is my brother Phillip and he's retarded"—almost as if she were proud of the fact. Another common problem with siblings is dealing with the questions that arise when the retarded child is placed in a residential setting or a foster home. Questions about the parents' motivation for placement are not unusual and can be guilt-producing to the

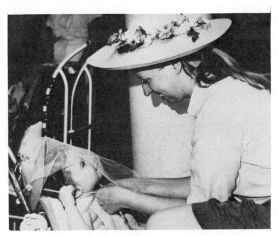

Getting ready for a party at a residential care facility

parents. Placement may arouse fears on the part of the normal children about whether they too will be sent away from home.

Pressures from extended family may also pose problems for parents of retarded children. As the Jacobsons mentioned, the grandparents may have definite expectations about the responsibilities of child rearing and these may not include finding alternate care for a retarded child. One parent in a group mentioned that her mother left books around that talked about the joys of having a retarded child the minute she found out the parents were considering foster care. Another had a sister who offered to take her retarded child in addition to her own six children rather than have the child placed in an institution.

This session can be a problem-solving session where parents learn techniques of handling these difficult situations from one another. The emotional reactions mentioned before also occur. Parents dissipate feelings and identify their problems as being similar to those of other parents.

Session 3—This session should be geared toward whatever goal the social worker wishes to accomplish, and can stretch out to

two or three sessions if agreed on in advance by the parents and social workers. People in early childhood and other educational settings have used it to teach parents the basics of behavior management, speech development, and structuring of leisure time for the retarded. It can also be used to familiarize parents with changes and help them adjust to those changes. Our goal is to help the parents adjust to eventual placement of their child in a residential setting. These parents have made the decision to place, but have a lot of ambivalence because of societal pressures and their own expectations of parenting and what that involves.

A set of parents who have already placed their child are often invited into the group at this point to answer questions and talk about their own ambivalence and their resolution of that over time.

Final session—Parents of newly diagnosed retarded children are not likely to become concerned about the issues and services that affect the general population of retarded individuals. Problems like guardianship or development of semi-independent living situations as these relate to the adult retarded are beyond the comprehension of very young parents or even of some parents who are several years into the grieving process but still feeling very intensely. All parents, however, should be aware of organizations for parents of retarded children, such as the Association for Retarded Citizens. This final session is used to familiarize parents with this organization so that at the point when they wish to become active or need an advocate, they know where to turn.

Although not every setting lends itself to group work as an intervention technique, each setting should be examined periodically with this mode of intervention in mind. It is my firm belief that with a skillful group leader, parents can get more assistance in coping with having a retarded child in four to six sessions than they can get in many sessions with a social worker on a casework basis.

SUMMARY

Regardless of the cause of retardation, parents who have a child with problems are grieving. The loss they mourn is that of the perfect child, the super athlete, beauty queen, or leader of the country. Even normal children fail to live up to the expectations of their parents, but parents of normal children have many years to know and adjust to the shortcomings of their children. Parents of retarded children, on the other hand, know and must adjust (daily) to the limitations of their children from the time they are diagnosed.

The social worker can play a significant role in helping parents adjust to their retarded child. The Jacobsons suggest that we assist parents in this process by being listeners, clarifiers, and co-conspirators in systems where services might be available but difficult to find. They also suggest that we help parents to focus on what can be done to help the child develop to his/her full potential.

In order to effectively work with parents of retarded children, the social worker must continually grow in his/her awareness of the reactions of parents to having a retarded child and the process of grief over time.

Whether or not a social worker plans to specialize in the area of mental retardation in his/her professional work, it is important for every social worker to have some basic knowledge about retardation and its effects on the person, the family, and the commu-nity. Adjusting to a retarded child and meeting those extra needs places a stress on the child's family, the neighborhood, the school, and the larger society. All areas of social work practice play a role in the care and development of the retarded.

Along with this base of knowledge, the social worker must be able to listen with compassion to a family who must struggle with their reactions to their retarded child. Even though the worker may deal with many such families, it is important to remember that each family faces an experience which for them is unique. The resolutions they come to in their relationship with their child, and the decisions they make regarding their child's present and future must fit with their values and coping abilities. The social worker can play a valuable role in helping parents reach a resolution that is comfortable for them, realizing that this process will be repeated over time as new information is available about the child, new resources become available, or new crises occur. The worker can be most effective in this role if he/she does not harbor preconceived notions about what is "best" for the family and child. The family knows what is best for them; the worker's job is to help them discover that fact.

NOTES

1. Herbert J. Grossman, ed., *Manual on Terminology and Classification in Mental Retardation*, rev. ed. (Washington, D.C.: AAMD, 1975), p. 11.
2. U.S. Public Law 91–517, *United States Statutes at Large*, 91st Congress, vol. 84, part 1 (Washington, D.C.: U.S. Government Printing Office, 1971), pp. 1316–27.
3. Ruth E. Little, "Drinking during Pregnancy: Implications for Public Health," *Alcohol Health and Research World* 4, no. 1 (1979): pp. 21–29.

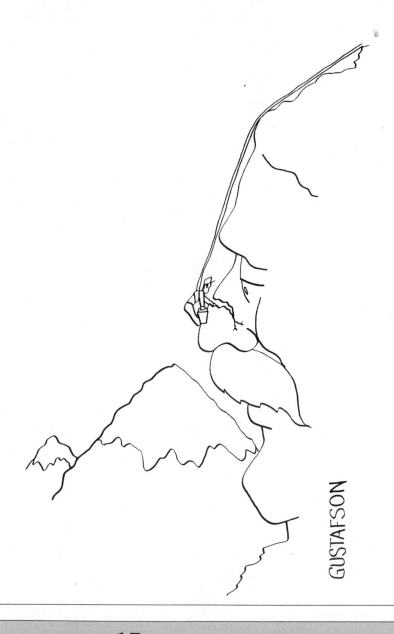

GUSTAFSON

chapter **15**

EXTENT OF THE PROBLEM

According to the National Arts and Handicapped Information Service, there are over 50 million handicapped people in the United States, nearly 1 out of 4 persons.[1] The number of handicapped include:

12.5 million temporarily injured (severe burns, injuries to back or spine, broken limbs).

11.7 million physically disabled (including people who use canes, crutches, walkers, braces; who are in wheelchairs; the mobility-impaired elderly; and people with illnesses such as severe cardiovascular disorder, cerebral palsy, and chronic arthritis).

11.0 million hearing impaired.

8.2 million visually impaired.

6.8 million mentally disabled (severely emotionally disturbed, retarded, brain damaged, severely learning disabled).

2.4 million deaf.

2.1 million institutionalized (mentally retarded, mentally disturbed, terminally ill).

1.7 million homebound (degenerative illnesses like multiple sclerosis, chronic health disorders).

1.3 million blind.[2]

HISTORY OF REHABILITATION PRACTICES

Society's willingness to tend to the needs cf those impaired has always been largely determined by the perceived causes of the impairments, the existing medical knowledge, and the general economic conditions.

When the early Greek civilization prospered, a few thousand years ago, the Greeks had the philosophy of the unity of body and soul, with a blemish on one signifying a blemish on the other.[3] This philosophy led to a negative attitude toward the disabled, with the extreme implication of this doctrine being found in Sparta where "the immature, the weak, and the damaged were eliminated purposefully."[4] Centuries later in Rome, the Romans also put to death some of the disabled who were considered "unproductive."[5] In ancient history there were almost

Physical/mental handicaps and rehabilitation

Testing the extent of a hearing impairment

no organized efforts to meet the needs of the mentally retarded. In early Greece and during the reign of the Roman Empire, mental illness was seen as being due to demons entering the body, with exorcism being the primary treatment.[6]

During the Middle Ages disability was either seen as the result of demonic possession, or as God's punishment.[7] Modern Christian values of charity and humanitarian treatment were generally absent during this period, partly as a result of poor economic conditions. About the only employment for the handicapped provided by feudal lords was that of court jester, a position considered suitable for the mentally retarded and for the physically disabled.[8] The mentally ill continued to be viewed as being possessed by demons, and cruelty was advocated and used to punish and drive out the devil in residence.

The Elizabethan English Poor Laws of 1601 provided financial support for the involuntary unemployed (including the handicapped). These Poor Laws were the first major secular based relief effort for the poor and the handicapped.[9]

In early colonial America conditions were not yet suitable for the development of reha-

bilitation programs as the colonists were barely able to earn a living from the soil, and because disability was viewed as the result of God's punishment.[10]

The 19th century finally saw a gradual recognition being given to the needs of the disabled in the United States. A few of the efforts to develop programs will be mentioned. Thomas Gallaudet opened the first school for educating the deaf in this country in 1817 in Hartford, Connecticut.[11] Gallaudet demonstrated that the deaf could be taught to read and speak, which led to the opening of other schools for the deaf. The first school for the blind was opened in 1832 in Massachusetts.[12] The first sheltered-type work situation for the employment of the blind was established in 1850 in Massachusetts.[13]

Mental retardation, prior to and during the early part of the 19th century, was thought to be inherited and therefore incurable.[14] In the first half of the 19th century most of the mentally retarded "were relegated to lunatic asylums, poorhouses, almshouses, or local jails."[15] Interest in providing services to the retarded began in France, especially after the physician Jean Itard made considerable progress over a five-year period in the early 1800s in educating a 12-year-old "wolf child" found in a forest who was diagnosed as severely retarded. When found, the child was unsocialized, and walked on all fours.[16] The philosophy of providing services to the retarded gradually spread to this country. In 1848 the first residential school for the retarded was opened in Barge, Massachusetts.[17] Unfortunately, the orientation toward the retarded during the latter half of the 19th century switched from one of education and training to custodial care. One of the major reasons for this change was the popularity of Social Darwinism which asserted that if was far better for society to allow the poor and the weak to perish rather than to sustain their existence and encourage their multiplication through government-supported programs.[18] The mentally retarded were viewed as having defective genetic strains, and as a result sterilization was extensively used at the end of the 19th century.[19]

The first mental hospitals for the mentally ill were built in this country in the 1850s and 1860s.[20] Prior to this time Dorothea Dix had visited many locations documenting that the mentally ill were either kept "out of sight" in the homes of their families or confined in almshouses and local jails.[21] It should be noted the living conditions of almshouses and mental hospitals were deplorable and would make even our worst present-day prisons and jails look like country clubs in comparison.

The physically disabled, up until the latter half of the 19th century, were either taken care of by their family or placed in almshouses. Toward the end of the 19th century the disabled first began to benefit from medical advances—antiseptic surgery, orthopedic surgery, heat and water therapy, use of braces, and exercise programs.[22] Near the end of the 19th century public funds began to be used for the education and training of handicapped children.[23]

The Charity Organization Movement during the latter part of the 19th century created a structure not only for future social work practices, but also for vocational rehabilitation casework.[24] These early organizations had a rehabilitation focus, rather than maintenance. The movement also advocated extensive investigation of each case, and the utilization of individualized treatment determined by the needs of each client. Unfortunately, the volunteers who provided the services of the Charity Organization Movement operated from the premise that the causes of poverty and being handicapped had moral roots, and that the primary way to be helped was through spiritual means.[25]

During the late 19th and early 20th centuries, few precautions were taken by industries to improve worker safety. As a result, a large number of people suffered impairments from poor working conditions and industrial accidents. To meet the tolls being taken by the Industrial Revolution, the first worker's compensation law was passed in 1910 in New York.[26]

In the early 20th century large numbers of unskilled rural youths began flocking to cities seeking employment. There were also increasing numbers of dislocated industrial workers who needed retraining. The federal government in 1917 therefore passed the Smith-Hughes Act which made federal monies available for vocational education programs, and also created the Federal Board of Vocational Education.[27] The next year (1918) the Soldier's Rehabilitation Act was passed, which was a program designed to rehabilitate disabled veterans.[28]

The federal Social Security Act of 1935 established the permanency of rehabilitation programs, and established public assistance programs for the blind and for the disabled.

The Barden-LaFollette Act of 1943 extended rehabilitation services to the mentally ill and to the mentally retarded.[29]

During World War II there was a severe labor shortage which provided the disabled with work opportunities in which the disabled successfully demonstrated to thousands of employers that if placed in an appropriate job, they could perform well. This growing realization led in 1945 to the establishment of the President's Committee on Employment of the Handicapped.[30]

After World War II there were a number of federal programs passed which underscored society's growing belief that those with impairments could be productive workers, and should be given the opportunities and training to demonstrate their work capacities.[31]

Spurred by the Civil Rights Movement in

Paid work—packaging materials—at a sheltered workshop

paried, and in helping those impaired to live satisfying and productive lives.

Impaired people are now making it to the top in many careers

Criss Cole is a judge in Houston, Texas and is blind.

Dana Wakefield is a juvenile-court judge in Denver and is blind.

W. Mitchell is mayor of Crested Butte, Colorado, and is a paraplegic.

Phyllis Frelich won the Tony Award as the best broadway actress in 1980 and is deaf.

S. Craig Kiser is chief counsel for Florida's Department of Banking and Finance and is blind.

Shirley K. Price is an employment executive at the Johnson Space Center in Houston and is a dwarf with no arms.

Max Cleland, heads the U.S. Veterans Administration Department and lost his legs and one arm in Vietnam. Similar to a growing number of other people who are impaired, he drives his car to work, travels widely, and participates in sports.

SOURCE: "For Disabled, Jobs Few—But Many Make It," *U.S. News & World Report*, September 8, 1980, p. 45.

the 1950s and 1960s, a new minority group began to be heard in the late 1960s and in the 1970s. Persons with physical disabilities began speaking out, marching forth, and demanding equal rights. They have been seeking, including through legislation and lawsuits, an end: to job discrimination, to limited educational opportunities, to architectural barriers, and to societal discrimination. In 1973 Congress passed the Vocational Rehabilitation Act, one section of which prohibits discrimination against the handicapped by any program or organization receiving federal funds. Included in this nondiscriminatory policy is an affirmative action policy (described in Chapter 8) in which employers who receive federal funds must demonstrate extensive efforts to hire those with impairments.

The 20th century has seen the development of numerous programs and technological advances to help the physically disabled, the temporarily injured, the deaf and the hearing impaired, the blind and the visually impaired, the mentally disabled, and those with chronic health disorders. Yet, as will be discussed, much remains to be done in changing society's attitudes toward the im-

SOCIETY'S REACTIONS TO DISABILITIES

Our culture places a high value on having a beautiful body. There are a number of physical fitness health clubs, and Americans spend large proportions of their budgets on clothes, cosmetics, exercise programs, and special diets to look more attractive. Beauty is identified with goodness, and physical ugliness with evil. Movies, television, and books portray heroes and heroines as being physically attractive, and villains as being ugly. Snow White, for example was beautiful, while the evil witch was ugly. Children are erroneously taught that being physically attractive leads to the good life, while having unattractive features is a sign of being inferior. Richardson found that young children rated people with disabilities as being "less desirable" than people without impairments.[32]

Unfortunately this emphasis on the body beautiful has subjected those with impairments to be the object of cruel jokes and has occasionally led to the disabled either being shunned or being treated as being inferior. According to Cooley, if the impaired are related to as if they are inferior, second-class citizens, they are apt to come to view themselves as being inferior and to have a negative self-concept.[33] Our society needs to reassess its values about the perfect physique. It would seem other traits ought to weigh more—honesty, integrity, personality, being responsible, kindness, and helpfulness.

Wright has noted the emphasis on the body beautiful has led society to also believe that the impaired "ought" to feel inferior.[34] Wright has coined the term *the requirement of mourning* for this expectation of society. An able-bodied person who spends a great deal of time, money, and effort to be physically attractive psychologically wants an impaired person to mourn the impairment, because the able-bodied person needs feedback that it is worthwhile and important to strive to have an attractive physique.

Another consequence of the "body beautiful" cult is that disabled persons are sometimes pitied as being less fortunate and given sympathy. Many of the impaired decry receiving pity and being patronized. They seek to be treated as equals.

HOW MUCH FOR REHABILITATION? Our society continues to face a dilemma regarding how much money to spend for rehabilitation. Advocates of increased expenses use such arguments as those summarized by Salvatore DiMichael in the 1960s:

> The average cost of rehabilitation is returned fivefold in income taxes paid by the employed handicapped worker; the average rate of income after rehabilitation is seven to ten times greater for the average person than before rehabilitation; and vocational rehabilitation of a handicapped person on public assistance can be effected at a one-time cost comparable to the cost of supporting him on welfare during a one-year period.[35]

Fiscal conservatives argue our economy cannot afford to increase expenditures. They point to cases such as that of Geri D. which they say documents too much money is already being spent in some areas.

Geri D. is now five months old and is residing in a residential facility for the retarded at an annual cost of $30,000 per year. She has severe medical problems, including cardiovascular dysfunctions. She is so profoundly retarded that she will never be able to sit up, a developmental milestone that children of average intelligence achieve at six months of age. Geri was born premature, with multiple medical problems. Lifesaving technology kept her alive. Already over $250,000 has been spent in keeping her alive.

With medical advances, our society will face increasingly difficult issues regarding where financial resources should be used.

There is also a tendency in our society to conclude that because a person is handicapped in one area, they are also handicapped in other areas. Weinberg has noted that people talk louder in the presence of someone who is blind, as it is erroneously assumed that people who cannot see also have hearing problems.[36] People with physical impairments are also erroneously at times assumed to be mentally and socially retarded. A 22-year-old college student in a wheelchair describes one example of this tendency:

> I'm in church with my father and my father is standing beside me and I'm in a wheelchair. I'm relatively intelligent, but I'm disabled. I'm sitting there like anyone else. And somebody comes up to my father and they're about as far away from me as from him and they say to my father, "How's he doing?" "Well he's looking pretty good." And I just want to kick him in the stomach.[37]

Unfortunately, relating to the impaired as if they are socially and mentally retarded may lead the impaired to believe they are less intelligent and less effective in social interactions.

Studies have found that people end interactions sooner with impaired people than with nonimpaired people.[38] Many people are uncomfortable when a handicapped person is near because they are uncertain what is appropriate and inappropriate to say. They fear saying something that may offend the handicapped person. They do not want to make any direct remarks about the disabling condition. Yet, if they try to ignore the disability they may make impossible demands on the impaired person (for example, conversing while moving along a hallway with a person in a wheelchair and then being confronted by a flight of stairs). People show their discomfort in a variety of ways—abrupt and superficial conversations, fixed stares

away from the impaired person, compulsive talking, or an artificial seriousness. Impaired people are sensitive to such artifical interactions. Fred David describes a set of encounters about these interactional strains.

> I get suspicious when somebody says, "Let's go for a uh, ah [imitates confused and halting speech] push with me down the hall," or something like that. This to me is suspicious because it means that they're aware, really aware, that there's a wheelchair here, and that this is probably uppermost with them. . . . A lot of people in trying to show you that they don't care that you're in a chair will do crazy things. On, there's one person I know who constantly kicks my chair, as if to say "I don't care that you're in a wheelchair. I don't even know that it's there." But that is just an indication that he really knows it's there.[39]

Impaired people detest being treated socially different simply because they have a physical impairment.

CURRENT SERVICES

There are a number of programs (some of which are federally funded and administered at state or local levels) which provide funds and services to the disabled. A few of these programs will be briefly described.

Sheltered workshops. These workshops provide a variety of services which generally include vocational evaluation, sheltered employment, work adjustment, counseling services, and placement services. Each of these services will be briefly described.

Vocational evaluation. Clients are assessed on the basis of work behavior, physical capacities, social interaction, psychological functioning, and vocational goals and interests. Emphasis is placed on identifying the client's vocational assets and limitations.

Packaging samples of laundry detergent at a sheltered workshop

Sheltered employment. A work environment is provided for individuals unable to immediately secure or maintain jobs in the community. Clients are paid (often below the minimum wage level) for work produced. Work tasks consist of various subcontract jobs from industries in the community that allow for long-term vocational development and possible placement into competitive employment. There is periodic evaluation of client's progress in meeting rehabilitation objectives to ensure maximum vocational and personal development.

Work adjustment training. Vocational training experiences are provided to clients who are not yet ready for competitive employment following their initial vocational evaluation. The program is conducted in a work setting, utilizing various types of subcontract jobs secured from industries in the community. The work is used to train individuals in developing good work skills and appropriate behavior on the job. Counselors are available to discuss problems, assist in learning new tasks, and to help develop better work habits.

Counseling services. Counseling services include individual, group, parent, and vocational guidance. Individual counseling stresses treatment goals applied to mutually determined problem areas. Group counseling focuses on the stimulation of peer interaction and development of social skills. Parent counseling acquaints parents with treatment objectives, thus providing support for the total rehabilitation objectives in the home. Exposure to the work world, development of job seeking skills, and identifying realistic goals are the major emphases of vocational counseling.

Placement services. This program assists clients in securing competitive employment. Clients' work habits and skills are first assessed. Then clients receive training in the proper skills for job seeking, applying for a job, and holding a job. Counselors then seek together with clients, to place the clients with local employers. After placement, contact is maintained for a period of time to handle work adjustment problems that may arise.

Educational programs. Historically, many public schools either refused to serve the severely impaired, or segregated them in special programs. In 1975 Congress enacted the Education for All Handicapped Children Act. This statute mandates that all local school districts must provide full and appropriate educational opportunities to all impaired children. An individualized educational program designed to meet the unique needs of each impaired child must be developed which provides for instruction in the least restrictive environment that is feasible.

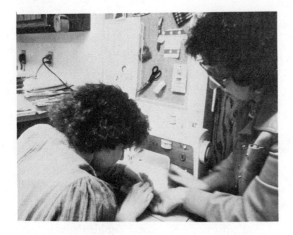

Teaching a person how to sew at a sheltered workshop

The intent is to "mainstream" each impaired child so that each can participate as much as possible in regular educational programs. Most school districts now have "Special education programs" designed to meet the educational needs of the retarded, the emotionally disturbed, those with learning disabilities, and the physically handicapped.

Specialized schools. Most states have schools for the hearing-impaired, and schools for the visually-impaired. Often these specialized schools also provide state-wide consultation for young children.

Teaching a person to use a telephone

Group homes, halfway houses, and nursing homes. There are a number of these facilities that provide living arrangements for the mentally retarded, emotionally disturbed, and physically handicapped who for a variety of reasons are unable to live with their parents.

Residential treatment centers. There are a variety of treatment centers that provide residential care and treatment, such as mental hospitals, residential treatment centers for the emotionally disturbed, and developmental training centers for the mentally retarded. Average length of stay varies between facilities, and may range from several days to permanent care. Some of these residential facilities also serve clients on an outpatient basis, providing diagnostic, evaluative, and planning services.

Day-care centers. These centers provide day-care services to the retarded, emotionally disturbed, or physically disabled. The centers not only serve to give the parents some free time, but also provide training in the areas of self-help, socialization, homemaking, communication, and leisure-time activities.

Hospital services. Hospitals provide a variety of rehabilitation services for those impaired, such as medical services, physical therapy, and speech therapy. For those who are severely injured, or have a serious chronic illness, hospitals are often the entry point into the rehabilitation system.

Meals on wheels. This program provides hot and cold meals to housebound recipients who are incapable of obtaining or preparing their own meals, but who can feed themselves.

Home health services. Services provided under such programs include visiting nurse services, drugs, physical therapy, laboratory services, and sickroom equipment.

Homemaker services. In some communities homemakers are available to take care of

Teaching a worker to operate a printing press at a sheltered workshop

household tasks that the impaired are unable to do for themselves.

Vocational rehabilitation funding. Federal funding for rehabilitation programs has gradually evolved in this country. Two of the key statutes were the Vocational Rehabilitation Act Amendments of 1954 and the Rehabilitation Act of 1973.[40] At the present time there are federal matching funds available to states for basic rehabilitation programs at the matching rate of 80 percent federal, and 20 percent state. Individuals are eligible for vocational rehabilitation services if they have a mental or physical disability that substantially interferes with their ability to obtain employment, and if there is a reasonable expectation that services will enable them to obtain employment. Potential clients receive medical testing free of charge to assess the extent of their disability, and to check their overall health. Rehabilitation counselors employed by the state review these results. Applicants found eligible may then receive, at state and federal expense, a variety of services:

a. Special equipment, such as hearing aids, guide dogs, wheelchairs, canes, or prosthetics.
b. Special training in such areas as sign language, vocational training, reading, or social adjustment. This training may take place at a sheltered workshop, vocational school, public or private college, or on the job.
c. Money, for transportation and living expenses during the period of training.
d. Medical, surgical, and other services that will lessen the extent of the client's impairment.
e. Individual counseling and guidance.
f. Assistance in finding a suitable job and essential equipment, licenses, tools, or stock for a small business.
g. Follow-up to smoothen the client's entrance into employment.

Under this program states are able to set priorities for categories of eligible clients who will be served when financial resources are limited—for example, states may assign a higher priority to clients who need medical restoration over those who need psychological counseling. Each state also has the option of whether an economic means test should be used to determine the applicant's entitlement for certain services.

Medicaid. A program covering medical expenses for low-income people (described in Chapter 4).

Old-Age, Survivor's, and Disability Insurance. A social insurance program for those who are no longer able to work, following several years of covered employment (described in Chapter 4).

Supplemental Security Income. A public assistance program for the visually impaired and disabled (described in Chapter 4).

Food stamps. A program to offset some of the food expenses for low-income people who qualify (described in Chapter 4).

Worker's Compensation program. Workers injured or disabled on the job, as well as the surviving dependents of workers who die as a result of such injury, are provided financial assistance as compensation for lost wages and to pay for the cost of any required medical or rehabilitative care.

ROLES OF SOCIAL WORKERS

Social workers encounter the impaired in two general ways. First, the impaired are encountered in settings where the primary service focus is other than rehabilitation. For example, workers at family counseling agencies primarily see families with marital and interpersonal problems. Yet, at times, one or more of the family members may be handicapped. The impairment may be unrelated to the family problems, or may be an important contributing factor. When the latter occurs, the social worker's role is to help the family assess and understand the nature and impact of the impairment, and then help the family develop more effective strategies for handling the difficulties associated with the impairment.

Second, social workers are employed in settings which primarily serve the handicapped: such as sheltered workshops, nursing homes, general hospitals, day care centers for the handicapped, rehabilitation hospitals, and specialized schools (such as schools for the visually impaired).

Rehabilitation of the impaired can be defined as "restoration of the handicapped to the fullest physical, mental, social, vocational, and economic usefulness of which he or she is capable."[41] Rehabilitation involves several focuses: vocational training, vocational counseling, psychological adjustment, medical and physical restoration, and job placement. Clients, of course, differ in which of these services focuses are needed. Some clients required services in all of these areas.

There are a wide range of professionals providing rehabilitation services: physicians, nurses, clinical psychologists, physical therapists, psychiatrists, occupational therapists, recreational therapists, vocational counselors, speech therapists, hearing therapists, industrial arts teachers, social workers, special education teachers, and prosthetists. Most of these therapists focus on the physical functioning of clients, while social workers primarily focus on the social functioning of clients. In most rehabilitation settings a team approach is used.

In rehabilitation settings the major functions of social workers include:

Counseling clients. Such counseling involves helping clients adjust to the impairment, and adjust to the rehabilitation program at the agency. A wide range of problems may be covered: personal, interpersonal, family, financial, vocational adjustment, and educational adjustment.

Counseling families. In some rehabilitation settings a worker is primarily involved in working with the family, and not the client, especially if the client is a young child. Counseling with the family involves helping the family to understand the nature of the handicap and the prognosis, helping the family members to make the essential adjustments to better help the client, and providing counseling on personal and interpersonal concerns associated with the disability. In such a role a worker provides information, comfort, understanding, counseling on specific concerns, and sometimes referral services.

Taking social histories. A social history contains information about the client's family background and present status. The history contains information about what the client's family life was like prior to contact with the agency, what it is like now, and what it will probably be like in the future. A social history contains: a history of the disability, positive and negative reactions of family members to the disability, significant family relationships, summary of strengths and weaknesses within the family for handling the impairment, information on social skills of the client, a history of the client's functioning at school and at work, a history of services provided in the past, and a summary of the problems and concerns of family members associated with the handicap. Information for the social history is gathered from the client, from family members, and from case records of other social and medical agencies that the client has had contact with.

Serving as liaison between the family and the agency. Keeping the lines of communication open is essential in any human service setting. In a rehabilitation setting social workers generally have the responsibility to serve as liaison between the agency staff and the family. At times a worker arranges meetings between the staff and the family to discuss the client's impairment, factors affecting rehabilitation, and to discuss future plans and services. In a hospital setting it is the physician's responsibility to explain the particular medical condition to the client, but a social worker often has the responsibility to discuss the implications of the medical condition with the client and the family. Implications covered include the likely effect the

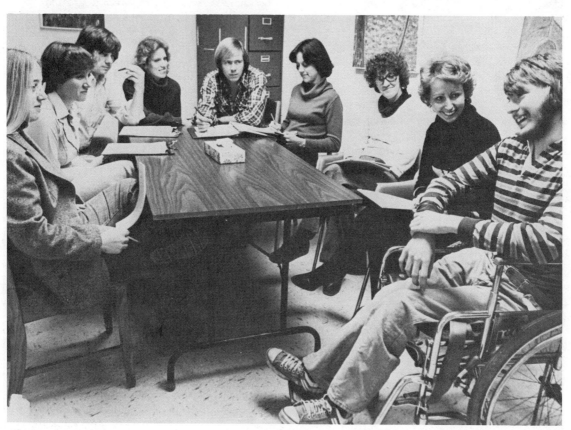

Social workers and other professionals staffing a client at a sheltered workshop

SOCIAL HISTORY OF A CLIENT AT A VOCATIONAL TESTING DIVISION OF A SHELTERED WORKSHOP

Hillside Vocational Training Center
Columbus, Ohio

Name: Jim Frey

Date of Birth: 6-30-60

Address: 550 S. Adams, Columbus

Telephone: 478-2346

Religion: Lutheran

Occupation: Unemployed

Race: Black

Marital Status: Single

Height: 5'10"

Weight: 180

REASON FOR TESTING

Three years ago on April 30, 1977 Jim Frey was involved in an automobile accident with his older brother, Bob. Bob was killed in the accident, and Jim's spine was severed. Mr. Frey was hospitalized for three months, spent five more months convalescing in a nursing home, and since that time has been living with his parents. Mr. Frey is paralyzed from the waist down. Following the accident he was also severely depressed. He was referred to this agency by Lakeland Counseling Center, an agency that Mr. Frey and his parents have been receiving counseling from. Mr Frey's depression has gradually decreased, and he is now seeking testing and vocational counseling to explore career opportunities.

Family background and early history. Mr. Frey's father, Donald Frey, has been an insurance salesman for the past 27 years. His mother, Joan Frey, has been a real estate broker for the past 14 years. Both Mr. and Mrs. Donald Frey appear to be very concerned about their son's future, and both stated they are willing to do whatever they can to help. The Freys live in a middle-class neighborhood, and have a home that is clean and well kept. The Freys appeared to have considerable respect for each other, and a good relationship.

The only children that the Donald Frey's had were Jim and Bob, with Bob being two years older. The Freys reported both their children did well academically in school, and each had a number of friends. The boys were both active in intramural sports, with Bob being a second-string player on the basketball team in his junior and senior years. The most serious trouble that either of the boys had gotten into prior to the accident was Bob being arrested for setting off fire crackers around the 4th of July five years ago.

The automobile accident occurred after Jim and Bob had left a party late one evening in which alcoholic beverages were served. Their car hit a bridge abutment. Bob was killed instantly. The parents reported they were extremely distraught following this accident and felt their whole world had shattered. They indicated they had few friends they socialized with, as they spent most of their time prior to the accident with their work and their children. They received counseling for grief and depression for 18 months from Lakeland Counseling Center. They indicated they discontinued counseling when the person they were seeing made a job transfer to the West Coast.

For nearly the past two years Mr. and Mrs. Donald Frey have been caring for Jim at home. Mrs. Frey indicated she has taken a leave of absence from her real estate position in order to care for her son. They acknowledged caring for Jim has been "taxing," as he has been quite depressed and has required considerable physical attention. Only recently has he been able to get into and out of a wheelchair without assistance. The parents still mourn the loss of Bob, but are increasingly becoming optimistic with the progress that Jim has been making: including a decrease in his depression, increased physical agility, and now a motivation to receiving training for a career.

School performance. Jim Frey attended Franklin Elementary School, Stevens Junior High, and Randal High School. At the time of his accident, Jim was a senior. He was near graduation, but as yet has not completed the course work. School records show Jim generally received As and Bs, with a few Cs. Jim had an intelligence test in his sophomore year in which he achieved a score of 122. Prior to the accident Jim was planning to attend college. He reportedly had a number of friends, and most continued to visit him for the first several months following the accident. But as time passed, and as Jim's depression continued, his friends gradually stopped coming by to see him. At the present time he has no close friends.

General health. Up until the accident his health was generally good. He had a hernia operation at age 10, and a broken collar bone at age 12. During the accident Mr. Frey suffered a severed spine and is now partially paralyzed. He also had a variety of cuts from glass that required over 80 stitches. Since the accident he at times has experienced considerable pain connected with his injury, and has been prone to catch flus and colds. Medical reports indicate Mr. Frey received intensive physical therapy while at the hospital, and while convalescing in the nursing home. Upon returning to his home, Mr. Frey's parents were instructed on giving him a variety of exercises.

Dating history. Mr. Frey indicated he dated a number of young women prior to the accident. At the time of the accident he was dating someone steadily, during his senior year. At first this person showed considerable interest in Mr. Frey and his circumstances. However, Mr. Frey stated after a few months she started dating others, and her interest in continuing their relationship rapidly declined.

Employment history. Mr. Frey was a paperboy for a few years. Prior to the accident he worked part-time as a busboy at a restaurant. He has not worked since the accident.

Prior contact with social agencies. Mr. Frey was hospitalized in 1977 for three months at St. Mary's hospital. Records show he received extensive physical therapy, and counseling for depression from the social work staff. Following this hospitalization he was transferred to Countryside Nursing Home where he continued to receive physical therapy and counseling. Mr. Frey had fallen asleep on the fateful night when his brother was killed. For months after that, Mr. Frey was depressed and continued to feel guilty because he felt if he had stayed awake he might have kept his brother awake—the police concluded that the accident occurred after Bob Frey had fallen asleep. Jim Frey also has been depressed over the breakup with his girl friend, the loss of other friends, and particularly over the hopes and expectations for his future being shattered. After Jim Frey returned home, his parents made arrangements with the referring agency (Lakeland Counseling Center) for Jim to receive counseling associated with his depression and also focused on his future. Reports received from Lakeland Counseling Center also indicated that Mr. Frey's parents have expressed concerns in the past year that Jim may be drinking beer and other alcoholic beverages to excess.

General impressions. Mr. Frey has made gradual progress in putting his life back together since his auto accident three years ago. At times he is still somewhat depressed, but he now is making efforts to stop brooding about his past, and is motivated to make efforts to improve his situation. He is looking forward to the test results at this center as he wants to receive training for a career. At the present time he is uncertain which career he desires to pursue, and is uncertain which vocations or professions he is qualified to pursue. He is articulate, personable, and appears to possess a high intellect. He has expressed a strong interest in graduating from high school, and wonders whether he might have the capacities and financial resources to attend college. His parents appear supportive of his desires to seek a higher education, and stated they would be willing and able to provide some financial support.

Mr. Frey stated he is also interested in learning to drive, and hopes to be able to secure a driver's license, and an auto with assistive devices that would enable him to drive.

Mr. Frey's drinking was discussed with him. He stated he may at times drink to excess, but he said this only happens when he is bored, depressed, or has nothing to do. It would seem that Mr. Frey's drinking is a potential difficulty that should be monitored.

Mr. Frey, after three years of brooding about the accident and his problems, is now enthusiastically looking forward to the testing results at this Center and is highly optimistic about the future. This enthusiasm is indeed a positive sign. However, it is important for Mr. Frey to realize that testing is only the first step. Mr. Frey hopes to acquire the necessary training, employment, and financial resources to live independently of his parents. While his parents are supportive, there are occasional conflicts between Mr. Frey and his parents, such as over his drinking. Mr. Frey may occasionally get discouraged when obstacles are encountered in arriving at the goals that he has set. It is at these times that Mr. Frey may need continued counseling to prevent the return of a long-term depression.

Respectfully submitted,

Frank Lia
Social Worker

impairment will have in the future on the capacity of the impaired person to function at work, at school, in social situations, and within the family. To be an effective liaison, a social worker in a rehabilitative setting needs a basic knowledge of a variety of medical conditions, of medical terminology, and an awareness of the implications of these medical conditions for emotional, physical, and social functioning.

Being a broker. Often a social worker serves a linkage function in helping families to make use of other community resources. To be an effective broker a worker needs a knowledge of other community services, including the programs provided, eligibility requirements, and admission procedures. Clients may need a variety of services from other community agencies, such as financial assistance, wheelchairs, prosthetic services, day-care services, special job training, visiting nurse services, and transportation.

Discharge planning. In some rehabilitation settings, such as hospitals, social workers have major responsibility for discharge planning. If a client is unable to return home, arrangements have to be made for placement in some other setting, such as a nursing home or a group home. Social workers often help clients and their families to prepare for returning home or to some other facility. Involved in such arrangements are making plans for financial aid, and for such specialized care as visiting nurse services, day care, physical therapy, and job training.

REACTIONS TO HAVING AN IMPAIRMENT

To work effectively with the handicapped and their families requires that the social worker understand and effectively deal with the emotional reactions to having an impairment. Clients and their families have a variety of reactions upon being informed an impairment exists. The effectiveness of counseling frequently depends on the social worker understanding such emotional reactions in order to assist clients and their families in acknowledging an impairment exists, and that they can generally be helped with available services.

In spite of the importance of understanding the emotional reactions of clients to having an impairment, there has been little research and theoretical attention in this area. An important contribution, however, has been made by Elisabeth Kübler-Ross. In *On Death and Dying,* Kübler-Ross presents five stages of dying that terminally ill people typically proceed through.[42] These five stages are summarized in Chapter 13 and include: denial, rage and anger, bargaining, depression, and acceptance. These stages are not absolute as not everyone goes through each stage. Some people also waver back and forth from one stage to another. But, used in a flexible, insight-producing way, professionals who counsel the terminally ill have found this paradigm to be a valuable theoretical framework in understanding why patients are displaying a variety of emotional reactions.

It appears to this writer that Kübler-Ross's five stages are emotional reactions which are not unique to the terminally ill but are common emotional reactions which all clients typically display when confronted with evidence that they have a personal problem, including being informed they have an impairment.

Denial, rage and anger, bargaining, depression, and acceptance are in the author's experiences common reactions in the following situations: a couple is informed their 1-year-old daughter is mentally retarded; a 20-year-old male is informed he will be paralyzed for the rest of his life as the result of an auto accident; a couple is informed their 6-month-old son has cerebral palsy; a 33-year-old business executive has a massive heart attack and is informed he will have to make major changes in his lifestyle; a husband is informed his wife will be severely visually impaired following an accident at work; a 26-year-old woman is informed she has multiple sclerosis; a 28-year-old farmer is informed his leg must be amputated following an accident; a couple is informed their 2-year-old son has a severe hearing impairment; a 17-year-old is informed she has rheumatoid arthritis. This list could perhaps be infinitely expanded.

The role of the social worker in constructively handling these five emotional reactions will briefly be described.

Stage 1—Denial ("No, not me"). For clients (or the families of clients) to admit they have an impairment is difficult as they may often (erroneously) perceive themselves as sinful, weak, or irresponsible. In our society which glorifies "the body beautiful" acknowledging that an impairment exists is often erroneously interpreted by clients as indicating they are less important or worthy. Also, recognizing an impairment exists means a client has to acknowledge that his/her life will have to change. When such change is inevitable clients often mourn the loss of that which must be changed. For example, a young successful businessperson may have to change his/her whole life following a heart attack, including pursuing some other career with fewer pressures. Denial is often important and necessary as it helps cushion the impact of the client's awareness that change is inevitable.

Social workers need to understand that there are reasons, similar to the above, why clients are denying an impairment when first informed. For people who deny a problem exists, constructive changes are not apt to occur, unless the worker finds a way to convince them that an impairment exists. When a client denies a problem exists, counseling needs to focus on this denial by exploring why the person believes a problem does not exist and by gathering evidence to document the existence of the problem to the client. The client then needs to be confronted, in a tactful manner, with this evidence.

Stage 2—Rage and anger ("Why me?"). Clients (or their families) resent the fact that others remain the same, while they are afflicted with an impairment. Clients feel it is "unfair" that they are afflicted. Also, clients may resent the fact that relatives, old friends, and others are doing the things that they can no longer do. Anyone may be the target of the anger. At times the anger may be directed at the social worker for confronting them with the reality of their handicap.

The underlying reasons generating the client's anger need to be remembered during this stage. Conveying emotional support and empathy helps create an atmosphere where they feel more comfortable in coming to terms with their impairment. Allowing clients to ventilate their anger serves to reduce the intensity of the anger; and once the intensity is reduced they are better able to realistically examine their difficulties. During this stage it is helpful for professionals to realize that when clients are angrily attacking them, the reason for the anger is probably being generated by the clients saying "Why me?" and should not be personalized by helping professionals. Reacting personally or negatively to the clients' anger will only feed into clients' hostile behavior.

Often during this stage clients feel overwhelmed by their problems, which is a factor in their intensely feeling "Why me?" If clients feel overwhelmed, they need to see that there is help available in handling the impairment, and that by taking things one step at a time, one day at a time, they can gradually make the adjustments that will lead them to live a fulfilling life and minimize the negative effects of their impairment. At times it is helpful for clients at this stage to talk to others who have had similar impairments and have made the necessary adjustments to put their lives back together.

It is sometimes also useful to help clients realize that expecting "justice and fairness" in the world is irrational.[43] People are not created equally. Everyone has strengths, and everyone has weaknesses. It is self-defeating to brood about one's weaknesses and impairments. Because humans are fallible, injustices and unfair circumstances can be expected to occur. To expect fairness is unrealistic. All we can do is to seek to develop our capacities to the fullest and to seek to live a satisfying life in spite of the shortcomings we have. When we realize that it is impossible to change an "unfair" situation, the most productive approach is to acknowledge that the situation exists, and to stop telling ourselves how awful it is.[44]

Stage 3—Bargaining ("Yes, me, but . . ."). During this stage clients are beginning to accept the existence of the impairment, but will bargain for a wide variety of things: getting a second opinion, substituting cigar smoking for cigarette smoking for someone who has emphysema, working two more weeks to organize things at the office prior to taking an extended period of relaxed recovery for someone who has had a heart attack, and so on. Clients promise to be good or to do something in exchange for another week or month before they use the alternatives presented to them to change. Or, they hope that there will be scientific breakthroughs that will fully cure the impairment.

During the bargaining stage clients will usually try to change a few circumstances in their life, and they then hope that these changes will miraculously eliminate the impairment. Parents of a severely retarded child may hope, for example, that increased training and education will enable their child in several years time to be of "normal" intelligence. Bargaining is a common reaction. During this stage a social worker should confront clients with the realities of the impairment and also indicate what the prognosis is. The hopes of clients and their families should not be devastated, but clients need to be fully informed of the realities of the impairment. For example, parents of a severely retarded child need to be informed it is unrealistic to expect their child will someday be of normal intelligence but that there are a variety of services (special education programs in schools, day-car centers, sheltered workshops, work training programs) to help their child live a fulfilling life.

Stage 4—Depression ("Yes, me"). Clients (and their families) at this stage have stopped denying the existence of their impairment. Their anger has subsided, and they no longer try to bargain. They understand the nature of their impairment and realize they will need to make changes in their lives. However, they as yet are not ready to put forth the efforts to improve their circumstances. They tend to brood about having an impairment and convey an attitude of "Woe is me," "How awful this is," and "Poor me." Often they blame themselves for having the impairment. Frequently they mourn about how the impairment will affect their future, and they mourn the loss of what they will have to change in their lives.

During this stage counselors need to convey empathy and help clients see that their impairment will not affect their lives as drastically as they perceive. At this stage clients need to be given realistic hope that they can make the adjustments that will enable them to lead a meaningful life. Frequently this can be facilitated by describing available services for rehabilitation and by helping them to make arrangements to use such services. Again, at this stage it is often useful for them to talk to others that have had a similar impairment. Perhaps there may be a self-help group focusing on their impairment in the community that clients can join to share and discuss experiences and problems and to learn about the specific steps that others have taken to minimize the effects of the impairment.

Stage 5—Acceptance ("I have a problem, but it's all right," "I can"). Clients now, for the first time, make a concerted effort at this stage to minimize the effects of the impairment, and to put their lives back together. They have the attitude now of, "I can do it." There is hope. A plan for rehabilitation can be presented at this stage if one was lacking or dismissed in earlier stages. Fear and apprehension is still present but very much reduced. Clients now have the motivation to do what they can to put their lives back together. Only when clients reach this stage are they ready to work on a rehabilitative program.

With an understanding of the above paradigm, social workers are better able to understand why clients are reacting in various ways to their impairments. With this awareness, workers are then better able to intervene in the ways suggested in order to have clients reach the fifth stage of acceptance. Clients need to reach the "acceptance" stage before they will be motivated to commit themselves to participating in a rehabilitative program.

It should be noted these are not the only reactions that clients (and their families) may display to having an impairment. Some other reactions that may be displayed include guilt, frustration, shame, fear, and disappointment.

Parents, for example, who have a child born with an impairment may feel guilty for a variety of reasons. They may feel guilty because they believe they caused the impairment through sinning. Because sex and reproduction are closely associated, they may believe God is punishing them for some transgression. Or, the parents may feel guilty because the mother may have lifted some heavy objects while pregnant, or because the mother took drugs or drank alcoholic beverages while pregnant.

The parents may also feel embarrassed or ashamed of the child's impairment and fear being rejected by others because of the child. Or, the parents may feel a special sense of worthiness—they may feel they have been given a special child, and that they now have a divine mission to devote themselves to caring for the child. Or, the parents may feel intense disappointment in not having a "normal child" and now resent the added burden of having to raise a child that will require increased care and attention. Or, the parents may fear they will be rejected by others because of the child.

In helping clients handle these various emotional reactions it is helpful for workers to help clients identify those emotions that are interfering with a habilitative or rehabilitative program. For those emotions that are interfering, strategies can then be developed to counter such emotions. For example, if a mother of a child born with Downs syndrome feels guilty because she thinks she caused this impairment during the pregnancy by lifting too much, arrangements may be made with a physician or a genetics counselor to explain the etiology of the disorder and to assure her that her concerns over lifting something heavy had nothing to do with causing the disorder.

It should also be noted that Kübler-Ross's paradigm may not always apply to young children. Children born with an impairment are generally not initially aware of their handicap. Awareness gradually comes through interacting with others over a lengthy period of time. Handicapped children gradually learn they are different and that others often place negative values on their handicap. In the following excerpt from an autobiography, Christy Brown, born with cerebral palsy, describes some of his feelings. Christy Brown used to ride in a wagon that was pulled by his brothers and sisters, but when it broke, he was unable to get around:

> I was now just ten, a boy who couldn't walk, speak, feed or dress himself. I was helpless, but only now did I begin to realize how helpless I really was. I still didn't know anything about myself: I knew nothing beyond the fact that I was different from others. I didn't understand what made me different or why it should be I. . . .
>
> I couldn't reason this out. I couldn't even think clearly about it. I could only feel it, feel it deep down in the very core of me, like a thin sharp needle. . . .
>
> Up to then I had never thought about myself. True, there had come sometimes a vague feeling that I wasn't like the others, an uneasy sort of stirring in my mind that came and went. But it was just one dark spot in the brightness of things; and I used soon to forget it. . . .
>
> Now it was different. Now I saw everything, not through the eyes of a little boy eager for fun and brimming with curiosity, but through those of a cripple, a cripple who had only just discovered his own affliction.
>
> I looked at Peter's hands. They were brown, steady hands with strong, square fingers, hands that could clasp a hurley firmly or swing a chestnut high into the air. Then I looked down at my own. They were queer, twisted hands, with bent, crooked fingers, hands that were never still, but twitched and shook continually so that they looked more like two wriggling snakes than a pair of human hands.
>
> I began to hate the sight of those hands, the sight of my wobbly head and lopsided mouth. . . .[45]

Christy's awareness of his impairment involved four steps: (1) an avoidance of thinking about himself and his handicap, (2) a vague sense that he was different from others, (3) a critical incident—not being able to go out—that forced Christy to acknowledge that he had an impairment, and (4) a self-depreciation because of his impairment.

There is a tendency for parents to overindulge and overprotect a handicapped child. The child is given less responsibility, fewer limits are placed on unwanted behaviors, personal whims of the child are indulged more, and the child is often punished less, partly because there is sympathy for the suffering the child is undergoing. Children become aware of this special status, and sometimes use this sympathy to manipulate those they come in contact with. Louise Baker describes how she manipulated others at age eight, shortly after a leg was amputated following an automobile accident.

> Even before I left the hospital my sudden power over people was showing itself. First of all, with completely unconscious brilliance, I chose rather inspired subjects to discuss during my five days of postoperative delirium. I rambled on feverishly but with moving feeling about a doll with real golden hair and blue eyes that opened and closed. I even conveniently mentioned the awesome price and just where such a doll might be purchased, and I sighed over my father's attested poverty which prevented him from buying this coveted treasure. . . . The news spread: "The poor little crippled child in the hospital . . . wants a doll. . . ." When I left the hospital it took two cars to transport my loot.
>
> Very soon after I came home from the hospital I realized that all I had to do was mumble the magic words . . . "I'll never be able to run again, will I?" This sad little speech—then the moment was ripe to make almost any demand . . .
>
> Three months before, I was a reasonably well-mannered child . . . now I was a precocious golddigger, and anyone was fair game.[46]

When clients or members of their family are reacting (emotionally or behaviorally) in ways that substantially interfere with the rehabilitation process, the social workers have a responsibility to tactfully confront the clients or their families about this. Sometimes considerable evidence will have to be presented, perhaps over a period of time, to have the clients and family members acknowledge that certain reactions are intensifying the effects of the impaired. Once the acknowledgment occurs, then strategies for changing the reaction patterns can be discussed, and one or more approaches selected and implemented to change the destructive reaction patterns.

SUMMARY

Those who are handicapped include the temporarily injured, the physically disabled, the deaf and hearing impaired, the blind and visually impaired, the mentally retarded and emotionally disturbed, and those with degenerative illnesses and chronic health disorders.

Throughout history the willingness of societies to care for the needs of those impaired has always been largely determined by the perceived causes of the impairment, the existing medical knowledge, and the general economic conditions.

Throughout much of history disability was often viewed as the result of demonic possession or as due to God's punishment.

In this century our society has made progress in better understanding the needs of the impaired, and in designing services to meet these needs. Yet, there still is a general lack of acceptance of the disabled, which is often related to the emphasis on the "body beautiful" in our society. The impaired are still frequently given pity, shunned, or made the brunt of jokes. Our society has yet to learn that the disabled are people, who want to be treated as peers. Until the impaired are given an opportunity, not only legally but socially, to be treated as peers, social services will only be partially effective. Ideally, the impaired should only be limited by the physical restrictions of their impairment. Sadly the psychological and social obstacles faced by disabled persons often are greater than their actual physical limitations. Our society has yet to learn that an impaired person is a person—a person who happens to have an impairment.

As is true for many social service programs, rehabilitative services is limited by the amount of money society is willing to spend for such services.

Social workers are only one of numerous professionals that provide services to the impaired. The roles of social workers in providing rehabilitative services are not limited to, but include counseling the impaired, counseling family members of the impaired, gathering information through social histories, serving as liaison between the family and the agency, being a broker, and discharge planning.

Another role of a social worker is to help the impaired and their family members change emotional and behavioral reactions that are interfering with the rehabilitative process. A useful paradigm in understanding reactions to having an impairment is the theoretical framework originally described by Kübler-Ross which includes the five stages of: denial, rage and anger, bargaining, depression, and acceptance.

NOTES

1. Nancy Weinberg, "Rehabilitation," in *Contemporary Social Work*, ed. Donald Brieland, Lela Costin, and Charles Atherton, 2d ed. (New York: McGraw-Hill, 1980), p. 302.

2. Ibid., pp. 301–2.

3. G. L. Dickinson, *Greek View of Life* (New York: Collier, 1961), p. 95.

4. S. Nichtern, *Helping the Retarded Child* (New York: Grosset & Dunlap, 1974), p. 14.

5. J. F. Garrett, "Historical Background," in *Vocational Rehabilitation of the Disabled*, ed. D. Malikin and H. Rusalem (New York: New York University Press, 1969), pp. 29–38.

6. J. C. Coleman, *Abnormal Psychology and Modern Life*, 3d ed. (Glenview, Ill.: Scott, Foresman, 1964).

7. C. E. Obermann, *A History of Vocational Rehabilitation in America* (Minneapolis: Dennison, 1964).

8. L. Kanner, *A History of the Care and Study of the Mentally Retarded* (Springfield, Ill.: Charles C Thomas, 1964), p. 6.

9. M. Judge, "A Brief History of Social Services," part I, *Social Rehabilitation Record* 3, no. 5 (1976): 2–8.

10. Stanford Rubin and Richard Roessler, *Foundations of the Vocational Rehabilitation Process* (Baltimore: University Park Press, 1978), p. 4.

11. A. F. Tyler, *Freedom's Ferment* (New York: Harper & Bros., 1962), pp. 294–96.

12. J. Lenihan, "Disabled Americans: A History," *Performance* 27, Bicentennial Issue, The President's Committee on Employment of the Handicapped (Washington, D.C.: U.S. Government Printing Office, 1977).

13. Obermann, *History of Rehabilitation*, p. 333.

14. L. M. Dunn, "A Historical Review of the Retarded," in *Mental Retardation*, ed. J. Rothstein (New York: Holt, Rinehart & Winston, 1961), pp. 13–17.

15. Obermann, *History of Rehabilitation*, p. 80.

16. Kanner, *History of the Mentally Retarded*.

17. Ibid., p. 39.

18. Rubin and Roessler, *Foundations*, pp. 12–13.

19. Ibid., pp. 13–14.

20. Lenihan, "Disabled Americans.

21. Tyler, *Freedom's Ferment*, p. 306.

22. Rubin and Roessler, *Foundations*, pp. 8–9.

23. Ibid., pp. 10–11.

24. R. Lubove, *The Professional Altruist* (Cambridge, Mass.: Harvard University Press, 1965).

25. Ibid.

26. Obermann, *History Rehabilitation*, p. 121.

27. Rubin and Roessler, *Foundations*, pp. 22–23.

28. Obermann, *History Rehabilitation*, pp. 155–57.

29. R. Thomas, "The Expanding Scope of Services," *Journal of Rehabilitation* 36, no. 5, (1970): 37–40.

30. Rubin and Roessler, *Foundations*, pp. 30–32.

31. Ibid., pp. 32–45.

32. S. Richardson et al., "Cultural Uniformity in Reaction to Physical Disabilities," *American Sociological Review* 26, (April 1961): 241–47.

33. C. H. Cooley, *Human Nature and the Social Order* (New York: Scribner, 1902).

34. Beatrice A. Wright, *Physical Disability: A Psychological Approach* (New York: Harper, 1960), p. 259.

35. Salvatore G. DiMichael, "The Current Scene," in *Vocational Rehabilitation of the Disabled: An Overview,* ed. David Malikin and Herbert Rusalem (New York: New York University Press, 1969).

36. Weinberg, "Rehabilitation," p. 310.

37. Ibid., p. 310.

38. R. Kleck, H. Ono and A. H. Hastorf, "The Effects of Physical Deviance upon Face-to-Face Interaction," *Human Relations* 19 (1966): 425–36.

39. Fred David, "Deviance Disavowel: The Management of Strained Interaction by the Visibly Handicapped," in *The Other Side: Perspectives on Deviance,* ed. Howard S. Becker (New York: Free Press, 1964), p. 123.

40. Rubin and Roessler, *Foundations,* pp. 32–44.

41. *Symposium on the Process of Rehabilitation* (Cleveland: National Council on Rehabilitation, 1944), p. 6.

42. Elisabeth Kübler-Ross, *On Death and Dying* (New York: Macmillan, 1969).

43. W. W. Dyer, *Your Erroneous Zones* (New York: Funk & Wagnalls, 1976).

44. A. Ellis and R. Harper, *A New Guide to Rational Living* (North Hollywood, Calif.: Wilshire Book, 1977).

45. Christy Brown, *The Story of Christy Brown* (New York: Pocket Books, 1971).

46. Louise Baker, *Out on a Limb* (New York: Whittlesly House, 1946), pp. 4–5.

chapter **16**

INTRODUCTION

This chapter will focus on chemical use, abuse, dependency, and treatment. Since alcohol is the most widely used, abused, and addictive drug today a good portion of the chapter will be devoted to a discussion of alcohol, abusive drinking (drunkenness), and alcoholism. Included will be a discussion about personality defects or emotions which contribute to the use, abuse, or dependency. The latter part of this section will speak of treatment and methods of counseling the problem drinker or the alcoholic. The latter part of the chapter will also deal with the use, abuse, dependency, and treatment for drugs: the depressants, stimulants, hallucinogens, volatile chemicals and marijuana (*Cannabis sativa*).

There are a number of reasons for separating the discussion of alcohol from other drugs. It should be mentioned first that alcohol is the most widely used and abused drug

---

* This chapter was written for this text by Tim Bliss, Ms. Ed., former director of an alcoholism/drug abuse service.

in our society today. While alcohol is highly condoned, even in abuse situations, other drugs are condemned; and where narcotics, depressants, and stimulants have legitimate medical use, alcohol has none. Presently most treatment modalities separate alcohol dependency from drug dependency because most believe treatment is different. However, mention must also be made that some treatment modalities such as therapeutic communities have the general belief that the chemical of choice is only a symptom and that treatment should focus on changing the lifestyle.

For those of us in the field of chemical dependency, there is often a tendency to generalize by classifying the alcoholic as having a passive-aggressive personality, and the drug abuser as displaying antisocial behavior. Definitions are needed at this point to understand why these terms are generally accepted. It must be mentioned, however, that although these terms are used loosely, other diagnoses are made.

A passive-aggressive personality is characterized by passively expressed aggression;

Drugs—Use, abuse, and treatment*

for example, by obstructionism, pouting, procrastination, intentional inefficiency or stubbornness. The behavior commonly reflects hostility which the individual feels s/he dare not express openly. Often the behavior is one expression of the patient's resentment at failing to find gratification in a relationship with an individual or institution upon which s/he is overdependent.[1]

The antisocial behavior fits those individuals who are unsocialized and whose behavior patterns bring them repeatedly into conflict with society. However, a mere history of offenses is not sufficient to justify this diagnosis. They are incapable of significant loyalty to individuals, groups, or social values. They are grossly selfish, calloused, irresponsible, and impulsive. The antisocial person is unable to feel guilt or to learn from experience and punishment; and thus tends to blame others or offer rationalizations for his/her behavior.[2]

ALCOHOL—ETHYL ALCOHOL/ GRAIN ALCOHOL

Ethyl alcohol or grain alcohol is a colorless liquid used and abused for centuries. But alcohol itself is no more harmful than soft drinks; it is a person's attitude toward alcohol that causes the majority of problems. "Devil's Brew, hooch, sauce, juice" exemplifies the negative connotations associated with alcohol.

In use, alcohol causes several kinds of physical reactions as determined by the amount consumed. Contrary to popular belief, alcohol is not a stimulant; it is a central nervous system depressant. Initially, however, it may appear to react as a stimulant in that it relaxes tensions and lowers inhibitions. However, as drinking continues, mental and physiological processes of reasoning, perception, speech, muscle coordination, and respiration slow down. In small amounts

it can act as a sedative relieving nervous tension and inducing a sense of calmness. Alcohol also acts as an analgesic in these small amounts by relieving minor pain without inducing sleep. As the level of alcohol increases in the blood, effects on the body change. In large amounts it acts as a narcotic and induces sleep, thus relieving physical and mental pain. In even larger amounts it can act as a toxin as a result of a lethal dose in the bloodstream.

Roughly, 20 percent of alcohol consumed is absorbed immediately and directly through the stomach walls into the bloodstream. Unlike food, alcohol doesn't need to be digested. When alcohol is absorbed through the stomach walls into the bloodstream, it is carried directly to the brain, depressing its activity. It rushes so fast into the bloodstream that moments after it is consumed it can be found in almost all the tissues, organs, and secretions of the body. The remaining 80 percent is processed at a slower rate through the liver and gastrointetinal tract.[3]

The history of public attitudes toward alcohol, including social control, is remembered most with such organizations as the Women's Christian Temperance Union (WCTU).[4] This organization campaigned for alcohol's prohibition. WCTU believed alcohol was responsible for many social problems, including crime and unemployment. The "skid row" image evolved during this time period as immigrants and the working or lower class males were seen drinking in taverns and in public. As a result, public attitudes associated alcohol consumption with these classes of people and it was viewed negatively by groups of higher social status.

In 1920 the Eighteenth Amendment to the U.S. Constitution was ratified by a number of states outlawing the sale of alcohol. Prohibition began. Soon the Eighteenth Amend-

A "good time" at a bar

The morning after

ment was to become one of the most unenforceable laws ever to be passed. People continued to drink at all social levels. Organized crime associations competed with each other for the biggest share of the illicit liquor market. Finally in 1933 the Eighteenth Amendment was repealed.

Today, as the use of alcohol has become more widespread and accepted among the middle and upper classes, public attitudes toward alcohol certainly have changed. It is no longer viewed as society's drink of destruction. Instead, alcohol today is widely accepted, and it is usually considered good manners to offer guests alcoholic beverages at a party.

Drinking

If you view alcohol as the "Devil's Brew" you've already condemned nearly 50 percent of the population in our society who drink. And if you drink and view nondrinkers as "teetotalers" you've condemned the other 50 percent of the population.

Drinking serves many positive functions as well as negative. The conduct of social life often requires that persons with divergent lifestyles come into contact with each other for social as well as instrumental reasons. Cocktail parties are good examples of this and the relaxing effects of alcohol can greatly reduce the potential tension in such circumstances. Even when good friends get together social interaction can flow more smoothly than would be the case in its absence. Taverns and similar types of "watering holes"[5] which are patronized by all social classes provide a center for social interaction and relaxation.

People have the choice to not drink, to drink, or to abuse. If you don't drink, all it takes is a polite "No thank you"; but how is this generally accepted by our society? For example, a party is given and there is a toast to good health and happiness. The host pours the wine and one individual says "No thank you," thus leaving the wine glass empty. The host then proposes a toast, all the wine glasses are raised and suddenly the wine glass that is full reaches across the table and fills the empty glass with wine. The toast is made. What is wrong here? Does it say something about society's attitude toward the nondrinker? Of course it does, and it is that attitude that makes alcohol such a potentially dangerous drug. Also think of the consequences if the nondrinker was a recovering alcoholic.

What about those who drink? It is generally agreed people drink to relax and relieve social insecurities. This, for those who drink responsibly, is a proper and controlled use of alcohol. Drinking has also been a part of religious ritual and cultural tradition for centuries. Use of alcohol in religious ceremony is a custom among Jews, and they have a low rate of alcoholism. It is used to "gladden the heart," and abuse just doesn't occur. Again, attitude plays a significant role. Roman Catholics, on the other hand, have mixed feelings or attitudes toward drinking and have a high rate of alcoholism. Buddhists or Mormans are a few who condemn the use of alcohol, and consequently, also have high rates of alcoholism. The use of alcohol by native American Indians is another example. The West wasn't won by the Winchester or Colt 45; it was won by "Old Grand Dad" and some of those "spirited" folks. The white man introduced alcohol to Indians, and abuse and addiction ran rampant.

Why do we drink? There are many reasons, but let us first focus on the emotional aspects which lead into use, abuse, and addiction. Let's look at six or seven emotions which cause problems. If we look at these emotions as characters, we should be able to have a better understanding of each.[6]

1. Lonely—She is wrapped up in a world of her own. She believes no one likes her and therefore goes into seclusion many times displaying a passive-aggressive personality.

2. Fearful—He is afraid of everything and everybody. Fearful won't change because he is afraid that he might get hurt.

3. Inadequate—He loves to downgrade himself and is full of self-pity. He always displays the "poor me" image.

4. Insecurity—She clings to everybody, is always very anxious, is unable to make decisions.

5. Guilty—Believes she is to blame for every bad thing that happens to her or around her.

6. Resentment—Is always walking around with a chip on his shoulder.

7. Immaturity—Is the one who always has the easy way out. He will get out of any situation with as little effort as possible.

These innate emotions reside within us all. Some people drink to make these emotions disappear, until the opposite occurs and drinking magnifies these problems.

Drunkenness

How do you view the drunk at a party? Is s/he funny? If you condone or ignore drunkenness, usually the person will get drunk again. And if you laugh at the drunk, what usually happens? You guessed it, s/he gets drunk again. How do you react to a story about a drunk? A lady walked into a bar with a goose under her arm and the drunk made the remark, "What are you doing with that pig in here?" The lady said "That isn't a pig, it's a goose." The drunk replied, "I was talking to the goose!" The drunk went down a one-way street and was stopped by a police officer who said "Mr., what's wrong with you, didn't you see the arrows?" And the drunk replied "Arrows, I didn't see the Indians!"

Now is there a difference between laughing at a drunk and a story about a drunk? Of course there is! What is funny about a drunk? Possibly s/he could drive a car and kill someone or accost your best friend's wife (or husband), and on and on.

A story about a drunk is funny as long as it doesn't hurt anyone.

Why abuse? People abuse because of those emotions discussed earlier. Adolescents try to ease "growing pains" and the process of "fitting in" by drinking. Abuse is the result of the social pressure coupled with lack of understanding and education about alcohol.

Alcoholism/addiction

Alcoholism is a simple illness to understand. The alcoholic drinks because s/he has to. The individual who has a problem as a result of his/her drinking is alcoholic. S/he will not get better unless the drinking stops, because alcoholism is a progressive disease as defined by the American Medical Association in 1956.

How do you view alcoholism? Is it a moral judgment on your part; do we judge? Again, our attitude has a great deal to do with it. Attitudes are perhaps the hardest things to change and many times people aren't able to change them. Do you view the alcoholic as being an equal? Many of us don't; somehow we are up here and they are down there. And how does the alcoholic perceive this?

Alcoholism is a progressive disease that, without sobriety, ends up in institutionalization, mental and/or physical deterioration, possibly to the point of death.

Alcoholism is a major health problem throughout such countries as the Soviet Union, Scandinavia, Ireland, and the United States.[7] Alcoholism is listed as the third major public health problem. It is the chief cause of traffic accidents, liver disease, and divorce.[8]

Once alcoholism sets in, one can never again regain control. This has probably been tested and validated by every alcoholic at one time or another. There are over 10 million alcoholics in America, each one affects at least four other key individuals, including the spouse, family, or employer.

If we were to break down costs, in general this is what it would look like. It is estimated that $9 billion is lost annually in business and industry due to alcoholism.[9] This figure reflects cost in terms of absenteeism, sick leave, on-the-job accidents, and missed or late work assignments. It is generally accepted by those in the field of alcoholism and drug abuse that 6 to 10 percent of the total work force experience personal problems to such a degree that it affects their job performance.

If the employee is identified early enough through documentation of poor work performance, that person has a 60–70 percent chance of total recovery. This is primarily accomplished by industry implementing an employee assistance program, sometimes known as a troubled employee program. Usually an employee assistance program starts with a policy drawn up by management describing sociomedical problems; that is, alcoholism/drug dependency, emotional and physical problems.

The policy statement defines these illnesses and sets a procedure for dealing with employees whose job performance has deteriorated. The procedure indicates the importance of documenting a pattern of poor work performance; that is, sick leave or absenteeism. The way the program works is by confronting the employee through the normal three- or four-step disciplinary procedure. In addition, the supervisor offers a referral for help to the troubled employee. The referral for help should be an outside agency, such as the local Alcohol Information and Referral Center.

If job deterioration continues without the offer to help, the employee is usually termi-

One for the road–Is it worth it?

nated. This may drastically affect the individual's life. Therefore, it is important this pattern of job deterioration is identified and dealt with. The supervisor at work should only focus on performance as he or she is not a diagnostician.

Complications that exist in identifying poor work performance are the absence of supervision as well as low visibility of job performance. Either type can result in a failure to make appropriate referrals and also lead to inappropriate referrals to employee assistance programs. These complications exist in nearly all work organizations and may stem from the organizational structure or from supervisory incompetency. Low visibility of job performance may result because of minimal interdependence among jobs. In other words, jobs performed independently may allow for simultaneous development and cover-up of deviant drinking or drug use patterns. Jobs that have low visibility often do not have clear goals established by the employer. When goals aren't established, anxiety is produced and the employee may find alcohol or drug use an effective release for tension. Therefore, if the organization does not evaluate and have clear production goals itself, there is little means of identifying deviant work performance.[10]

Treatment

The symptom that is most common among alcoholics is denial. None of us like to think we are different, and it isn't surprising that drinking for the alcoholic is characterized by innumerable, egotistical attempts to prove that s/he can drink like other people drink. Many attempts are made through sneaking drinks, excusing drinking behavior, or by blaming others (If you had a wife like mine, you'd drink too!) Alcoholism is highly stigmatized. The alcoholic doesn't see him/herself as the down-and-out skid row bum, and that is legitimate because only 3 percent of the alcoholic population is skid row. Most alcoholics do have jobs, families, and lead fairly normal lives. Not until these rationalizations are broken down, can we, as counselors, begin to treat alcoholics and their families.

Going back to the question, how does the alcoholic perceive the sometimes superior attitude of the counselor? The alcoholic would feel resentful just as you or I would, and the excuse to drink would become much more justified. One must first take a very close and careful look at personal attitudes for effective treatment. Then an educational approach should be taken with the alcoholic and family. This means defining what alcoholism is, how it affects others, and what can be done to arrest it.

Jellenick, the well-acknowledged alcoholigist, proposes that the etiology can very tremendously depending on the alcoholic's use of alcohol.[11] He further states that the best way to understand alcoholism is by the disease concept in which various body systems are progressively involved. Jellenick stresses that in educating the alcoholic and his/her family (or whoever else is important to that person) it is beneficial to relate that, although psychological causes vary, physical signs and symptoms can be generally agreed upon.

The second and perhaps most crucial point to be emphasized is confrontation. Again, one of the most difficult aspects of breaking through alcoholism is denial. The alcoholic has had many years experience with denial (10 to 20 in males, 5 to 7 in females and 12 to 18 months with teenagers). Therefore, it becomes extremely important for the counselor to know how to confront the alcoholic, utilizing as many tools as possible. Family, friends, and employers are the primary tools. In confronting the alcoholic, documentation of incidents that occurred while drinking becomes extremely important. This is particularly important because the alcoholic may have blackouts. These are periods of amnesia as opposed to passing out or unconsciousness. Both are due to excessive drinking. Many times during confrontation it is important that the entire family be present to reinforce the incident. In documenting the incident it is immensely useful to write down the date and time, and to be as specific as possible in describing the situation. The counselor can be present during this confrontation to act as a facilitator; however, the primary responsibility in breaking through denial is with the spouse, family or employer.

Many times the practicing alcoholic has been threatened with divorce, job discipline, and so on. It is important not to continue these threats; action must occur if the alcoholic continues to drink after confrontation. Perhaps recovery will then take place because the alcoholic realizes the spouse or employer is serious about treatment. If the alcoholic agrees to seek help, the following steps should be taken:

We know that one of the most effective therapies for alcoholism today is a self-help approach known as Alcoholics Anonymous. Briefly, AA was founded by two individuals, both of whom were alcoholics. Bill Wilson was a stock analyst, and after losing much of his money in the Stock Market Crash of 1929,

he took to the bottle. After having been warned that his health was in jeopardy unless he stopped drinking, Bill W. underwent what seemed to be a spiritual experience and he made up his mind to stop drinking. He learned that by discussing his drinking problem with other alcoholics, it helped him to remain sober. He spent a considerable amount of time with Robert Smith, an Ohio doctor, also alcoholic, and together they formed Alcoholics Anonymous. Today AA has in its membership 800,000 recovered alcoholics in 92 countries.[12] Bill W. and Dr. Bob, as they were known within AA, remained anonymous until their deaths. Today AA functions as it did with Bill W. and Dr. Bob; the sharing of similar experiences to abstain from the one drink that is too many and the thousand drinks that are not enough.

AA should be established within the treatment plan as soon as possible with the attendance of as many meetings as necessary. A list of AA meetings can generally be found within most alcoholism treatment programs at local mental health centers. Counseling services should be provided to discuss marriage problems and to better understand one's individuality. Al-Anon, an organization for the spouse of the alcoholic should also be utilized. This helps the spouse become more familiar with personal problems and better acquainted with the alcoholic's problem. Alateen is still another organization that can be used for the teenagers, whose parents are alcoholic.

When an alcoholic becomes involved in counseling, the primary course of treatment, generally the first 6 to 12 sessions, should concentrate strictly on the drinking behavior and the thoughts, feelings, and emotions which surround that behavior. The spouse, family, and others who are involved with the alcoholic should be well educated about the disease and its treatment because these people often need as much help as the alcoholic. They, too, have been caught up in excusing behavior and making threats, very similar to the alcoholic's way of life.

Generally treatment is based either in an inpatient or outpatient setting. If a client is reached at an early stage of alcoholism or alcohol abuse, s/he can be treated on an outpatient basis. Outpatient treatment usually works with the client who can work and live at home without any significant problems. If on the other hand, the client is unable to live at home (if s/he is drinking), usually inpatient treatment will be recommended. Both modes of treatment are interrelated in that after a client has gone through an inpatient program s/he will be followed up on an outpatient basis.

Inpatient treatment can last anywhere from two weeks to three months depending on the treatment center. Staff are usually: (a) recovered alcoholics/addicts as lay counselors, and (b) professional staff such as social workers, psychologists and physicians. Treatment usually is intense, including group therapy, one-on-one therapy, an orientation to Alcoholics Anonymous, and occupational and recreational therapy.

Psychodrama treatment for a chemically dependent group

Outpatient, which is not as intense as inpatient, usually lasts from three to six months and offers the same forms of treatment. Outpatient usually has lay counselors or recovered alcoholics/addicts, professional staff, and physicians. In addition to working with the alcoholic, many times outpatient provides community education to aid in prevention or early intervention.

Halfway houses are still another mode of treatment used to house the alcoholic who is not yet ready to live alone in the community. Halfway house care usually lasts from one month to a year.

DRUGS

Drugs are chemical substances, solid, liquid, or gaseous, that are frequently used in the treatment of a medical disorder. It is any substance which affects the mind and/or body, resulting in physical or behavioral changes. The etiology of drug abuse varies considerably depending on the environmental circumstances, feelings of isolation, insecurity, inadequacy, and so forth. Behavioral changes vary according to dosage, situational circumstances, personality characteristics, to name a few. Drugs can and do lead to compulsive abuse and physical dependence, which is perhaps the worst feature about drug abuse.

Perhaps the strongest barrier in community prevention and early intervention lies in the stereotyped "drug fiend" that casts the drug user as "out of this world," shiftless, and dominated by a bizarre value system. Today's "drug fiend"[13] is seen as both a menace to society and a leech on society's resources (the criminal justice system and welfare). Society's reaction toward this image is one of hatred and rejection, calling for severe punishment as they are thought to be hopelessly incurable. Along with this stereotyped image is the long-haired hippie who is

Drugs seized in a raid

usually classified as the radical whose only purpose in life is to have sex, use marijuana of LSD, and to overtake the government.

This stereotype provides for inappropriate discrimination for those who fit the image but are not users. This image also tends to be a problem for treatment staff who tend to believe it, when they try to treat the abuser who is considerably impaired. Most deviant drug users are very much aware of the consequences they will receive if caught or discovered.

Psychological dependence is a state in which a person feels a need to take a drug. This may occur with or without physical dependence. The seriousness of dependence varies with the personality, the length in which the drug is taken, and the type of drug.[14]

Physical dependence or addiction results when certain drugs are taken on a regular basis over a period of time in which the body begins to need the drug to carry on normal functioning.[15]

If a person discontinues a drug s/he may experience physical withdrawal reactions. The severity of withdrawal depends on the type, amount, and duration in which the drug was used.

In many instances a tolerance develops which causes a need for larger amounts of the drug to produce the same type of euphoria that lesser amounts once produced. Tolerance can develop to such a degree that an overdose may occur.

Stimulants

Stimulants are drugs that stimulate the central nervous system. These drugs (depending on the individual) can provide relief from fatigue, increase alertness, elevate ones' mood, and heighten one's sense of excitation and well-being. Two of the most widely used drugs in America today are tobacco and caffeine. Neither of these are generally considered to be psychoactive—thus, few people view them as being drugs.

But tobacco has many people concerned about its detrimental health effects. It has been associated with some forms of cancer, heart disease, emphysema, and many other serious health disorders. According to a report by the U.S. Surgeon General's Office, cigarette smoking is estimated to result in 80,000 deaths a year from lung cancer, 19,000 from chronic pulmonary disease, and 22,000 deaths from other cardiovascular disease.[16] It is clear that the toll in human lives and suffering from the use of tobacco is startlingly high—far higher than for any other drug with the possible exception of alcohol. In recent years cigarette smoking has become a major public concern, and smoking is now restricted in public areas, such as in restaurants and on airplanes. The American Cancer

Society has had a tremendous impact on encouraging those who do smoke to quit. These and other efforts have helped considerably in making smoking socially and personally unacceptable.

The other commonly used stimulant is caffeine. Its effects are relatively mild and socially acceptable. Caffeine-loaded soft drinks advertise that you can expand your accomplishments through such ads as, "You've got a lot to live and Pepsi's got a lot to give."[17] Because caffeine is so widely accepted, we often don't think about the fact that it may be a contributing factor in heart disease and other health-related problems.

Amphetamines

Amphetamines are generally used for treating narcolepsy and minor chemical depression.[18] Amphetamines have also been used in the past to treat overweight clients; however, in recent years, prescriptions have been discouraged due to the overall dangers amphetamines can produce when abused. These dangers include possible drug psychosis resembling paranoid psychosis, violent behavior as a result of overreacting to normal stimuli, unpredictable mood changes, malnutrition, and a high susceptibility to infection.

During the middle and late 60s illegal amphetamine use was rampant among youth and was frequently a factor in leading to violent crimes. A World Health Organization report in 1965 unequivocally stated concern over the worldwide spread of amphetamines among the young.[19] Moreover the Select Committee on Crime of the House of Representatives clearly implied an increase when it reported, "There is an incredible overproduction of speed by legitimate manufacturers. Eight billion speed pills are being spewed out upon this country every year. This is enough for 40 doses for every man,

woman, and child in the United States."[20] Later, the committee report stated "Testimony uniformly attested to the relationship between abuse of amphetamine-type drugs and violence and crime."[21] Witnesses testified at a Senate hearing that truck stops on major highways were the major centers of distribution of illegal amphetamines and that at least half of the 9 million doses of amphetamines and barbiturates produced in 1962 had found their way into the black market.[22] Since that time, many governmental restrictions have been placed on the manufacturing and distribution of amphetamines. Yet, the black market continues to distribute illicit amphetamines.

Amphetamines are used by truck drivers, professional athletes, executives, and students, and are controversial from a legal, ethical, and medical standpoint.[23]

The effects of this drug are as follows: increased concentration and aggressiveness, a heightened sense of exhilaration, and severe depression after prolonged use.

With voluntary action on the part of physicians and drug manufacturers, as well as restrictions on prescribing and manufacturing amphetamines, efforts are being made to minimize dependence and to cut off a major supply to the black market.

Depressants

Barbiturates are used to sedate, relieve anxiety, and induce sleep. Without a doubt, of all drugs abused, barbiturate withdrawal is most severe and dangerous. Indirect evidence suggests that barbiturate abuse is increasing.

Nembutals and Seconals have been found in abuse situations, especially in conjunction with alcohol. Smith found barbiturate use to be a correlate of amphetamine abuse, with Secobarbital (reds) employed as a way to come down from amphetamine stimulation.

(Tranquilizers are also becoming popular as "downers.")[24]

Barbiturates basically have the same effects as alcohol. The sense of well-being or euphoria depends on the psychological state the user is in, the conditions under which the drug is taken (setting), and the pharmacological properties of the drug. Judgment is considerably impaired and body functions lack normal control.

The most widely preferred barbiturates are short to intermediate acting in nature (four to six hours) by those individuals wishing to get high.

Individuals generally involved in barbiturate abuse range in age from 30 to 50 years old. Adolescents use barbiturates as a result of wanting to experiment or as an accessory to other drugs whose effects they value more highly.[25]

Most individuals who abuse barbiturates are not involved in the drug subculture. They obtain their supply through physicians rather than the black market. Usually the abuser complains to several physicians of sleepless nights and a great deal of nervousness. Often, because of his/her middle-class image, the abuser doesn't have any problem refilling prescriptions; this results as some pharmacists don't bother to notify the physician when refilling the prescription.

Usually the abuser goes undetected until he or she demonstrates confusion and an inability to perform as exemplified by slurred speech or a staggering gait.

Barbiturates are generally taken orally, but in some cases they are injected intravenously. Barbiturate injection is more often seen in the drug subculture. Shortly after injection an immediate sense of euphoria is felt. This method is by far the most hazardous.

The following example represents a barbiturate overdose. A 35-year-old male was referred for psychiatric treatment following an

A suicide from an overdose of barbiturates

overdose of barbiturates, which had resulted in a three-day hospitalization. He related an episodic use of intravenous methamphetamine over a period of three years. His wife, a nurse, supplied clean syringes and occasionally would also use the drug, so that "we could be together." Three months before coming into treatment he had reestablished contact with an old friend and they began tripping together on reds. Because his tripping partner was female, numerous arguments with his wife resulted. Whenever she would complain about his activities, he would respond by shooting more reds. Following one of the domestic quarrels, he left home in anger and was discovered the next morning dead from an overdose of reds. The coroner could not determine whether the overdose was intentional or accidental.[26]

Barbiturates are also the number one suicide drug, usually preferred by women but also used by men. The following illustrates this. A few years ago this author knew an individual quite well. The individual was heavily involved in the drug subculture. Several times in his remaining months alive, he had verbally threatened suicide. His drugs of choice were alcohol and Seconals. One night he again threatened suicide in a drunken stupor and the next morning was found dead in a bedroom. Beside him was a suicide note.

Many abusers also use "barbs" for self-medicating purposes. These include easing symptoms of withdrawal from heroin, to relieve muscular aches from LSD, and to enable one to come down from a speed run.

Inpatient treatment is almost always recommended for barbiturate withdrawal. Mild withdrawal usually takes the form of anxiousness, disruption of sleep, and irritability. Severe withdrawal usually includes convulsions, psychosis, and death.

Treatment should consist of a slow withdrawal in a detoxification center and a long-term therapy approach. Long-term residential care lasts 6 to 12 months in a drug-free environment. Treatment should focus on changing the lifestyle as many times he or she wants the drug long after detoxification to relieve the anxiety or frustrations you or I could normally cope with. The drinking behavior should also be closely observed if the individual chooses to drink, as in many instances the addict switches to alcohol for self-medication.[27]

Narcotics

Narcotic drugs are some of the most valuable medicines known. However, they are also widely abused. Narcotics are synonymous with opium, morphine, heroin, and codeine. Morphine is probably the most effective pain reliever. Morphinelike drugs depress the central nervous system to produce a marked reduction in the feelings associated with pain. Morphine also produces a sense of euphoria, and the addict or abuser is usually lethargic and indifferent to the environment. Chronic use leads to physical and psychological dependence. As the need increases the addict usually becomes more involved in criminal activity to support the habit.

Withdrawal includes nervousness, anxiety, running eyes and nose, sweating, dilated pupils, gooseflesh, muscle aches, high blood pressure and a fever. Most addicts are obsessed with securing a fix. The severity of withdrawal depends on the physical dependence and the amount of the drug used. Usually 8 to 12 hours after the last fix, withdrawal symptoms appear. Detoxification usually lasts from 3 to 21 days.

Most addicts neglect themselves and are highly susceptible to infection and malnutrition. Because most morphinelike drugs are usually injected, unsterile injections occur frequently. This may result in serious or fatal septicemia, hepatitis, and abscesses at the point of injection as well as in internal organs.

Heroin tolerance also develops rapidly and increasing doses are needed to produce the desired effect. It is administered under the skin (skin popping), sniffing (snorting), or directly into the vein (mainlining). Heroin is a white or brown powder and is liquefied when skin popping or mainlining.

Heroin is synthesized from morphine and is roughly 10 times as potent in pure form. Heroin in pure form on the street is rare. Most heroin is cut or diluted by the distributor. It usually contains one part heroin and nine or more parts of other substances including quinine or powdered milk.[28]

Codeine is most commonly abused in the form of cough medicine and is less addictive than morphine and heroin, and withdrawal symptoms are less severe.

Heroin was originally invented to treat morphine withdrawal. When this was found to be ineffective, methadone was used to treat heroin addiction. Methadone is highly controversial today as opinions vary considerably. It seems methadone detoxification has been fairly successful, while methadone maintenance continues to be highly questionable.

Federal law classifies cocaine as a narcotic although its effects resemble a stimulant. Cocaine will be discussed later in this chapter.

Hallucinogens

Hallucinogenic drugs distort objective reality. Various senses are involved and in large doses these drugs produce auditory and visual hallucinations. Hallucinogenic drugs are either produced from plants or synthetically. Effects consist of restlessness, distortion of reality, possible psychosis, and possible psychological dependence. Physical dependence does not develop.

LSD-25, lysergic acid diethylamide, or "acid," as it is known in the drug subculture, is derived from the ergot fungus. The ergot fungus is a disease that develops on rye and wheat grain. Usually a "trip" will last 8 to 16 hours. Physical reactions include increased heartbeat, dilated pupils, goose bumps, profuse perspiration, and nausea. While tripping, reality is considerably distorted. The aftereffects are acute anxiety or depression. Flashbacks can occur months after the actual drug experience.

Another hallucinogenic drug is mescaline (peyote) derived from the buttons of the mescal cactus plant. It usually is ground into a powder and taken orally, with the effects lasting 6 to 12 hours. Psilocybin and psilocyn are obtained from certain mushrooms grown in Mexico; these drugs basically create the same effects as mescaline except the experience lasts around six hours. DMT (dimethyltryptamine) is a short-acting drug found in

seeds of certain plants in the West Indies and South America. It is produced synthetically and its vapor is inhaled by mixing it with marijuana or tobacco. The "high" lasts from 45 minutes to an hour. DET (diethyltryptamine) is similar to DMT; however, it has not been found in plants. DET is produced synthetically, and the effects last up to three hours. DET is usually smoked with marijuana or tobacco. DOM (dimethoxyamphetamine), popularly known in the drug subculture as STP (serenity, tranquility, and peace), lasts six to eight hours. The high is similar to amphetamines in small doses; in greater doses, the effects are similar to mescaline, and it potentially can produce convulsions. Little is actually known about the pharmacological, psychological or therapeutic effects.

PCP (phencyclidine) is produced as an exotic veterinary anesthetic for large animals such as bears and big cats. Commonly known as "Angel Dust" or "Wack" in street language, the high includes feelings of weightlessness and being out of touch with the immediate environment. It will intensify overt or latent psychotic tendencies, as will most other hallucinogenic drugs. This drug has many serious consequences, with flashbacks being a common side effect. Because of its strong anesthetic effect, an undetermined amount can cause death. Visual effects are very similar to LSD.

Volatile chemicals

Volatile chemicals come in several forms: glue, gasoline, lighter fluid, paint thinner, and aerosol propellants. Usually the drug effects last up to two hours and can cause severe brain, liver, lung, and heart damage. These drugs distort perception and create dreamlike images and hallucinations. They can create a psychological dependence but not a physical addiction. A shocking example of this type of abuse was related by an applicant for a position at our agency. In a small town in Arizona children were coming to school high, and the incidence of brain damage among youth was soaring at the local hospital. The problem was identified as being due to children sniffing gasoline from auto tanks. The townspeople had to lock their gas caps as the problem became so widespread.

Cocaine

Cocaine, commonly known as "coke" or "snow," is listed as a narcotic, but its effects are similar to a stimulant. This drug is known as the "rich man's high" as it street price is quite costly. The effects sought by most users (unlike LSD or heroin which increases orientation toward self and one's internal processes) is that cocaine can facilitate social interaction.

Cocaine originates from the coca leaf which grows mainly on the western side of South America. Cocaine can be snorted or injected at a cost of around $50 a gram or $500 to $1,200 an ounce.[29] The high consists of one to two hours of pleasurable exhilaration and euphoria. Its reaction is similar to amphetamines; however it is not as damaging as amphetamines. A frequent side effect caused by snorting is damage to the nasal membrane.[30] Chronic use increases the severity of cocaine's stimulating effects. After a few days the pleasurable effect gives way to an intense feeling of anxiety, with possibly a gross paranoid feature. Usually after coming down, severe depression occurs. Although physical addiction isn't present, the psychological dependence often leads the chronic abuser to believe that more cocaine will remedy the depression.

Marijuana

Marijuana, "pot," or "grass," comes from the plant *Cannabis sativa L.* It grows through-

out the world and its fibers are legitimately used to produce twine, rope, and paper. The seeds are used in various feed mixtures, such as in birdseed.

Marijuana is the most controversial drug today. It is also the most profitable import that is smuggled into this country. A five-ton load of marijuana purchased in Colombia for $500,000 can be resold in a day or so to drug wholesalers for $2.5 million in cash. After the load has passed from the wholesaler to many middle distributors, its eventual street value will be some $10 million to $11 million. With tax free profits like this the type of people participating in the take include lawyers, law enforcement officers, as well as many other "professionals."

One gang was organized by two boyhood friends, and at its peak was bringing into this country more than a million pounds of marijuana. The gross take in a three-year period was over $250 million! The gang was eventually put out of commission falling to charges of racketeering and a variety of miscellaneous charges. It is estimated, however, by federal enforcement agents that 20 other big smuggling gangs exist, operating out of isolated airstrips in southern Florida.

Marijuana is smuggled into this country using a fleet of planes and luxury yachts, converted into minifreighters. Gang-owned mansions on Miami's Intra Coastal Waterway serve as "stash houses." The marijuana is then picked up by wholesalers in armed vans. Hijacking is rare as these gangs have reputations for being extremely tough and reckless. Recruitment for technicians who are needed for various job functions is an easy task, as affluence becomes an overpowering lure. One former gang member revealed that in one $300-a-day duplex, an eight-foot-long table was completely covered with money, in denominations of up to $50 stacked eight inches high. They told this member there was $8 million on the table.[31]

While marijuana smuggling looks

"Taking a hit"

profitable, some of these gangs disband due to police arrests and convictions. The problem seems to be that many gangs can evade government detection through sophisticated tactics and electronic equipment, oftentimes more sophisticated than what the government is using.

The effects of marijuana and hashish (a concentrated resin from the plant) varies as does any other drug according to mood, circumstances, and the quality of the drug. The effects commence in about 15 minutes after inhaling the smoke from a joint (cigarette) or a pipe. It produces intoxication accompanied by a feeling of well-being, relaxation, sociability, talkativeness, laughing, and in a sizable majority of users, a feeling of floating.[32] There isn't any evidence of physical addiction, and psychological dependence is minimal as indicated by Goode.[33]

Within the last 15 years there has been a marked increase in the use of marijuana in the United States. Reasons for this are many, but probably the most significant cause was the social upheaval caused by the war in Vietnam. There was a rejection of established values, and most young people were symbolizing marijuana as their freedom from the traditional values. To the establishment it meant radicalism and wasn't viewed as a mild intoxicant.

In 1971 an organization named NORML (National Organization for the Reform of Marijuana Laws) was established with the support of the Playboy Foundation. NORML started as a slipshod organization but in recent years has had a significant impact on marijuana legislation throughout the United States. Currently, NORML supports decriminalization, which advocates that laws should be changed so that a smoker would not be arrested or jailed, and that smoking marijuana would not be a misdemeanor or a felony (a fine for possession would be enforced rather than arrest).

NORML has aided in the decriminalization of marijuana legislation in several states including: Oregon, Alaska, Maine, Colorado, California, and Ohio. Several other states have bills pending dealing with decriminalization.

Is marijuana harmful? In March 1972, the National Commission of Marijuana and Drug Abuse conducted one of the most extensive studies on marijuana use, spending two years and $4 million, and concluded that it was relatively harmless when smoked in moderation. The commission recommended decriminalization.[34]

One should remember that (as with any other drug) whenever it is used to cover emotions or to cope with life, it becomes harmful and warrants treatment.

What's the thrust for solving America's drug problem? It lies in education, prevention, and early intervention. Professionals in the field today have learned a great deal about education, and they know that scare tactics, war stories, and information in general aren't the answers. Education of alcohol and drug abuse should present current information, involve discussions of attitudes and values about using drugs, and offer alternatives other than drugs, to learn and experience from. It is extremely important that educators don't give the idea it's "OK" to do certain types of drugs, especially when working with youth. Young people today are developing coping devices to survive in a world of tremendous pressure; a drug will only complicate their lives if they use it to gain temporary relief from unwanted emotions.

SUMMARY OF TREATMENT PROGRAMS

1. Public or private alcohol and/or drug abuse services usually consist of detoxification facilities and inpatient and/or outpatient services. Detoxification lasts from 24 hours to 21 days depending on the severity of withdrawal. Inpatient care lasts two to three weeks in a chemically free environment. This structure is designed for those chemically dependent individuals who are unable to function in the community. Outpatient care lasts three to six months. Outpatient care usually is not as intense as inpatient, as the chemically dependent person has already been detoxified or is able to stop using drugs on his/her own. Outpatient consists of counseling, medical services, and vocational services. Many hospitals and a number of mental health centers provide this type of treatment program. Usually clients and their families are referred to AA, Al-Anon, and Alateen, respectively, in conjunction with counseling appointments.

2. Alcoholics Anonymous (AA) is a fellowship of men and women who meet to find and maintain sobriety. The only requirement for membership is the sincere desire to stop drinking.

There are no formal rules or dues. Members are encouraged to avoid all controversy and affiliation with causes; AA's only concern is to help people who have a drinking problem.

Generally groups meet once a week for a closed meeting for members only; some hold open meetings that the public and especially

Drug abuse counseling

the spouses may attend. In addition, many open meetings are periodic social gatherings which include the members' families. At many open meetings speakers tell their own stories and the way that AA has helped them. Each new member of AA receives a copy of the program's 12 steps for arresting alcoholism, and quite often a sponsor will help him/her adjust to the group.

3. Al-Anon is an organization formed to help the families of alcoholics. Al-Anon family groups are fellowships of men and women who are husbands, wives, relatives, or close friends of alcoholics. Al-Anon offers a new way of life to families in understanding their own problems. Oftentimes one or more members will give short talks on one of the 12 steps as applied to themselves. Sometimes there are question and answer meetings with general discussion afterward.

CASE HISTORY OF A HEROIN ADDICT

Many times the drug counselor feels he/she isn't making any progress in the recovery process of the heroin addict. Counseling the heroin addict takes a special type of counselor—one who can walk the walk and talk the talk, so to speak. To counsel, first off, it takes an extreme amount of dedication, concentration, and effort.

The client I worked with was a 30-year-old black, married male with three children. The history was as follows. The client will be referred to as Bob. Bob was raised in an urban area; he was the middle child and seemingly led a normal childhood. As he reached his early teens he got more and more involved with drinking and drugs. He graduated from high school and went into the army soon after graduation. This is where many problems arose. Bob had several bouts with the army ranging from insubordination to disorderly conduct. He started chipping heroin and became quite involved in the drug culture overseas in Germany. He then married a white German girl and brought her back to the United States where they have lived for the past ten years. Bob then became involved in an armed robbery and claimed he was innocent; yet he spent three years in prison. After his prison time ended, Bob secured a job at a local factory; this lasted approximately one and one half years at which time he was fired for excessive absenteeism. The excessive absenteeism was a result of episodic drinking and drug abuse.

Prior to Bob's going to prison he was involved in the Black Panthers. What was interesting was that he was married to a white, which had to be a conflict with Bob.

In general Bob seemingly had quite a conflict being black. He wanted at times to be white, and yet at other times wanted to be married to a black instead of a white.

Bob became increasingly involved with drugs, and in time developed a habit with heroin. This led to his involvement in both the criminal justice system and treatment.

Fortunately, there was a federal grant at this time that could divert criminal justice clients to alcohol or drug treatment centers. Bob became involved in a local alcohol treatment center while on probation. However, due to the fact he was a heroin addict, treatment was ineffective. Within a very short period of time after discharge, Bob was back to "junk." He was then involved in another armed robbery and this time was facing 7 to 10 years for several counts of armed robbery and burglary. At this point I became involved with the client. Bob was out on bond and was awaiting his court date. Throughout this time period Bob was seen on an outpatient treatment basis. Urine drug screens were taken and all turned up negative for opiates for about four weeks. Then Bob started chipping (using heroin on occasion). A therapeutic community which treated heroin addicts had been contacted to arrange an intake interview with Bob. The therapeutic community was a six- to nine-month intensive inpatient treatment program. Their philosophy was that the drug of choice was only a symptom and what needed to be changed was the lifestyle.

The court date was finally reached and it was time for Bob to "face the music." The therapeutic community had interviewed Bob and he was accepted into their program. I had arranged for a psychologist to run a series of tests on Bob to determine statistically his chances of succeeding in treatment. The results of this testing were that Bob would have one third of a chance of succeeding in treatment, one third not succeeding, and one third of no change at all. Obviously statistics were against Bob, but in outpatient treatment he had demonstrated that he was sincere and did want to change. So with that, this author and Bob's probation officer felt treatment was the best alternative rather than incarceration. The presiding judge was approached with this alternative and he accepted it. However, Bob was found guilty so the judge imposed a stayed sentence of seven years to be served if Bob did not successfully complete treatment.

The following week Bob was transferred to the therapeutic community. He stayed there approximately six months at which time the community voted that he be terminated, unsuccessfully completing treatment. Bob was voted out for a number of reasons: (a) he wasn't following instructions when reprimanded by staff, (b) overall he was an extremely bad influence on the rest of the community as he was always gaming people, not being able to be honest with himself or others, (c) he was breaking cardinal rules which meant that when he would get angry other members of the community were actually afraid to be around him as they were afraid he might get physically violent. The incident that resulted in Bob's termination was that he was reprimanded for an incident that involved a female client. Supposedly Bob had intercourse with the female and the female admitted this to staff in one of the community's "cop to" groups. (A "cop to" simply means people in the community that have done something wrong, or are feeling guilty, talk about it in one of these groups.)

The staff told Bob he was on a communication ban (no talking) the following day; they also requested he wear a five-foot sign with some writing on it. This kind of reprimand might seem ineffective or silly to some of us; however, it is quite effective in an atmosphere like a therapeutic community, especially on a long-term basis. Bob didn't follow through the next day and a vote was taken and he was transferred to the county jail where he would await a decision by the probation officer, the judge, and the original referring agent.

We had decided Bob was still amenable to treatment. However, this would entail a more highly structured treatment environment, a facility that dealt more with the hard-core heroin addict.

Meanwhile Bob was becoming increasingly bitter sitting in jail thinking about what had occurred, and also becoming anxious due to the fact he was facing seven years in prison.

The probation officer and original treatment staff involved with Bob found a treatment facility that would be most favorable to any kind of successful treatment for Bob. The judge also went along with this.

Bob, after about two weeks of sitting in jail was transferred on a Friday afternoon to this treatment facility. Friday evening he called his wife and absconded from treatment. He has not been heard of since, and consequently his probation has been revoked and when caught, he will be sent to prison.

I have heard unofficial reports he is still around, back to heroin in his old way of life.

This is not a success story, obviously, but all too often that's all we ever hear. The field is challenging; however, this case history is also a real part of treatment that oftentimes a therapist has to realize his/her own limitations and accept reality as it is. Not everyone is a success and no matter what you do, *you* can't change that. All we can do is seek as much knowledge about the field as possible and utilize every tool available to motivate clients in changing their behavior. Only after this can we say, "I gave it my best shot, and that's all there is."

4. Alateen groups are established for adolescent children of alcoholics. The groups attempt to help adolescent members accept the parents' alcoholism as an illness. Special attention is devoted to problems of bringing friends or dates into the home, and learning how to cope with an alcoholic parent and with the reactions of the neighborhood and community.

5. Adolescent therapeutic community group homes are long-term (around three months) treatment programs. A variety of activities are offered (physical, social, personal) to help the chemically dependent adolescent adjust to a chemically free lifestyle. Camping, exercise, meditation are a few examples of activities teenagers participate in. Staff usually try to build the adolescents' self-concept as usually most of the teen-

agers have poor self-concepts upon admission. Signs are sometimes worn stating for example, "Don't be misled, I like people" to emphasize certain character defects that need to be removed. Seemingly these programs are successful as they teach adolescents independence, creativity, and caring about themselves and others.

6. Therapeutic communities are long-term residential treatment programs, usually 12 to 18 months in length. The age range of program participants ranges from 18 to 65. Therapeutic communities attempt to focus on lifestyle changes, molding a person so that he or she can function appropriately in society. The environment is one of constant confrontation that aims at breaking down walls that cover up the real person. An individual might, for example, come on as a

Occupational therapy at a drug treatment center

"tough guy" as a result of leading the street life. Actually, this image needs to be broken down. Feelings that are painful (for example, loneliness, fear, depression) are allowed to be expressed, eventually allowing the individual to be honest with him/herself, and thus not needing to wear a mask. Many graduates of therapeutic communities remain in close contact for support purposes. It is difficult to measure the success of these programs because there is a high rate of dropouts. However, for those that graduate there is evidence they are successful in obtaining employment and remaining chemically free.

SUMMARY

This chapter has focused on alcohol and other drugs. A wide range of drugs have been described—including their medical uses, their psychological and physiological effects, the extent to which they are abused, and the costs of their use and abuse to individuals and to society. Current treatment programs for alcohol and drug abusers were also described.

As professionals going into the field of alcoholism and drug abuse, it is important to keep an open mind toward available therapies and to constantly search to learn more about the field. In keeping an open mind we will be able to educate our community, as this is where we will begin to solve the problems associated with use, abuse, and dependency.

NOTES

1. American Psychiatric Association, *Diagnostic and Statistical Manual of Mental Disorders,* 2d ed. (Washington, D.C.: The Association, 1968), p. 43.
2. Ibid., p. 43.
3. Richard F. Buckley, *Alcoholism and the Helping Professions* (Madison, Wis.: University of Wisconsin, Extension Division, Department of Social Work, 1967), p. 14.
4. Thomas Sullivan et al., *Social Problems: Divergent Perspectives* (New York: Wiley, 1980), p. 616.
5. Harrison M. Torice and Paul M. Roman, *Spirits and Demons at Work* (Ithaca, N.Y.: Cornell University Press, 1972), p. 38.
6. *The Alcoholic within Us* (Santa Monica, Calif.: Pyramid Films, 1973).
7. Buckley, *Alcoholism,* p. 2.
8. Ogden Tanner, *Stress* (New York: Time/Life, 1976), p. 142.
9. Donald Light, *Society Magazine,* September 1975, p. 13.
10. Torice and Roman, *Spirits and Demons,* p. 105.
11. Eva Maria Blum and Richard H. Blum, *Alcoholism—Modern Psychological Approaches to Treatment* (San Francisco: Jossey Bass, 1974), p. 42.
12. Robert Campbell, *The Enigma of the Mind* (New York: Time/Life Books, 1976), p. 20.
13. Torice and Roman, *Spirits and Demons,* p. 42.
14. The City of Milwaukee Health Department, drug information wall poster.
15. Ibid.
16. Sullivan, et al., *Social Problems,* p. 624.

17. David E. Smith and Donald R. Wesson, *Uppers and Downers* (Englewood Cliffs, N.J.: Prentice-Hall, 1973), p. 41.

18. Drug Enforcement Administration, U.S. Department of Justice *Fact Sheets* (Washington, D.C.: U.S. Government Printing Office, 1975), p. 40.

19. Torice and Roman, *Spirits and Demons*, p. 72.

20. Ibid., p. 72.

21. Ibid.

22. Ibid.

23. Ibid., p. 72.

24. Smith and Wesson, *Uppers and Downers*, pp. 87, 89.

25. Ibid., p. 80.

26. Ibid., p. 92.

27. Ibid., p. 96.

28. Drug Enforcement Administration, *Fact Sheets*, p. 33.

29. Smith and Wesson, *Uppers and Downers*, p. 80.

30. Ibid., p. 81.

31. Stanley Penn, "The Pot Trade: How a Ring Turns Smuggling into Riches: For a While," *The Wall Street Journal*, July 22, 1980.

32. Torice and Roman, *Spirits and Demons*, p. 61.

33. Ibid., p. 66.

34. "Playboy Interview: Keith Stroup," *Playboy*, February 1977, p. 64.

chapter 17

It has been suggested that most people spend more time thinking about sex than anything else. While that would be difficult to prove, it seems clear that sexuality, and all that it implies, is a significant area in the lives of almost all people. This chapter will discuss the social worker's role in helping persons alleviate their problems and maximize their potential as sexual human beings. The first part will examine sexual counseling; sex therapy will be discussed in the second part.

What is the difference between sexual counseling and sex therapy? Sexual counseling is defined as short-term, often crisis-oriented counseling directed toward the alleviation of some immediate difficulty related to sex, such as problem pregnancy, rape, surgery which affects sexual response, or sexual behavior which society deems inap-

---

* This chapter was specially written for this text by Lloyd G. Sinclair, M.S.S.W., A.C.S.W. Mr. Sinclair is a sex therapist at Midwest Center for Sex Therapy, Madison, Wisconsin, and an instructor at the University of Wisconsin—Whitewater, Department of Social Welfare, Whitewater, Wisconsin. He is certified as a sex educator and a sex therapist by the American Association of Sex Educators, Counselors, and Therapists (AASECT).

propriate. Sex therapy, on the other hand, deals with the alleviation of sexual dysfunction, such as erectile difficulty or failure to achieve orgasm, and implies a planned change sequence involving several contacts between the client(s) and the therapist(s). This sequence generally consists of several stages, including problem definition, history gathering, physical examination, information dissemination, prescribed sexual experiences, and ongoing evaluation.

SEXUAL COUNSELING

Social workers have long been recognized as resources for persons suffering from problems related to sex. Alfred Kinsey, author of the classic Kinsey reports: *Sexual Behavior in the Human Male*[1] and *Sexual Behavior in the Human Female*,[2] observed that social workers were sought out by persons with sexual concerns more than any other professional group. Further, most sexual counseling done by social workers is performed by persons whose primary professional role is not that of sexual counselor. Probation and parole

Sexual counseling and sex therapy*

officers, group home supervisors, school, medical, and psychiatric social workers are frequently confronted by persons with problems related to sex, demanding their skills as sexual counselors.

Prerequisites to effective counseling

In addition to the requirements of the specific professional position, there are two basic prerequisites to becoming an effective sexual counselor: comfort and knowledge.

In order to be effective as a social worker, one must be professionally comfortable with the subject matter. This is absolutely essential in the area of sex, where most people tend to be anxious and embarrassed. This certainly doesn't mean the counselor would feel comfortable *experiencing* all the various sexual behaviors her/his clients might report. Rather, it means the counselor should be comfortable enough with her/his own sexuality that the behaviors reported by clients, however aberrant, don't threaten the worker's personal sexuality. Further, as in all helping relationships, when the counselor is confronted with a situation which demands additional expertise or comfort, ethics dictate that the worker identify the situation honestly and make an appropriate referral. Social workers can be effective as role models to their clients, demonstrating that sex can be addressed directly, clearly, and without embarrassment.

Since social workers aren't inherently more comfortable in the area of sex than anybody else, comfort needs to be developed. While there are many ways to do this, some of the most effective include examination of one's own sexual history and values, talking frankly with others about sex, exposing oneself to sexually explicit material, and gaining as much knowledge—the second prerequisite—as possible.

It is generally assumed that knowledge and training about a subject is a requirement to be helpful to others in that area. Surprisingly, many people seem not to apply this premise to sex. They consider themselves to be self-taught *sexperts*, believing that their own personal experience provides them with as much knowledge as they need. This assumption not only is incorrect but is downright dangerous and unethical. Particularly in the past two decades, we have learned a great deal about sex; the responsible, competent sexual counselor will take it upon her/himself to gain as much of this knowledge as possible.

We will now examine, in some depth, four specific examples of professional sexual counseling. As you read them, think about the comfort and knowledge that would be required to most effectively resolve the problems presented.

The nursing home

Fran was a social worker in a nursing home. A nurse who worked nights had become very upset the previous evening because she had walked into the room of an elderly resident and found him masturbating. She had scolded him for his behavior and had made the incident known to several other people.

Fran decided that this was something that shouldn't be ignored. She spoke first to the nurse to learn more about the incident. The nurse thought the behavior was abhorrent, using words like "perverted," "juvenile," and "animalistic" in her description.

Fran then spoke to the resident. He expressed regret and embarrassment about the incident, felt his privacy had been severely violated, but conceded that "he really should act his age."

Fran knew that masturbation was a healthy, normal sexual outlet for all people, regardless of age. Indeed, for this man, masturbation was perhaps the only reasonable means presently available to express his sexuality; his wife of 45 years had died a few years before. Fran was also aware that many people, including older persons themselves, believe that sex is for the young, and that the only legitimate sexual expression is that which is shared by a heterosexual couple.

Fran offered the resident information about the normalcy of self-stimulation, and reassurance that it was not his behavior, but the nurse's, that was the problem. They discussed ways that he could enjoy more privacy, in order to honor his right to personal, solitary space. The resident appeared grateful for the recognition of his personhood. Fran spoke again to the nurse. She obviously had strong ideas about masturbation, and Fran knew she wasn't going to change them. She knew that people who have fixed, powerful emotions in response to behavior which is enjoyable *to others*, and doesn't affect them, are often responding to something in themselves that is threatening.

Fran's goal, instead, was to encourage the nurse to recognize the resident's need for privacy to maintain self-esteem. The nurse agreed that living in a nursing home stripped residents of most of what they had enjoyed throughout their adult lives—self-determination, property, privacy. Because the nursing home was, in part, a medical care facility, there were good reasons why many of the residents' personal needs had to be compromised—but there were also simple ways to respect their rights. Fran and the nurse agreed that residents should not lock themselves into their rooms, but a closed door could be respected by a knock and an invitation to enter, rather than the staff's current habit of merely barging in. They took this idea to the nursing home director who agreed to have the staff implement the policy for a trial period.[3]

The adolescent group home

Pat, a social worker in a group home for adolescent women, became concerned about Tina, a 16-year-old resident. Tina had confided to some of the other women in the house that she and her friend, Dennis, were having intercourse regularly. Pat was faced with several dilemmas: (a) in wanting to respect their privacy, was it appropriate to confront her on the subject? (b) if she did confront her, should Pat try to change her behavior by attempting to stop Tina from having intercourse? or (c) should she respect Tina's right to make her own decisions and suggest that they use birth control?

Pat decided that while ignoring the entire issue would certainly be easiest for *her*, it probably would not be in Tina's best interests. Pat was most concerned that Tina might become pregnant, causing negative consequences for herself, Dennis, the potential child, and others.

Pat examined her values and her knowledge about teenage sexuality. She was aware that Tina might be, among her immediate peer group, in the majority in that she was having intercourse. A recent study indicated that 31 percent of 16-year-old women in the United States have had intercourse, and the sexually active group is growing in number.[4] While a 16-year-old might be viewed by Pat as inappropriately young to be sexually active, she realized that Tina's values were different from hers and that, practically speaking, there was little that Pat could do to force Tina to stop even if she wanted to do so.

But birth control seemed like another matter. Pat believed that the aspects of Tina's behavior that affected her alone were largely her business. But the prospect of a child being born to a 16-year-old was another concern. Pat knew that 1 million teenagers in the United States became pregnant each year and that one fifth of all births in this country are to teenage mothers.[5] She didn't want Tina to be among those statistics. She decided it was appropriate to encourage Tina to protect herself from an unwanted pregnancy.

Pat approached Tina to discuss the issue. While Tina was initially reluctant to talk about it, Pat was able to draw her out with some perseverence. Tina confided that she was, indeed, engaging in regular sexual activity with Dennis, that they were not using a contraceptive, and that she certainly did not want to get pregnant. She felt they were very much in love with each other, and considered their sexual activity to be a testimony of their love.

Tina's statements seemed reasonable to Pat—most people believe that sex *is* a statement of love. But Tina was only 16. Could her love be as real as someone's who was older? Pat reflected on her own history, remembering when she was 16, feeling very much in love. She had waited to have intercourse until later—she hadn't even considered it at age 16—but Tina was living in a different environment.

Pat encouraged Tina to talk more about love and sex. Was the sexual aspect of their relationship enhancing other aspects? Did she feel it was good for each of them as individuals?

After considerable discussion, Tina observed that sex really wasn't that important to her, and that while it was somewhat pleasurable from an emotional standpoint, it wasn't as physically exciting as it had been early in the relationship. Lately she had felt trapped by the expectation of intercourse whenever she and Dennis were alone together. Sex had, in her mind, taken on entirely too much importance. She feared that their sexual life was the major reason for Dennis's interest in her.

The more she talked, the clearer it became that Tina wanted permission *not* to have intercourse. Both she and Dennis had been under tremendous peer pressure to "grow up," and she thought they had become involved in intercourse because it was expected behavior. She wondered if Dennis was really that interested in sex, or if perhaps he just had to act out a role. This uncertainty had allowed her to put off decision making about birth control—she might stop having intercourse, so she wouldn't need it—and confronting Dennis directly—if sex *was* that important to him, maybe he would break up with her if he knew her true feelings.

Pat suggested that Tina discuss her feelings with Dennis, to stop assuming sex was something too volatile to talk about. She encouraged Tina to be assertive about what was good for her, that no one should engage in sexual activity primarily for *someone else*. Pat further encouraged Tina to think about possible alternatives to intercourse—sexual and nonsexual—which Tina might feel more comfortable with and Dennis would enjoy. She agreed to bring it up with Dennis the next weekend, and she and Pat would talk further after that. In the meantime, Tina agreed that if intercourse occurred, she would insist they use a condom.

Counselors should be aware that often a sexual problem is really another kind of problem. This is particularly common with children, adolescents, or persons who live in institutions who may be deprived of adequate attention.

Children learn quite early in life that perhaps the most effective way to generate attention is to do something which is sexual and inappropriate. Since many adults are anxious about sexual matters, the tendency is to overreact when forced to confront them. When one adds the fact that most persons, particularly, the young, have very limited access to good information about appropriate sexual behavior, the result is often sexual experimentation which is seen by society as inappropriate.

Couple in moonlight

The foster home

Jim was a 14-year-old boy who lived in a foster home. His history included many short-term living situations with relatives, and foster and group homes. Jim's foster parents became aware, through the parents of 10-year-old Steve, that Jim had repeatedly pressured Steve into exploring and touching each other's genital areas, and Jim had suggested that they experiment with oral sex. Steve was frightened, but couldn't seem to say "no" to Jim.

Jim's social worker intervened in this situation by talking first with Steve's parents to determine what their reaction had been when Steve first reported the incidents to them. They had not, fortunately, overreacted with alarm (a not uncommon reaction which is usually more damaging to the child than the behavior itself). They commended Steve for telling them about it, assured him that he was not at fault, answered his questions, and told him that while it wasn't that serious, he shouldn't do anything that was being forced on him or otherwise did not seem right. The social worker chose not to meet directly with Steve and encouraged his parents to continue to be *askable* with Steve. They could, further, suggest ways for Steve to avoid a compromising situation with Jim, should the incident recur.

The social worker then met with Jim's foster parents. When informed of Jim's behavior, they had reacted with alarm, reprimanded him and confined him to the house afternoons and evenings for several days. The parents remained confused, upset, and angry about Jim's behavior. The social worker acknowledged that forced sexual behavior is clearly inappropriate, but encouraged the parents to view same-sex behavior as relatively normal for an inquisitive, maturing adolescent. In fact, in boys under the age of 15, homosexual contact is more common than heterosexual contact.[6] They seemed relieved when the social worker offered to meet with Jim.

When talking to Jim, the social worker informed him of his awareness of the situation and asked him about it. Jim told the worker that he had explored genitals with Steve but initially denied having been the aggressor. When Jim realized that he would not be punished by the social worker for being honest, he conceded that the behavior had been at his initiation.

The social worker pondered the most appropriate method of approaching the problem. What was Jim's behavior indicating? Was he merely curious? Was he a homosexual? Was he exercising power and dominance over his young friend? Did he not know the behavior was inappropriate?

After a lengthy, frank discussion, the social worker concluded that Jim did, indeed, know that forcing sexual behavior on someone else was wrong. The social worker stressed the importance of consent in sexuality. There did seem to be elements of curiosity operating, but they didn't seem to account entirely for the behavior.

Jim stated that he was as interested sexually in girls as he was in boys; the choice of Steve seemed to be more due to accessibility than anything. The social worker was aware that a majority of adolescents engage in sex play with members of their own gender, and that the label *homosexual* can safely be applied only to adults who have and prefer sexual relationships with members of their own sex.[7]

Jim seemed to have chosen Steve partly because, being older, he had more likelihood of pressuring him to get what he (Jim) wanted. But the most important element seemed to be the attention he was likely to generate in adults—foster parents, social workers, and others—when the behavior was reported.

Had the social worker seen these incidents solely as a sexual problem, or indeed primarily as a sexual problem, he would likely experience little success in dealing with Jim. If attention is the reward, Jim is likely to act out more and more to continue the shower of concern and attention from significant adults. The more therapy the social worker would do, the more Jim is likely to continue, even if punishment was involved.

The social worker was aware that human beings' need for attention and recognition is one of the strongest of emotional needs. When people are feeling unnoticed, rejected, or discounted, they have been known to experience huge amounts of pain, to the point of threatening their lives, to gain attention.[8] This is a process the person is usually not consciously aware of. Punishment is not necessarily a negative consequence—at least when one is being punished, he/she is being recognized by the punisher.

The treatment plan developed by the social worker was designed to encourage Jim's foster parents to give him attention for appropriate, positive behavior. If inappropriate sexual incidents were to occur, the par-ents agreed to reprimand Jim briefly and drop further discussion or punishment. The social worker further encouraged the foster parents to talk with Jim about sex, independent of the incidents, to give him information and help him make healthy decisions.

The social worker informed the parents of the possibility of increased attention-getting sexual acts, particularly once the activity following the most recent one died down. A well-known pattern for behavior which gains a reward (in this case, attention) is to undergo a radical increase once the reward is removed.[9] Sometimes persons, in desperation for attention, escalate their behavior in a vain attempt to force the response they are seeking when they are deprived of it. Usually the behavior will disappear quickly once the previously expected reward is consistently withheld.

In fact, this escalation did not occur. The social worker continued to be in contact with Jim and his foster family, and no further inappropriate sexual acts were reported.

Words

When talking with clients about sex, careful consideration should be given to the use of words. Sex words can be categorized roughly into three groups: slang, colloquial, and scientific. Slang words and expressions, like "tits" and "getting laid," are used to describe things vigorously and often demeaningly. Colloquial language, such as "making love" or "coming," define things clearly, relatively uneuphemistically, and usually with a pleasant tone. Scientific language, like "coitus" and "testicles," connotes precision and a certain value-free detachment.

It is important to realize that most people use slang terms when talking about sex. Warren R. Johnson captured this when he wrote, "Fuck, screw, jack-off, cock, pussy, wet dream, and the like are, perhaps, regrettably vulgar, but they are the dominant linguistic sex vehicles of American English."[10]

This is not to suggest that helping professionals should necessarily use slang terms when talking with clients. Sex counselors must, however, *understand* the meaning of slang terms and be *comfortable* when hearing them. This is particularly critical when working with certain groups of people, such as mentally retarded persons, where the language barrier may be severe. The vocabulary which is most comfortable to the counselor may be completely misunderstood by the client. In these cases, the use of slang terms may be essential to communicate effectively.

Most counselors develop a vocabulary which is comfortable for them, somewhere between slang and scientific. When the words used are overly technical, they tend to be misunderstood or the language may be a mask for the counselor's discomfort. The major problem with slang words is that they may be interpreted as vulgar by many clients.

Emma Lee Doyle, a sex therapist from Dallas, Texas, illustrates the problem of sex words in a colorful case example. When interviewing a woman client, Doyle asked her what her husband did sexually which she really disliked. The woman replied. "He insists on referring to my genital area as my 'pussy.' I hate the word 'pussy,' it's so demeaning and vulgar." When Doyle asked what words she preferred for him to use, she said, "I wish he'd call it my 'cunt,' it's so much more refined." The sensitive therapist is cautious in her/his use of words, taking care to listen to clients for the connotations they place on the words they use.

Abortion counseling

Reputable medical clinics providing abortion services offer patients the option of counseling, either individually or in groups. Prior to the early 1970s, abortions were illegal in the United States, and it was not until 1973 that the Supreme Court struck down state laws prohibiting abortions. Therefore, abortion counseling is relatively new as a specialization. While the question of whether abortion should be available to persons remains a hotly contested issue due to peoples' deep moral and religious feelings, abortion remains available to those who are able to pay for the procedure.

Most abortion counseling is done immediately prior to the medical procedure. Counseling should involve the discussion of at least three areas: the decision to terminate the pregnancy, the medical procedure, and birth control.

Since abortions have, until recently, often been performed by unqualified persons in unsafe surroundings, many people have

Single and pregnant: What to do?

fears and misinformation about the safety of the medical procedure. The abortion counselor can point out that abortion, when performed early in pregnancy by a physician, is considerably safer than carrying the pregnancy to term.[11] She/he should answer whatever questions the patient has about the medical procedure—how she is likely to feel, for what amount of time, what her recovery will involve, aftercare, and so forth.

The decision to terminate a pregnancy is a difficult one for most persons, although not for everyone. A sensitive counselor will probe the patient's feelings and thoughts regarding her options. Particularly for the woman who is undecided, it is critical to provide a calm and supportive atmosphere to promote her making the best decision.

The abortion clinic

Carri came to the abortion clinic requesting to speak to someone regarding her pregnancy. She had missed her period and received a positive pregnancy test.

Carri told the counselor she had been in a relationship with Bruce for two years, and lately they had been distant and argumentative. She was feeling little support from him in general and had, for that reason, not revealed to him that she was pregnant. It was clear to her that she hadn't wanted to conceive, but they had been irregular users of birth control, assuming a pregnancy wouldn't happen to them.

The counselor asked her to discuss her thoughts about her alternatives. Carri was 19, a sophomore in college, and was interested in continuing her studies through a graduate degree in journalism. One of her major concerns was that her pregnancy, if continued, would interrupt her career goals.

She was worried about her relationship with Bruce. They had discussed ending it, but neither seemed to have the courage to do

so. Carri felt that if the relationship had continued like it started—warm, loving, supportive—she would consider getting married to Bruce. But not now. Besides, she felt that a pregnancy was a poor reason to get married.

Carri talked about putting the child up for adoption. While this would allow her to resume her studies relatively quickly without feeling pressure to get married, she was terrified of her parents' reactions. She felt they might reject her, or influence her to get married, or at the very least, be extremely disappointed. Carri feared those reactions greatly.

The circumstances seemed to point to abortion as the best alternative. But was abortion murder? She had always abhorred the idea of abortion, and never thought she would consider it for herself. Abortion was certainly not an alternative she would feel good about.

The counselor spent a great deal of time simply listening. Carri needed to talk with someone, and had not yet trusted her dilemma with a friend. It was also clear that she had spent a large amount of time probing her predicament. The counselor helped Carri sort her alternatives—*would* her parents reject her, *would* suspending her studies for a semester or two be that serious of a problem, what about the option of keeping the child and returning to school once the child could be taken care of by a babysitter?

Carri worried about whether getting an abortion was selfish, or if it meant she disliked children. They talked about the quality of life as being important, and if Carri were to raise the child herself, she might not be as able to give time, love, and energy as fully as if she had planned the pregnancy. Another stark reality was economic; Carri was aware that her lack of financial resources would pose an ongoing problem should she decide to keep the child. They agreed it wasn't exactly an act of selflessness to give birth to someone she didn't have time for, couldn't feed or read to, someone who might grow to feel lonely and resented. The counselor encouraged Carri to recognize her own needs as important and the validity of wanting what seemed best for herself.

The counselor raised the question of whether to share the dilemma with Bruce. While Carri feared rejection from him, they both agreed he had some right to know about the pregnancy. Since Carri was the one who was ultimately likely to be most affected by the pregnancy, the primary decision should rest with her. But a part of her decision might be determined by his response. Further, Carrie felt she needed someone close to talk with about her feelings and share her burden. With some encouragement from the counselor, Carri decided to discuss it with Bruce. The counselor suggested, further, that it might be helpful to talk with another close friend.

After an intense, 90-minute discussion, the counselor suggested that Carri go home, talk with Bruce, think about it more, and come back in a couple of days for further discussion. She was early enough in her pregnancy that time was not critical. While Carri was eager to make her decision, additional time would probably help her find the best one.

As the counselor left the session, she was aware of being emotionally drained. While she had talked with many women in a very similar predicament before, she was struck by the pain in each individual. These are almost never simple decisions, and she realized how important it was to present options fairly and accurately, guiding the client but not deciding for her.

Occasionally the decision seemed pretty obvious—the 16-year-old rape victim, the 13-year-old incest case, the woman who had been exposed to German measles. But these cases were rare. Most of the persons she saw

who were coping with an unwanted pregnancy would be able to have the child and would probably be at least adequate parents. But should they be forced into parenthood because they accidentally got pregnant? The court has said they shouldn't but each individual needs to decide for herself.

Carri returned one week later, had talked several times with Bruce, and decided to get an abortion. He accompanied her on the day of her appointment. They decided to postpone any decisions about the future of their relationship until this crisis had passed. The counselor explained the medical procedure to them, discussed birth control, and Carri would start on oral contraceptives following the abortion.

SEX THERAPY

Until the late 1960s, most helping professionals assumed that sexual functioning was an entirely natural activity and any dysfunction was merely a by-product of other individual or relationship problems. Therefore, the resolution of sexual problems would be a natural outcome of the resolution of other problems. Indeed, if one set out to resolve *only* the sexual problem, and was successful, some other problem would surface since the sexual problem was seen as a symptom of a larger pathology.

Depending on the therapist's theoretical framework and philosophical beliefs, these psychological problems might be the result of unresolved conflicts, incomplete growth in a particular stage, communication problems, or perhaps faulty learning. When a client sought therapeutic help with a sexual problem, the therapist set out to improve functioning in her/his life in general, assuming sexual functioning would follow suit. Often it did.

But alarmingly often it did not. Persons would undergo psychoanalysis or another form of psychotherapy, gain insight into themselves and their problems, but would continue to suffer from premature ejaculation, or nonorgasmic response, or some other sexual problem.

Masters and Johnson

In 1957, William Masters and Virginia Johnson began their classic study of the physiology of human sexual response. Their research in this area was the finest performed ever before or since. Their contribution to the scientific understanding of human sexual response was enormous. Perhaps the most complimentary statement to the quality of their research is that it has, with minor and rare exception, stood the test of others' replication in the two decades following. Masters and Johnson's findings were reported in their book, *Human Sexual Response*.[12] While *Human Sexual Response* is a medical text and therefore difficult for most persons who lack a familiarity with medical terminology, excellent synopses of their findings, written for lay persons, are available. One such condensation is *An Analysis of Human Sexual Response*.[13]

Upon completion of their research on human sexual response, Masters and Johnson set about, beginning in 1959, to treat persons with sexual dysfunctions. They departed radically from the prevailing thinking of the day, discussed above, which suggested sexual problems were merely manifestations of other problems. They identified the relationship of the two partners as the client, rather than one person or the other, and indeed *required* both partners to participate in the process of therapy. They did what many others had thought untenable—they isolated the sexual problem, dealt with it directly in short-term therapy, and generated extremely successful results. Virtually all forms of sex therapy developed since Masters and John-

son's methods were reported in *Human Sexual Inadequacy*[14] (a condensation for the lay person is *Understanding Human Sexual Inadequacy*[15]) have been variations on their original approach. Further, there is no evidence that relief of a sexual problem leads to the formation of a replacement problem.

Why sexual dysfunction?

It is generally agreed that all sexual dysfunctions (except the minority which are caused by physical problems such as diabetes or spinal cord injury) are the result of a single, pervasive cause: anxiety. This anxiety can be as straightforward as a fear of a specific sexual failure, such as an inability to reach orgasm. It may be much more complex, such as a fear of becoming close to another person which relates back to negative experiences in early childhood. Or, perhaps most commonly, it may be a combination of a variety of anxiety-producing factors. In any case, anxiety is the common element which, for almost everyone, interrupts the ability to fully function sexually.

Every person defends against anxiety-producing situations differently. Some people are quick to respond; others slow. Some have many physical reactions such as palm sweating or mouth dryness; others want to talk or be quiet. These differences account for why anxiety can result in a problem of erectile difficulty for one person, inability to have orgasm for another, and a lack of sexual interest for a third. We all choose to avoid unsafe situations, so as we approach danger, we avoid. If you have learned that being sexual with a particular partner is "dangerous," you are likely to feel little desire to be with that person. If you have found that being sexual with all partners is dangerous, you might develop an inhibition of sexual desire for partner-sex and instead express your sexuality by looking in windows, exposing your genitals to strangers, becoming sexually aroused by certain objects, or a multitude of other variations.

Helen Singer Kaplan, a noted psychiatrist and sex therapist, has identified three phases of sexual response: desire, excitement, and orgasm.[16] Anxiety can produce dysfunctions in each phase. The principal desire phase disorder is hypoactive desire—lack of sexual interest. Excitement phase disorders include erectile difficulty in men and lack of arousal in women, which results in little vaginal lubrication or other normal physical responses to sexual stimulation. These are discussed later in this chapter. Orgasm phase dysfunctions include premature ejaculation or retarded ejaculation in men, and orgasmic dysfunction in women. Two dysfunctions which are not associated with a particular phase of sexual response are (1) vaginismus in women—a painful, spastic contraction of the pelvic muscles which prohibits vaginal penetration, and (2) the male counterpart to vaginismus, ejaculatory pain due to muscle spasms.

Because some situations may be perceived as safe and others dangerous, all these dysfunctions can be present in some situations or with some partners and absent at other times or with other partners. And because sexual problems are almost always relationship problems, the dynamics of the relationship have a profound effect on the success or failure of treatment. This is why treating some sexual problems is straightforward and simple, and treating others is extremely complex.

Levels of therapeutic intervention

Jack S. Annon, a psychologist and sex therapist from Honolulu, Hawaii, has developed an extremely useful conceptual scheme for the treatment of sexual problems.[17] He rejects the notion that the alleviation of sexual dysfunction demands, in every case, intensive therapy. Rather, he suggests a model providing four levels of approach: permission, limited information, specific suggestions, and intensive therapy. The acronym for the model is PLISSIT.

Annon suggests the largest number of sexual problems can be treated effectively by the helping professional simply giving the client well-placed, accurate *permission*. Permission, used in this model, implies a kind of professional reassurance, letting clients know they are normal, OK—not perverted or deviant. Many people are not bothered by the specific behavior they are engaging in, but are concerned that it is seen by most other people as wrong or aberrant. These concerns frequently involve masturbation ("it's only for kids"), fantasies and dreams ("to think about it is equal to doing it"), or behaviors expected by society but not desired by the individual ("anal intercourse is the latest thing"). The case example of Tina, discussed above, is an illustration of a client seeking permission *not* to engage in a certain sexual activity.

A smaller group of persons suffering from sexual problems can be treated by the helping professional disseminating *limited information*. Limited information, usually expanding on permission, provides the client with "specific factual information directly relevant to the particular sexual concern."[18] An example of this, from my experience, was presented by a 68-year-old client who had believed, for as long as he could remember, that human beings were capable of a certain number of orgasms in life, and no more. So he had *rationed* them, always confining orgasms to a single intercourse experience each weekend. The therapist informed him that what he had believed was incorrect. In fact, he could enhance his ability to respond sexually by maintaining a frequency and regularity of response. Since this client received this information, he has been making up for a great deal of lost time. His need in this area was for a specific piece of accurate information. Because so many people suffer from misinformation about sex, examples of persons needing this level of intervention abound. Often they involve myths about averages (sizes, frequencies), masturbation, menstruation, and aging.

A still smaller number of clients need intervention at Annon's next level, *specific suggestions*. The therapist offers the suggestions only after he/she has taken a *sexual problem history*. The sexual problem history includes (1) description of the current problem, (2) onset and course of the problem, (3) client's concept of the cause and maintenance of the problem, (4) past treatment and outcome, and (5) current expectancies and goals of treatment.[19]

This history, short of a complete sexual history but providing more background than is generally needed for permission or limited information, is important to maximize the likelihood that the specific suggestions will be effective in the alleviation of the sexual distress. Specific suggestions are often given to relieve performance problems. For example, the woman who finds intercourse painful due to lack of lubrication might benefit from suggestions encouraging the couple to slow down, allowing her adequate time for arousal, and identifying verbally to her partner behaviors which are pleasurable to her.

The final level, *intensive therapy*, is required by a very small number of persons with sexual complaints. Their dysfunctions are sufficiently involved and complicated that intervention using permission, limited information, and specific suggestions is not sufficient to alleviate the dysfunction.

Principles of sex therapy

The basic tenets of most common forms of sex therapy are outlined below:

1. Sexual behavior, while being a natural physiological process, is largely governed by learned behavior. Many persons who suffer from sexual dysfunction have experienced inadequate or inaccurate learning. Further, the more information one has (about sex or anything else), the more likely is that individual to make healthy decisions and function in the most satisfying way.
2. The vast majority of sexual problems are psychological in origin, not organic. While most have physical manifestations (spastic contractions of the pelvic musculature, erectile difficulty), they originate from mental preoccupations which interrupt sexual response: performance anxiety, fear of failure, unreasonable expectations, focusing on a goal, and so on.
3. Persons benefit from verbal communication with their partners regarding their sexual behavior preferences.
4. The most effective way to learn about one's own sexual response is through masturbation, an activity that provides immediate, accurate feedback. Only when one is familiar with her/his own response can one accurately communicate it to a partner.
5. In a sexual relationship, both persons contribute positively and negatively to the interaction. There is no such thing as an uninvolved partner.[20]
6. Virtually all sexual dysfunctions are either correctable or adaptable; the symptoms can be reversed or behaviors can be adapted to accommodate performance problems, enabling the persons to obtain sexual gratification.

The sex therapy clinic

Bill, age 36, and Mary, 33, had been married for 10 years when they first telephoned the sex therapy clinic. Bill is an attorney;

Mary is, at present, primarily responsible for the care of their children, age six and three, and is active in civic organizations.

Bill and Mary were each aware of sexual problems in their marriage from almost the beginning, but for years they were never discussed except in an argument. Mary was quite sure she had never experienced orgasm, and Bill had, early in their sexual relationship, been unable to control his ejaculation. His response resulted in his reaching orgasm almost immediately at the commencement of intercourse. More recently, Mary had become almost completely turned off to sex, and Bill found he was experiencing increasing difficulty maintaining his erection so intercourse could occur at all. Both seemed aware, although it had not been stated outright, that the tensions in the sexual area were carrying over into other areas of their relationship. Further, if the sexual problems did not get resolved, the relationship would probably continue to deteriorate and eventually end in separation and divorce.

Acknowledging these rather grim realities, Mary finally gathered enough courage to ask her gynecologist for help. He examined her, found no physical problems, reassured her that help was available, and suggested that she call a sex therapy clinic where he had referred patients before.

Mary and Bill discussed the doctor's advice and agreed that something needed to be done. Since Mary felt the problem was largely *hers*, she made the telephone call.

Mary's inquiry was referred to a woman therapist. The therapist, realizing the anxiety which almost always accompanies the initial contact, projected a reassuring tone as she briefly explored the problems with Mary. She explained that both of them would be seen by a male-female co-therapy team should they decide to participate in sex therapy. After answering all of Mary's questions, the therapist suggested that she discuss it

with Bill, and if they desired, set up an evaluation meeting.

The evaluation session

Bill and Mary made a preliminary decision to proceed, so the evaluation session was scheduled.[21] The purposes of this initial meeting were (1) to provide an opportunity for the clients to meet the co-therapists who would be seeing them should they enter therapy; (2) to provide for the therapists, through discussion with each client, the background and current assessment of the problems to determine if therapy would likely be helpful, what level might be most appropriate, or if referral to another agency might be more fruitful; (3) to describe the treatment plan which might be used; and (4) to answer all questions before a further decision to proceed was made. The male therapist suggested a physician for Bill to see to rule out any organic or physiologic reason for his erectile difficulty. While he suspected strongly the erectile problems were anxiety related and not caused by physical problems, he wanted to be sure he wasn't attempting to treat a biological problem with counseling. Bill agreed to see this physician. Bill and Mary left the sex therapy office feeling greatly relieved; they had begun to deal with the situation after 10 years of avoidance, and the therapists had reassured them that their problems were neither unique nor hopeless.

The sexual history

In the next therapy meeting, the sexual history was gathered. The couple was separated, each meeting with the therapist of their own gender. Each therapist explored their client's childhood and adolescent experiences, goals of therapy, patterns in their family of origin, sexual value systems, the history of the sexual problems, strengths and weaknesses of the marriage, and much

Sex therapy

more.[22] The purposes of the history-taking session are twofold: (1) for the therapist to understand, as accurately and completely as possible, the client he or she will be principally representing in treatment (the client of the same gender), and (2) for the client to establish "comfort" with that therapist which will facilitate the entire treatment process.

During the history-taking session, the therapists were particularly careful to ask specific questions and press for specific, detailed answers. A very important rule for sexual counselors and therapists to observe is to avoid *assuming* anything. Because specific, personal sexual experiences are not something people tend to talk about, particularly if there is a sexual problem involved, persons often assume their behaviors are similar to everybody else's. The thorough, careful therapist will avoid serious pitfalls that will sabotage the success of therapy if they are not noticed. Two examples, drawn from my clinical experience, illustrate this point.

One couple reported that when the woman had an orgasm, she "really came."

The therapists pressed for more information—the man said she "ejaculated so much it made a puddle on the bed." If the therapists had assumed he was talking about copious lubrication, they might have been pleased to know her body was responding so well. She was, to the couple's shock, suffering from urinary incontinence; her pelvic musculature was so poor that when she experienced orgasm she was voiding her bladder. While, with the correct diagnosis, this turned out to be a relatively simple problem to treat, the couple would not have known what to do without the therapists' guidance, which begins with specific, accurate information.[23]

Another client who had recently been divorced, in part because of the couple's inability to have children, reported that he could have orgasms through masturbation and intercourse. When the therapist asked for more specific information, he learned that what the man was defining as orgasm and ejaculation was, in fact, the secretion of Cowper's gland fluid, a clear substance which drips out the end of the penis during arousal but *prior to* ejaculation and orgasm. He had developed a lifelong pattern of stimulation to arousal but always stopped prior to orgasm; he didn't realize there was more he could experience. Previous psychotherapists had taken his report of orgasm at face value. The sex therapist suggested that he continue the stimulation, and he reported a very pleasant surprise with his next sexual experience.

It may be tempting to assume that people who suffer from such gross misinformation would be people who might be misinformed in a lot of other areas. Beware—general intelligence is not a measure of sex intelligence. The couple in the incontinence example were college graduates; the man who was misinformed about his orgasm was a prominent and highly respected professional person.

The round table

Bill and Mary met with the therapists for the next meeting, the round table. The purposes of the round table meeting are (1) to review each client's history as it relates to the sexual problem, (2) to trace and account for the development of the problem, (3) to outline the treatment plan, (4) to dispell myths and correct misinformation which were uncovered in previous meetings, and (5) to assign the initial home experiences and communication exercise.

The male therapist, in reviewing Bill's history, discussed how Bill *learned* a pattern of quick ejaculation from sexual experiences as a teenager. Since he was fearful at that time that he might be caught, it was functional for him to come to orgasm quickly. This was long before he learned that prolonging his arousal would be more pleasurable for both his partner and himself. When he entered marriage, he expected his response to slow down as he became more familiar with Mary. But Bill seemed to have learned the pattern of speedy response so thoroughly that he was utterly unable to respond any other way. The more he worried about the problem, the more anxiety he experienced, causing him to have even less control. Eventually, he started experiencing difficulty with erection. He had become so preoccupied with his performance that he was blocking all erotic stimulation—a necessary condition for erection to occur in a sexual encounter.

Mary, on the other hand, had learned as a teenager to be *sexy*, but not *sexual*. That is, she was expected to attract men, but not to "go too far." She became adept at kissing, hugging, and petting—becoming very aroused—but then stopping the sexual encounter. This pattern, arousal followed by turnoff, later victimized her in marriage, long after she had to worry about getting pregnant, venereal disease, or ruining her reputation. Not surprisingly, she described her teenage petting experiences as the best sexual encounters of her life.

For the first several years of marriage, Mary remembered experiencing high arousal, but short of orgasm, and then "going numb, feeling nothing." In the more recent past, her body felt less and less aroused, as if to say, "I'm not going to reach orgasm anyway, so why bother?"

The therapists pointed out these patterns, emphasizing that the sexual problems were neither person's fault. New, more functional patterns could be learned to replace the old, dysfunctional ones.

The woman therapist gave Mary a beginning self-pleasuring assignment. This was to help her learn her own sexual response, so that later she could share it with and teach it to Bill. Both agreed there was no way Bill could automatically *know* what was pleasurable to Mary, particularly if she didn'd know herself. Mary had never masturbated, and with encouragement and specific, graduated instructions, she agreed to try.[24]

The male therapist instructed Bill to continue masturbating, something he had been doing since childhood. He suggested for Bill to slow down, however, to learn as much about his various levels of arousal as possible.

Touching

The couple was instructed to abstain from intercourse, in order to eliminate the anxiety which had invariably surrounded that activity. In place of intercourse, they were given the following instructions:

> To many persons, the idea of touching any part of the body is thought of only as a preliminary to orgasm. Thinking of touching in this way often causes the touching to become less valued in and of itself. Although the entire body may be pleasant to touch and to have touched, emphasis is usually placed on the

breasts, vaginal area, penis, and testicles. Touching need not be explicitly genital or goal-oriented to be pleasurable. Touching, by yourself or with a partner, can be a joyful expression of discovery and exploration, of giving and getting.

Plan ahead and prepare, together, a quiet, private, warm, and comfortable place. Create an atmosphere that is pleasant for you. It may include soft colored lights, or candles and music, or other things which help you relax. Get really comfortable by removing your clothing and assuming positions which will permit relaxation during long periods of touching. Give yourselves a lot of time. Slowly become very familiar with your partner's entire body. Remember, this experience is not one of trying to sexually arouse one's partner; but it is an experience which is designed to give you time and space to explore your own feelings about touching and being touched. Touch, stroke, squeeze, and caress your partner for your own pleasure. The feeling you receive need not be an arousing one. You will feel something; get in touch with whatever that feeling is.

You may wish to shower together, using pleasant soaps on one another's body, or try a shower in the dark (you must then really rely on touch). When you do come together for a touching experience it is suggested you use a pleasant tasting, nonalcohol based lotion or oil, or a baby powder, which is particularly nice in warm weather. These facilitate the movement of skin on skin and reduce friction. Oils or lotions should first be poured in your hands to be warmed or warmed on a stove or candle stand.

Use your fingers, fingertips, your palms and your full hand to touch and caress in different ways. This is not a massage. Massage is designed primarily to give pleasure to the other person. Remember, the major purpose of this touching experience is to discover feelings for yourself through touching your partner. It may be pleasant to close your eyes while touching so you can "get into" your own feelings without observing your partner's response. Try a joyful fantasy, if you like; or pretend you've lost the use of your sight for awhile and must rely on touch alone. The person being touched has only to lie there and concentrate on his or her own feelings of being touched. Sometimes, too, you may want to visually explore your partner's body while you are touching and would feel more comfortable if your partner were to close his or her eyes. If so, ask your partner to do so. If it would be pleasant to comb your partner's hair, do so. Since you are touching your partner for yourself, you need not concern yourself with your partner's reaction, unless it is one of discomfort or pain (if so, your partner must tell you). After each touching experience discuss your feelings with one another; not in a directive or accusatory fashion but with an effort toward understanding each others feelings about touching and being touched. Do not make assumptions about your partner's feelings. It is important to remember to communicate with one another and not to move faster than your comfort levels.

The first week we ask you to have "touching experiences" a minimum of three times during the week to reenforce comfortable feelings. We will discuss with you which partner should initiate the first touching experience. After the "initiator" has fully explored his or her partner's body for their own pleasure, he or she will change off and the person who was touching for his or her own pleasure will then become the one who is touched. During this first week we do not want the man to touch his partner's breasts, nipples, or vaginal area, nor do we want the woman to touch her partner's nipples, penis, or testicles. Touching should be done only with the hands during this week.

Verbal communications

Bill and Mary were also given the following instructions to enhance their verbal communications:[25]

Most sexually intimate couples think they know considerably more about each other's feelings, attitudes and behaviors than they, in fact, really do know. They take pride in out-guessing and in predicting their partner's responses without adequately communicating with each other. They believe "If he/she loved me—he/she would *know* how I feel."

Responsibility for self:

We are each responsible for our own sexuality. We should not wait for someone else to discover it for us. We need to explore, discover and understand our own sexual responses. We are then free to share or not to share our sexuality with another person. If we decide to share our sexuality, we need to be willing to communicate with our partner what we have learned about ourselves, to be open and vulnerable, to risk. We also need to be willing to learn about our partner's sexuality *from our partner*. We cannot make assumptions about his/her needs, feelings, or thoughts, without asking. Too often we are wrong. In order to share a sexual experience on an equal basis we must both have and express knowledge, comfort and responsibility for our own sexuality. This responsibility is necessary to take ownership for our own feelings, attitudes and ideas as well as our behavior.

Representation of self:

Once we are responsible for our own sexuality and have made a decision to share our sexuality with another person, we need to learn functional ways to represent ourselves clearly to our partner. Perhaps the simplest and most effective verbal communication method is "I language."

I language:

a. "You make me so angry when you don't pick up your clothes."
(an accusatory statement which is most likely to place your partner on the defensive.)

b. "I'm angry because in addition to picking up my own clothes I feel I have to pick your clothes up too."
(permits further communication and represents your feelings.)

a. "Let's go out to dinner."
(a confused message that takes over your partner's response.)

b. "I'd like to go out to dinner and wonder if you would like to also."
(much clearer)

a. "You're so clumsy when you touch my breasts."
(another accusatory message likely to shut down communication—not open it up.)

b. "I get turned off when you touch my breasts that way because it hurts; I'd like to show you what kind of touch feels good."

a. "Do you want to go to the movies tonight?"
(answer: "I don't know, do you?"—next response—"I don't know, I asked you first"—result: confusion)

b. "I would like to see ___ tonight, and wonder if you would also like to see that film?"
(extremely clear)

The purpose of "I" language is not to promote agreement but rather to promote accurate communication and understanding. Only with accurate understanding can you ever know if you agree or disagree. When you use "I language" you must first be aware of your own feeling, attitude, idea, or thought, before you can clearly state it to your partner. Thus, the use of "I language" helps you to get in touch with your own feeling first. All feelings are real for you—they exist—they may not always be rational—but you have them. It is your responsibility to represent *your* feeling. Do not expect your partner to know your feelings clearly unless you represent them. Through the use of "I language" you minimize putting your partner in a defensive position. You also optimize opening further communication. You speak for *you*, not for someone else. Hopefully, you know yourself better than anyone else because you have given yourself permission to know and to represent yourself. By honestly expressing your feelings you encourage your partner to do the same. Honesty often seems risky when used with someone you care about; but the alternative may be confusion.

The physiology session

The next therapy meeting followed the round table by one week. The purposes of this meeting are: (1) to review and evaluate the couple's experiences in touching and communication, (2) to make new assignments, and (3) to discuss the physiology of human sexual response.

The therapists asked Bill and Mary about their first week's assignments, focusing on relaxation, learning, and comfort as the goals, not sexual arousal. Both reported feeling awkward during the first touching experiences, but the awkwardness soon passed and both enjoyed the experience of performance-free touching.

Since Bill and Mary seemed comfortable, they were given the next touching assignment. They were instructed to do exactly as they had done the previous week, except now they could include breasts, nipples, and genitals in the touching. These areas were not to become the focus of the sessions, nor was there an expectation of arousal. In fact, if arousal did occur, they were instructed to move the touching to another area. And, of course, they were not to have intercourse.

The therapists asked about "I language." Mary had found it particularly useful in communicating anger to Bill; he had largely forgotten to use it. The therapists reemphasized its importance, particularly following a touching experience.

Bill reported that he was able to slow his arousal in masturbation as much as he wanted. This didn't seem significant to him—his lack of control was associated with intercourse—but he was becoming more aware of his levels of arousal. He was learning to recognize the point of ejaculatory inevitability, the few-second period immediately preceding orgasm. The therapist informed him that his efforts at slowing his response will need to be focused prior to ejaculatory inevitability; once he is in that stage, orgasm is, as it states, inevitable.

Mary had spent some private time each day exploring her body. She had many questions for the woman therapist and seemed eager to continue her exploration.

The therapists gave Bill and Mary two additional assignments. They taught the couple the use of the *squeeze technique* for controlling premature ejaculation,[26] and Mary was given exercises designed to strengthen her vaginal muscles, thereby increasing vaginal sensations.[27]

The therapists then presented, using slides, factual information on human sexual response. This educational experience is used to promote knowledge and understanding of physical changes which occur in the body as a result of sexual arousal. Much of this data was gathered by Masters and Johnson in their famous studies of the physiology of human sexual response.

In their discussion of sexual response, the male therapist assumed primary responsibility for presenting male response, the female therapist for presenting female response. They paid particular attention to the physiological components of Bill and Mary's sexual dysfunctions—nonorgasmic response, premature ejaculation, and erectile dysfunction.

Masters and Johnson identified four stages of sexual response in females and males: excitement, plateau, orgasm and resolution. There are many similarities in the physical responses of men and women. These include the two major body changes which result from sexual stimulation—myotonia, or muscle tension, and vasocongestion, or blood engorgement.

The male therapist explained the genital response in the male, using slides and models to illustrate the physical changes. In *excitement,* blood flows into the erectile tissue of the penis (vasocongestion), resulting in erection. The scrotum (the sac surrounding the testicles) becomes thicker, more wrinkled, and the testicles move up closer to the body.

Plateau response is characterized by the continuation of erection, although it often waxes and wanes during sex play with a partner. The testicles become fully elevated, rotate toward the front, and become blood engorged causing expansion in their size. The Cowper's gland secretes a small amount of clear fluid which comes out the tip of the penis. The purpose of this fluid is generally thought to be to cleanse the urethra of urine, thereby neutralizing the chemical environment for the passage of sperm.

The *orgasm* stage in men consists of two phases. The first is ejaculatory inevitability, a short period during which stimulation sufficient to trigger orgasm has occurred, and the resulting ejaculation becomes inevitable. The second phase, ejaculation, results from rhythmic contractions (myotonia) forcing sperm and semen through the urethra. Simultaneous with this is the very pleasant physical sensation of orgasm.

The final stage, *resolution,* represents a return to the unstimulated state. In resolution, the penis loses its erection, and the testicles lose their engorgement and elevation.

In women, the *excitement* stage of sexual response ushers in many changes. The process of vaginal lubrication begins. This response is analogous to the male erection; it is caused by sexual stimulation and is, physiologically, a blood engorgement response. The uterus and cervix begin to move up and away from the vagina. The clitoris and labia minora (inner lips) enlarge and the labia majora (outer lips) spread. Breast size increases slightly and the nipples become erect.

In *plateau,* the uterus continues in its movement up and back, the vagina lengthens and balloons at the rear, and the outer third of the vagina contracts, causing a gripping effect. The clitoris retracts under its hood, making it seem to disappear.

At *orgasm,* the uterus and vagina become involved in wave-like muscular contractions. This response, as well as the subjective pleasure of orgasm, are very similar to the experience of the male.

In *resolution,* the cervix and uterus drop to their normal positions, the outer third of the vagina returns to normal, followed by the inner two thirds. The clitoris and the breasts also return to normal.

The therapists also discussed the many involuntary *extragenital* physical responses in men and women. These include muscle tension responses such as facial grimmace, spastic contractions of the hands and feet, and pelvic thrusting. Extragenital blood engorgement responses include sex flush, blood pressure and heartrate increases, and perspiration on soles of feet and palms of hands.

Finally, the therapists discussed how aging affects sexual response. They emphasized that persons are capable of experiencing pleasurable sexual response throughout life; while their bodies may slow down, they do not need to stop. The effects of aging on sexual response are summarized in Figures 17–1 and 17–2.

Sex therapy for Bill and Mary continued for eight additional weekly meetings. Progress of Mary occurred dramatically in the fourth week; she experienced her first orgasm in self-stimulation, and she continued in her ability to stimulate herself to orgasm.

During one of the couple touching experiences, Mary stimulated herself to orgasm. Sporadically at first, and then consistently by week six, each were able to bring the other to orgasm through hand stimulation. Touching experiences in the later weeks of therapy emphasized whole-body touching, genital touching, female-active intercourse with si-

FIGURE 17–1 Aging aspects of sexual response in men

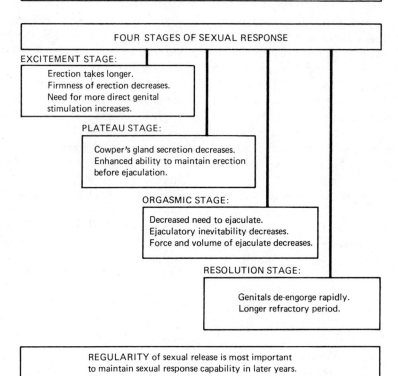

Bodily processes slow down BUT THEY DO NOT STOP
A natural slowing down DOES NOT mean a loss of interest

FOUR STAGES OF SEXUAL RESPONSE

EXCITEMENT STAGE:

Erection takes longer.
Firmness of erection decreases.
Need for more direct genital
stimulation increases.

PLATEAU STAGE:

Cowper's gland secretion decreases.
Enhanced ability to maintain erection
before ejaculation.

ORGASMIC STAGE:

Decreased need to ejaculate.
Ejaculatory inevitability decreases.
Force and volume of ejaculate decreases.

RESOLUTION STAGE:

Genitals de-engorge rapidly.
Longer refractory period.

REGULARITY of sexual release is most important
to maintain sexual response capability in later years.

multaneous clitoral stimulation, and lots of verbal feedback.

Bill practiced the penile squeeze (the technique to delay ejaculation) in self-stimulation and Mary applied it during their couple experiences. They found he could experience increased stimulation with less need for the squeeze. In the seventh week, Bill was able to control his orgasm, assuming there had not been a period of abstinence from orgasm, as he desired.

Not surprisingly, once Bill understood the mechanisms that were previously precluding his erection, and he and Mary were comfort-

able in their sexual interactions, erectile difficulty was seldom a problem. When problems did occur, Bill was able to identify the cause, take it in stride, and have a better experience the next time.

At the termination of therapy, Mary and Bill reported that they were both enjoying their sexual experiences and that improvement in their sexual intimacy had relieved many other tensions in the relationship. Their communication had also improved greatly. They were interested in Mary achieving orgasm in intercourse through penile thrusting alone, but this certainly wasn't

FIGURE 17–2 Aging aspects of sexual response in women

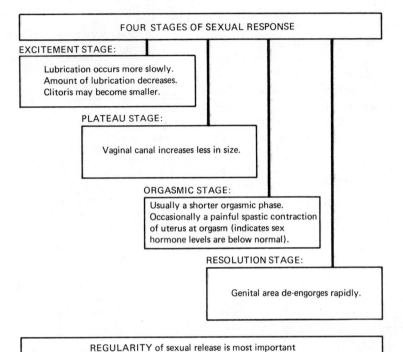

Bodily processes slow down BUT THEY DO NOT STOP
A natural slowing down DOES NOT mean a loss of interest

FOUR STAGES OF SEXUAL RESPONSE

EXCITEMENT STAGE:
Lubrication occurs more slowly.
Amount of lubrication decreases.
Clitoris may become smaller.

PLATEAU STAGE:
Vaginal canal increases less in size.

ORGASMIC STAGE:
Usually a shorter orgasmic phase.
Occasionally a painful spastic contraction
of uterus at orgasm (indicates sex
hormone levels are below normal).

RESOLUTION STAGE:
Genital area de-engorges rapidly.

REGULARITY of sexual release is most important
to maintain sexual response capability in later years.

an all-important goal. Further, they know what they could do to work toward that, and looked forward to the process.

A major thesis of this chapter is that almost all social workers, regardless of their specific professional responsibilities, are sometimes called upon to be sexual counselors. Further, the levels of treatment of sexual problems require varying degrees of knowledge, comfort, and experience. Since most social workers are not sex therapists, the need for responsible referral arises. To assist persons in locating competent, experienced sex therapists, the American Associa-

tion of Sex, Educators, Counselors, and Therapists (AASECT) certifies qualified sex therapists. The association will, by writing their office at 5010 Wisconsin Avenue, N.W., Suite 304, Washington, D.C., 20016, provide the names of knowledgeable, ethical, and experienced sex therapists.

SUMMARY

In this chapter, we have examined the role of the social worker as a helping agent to persons suffering from sexual problems. The social worker is frequently called upon to step out of her/his primary professional role to become a sexual counselor. In this role, the worker performs short-term, often crisis-oriented counseling directed toward the alleviation of some immediate difficulty related to sex. We explored four such situations: problems resulting from a nursing home resident being caught masturbating, a teenage woman making decisions about sexuality with her partner, an adolescent boy who was caught making sexual advances to another younger boy, and a woman struggling with decisions about an unwanted pregnancy. Issues specific to effective sexual counseling, such as the counselor's vocabulary, were highlighted in this section.

Sex therapy focuses on the alleviation of sexual dysfunction, implying a planned change sequence involving several contacts between the client(s) and therapist(s). The stages of intensive sex therapy are problem definition, history gathering, physical examination, information dissemination, prescribed sexual and communication experiences, and ongoing evaluation.

The historical and theoretical underpinnings of current sex therapy were discussed. Critical issues in sex therapy, such as the therapist's need to avoid making assumptions, were examined. Jack S. Annon's conceptual model for defining levels of intervention—permission, limited information, specific suggestions, intensive therapy—was discussed. An example of intensive sex therapy was given which paid particular attention to prescribed sexual and communication experiences.

NOTES

1. Alfred Kinsey et al., *Sexual Behavior in the Human Male* (Philadelphia: W. B. Saunders, 1948).

2. Alfred Kinsey et al., *Sexual Behavior in the Human Female* (Philadelphia: W. B. Saunders, 1953).

3. For an excellent discussion of the sexual needs and problems of persons society tends to ignore, see Harvey L. Gochros and Jean S. Gochros, *The Sexually Oppressed* (New York: Association Press, 1977). A film which portrays many issues related to intimacy, sexuality, and loneliness in institutions is *Rose by Any Other Name,* available from Adelphi University Center on Aging, Garden City, New York.

4. The Alan Guttmacher Institute, "Eleven Million Teenagers—What Can Be Done about the Epidemic of Adolescent Pregnancies in the United States" (New York: Planned Parenthood Federation of America, 1976), p. 9.

5. Ibid., pp. 10–11.

6. Gary F. Kelly, *Learning about Sex* (Woodbury, N.Y.: Barron's Educational Series, 1976), p. 168.

7. Sol Gordon, "Ten Heavy Facts about Sex" (Syracuse, N.Y.: Ed-U Press, 1975). This is an exceptionally creative pamphlet designed for adolescents, which answers frequently asked questions about sex.

8. A. J. Bachrach, W. J. Erwin, and J. P. Mohr, "The Control of Eating Behavior in an Anorexic by Operant Conditioning Techniques," in L. P. Ullman and L. Krasner, *Case Studies in Behavior Modification* (New York: Holt, Rinehart, & Winston, 1965), pp. 153–63.

9. James Deese and Steward H. Hulse, *The Psychology of Learning* (New York: McGraw-Hill, 1967).

10. Warren R. Johnson, "Sex Education of the Mentally Retarded," in Felix de Cruz and Gerald D. LaVeck, *Human Sexuality and the Mentally Retarded* (New York: Brunner-Mazel, 1973), p. 64.

11. C. Tietze, "Induced Abortion," in J. Money and H. Musaph (eds.), *Handbook of Sexology* (Amsterdam: Elsevier/North Holland Press, 1977), pp. 605–20.

12. William H. Masters and Virginia E. Johnson, *Human Sexual Response* (Boston: Little, Brown, 1966).

13. Ruth Brecher and Edward Brecher, *An Analysis of Human Sexual Response* (New York: Signet Books, 1966).

14. William H. Masters and Virginia E. Johnson, *Human Sexual Inadequacy* (Boston: Little, Brown, 1970).

15. Fred Belliveau and Lin Richter, *Understanding Human Sexual Inadequacy* (New York: Bantam Books, 1970).

16. Helen Singer Kaplan, *The New Sex Therapy* (New York: Brunner-Mazel, 1974), p. 290; and Helen Singer Kaplan, *Disorders of Sexual Desire and Other New Concepts and Techniques in Sex Therapy* (New York: Simon Schuster, 1979).

17. Jack S. Annon, *Behavioral Treatment of Sexual Problems* (Hagerstown, Md. Harper & Row, 1976).

18. Ibid., p. 65.

19. Ibid., p. 77.

20. Masters and Johnson, *Human Sexual Inadequacy*, pp. 2–3.

21. This case history illustrates the method used by the author when seeing couples in intensive sex therapy. As stated above, virtually all forms of sex therapy currently in practice are based on psychotherapeutic techniques pioneered by William Masters and Virginia Johnson, described in *Human Sexual Inadequacy*. These techniques have been expanded upon by many sex therapists, the most notable of whom is Helen Singer Kaplan. Her ideas are described in *The New Sex Therapy* and *Disorders of Sexual Desire and Other New Concepts and Techniques in Sex Therapy*. I wish to credit them.

22. An excellent outline for a sexual history can be found in Masters and Johnson, *Human Sexual Inadequacy*, pp. 34–51.

23. Arnold Kegel, "The Physiologic Treatment of Poor Tone and Function of the Genital Muscles and of Urinary Stress Incontinence," *Western Journal of Surgery, Obstetrics and Gynecology* 56 (1949): 527–35.

24. Lonnie Garfield Barbach, *For Yourself* (Garden City, N.Y.: Doubleday, 1975).

25. "I language" is a communication technique suggested by many helping professionals. For a more thorough treatment, see Thomas Gordon, *Parent Effectiveness Training (The Tested New Way to Raise Responsible Children)* (New York: Wyden, 1970).

26. Masters and Johnson, *Human Sexual Inadequacy*, pp. 101–15.

27. Georgia Kline-Graber and Benjamin Graber, *Woman's Orgasm* (New York: Bobbs-Merrill, 1975), pp. 77–80.

chapter *18*

THE PROBLEM

There are now over 4.5 billion people living on earth.[1] In 1930 there were 2 billion.

TABLE 18–1   Doubling times of the world's population

Date	Estimated world population	Time required for population to double
8000 B.C.	5 million	
1650 A.D.	500 million	1,500 years
1850.	1 billion	200
1930.	2 billion	80
1975.	4 billion	45
		35

SOURCE: Paul R. Ehrlich, Anne H. Ehrlich, and John P. Holdren, *Human Ecology: Problems and Solutions* (San Francisco: W. H. Freeman, 1973), p. 21.

Assuming a continued doubling rate of 35 years, by 2010 there will be 8 billion people. If this growth continued for 900 years, there would be 60,000,000,000,000,000 (60 million billion) people! This would mean there would be about 100 persons for each square yard of the earth's surface, both land and water.[2]

Doubling time is based on the extent to which the birthrate exceeds the death rate. Doubling times have a compound effect. Just as interest dollars earn interest, people added to the population produce more people. Table 18–2 shows the relationship between the annual population growth rate and the doubling time of the population.

TABLE 18–2   Rate of population growth and doubling time

Annual percent increase	Doubling time
1.0	70 years
2.0	35 years
3.0	24 years
4.0	17 years

SOURCE: Paul R. Ehrlich, *The Population Bomb* (New York: Ballantine Books, 1971), p. 10.

Thus, what seems a small population growth rate of 2 percent per year (the current rate in the world), leads to a dramatic doubling time of 35 years. With an annual growth rate of 2

Overpopulation and family planning

Under the new law [the news article reports], which has had its title changed from "compulsory sterilization" bill to "family size limitation" bill, men up to age 55 and women up to age 45 must be sterilized within 180 days of the birth of their third living child. The first obligation rests on the men, and affects the woman only "if a vasectomy would endanger her husband's life." Prison terms of up to two years are provided for those who fail to comply with the measure. In practice, however . . . offenders would be sterilized and paroled. . . . [the state's] leading exponent of compulsory sterilization said that one million men would become eligible for vasectomies as soon as the law became effective, and declared his willingness to stake his reputation on the state's ability to sterilize more than a million a year. "Society," he said in an . . . interview, "has a duty to act against 'people pollution' just as it removes latrines built on a river used by people."

Note: This law was rescinded with the fall of Prime Minister Indira Gandhi's government in 1976—a few years later she returned to power. Although rescinded, the law illustrates the extent to which some people will go to alleviate the pressures of unwanted population growth.
SOURCE: "Maharashtra Passes Family Size Limitation Measure," *Intercom 9* September 1976, p. 5. The official quoted is G. N. Pai, one of India's leading exponents of compulsory sterilization.

percent, 70 to 75 million people are being added to the world's population annually.[3]

The countries experiencing the most severe doubling time problems are the "underdeveloped countries." Sadly, population growth is greatest in the countries that can least afford increases; the countries that need to spend their resources on improving their economic conditions. Underdeveloped countries have about twothirds of the world's population, and doubling times around 20 to 35 years.[4] People are "hungry"; many are starving in these countries. Underdeveloped countries tend to have primitive and inefficient agriculture, small gross national products, and high illiteracy rates. The bulk of the population in such countries spend most of their time in trying to meet basic, subsistence needs.

Underdeveloped countries are characterized by high birthrates and declining death rates. Unfortunately, the trend in the past has been that when a country begins to industrialize, the death rate drops (people live longer) while the birthrate tends to remain high for a substantial period of time. The result is a rapid population growth rate.

Lee Rainwater has noted "the poor get children."[5] There is a vicious circle involving rapid population growth and poverty. Rapid population growth places an increasing strain on a nation's ability to feed and clothe its growing masses. Thus, rapid population growth strains resources, which leads to poverty. Poverty, in turn, leads to a high birthrate, which leads to further population growth. World Bank President Robert S. McNamara warns: "Short of thermonuclear war itself, rampant population growth is the gravest issue the world faces over the decades ahead."[6]

Developed or industrialized countries have doubling times in the 50–200-year range.[7] In the United States the birthrate has in recent years steadily decreased and is nearly a zero population growth rate (an average of two children per family). The basic reason the doubling time in developed countries is longer is because people decide to have fewer children (for financial and other reasons). It now costs over $50,000 to raise a child from birth to adulthood in this country.[8] Developed nations are characterized by low birthrates and low death rates.

The slower doubling times in industrialized countries in no way means such nations are not part of the problem. If one looks at consumption rates of raw materials, they are the major culprit. The United States, for example, uses about one third of all the raw materials consumed each year, but has less than one fifteenth of the world's population.[9] The United States is therefore using five times its "fair share" of raw materials.

On a positive note recent studies show the world's population explosion is now slowing down. In one impoverished country after another, investigators report a "dramatic and unexpected decline" in the birthrate.[10] Some authorities are now predicting the global population may stabilize around 8 billion people early in the next century.[11] If these projections hold, the global devastation due to population growth which has been widely forecast may not occur.

A number of reasons are being cited for recent reductions of birthrates in some overpopulated countries. These reasons include an increased availability of contraceptives and a rise in the average age at which couples marry. Educational programs and family planning programs apparently are being effective in changing the traditional peasant attitude that large numbers of children are needed to help till the soil and support their families.[12]

Whether the recent reduction in the birthrate is temporary, or will be a more permanent trend, is uncertain.

An optimal population size. A frequent question is "What is the capacity of the world to support people?" Asserting that a country's population is too large or too small implies there is an optimal size. Such a conception may be in error; probably no exact figure can precisely determine the optimum population for the world.

Many variables and values would enter into specifying an optimal world population size; including preserving a certain standard or quality of life, rate of consumption of nonrenewable raw materials, future technological breakthroughs in finding new energy sources and new food sources, specifying and maintaining "safe" levels of clean air and water, and public acceptance of the government's role (perhaps compulsory) in population control. The industrialized nations, with their high consumption and high waste economies are using up more of the earth's raw materials and generating more pollution than underdeveloped countries. Because of consumption rates, adding 1 million people to industrialized countries is comparable to adding 30 million people to underdeveloped countries.[13]

Too little food. An estimated half-billion people today are undernourished—that is, slowly starving—while another billion are malnourished.[14] Erhlich estimates 10–20 million people, mostly children in underdeveloped countries, are dying of starvation each year in the world.[15] Even in the United States, a number of people are undernourished, with some dying of starvation.[16]

There has been an ongoing, heated controversy among scientists whether technology will be able to substantially increase the world's food supply. Thomas Malthus theorized in 1798 that population growth, if left unchecked, would eventually outstrip the food supply.[17] Some scientists are claiming at the present time that we have already

Now, and forever?

reached the limit where technology will no longer be able to increase the food supply to meet the food needs of even a slowly growing world population, while others are predicting technology can probably provide food for a population 10 times as large as our current population.[18]

Can technology meet increasing food needs? The verdict is not yet in. For example, several years ago a technological breakthrough led to a dramatic improvement in the yield of new strains of wheat and rice. This so-called green revolution, however, requires increased use of fertilizers and water. Fertilizers are becoming scarce and in-

creasingly expensive, and many of the underdeveloped countries cannot afford expensive irrigation systems. Because of such variables, the beneficial effect of the green revolution is not as yet precisely known.

Research on increasing the food supply is taking other approaches. One effort is to investigate the feasibility of cultivating the tropical rain forests of Africa, South America, and Indonesia. Such areas have large amounts of sunshine and water, but poor soil (requiring large quantities of fertilizer) and insect infestation. Another effort is geared to finding new ways to harvest increased amounts of fish and plant life from the sea. The sea contains huge quantities of food, much of which is currently not palatable.

Too little energy. The consumption of energy has doubled every 12 years in our recent history.[19] Over nine tenths of the world's energy consumption is provided by fossil fuel sources: oil, coal, and natural gas. Natural gas sources are rapidly being depleted. The domestic supply of oil in the United States is incapable of meeting our needs, and therefore this country is heavily dependent on foreign sources. In recent years the price of gasoline at service stations has skyrocketed. It has been estimated that petroleum and natural gas reserves will be substantially depleted in a century.[20]

The energy crisis is changing lifestyles of Americans. There has been a dramatic shift to buying smaller, energy efficient cars. Less heat is being used in the winter time, and some families are returning to burning wood. There has also been a trend to take fewer vacations, and to travel shorter distances during vacations. Distant friends and relatives are being visited less. To many Americans it appears that our economy, which is heavily dependent on energy, is being held hostage by foreign oil-producing nations. Certain industries, such as the automobile industry, are in serious financial trouble because of the impact of the energy crisis. The highway speed limit has been reduced to 55 miles per hour, car pooling is increasing, and more people are walking or using a bicycle instead of a fuel-powered vehicle. Solar products, including solar heated homes, are becoming more popular.

The world today is confronted with an energy problem of major proportions. New sources of energy that work as well as fossil fuel sources will have to be found.

Nuclear energy is a possibility, but con-

cerns over controlling the safety of nuclear power plants have slowed construction. In March of 1979 there was a near disaster at a nuclear power plant at Three Mile Island in Pennsylvania. Radioactive steam escaped, and there was a danger of a meltdown which probably would have killed many in the area from lethal overdoses of radiation. The accident emphasized that safety in any nuclear energy plant cannot be taken for granted. Nuclear energy out of control has the potential for a large-scale disaster. Another unresolved concern over nuclear energy is how to safely dispose of radioactive nuclear waste products—such nuclear waste generates radiation for centuries which can cause cancer and other health problems to those exposed. High-level nuclear waste gives off intense heat, initially as high as 900°F., and some of its substances remain toxic for millions of years.

In 1980 the federal government passed legislation to finance and create a synthetic fuel industry. The raw materials for synthetic fuel are in oil shale formations, coal deposits, and gooey tar sands. The term *synthetic fuel* is a misnomer, since its components have the same carbon base as crude oil. Coal, for example, will become gas if it is pulverized, and then mixed with oxygen and steam under extreme heat. Shale is a dark-brown, fine-grained rock that contains carbon. Production problems are considerable, as it is estimated that it takes 1.7 tons of shale to produce a barrel of oil, and a ton of coal to produce two barrels of oil.[21] On a positive note it is estimated that the United States has a 600-year supply of the raw materials for synthetic fuel.[22]

Solar energy is another hope. Some 12,000 U.S. homes now get all or part of their heating and cooling from the sun.[23] Even the White House has a solar water-heating system installed on its roof. Another potential use of sunlight is direct conversion to electricity. Sunlight can be converted directly into electricity with photovoltaic cells.

Gasohol is another hope to ease the energy crisis. Gasohol is a mixture of nine parts unleaded gasoline to one part alcohol. Raw materials for the alcohol part—methanol and ethanol—are virtually inexhaustible. Methanol can be produced from coal, municipal garbage, and waste wood products. Ethanol can be distilled from grain, sugar crops, and almost any starchy plant.

Another potential energy source is wind power. Windmills can be used to generate electrical power, and are having a revival on some farms and in some small towns.

Still another potential source of energy is the burning of garbage and agricultural wastes, including manure. Questions remain whether this source is feasible, and also whether returning agricultural wastes to the soil is not preferable to burning the material.

Other nonrenewable resources.   Mineral resources other than fuels have become essential elements for industrial production. Essential elements include copper, lead, zinc, tin, nickel, tungsten, mercury, chromium, manganese, cobalt, molybdenum, aluminum, platinum, iron, and helium. Consumption of such minerals is proceeding so rapidly that reserve sources will be eventually depleted, substitutes will have to be found, and expensive mining of low-quality ores will have to be undertaken. As the under-

A solar heated home

Another approach to conserving heat and energy: An earth covered home

A geyser: Such geothermal activity may be a future source of energy

developed countries begin to industrialize, the demand for these nonrenewable minerals will far exceed the supply.

Too little water. Somewhat surprisingly, fresh water is also in short supply in the world. Ninety-seven percent of the world's water is salt water, with only 3 percent being fresh water.[24] Of this fresh water 98 percent is tied up in ice caps, particularly in Greenland and Antarctica.[25] Developed nations are using substantially more water per person than undeveloped nations. It has been estimated that an African uses 0.8 gallons of water a day, compared to 270 gallons for a New Yorker.[26]

Water is also needed in large quantities to produce food. A pound of wheat requires about 60 gallons of water, while a pound of meat requires from 2,500 to 6,000 gallons.[27] If irrigation efforts are expanded in the world to grow food, freshwater resources will obviously be depleted at a faster rate. Removing salt from water (desalinization) is now being done on a small scale, but it is so expensive that it is currently only being used for drinking purposes.

Air pollution. Industrialized nations, with high-consumption patterns, also have corresponding waste disposal problems. Environmental damage is most severe in large, densely populated, industrial centers. Some cities (such as Los Angeles) occasionally have such dense smog that even on some clear days there is a haze over the city. Moreover, it is not only the air over cities that is polluted, but the entire atmosphere of the earth is affected to some degree.

Air pollution not only rots windshield wiper blades and nylon stockings, blackens skies and clothes, damages crops, corrodes paint and steel, but is also a killer of people. Death rates are higher when and where smog occurs; especially for the very old, the very young, and those with respiratory ailments. Pollution contributes to a higher incidence of pneumonia, emphysema, lung cancer, and bronchitis. In 1952 the London smog disaster was directly linked to some 4,000 deaths. Such disasters are of substantially less significance than the far-reaching effects of day-to-day living in seriously polluted cities.

In the United States the national Public Health Service estimates that more than 140 million tons of carbon monoxide are being added annually to the atmosphere—about three quarters of a ton per person annually![28] Cars emit about 66 million tons of these pollutants, industrial centers (particularly pulp and paper mills, petroleum refineries, chemical plants, iron and steel mills) add a large share, and so does burning trash and burning fuel for heating homes and offices. Carbon monoxide is not the only pollutant being released into the air, others include nitrogen oxides, sulfur oxides, and hydrocarbons.

Air pollutants also have the potential for altering the earth's atmosphere and climate. Whether added pollutants will cause the climate to become warmer, or cooler, or have no effect is currently being debated. By reflecting sun rays away from the earth while in the atmosphere, pollutants could cause the earth to become cooler; on the other hand, by forming a layer over the earth, they could prevent heat from escaping.

Water pollution. The U.S. Public Health Service recently rated the water supply of 60 American cities as being a "potential health hazard" or as "unsatisfactory."[29] Reasons included tap impurities, infrequent testing for bacteria, and impure water sources. As the population grows in an industrial center, so does industry, which pours into the water a vast array of contaminants: detergents, sulfuric acid, lead, hydrofluoric acid, ammonia, and so on. Increased agricultural production also pollutes water via insecticides, herbicides and nitrates (from fertilizers). The result is the spread of pollution in creeks, streams, lakes, along coastlines (and most seriously) in groundwater where purification is almost impossible. Water pollution poses the threat of epidemics through hepatitis, dysentery, and poisoning by exotic chemicals. Some rivers and lakes are now

Smog in Los Angeles on a sunny day: Mountains a short distance away are obscured

so polluted they cannot support fish and other organisms which require relatively clean, oxygen-rich water; such lakes and rivers are accurately described as "dead."

There is a growing concern over acid rain. Formed from emissions from automobiles and industrial plants, acid rain has become a serious problem in eastern Canada and the northeastern United States. Acid rain is killing fish in lakes and streams, and is reducing the number of plant nutrients in the ground and thereby is making soil less fertile. It has also damaged timber, and may eventually start damaging man-made structures, including classic architecture and sculptures. Scientists estimate 50,000 lakes in the United States and Canada are now so polluted by acid rain that fish populations have either been destroyed or severely damaged.[30]

Canada Environment Minister John Fraser has called acid rain his country's "worst environment problem."[31] Acid rain is created when sulfur and nitrogen oxides emitted from automobiles and industrial plants combine with moisture in the air to form sulfuric and nitric acids.

General pollutants. Some substances— such as chlorinated hydrocarbons, lead, mercury and fluorides—reach us in so many ways that they are considered general pollutants. Of the chlorinated hydrocarbons, DDT has been used the longest, but now is banned. DDT is a synthetic insecticide. DDT as a chemical breaks down slowly; it will last for decades in soil. Unhappily, the way DDT circulates in ecosystems leads to a concentration in carnivores (flesh-eating animals and humans); that is, it becomes increasingly concentrated as it is passed along a food chain. Following World War II DDT was widely used as an insecticide until research involving laboratory animals showed DDT affects fertility, causes changes in brain functioning, and increases the incidence of cancer.[32] The long-term effects of DDT (and of many other general pollutants) are still unknown. DDT has a poisoning effect that may (or may not) lead to subtle physiological changes. Most mother's milk in the United States now contains a high enough level of DDT that it would be declared illegal in interstate commerce.[33] DDT was used extensively before research indicated it had dangerous long-term effects. An important question is: Among the thousands of chemicals currently being used, which ones have unknown toxic side effects?

In the 1970s Life Science Products Company and Allied Chemical Corporation were found guilty of safety violations in producing Kepone and of contaminating the James River in Virginia with Kepone through dumping.[34] Kepone is a chemical pesticide and a hydrocarbon similar to DDT. Production processes were so appalling that gray powdery Kepone dust covered everything in the small town of Hopewell, Virginia, where it was being produced. There were times when traffic was slowed by poor visibility caused by the blowing dust. Kepone causes a variety of detrimental effects—tremors, loss of weight, infertility, symptoms similar to alcoholism and drug addiction, and possibly cancer. The James River had to be closed to fishing because of contamination, and the Virginia fishing industry lost over $10 million in 1976 alone. The long-term effects of this Kepone contamination are as yet unknown.

Many other examples could be cited. In 1980 residents of Love Canal (a section of Niagara Falls, New York) were forced to abandon their homes because it was discovered that buried underground were 20,000 tons of toxic substances including highly lethal dioxin—dumped by Hooker Chemical & Plastic Company over a 25-year-period until 1953.[35] Studies found that residents of Love Canal were subject to higher rates of cancer, birth defects, miscarriages, and chromosome damage.

Chronic lead poisoning is also serious; it leads to loss of appetite, weakness, and apathy. It causes lesions of the neuromuscular system, circulatory system, gastrointestinal tract, and the brain. Exposure to lead comes from a variety of sources: combustion of gasoline, pesticides, lead pipes, from food and water, but perhaps is most hazardous when children eat paint containing lead.

Exposure to high concentrations of mercury may cause blindness, deafness, loss of coordination, severe emotional disorders, or even death. Mercury is added to the environment in many ways. It may leak into the water from industrial processes that produce chlorine. It is emitted by the pulp and paper industry. It is a primary ingredient of agri-

cultural fungicides. Small amounts are released when fossil fuels are burned.

Several problems. The above material highlights several national and international problems: large-scale starvation and malnourishment, rapid consumption of nonrenewable fossil fuels and minerals, food shortages, energy shortages, need to develop new energy sources, assuring the safety of nuclear energy power plants, shortage of water reserves, air pollution, water pollution, and general pollutants (some yet unknown) that cause slow, subtle physiological changes. Approaches to resolve these problems go well beyond the scope of this chapter. However, all are closely related to overpopulation. If the population growth rate is reversed to head toward a zero growth rate,

Modern burial mound

and even to go negative, it may give us the necessary time to find solutions to the above problems.

WHAT NEEDS TO BE DONE

Paul Ehrlich summarizes what is needed:

> We must rapidly bring the world population under control, reducing the growth rate to zero and eventually making it go negative. Conscious regulation of human numbers must be achieved. Simultaneously we must greatly increase our food production. This agricultural program should be carefully monitored to minimize deleterious effects on the environment and should include an effective program of ecosystem restoration. The world's supply of nonrenewable resources must be assessed and plans made for the most economical and beneficial management and use of what remains of them. As these projects are carried out, an international policy research program must be initiated to set optimum population-environment goals for the world and to divise methods for reaching these goals. So the answer is simple. Getting the job done, unfortunately, is going to be complex beyond belief—if indeed it can be done.[36]

Ehrlich then provides some specific recommendations for reaching this goal.

1. Being the most affluent and influential superpower, the United States should first "get its house in order" and set a model for population control.
2. Set a goal of a stable optimum population size for our country and display our determination to rapidly achieve this goal.
3. Reverse the government's current "reward" system for having children. Specific measures include:
   a. No longer allowing income tax deductions for children.
   b. Placing a luxury tax on layettes, diapers, cribs, expensive toys, and diaper services.
   c. Rewarding small-sized families by such measures as giving "responsibility prizes" to each man who had a vasectomy before having more than two children.
4. Subsidize adoptions and simplify adoption procedures.
5. Guarantee the right of any woman to have an abortion.
6. Enact a federal law requiring sex education in schools—sex education that includes material on the need for regulating the birthrate and the techniques of birth control.
7. Develop new contraceptives that are reliable, easy to use, and do not have harmful side effects.[37]

Bernard Berelson compiled a list of other proposals to control population, including:

1. Adding temporary sterilants to water or food supplies. Doses of an antidote would be carefully rationed by the government to produce the desired population size (such sterilants are not as yet in existence).
2. Compulsory sterilization of men with three or more living children.
3. Raising the minimum age of marriage.
4. Providing benefits (money, goods, or services) to couples not bearing children for extended time periods.
5. Requiring that foreign countries must establish effective population control programs before *any* foreign aid will be provided.[38]

Some of these proposals appear "too radical" and conflict with moral and ethical values. But will we reach such an overpopulation crisis that they may be necessary in the future? At our present growth, the world's population will double in 35 years.

As indicated previously, many underdeveloped nations are now providing sex education and family planning programs to their people, which (at least temporarily) is showing evidence of lowering birthrates. Hopefully, the population control measures recommended by Berelson can be avoided.

Paul Ehrlich et al. provide an elegant summary of the need to establish a worldwide vision of the future of the human race:

> Perhaps the major necessary ingredient that has been missing from a solution to the problems of both the United States and the rest of the world is a goal, a vision of the kind of Spaceship Earth that ought to be and the kind of crew that should man her. Society has always had its visionaries who talked of love, beauty, peace, and plenty. But somehow the "practical" men have always been there to praise smog as a sign of progress, to preach "just" wars, and to restrict love while giving hate free rein. It must be one of the greatest ironies of the history of the human species that the only salvation for the practical man now lies in what they think of as the dreams of idealists. The question now is: can the self-proclaimed "realists" be persuaded to face reality in time?[39]

THE ABORTION CONTROVERSY

If the world's population continues to grow at or near its present rate, the current controversy over voluntary abortions may look "pale" compared to controversies that will be generated if compulsory population control measures are needed.

The abortion controversy has now been going on for nearly two decades, but was heightened when in January 1973 the U.S. Supreme Court in a 7 to 2 decision overruled state laws that prohibited or restricted a woman's right to obtain an abortion durig the first three months of pregnancy. States still have the authority to impose increasing restrictions after the third month. In the last 10 weeks of pregnancy (a time when there is a good chance that the fetus will live) states may prohibit abortions if they desire, except where the life or health of the mother is endangered.

In 1977 Congress passed and President Carter signed into law the so-called Hyde Amendment (named for its original sponsor, Representative Henry Hyde from Illinois). This amendment bars Medicaid spending for abortions except when a woman's life would be endangered by childbirth or in cases of promptly reported rape or incest. In June 1980, this amendment of a 5–4 vote was upheld as constitutional by the U.S. Supreme Court. The ruling means that the federal government and individual states do not have to pay for most abortions wanted by women on welfare.

The Hyde Amendment is significant because between 1973 and 1977 more than one third of the legal abortions performed in the United States were for women on welfare.[40] The passage of the Hyde Amendment shows the strength of the anti-abortion forces in this country. Opponents of the Hyde Amendment fear that illegal "back alley" abortions may again be performed, with some women dying from medical complications.

One of the Republican platform positions in 1980 was to support a constitutional amendment to ban all abortions, except those needed to save a woman's life. In 1980 a number of liberal Democratic political leaders were defeated, partly because of their support for legalized abortions and their support for federal financing of abortions for those unable to pay. With the election of a number of conservatives in 1980, there are apt to be renewed efforts to restrict (or ban) access to legal abortions.

The major objection to permitting abortions is based on moral principles. The Roman Catholic Church views the abortion issue as one of the most important, current moral issues. This church, and the "right to life" groups condemn abortions as being synonymous to murder. They assert life begins at conception, and point out there is no phase during pregnancy in which there is a distinct, qualitative difference in the development of the fetus. The only reason the Roman Catholic Church views as acceptable for an abortion is when it is done to save the physical life of the mother. They justify this type of abortion on the principle of "double effect." The principle of double effect states that a morally evil action (an abortion) is allowable when it is the side effect of a morally good act (saving the life of the mother).

There are a number of arguments that have been advanced for permitting abortions: (*a*) If abortions were prohibited again, women would seek illegal abortions as they did in the past. Performed in a medical clinic or hospital, an abortion is a relatively safe operation, but performed under unsanitary conditions, perhaps by an inexperienced or unskilled abortionist, the operation is extremely dangerous and may even imperil the life of the woman. (*b*) If abortions were again prohibited, some women would again attempt to self-induce abortions. Attempts at self-induced abortions can be extremely dangerous. Women have tried such techniques as severe exercise, hot baths, pelvic and intestinal irritants, and even attempted to lacerate the uterus with such sharp objects as hatpins, nail files, and knives. (*c*) Recognizing abortions as being legal helps prevent the birth of unwanted babies; such babies have a higher probability of being abused or neglected. (*d*) Permitting women to obtain an abortion allows women to have greater freedom as they would not be forced to raise a child at a time when they had other plans and commitments.

Personal opinion. Fifteen years ago I was opposed to allowing abortions on the "right

A pro-abortion demonstration

to life" principle. At that time I felt that the "right to life" was *the* most basic right that anyone had and should in no way be infringed upon. Then, our society became increasingly informed about the dangers of overpopulation and its associated problems. It gradually dawned on me that there may be a more basic right than the right to life; that is, the preservation of the quality of life. Given the overpopulation problem and given the fact that abortion is a necessary population control technique (in some countries the number of abortions is approaching the number of live births); I arrived at the conclusion that abortions are a

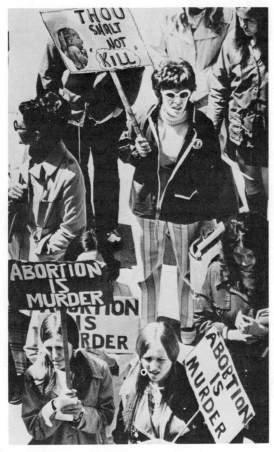

An anti-abortion demonstration

necessary measure (although less desirable than contraceptives) to preserve the quality of life. Unless life has quality, the right to life is meaningless.

FAMILY PLANNING

Family planning services are obviously essential programs for population control. Such services include providing birth control information and contraceptives, pregnancy testing, infertility counseling (family planning includes helping couples who desire children to have children), sex education,

abortion counseling and abortions, counseling on child spacing, sterilization—information and techniques, and helping couples to prepare for parenthood. Such services not only are important for populaton control, but also help individuals and couples with personal needs and circumstances.

Governmental programs. National family planning programs are governmental efforts to lower birthrates by funding programs that provide birth control information and services. With family planning programs families voluntarily decide whether to limit the number of children they have. Most countries, including underdeveloped and developed nations, now have official family planning programs. This is a remarkable achievement since 25 years ago no underdeveloped country had a governmental family planning program.[41] (In fact, 25 years ago several countries had programs with the opposite objectives—programs designed to increase the birthrate and the rate of immigration). These statistics indicate that concern about world population growth is a recent phenomenon.

In spite of these advances no nation has established a comprehensive population policy that sets population goals (limits). No country has yet adopted zero population as a policy goal. In popular usage zero population means that the birthrate is equal to the death rate. Zero population growth is roughly equivalent to an average of two children per family.

The only country to establish a population control policy is India.[42] Population control is the deliberate regulation of the size of the population by society. (Family planning, in contrast, is the regulaton of births by individual families.) India launched a population control program in 1976, but it did not last long. In 1976 India passed legislation which urged individual states to establish a compulsory sterilization program. The only state to pass such a bill was Maharashtra, which contains the city of Bombay. Sterilization was required after the birth of three children. From April through December 1976, more than 7 million sterilizations were reportedly performed in India.[43] However, resistance to the policy arose, and in some instances rioting resulting in fatalities occurred. The government of Indira Gandhi was toppled, partly as a reaction to the compulsory sterilization program. The officials who replaced Gandhi then returned to advocating a voluntary family planning program. (Indira Gandhi has since returned to power.) Whether India will attempt to enact another population control policy is unclear—future population growth may be a decisive factor in determining whether population control is necessary.

Until President Lyndon Johnson's 1965 State of the Union address, family planning was not considered a proper concern for our government. In his address, President Johnson stated that $5 spent on family planning was worth $100 invested in some other area of world economic development. In 1966 the Department of Health, Education and Welfare developed regulations which for the first time allowed federal funds to provide family planning services to welfare clients on a voluntary basis. Unfortunately, the avowed purpose of this policy (which was widely criticized) was not phrased in terms of family planning goals, but instead had the objectives of reducing the welfare burden by lowering the illegitimacy rate and of breaking the poverty cycle by decreasing the transmission of poverty from one generation to another.

The National Center for Family Planning Services was established by the passage of the Family Planning Services and Population Research Act of 1970. This act recognized that family planning was part of the delivery of comprehensive health services for all. In 1972 Congress mandated that family planning services must be provided to all welfare recipients who desired them. At that time contraceptive policy changes were also made which lifted restrictions on marital status and age for receiving birth control information and devices.

Private agencies. In the United States most family planning services have in the past been provided by private agencies and organizations. The largest and best known organization is Planned Parenthood. This organization was founded in 1916 by Margaret

---

HUMOROUS, TRUE, AND SAD	One of the reasons for India's overpopulation problem is that it is often difficult to make the natives understand how to use birth control methods properly.
	Recently, a family planning worker showed residents of a rural village how to use condoms by unrolling one over a broomstick handle.
	Returning to the village a year later, the worker found a large number of new babies.
	The natives were as puzzled as he. Before intercourse, they had dutifully put condoms on their broomsticks.
	SOURCE: "Facts," *National Lampoon,* November 1976, p. 34

Sanger with the opening of the first birth control clinic in Brooklyn. The organization now has clinics located throughout the nation. Planned Parenthood now offers: (*a*) Medical services—physical examinations, pap smear tests, urine and blood tests, venereal disease screening, all medically approved methods of contraception, pregnancy testing. (*b*) Counseling services—infertility, premarital, contraceptive, pregnancy, sterilization for males and for females.(*c*) Educational services—sex education, contraceptive information including effectiveness and side effects of the varied approaches, breast self-examinations.

Family planning services are presently available in practically all areas in the United States from a variety of public and private organizations, including: health departments, hospitals, physicians in private practice, Planned Parenthood affiliates, and other agencies, such as community action groups and free clinics.

Ranking of effectiveness of contraceptives in preventing pregnancies

1. Sterilization
2. Oral progestin-estrogen (the pill)
3. Intrauterine devices
4. Diaphragm and spermicide
5. Condom
6. Withdrawal
7. Spermicide alone (spermicides are agents such as contraceptive creams, foams and jellies that destroy sperm cells)
8. Rhythm
9. Douche

Note: After the first four or five listed contraceptives, the risk of pregnancy for sexually active users is sharply increased.
SOURCE: William Petersen, *Population*, 3d ed. (New York: Macmillan Publishing Co., 1975).

Is the Pill safe?

The most frequently used method of contraception is the pill. However, considerable concern has been raised in recent years about the adverse medical effects of birth control pills. Estrogens are a major ingredient of birth control pills, and are primarily responsible for the side effects that may occur. But estrogens are also used for other purposes—to treat the symptoms of menopause, and later as a postmenopausal pill as some women believe estrogen helps make them feel and look better.

In 1976 Alexander Schmidt, commissioner of the Food and Drug Administration, summarized what is known about the benefits and side effects of estrogens and birth control pills.[44]

1. Except for sterilization procedures, the pill is the most effective means of contraception. It is over 99 percent effective when used properly. It is somewhat more effective than an intrauterine device, and much more effective than the diaphragm and the condom.
2. The pill can help regulate a woman's menstrual cycle and is free of all but minor side effects for most women.
3. The most serious risk is an increased tendency for blood clots to form. A clot that forms in a vein may break off, travel to the lungs, and cause a pulmonary embolism, which may be fatal. Blood clots that form in arteries may travel to the heart (causing a heart attack) or travel to the brain (causing a stroke).
4. If the pill fails to prevent pregnancy (although it seldom does) it may harm the fetus. Any woman on the pill who believes she is pregnant should see a doctor immediately.
5. Birth control pills may on rare occasions cause liver tumors, nearly all of which are benign.
6. Birth control pills approximately double the risk of developing gallstones.

7. In some women the pill may increase blood pressure, although the blood pressure usually returns to normal when use of the pill is discontinued.

8. Minor side effects that are not dangerous may include nausea, vomiting, tender breasts, weight gain or loss, unexpected vaginal bleeding or change in menstrual cycle.

9. The actual number of women who have serious side effects is very small. Of all women using the pill, about three out of every 100,000 will die each year from complications of the pill. In contrast, the death rate with the intrauterine device is about one per 100,000 per year.

10. For sexually active women the pill is safer than using no contraceptives, because about 25 women per 100,000 who are pregnant die from complications of pregnancy.

11. The rate of blood clotting and heart attacks while using the pill increases with age, especially for women in their late 30s and early 40s. The risks of other contraceptives are unrelated to age. For these reasons the Food and Drug Administration (FDA) recommends that women over 40 should use some other method of contraception.

12. Any woman taking the pill should be examined regularly by a physician.

13. The FDA recommends that women with a history of breast cancer or cancer of the uterus or of blood clotting should not take a pill.

14. A number of physicians also recommend that the following women should not use the pill: those with migraine headaches, mental depression, fibroids of the uterus, heart or kidney disease, asthma, high blood pressure, diabetes, and epilepsy.

15. When women cease taking the pill, there may be a delay in the return of menstruation and lactation, as well as a loss of hair and a recurrence of acne in rare cases.

The FDA feels strongly that women should understand the purposes of the pill, the benefits, the risks, and the alternatives, and then personally be involved in the decision whether to take the pill. Every medicine has risks as well as benefits, and it is partly up to the individual to decide whether the benefits outweigh the risks.

Social work and family planning

Social workers tend to be concerned about overpopulation and the problems it is creating now, and the even greater problems it may create in the future. In almost every social service agency, social workers come in contact with clients who want and need family planning information. In their work social workers also must respond to controversial issues: for example, possible racist implications when family planning services are directed at serving the poor, providing abortion information and making referrals, providing contraceptive information to teenagers, and responding to those who advocate involuntary sterilization of people who are seriously handicapped with hereditary conditions.

An emerging career opportunity. Few social workers are now employed in settings where the primary service is family planning. Yet, many roles in family planning are well suited for social workers: premarital counseling, pregnancy counseling, providing contraceptive information including effectiveness and side effects of the varied approaches, sex education services, VD counseling, abortion counseling, counseling for couples who are sterile and desire children, and community organization efforts to develop family planning services in the area and create a community atmosphere that is accepting of family planning as a legitimate service. Now, family planning counseling is fragmented in many communities, with a wide variety of agencies providing counseling on a few of the above areas—public health departments provide VD counseling, adoption agencies provide counseling for couples who are sterile, medical clinics which perform abortions provide abortion counseling, public welfare departments provide contraceptive information for clients, Family Service agencies provide premarital counseling, and so on.

There are several reasons for anticipating that family planning services will be expanded in future years, thereby creating new career opportunities for social workers. The general public is increasingly becoming aware of the dangers of overpopulation. There has been a growing acceptance and utilization in our society of contraceptives, sex education, and abortions. The federal government has in recent years recognized that family planning services need to be expanded and further developed. The recently created National Center for Family Planning Services is anticipating an expansion of family planning services through existing social and health-related agencies, and is predicting new career opportunities for social workers in family planning.[45]

Increasingly social workers are being hired in specialized agencies that deal with family planning—Planned Parenthood, maternal and child health clinics, and agencies providing abortions and abortion counseling.

School social workers have become increasingly involved in family planning activities in connection with sex education for sexually active teenagers. Social workers in single-parent units of social services departments (also called public welfare or human services departments) are heavily involved in providing family planning services. Social workers in many other settings are also heavily involved in providing family planning services; for example, in pediatrics and gynecology departments in hospitals and clinics, child welfare agencies, and residential treatment facilities for teenagers.

Family planning education. Unfortunately very few undergraduate and graduate social work programs have family planning courses. A number of programs do provide some family planning instructional units in other courses. In reviewing the extent of family planning education in social work, Ketayun H. Gould concludes, "If social work is to play a significant role in family planning and in social policy related to population problems, the schools of social work have to provide effective educational programs."[46]

In-service training in family planning is also needed and being requested by practicing social workers. Since family planning information for clients is provided to some extent by most social agencies, an extensive in-service training effort is probably needed. A survey of two country welfare departments in Michigan and Illinois conducted a few years ago found that 84 percent of the social workers felt family planning in-service training would be helpful.[47] Specific content areas requested were factual information about birth control methods, clarification of the agency's family planning policy, counseling techniques for family planning, and information about other family planning services in the community.

The future. A national policy on family planning is needed. Currently, there is considerable controversy on a number of issues associated with family planning: sex education in schools, abortions, providing birth control information and devices for teen-agers, and the issue whether the federal government should pay for abortions for those who cannot afford them.

In the United States public family planning centers have been concentrated in poor communities and in nonwhite communities. Middle-class families primarily receive family planning services from private agencies and from private physicians. Some leaders of nonwhite communities have charged that public family planning centers have a "geno-cide" objective—that is, the objective of reducing the size of the nonwhite community.[48] Social workers need to recognize that family planning is not an antipoverty measure, and need to understand that our country's historical treatment of nonwhite groups justifiably makes nonwhites suspicious of outside efforts to limit the number of births. Family planning should not simply seek to limit births, but should be part of a comprehensive approach to health care.

If problems associated with overpopulation continue to intensify, a national policy on population control may also need to be developed. Populaton control is the deliberate regulation of populaton size by a society. A number of authorities are predicting dire consequences for the future of the world unless population control measures are implemented immediately. Other authorities discount overpopulation concerns and predict technological advancements will prevent cataclysmic effects from rapid population growth. If the latter are mistaken, a few years from now we may be forced to apply population control measures that now seem unethical and "inhumane." Whatever the future it is essential that social workers are prepared to function as practitioners and advocates of family planning. Being prepared not only involves acquiring the necessary knowledge of family planning information and counseling techniques, but also an examination of one's value structure (toward such issues as sex education and abortions) and the development of a value system that is consistent with family planning objectives.

SUMMARY

Problems associated with overpopulation are very serious and may have an adverse, dramatic effect on the quality of life in the future.

The world's population has more than doubled in size since 1930. At current growth rates, the population will again double in size in the next 35 years. Already we are experiencing resource crises. Some of the problems associated with overpopulation are:

1. Too little food—At the present time a large proportion of the people in the world are undernourished.
2. Too little energy—We currently have an energy crisis. Fossil fuel resources (oil, coal, and natural gas) which provide over nine tenths of the world's energy consumption are rapidly being depleted.
3. Too little water—Fresh water is in short supply.
4. Mineral resources are being depleted—Essential elements such as copper, zinc, iron, and manganese are increasingly becoming in short supply.
5. Air pollution—In large industrial centers air pollution is increasingly becoming a health hazard.
6. Water pollution—Water pollution is also a serious health hazard; some rivers and lakes are now so polluted they cannot support fish and other organisms.
7. General pollutants—Increasingly we are becoming aware of the harmful effects of such pollutants as lead, mercury, DDT, and other chlorinated hydrocarbons.

Unless the size of the world's population is brought under control, the above problems are apt to intensify. A number of proposals have been advanced to curtail the growth of the world's population, some of which if implemented would radically change current lifestyles.

Family planning services are essential programs for population control. Social workers are increasingly being employed in settings that offer family planning services. Family planning appears to be an emerging career field for social work as many roles are well suited for social workers: premarital counseling, pregnancy counseling, providing contraceptive information, sex education services, abortion counseling, VD counseling, and community organization efforts to further develop family planning services.

NOTES

1. Bernard D. Nossiter, "World Population Growth Falling," *Wisconsin State Journal*, June 15, 1980, sect. 1, p. 16; and Paul R. Ehrlich, Anne H. Ehrlich, and John P. Holdren, *Human Ecology: Problems and Solutions* (San Francisco: W. H. Freeman, 1973), p. 21.

2. Paul R. Ehrlich, *The Population Bomb* (New York: Ballantine Books, 1971).

3. Ketayun H. Gould, "Population and Family Planning," in *Contemporary Social Work*, ed. Donald Brieland et al. (New York: McGraw-Hill, 1975), p. 127.

4. Ehrlich, *Population Bomb*, p. 7.

5. Lee Rainwater, *And the Poor Get Children* (Chicago: Quadrangle Books, 1960).

6. Donald C. Bacon "Poor vs. Rich: A Global Struggle," *U.S. News & World Report*, July 31, 1978, p. 57.

7. Ehrlich, *Population Bomb*, p. 8.

8. John D. Moorhead, "Cost of Children Soars," *Wisconsin State Journal*, January 16, 1979, sect. 3, p. 1.

9. Ehrlich, *Population Bomb*, p. 129.

10. "Where Population Bomb Has Stopped Ticking," *U.S. News & World Report*, November 26, 1979, p. 94.

11. Ibid., p. 94.

12. Ibid., p. 95.

13. Rufus E. Miles, Jr., statement made at the hearings of the President's Commission on Population Growth and the American Future, April 15, 1971, *Population Bulletin* 27 (June 1971), p. 13.

14. Bacon, "Poor vs. Rich," p. 58.

15. Ehrlich, et al., *Human Ecology*, p. 227.

16. Gould, "Population and Family Planning," p. 129.

17. Thomas R. Malthus, *On Population*, ed. Gertrude Himmelfarb, (New York: Modern Library, 1960), pp. 13–14. (Original edition in 1798.)

18. Roger Revelle, "Food and Population," in *The Human Population: A Scientific American Book*, ed. Scientific American editors (San Francisco: W. H. Freeman, 1974), pp. 119–30.

19. Gould, "Population and Family Planning," p. 130.

20. M. King Hubbert, "Energy Resources," in *Resources and Man* (San Francisco: W. H. Freeman, 1969).

21. "Fuels for America's Future," *U.S. News & World Report*, August 13, 1979, p. 33.

22. Ibid., p. 32.

23. Ibid., p. 33.

24. Paul R. Ehrlich and Anne H. Ehrlich, *Population, Resources, Environment* (San Francisco: W. H. Freeman, 1970), p. 65.

25. Ibid., p. 65.

26. "Warning: Water Shortages Ahead," *Time*, April 4, 1977, p. 48.

27. Gould, "Population and Family Planning," p. 130.

28. Ehrlich and Ehrlich, *Population, Resources, Environment*, pp. 118–19.

29. Ibid., p. 126.

30. "The Growing Furor over Acid Rain," *U.S. News & World Report*, November 19, 1979, p. 66.

31. Ibid., p. 66.

32. Ehrlich, *Population Bomb*, pp. 31–35.

33. Ehrlich et al., *Human Ecology*, p. 132.

34. Thomas Sullivan, et al., *Social Problems* (New York: Wiley, pp. 155–62.

35. Robert A. Kittle, "Living with Uncertainty: Sage of Love Canal Families," *U.S. News & World Report*, June 2, 1980, p. 32.

36. Ehrlich, *Population Bomb*, p. 127.

37. Ibid., pp. 127–45.

38. Bernard Berelson, "The Present State of Family Planning Programs," *Studies in Family Planning* 57 (September 1970), p. 2.

39. Ehrlich, et al., *Human Ecology*, p. 279.

40. "Abortion Foes Gain Victory," *Wisconsin State Journal*, July 1, 1980, sect. 1, p. 1.

41. W. Parker Mauldin, "Family Planning Programs and Fertility Declines in Developing Countries,"

Family Planning Perspectives 7 (January–February 1975): 32.

42. Lynn C. Landman, "Birth Control in India: The Carrot and the Rod?" *Family Planning Perspectives* 9 (May–June 1977): 102.

43. Ibid., p. 102.

44. Alexander M. Schmidt, "Estrogens and the Pill," *Parade Magazine,* September 19, 1976, pp. 10–12.

45. National Center for Family Planning Services, *Family Planning Digest* (Washington, D.C.: U.S. Department of Health, Education and Welfare, March 1972).

46. Gould, "Population and Family Planning," p. 136.

47. Alice A. Varela, "Developing an In-Service Training Program for Social Workers on Family Planning," in *The Social Worker and Family Planning,* ed. Joanna F. Gorman (Berkeley, Calif.: University of California Press, 1970).

48. Gould, "Population and Family Planning," p. 138.

chapter 19

"THE BEST YEARS OF YOUR LIFE"	This is Tom Townsend. He had been with the iron works plant 42 years. Being promoted to foreman 16 years ago had fulfilled his dreams, and there was nothing he desired more than to be on the job and managing his crew. He had been married to Laura for the past 37 years. At first their marriage had some rough moments, but Laura and Tom had long since grown accustomed and comfortable with each other. She was a fine woman, and her main job was managing the home. They had had two children who had grown up, moved away, and now had homes of their own.

Life was at the factory for Tom. He didn't have time to develop other hobbies and interests, nor was he interested in picnics or socials. When he had time off from work he used it to repair things around home and to "tool up" for getting back to work.

Television replaced talk in his home, and Tom usually spent weekends watching a variety of sports programs.

One day it was May 18, and Tom was 70. The company marked the occasion with a dinner that was well attended. Tom and Laura were there, along with their children and families, the members of Tom's crew and their wives, and the company managers and their wives. Everyone at first was a little anxious as these people did not often get together with each other socially. The dinner, however, went fairly well. Tom was congratulated by everyone, received a gold watch, and made appropriate remarks about his positive feelings about the company. After a few more cocktails everyone went home. Tom was feeling sentimental, but also good about himself because everyone was acknowledging his contributions.

Problems experienced by the elderly; gerontological services

Tom awoke at 7 o'clock the next morning, the usual time for him to get ready for work. Then it hit him. He was retired, with nowhere to go and no reason for rising. His life at the plant was over. What should he now do? He didn't know.

He spent the next week following Laura around the house, getting on her nerves. At times he complained about feeling useless. Twice he commented he wished he were dead. He went back to the plant to see his men, but they were too busy to talk. Besides, there was Bill who had been promoted to foreman who enjoyed showing Tom how the department's productivity had increased, and bored Tom with his plans for making changes to further increase production.

Long walks didn't help much, either. As he walked he thought about his plight and became more depressed. What was he going to do? What could he find to meaningfully occupy his time? He looked into a mirror and saw his receding hairline and numerous wrinkles. More and more he started to feel a variety of aches and pains. He thought to himself, "I guess I'm just a useless old man." He wondered what the future would hold. Would his company pension keep pace with increasing bills? Would he eventually be placed in a nursing home? What was he going to do with the remainder of his life? He just didn't know.

Tom Townsend, at least at the present time, had no serious financial concerns. Gordon and Walter Moss describe the plight of someone who is old and poor:

An old woman turned quickly away from the dismal scene outside her Florida hotel room window. Listlessly, she mixed her own breakfast: a cup of Sanka and a small glass of Tang. After finishing her breakfast, she looked at her wardrobe. It contained a few unwanted dresses given to her by a relative, and one she had bought herself seven years ago. After choosing one, she made her bed and dusted her dresser, two small tables, and their lamps. She then turned on a small fan in anticipation of a hot muggy day, wound her clock, straightened her small pile of old books, blew dust from the artificial flowers in a cheap vase, and sat down in her only chair to watch television. Finally, it was noon, time for her to go down to the church for a hot lunch. In the afternoon, she would watch television soap operas, or perhaps spend an hour or two visiting with the many other widows in the hotel.

All the while, uncertainty gnawed at her. Already she was paying over half of her small retirement and welfare income for rent; and if the rent went up anymore she would be unable to stay. The hot lunch, sponsored by the federal government, cost her only 50 cents and helped a little. Nevertheless, due especially to medical bills, she frequently ran out of money before the end of the month.

Her ulcer was her biggest worry. A few weeks earlier, it had started to bleed, and she had passed out. She had lain helpless for some time before finally managing to crawl to the phone. The desk clerk and some friends had then helped her get to the hospital. She had been more fortunate than some others in the hotel. Their lives had ended in their rooms because they had been too weak from malnutrition to crawl for help.[1]

Do these two stories sound like sentimental fiction? We wish! Sadly, however, these accounts are typical retirements turned into nightmares.[2]

Throughout time, some primitive societies have abandoned their enfeebled old. The Crow, Creek, and Hopi Indians, for example, built special huts away from the tribe where the old were left to die. The Eskimos left the incapacitated elderly in snowbanks, or forced them to paddle away in a kayak. The Siriono of the Bolivian forest simply left them behind when they moved on in search of food.[3]

Although we might consider such customs to be shocking and barbaric, have we not also abandoned the old? We force them to retire when many are still productive. All too often, when a person is forced to retire, his/her status, power, and self-esteem are lost. Also, in a physical sense we seldom have a place for large numbers of older people. Community facilities—parks, subways, libraries—are oriented to serving children and young people. Most housing is designed and priced for the young couple with one or two children and an annual income in excess of $15,000. If the elderly are not able to care for themselves (and if their families are unable to care for them) we "store" them away from society in nursing homes. Our abandonment of the elderly is further indicated by our taking little action to relieve financial problems of the elderly as 27 percent of the elderly who live alone are in poverty.[4]

WHAT IS OLD AGE?

Elizabeth Ferguson describes some of our myths and stereotypes about the elderly:

Stereotyped notions about aging and the elderly exist in all segments of the population. Many of them are myths, but they are held tenaciously, and sound data to rebut them are scarce. The aging are generally thought to be less intelligent, less able to learn, more rigid, riskier as employees, less ambitious, and therefore more easily satisfied, less able to adapt and cope. How often these stereotypes turn into self-fulfilling prophecies is not known, but the existence of those who refute all the myths should be more widely publicized.[5]

Age need not be a barrier to making major contributions

At age 80 George Burns received his first academy award for his role in *The Sunshine Boys.*

At 81 Johann Wolfgang von Goethe finished writing *Faust.*

At 81 Benjamin Franklin mediated the compromise that led to the adoption of the U.S. Constitution.

At 82 Leo Tolstoy wrote *I Cannot Be Silent.*

At 82 Winston Churchill finished his four-volume text, *A History of the English-Speaking Peoples.*

At 84 W. Somerset Maugham wrote *Points of View.*

At 88 Konrad Adenauer was Chancellor of Germany.

At 88 Michelangelo designed the Church of Santa Maria degli Angeli.

At 88 Pablo Casals was presenting cello concerts.

At 89 Artur Rubinstein gave a critically acclaimed recital in Carnegie Hall, New York City.

At 89 Mary Baker Eddy was heading the Christian Science Church.

At 89 Albert Schweitzer was directing a hospital in Africa.

At 90 Pablo Picasso was producing engravings and drawings.

At 91 Eamon de Valera was president of Ireland.

At 91 Adolf Zukor was chairman of Paramount Pictures.

At 93 George Bernard Shaw wrote a play entitled "Farfetched Fables."

At 94 Bernard Russell headed international peace drives.

At 100 Grandma Moses was still painting.

SOURCE: *U.S. News & World Report,* September 1, 1980, pp. 52–53.

On the other hand, the mass media portray retired people as able to travel and play golf, in good health, sunning themselves in warm climates in the winter, and free of money worries. For the "young aging," particularly those in upper income groups, there is some validity to this stereotype.

Attention to the social and physical needs of the elderly is a relatively new field. In prior societies few persons survived to advanced ages. Life expectancy has increased dramatically in America since the turn of the century—up from 49 years in 1900 to 72 years in 1977.[6] Also, in most other societies, in contrast to ours, the elderly had some meaningful role to perform; as arbitrators and advisers, as landowners and leaders, as repositories of the wisdom of the tribe, as performers of tasks within their own capabilities.

Members of primitive tribes often do not know how old they are. In contrast, chronological age is very important to us. Our passage through life is partially governed by our age. Chronological age controls when we are old enough to go to school, to drive a car, to marry, or to vote. Our society has also generally selected 65 as the beginning of old age.

In primitive societies "old age" is generally determined by physical and mental conditions rather than by chronological age. Primitive societies' definition of "old age" is more accurate than ours. Everyone is not in the same mental and physical condition at age 65. Aging is an individual process which occurs at differing rates in different people, and social-psychological factors may retard or accelerate the physiological changes.

The process of aging is called *senescence.* Senescence is the normal process of change in the body that accompanies aging. Senescence affects different persons at different rates. Also, the processes affected by aging vary between persons. Visible signs of aging include the appearance of wrinkled skin, graying and thinning of hair, and stooped or shortened posture from compressed spinal disks.

As a person ages, blood vessels, tendons, the skin, and connective tissue lose their elasticity. Hardening of blood vessels and stiffening of joints occur. Many of the health problems faced by the aged result from a general decline of the circulatory system. Reduced blood supply impairs mental sharpness, interferes with balance and reduces the effectiveness of the muscles and body organs. The probability of strokes and heart attacks also increases.

As a person ages, the muscles lose some of their strength, and coordination and endurance become more difficult. There is also a decline in the functioning of such body organs as the lungs, kidneys, and to a lesser extent the brain. Fortunately, the degree to which one's body loses its vitality can be influenced by one's lifestyle. People who are mentally and physically active throughout their younger years remain more alert and vigorous in their later years.

As senescence proceeds, hearing and vision capacities decline, food may not taste the same, the sense of touch may become less sensitive, and there may be a loss of memory of recent and past events.

A key notion to remember about senescence is that no dramatic decline need take place at one's 65th birthday or at any other age. We are all slowly aging throughout our lives. The rate at which we age depends on many factors. A large number of elderly are physically active and mentally alert. Unfortunately, in describing the process of aging, it gives the impression that the physical and mental functioning of the elderly person are reduced to a minimal level. Although the functioning of these processes may be at a somewhat lower level, the processes are functioning at a high enough level to enable a large number of elderly to be physically active and mentally alert!

In defining "old age" the federal government generally uses a chronological cutoff

---

AGE NEED NOT BE A BARRIER TO ATHLETIC EXERCISES

Jodi Durkee celebrated her 70th birthday last week by swimming across Lake George. She said she was thinking of swimming over and back for next year's birthday. "I feel great," Mrs. Durkee, a great-grandmother, said after completing the mile and a half swim in an hour and 20 minutes. "I just want to prove that just because you get old, you don't have to put yourself on a shelf somewhere." Mrs. Durkee, aquatic director at the Glens Falls, N. Y. YMCA, said before churning across the lake.

Wisconsin State Journal, **August 8, 1977.**

---

point—age 65—to separate elderly adults from others. There is nothing magical or particularly scientific about age 65. In 1883 the Germans set age 65 as the criterion of aging for the world's first modern social security system for the elderly.[7] When the Social Security Act was passed in 1935, the United States also selected age 65 as the eligibility age level for retirement benefits, based on the German model.

WHY IS OLD AGE A PROBLEM TODAY?

Old age is a problem because our society is creating a large elderly population that has little practical use to our society.

An increasing aged population. The aged are partially a problem for our society because there are now eight times as many people age 65 and older than there were at the turn of the century. Table 19–1 shows the number of older people has steadily been increasing.

There are several reasons for the phenomenal growth of the older population. The improved care of expectant mothers and newborn infants has reduced the infant mortality rate, allowing an increased proportion of those born to live to old age. New drugs, better sanitation, and other medical advances have increased the life expectancy of Americans from 49 years in 1900 to 72 years

TABLE 19–1 Composition of U.S. population age 65 and older

	Year			
	1900	*1950*	*1970*	*1980*
Number of older persons (in millions)...............	3	12	20	25
Percent of total population ..	4	8	9.5	11

SOURCE: Matilda W. Riley and Anne Foner, *Aging and Society,* vol. 1: *An Inventory of Research Findings* (New York: Russell Sage, 1968), p. 18; and "How Population Shifts Are Changing America," *U.S. News & World Report,* March 5, 1979, pp. 76–79.

in 1977.[8] Another reason for the increasing proportion of the aged is that the birthrate is declining, fewer babies are being born.

Low status. The aged are also a social problem because we have generally been unsuccessful in finding something important or satisfying for the old to do. In most primitive and earlier societies, the old were respected and viewed as useful to their people to a much greater degree than is the case in our society. Industrialization and the growth of modern society have robbed the old of a high status in our society. Prior to industrialization, older people were the primary owners of property. Land was the most important source of power, and therefore the elderly controlled much of the economic and political power. Now, people primarily earn their living in the job market, and the vast majority of the aged own little land and are viewed as having no salable labor.

In earlier societies the elderly were also valued because of the knowledge they possessed. Their experiences enabled them to supervise planting and harvesting, and to pass on knowledge about hunting, housing, and craft making. The elderly also played key roles in preserving and transmitting the culture. But when books became widespread and with the rapid advance of science and technology, old people became less valuable as storehouses of culture and records.

The low status of the elderly is closely associated with "agism." The term *agism* refers to the negative image and attitudes toward an individual simply because he or she is old. Today the reaction to the elderly by many people is a negative one. Agism is like sexism or racism because it involves discrimination and prejudice against all members of a particular social category. Two hundred years ago the elderly had a high status in our society. The status of the elderly has declined for several reasons. The elderly no longer hold positions of economic power. Children no longer learn their future profession or trade from their parents—instead such skills are learned through other institutions such as the school system. In addition, the children of the elderly no longer are dependent on their parents for their livelihood as they generally are capable of making a living through a trade or profession that is independent of their parents. Finally, the elderly no longer perform tasks that are viewed as essential by society—often the older workers' skills are viewed as outmoded even before they retire.

The prejudice against the elderly is shown in everyday language by the use of terms that no racial or ethnic group would ever accept—"old buzzard," "old biddy," "old fogy."

From a rational view agism makes no sense because those who delight in discriminating against the elderly will one day be old themselves.

Early retirement. The maintenance of a high rate of employment in our society is a major goal. One instrument that our society uses to keep the work force reduced to a level in line with demand is mandatory retirement at a certain age, such as 65 or 70. In many occupations the supply of labor is exceeding the demand. An often used remedy for the oversupply of available employees is the encouragement of ever earlier retirement. Forced retirements often create financial and psychological burdens that retirees usually face without much assistance or preparation.

Our massive social security program supports early retirement, as retirement can some as early as 62. Pension plans of some companies and craft unions make it financially attractive to retire as early as 55. Perhaps the extreme case is the armed forces which permits retirement on full benefits after 20 years' service as early as age 38.

Many workers who retire early supplement their pension by obtaining another job, usually of a lower status.

More than 80 percent of Americans 65 years of age and older are retired even though many are intellectually and physically capable of working.[9]

Early retirement has some advantages to society, such as reducing the labor supply and allowing younger employees to advance faster. But there are also some serious disadvantages. For society the total bill for retirement pensions is already huge and still growing. For the retiree it means facing a new life and status without much preparation or assistance. While our society has developed educational and other institutions to prepare the young for the work world, it has not developed comparable institutions to prepare the elderly for retirement. Being without a job in our work-oriented society is often a reality shock for older people.

In our society we still view a person's worth partly in terms of his/her work. People often develop their self-image (their sense of who they are) in terms of their occupation— "I am a teacher," "I am a barber," "I am a doctor." Because the later years generally provide no exciting new roles to replace the occupational roles lost upon retirement, a retiree cannot proudly say "I am a. . . ." Instead, s/he must say, "I *was* a good. . . ." The more a person's life revolves around work, the more difficult retirement is apt to be.

There are several myths about the older worker that have been widely believed by employers and the general public. Older workers are thought to be less healthy, clumsier, more prone to absenteeism, more accident prone, more forgetful, and slower in task performance.[10] Research has shown these myths to be erroneous. Older workers have lower turnover rates, produce at a steadier rate, make fewer mistakes, have a more positive attitude toward their work, and exceed younger employees in health and low-on-the-job injury rates.[11] However, if the older worker does become ill, s/he usually takes a somewhat longer time to recover.[12]

Proponents of mandatory retirement advance several reasons for maintaining this system. First, there are simply not enough jobs for everyone. If the system were abolished, some older persons would probably work longer and thereby prevent some younger persons from obtaining those jobs. Second, younger employees would find promotions less frequent as the better positions would be held for a longer period by older workers. Third, some employers argue that

abolishing mandatory retirement would force them into the unpleasant task of firing older workers who no longer are productive. They assert mandatory retirement now serves as a socially acceptable way to remove unproductive older workers. Fourth, because of seniority and pay increases over the years, older workers are generally paid more than younger workers. Some employers argue that being forced to continue to employ older workers would increase production costs, and thereby force companies to either raise prices or employ fewer people.

Proponents of eliminating mandatory retirement argue that the system is clearly discriminating against the elderly. They assert a person's ability should be the main criterion of who works. Mandatory retirement often results in forcing older people into unwanted idleness and a reduced standard of living.

It would seem far better if workers who are still productive could stay on the job longer on a part- or full-time basis, rather than being unemployed on a pension plan, or being forced to take another job of a lower status.

Emphasis on youth. Our society fears aging and old age more than most other societies. Our emphasis on youth is indicated by our dread of getting gray hair and wrinkles, or becoming bald. The youth emphasis is also indicated by our being pleased when someone guesses our age to be younger than it actually is. More than other societies, we place a high value on change and new programs. European societies, on the other hand, place a higher value on tradition and preserving customs and lifestyles from the past.

Our society places a high value on mobility, action, and energy. We like to think we are doers. For many, John F. Kennedy symbolized the vigor and energy we like to think of as being "American."

In a society focused on youth, the elderly are assigned a lower status. But why this emphasis on youth in our society? The reasons are not fully clear. There appear to be several factors. Industrialization has resulted in a demand for laborers that are energetic, agile, and have considerable strength. Rapid advances in technology and science has made obsolescent past knowledge and certain specialized work skills (for example, that of a blacksmith). Pioneer living and the gradual expansion of our nation to the West required "brute" strength, energy, and stamina.

Then there are a number of values that underly our emphasis on youth. The following values are not indigenous to America, but have found their strongest expression here. Competition has always been emphasized, and has been reinforced by Darwin's notions on evolution which highlighted survival of the fittest and the need of a struggle for existence. Benjamin Franklin asserted that hard work was noble and idleness was dangerous, and Americans generally agreed. Individualism (the notion that one is master of one's own fate) has also influenced our views of the elderly. Often in the past if a retiree found him/herself impoverished, it was thought to be due to some moral flaw, such as not having worked hard enough, or saved enough, for old age.

Health problems and cost of care. Old age is partly a social problem because of the high costs of health care. Over three quarters of the aged have one chronic condition, and almost half have two or more.[13] Almost 1 in 10 is bedridden.[14] Four out of 10 have physical impairments that interfere with performing major self-care tasks.[15] Older people see their doctor more often, spend a higher proporton of their income on prescribed drugs,

and once in the hospital they stay longer. The health status of the "old" old (75 and older) is worse than for the "young" old (65 to 74).[16]

The physical process of aging (senescence) is one reason for the elderly having a higher rate of health problems. However, research in recent years has demonstrated social and personal stresses also play a major role in causing diseases. The elderly face a wide range of stressful situations: loneliness, death of friends and family members, retirement, changes in living arrangements, loss of social status, reduced income, and a decline in physical energy and physical capacities. Medical conditions also may result from substandard diets, inadequate exercise, cigarette smoking, and excessive drinking of alcoholic beverages.

Flynn further notes:

> Studies of long-living peoples of the world show that neither heredity nor low prevalence of disease is a significant determinant of longevity. Four other factors are much more likely to predict long-term survival: (1) a clearly defined and valued role in society; (2) a positive self-perception; (3) sustained, moderate physical activity; and (4) abstinence from cigarette smoking. Studies in this country indicate that secure financial status, social relationships, and higher education are also important.[17]

Old people are older. Old age is also a problem because an increasing number are "older." Over a million people in the United States are 85 or older. It is estimated that the number of people over 80 in America will nearly double in the current generation.[18] The "old old" have the lowest incomes and require the most medical and nursing care. Approximately 13,000 "older Americans" are thought to be past the age of 100.[19]

In comparing the "old" old to the "young" old, the former are substantially more apt to be widowed, to have more serious health problems, and to be depressed.[20]

Inadequate income. Many of the elderly live in poverty. A fair number lack adequate food, essential clothes and drugs, and perhaps a telephone in the house to make emergency calls.

In 1977 the median income of men over 70 was $5,007, while the median income for women of the same age was $3,108.[21] Both of these figures are close to the nationally established poverty line, which means many of the elderly are living in poverty.

The financial problems of the elderly are compounded by additional factors. One factor is the high cost of health care which has previously been discussed. A second factor is inflation. Inflation is especially devastating to those on fixed incomes. Most private pension benefits do not increase in size after a worker retires. For example, if living costs rise annually at 7 percent (recent years have been higher) a person on a fixed pension would in 20 years be able to buy only one fourth as many goods and services as s/he could at retirement.[22] Fortunately, Congress in 1974 enacted an "automatic escalator" clause in social security benefits, providing a 3 percent increase in payments when the Consumer Price Index increased a like amount. However, it should be remembered social security benefits were never intended to make a person financially independent—it is nearly impossible to live comfortably on monthly social security checks.

The most important source of income for the elderly is social security benefits, primarily (a) the Old Age, Survivors, Disability Insurance, and Health Insurance Program, and (b) the Supplemental Security Income Program (see Chapter 4 for descriptions). Over one third of the income of the elderly comes from social security, and nearly half of

the elderly have no other income.[23] Yet, social security payments do not provide a level of living much above subsistence.[24]

The importance of financial security for the elderly is emphasized by Sullivan et al.:

> Financial security affects one's entire lifestyle. It determines one's diet, ability to seek good health care, to visit relatives and friends, to maintain a suitable wardrobe, and to find or maintain adequate housing. One's financial resources, or lack of them, play a great part in finding recreation (going to movies, plays, playing bridge or bingo, etc.) and maintaining morale, feelings of independence, and a sense of self-esteem. In other words, if an older person has the financial resources to remain socially independent (having her own household and access to transportation and medical services), to continue contact with friends and relatives, and to maintain her preferred forms of recreation, she is going to feel a great deal better about herself and others than if she is deprived of her former style of life.[25]

Loss of family and friends. Single old people are generally less well off than married elderly. The longer life span of women has unfortunately left more than half of them without a spouse.[26] Gordon and Walter Moss comment about the value of marriage for older persons:

> They now have much more time for and are more dependent upon each other. Some marriages cannot handle this increased togetherness, but those that can become the major source of contentment to both partners. The understanding wife can be enormously important in helping her husband adjust to retirement. The understanding husband can help his wife adjust to a new role when all the children have left home. A good marriage, or a remarriage, provides the elderly person with companionship and emotional support, sex, the promise of care if he is sick, a focus for daily activities, and frequently greater financial independence. Sex roles often blur, and the husband actively helps in household chores.[27]

The elderly person's life is made more isolated and lonely when close friends and relatives move away, or pass away. Old age is a time when close friends are most apt to die.

The needs of aging parents can present some painful dilemmas for their children, especially if the parents are poor or in ill-health. The children may have families of their own requiring heavy responsibilities on their time and finances. For children on tight budgets, deciding how to divide their resources among their parents, their own children, and themselves can be agonizing. Some children face the difficult question of whether to maintain a parent within their home, to leave the parent live alone, or to seek to place the parent in a nursing home.

A new high-rise apartment complex (retirement community) for the elderly

Where the elderly live. We have heard so much about nursing homes in recent years that few people realize that 95 percent of the elderly do not live in nursing homes or any other kind of institution.[28]

About 70 percent of all elderly males are married and live with their wives.[29] Because females tend to outlive their spouses, nearly two thirds live alone.[30] Nearly 80 percent of older married couples maintain their own households—in apartments, mobile homes, condominiums, or their own houses.[31] In addition, nearly half of the single elderly (widows, widowers, divorcees, never married) live in their own homes.[32]

Old people who live in rural areas generally have a higher status than those living in urban areas. People living on farms can retire gradually. When a person's income is in land rather than a job s/he can retain importance and esteem to an advanced age.

However, almost three quarters of our population live in urban areas,[33] and the elderly often live in poor-quality housing. They may find themselves trapped in decay-ing, low-value houses needing considerable maintenance and surrounded by racial and ethnic groups different from their own. Many of the urban elderly live in hotels or apartments in the urban inner cities with inadequate living conditions. Their neighborhoods may be decaying and crime-ridden, and such elderly are easy prey for thieves and muggers.

Fortunately many mobile-home parks, retirement villages, and apartment complexes geared to the needs of the elderly are being built throughout the country. Many such communities for the elderly provide a social center, security protection, sometimes a daily hot meal, and perhaps a little help with maintenance.

When the aged do not maintain their own households, they most often live in the homes of relatives, primarily one of their children.

Transportation. Owning and driving a car is a luxury only the more affluent elderly and

Old man with shopping cart

physically vigorous can afford. The lack of convenient, inexpensive transportation is a problem faced by most elderly.

Crime victimization. Having reduced energy, strength, and agility, the elderly are more easily victimized by crime, particularly robbery, aggravated assault, burglary, larceny, vandalism, and fraud. Many of the elderly live in constant fear of being victimized. Some are extremely hesitant to leave their homes for fear they will be mugged, or from fear their homes will be burglarized while they are away.

Sexuality in old age. There is a common misconception that older people lose their sexual drive. If an older male displays a sexual interest he is labeled a "dirty old man." When two older people exhibit normal heterosexual behavior, someone is apt to comment "Aren't they cute?" Yet many older people have a strong sexual interest and a satisfying sex life.[34] Sexual capacities, particularly in women, show little evidence of

aging, and a large percentage of elderly males are capable of sexual relations.[35]

Masters and Johnson see no reason why sexual activity cannot be enjoyed by elderly couples.[36] If sexual behavior does decline, it probably is due more to social reasons than physical. According to Masters and Johnson the most important deterrants to sexual activity when one is older are: the lack of a partner; overindulgence in drinking or eating; boredom with one's partner; attitudes toward sex, such as the erroneous belief that sex is inappropriate for the elderly; poor physical or mental health; attitudes toward menopause; and fear of poor performance.[37]

The attitudes of the "younger generation" often create problems for the elderly. A widow or widower at times faces strong opposition from other family members against remarrying. Negative attitudes are often strongest when an elderly person becomes interested in someone younger who will become an heir if the older person dies. Old people are sometimes informed they should not be interested in members of the opposite sex, and that they should not establish new sexual relationships.

Fortunately, the attitudes toward sexuality in old age are changing. Taber notes:

> With the changing attitudes of younger people to alternatives to the traditional family, some older people are finding informal arrangements for living together attractive. The couple who do not have a marriage ceremony can share all the companionship and sexual satisfactions without upsetting inheritance rights and retirement benefits. When they become aware of it, their children may accept such a pattern because they find it preferable to remarriage. We have no idea of the numbers that are involved, but the old as well as the young have new options as societal norms change. The popularity of living together without marriage will probably increase.[38]

Malnutrition. "The elderly are the most uniformly undernourished segment of our population," according to Senator George McGovern, chairman of the Select Committee on Nutrition and Human Needs.[39] There are a number of reasons for chronic malnutrition of the elderly: transportation difficulties in getting to grocery stores; lack of knowledge about proper nutrition; lack of money to purchase a well-balanced diet; poor teeth and lack of good dentures which greatly limits the diet; lack of incentive to prepare an appetizing meal when one is living alone; and inadequate cooking and storage facilities.

Emotional problems. Depression is the most common emotional problem. The suicide rate of white men in their 80s is four times as high as men in general.[40] Given the problems of the elderly (many created by our society by making old age largely a "useless" role), the high rate of depression is understandable.

Those who have emotional problems in earlier life, unless resolved, will continue to have them when older. Often these problems will be intensified by the added stresses of aging.

The National Institute of Mental Health, after an 11-year study, identified two major barriers to good mental health in the later years: (1) failure to bounce back from psychosocial losses, and (2) failure to have "meaningful" life goals.[41] Old age is a time when there are drastic changes thrust upon the elderly that emotionally may create problems: loss of a job and its accompanying status; loss of a spouse; loss of friends and relatives through death or moving; poorer health; loss of accustomed income; and changing relationships with one's children and grandchildren.

Unfortunately there is an erroneous assumption that "senility" and "mental illness" are inevitable and untreatable. Robert Butler has found, on the contrary, that old people respond well to both individual and group counseling.[42]

Death. Preoccupation with dying, particularly with the circumstances surrounding it, is an ongoing concern of the elderly. They see their friends and relatives dying. The elderly's concern about dying is most often focused on dreading the disability, the pain, and long periods of suffering that may precede death. They generally would like a death with dignity, where they could die in their own homes, with little suffering, with mental faculties intact, and with families and friends nearby.

Old people are also concerned about the costs of their final illness, the difficulties they may cause others by the manner of their death, and whether their resources will permit a dignified funeral.

In our society we tend to wall the dying off with silence. Apparently we try to do this in order not to have to confront our own mortality. We often force people to die alone. In hospitals great efforts are made to separate the dying from the living. Dying patients are moved into separate rooms. Often the medical staff attempts to shield the dying person from becoming aware of his/her impending death. Families, too, also begin to treat the patient differently when they know the end is near. (Being treated differently by medical staff and family often subtly informs the dying that death is imminent.)

Death is taboo as a topic of conversation in our society. Our society is structured to prevent death from being disruptive. For example, it has been suggested that a major reason for mandatory retirement is that it helps businesses to avoid disruption by the death of key personnel.[43]

A number of authorities have urged our society to treat death more openly.[44] It would enable the dying person to better prepare for death, perhaps by having additional time to reassess his/her life and to come to some conclusions about what has been accomplished and what life has meant. It would also give the dying person more time to become accepting of death, and time to make financial arrangements, such as making a will. For family members it would give them time to make necessary arrangements (including financial), and time to redress old wrongs and heal misunderstandings. For all members of society, it would better enable them to face and psychologically come to terms with their eventual death. The recent popularity of courses in death and dying at college campuses shows people feel a need to psychologically become more comfortable with facing death.

The hospice movement is an emerging social welfare program. Hospices allow the terminally ill to die with dignity—to live their final weeks in the way they want to. Hospices have their origin among European religious orders in the Middle Ages who welcomed travelers who were sick, tired, or hungry.[45] Hospices are located in a variety of settings—in a separate unit of a hospital, in a building independent of a hospital, or in the dying person's home. Medical services and social services are provided in hospices, and extensive efforts are made to allow the terminally ill to spend their remaining days as they choose. Hospices sometimes have educational and entertainment programs, and visitors are common. Pain relievers are extensively used so that the patient is able to live out the final days in relative comfort.

CURRENT SERVICES

Present services and programs for the elderly are primarily "maintenance" and "Band-Aid" in nature.

There are a number of programs, often federally funded, to provide services needed by the elderly.

Older Americans Act of 1965. This federal law created an operating agency (Administration on Aging) within the former Department of Health, Education, and Welfare. This law and its amendments are the bases for financial aid by the federal government to assist states and local communities to meet the needs of the elderly. Ten objectives of the act are to secure for the elderly:

1. An adequate income.
2. Best possible physical and mental health.
3. Suitable housing.
4. Restorative services for those who require institutional care.
5. Opportunity for employment.
6. Retirement in health, honor, dignity.
7. Pursuit of meaningful activity.
8. Efficient community services.
9. Immediate benefit from research knowledge to sustain and improve health and happiness.
10. Freedom, independence, and the free exercise of individual initiative in planning and managing their own lives.[46]

Although these objectives are commendable, the reality is that these goals have not been realized for many of the elderly.

Illustrations of programs. The problems of the elderly have now been focused upon by the public spotlight, and have become a popular cause. There have been two White House Conferences on Aging, in 1961 and in 1971. Many states now have a state office on aging, and some municipalities and counties have established community councils on aging. Universities are establishing centers for the study of gerontology; and nursing, medicine, social work, architecture, and other professions are establishing fields of study on gerontology. Government research grants are being given to encourage the study of the elderly by academicians. Publishers are now producing books and pamphlets to inform the public about the elderly, and a few high schools are beginning to offer courses to help teenagers understand the elderly and their circumstances.

There are a number of programs, often federally funded and administered at state or local levels, to provide funds and services needed by the elderly. A few of these will be briefly described.

Medicare—A health insurance program described in Chapter 4.

Old Age, Survivors', and Disability Insurance—A social insurance program (described in Chapter 4).

Supplemental Security Income—A public assistance program (described in Chapter 4).

Medicaid—Pays for medical expenses for low-income people (described in Chapter 4).

Food stamps—A program to offset some of the food expenses for low-income people who qualify (described in Chapter 4).

Nursing Home Ombudsman Program—A program to investigate and act upon concerns expressed by residents in nursing homes.

Meals on wheels—Provides hot and cold meals to house-bound recipients who are incapable of obtaining or preparing their own meals, but who can feed themselves.

Retired Senior Volunteer Program (RSVP)—A program which seeks to match work and service opportunities with the elderly volunteers seeking them.

Foster Grandparent Program—Pays the elderly for part-time work in which they provide individual care and attention to ill and needy children and youths.

Service Corps of Retired Executives (SCORE)—Provides consulting services to small businesses.

Senior citizen centers, golden age clubs and similar groups—Provide leisure-time and recreational activities for the elderly.

Special bus rates—Reduces bus transportation costs for the elderly.

Property tax relief—Available to the elderly in many states.

Special federal income tax deduction—For people over 65.

Housing projects for old people—Built by local sponsors with financing assistance by the Department of Housing and Urban Development.

Movie theaters and other places of entertainment—May charge the elderly reduced rates.

Home health services—Includes visiting nurse services, physical therapy, drugs, laboratory services, and sickroom equipment.

Nutrition programs—Provide meals for the elderly at group "eating sites." These meals are generally provided four or five times a week, and usually are luncheon meals. These programs improve the nutrition of elderly persons and offer opportunities for socialization.

Homemaker services—In some communities homemakers take care of household tasks that the elderly are no longer able to do for themselves.

Day-care centers for the elderly—Such centers provide activities that are determined by the needs of the group. This service gives the family some relief from

A foster grandparent at a residential care facility for the retarded

24-hour-a-day care. Programs such as home health services, homemaker services, and day-care centers prevent or postpone institutional care.

Telephone reassurance—Volunteers, often older persons, telephone elderly people

A visiting nurse

who live alone. Such calls are a meaningful form of social contact for both parties and also ascertain whether any accidents or other serious problems have arisen which require emergency attention.

Nursing homes—Provide residential care and skilled nursing care when independence is no longer practical for the elderly who cannot take care of themselves or for the elderly whose families can no longer take care of them. Because of the national attention given to nursing homes, a closer look at these homes will be taken.

NURSING HOMES

Nursing homes were created as an alternative to expensive hospital care and are substantially supported by the federal government through Medicaid and Medicare. Over half a million older people now live in extended care facilities, making nursing homes a $1 billion industry.[47] There are now more patient beds in nursing homes than in hospitals, and over 40 cents of each Medicaid dollar goes to nursing homes.[48]

Nursing homes are classified according to the kind of care they provide. At one end of the scale there are residential homes that provide primarily room and board, with some nonmedical care (such as help in dressing). At the other end of the scale are nursing care centers that provide skilled nursing and medical attention 24 hours a day. The more skilled and extensive the medical care given, the more expensive the home. The costs vary from a few hundred to more than $1,000 per month. Although only a small percent of the elderly live permanently in homes (about 5 percent), many spend some time convalescing in them.

A few years ago Ralph Nader released a report highly critical of nursing home care. The report cited: instances of patients heav-

Pool at a nursing home

ily tranquilized in a stuporous state so that they were easier to manage; use of patients as guinea pigs in drug experiments; abysmal neglect and dehumanization; and kickbacks to nursing home administrators from druggists.[49]

One scandal after another characterizes care in nursing homes. A few years ago in Houston an elderly woman was so neglected in a nursing home that her death was not discovered until rigor mortis had set in, and another woman was hospitalized from rat bites.[50] In another area of the country one doctor received $42,000 one year for giving 8,275 injections to 149 nursing home patients.[51] In 1980 a nursing home in Madison, Wisconsin, strapped a 37-year-old stroke patient into her wheelchair for over 40 minutes at a time when the patient had no bladder or bowel control, and she was not assisted to the toilet in spite of her repeated cries for help.[52]

Robert Butler, a recent director of the National Institute on Aging, has visited a number of nursing homes and has found patients lying in their own feces or urine.[53] He also found that the food was so unappetizing that residents at times refused to eat it,

that many homes had serious safety hazards, and that boredom and apathy was common among staff as well as residents.

In spite of the criticism, nursing homes are needed, particularly for the elderly who require medical and nursing care. If nursing homes were abolished, some other institution such as a hospital would have to serve the elderly who can no longer live independently or with their families.

At the present time people of all ages tend to be prejudiced against nursing homes, even those that are well run. Frank Moss describes the elderly person's view of nursing homes:

> The average senior citizen looks at a nursing home as a human junkyard, as a prison—a kind of purgatory, halfway between society and the cemetery—or as the first step of an inevitable slide into oblivion.[54]

To some degree there is reality to the notion that nursing homes are places where the elderly wait to die.

The assertion that nursing homes are needed does not mean all of the residents in nursing homes need to be there. Sadly, it is

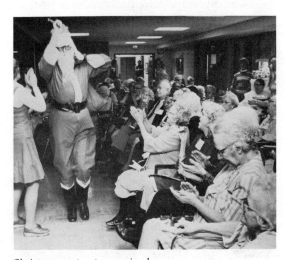

Christmas party at a nursing home

estimated that fewer than half of the current residents would have to enter a home if occasional medical and personal assistance could be provided.[55]

According to one estimate, about 30 percent of nursing homes are really undesirable places to live, about 40 percent are good, and 30 percent are reasonably adequate.[56]

The most common complaint against nursing homes appears to be the lack of well-trained professional staff.[57] Nurses trained in the special needs of the aged are in short supply. Nursing home administrators in some states need only be 18 years old and have taken a six-month training course in nursing home administration. Few homes have social workers, occupational therapists, physical therapists, or other rehabilitative services.

Because most nursing homes are profit-making businesses, a number of other problems may arise. There is an effort to keep salaries down and to have a minimum number of staff. A home may postpone repairs and improvements on the facilities. Food is apt to be inexpensive, such as macaroni which is high in fats and carbohydrates. Congress has provided that every nursing home patient on Medicaid is entitled to a monthly personal spending allowance. The homes have control over these funds and some homes keep this money.[58]

Gordon Moss and Frank Moss discuss additional complaints:

> The quality of care from both particular staff members and from the institution as a whole is another major source of problems and complaints. There may be much delayed or no response to calls for help. Patients may be left sitting for a long time on bedpans. The staff may harass patients they dislike or consider to be insufficiently docile by doing these things, or by withholding services, isolating them in separate rooms in little-used parts of the building, or forcing them to remain bedridden.[59]

There also are occasional complaints about the physical facilities. There may not be enough floor space, or too many people in a room. The call light by the bed may be difficult to reach, or the toilets and showers may not be conveniently located. The building may be decaying.

Nursing home patients may also have complaints about some of the other patients who cause problems by being noisy, by stealing, and by disrupting others' privacy.

It has been charged that as high as 40 to 50 percent of nursing home drugs may be administered in error, resulting in adverse reactions and occasional death.[60] A Senate Committee on Aging reported in 1977 after eight years of investigation that,

> the evidence is overwhelming that many pharmacists are required to pay kickbacks to nursing home operators as a precondition of obtaining a nursing home's business.[61]

Frank Moss, along with a number of other authorities, is critical of our society's response to the problems of the elderly:

> The phenomenon of large numbers of ill elderly is a comparatively recent problem in the United States, as is our "solution"—nursing homes. The solution reflects today's society: the sick and the aged are an embarrassment; they remind us of our own mortality and therefore should be removed from view.[62]

Social work and the elderly*

Social work education is taking a leading role in identifying the problems of the aged, and by beginning to develop gerontological specializations within their curricula. Although in the past social workers have not been a significant part of the staff of most

---

* A fuller discussion is by Louis Lowy, *Social Work with the Aging: The Challenge and Promise of the Latter Years* (New York: Harper & Row, 1979).

agencies serving the aging, this is changing. Some states, for example, are now requiring that each nursing home must employ a social worker.

Social work has a number of skills to help meet the special needs and concerns of the aged. Social workers are needed as brokers to link the elderly with available services. In any community there are a wide range of services available, but few people are knowledgeable about the array of services and about various eligibility requirements. The social worker's knowledge of community resources prepares him/her for this broker role. The elderly are in special need of this "broker" service as some have difficulty with transportation and communication, and others may have outmoded prejudices against seeking assistance.

Counseling is another function social workers can provide to the elderly, or to the families of the elderly. Areas involved include counseling on emotional problems, employment counseling for another job, counseling to find new "meaning" in living, counseling on coping with health problems, counseling on death and dying, and counseling on whether to enter a nursing home.

Outreach is another role for social workers, including identifying and offering services to the aged who need: financial assistance, better housing, health care services, recreational and leisure-time services, transportation, companionship, consumer protection services, sex education, hot meal programs.

There are other roles that are opening up for social workers in the field of aging: consultants, community planners, researchers, and administrators of services. However, the role of advocate may in the future be the most crucial role. Kosberg makes the following comments about this role:

Some time in the not-too-distant future there may well be a thundering outcry against the conditions in which the aged live. Call it an eruption of social conscience. Such a phenomenon has occurred in regard to racial prejudice, poverty, the status of women, pollution, and overpopulation. Social workers have the motivation and responsibility to care for the disadvantaged; this care is the raison d'être of their profession. If they are not in the vanguard of such a movement on behalf of the aged—making sure that it is a long-range effective effort—they will be denying their commitment to their profession and to society.[63]

THE FUTURE FOR THE ELDERLY

In spite of all the maintenance and "Band-Aid" programs that are now available for the elderly, the key problems of the elderly remain to be solved. A high proportion of the elderly do *not* have: "meaningful" lives, a respectful status, adequate income, adequate transportation, good living arrangements, an adequate diet, and adequate health care.

Currently we hear a great deal about various kinds of discrimination: racism, sexism, anti-Semitism, ethnocentrism. There is another that we may soon hear about, and that many of us (perhaps unknowingly) are guilty of, namely agism-prejudice against the elderly. How can we defend forcing people to retire when they are still productive? How can we defend the living conditions within some of our nursing homes? How can we defend our restrictive attitudes toward sexuality among the elderly? How can we defend providing services to the elderly that are limited in scope to primarily having maintenance and subsistence goals, while for all other age-groups a wide range of services are being provided to help younger people live gratifying and fulfilling lives? Gordon and Walter Moss comment:

Just as we are learning that black can be beautiful, so we must learn that gray can be beautiful, too. In so learning, we may brighten the prospects of our own age.[64]

If in reading this you say to yourself, "This writer must be crazy, old age is ugly, not beautiful," then stop and think, you are obviously guilty of agism as you are prejudiced against the elderly.

In the past, prejudice has been most effectively combated when those being discriminated against join together for political action. It therefore seems apparent that if major changes in the elderly's role in our society are to take place, the elderly will have to join together into political efforts.

Older people are in fact becoming increasingly involved in political activism and in some cases even radical militancy. Two prominent organizations are the American Association of Retired Persons and its affiliated group, the National Retired Teachers Association. These groups, among other projects, are lobbying for the interests of the elderly at local, state, and federal levels of government.

A more radical group that has caught the public's attention is the Gray Panthers. This organization argues that the fundamental flaw in our society is the emphasis on materialism and on the consumption of goods and services rather than on improving the quality of life for all citizens (including the elderly). The Gray Panthers seek to end agism and to advance the goals of human freedom, human dignity, and self-development. This organization emphasizes using social action techniqes, including getting the elderly to vote as a bloc for their concerns. The founder of the group, Maggie Kuhn states, "We are not mellow, sweet old people. We have got to effect change, and we have nothing to lose.[65]

There are clear indications that the politics of age have arrived, and will be felt in future elections. The elderly are likely to have a say in the future on many social and political issues. At age 69 Ronald Reagan in 1980 was elected president, the oldest person ever elected to this office. Reagan received exten-

sive support from elderly voters and has made political promises to improve the status and living conditions of the elderly in our society.

Preparing for old age

Growing old is a lifelong process. Becoming 65 does not destroy the continuities between what a person has been, presently is, and what s/he will be. Recognition of this fact should lessen the fear of growing old. For those of modest means who have prepared thoughtfully, old age can be a period, if not a luxury, then at least of reasonable comfort and pleasure.

Gordon and Walter Moss indicate,

> A couple in good health who own their home out-right and have only ordinary upkeep on house and car, who have accumulated through careful nurturance savings of a few thousand dollars, and who receive a Social Security and pension income of between $400 and $500 per month can expect to pass the time quite agreeably. . . .
>
> Those a little better off may find group travel plans within their means. For these, the dream trip to Hawaii or Europe can become a reality. The occasional shopping trip with lunch at a favorite restaurant, a visit to the beauty parlor, and season tickets for the local concert or theatre series may spice up their days.[66]

Others may be able to start small home businesses focused on their hobbies, or become involved in meaningful activities with churches and other organizations. Still others may relax with fishing, and slowly traveling around the country. Others may continue such interests as painting, writing, woodworking, weaving, needlework, reading.

Our lives largely depend on our goals and our motivations to achieve those goals. How we live prior to retiring will largely determine whether old age will be a nightmare, or whether it will be fulfilling and gratifying. There are a number of areas we should attend to in our younger years:

1. Health: A sound exercise plan is critical, and so are periodic health examinations to prevent the development of chronic health problems. Also critically important in maintaining health is learning and using approaches to reduce psychological stress. (Some stress reduction approaches are described in Chapter 13.)

2. Finances: Saving money for later years is important, and so is learning to manage (budget) money wisely.

3. Interests and hobbies: Psychologically people who are traumatized most by retirement are those whose self-image and life interests center around their work. People who have meaningful hobbies and interests look forward to retirement in order to have sufficient time for their hobbies and interests.

4. Self-identity: People who are comfortable and realistic about who they are and what they want out of life are better prepared, including in later years, to deal with stresses and crises that arise. (Some guidelines on how to develop a positive identity are presented in Chapter 2 of this text.)

5. Looking toward the future: People who dwell in the past, or rest upon past achievements are apt to find the older years depressing. On the other hand, a person who looks to the future generally has interests that are alive and growing, and is thereby able to find new challenges and new satisfactions in later years. Looking forward the future in-

Old man fishing

volves planning for retirement, including deciding where you would like to live, in what type of housing and community, and what you look forward to doing with your free time.

6. Coping with crises: If a person learns to cope effectively with crises in younger years, these coping skills will remain when a person is older. Involved in effective coping is learning to approach problems realistically and constructively.

SUMMARY

Aging is an individual process which occurs at differing rates in different people. Chronological age is an inaccurate measure of how physically fit and mentally alert an elderly person is.

Old age is a social problem because our society is creating a large elderly population that at the present time has little practical value to the society. People 65 and older now compose over one tenth of our population.

A number of problems are encountered by the aged in our society: a low status, mandatory retirement when many are still productive, lack of a meaningful role, the emphasis on youth in our society, health problems, inadequate income, loss of family and friends, inadequate housing, transportation problems, restrictive attitudes on expressing their sexuality malnutrition, crime victimization, emotional problems such as depression, and concern with the circumstances surrounding dying.

A wide array of services are available to the elderly, but these are primarily geared to maintaining the elderly, often at or slightly above a subsistence level of existence. Services provided in some of our nursing homes are inadequate, and the level of care provided in some of these homes has been sharply criticized. Nursing homes have also been criticized as being "storage centers" for the elderly so that members of our society can avoid coming face-to-face with their own mortality.

Although the level of care needs to be substantially improved in some of them, nursing homes are needed for the elderly who cannot take care of themselves and/or for those whose families can no longer provide care. (It is generally unknown that 95 percent of the elderly live independently or with relatives, and not in nursing homes.)

In many ways the elderly are victims of agism (for example, being forced to retire when still productive). Social workers have numerous skills and roles in serving the elderly, including that of being an advocate to secure system chances to better serve the elderly. In the future we are apt to see the elderly increasingly joining together for political action to work toward ending agism.

NOTES

1. Gordon Moss and Walter Moss, *Growing Old* (New York: Pocket Book, 1975), pp. 17–18.

2. Eric Sharp, "The 'Retirement in Florida' Dream Can Become a Nightmare for Some," *Detroit Free Press*, September 9, 1973.

3. Moss and Moss, *Growing Old*, p. 18.

4. "Rich New Market among Nation's Elderly," *U.S. News & World Report*, November 12, 1979, p. 80.

5. Elizabeth Ferguson, *Social Work: An Introduction*, 3d ed. (Philadelphia: Lippincott, 1975), p. 238.

6. Moss and Moss, *Growing Old*, p. 20; and "How Population Shifts Are Changing America," *U.S. News & World Report*, March 5, 1979, pp. 76–79.

7. Thomas J. Sullivan, et al. *Social Problems* (New York: Wiley, 1980), pp. 335–70.

8. Moss and Moss, *Growing Old*, p. 20; and "Population Shifts," pp. 76–79.

9. Sullivan et al., *Social Problems*, p. 343.

10. Robert N. Butler and Myrna I. Lewis, *Aging and Mental Health: Positive Psychosocial Approaches*, 2d ed. (St. Louis, Ill.: Mosby, 1977).

11. Ibid.

12. Ibid.

13. U.S. Department of Health, Education and Welfare, Social Security Administration, *The Size and Shape of the Medical Care Dollar* (Washington,

D.C.: U.S. Government Printing Office, 1971), p. 30.

14. Marilyn L. Flynn, "Aging," in *Contemporary Social Work,* ed. Donald Brieland, Lela Costin, and Charles Atherton, 2d ed. (New York: McGraw-Hill, 1980), p. 352.

15. Ibid., p. 352.

16. Ibid., p. 352.

17. Ibid., p. 353.

18. Merlin Taber, "The Aged," in *Contemporary Social Work,* ed. Donald Brieland, Lela Costin, and Charles Atherton (New York: McGraw-Hill, 1975), p. 356.

19. Rex A. Skidmore and Milton Thackeray, *Introduction to Social Work,* 2d ed. (Englewood Cliffs, N.J.: Prentice-Hall, 1976).

20. Flynn, "Aging," pp. 344–70.

21. Sullivan et al., *Social Problems,* p. 336.

22. "Will Inflation Tarnish Your Golden Years?" *U.S. News & World Report,* February 26, 1979, p. 57.

23. Moss and Moss, *Growing Old,* p. 39.

24. Sullivan et al., *Social Problems,* pp. 357–58.

25. Ibid., p. 347.

26. Moss and Moss, *Growing Old,* p. 47.

27. Ibid., p. 47.

28. Ibid., p. 56.

29. Flynn, "Aging," p. 352.

30. Ibid., p. 352.

31. Moss and Moss, *Growing Old.*

32. Ibid.

33. Taber, "The Aged," p. 357.

34. Ibid., p. 359.

35. Bert K. Smith, *Aging in America* (Boston: Beacon Press, 1973), pp. 31–32.

36. William H. Masters and Virginia E. Johnson, "The Human Sexual Response: The Aging Female and the Aging Male," in *Middle Age and Aging,* ed. B. L. Neugarten (Chicago: University of Chicago Press, 1968).

37. Ibid., p. 269.

38. Taber, "The Aged," p. 359.

39. Ferguson, *Social Work,* p. 241.

40. Ibid., p. 253.

41. Skidmore and Thackeray, *Introduction to Social Work,* p. 225.

42. Robert N. Butler, "Myths and Realities of Aging," address presented at the Governor's Conference on Aging, Columbia, Md., May 28, 1970.

43. Moss and Moss, *Growing Old,* p. 72.

44. See, for example, Elisabeth Kübler-Ross, *On Death and Dying* (New York: Macmillan, 1969).

45. Sullivan et al., *Social Problems,* p. 363.

46. U.S. Department of Health, Education and Welfare, *Older Americans Act of 1965, as Amended, Text and History* (Washington, D.C.: U.S. Government Printing Office, November 1970).

47. Taber, "The Aged," p. 363.

48. Abigail Trafford, "The Tragedy of Care for America's Elderly," *U.S. News & World Report,* April 24, 1978, p. 56.

49. Claire Tounsend, *Old Age: The Last Segregation* (New York: Grossman, 1971).

50. Trafford, "Tragedy of Care," p. 56.

51. Robert N. Butler, *Why Survive? Being Old in America* (New York: Harper & Row, 1975) p. 264.

52. Dianne Paley, "Nursing Home Is Cited Again," *Wisconsin State Journal,* May 23, 1980, sect. 4, p. 1.

53. Butler, *Why Survive?* p. 264.

54. Frank Moss, "It's Hell to Be Old in the U.S.A.," *Parade Magazine,* July 17, 1977, p. 9.

55. Moss and Moss, *Growing Old,* p. 61.

56. Ibid., p. 66.

57. Ibid., p. 64.

58. Moss, "It's Hell," p. 9.

59. Moss and Moss, *Growing Old,* p. 65.

60. Moss, "It's Hell," p. 9.

61. "Medicaid Kickbacks Called 'Way of Life," *Wisconsin State Journal,* July 17, 1977, sect. 1, p. 11.

62. Moss, "It's Hell," p. 9.

63. Jordan J. Kosberg, "The Nursing Home: A Social Work Paradox," *Social Work* 18, no. 2 (March 1973): 109.

64. Moss and Moss, *Growing Old,* p. 79.

65. Butler, *Why Survive?* p. 341.

66. Moss and Moss, *Growing Old,* p. 73.

GUSTAFSON　　*part three*

Social work practice

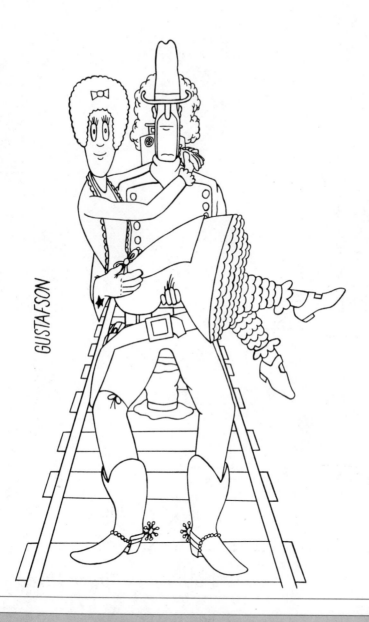

GUSTAFSON

The preceding chapters have focused on describing prominent social problems and discussing current social services to meet these problems. The focus of this chapter, and the following two, will be on social work practice. This chapter will discuss working with individuals. The next two chapters will discuss working with groups, and social work community practice. Traditionally, working with individuals in social work has been called social casework. This chapter will describe the casework process, summarize essential skills needed by caseworkers, and describe typical casework activities.

There used to be an erroneous concept that a social worker was either a caseworker, a group worker, or a community organizer. Practicing social workers know such a concept is faulty, because every social worker is involved as a change agent in working with individuals, groups, and community groups.

* This chapter was jointly written by Charles Zastrow and Ursula Sennewald Myers. Ms. Myers was a social worker superviser of a single-parent unit at Rock County Social Services Department (Janesville, Wisconsin) and now is executive director of this agency.

The amount of time spent at these levels varies from worker to worker, but every worker will, at times, be assigned and expected to work at these three levels and therefore needs training at all of them.

A majority of social workers spend most of their time working with individuals in public or private agencies, or in private practice. Social casework is aimed at helping individuals, on a one-to-one basis, to meet personal and social problems. Social casework services are provided by nearly every social welfare agency that provides direct services to people. Social casework encompasses a wide variety of activities, such as counseling runaway youths, helping unemployed people secure training or employment, counseling someone who is suicidal, placing a homeless child in an adoptive or foster home, providing protective services to abused children and their families, finding nursing homes for stroke victims who no longer need to be confined in a hospital, counseling individuals with sexual dysfunctions, helping alcoholics to acknowledge they have a drinking problem, counseling those with a terminal

Social work practice with individuals*

illness, being a probation and parole officer, and providing services to single parents.

All of us at times face personal problems that we cannot resolve by ourselves. Sometimes other family members, relatives, friends, or acquaintances can help. At other times we need more skilled help to handle emotional problems, or to obtain resources in times of crises, or to handle marital or family conflicts, or to deal with problems at work or school, or to cope with a medical emergency. Furnishing skilled, personal help is what social casework is all about.

Caseworkers provide a number of different services. At times they are "brokers" when they help link an individual who needs help with community services. Another role is "public education" in which they seek to inform other individuals or groups about current problems and services. Another role is that of an "advocate" for clients to secure needed services when such services are not readily available. Other roles are "outreach," "teacher" of new information and skills, "behavioral specialist," and "consultant." But the primary skill and role of a caseworker is that of counseling. As previous examples in this book indicate, social workers counsel people with a wide variety of personal and social problems.

The authors of this chapter dislike some of the negative connotations associated with the term *caseworker*. *Webster's New Collegiate Dictionary* (1973) defines a case as "a set of circumstances or conditions;" "a situation requiring investigation or action, as by the police;" "the object of investigation or consideration." With such definitions, the term *caseworker* connotes someone who performs primarily an investigative function. The term thereby does not convey the respect that should be given to clients, nor does it convey the importance of building a working relationship with clients. The authors believe a term such as *counselor* conveys a more realis-

tic image of the skills, functions, and approach of social work with individuals.

THE COUNSELING PROCESS

Accountability is increasingly becoming an important emphasis in social welfare. Social service programs that are unable to demonstrate their effectiveness are gradually being phased out. In January 1973, Joel Fischer raised the question whether casework is effective.[1] He reviewed outcome studies on casework services, and concluded that such services failed to be able to document they are effective. Critics of Fischer's review have criticized his methodology. Yet, the question has been raised—is casework effective? As yet, research has *not* demonstrated that casework is effective!

Counseling is the core of casework practice. Chapter 5 in this text has conceptualized the counseling process from the counselor's perspective. The process was conceptualized as involving three phases: (1) building a relationship, (2) exploring problems in-depth, and (3) exploring alternative solutions.

The counseling process can also be conceptualized from the client's point of view. In order for counseling to be successful, clients must give themselves a progressive series of "self-talk." These self-talk stages will briefly be presented.

Stage I—Problem awareness. At this initial stage clients must say to themselves, "I have a problem," "I need to do something about my situation." If people with problems refuse to acknowledge they have a problem they will of course not be motivated to make the efforts needed to change. In some areas of social work, for example working with problem drinkers, it is sometimes difficult to have people acknowledge they have a problem. For people who deny a problem exists,

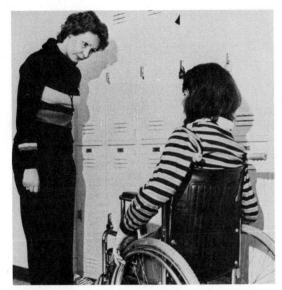

Brief counseling at a sheltered workshop

constructive changes are not apt to occur, unless the counselor finds a way to convince them that a problem exists. When a person denies a problem exists, counseling needs to focus on this denial by exploring why the client believes a problem does not exist, and by gathering evidence to document the existence of the problem to the client.

Stage II—Relationship to counselor. The next stage of the counseling process is where the client arrives at the point where his/her self-talk is, "I think this counselor will be of help to me." If the client instead has the self-talk, "This counselor can't help me. I don't need a head shrinker. I just don't trust this counselor." then counseling is apt to fail. Chapter 5 in this text discusses in some detail helpful guidelines for "how to" establish a working relationship with clients.

Stage III—Motivation. Clients must come to say to themselves, "I think I can improve my situation," "I want to better myself."

Unless a client becomes motivated to change, constructive changes are not apt to occur. Helping a person become motivated to improve his/her situation is a key to effective counseling. Chapter 4 in this text provides a number of guidelines and suggestions on how to motivate "discouraged" or "apathetic" people.

Stage IV—Conceptualizing the problem. In order for counseling to be effective a client needs to recognize, "My problem is not overwhelming, but has specific components that can be changed." Many clients tend to initially view their situation as being so complex that they become highly anxious or emotional, and thereby are unable to see that their problem has a number of components that they can change in a step-to-step fashion. Three years ago, for example, one of the authors of this chapter counseled a teenager who had missed her menstrual period for the past three months, and was so overwhelmingly afraid of being pregnant that she was unable to figure out on her own that the first step was to have a pregnancy test. In order to help clients conceptualize their problems, the counselor needs to explore the problems together in-depth with the client. Guidelines on how to explore problems in-depth with clients are presented in Chapter 5.

Stage V—Exploration of resolution strategies. One of the steps of the counseling process is for the client and counselor to jointly explore resolution strategies. Each client is unique, and so are his/her problems. What works for one client may not be in the best interest of another. An abortion, for example, may be compatible with one client's values and circumstances, but may well be undesirable for another unmarried pregnant woman who has a different set of values and goals. If counseling is going to be effective the client needs to say to him/herself, "I see there are several courses of action that I might try in order to do something about my situation." Unless a client comes to realize there are some resolution strategies, counseling is apt to fail.

Stage VI—Selection of a strategy. As indicated in Chapter 5, the counselor and client need to discuss the probable effects and consequences of possible resolution strategies. If counseling is going to be successful the client must conclude, "I think this approach might help me and I am willing to try it." If a client is indecisive or refuses to make an honest commitment to trying a course of action, constructive change will not occur. For example, if a client says to him/herself, "I know I have a drinking problem, but am unwilling to take any action to cut down on my drinking," counseling probably will not be successful.

Stage VII—Implementation of the strategy. Counseling will only be successful if the client follows through on his/her commitment and then concludes, "This approach is beginning to help me." If the client follows through on the commitment, but instead concludes, "I don't believe this approach is helping me," counseling again is failing. If this occurs, the reasons for no gain need to be examined, and perhaps another resolution strategy needs to be tried.

Stage VIII—Evaluation. If constructive change is apt to be long-lasting or permanent, the client must conclude, "Although this approach takes a lot of my time and effort, it's worth it." On the other hand, if he/she concludes, "This approach has helped a little, but it's really not worth what I'm sacrificing for it," then counseling will either be ineffective, or an alternative course of action needs to be developed and implemented.

The advantage of this conceptualization of the counseling process is that it presents a framework for improving the effectiveness of counseling. When counseling is not being of help, this framework indicates that by examining the self-talk of clients about the counseling they are receiving, the reasons for no progress can be identified and then needed changes made in the counseling process. (It should be noted there is some overlap between these stages; for example, stage II involving the relationship between client and counselor needs to be given attention to throughout the counseling process).

Essential skills needed by caseworkers

Capacity to build a working relationship. Counselors need to establish a nonthreatening atmosphere where the client feels safe to communicate his/her troubles. In initial meetings the counselor needs to "sell" him/ herself as an understanding, knowledgeable person who might be able to help. The counselor needs to show respect and genuine interest in the client, and convey that the client (in spite of perhaps shocking behavior) is a worthwhile person. Generally, a counselor is nonjudgmental; respect is shown for the client's values without the counselor trying to sell his/her own value system.

Capacity to explore problems in depth. A counselor needs to have interviewing skills to help a client tell his story; to encourage him/her; and to be able to identify hidden meanings between verbal and nonverbal messages. To be a competent interviewer requires the capacity to listen and view what the client is saying from the client's perspective. Also, it requires empathy which is the capacity to convey that the counselor is understanding and cares about what the client is thinking and feeling. Finally, a knowledge

Counseling a runaway youth

of human behavior (how people think and feel about events that happen to them) is needed.

Capacity to explore alternative solutions. Once the client's set of problems are explored in depth, resolution approaches must jointly be discussed. It is the counselor's responsibility to have a knowledge of numerous treatment approaches and community resources, so that appropriate courses of action can be shared and discussed with the client. The probable effects and consequences of various courses of action need to be carefully explored with the client. The client generally has the right of self-determination; that is, the right to choose the course of action among possible alternatives.

A variety of treatment approaches

To be an effective counselor a social worker must have a working knowledge of: (a) interviewing principles, and (b) a variety of treatment approaches. Casework is not a single method. In fact, there are numerous treatment approaches that are used. Table 20–1 provides a partial list of comprehensive counseling approaches. (Comprehensive treatment approaches are designed to treat a wide range of emotional and behavioral problems.)

In addition to these large-scale or comprehensive approaches to casework, there are a growing number of specialized approaches for specific problems: for example, sexual therapies for sexual problems, assertive

TABLE 20–1 Comprehensive theoretical approaches to doing casework

Casework or counseling approach	Name of primary developer
Psychosocial model	Gordon Hamilton
Functional model	Jessie Taft
Problem-solving model	Helen H. Perlman
Task-centered model	William J. Reid
Family therapy	Numerous theoreticians
Psychoanalysis	Sigmund Freud
Client-centered therapy	Carl Rogers
Transactional analysis	Eric Berne
Gestalt therapy	Frederick Perls
Rational-emotive therapy	Albert Ellis
Reality therapy	William Glasser
Crisis intervention	Numerous theoreticians
Behavior modification	Numerous theoreticians
Provocative therapy	Frank Farrelly
Radical therapy	Numerous theoreticians
Adlerian therapy	Alfred Adler
Analytical therapy	C. G. Jung
Existential therapy	Numerous theoreticians
Encounter therapies	Numerous theoreticians
Ego psychology approaches	Numerous theoreticians
Cognitive approaches	Numerous theoreticians
General systems approaches	Numerous theoreticians
Role theory approaches	Numerous theoreticians

Note: A summary of each of these approaches is well beyond the scope of this text. These therapies are summarized in *Social Work Treatment,* ed. Francis J. Turner (New York: Free Press, 1979); *Current Psychotherapies,* ed. Raymond Corsini (Itasca, Ill.: F. E. Peacock, 1979); and in Charles Zastrow, *The Practice of Social Work* (Homewood, Ill.: Dorsey Press, 1981).

training for aggressive or shy people, parent effectiveness training to improve effective parenting, specialized drug counseling approaches, alcoholics anonymous, parents anonymous, and so on. Table 20–2 contains a partial listing of a variety of specialized treatment approaches.

It is impossible for any social worker to have an effective working knowledge of all of these comprehensive and specialized treatment approaches. What a social worker should do, however, is to continue throughout his/her career to learn additional approaches and to continue to learn to more effectively apply those approaches s/he is already acquainted with. Social work agencies encourage this continual learning through offering in-service training, workshops, sending workers to conferences, and

by encouraging workers to take additional college courses in the helping professions.

A worker should continue to learn a wide variety of intervention approaches so that the worker can select from his/her "bag of tricks" which intervention approach—given each client's unique set of problems and circumstances—is apt to be most effective. It should be noted that the selection of an intervention approach is also based on a worker's personality. Counselors soon become aware that their personality partially determines which therapy approaches they are more comfortable in applying.

At first glance Tables 20–1 and 20–2 present such a long "shopping list" of intervention approaches that the reader is apt to be bewildered about which treatment approaches s/he should attempt to learn. Prac-

TABLE 20–2   Specialized treatment approaches

Treatment approach	Treatment approach
Psychodrama	Muscle relaxation
Assertiveness training	Deep breathing relaxation
Token economies	Imagery relaxation
Contingency contracting	Meditation
Systematic desensitization	Hypnosis
In vivo desensitization	Self-hypnosis
Implosive therapy	Biofeedback
Covert sensitization	Encounter groups
Aversive techniques	Marathon groups
Thought-stopping	Sensitivity groups
Sex therapy	Alcoholics Anonymous
Milieu therapy	Parents Anonymous
Play therapy	Weight Watchers
Parent effectiveness training	

Note: These therapies are summarized in *Social Work Treatment*, ed. Francis J. Turner (New York: Free Press, 1979); and in Charles Zastrow, *The Practice of Social Work* (Homewood, Ill.: Dorsey Press, 1981).

tice or methods courses in social work programs provide an overview of many of these approaches so the reader will begin to become aware which approaches s/he will be comfortable in applying.

Furthermore, the employment area that one seeks in social work will also be a factor in focusing the reader's attention on which treatment approaches to learn about. If you're working with shy or aggressive people, assertiveness training is recommended. Alcoholics Anonymous is recommended for people with drinking problems, rational therapy for people who are depressed, systematic desensitization for people who have phobias, and so on.

A useful guideline in deciding which intervention approach to use when you have a client in front of you is to place yourself in "the client's shoes" and ask yourself, "given this client's unique set of problems and circumstances, which intervention approach is apt to be most helpful?"

At the present time the needed research as yet *not* been conducted to determine the effectiveness of most of the approaches listed in Tables 20–1 and 20–2.[2]

Obviously, with this wide array of approaches to casework or counseling, some approaches are going to be found more effective than others. For example, from 1920 to 1950 casework practice was heavily influenced by psychoanalytic theory. Since 1950 a number of studies have found psychoanalytic approaches to be generally ineffective,[3] and counselors are increasingly using approaches other than those suggested by psychoanalytic theory.*

Increasingly federal and state governmental units are requiring that the effectiveness of treatment approaches be measured. Gradually, programs found to be ineffective are being phased out.

The trend for the future seems clear. Increasingly social workers will have to document the quantity of services they provide, as well as the effectiveness of their services.

---

* It should be noted that psychoanalytic theories on personality development are still fairly widely taught at undergraduate and graduate schools of social work. These theories are useful in helping to understand human behavior and personality dynamics. However, psychoanalytic treatment techniques are now taught in only a few social work programs.

MEDITATION—AN EXAMPLE OF A SPECIALIZED TREATMENT APPROACH

Recorded accounts of meditative practice date back over 2,000 years among Judaic spiritual leaders, Zen monks, Indian yogis, and Christian monks. The earliest Christian meditators were hermits during the 4th century A.D. in the Egyptian desert. The meditative practices of these Christian monks were strikingly similar (suggesting a cultural exchange) to Hindu and Buddhist meditators in India at that time. These Christian meditators repeated silently or quietly a phrase from the Bible. The most popular phrase or mantra was "Lord Jesus Christ, Son of God, have mercy on me, a sinner."

There are numerous meditation approaches that are practiced today. A partial list includes Yoga, Transcendental meditation, Zen, and Tibetan Buddhism.[4]

Practically all meditation approaches seek to achieve a meditative state by having a person concentrate on and repeat a mantra. Examples of mantras include a chant, a sound, a word, a phrase, a spiritual value, imagery of a relaxing place, and so on. Different approaches use different mantras, different rituals, seek to produce somewhat different meditative experiences, and have somewhat different goals to be attained through meditation.

Transcendental meditation (TM) will be used as an illustration as it is the most popular meditation approach in this country. TM was developed by Maharishi Mahesh Yogi (a Hindu spiritual leader) and gained popularity in the 1960s in America when it was practiced by such celebrities as the Beatles.

In TM meditators repeat to themselves a mantra over and over in their mind, while seating comfortably in a quiet place. The mantra in TM is a Sanskrit sound or word that is given to the meditators by TM instructors. The mantras come from Sanskrit sources used by many Hindus, and are not unique to TM. (Benson has found any word or phrase will work just as well as the words given by TM instructors. Benson, for example, states the word "one" repeated over and over will have the same meditative effect as the words given by TM instructors).[5] Two examples of mantras given by TM instructors are "Aing" (a sound sacred to the divine mother) and "Shyam" (a name of Lord Krishna). TM meditators are advised to meditate 20 minutes in the morning and 20 minutes in the evening, usually before breakfast and dinner.

Among other merits, research evidence shows meditation is effective in reducing stress and anxiety, and thereby useful in treating a wide range of psychosomatic disorders—including headaches, ulcers, diarrhea, constipation, and hypertension.[6]

Meditation appears to have therapeutic value as it successfully stops a person from thinking about (and worrying about his/her day-to-day problems). Meditation does this by having a person sit in a quiet place, in a comfortable position, and especially by encouraging a person to stop thinking about day-to-day concerns and instead concentrating on repeating a mantra over and over.[7]

JOB DESCRIPTION	Title of Position: Social Worker III–Single-Parent Counselor Department: County Department of Social Services Division: Child Welfare

1. Duties and responsibilities: (Indicate the approximate percentage of time devoted to each major task or group of tasks).

70% A. Direct services include:

1. Counseling, providing therapeutic services, and information-sharing with single parents (pregnant females, unwed mothers, and alleged fathers) and their families, utilizing home visits, office interviews, and telephone contacts. Counseling services include premarital, marital, parental, sexual, educational, fertility control, and general family planning counseling, as well as parenting child care, and money management skills. Therapy is provided in conjunction with the counseling and may be on a one-to-one, group, or co-counseling basis. The counseling modality is the choice of the worker and may include Rogerian, Gestalt, rational emotive therapy, provocative therapy, confrontive therapy, transactional analysis, crisis-intervention, conjoint family therapy, as well as any others and/or an eclectic approach.

2. Ongoing evaluation of physical, social, psychological, and emotional environments existing in the family constellation, thereby assessing the level of maximization of individual potentials and assisting the client to meet same. Counseling and planning, as well as expediting such plans, for the unborn (keeping the child, terminating parental rights, placement in foster care, explanation of adoptive procedures, legal rights, and so forth.)

3. Placement of children in foster homes and working with the foster parents in terms of child development and child care (related to specific children's needs). Working with the parents toward rehabilitating the home and the return of the minor to the natural parents. Supervising visits between the natural parent and the minor child.

4. Relicensing foster homes.

5. Counseling and "supervising" single-parent families where the intake assessment has been one of child neglect, focusing on the protection of the child as well as the rehabilitation of the parent.

6. Knowledge of and the ability to use appropriately the Wisconsin Child Welfare Statutes (Chapter 48), Health and Social Services Statutes (Chapter 49), and court proceedings revolving around same.

5% B. Use of community services, resources, and professionals when deemed appropriate. These include, but are not limited to, county courts, child-care facilities, foster homes, group homes, County

Guidance Clinic, the County Youth Shelter, educational and training facilities, institutions providing residential and/or medical resources including long-term treatment centers, hospitals, clinics, private practitioners, public health and school nurses, family planning clinics, medically approved abortion clinics, juvenile and adult probation and parole offices, and so on.

10% C. Complete narrations, agency forms and related documents, prepare court reports and general correspondence, following prescribed formats.

3% D. Participate in training and educational opportunities, staff and unit meetings, supervisory conferences and community conferences.

5% E. Provide training courses for agency staff; public relations presentations as assigned or self-originated and approved; supervise student interns as assigned.

7% F. Implement and assume responsibility for completion of special assignments and/or projects as assigned by supervisor and/or agency administration.

G. Other duties as assigned.
(Transportation time is required in all sections above.)

2. Qualifications required: (Indicate the more important qualifications that would be required for filling a vacancy—such as education, experience, knowledge, skills, abilities, and special physical and personality characteristics, etc.)

Must comply with Wisconsin Merit System requirements. The agency requires B.S. in Social Work Degree; at least three years' experience as a social worker; 255 in-service training credits; 12 graduate credits from an accredited School of Social Work or extension program; must have a car and a valid driver's license; should have a sophisticated level of expertise and practice skills; must be a mature and perceptive person with a strong sense of self. Counselor must be able to develop and expedite creative problem solving. Assigned most difficult cases in the agency (in general) as well as being expected to manage a caseload as well as special assignments.

3. Supplementary information: (Indicate any other information which further explains the importance, difficulty, or responsibility of the position.)

On meeting the prerequisites of this position, the social worker is expected to be assigned the most complex cases, particularly involving problems related to her/his high level of expertise. The worker may provide services via group work, co-counseling with one of his/her peers, initiate and preside over staffings, and is expected to function autonomously in terms of the use of social work skills.

SOURCE: Ursula Meyers, "Job Description: Social Worker III," Rock County Department of Social Services, Janesville, Wisconsin, 1977.

Extensive paperwork is involved in this accountability process. An effective social worker generally has a working knowledge of a variety of treatment approaches. In working with clients, the worker should focus on selecting the most effective treatment approaches to help the client solve the problem(s), rather than trying to redefine the client's problem so as to be able to use the worker's favorite treatment approach.

Sample job description

The preceeding two pages contain an actual job description for a social work position. The job description is for a single-parent counselor at a county social services (public assistance) agency in the state of Wisconsin. The description is "typical" in the sense that it specifies need, knowledge of certain treatment approaches, specifies the task assignments for the position, and specifies the training and experience required for the position. (The position is for a "third"-level position in social work practice and therefore requires training and work experience beyond the baccalaureate degree.)

TYPICAL SOCIAL WORK ACTIVITIES

A social worker is a multiskilled person, having training and expertise in a wide range of areas. Caseworkers, of course, counsel individuals who have problems. They have contact with other family members to obtain additional information and to enlist their support in a treatment plan. Many times the family itself becomes the focus of treatment rather than the initial client. They seek services for clients from other agencies in the community and also respond to service requests from other agencies. They relate to day-care centers, schools, hospitals, probation department, and other community service agencies, as well as to banks, busi-nesses, and churches. They deal with the court and at times are required to provide reports to the court as well as testify in court and to carry out judicial decisions. They sometimes form and lead groups. They interpret their services through speeches to community organizations, and by providing reports and interviews to the press. Gaps in services are at times identified, and often social workers are involved in the development of new services.

The following material provides case illustrations of the multifaceted functions, duties, and roles of a social worker. The material is a hypothetical summary of the experiences of a supervisor of a single parent unit at a county social services agency.

Examples of referrals

Mary M _____
Address _____
Age 28
Circumstances precipitating request for services: Two months pregnant, plans to keep baby and remain single; employed but afraid she'll be fired; alleged father age 19 and said to be drug dependent; was in foster care as child. Wishes to see Single-Parent Worker immediately.

Jean P _____
Address _____
Age 16
Alleged circumstances precipitating request for services: Five months pregnant; single; living in parental home (alleged father also living there); parents refuse to permit marriage although they know couple have intercourse. Jean wishes services of Single-Parent Counselor to help her get married.

Betty O _____
Address _____
Age 13

Circumstances precipitating request for services: Referred by VD Clinic as potential Child Welfare case (was taken to the clinic by an older brother when a male friend told him he thought Betty had VD); two months pregnant; has active syphilis; indicates she has been sexually active since she was ten; is on amphetamines and barbiturates, some experience with cocaine; Indicated at clinic that mother physically abusive in disciplinary methods; father deceased; no previous record. Immediate assessment required: Child Welfare Unit referral.

Bill _____
Address _____
Age 17

Circumstances precipitating request for services: Thinks his girl is pregnant; wants to see a counselor and will bring girl with him; appeared to be distraught. Wishes to talk to male Social Worker on one-to-one basis.

Some of these referrals may be early intervention, short-term involvements, but some may require intensive, long-term counseling. Let's look at how a casework narration might work up over a period of time.

Case examples of the intervention and therapy process

LYNN: Age 13, referred to Social Services Assessment Section by the School Social Worker; is six-and-one-half months pregnant. Medical attention began at five months when parents became aware of pregnancy.

Initial assessment: Precipitating problem—adolescent pregnancy; focus of social services—resolution of problems relating to and arising out of high-risk, single pregnancy; primary target system is Lynn, with secondary target systems her immediate family and the alleged father of the pregnancy. This case is designated a protective

services case under the child welfare statutes and will be provided social services at Lynn's request on an intensive level until such time as Lynn and her social worker mutually agree to terminate their social services relationship.

Lynn is a brown-eyed brunette, a slight and physically immature girl. Both parents are living. She has indicated that she would like to work on the following problem areas immediately: how she became pregnant and the physiology of pregnancy, what happens when you have a baby, what she will do with the baby after it is born. Her educational program is apparently not an immediate problem, as she has indicated quite strongly that she plans to stay in school and is going to graduate and become a beauty operator. She is attending the alternate classroom program for pregnant girls and is doing well, according to Lynn and the school social worker.

As indicated, Lynn is interested in and requires input in the areas of health and human development, with perhaps some discussion of adolescent sexuality, the birth process, and postnatal planning. It is expected other areas of mutual concern will open up during counseling sessions. Case is being transferred to the Single-Parents Services Unit for assignment.

SOCIAL WORKER BOHL: Date of summary narration: ____. Focus of casework relationship—resolution of problems arising from high-risk teenage pregnancy of single, 13-year-old female. Social worker role—counseling and advocacy. Counseling took place at Lynn's house after school, or after evening meal if parents were included. Both parents are employed full time. I have been seeing Lynn on a weekly basis since date of assignment. She is now three months postpartum, having prematurely delivered a female child on ____, three weeks prior to due date. It was a normal delivery, although the infant weighed four pounds seven ounces at birth and was kept in the high-risk nursery in an incubator until she weighed five pounds, a matter of six days.

Summary of events and contacts: The initial focus was to respond to Lynn's designated problem areas. Methods used were tutorial as well as response to direct questions, involvement of health professionals, and nondirective reality-based counseling. We used *Our Bodies, Ourselves*[8] as our text, plus discussions, films and books provided by me and the public health nurse, Mrs. ___ and the maternity unit at ___ Hospital. A tour of the maternity wing and delivery room fortunately took place before her early delivery. It was evident, from Lynn's many questions about sexuality, that she was aware of the basic plumbing involved in becoming pregnant but was uninformed about the essence of male and female sexuality. (We continue to cover this in bits and pieces as she brings it up, or as I see the opportunity to incorporate it in the learning process. It is apparent to me that Lynn is just beginning to find her self, her identity. It is interesting to note that she has never spoken of herself as a "mother," even though we are confronting this issue in our reality therapy.)

I had advised Lynn early on that I would be involving her parents in the counseling program, and that the alleged father of the child would also be a primary person in our casework relationship. There was little affective response to this information. In fact, a major concern of mine is the quality of family interaction, and the apparent arms-length relationship they have with one another. Perhaps one of the peripheral results of this unexpected and probably unwanted pregnancy will be to initiate a viable communications system between family members. I see this as an objective, even though the need for open communication does not yet seem apparent to the family.

Interspersed, then, with the one-to-one visits with Lynn were counseling sessions with Lynn and her parents. The primary focus of these was to respond to Lynn's request for postpartum planning. Secondary focus was enhanced communications among family members. Both individually and with her parents we explored the alternatives available—whether to keep the baby and raise it as a single parent (we agreed that this would be a most difficult task) or to terminate parental rights and free the baby for adoptive placement. (We agreed that this would also be difficult.) The pros and cons of both these decisions were explored. Lynn's comment was that no matter what she decided, she was growing up faster than she really wanted to. During one of the last decision-making visits, she began to cry uncontrollably. This was the first real breakthrough, for I now began to have hope that this youngster could start accepting herself as a feeling person, even though the feelings coming out were essentially unhappy ones. We talked for a long time that night, and it was the best use of overtime that I've made in many a workweek. We examined her feelings of denial and anger, and the tasks she would be working on after the baby's birth. It was a rewarding session for both of us.

On ___, during Lynn's eighth month of pregnancy, I was thrown a real curve. Lynn's mother called me at the office and asked me to stop over on my way home from work as she had something to discuss with me. I did, and was greeted with an announcement that she and her husband had decided that they "would really like to have another baby around the house," and that she felt she had worked long enough, was "quitting" and staying home to take care of "our baby." Lynn was sitting on the couch looking at her feet and crying. I (tactfully, I hope) advised her mother that Lynn, as the mother, was the only person legally able to make any decision in regard to the baby, and that the alleged father, with whom we had met several times during the course of the past two months, also had certain rights and responsibilities. Her mother then informed me that they had become aware of Lynn's pregnancy during her second month, not her fifth, and had refused to discuss the alternative of abortion with her because abortion was against their moral beliefs, and that they also did not believe in giving away "your own flesh and blood." They had apparently been spending most of our very quiet counseling sessions coming to their recent decision.

At that point, my role shifted into that of an advocate for Lynn and the baby and their personal and legal rights. Much of the next two hours was spent stressing the urgency of actively permitting Lynn to make her own choice. I was not successful.

The following day the alleged father, Tom, age 17 and a high school senior, came in to see me, visibly upset. He said that he had a part-time job and was willing to help pay for the expenses, but that he had thought all along that Lynn was going to give up the baby and that he would be "signing the papers" for termination of his parental rights. He liked Lynn and thought she was a nice girl to be with but he was "sure not about to mess up his life." I tried as tactfully as I could to let him know that while he had not necessarily "messed up" his life, he had to deal with some hard facts as to responsibilities, and that he also had some rights as well. As it stands now, his parents are going to hire an attorney to fight any paternity action taken by her parents. I have also involved Bill Adler as co-counselor and Tom's advocate, with Tom's consent.

Lynn was unable, even with my support, to fight her parents. She is, after all only 14, having had a birthday recently, and still a very dependent minor. The pressures at home were apparently too much for her, and

she decided to keep the baby. After the decision was made, we focused on making every effort to ensure the success of her revised plan. Lynn was referred to the high-risk center for maternal care and fortunately was able to deliver there in spite of her precipitous delivery. We involved the public health nurse in a schedule of regular visits to teach prepartum and assist in postpartum child care. Lynn is eligible for child care monies, since the family income has been reduced. Her mother is providing infant care while Lynn is in school.

In fact, Lynn's mother is assuming more and more of the mothering role for the new baby. Indeed, after an initial spurt of "playing mother" following her release from the hospital, Lynn is drawing away from her parenting responsibilities. She is expressing some hostility toward her mother for taking over the baby, and yet has also told me that she does not want to bother with the baby any more. "My mother and father got what they wanted."

It is apparent that at this point, Lynn is experiencing some normal ambivalence toward what she is biologically—a mother—and what she is emotionally and developmentally—a 14-year-old girl in process of becoming a person. We have agreed that this is going to be the focus of our casework relationship for the next several months. Contraception will continue to be a discussion point. I expect that Lynn will draw further and further away from her biological role, prematurely imposed, and become emerged in the process of becoming a person. This will be our joint goal, time-frame open-ended, with counseling appointments on a weekly basis for now. End of narration. Review date: three months.

JEAN: This is a short-term involvement, as I have been called in by the hospital to see a 19-year-old girl who has just delivered and wishes to TPR (terminate parental rights).

She is apparently quite bright, because she is an advanced student at ___ and has been in college since she was 16.

Initial Assessment: Jean X. is certainly bright academically. She is in her last year at ___ University, having completed high school on an accelerated program, and is planning to go on to medical school, having already been accepted under a special program for disadvantaged persons. She is a physically mature young woman, short and small-boned, who has just been through what she described as a "rotten experience." Jean wishes to have the services of our agency to assist her in terminating her rights to her "accident" and to avoid any publicity in the matter. In checking with the nurse, I find that although the delivery was extremely difficult, the child is a healthy boy, and weighs seven pounds, four ounces. Jean has not named the father of the child.

I will be the primary social worker on the case because of its short-term nature and its crisis orientation.

Focus of the therapeutic relationship: Resolution of problems precipitated by problem pregnancy. Social worker role: Counselor, advocate, and expeditor. During my initial visit with Jean, she literally exploded with information, and used four-letter words to describe her condition. She is a motivated young woman, and indicated to me that she was not letting this accident of birth stand in her way of achieving her life goals. She informed me that she had been on contraceptives, had been sexually active with several friends, white and nonwhite, had no idea who the father of the child was and was extremely angry at the contraceptive failure she had experienced. I asked about abortion, and she said that she had denied the pregnancy and that by the time she realized she was really pregnant, it was too late to do anything "easy." (Because of the second-naturedness of my alternatives discussion, I did discuss them all. Jean is determined to TPR.)

By the time I explained the process of terminating both parent's rights, she was quite depressed. Publication and all those legal requirements would make it very difficult for her to remain anonymous. I tried as tactfully as possible to mention that her pregnancy may have been obvious; she said it was not as she hardly showed.

I left her with a list of procedures for TPR, and said that I would stop by to see her the next day, explaining also that I would be her support throughout the entire process.

When I saw her the next day we talked a long while about the strength it would involve on her part to go through the emotionally rigorous procedure of termination, particularly because there would be publication for all possible fathers. She seemed determined, and at the end of our discussion we both thought and felt that she was making the right decision.

Jean returned to her studies after agreeing to meet as needed because of legal procedures or personal problems. I saw her several times prior to the hearing, primarily to provide information and support.

The termination hearing took place yesterday after the routine 10-day publication in an area newspaper for the unknown fathers. The hearing went well and quickly. Jean is a staunch young woman. She had said hello and goodbye to the baby in the hospital and saw it off to its foster home. She knew he would be there only temporarily, and asked me to let her know something about the adoptive parents when he is placed in a permanent home. I will.

End of narration. Case closed; to be reopened only at request of client. Referral was made to the Family Planning Clinic at Jean's request for postdelivery contraception.

DORIS: Age 16, a high school junior at The ___ School; referred to us by Information and Referral Service for abortion information and counseling. Initial contact was by telephone, directly to me. I will be the social worker on the crisis intervention situation as requested by the client.

Focus of the relationship: Resolution of problems resulting from unwanted pregnancy. Client's objective: Termination of the pregnancy by abortion. Social worker's role: Counseling and advocacy.

Summary of contacts: On Monday I received a telephone call from Doris indicating she had called I&R for a resource to help her get an abortion and that our agency was among the resources suggested. She told me her age and that she thought she was pregnant, definitely wanted an abortion, did not want anyone to know anything about the pregnancy, did not want me to know her last name. She "just wanted a good, safe place to go." I told her I would respect her desire and right to privacy and that we could discuss her concerns right then if she had time.

She did. She then informed me that she was across the street in a telephone booth. Could she come over and talk to me? Yes, she could.

Doris is a heavy-set, open-faced and matter-of-fact girl. She had not, however, had a confirmation of pregnancy. This came out in our discussion and we promptly arranged for the test at the Family Planning Clinic. She told me that she had been "screwing around since she was 14," did not think she would ever become pregnant because she had not become pregnant yet, and would not under any circumstances have a baby even if she did become pregnant. She didn't like kids. These comments led to a discussion of alternatives to abortion, verification that abortion was by free choice on her part, should she actually be pregnant, and general information as to medical clinics available in the area, procedures used by these clinics, the actual process of abortion from the patient's standpoint, and after care. Doris left for her pregnancy test and was to call me if it was positive. She did and it was.

Arrangements were made for a therapeutic abortion in three days. As the client wishes complete confidentiality, I will drive her to her appointment. This will enable me to, hopefully, do some counseling in the areas of birth control, self-concept, and responsibility. I see the primary need at this time to be contraceptive-oriented, and Doris is in agreement that she could use some help in this area.

On Saturday Doris and I drove to Madison, and she had a first trimester abortion. She experienced no difficulty other than slight fatigue. She will have a follow-up visit in two weeks, barring any unusual problems. She appeared quite relieved and was relaxed and talkative on the return trip. We discussed birth control and made an appointment for a more in-depth counseling session in four days. It was also agreed that she would use the family planning clinic "now that she knew where it was." I gently reminded her that it had been listed in the telephone book for over a year.

Just as I dropped Doris off around the corner from her home, she asked me if I would "help her get her head together" about herself. I told her to think about the things she wanted to talk about before our next session, and that we would go from there to wherever she chose.

We have moved from an objective-and-time-limited contract to an open-ended one. It will be exciting and interesting to see what areas this young woman wishes to explore and in what direction she will eventually move.

End of narration. Contacts to be initiated by client.

Since reduction in the incidence of premature parenthood among teenagers is a primary objective of single-parent social work,

TELEPHONE LOG   A hypothetical telephone log kept by a Single-Parent Unit Supervisor might read something like this stream-of-consciousness account of one day's calls: Telephone contacts, Week of August 16: Supervisor's notes—

A.M.—Early call today. The young man sounded very young and unsure. Wanted to know where to go to get some counseling on contraceptives "and sex." I told him about our "men only" clinic for family planning and the Blue Bus, and also let him know that we had staff people that would be available to him should he wish to become involved in more long-term counseling than was available at the clinic. He finally asked about VD testing and I gave him a list of our resources, again mentioned the clinic, and suggested he might want to call ahead to make a longer appointment with the social worker there. I also let him know that a supply of free condoms was available for persons coming to the clinic for their initial visit, and that the clinic was free. He said thank you very much, and hung up before I could say much more. I hope he gets to the clinic, that he doesn't have VD, and that he starts practicing contraception immediately. I can't stop being frustrated about the boy's reliance on the girls to practice birth control. Hope the Family Planning Clinic for men takes off and can become a viable part of our preventive programming for next year, too.

A.M.—Marilyn calls with some great news—the Ortho "detail" man is coming to do a two-hour presentation on contraception for the staff, complete with film, samples, and experience in counseling men. What perfect timing, and what a "creative concepts" person she is. (If she ever wants to leave single-parent services, I'll throttle her.) We will use this as an in-service training program for the staff and a brushup for the single-parent workers. It helps to have our continuing education programs take place here at the office. The caseloads are so intensive that I am loathe to have the social workers leave for two or three days' training away from home base, even though it is a necessary part of their job responsibilities.

A.M.—Liz called and is in conference with a 23-year-old pregnant woman who was due last week and is planning to give up her child for adoption. She has had no previous contact with our agency. Can I get someone to handle the termination of parental rights, foster placement of the infant, contact of adoption agency of client's choice, and crisis counseling of the mother once Liz completes the initial stages of intake? I say "yes," check my assignment book (everyone has so many new cases), and tell her I will contact Sherry. "Good," she says. "I'll talk to you in a little while about the fine print." I call Sherry.

A.M.—The newspaper is on the line and wants to know about the recent case of the baby found abandoned in a nearby college dormitory. I refer them to our Public Information Specialist, as I can't discuss confidential cases with anyone (Agency regulations and common sense).

A.M.—The mother of a young client calls and tells me that the local school system is dragging its feet on programming her daughter for special education classes. "Does she really need Special Education classes?" I ask. This leads to a long discussion on what is best for the daughter in today's school environment versus what the mother's experience was in her day. As it turns out, mother is anxious, not the pregnant girl. She likes being in the regular classroom structure, is doing well, and won't be delivering until well after school is out for the semester. We leave it that the mother will call the school and withdraw her request for special programs. We have had a good exchange of ideas (I can certainly understand where she is coming from) and we are both the wiser for our conversation.

A.M.—The student social work intern is due in five minutes and I need some coffee.

P.M.—The YWCA called and would like to have B___ speak to their Alternate Classroom for pregnant teens on adolescent sexuality. Can she come next week? Fine with me, but please double check with Public Information and B___. Next week may be all booked with client appointments.

P.M.—An alleged father with whom we have had a very good working relationship is waiting on my other line. He is worried about Ann and the baby. Ann seems to be going into a severe depressive state and is not taking care of the baby. He is working the second shift and can't be at home in early evening when the depression seems to peak. Can I get in touch with the social worker and ask her to stop by to see Ann after work today? I will try, but someone will call on Ann, one way or another. I try to determine whether this depression seems to be of a normal postpartum variety, or exaggerated postpartum, or something more. He doesn't know. She just sits and cries a lot. Sometimes he does too, he says. I reassure him that if no one else can get over to see her, I will go. Good, he says and hangs up. (Nineteen—perhaps too young to be a father. She is 18. They are having a trial marriage without the ceremony. Much work ahead for everyone. Better leave a call in for S___.)

P.M.—Edna (my secretary) alerts me to a call on her line, and that the woman has been waiting for 10 minutes to talk to me. It is a mother with a 12-year-old daughter allegedly pregnant by her step-father. She wants to come down to see me right away, needs abortion counseling for her daughter and divorce counseling for herself. I block out the rest of the afternoon and tell her to come right away. (We will bypass the intake worker this time, but I call the Protective Services Units for standby on this one, as there may be a child abuse situation on the basis of the mother's statement.) I think I need some more coffee and a Gelusil.

practice skills must include strong abilities in public speaking and "consumer" education. Social workers are given ample opportunity to demonstrate those skills by cooperative school systems, and it is not unusual for each Single-Parent Specialist to appear as guest "lecturers," group discussion leaders, or panelists at regular high school and middle-school classroom sessions.

The anonymous questions asked of such a panel by a large class of senior high school students give some indication of young adults' need for accurate information, and the fallacy of assuming that "by the time they are in senior high, they know it all."

Can kids under 18 get birth control? How? Do you have to pay for it?

How do most teenagers you've encountered feel about having a baby at such an early stage of life?

How can persons deal with society if they become pregnant?

If a girl is pregnant and wants to keep her baby can her parents make her give the child up?

What advice would you give to a girl about premarital sex and getting pregnant?

Are there places that take girls that want to have their baby but don't want anyone to know? How much do they cost? How do you find out about them? Where can a girl go if she gets kicked out of the house?

Why do you think there are so many unwanted pregnancies?

If an unwanted baby arrives, does it usually end up being messed up and abused?

Do you talk with the fathers? Any legal rights binding a guy to marry a girl he got pregnant if she's under age and he's legal age?

Is the boy obligated to pay for an abortion or the cost of having the child if his girl becomes PG? If you don't marry her and she keeps the kid, must you pay child support? What if he can't pay?

Why is it some boys when they find out that their girl is PG want to run, or tell the girl how do you know it's mine?

Do most guys desert the girl after the pregnancy is final?

Can you make the guy marry you even if he doesn't want anything to do with it?

In how many cases do parents adopt a teenage daughter's unwanted baby?

Hi there! If a girl gets pregnant and feels she does not want the baby does the guy get anything to say as to whether or not she has the child? Can he say she should not have it? Just how much say does a male have in this? Any?

How dangerous are the consequences of an abortion?

In the case of an abortion, can the male watch this or not? To see what a pain it is.

How do you think most guys would feel if his girl had an abortion?

If you are under 18 can you get an abortion without your parents' say so? If you are under 18 do you think that parents have any right to make you have an abortion or give up the child?

What is the best method of abortion? Is it unhealthy to have more than one? Is there any place around here where you can go? How much does it cost? Do you have to stay there long?

Has the population dropped since abortions were legalized?

What is the percentage of mistakes in abortions that cause damage?

Is there any place a girl can go around here if she is pregnant and doesn't want to tell her parents?

Who does a girl contact if she wants to give her baby up for adoption? Can she see the baby after that?

Do you think a 17-year-old girl can manage to have and keep her baby and bring it up the right way and how hard would it be, even if she is not living at home and on her own in all ways?

Responding to the needs and wishes of single parents with a comprehensive and cohesive program requires the cooperation of many community agencies and professionals. Public and private social service agency personnel, health care providers, school counselors, mental health professionals, child care providers, hospital personnel and family planning clinicians can become involved in a community organization program which focuses on comprehensive programming and information sharing among these professionals. (A letter "calling" for a meeting involving comprehensive programming is presented above.)

Every once in a while, a surge of creative thinking takes place, and the social work experience reaches out to design and establish an innovative preventive program. (Social work has long been accused of Band-Aid philosophies and practices, perhaps with some justification.) An example of an innovative proposal is presented below.

COORDINATION AND PLANNING

A "call" to a meeting involving comprehensive programming and information sharing:

Dear Counselor,

The next quarterly meeting of Single Parent Counselors and Care Providers will be held at the County Social Services Building on Monday, March 10 at 9 A.M. We will be updating on several issues, among them the impact of recent court decisions on minors' rights, the current status of the alternate school for pregnant girls program in ___ School District, and the issue of independent adoptions. We also have the credentials of a new abortion clinic located in ___ and will be relating this information to you.

The Supervisor of the Birth Department at ___ ___ Hospital will not be able to attend, but wanted me to let you know that effective yesterday, the alleged father may accompany the mother into the delivery room to observe the birth. Please advise your young mothers and fathers of this change in hospital policy.

If you cannot attend the meeting, please call Edna and let her know. Otherwise, we will be expecting you.

Sincerely yours,

Supervisor, Single Parent Services
County Department of Social Services

| INVOLVEMENT IN DEVELOPING NEEDED NEW PROGRAMS | A project proposal for preventive contraceptive programming for men became a reality in the Spring of 1980. The brief proposal for the clinic read: |

FOR MEN ONLY
FAMILY PLANNING PILOT PROJECT

Proposal writer: Ursula Myers, A.C.S.W., M.S.W.

Date: January, 7, 1980

Objective: To provide family planning education and counseling to men of any age seeking these services.

Counselors: Professional Social Workers from the staff of County Department of Social Services who have had special training and experience in Family Planning and Human Sexuality.

Location: County Family Planning Clinic.

Time frame: February 1, 1980 to June 30, 1980

Schedule: Weekly, beginning Thursday, February 6, and every week thereafter; hours—3:00 P.M. to 4:30 P.M.

Staff: Two male counselors.

Public information: Letters (from clinic) to schools and YMCAs; newspaper articles; posters.

Target system: All men of any age, particularly teenage and young adult males.

Goals: To effect an increase in male contraceptive use, an awareness of human sexuality, and a decrease in the number of single parent pregnancies, particularly among the teenage population.

Does this capsule description of the social work experience with single parents cover all bases? No, it does not. Does it satisfy the writer as to content? No, it does not. The essence of the social work relationship and the interpersonal dynamics between client and counselor do not translate too well into the printed word. It should be apparent to the reader that the material in this chapter is only intended to give an elementary introduction and a beginning experiential awareness of casework.

SUMMARY

Traditionally, working with individuals in social work is called casework. The primary skill and role of a caseworker is coun-seling. Other roles include: broker, public education, advocate, outreach, teacher of new information and skills, behavioral specialist, and consultant. Counseling, from the client's perspective can be conceptualized as involving these progressive stages:

1. Problem awareness.
2. Relationship to counselor.
3. Motivation.
4. Conceptualizing the problem.
5. Exploration of resolution strategies.
6. Selection of a strategy.
7. Implementation of the strategy.
8. Evaluation.

Questions have in recent years been raised whether casework and counseling are effective. In actuality, casework is not a single method; rather, there are many theoretical approaches to casework. Some approaches are more effective than others. In future years there will be considerable research on testing various approaches to casework, with the less effective approaches gradually being discarded. An effective caseworker has a working knowledge of a wide variety of treatment approaches.

To be effective at counseling, a caseworker needs skills in (a) establishing a working relationship with clients and (b) interviewing in order to explore problems in depth, and s/he also needs (c) a knowledge of various treatment approaches and community resources so that alternative resolution strategies can be explored with clients.

A caseworker is a multiskilled professional who is able to work effectively with troubled individuals, families, groups, the news media, and other community agencies and organizations. The chapter gave case examples of problems encountered and skills needed in social work practice.

NOTES

1. Joel Fischer, "Is Casework Effective? A Review," *Social Work* 18 (January 1973), pp. 5–20.

2. A. E. Bergin, "The Effects of Psychotherapy: Negative Results Revisited," *Journal of Counseling Psychology* 10 (1963), pp. 244–50; H. J. Eysenck, "The Effects of Psychotherapy," *International Journal of Psychiatry* 1 (1965), pp. 97–144; Joel Fischer, "Is Casework Effective? A Review;" R. B. Stuart, *Trick or Treatment: How and When Psychotherapy Fails* (Champaign, Ill.: Research Press, 1970).

3. H. J. Eysenck, "The Effects of Psychotherapy"; G. Heilbrunn, "Results with Psychoanalytic Therapy," *American Journal of Psychotherapy* 17 (1963), pp. 427–35; J. Leo, "Psychoanalysis Reaches a Crossroad," *New York Times,* April 4, 1968, sec. 1, pp. 1, 58; A. Salter, *The Case against Psychoanalysis* (New York: Citadel Press, 1963).

4. An expanded list of meditation approaches is presented and described by Daniel Goleman, "Meditation without Mystery," *Psychology Today,* March 1977.

5. Herbert Benson, *The Relaxation Response* (New York: Avon Books, 1975).

6. K. R. Pelletier, *Mind as Healer, Mind as Slayer* (New York: Delta, 1977).

7. Benson, *Relaxation Response.*

8. Boston Health Collective, *Our Bodies, Ourselves,* 2d ed. (New York: Simon & Schuster, 1976).

chapter 21

TYPES OF GROUPS IN SOCIAL WORK

A group generally is defined as

a plurality of individuals who are in contact with one another, who take one another into account, and who are aware of some significant commonality—an essential feature of a group is that its members have something in common and that they believe that what they have in common makes a difference[1]

Groups are increasingly being used in social work. The focus of groups has considerable variation as the following summary indicates.

Social conversation. Such conversation is often loose and tends to drift aimlessly. There is no formal agenda of topics to deal with. If the topic is dull, the subject is apt to change. Individuals may have some goal, perhaps only to establish an acquaintance-ship, but such individual goals need not become the agenda for the entire group. Social conservation is often employed for "testing" purposes, to determine how deep a relationship might develop with people we do not know very well. In social work, social conversation with other professionals is frequent, but groups involving clients generally have objectives other than conversation.

Recreation groups. The objective is to provide activities for enjoyment and exercise. Often such activities are spontaneous, and the groups are practically leaderless. The group service agency (such as YMCA, YWCA, or neighborhood center) may offer little more than physical space and the use of some equipment. Spontaneous playground activities, informal athletic games, and an open game room are examples. Some group agencies providing such physical space claim that recreation and interaction with others helps to build "character," and helps prevent delinquency among youth by providing an alternative to the street.

Recreation skill groups. The objective is to improve a set of skills, while at the same time providing enjoyment. In contrast to recreational groups, an adviser, coach, or instructor is generally present

Social work practice with groups

**AN EXAMPLE OF
A THERAPY
GROUP**

Several years ago when I was employed as a social worker at a maximum security hospital for the criminally insane, my supervisor requested that I develop and be a leader for a therapy group. When I asked such questions as "What should be the objectives of such a group?" and "Who shall be selected to join?" my supervisor indicated those decisions would be mine. He added that no one else was doing any group therapy at this hospital, and the hospital administration thought it would be desirable for accountability reasons for group therapy programs to be developed at this hospital.

Being newly employed at the hospital, and wary because I had never been a leader for a group before, I asked myself "Who is in the greatest need of group therapy?" and "If the group members do not improve, or even deteriorate, how will I be able to explain this; that is, cover my tracks?" I concluded that I should select those identified as being the "sickest" (those labeled as chronic schizophrenic) to invite as members of the group. Those labeled as chronic schizophrenic are generally expected to show little improvement. With such an expectation, if they did not improve, I felt I would not be blamed. However, if they did improve, I thought it would be viewed as a substantial accomplishment.

My next step was to invite those labeled as chronic schizophrenic to join the group. I met with each individually, and explained the purpose of the group and the probable topics that would be covered. I then invited them to join; 8 of the 11 who were contacted decided to join. Some of the eight frankly stated they would join primarily because it would look good on their record and increase their chances for an early release.

In counseling these group members, the therapy approach used was based on reality therapy as described in the following material.

At the first meeting the purpose and the focus of the group was again presented and described. It was explained that the purpose was not to review their past, but to help them make their present life more enjoyable and meaningful, and to help them to make plans for the future. Various topics, it was explained, would be covered: including how to convince the hospital staff they no longer needed to be hospitalized, how to prepare themselves for returning to their home community (for example, learning an employable skill while at the institution), what to do when they felt depressed or had some other unwanted emotion, and following their release what they should do if and when they had an urge to do something that would get them into trouble again. It was further explained that occasional films covering some of these topics would be shown and then discussed, and it was indicated the group would meet for about an hour each week for the next 12 weeks (until the fall when I had to return to school).

This focus on improving their current circumstances stimulated their interest, but soon they found it uncomfortable and anxiety-producing to examine what the future might hold for them. The fact that they were informed they had some responsibility and some control of that future also created anxiety. They reacted to this discomfort by stating they were labeled mentally ill, and therefore had some internal condition which was causing their strange behavior, and unfortunately a cure for schizophrenia had not yet been found. Therefore they could do little to improve their situation.

They were informed their excuses were "garbage" (stronger terms were used), and we spent a few sessions on getting them to understand that the label "chronic schizophrenic" was a meaningless label. I spent considerable time in explaining (as discussed in Chapter 5) that mental illness is a myth; that is, people do not have a "disease of the mind," even though they may have emotional problems. I went on to explain that what had gotten them locked up was their deviant behavior, and that the only way for them to get out was to stop exhibiting their strange behavior and to convince the other staff that they would not be apt to exhibit deviant behavior if released.

The next set of excuses they then tried was that their broken homes, or ghetto schools, or broken romances, or something else in their past had "messed them up" and therefore they could do little about their situation. They were informed such excuses were also "garbage." True, their past experiences were important in their being here. But it was emphasized that what they wanted out of the future, along with their motivation to do something about achieving their goals, were more important than their past experiences in determining what the future would hold for them.

Finally, after we had worked through a number of excuses we were able to focus on how they could better handle specific problems: how to handle being depressed, how to stop exhibiting behavior considered "strange," how to present themselves as being "sane" in order to increase their chances of an early release, how they would feel and adjust to returning to their home communities, what kind of work or career they desired upon their release, how they could prepare themselves by learning a skill or trade while at this institution, helping them to examine what they wanted out of the future and the specific steps they would have to take to achieve their goals, why it was important that they should continue to take the psychoactive medication that had been prescribed and so on.

The results of this approach were very encouraging. Instead of idly spending much of the time brooding about their situation, they became motivated to improve their situation. At the end of the 12 weeks the eight members of the group spontaneously stated that the meetings were making a positive change in their lives and requested that another social worker from the hospital be assigned to continue the group after I left to return to school. This was arranged. Three years later on a return visit to the hospital I was informed that five of the eight group members had been released to their home community and two of the others were considered to have shown improvement. The final group member's condition was described as "unchanged."

A recreation skill group at a YMCA

Headstart Halloween party: An educational group

and there is more of a task orientation. Examples of activities include golf, basketball, needlework, arts or crafts, and swimming. Competitive team sports and leagues may emerge. Frequently such groups are led by professionals with recreational training rather than social work training. Social service agencies providing such services include YMCA, YWCA, Boy Scouts, Girl Scouts, neighborhood centers, and school recreational departments.

A Boy Scout troop

Educational groups. The focus of such groups is to acquire knowledge and learn more complex skills. The leader generally is a professional person with considerable training and expertise in the topic area. Examples of topics include child-rearing practices, training in becoming a more effective parent, preparing for becoming an adoptive parent, and training volunteers to perform a specialized task for a social service agency. Educational group leaders often function in a more didactic manner, and frequently are social workers. These groups may resemble a class, with considerable group interaction and discussion being encouraged.

Problem-solving and decision-making groups. Both providers and consumers of social services may become involved in this type of group. Providers of services use group meetings for such objectives as developing a treatment plan for a client or a group of clients, deciding how to best allocate scarce resources, deciding how to improve the delivery of services to clients, arriving at policy decisions for the agency, deciding how to improve coordination efforts with other agencies, and so on.

Potential consumers of services may form a group to seek to find approaches to meet some current community need. Data on the need may be gathered, and the group may be used as a vehicle either to develop a program or to influence existing agencies to provide services. Social workers may function as stimulators and organizers of such group efforts. (See the following chapter on community organization.)

In problem-solving and decision-making groups each participant normally has some interest or stake in the process and stands to gain or lose personally by the outcome. Usually, there is a formal leader of some sort, and other leaders sometimes emerge during the process.

Self-help groups. Self-help groups are becoming increasingly popular and are often successful in helping individuals with certain social or personal problems. Katz and Bender provide a comprehensive definition of self-help groups:

> Self-help groups are voluntary, small group structures for mutual aid, and the accomplishment of a special purpose. They are usually formed by peers who have come together for mutual assistance in satisfying a common need, overcoming a common handicap or life-disrupting problem, and bringing about desired social, and/or personal change. The initiators and members of such groups perceive that their needs are not, or cannot be, met by or through existing social institutions. Self-help groups emphasize face-to-face social interactions and the assumption of personal responsibility by members. They often provide material assistance, as well as emotional support, they are frequently "cause"-oriented, and promulgate an ideology or values through which members may attain an enhanced sense of personal identity.[2]

Alcoholics Anonymous, developed by two former alcoholics, was the first to demonstrate substantial success. A number of other self-help groups have since been formed. Alan Gartner and Frank Riessman in a text entitled *Help* describe over 200 self-help groups that are now active,[3] illustrations of which are presented in Table 21–1.

Many self-help groups stress: (*a*) a confession to the group by each member that s/he has a problem, (*b*) a testimony to the group recounting past experiences with the problem and plans for handling the problem in the future, (*c*) when a member feels a crisis (for example, an abusive parent having an urge to abuse a child), that member is encouraged to call another member of the group who comes over to stay with the person until the crisis subsides.

There appear to be several other reasons why such self-help groups are successful. The members have an internal understanding of the problem which helps them to help others. Having experienced the misery and consequences of the problem, they are highly motivated and dedicated to find ways to help themselves and others who are fellow sufferers. The participants also benefit from the "helper therapy principle," that is, the helper gains psychological rewards by helping others.[4] Helping others makes a person feel "good" and worthwhile, and also enables the helper to put his/her own problems into perspective as h/she sees that others have problems that may be as serious, or even more serious.

Some self-help groups, such as the National Organization of Women, focus on social advocacy and attempt to make legislative and policy changes in public and private institutions. Some self-help groups (such as parents of the mentally retarded) raise funds and operate community programs. Many people with a personal problem use self-help groups in the same way that others use social agencies. An additional advantage of self-help groups is that they generally are able to operate with a minimal budget.

TABLE 21–1 Some self-help groups

Organization	Service focus
Abused Women's Aid in Crisis	For battered wives and other abused women
Adoptee's Liberty Movement Association	For adoptees searching for their natural parents
Alcoholics Anonymous	For adult alcoholics
American Diabetes Association	Clubs for diabetics, their families, and friends
Brain Tumor Support Group	For persons with brain tumors or their loved ones
Burns Recovered	For burn victims
Caesarian Birth Association	For those expecting a caesarian birth
Candlelighters	For parents of young children with cancer
Checks Anonymous	For persons in debt
Concerned United Birthparents	For parents who have surrendered children for adoption
Depressives Anonymous	For depressives
Divorce Anonymous	For divorced persons
Emotions Anonymous	For persons with emotional problems
Emphysema Anonymous	For those with emphysema
Fly without Fear	For people who are afraid of flying
Fortune Society	For ex-offenders and their families
Gam-Anon	For families of gamblers
Gray Panthers	An intergenerational group
Make Today Count	For persons with cancer and their families
Mensa	For persons of high IQs
Naim Conference	For widowed persons
The National Council of Stutterers	For adult stutterers
National Organization of Women	For women's equal rights
Overeaters Anonymous	For overweight persons
Parents Anonymous	For parents of abused children
Phobia Self-Help Groups	For persons with phobias
Prison Families Anonymous	For family members of prisoners
Resolve	A support group for infertile people
Stroke Clubs	For those who have had strokes and their families
Survivors of Suicide Victims	For the relatives and friends of suicide victims
We Care	Support group for divorced and separated persons

Socialization groups. Many authorities consider this type as being the primary focus of group work.[5] The objective generally is to develop or change attitudes and behaviors of group members to become more socially acceptable. Social skill development, increasing self-confidence, and planning for the future are other focuses. Illustrations include: working with a group of predelinquent youth in group activities to curb delinquency trends, working with a youth group of diverse racial backgrounds to reduce racial tensions, working with a group of pregnant young girls at a maternity home to make plans for the future, working with a group of elderly residents at a nursing home to remotivate them and get them involved in various activities, working with a group of boys at a correctional school to help them make plans for returning to their home community. Leadership of such groups requires considerable skill and knowledge in using the group to foster individual growth and change. Leadership roles of socialization groups are frequently filled by social workers.

Therapeutic groups. Therapy groups are generally composed of members with rather severe emotional or personal problems.

An outdoor work training group at a sheltered workshop: Some of the training involves socialization

Leadership of such groups generally requires considerable skill in being perceptive, in having a knowledge of human behavior and group dynamics, in having group counseling capacities, and in being able to use the group to bring about behavioral changes. Among other skills, the group leader needs to be highly perceptive regarding how each member is being affected by what is being communicated. Considerable competence is needed in being able to develop and maintain a constructive atmosphere within the group. Similar to one-to-one counseling, the goal of therapy groups is generally to have members explore their problems in-depth, and to then develop one or more strategies for resolving such problems. The group therapist generally uses one or more psychotherapy approaches as a guide for changing attitudes and behaviors; examples of such therapy approaches include psychoanalysis, reality therapy, learning theory, rational therapy, transactional analysis, client-centered therapy, and psycho drama.

Sensitivity groups. Encounter groups, sensitivity training and T (training)-groups (these terms are used somewhat synonymously) refer to a group experience in which people relate to each other in a close interpersonal manner, and self-disclosure is required. The goal is to improve interpersonal awareness. Jane Howard offers a typical description of an encounter group:

> Their destination is intimacy, trust, and awareness of why they behave as they do in groups; their vehicle is candor. Exhorted to "get in touch with their feelings" and to "live in the here-and-now," they sprawl on the floor of a smoky room littered with styrofoam coffee cups, half-empty Kleenex boxes and overflowing ashtrays. As they grow tired they rest their heads on rolled-up sweaters or corners of cot mattresses or each other's laps.[6]

An encounter group may meet for a few hours or for a longer period of time up to a few days. Once increased interpersonal awareness is achieved, it is anticipated that attitudes and behaviors will change. In order for these changes to occur a three-phase process generally takes place: unfreezing, change, and refreezing.[7]

Unfreezing occurs in encounter groups through a deliberate process of interacting in nontraditional ways. Our attitudes and behavior patterns have been developed through years of social experiences. Such patterns, following years of experimentation and refinement, have now become nearly automatic. The interpersonal style we develop through years of trial and error generally has considerable utility in our everyday interactions. Deep down, however, we may recognize a need for improvement, but we are reluctant to make an effort to seek improvement, partly because our present style is somewhat functional and partly because we are afraid to reveal things about ourselves.

Stewart L. Tubbs and John Baird describe the unfreezing process in sensitivity groups:

Unfreezing occurs when our expectations are violated. We become less sure of ourselves when traditional ways of doing things are not followed. In the encounter group, the leader usually does not act like a leader. He or she frequently starts with a brief statement encouraging the group members to participate, to be open and honest, and to expect things to be different. Group members may begin by taking off their shoes, sitting in a circle on the floor, and holding hands with their eyes closed. The leader then encourages them to feel intensely the sensations they are experiencing, the size and texture of the hands they are holding, and so forth.

Other structured exercises or experiences may be planned to help the group focus on the "here-and-now" experience. Pairs may go for "trust walks" in which each person alternatively is led around with his eyes closed. Sitting face to face and conducting a hand dialogue, or a silent facial mirroring often helps to break the initial barriers to change. Other techniques may involve the "pass around" in which a person in the center of a tight circle relaxes and is physically passed around the circle. Those who have trouble feeling a part of the group are encouraged to break into or out of the circle of people whose hands are tightly held. With these experiences, most participants begin to feel more open to conversation about what they have experienced. This sharing of experiences or self-disclosure about the here and now provides more data for the group to discuss.[8]

The second phase of the process is "change." Changes in attitudes and behavior is usually facilitated in sensitivity groups by spontaneous reactions or feedback to how a person "comes across" to others. In everyday interaction we almost never get spontaneous feedback and we tend to repeat ineffective interaction patterns as we lack knowledge of our effect on others. But in sensitivity groups such feedback is strongly encouraged. The following set of interactions illustrates such feedback:

Carl: Alright (in a sharp tone), let's get this trust walk over with and stop dilly-dallying around. I'll lead the first person around—who wants to be blindfolded first?

Judy: Your statement makes me feel uncomfortable. I feel you are saying this group is a waste of your time. Also, this appears to be your third attempt this evening to "boss" us around.

Jim: I also feel like you are trying to tell us peons what to do. Even the tone of your voice is autocratic and suggests some disgust with this group.

Carl: Really? I didn't realize I was coming across that way. I wonder if I do that at work and when I'm at home?

Such feedback provides us with new insights on how we affect others. Once problem interactions are identified, that member

Trust walk

is encouraged to try out new response patterns in the relative safety of the group.

The third and final phase is "refreezing." Unfortunately this term is not the most descriptive as it implies rigidity with a new set of response patterns. The goal of this phase involves the attitude of experimenting with new sets of behaviors so that the person becomes a growing, continually changing person who increasingly becomes more effective in interacting with others. In terminating a sensitivity group, the leader may alert the participants that they have to be "on guard" as old behavior patterns tend to creep back in.

Sensitivity groups usually generate an outpouring of emotions that are rarely found in other groups.

The goal of sensitivity groups provides an interesting contrast to those of therapy groups. In therapy, the goal is to have each member explore in depth personal or emotional problems that he/she has, and to then develop a strategy to resolve that problem. In comparison sensitivity groups seek to foster increased personal and interpersonal awareness and to then develop more effective interaction patterns. Sensitivity groups generally do not directly attempt to identify and change specific emotional or personal problems that people have (such as drinking problems, feelings of depression, sexual dys-

functions, and so on). The philosophy behind sensitivity groups is that with increased personal and interpersonal awareness, people will be better able to avoid, cope with, and/or handle specific personal problems that arise.

Sensitivity groups are increasingly being used in our society for a wide variety of purposes: to train professional counselors to be more perceptive and effective in interpersonal interactions with clients and with other professionals, to train people in management positions to be more effective in their business interactions, to help clients with overt relationship problems to become more aware of how they affect others and to help them to develop more effective interaction patterns, and to train interested citizens in becoming more aware and effective in their interactions.

Although encounter, marathon, and sensitivity groups are popular and have received considerable publicity, such groups remain controversial. In some cases inadequately trained and incompetent individuals have become self-proclaimed leaders and enticed people to join through sensational advertising. If handled poorly, the short term of some groups may intensify personal problems. Many authorities on sensitivity training disclaim the use of encounter groups as a form of psychotherapy, and discourage those

Contrasting goals of therapy versus sensitivity groups

Therapy groups

Step 1
Examine problem(s) in depth

Step 2
Explore and then select (from various resolution approaches) a strategy to resolve the problem

Sensitivity groups

Step 1
Help each person become more aware of him/herself and how he/she affects others in interpersonal interactions

Step 2
Help a person then to develop more effective interaction patterns

with serious personal problems from joining such a group. After reviewing the research on the outcome of sensitivity groups, Lieberman, Yalom and Miles conclude:

> Encounter groups present a clear and evident danger if they are used for radical surgery to produce a new man. The danger is even greater when the leader and the participants share this misconception. If we no longer expect groups to produce magical, lasting change and if we stop seeing them as panaceas, we can regard them as useful, socially sanctioned opportunities for human beings to explore and to express themselves. Then we can begin to work on ways to improve them so that they may make a meaningful contribution toward solving human problems.[9]

KEY GROUP DYNAMIC PRINCIPLES

Several key principles will be summarized in this section to give the reader a "flavor" of some of the unique aspects of groups.

Roles of leaders. Leaders may individually, or together with other members, fill a wide variety of roles:

Executive—the top coordinator of the activities of a group.

Policy maker—one who establishes group goals and policies.

Planner—decides the means by which the group shall achieve its goals.

Expert—source of readily available information and skills.

External group representative—the official spokesman for the group.

Controller of internal relations—leader controls the structure and may be a controller of in-group relations.

Purveyor of rewards and punishments—the leader promotes, demotes, and assigns pleasant or unpleasant tasks.

Arbitrator and mediator—the leader may act as both judge and conciliator and has the power to reduce or to increase factionalism within the group.

Exemplar—a model of behavior to show what the members should be and do.

Ideologist—the leader serves as the source of the beliefs and values of the members.

Scapegoat—the leader serves as the target for ventilating members' frustrations and disappointments.[10]

Authoritarian versus democratic leadership styles. The authoritarian leader has more absolute power than the democratic leader. He/she alone sets goals and policies, dictates the activities of the members and sets major plans. He/she is the purveyor of rewards and punishments and he/she alone knows the succession of future steps in the group's activities. In contrast the democratic leader seeks maximum involvement and participation of every member in all decisions affecting the group. He/she seeks to spread responsibility rather than to concentrate it.

Authoritarian leadership is generally efficient and decisive. One of the hazards, however, is that group members may do what they are told out of necessity and not because of any commitment to group goals. The authoritarian leader who anticipates approval from subordinates for accomplishments achieved may be surprised to find backbiting and bickering to be common in the group. Unsuccessful authoritarian leadership is apt to generate factionalism, behind the scenes jockeying and maneuvering for position among members, and lead to a decline in morale.

Democratic leadership, in contrast, is slow in decision making and sometimes confusing, but frequently proves to be more effective because of strong cooperation that generally emerges with participation in decision making. With democratic leadership interpersonal hostilities between members, dissatisfactions with the leader, and concern for personal advancement all become parts of the decision-making process. The danger of democratic leadership is that the private, behind the scenes complaining of the authoritarian approach becomes public conflict in a democratic approach. Once this public conflict has been resolved in a democratic group, a strong personal commitment develops which motivates members to implement group decisions rather than to subvert them. The potential for sabotage in an authoritarian group is high, and therein lies the advantage of the democratic style.

The democratic leader knows that some mistakes are inevitable, and that the group will suffer from them. Yet, such mistakes require the ability to stand by without interference because interference might harm the democratic process and impede the progress of the group in developing the capacity to make decisions as a group.

In some situations authoritarian leadership is most effective, while in others democratic leadership is most effective. As in any situation, the group will be more effective when members' expectations about the behavior appropriate for that situation are met. Where group members anticipate a democratic style, as they do in educational settings, classrooms, or discussion groups, the democratic style is usually found to produce the most effective group. When members anticipate forceful leadership from their superiors, as in industry or the military service, a more authoritarian form of leadership results in a more effective group.[11]

Task and maintenance specialists. Bales has conducted considerable research on problem-solving groups.[12] Two specific leadership functions have been identified. A task leader emerges because he/she is seen as having the best ideas and as doing the most to guide the discussion. Such a person concentrates on the task, and generally plays an aggressive role in moving the group toward the goal. For this reason, hostility is apt to arise and the task leader may be disliked. Concurrently, a second leader may emerge; the social-emotional specialist who concentrates on group harmony, and resolving tensions and conflicts within the group. In groups with official leaders, the leader is expected to be both the "task specialist" and the "social-emotional specialist." In groups without an official leader, these two functions are generally assumed by two different emergent leaders.

Characteristics of leaders. Krech et al. summarize the traits needed by a leader. A leader needs to be perceived as: (a) a member of the group he/she is attempting to lead, (b) as having to a special degree the norms and values which are central to the group, (c) as being the most qualified group member for the task to be accomplished, and (d) must fit the members' expectations about how he/she should behave and what functions he/she should serve.[13]

Research on personality traits indicate leaders, compared to followers, tend to be better adjusted, more dominant, more extroverted, more masculine, and to have greater interpersonal sensitivity. Other traits such as intelligence, enthusiasm, dominance, self-confidence, and equalitarianism are also frequently found to characterize leaders.[14]

Although potential leaders tend to have more of all positive attributes than any of the members in the group, they cannot be so extreme that they become deviates. At one campus, for example, it was found that "B" students were the campus leaders, while the more intelligent "A" students were considered a "grind" who occasionally were even considered outcasts for being "curve-wreckers."[15] Also, the person who does most of the talking has been found to win most of the decisions and becomes the leader, unless he/she talks so much that other group members are antagonized.[16]

Since the desired traits are dependent on the functions needed to be performed in a group, the best rule for leader selection is to select those individuals who have the necessary skills and are motivated to help the group accomplish its goals.

Effects of group on members. A number of studies have investigated conforming behavior. Conformity is the yielding to group pressures. For there to be conformity there must be conflict; conflict between the influences being exerted by the group and those forces in an individual which tend to lead a person to value, believe, act in some other way. For a member experiencing such conflict there are two available options: announce his/her own independent decision, or conform by announcing agreement with the group's position.

Conforming can take two forms. The expedient conformer outwardly agrees but inwardly disagrees. The true conformer both outwardly and inwardly is brought to agree with the group.

A number of conclusions have arisen from conformity research.[17]

1. Considerable amounts of yielding are produced by group pressure, even when the bogus group consensus to which the person conforms is obviously wrong. In one study, for example, a sample of 50 military officers were asked to indicate which of two figures, a star and a circle presented side by side, were larger in area. The circle was clearly

about one third larger, but under bogus group pressure 46 percent of the men agreed with the bogus group consensus.

2. Many people can be pressured into yielding on attitude and opinion items, even those having significant personal implications to them. For example, 50 military officers were asked privately and then later under bogus group consensus the question: "I doubt whether I would make a good leader." In private none of the officers expressed agreement, but under unanimous group pressure, 37 percent expressed agreement.

3. Yielding is far greater on difficult, subjective items than on easy, objective ones.

4. There are extremely large individual differences in yielding. A few people yield on almost all items; a few yield on none; while most people yield on some and not on others.

5. When people are retested individually and privately on the same items some time later, a major part of the yielding effect disappears as the person tends to revert to his/her own unchanged private judgment. Yet, a small part of the yielding effect does remain, indicating group pressure does have a lasting effect on changing attitudes.

6. As a group increases in size, the pressure for yielding increases, and more yielding occurs. When a person is opposed by a single other person, there is very little yielding.

7. Yielding is markedly reduced when a person has the support of one other person (a partner) in the group. Apparently a dissident opinion has a tremendous effect in strengthening the independence of like-minded people.

In a dramatic study involving conformity Milgram demonstrated that subjects in an experimental situation would administer electric shocks of dangerous strength to another person when instructed to do so by the experimenter.[18] (The other person unknown to the subject did not actually receive the electrical shocks.) Most of the subjects complied with the experimenter's commands, even when they were instructed to give increasingly strong shocks to the victim, in spite of the victim's protests and cries of anguish. This series of studies on obedience demonstrated people will yield to "authoritative" commands even when the behavior is incompatible with moral, normal standards of conduct. Milgram suggested his studies help us understand why the German people complied with the unethical commands of Hitler. Group pressures, especially when viewed as authoritative, have a tremendous effect on a person's actions, attitudes, and beliefs.

Group size. The size of a group has effects on member's satisfactions, interactions, and output per member. Smaller groups have generally been found to be rated more favorably.[19] Larger groups have been shown to create more stress, have more communication difficulties, and although successful in some tasks because of the greater number of skills available, to be generally less efficient or productive. In larger groups each person has less opportunity to talk, and some people feel inhibited and reluctant to talk. In discussion groups it has been shown that as the size of the group increases, the most frequent contributor assumes an increasingly prominent role in the discussion. The bigger the group, the greater the gap in amount of participation between the most frequent contributor and the other members of a group.

Slater found in one study that a group of five persons was the size that members were most satisfied with.[20] Observations of the interactions of smaller sized groups indicated the members were inhibited from expressing their ideas through fear of alienating one another and thereby destroying the group. Above the size of five, members felt restrictions on participating.

Groups of size two tend to avoid expressing disagreement and antagonism. This size also has high tension levels as each member is more "on the spot," as each is forced to react to what the other says. If a dispute arises in such a group, it becomes deadlocked as there is no majority and the group may break up.

Groups of even size tend to have higher rates of disagreement and antagonism than odd size groups, apparently because of the possible division of the group into two subdivisions of equal size.

Groups of size three have the problem of the power of the majority over the minority; that is, a 2-to-1 split leaves the minority feeling isolated.

To sum up, it appears probable that for any given task there is an optimal group size. The more complex the task, the larger the optimum size as the greater the number of needed abilities and skills.

Idiosyncrasy credits. Every member of a group gains credits (and rises in status) by showing competence and by conforming to the expectations applicable to him/her at the time. Eventually these credits allow a person to break norms and rules of the group without being chastized. To some extent, after credits have been accumulated, nonconformity to general procedures or expectations serve as a confirming feature of ones status, thereby enhancing ones status. Yet there is a limit on the number of earned idiosyncrasy credits. Nonconformity beyond this limit will result in a dramatic decrease in status and perhaps even rejection by the other group members.[21]

Stages in group development

Garland, Jones, and Kolodny have developed a model which identifies five stages of development in social work groups: (a) preaffiliation, (b) power and control, (c) intimacy, (d) differentiation, and (e) separation.[22]

This model seeks to describe the kinds of problems that commonly arise as groups begin to form and continue to develop. The model appears particularly applicable to therapeutic groups, socialization groups, and encounter groups. To a lesser extent the model is also applicable to problem-solving and decision-making groups, self-help groups, educational groups, and to recreation skill groups.

In the first stage of "preaffiliation" members are ambivalent about joining the group, so their interaction is guarded. New situations are often frightening, and the members seek to protect themselves from being hurt or taken advantage of. They seek to maintain distance, without revealing much of themselves and without risking much. On the other hand, members are also attracted to the group, as the group has the potential to meet some of their needs, and because they have had satisfying experiences in other groups. Given this ambivalence, members test out, often through approach and avoidance behavior, the extent to which they want to become involved. The first stage gradually ends when the members come to feel fairly safe and comfortable within the group, and make a tentative emotional commitment to join as they eventually decide the group will be rewarding.

The second stage of "power and control" emerges as group members struggle with each other to establish their places within the group. Struggles occur as members seek to take on certain roles and responsibilities, seek to establish norms and methods for handling group tasks, and seek to establish patterns of communication and alliances. Each member seeks power, partly for self-protection, and partly to gain greater control over the rewards and gratifications to be received from the group. Often these power struggles involve conflicts with the leader that need to be resolved: Does the leader or the group have primary control over the group's affairs? What are the limits of the power of the group, of the leader, and also of the extent to which the leader will use his/her power. Such power struggles create anxiety among members, and considerable testing by members to gauge the limits of power and to set norms for the power and authority of the leader and of the group. Rebellion by group members is not uncommon during this stage. If and when these power issues are satisfactorily resolved, trust is achieved, and group members make a major commitment to be involved in the group.

In the third stage of "intimacy" the group becomes more like a family, with the leader being viewed similar to a parent, and with sibling rivalry between members being displayed. Feelings about the group are now more openly expressed and discussed. The group is now viewed as a place where growth and change can take place. There is a feeling of "oneness" within the group, and members feel free to examine and make efforts to change personal problems, attitudes, and concerns. Struggle or turmoil during this stage involves examining "what this group is all about" and involves the members beginning to examine and starting to make changes in their personal lives.

During the fourth stage of "differentiation" the group is able to organize itself more efficiently. Leadership is now more evenly shared, and power problems are minimal.

Decisions are made and carried out on a more objective and less emotional basis. There is high communication between members and increased freedom for members to try out new and alternative behavior patterns. The differentiation stage is analogous to a healthy family unit in which the children have reached adulthood and are now becoming successful in pursuing their own lives. Relationships are between equals, and members are mutually supportive.

The fifth stage is "separation," and involves termination of the group. The purposes of the group have been achieved, and members have learned new, constructive behavioral patterns. However, termination is often difficult. Members may be hesitant to move on and may display regressive behavior in an effort to prolong the group. Some may even express anger over ending the group. The leader should give emotional support to members during this stage and help members to understand they now have the strength and capacities to move on to other social experiences. Informing reluctant members of other resources of support and assistance is at times also useful at this stage.

GROUP SERVICES AND SOCIAL WORK

Social group work's historical roots were in the informal recreational organizations—the YWCA and YMCA, scouting, Jewish centers, settlement houses, and 4-H clubs.

George Williams established the Young Men's Christian Association in London in 1844 for the purpose of converting young men to Christian values.[23] Recreational group activities and socialization activities were a large part of the early YMCA's programs. In 1851 YMCAs were first founded in this country in Baltimore and Boston. The Young Women's Christian Association began in Boston in 1866.[24]

Settlement houses which were established in many large cities of this country in the late 1800s are generally given a major share of the credit for being the roots of social group work.[25] Settlement houses sought to use the power of group associations to educate, reform, organize neighborhoods, preserve religious and cultural identities, and to give emotional support and assistance to newcomers from both the farm and abroad.

Now, almost every social service agency provides one or more of the following types of groups: recreation skill, education, socialization, and therapy. Most undergraduate and graduate social work programs provide methods courses to train students to lead groups, particularly training in leading socialization and therapy groups.

Group therapy is increasingly being used in counseling. It has several advantages over one-to-one therapy. The "helper" therapy principle generally is operative, where members at times interchange roles and sometimes become the "helper" for someone else's problems. In such roles, members receive psychological rewards for helping others. Groups also help members to put their problems into perspective as they realize others have problems as serious as theirs. Groups also help members who are having interaction problems to test out new interaction approaches. Research has also shown it is generally easier to change the attitudes of an individual while in a group than to change a person's attitudes individually.[26] Research discussed earlier on conformity demonstrated group pressure can have a substantial effect on changing attitudes and beliefs. Furthermore, group therapy permits the social worker to treat more than one person at a time, thus being a substantial savings in the use of professional staff.

In essence a group therapist uses the principles of one-to-one counseling (discussed in Chapter 5) and of group dynamics to work with clients to change dysfunctional attitudes and behavior. Generally a group therapist also uses the principles of certain comprehensive treatment techniques (such as reality therapy or client-centered therapy) and of certain specialized treatment techniques (such as parent effectiveness training and assertive training) to help clients resolve personal and emotional problems. The selection of which treatment techniques to use are generally based upon the nature of the problems.

The use of one of these specialized treatment techniques, assertive training, in group services will be illustrated in the following section. The principles of assertive training will first be briefly described.

HOW TO BECOME MORE ASSERTIVE*

Do you handle put-down comments well? Are you reluctant to express your feelings and opinions openly and honestly in a group? Are you frequently timid in interacting with people in authority? Do you react well to criticism? Do you sometimes explode in anger when things go wrong, or are you able to keep your cool? Do you find it difficult to maintain eye contact when talking? If you are uncomfortable with someone smoking near you, do you express your feelings? Are you timid in arranging a date or social event? If you have trouble in any of these situations, there is fortunately a useful technique—assertiveness training—that enables people to become more effective in such interpersonal interactions.

Assertiveness problems range from extreme shyness, introversion, withdrawal to inappropriately flying into a rage that results in alienating others. A nonassertive person is often acquiescent, fearful, and afraid of expressing his or her real, spontaneous feelings in a variety of situations. Frequently, resentment and anxiety build up, which may result in general discomfort, feelings of low self-esteem, tension headaches, fatigue, and perhaps a destructive explosion of temper, anger, and aggression. Some people are overly shy and timid in nearly all interactions. Most of us, however, encounter occasional problems in isolated areas where it would be to our benefit to be more assertive. For example, a bachelor may be quite effective and assertive in his job as a store manager but still be awkward and timid while attempting to arrange a date.

There are three basic styles of interacting with others: nonassertive, aggressive and assertive. Characteristics of these styles have been summarized by Alberti and Emmons:

> In the non-assertive style, you are likely to hesitate, speak softly, look away, avoid the issue, agree regardless of your own feelings, not express opinions, value yourself "below" others, and hurt yourself to avoid any chance of hurting others.
>
> In the *aggressive* style, you typically answer before the other person is through talking, speak loudly and abusively, glare at the other person, speak "past" the issue (accusing, blaming, demeaning), vehemently expound your feelings and opinions, value yourself "above" others, and hurt others to avoid hurting yourself.
>
> In the *assertive* style, you will answer spontaneously, speak with a conversational tone and volume, look at the other person, speak to the issue, openly express your personal feelings and opinions (anger, love, disagreement, sorrow), value yourself equal to others, and hurt neither yourself nor others.*

---

* This section on "How to Become More Assertive" is excerpted from an article written by this author with the same title in *The Personal Problem Solver*, ed. Charles Zastrow and Dae Chang. (Englewood Cliffs, N.J.: Spectrum Books, 1977) pp. 236–40. Reprinted by permission of Prentice-Hall, Englewood Cliffs, New Jersey.

---

* Robert E. Alberti and Michael L. Emmons, Stand up, Speak out, Talk Back! (New York: Pocket Books, 1975), p. 24.

STEPS IN ASSERTIVE TRAINING*

1. Examine your interactions. Are there situations that you need to handle more assertively? Do you at times hold opinions and feelings within you for fear of what would happen if you expressed them? Do you occasionally blow your cool and lash out angrily at others? Studying your interactions is facilitated by keeping a diary for a week or longer, recording the situations in which you acted timidly, those in which you were aggressive, and those which you handled assertively.

2. Select those interactions in which it would be to your benefit to be more assertive. They may include situations in which you were overpolite, overly apologetic, timid, and allowed others to take advantage of you, at the same time harboring feelings of resentment, anger, embarrassment, fear of others, or self-criticism for not having the courage to express yourself. Overly aggressive interactions in which you exploded in anger or walked over others also need to be dealt with. For *each* set of non-assertive or aggressive interactions, you can become more assertive, as shown in the next steps.

3. Concentrate on a specific incident in the past. Close your eyes for a few minutes and vividly imagine the details, including what you and the other person said, and how you felt at the time and afterward.

4. Write down and review your responses. Ask yourself the following questions to determine how you presented yourself:

(*a*) Eye contact—Did you look directly at the other person, in a relaxed, steady gaze? Looking down or away suggests a lack of self-confidence. Glaring is an aggressive response.

(*b*) Gestures—Were your gestures appropriate, free-flowing, relaxed, and used to effectively emphasize your messages? Awkward stiffness suggests nervousness; other gestures (such as an angry fist) signal an aggressive reaction.

(*c*) Body posture—Did you show the importance of your message by directly facing the other person, by leaning toward that person, by holding your head erect, and by sitting or standing appropriately close?

(*d*) Facial expression—Did your facial expression show a stern, firm pose consistent with an assertive response?

(*e*) Voice tone and volume—Was your response stated in a firm, conversational tone? Shouting may suggest anger. Speaking softly suggests shyness, and a cracking voice suggests nervousness. Tape recording and listening to one's voice is a way to practice increasing or decreasing the volume.

(*f*) Speech fluency—Did your speech flow smoothly, clearly, and slowly? Rapid speech or hesitation in speaking suggests nervousness. Tape recording assertive responses that you try out to problem situations is a way to improve fluency.

(*g*) Timing—Were your verbal reactions to a problem situation stated at a time closest to the incident that would appropriately permit you and the other person time to review the incident? Generally, spontaneous expressions are the best, but certain situations should be handled at a later time—for example, challenging some of your boss' erroneous statements in private rather than in front of a group he or she is making a presentation to.

(*h*) Message content—For a problem situation, which of your responses were nonassertive or aggressive, and which were assertive? Study the content and consider why you responded in a nonassertive or aggressive style.

5. Observe one or more effective models—Watch the verbal and nonverbal approaches that are assertively used to handle the type of interactions with which you are having problems. Compare the consequences between their approach and yours. If possible, discuss their approach and their feelings about using it.

6. Make a list of various alternative approaches for being more assertive.

7. Close your eyes and visualize yourself using each of the above alternative approaches. For each approach, think through what the full set of interactions would be, along with the consequences. Select an approach, or combination of approaches, that you believe will be most effective for you to use. Through imagery, practice this approach until you feel comfortable that it will work for you.

8. Role play the approach with someone else, perhaps a friend or counselor. If certain segments of your approach appear clumsy, awkward, timid or aggressive, practice modifications until you become comfortable with the approach. Obtain feedback from the other person as to the strengths and shortcomings of your approach. Compare your interactions to the verbal/nonverbal guidelines for assertive behavior in step 4. It may be useful for the other person to model through role playing one or more assertive strategies, which you would then, be reversing roles, practice using.

9. Repeat steps 7 and 8 until you develop an assertive approach that you believe will work best for you, and that you are comfortable with and believe will work.

10. Use your approach in a real-life situation. The previous steps are designed to prepare you for the real event. Expect to be somewhat anxious when first trying to be assertive. If you are still too fearful of attempting to be assertive, repeat steps 5 through 8. For those few individuals who fail to develop the needed confidence to try out being assertive, seeking professional counseling is advised—expressing yourself and effective interactions with others is essential for personal happiness.

11. Reflect on the effectiveness of your effort. Did you "keep your cool?"† Considering the nonverbal/verbal guidelines for assertive behavior discussed

in step 4, what components of your responses were assertive, aggressive, and nonassertive? What were the consequences of your effort? How did you feel after trying out this new set of interactions? If possible, discuss how you did in regard to these questions with a friend who may have observed the interactions.

12.   Expect some success, but not complete personal satisfaction, with your initial efforts. Personal growth and interacting more effectively with others is a continual learning process. Quite appropriately "pat yourself on the back" for the strengths of your approach—you earned it. But also note the areas where you need to improve, and use the above steps for improving your assertive efforts.

   * These self-training steps are a modification of assertive training programs developed by Robert E. Alberti and Michael L. Emmons. *Your Perfect Right* (Sar Luis Obispo, Calif.: Impact 1970) and by Herbert Fensterheim and Jean Baer, *Don't Say Yes When You Want to Say No* (New York; Dell, 1975).

   † Getting angry at times is a normal human emotion, and it needs to be expressed. However, the anger should be expressed in a constructive, assertive fashion. When expressed in a destructive, lashing out fashion, you are "blowing your cool."

Simply stated, assertive behavior is being able to express yourself without hurting or stepping on others.

Assertiveness training is designed to lead a person to realize, feel, and act on the assumption that he or she has the right to be him/herself and to express his or her feelings freely. Assertive responses generally are not aggressive responses. The distinction between these two types of interactions is important. If, for example, a wife has an overly critical mother-in-law, aggressive responses by the wife would include: ridiculing the mother-in-law, intentionally doing things that she knows will upset the mother-in-law (not visiting, serving the type of food the mother-in-law dislikes, not cleaning the house), urging the husband to tell his mother to "shut up," and getting into loud verbal arguments with the mother-in-law. On the other hand, an effective assertive response would be to counter criticism by saying: "Jane, your criticism of me deeply hurts me. I know you're trying to help me when you give advice, but I feel when you do that you're criticizing me. I know you don't want me to make mistakes; but to grow, I need to make my own errors and learn from them. If you want to help me the most, let me do it myself and be responsible for the consequences. The type of relationship that I'd like to have with you is a close, adult relationship and not a mother-child relationship."

(The processes of steps for learning to become more assertive are presented above in "Steps in Assertive Training.")

These steps systematically make sense, but are not to be followed rigidly. Each person has to develop a process that works best for him/herself.

Examples of behavior.   You are flying with a business associate to Los Angeles for a conference. The associate lights up a pipe; you soon find the smoke irritating, and the odor somewhat stifling. What are your choices?

1. Nonassertive response—you attempt to carry on a "cheery" conversation for the three-hour trip without commenting about the smoke.
2. Aggressive response—you increasingly become irritated, until exploding, "Either you put out that pipe, or I'll put it out for you—the odor is sickening."
3. Assertive response—in a firm, conversational tone you look directly at the associate and state, "The smoke from your pipe is irritating me. I'd appreciate it if you put it away."

At a party with friends, during small talk conversation, your husband gives you a subtle "put-down" by stating, "Wives always talk too much." What do you do?

1. Nonassertive response—you don't say anything but feel hurt and become quiet.
2. Aggressive response—you glare at him and angrily ask, "John, why are you always criticizing me?"
3. Assertive response—you carry on as usual, waiting until driving home, then calmly look at him and say, "When we were at the party tonight, you said that wives always talk too much. I felt you were putting me down when you said that. What did you mean by that comment?"

Assertive training in groups

Assertive training can be provided to almost any new or already existing group. There are several advantages of a group over individual training. A group provides a "laboratory" of other people to experiment with new assertive behaviors. A group has a broader base for social modeling as each person sees several others trying out a variety of assertive approaches. A wider variety of feedback is also offered by a group. Furthermore, a group is generally understanding and supportive. Finally, group pressure and expectations motivate members to conscientiously develop and practice new assertive responses.

A typical format for an assertive group is as follows. The number of members for a group generally ranges from 5 to 12 members. The first session is devoted to a lecture presentation on assertive behavior covering the differences between assertive, nonassertive and aggressive behavior. The specific steps in assertive training are then summarized. Several examples of typical situations are also given to illustrate that assertive responses are much more effective than aggressive or nonassertive responses.

In the following sessions specific situations involving assertive responses are then examined. At first it may be desirable to begin with situations that are not brought forth by members of the group (Group members may at first be reluctant to reveal personal situations they face.) Alberti and Emmons suggest the following situations be practiced:

1. Breaking into a small group of strangers already engaged in conversation at a party.
2. Starting a conversation with a stranger in a classroom, on a bus, at a meeting. Maintaining a conversation.
3. Returning faulty or defective items to a store.
4. Being assertive with significant others: parents, roommates, spouses, boy-girl friends.
5. Asking someone to turn down a stereo that is too loud or not talk so loudly in the library, theater, and so on.
6. Asking for a date/refusing a date on the telephone and face to face.
7. Expressing positive feelings; "soft assertions."
8. Speaking publicly.

ASSERTIVE TRAINING STEPS IN GROUPS

The following steps are recommended for group leaders in helping group members become more assertive:

1. Help each group member to identify the situations/interactions in which it would be to their benefit to be more assertive. Usually group members will bring up these situations themselves. For some, however, the members may be reluctant to reveal problem interactions, or be unaware they could better handle certain situations by being more assertive. Considerable tact and skill by the leader is necessary in initiating problem areas of the latter type.

2. When a problem interaction is identified each member of the group is asked to silently fantasize a response. For complicated situations with no simple resolution, considerable discussion may arise about possible ways of resolving the situation.

3. A member (often someone other than the person with the problem situation) is asked to role-play an assertive response. The member with the problem may be asked to play the role of the person he/she is having the problem with.

4. The group briefly then discusses the merits of the assertive strategy that was modeled in step 3.

If it is effective and the person with the problem is comfortable with it, that person is then asked to role-play the approach. If the group believes there may be a more effective approach, then steps 3 and 4 are repeated. If the person with the problem is uncomfortable about using a strategy that is effective, the reasons for the "uncomfortableness" are then explored. For example, for very shy people, certain attitudes, such as "don't make waves" or the "meek will inherit heaven" may need to be dealt with.

5. The person with the problem is asked to silently rehearse an assertive strategy, thinking what he/she will say and what are apt to be the consequences.

6. The person with the problem then is asked to role-play an assertive strategy.

7. Feedback is given by the group about the merits of the strategy. Generally the person is praised for the effective aspects, and coachd on how to improve other aspects. This approach is practiced via role-playing until the approach is perfected and the person with the problem becomes comfortable with it and develops sufficient self-confidence for the "real event." For feedback purposes, if possible, the approach is recorded on audio or video tape.

8. The person tries out the new response pattern in an actual situation.

9. The person describes at the next group meeting how the real-life test went. The person is complimented on the degree of success attained, and assistance is given on aspects that could be improved.

9. Learning how to argue with or stand up for oneself with a dominant or dogmatic and opinionated person.[27]

For each situation the following steps are used: (a) each member is asked to silently fantasize his/her response, (b) one member is selected to role-play an assertive response, (c) the group briefly discusses the strategy, (d) if a more effective response is desired, a new assertive response is role-played by a member, and (e) the group then discusses the strategy.

Following the examination of such situations group members are then encouraged to bring to the group real-life situations that are troubling them. Often such situations are complicated and involve close, intimate relationships. These situations may not have pat, simple resolutions.

A concluding remark about assertive training is that the structure of the technique is relatively simple to understand. Considerable skill (common sense and ingenuity), however, is needed to determine what will be an effective assertive strategy when a "real-life" situation arises. The joy and pride obtained from being able to fully express oneself assertively is nearly unequaled.

SUMMARY

Groups are increasingly being used in social work. Almost every social service agency now provides some group services. The focus of social work groups has considerable variation, including: social conversation, recreation, recreation skill development, problem solving and decision making, self-help, socialization, therapy, and sensitivity training.

The goal in therapy groups is generally to have each member explore in-depth personal or emotional problems that they have, and to then develop a strategy to resolve that problem. In contrast, sensitivity groups seek to foster increased personal and interpersonal awareness, and to then develop more effective interaction patterns.

Each group develops a unique character due to group dynamic principles, including: the particular roles played by the leader, an authoritarian or democratic leadership style, the handling of task and maintenance responsibilities, personality traits and characteristics of leaders, group conformity pressures on members, group size, and use of idiosyncrasy credits.

Many social work groups go through the following five developmental stages: (a) preaffiliation, (b) power and control, (c) intimacy, (d) differentiation, and (e) separation.

Group therapy is increasingly being used in counseling. In essence a group therapist uses the principles of one-to-one counseling and of group dynamics to bring about positive changes in attitudes and behaviors of clients. Generally a group therapist also uses the principles of comprehensive treatment techniques and of specialized treatment techniques to help clients. Assertive training is one such specialized change technique, and is increasingly being used to train people to be more effective in interpersonal interactions.

NOTES

1. Michael S. Olmstead, *The Small Group* (New York: Random House, 1959), pp. 21–22.

2. Alfred H. Katz and Eugene I. Bender, *The Strength in Us: Self-Help Groups in the Modern World* (New York: Franklin-Watts, 1976), p. 9.

3. Alan Gartner and Frank Riessman, *A Working Guide to Self-Help Groups* (New York: Franklin Watts, 1980.)

4. Frank Riessman, "The 'Helper Therapy' Principle," *Journal of Social Work,* April 1965, pp. 27–34.

5. Gerald L. Euster, "Services to Groups," in *Contemporary Social Work,* ed. Donald Brieland et al. (New York: McGraw-Hill, 1975), p. 220.

6. Jane Howard, *Please Touch: A Guided Tour of the Human Potential Movement* (New York: McGraw-Hill, 1970), p. 3.

7. Steward L. Tubbs and John W. Baird, *The Open Person* (Columbus, Ohio: Charles E. Merrill, 1976), pp. 48–50.

8. Ibid., p. 48.

9. Morton A. Lieberman, Ervin D. Yalom, and Matthew B. Miles, "Encounter: The Leader Makes the Difference," *Psychology Today* 6 (1973): 11.

10. David Krech, Richard S. Crutchfield, and Egerton L. Ballachey, *Individual in Society* (New York: McGraw-Hill, 1962), pp. 428–31.

11. A. Paul Hare, *Handbook of Small Group Research* (New York: Free Press, 1962), p. 309.

12. R. F. Bales, *Interaction Process Analysis: A Method for the Study of Small Groups* (Reading, Mass.: Addision-Wesley, 1950.)

13. Krech et al., *Individual in Society*, pp. 438–41.

14. Hare, *Handbook of Small Group Research*, pp. 292–93.

15. J. S. Davie and A. P. Hare, "Button-down Collar Culture: A Study of Undergraduate Life at a Men's College," *Human Organization* 14 (1956): 13–20.

16. J. G. March, "Influence Measurement in Experimental and Semi-Experimental Groups," *Sociometry*, 1956, pp. 260–71.

17. Krech et al., pp. 509–12.

18. S. Milgram, "Behavioral Study of Obedience," *Journal of Abnormal and Social Psychology*, 1963, pp. 371–78.

19. Hare, *Handbook of Small Group Research*, pp. 224–45.

20. P. E. Slater, "Contrasting Correlates of Group Size," *Sociometry*, 1958, pp. 129–39.

21. E. P. Hollander, "Conformity, Status, and Idiosyncrasy Credit," *Psychological Review*, 1958, pp. 117–27.

22. James A. Garland, Hubert Jones, and Ralph Kolodny, "A Model for Stages of Development in Social Work Groups," in *Explorations in Group Work*, ed. Saul Bernstein (Boston: Milford House, 1965) pp. 1–33.

23. Euster, "Services to Groups," p. 227.

24. Ibid., p. 227.

25. Ralph Dolgoff and Donald Feldstein, *Understanding Social Welfare* (New York: Harper & Row, 1980).

26. Kurt Lewin, "Group Decision and Social Change," in *Readings in Social Psychology*, ed. G. E. Swanson, T. M. Newcomb, and E. L. Hartley (New York: Holt, 1952).

27. Robert E. Alberti and Michael L. Emmons, *Stand up, Speak out, Talk Back!* (New York: Pocket Books, 1975), pp. 183–84.

chapter 22

Students considering a career in social work initially express disinterest in being a community organizer. Students indicate they would rather work directly with people, and have the erroneous belief that a community organizer uses skills and techniques that are too complex and too abstract for them to learn. Also, they view community organization as having too few rewards, and as involving a lot of boring, unenjoyable work. As an introduction to social work community practice it should be noted that the above beliefs are erroneous. The realities are: (1) the most basic skill that community organizer must have is to be able to work effectively with people, (2) an organizer spends most of his/her time in working together with individuals and with groups, (3) every practicing social worker occasionally becomes involved in community organization activities, (4) in working on a project an organizer becomes "ego involved," and seeing that project develop, approved, and implemented is immensely gratifying, and (5) community organization efforts are often "fun."

Workers in direct practice with individuals or groups are likely to become involved in community development activities when gaps in services or unmet needs are identified for clients they are working with. For example, if there is a rapid increase in teenage girls becoming pregnant in a community, a school social worker may become involved in efforts to establish a sex education program in the school system. If there are a number of terminally ill patients and their families complaining about the way they are treated in a hospital, a medical social worker may become involved in efforts to establish a hospice. If a juvenile probation officer notes a sharp increase in juvenile offenses, the officer may become involved in efforts to have juvenile offenders visit a prison and hear the consequences from inmates of what prison life is like (as depicted in "Scared Straight" programs).

Workers involved in developing needed new services are aware of the human benefits that will result. These payoffs, and the time and efforts workers put into community organization projects often lead them to be-

Social work community practice

Saul Alinsky, one of our country's most noted organizers, describes a tactic used by students at a private college to change the college's restrictive policies on social activities:

> I was lecturing at a college run by a very conservative, almost fundamentalist Protestant denomination. Afterward some of the students came to my motel to talk to me. Their problem was that they couldn't have any fun on campus. They weren't permitted to dance or smoke or have a can of beer. I had been talking about the strategy of effecting change in a society and they wanted to know what tactics they could use to change their situation. I reminded them that a tactic is doing what you can with what you've got. "Now, what have you got?" I asked. "What do they permit you to do?" "Practically nothing," they said, "except—you know—we can chew gum." I said, "Fine. Gum becomes the weapon. You get 200 or 300 students to get two packs of gum each, which is quite a wad. Then you have them drop it on the campus walks. This will cause absolute chaos. Why, with 500 wads of gum I could paralyze Chicago, stop all the traffic in the Loop." They looked at me as though I was some kind of a nut. But about two weeks later I got an ecstatic letter saying, "It worked! It worked! Now we can do just about anything so long as we don't chew gum."

SOURCE: Saul Alinsky, *Rules for Radicals* (New York: Random House, 1972), pp. 145–46.

come highly "ego involved." Obtaining success in establishing new services is experienced as a deeply gratifying political victory.

On a negative note, a reality is that the development of new services generally encounters a number of unanticipated obstacles, and requires several times as much time and effort as initially anticipated.

As yet there is no widely accepted definition of the terms *community organization* and *community development*. The modes of practice performed under these terms have a variety of labels: social planning, community planning, social planning, locality development, community action, and social action.

Community organization will be defined here as being the process of stimulating and assisting the local community to evaluate, plan, and coordinate its efforts to provide for the community's health, welfare, and recreation needs. A community organizer acts as a catalyst in stimulating and encouraging community action. Activities of a community organizer include encouraging and stimulating citizen organization around one or more issues, specifying the nature of the problem, coordination of efforts between groups, factfinding, formulating realizable goals, public relations and public education, research, planning, identifying financial resources, developing strategies to achieve the goal, and being a resource person. Agency settings that employ community organizers include community welfare councils, the United Way, social planning agencies, health planning councils, neighborhood councils, city planning councils, community action agencies, and occasionally some other private or public organization.

Community organizers become involved

in a wide variety of social issues, including civil rights, welfare reform, meeting the needs of poor people, education and health issues, housing, improving leisure-time services, race relations, minority-group employment, development of services to counteract alienation of youth, urban redevelopment programs, and developing services to teenage runaways and to those experimenting with drugs.

One out of every 20 professional social workers is employed in an agency whose main service focus is community organization.[1] There are a number of other disciplines in addition to social work that provide training in community organization: community psychology, urban and regional planning, health planning, corrections planning, recreation and public administration.

In recent years American citizens have organized around a number of issues. A few of the issues receiving national attention will be listed: unions striking for higher pay, truckers protesting the 55-mile-per-hour speed limit, returning the Panama Canal to Panama, farmers wanting higher prices, the abortion question, capital punishment, rights for homosexuals, tax cuts, school closings in many cities, national defense budget, nuclear energy, selective service draft, changing marijuana laws, massage parlors, nude dancing, affirmative action guidelines on hiring, financial loans to the auto industry, and environmental concerns.

BRIEF HISTORY OF COMMUNITY ORGANIZATION

People have organized to change social and political conditions for centuries. In the 1700s, for example, Americans organized to revolt against the British, and fought what has come to be called The Revolutionary War.

Community organization in social work had its roots in the 1800s in the Charity Organization Society movement and the Settlement House movement.[2]

In the 1800s private philanthropy bore the major responsibility for the relief of poverty and dependence in the United States. During the early 1800s a wide range of private health and welfare agencies were established to provide funds and services (which were generally combined with religious conversion efforts) to those in need. To avoid several agencies providing similar services to the same families, the Charity Organization Society was formed to *coordinate* efforts and to *plan* for meeting unmet needs.

The reformers associated with the settlement house movement based many of their programs on *social action* to promote social legislation for providing needed services to neighborhoods. The settlement house reformers also encouraged and stimulated neighborhood residents to work together to improve living conditions.

Community welfare councils were first organized in 1908.[3] Continuing the efforts begun by the Charity Organization movement, these councils served as coordinating organizations for voluntary agencies. The functions of these councils have continued to the present time and include planning, coordination, efforts to avoid duplication of services, setting standards for services, and efforts to improve efficiency and accountability.

Community Chests (now called United Way) were formed around 1920 to be centralized campaigns for raising funds for voluntary agencies.[4] In practically all communities United Way has been combined with Community Welfare Councils for the raising of funds, and for the allocation of funds to voluntary agencies.

All social welfare agencies and organizations become involved at times in community organization efforts. The successes, and

Off to a good start

failures, are well beyond the scope of this chapter. Instead, the remainder of this chapter will focus on describing the roles performed by community organizers, and describe two models of community organization.

ROLES OF ORGANIZER

There are several styles or roles for community organization activities. The role that is applied is ideally determined by the job to be accomplished. A given community issue may involve a variety of tasks, which usually necessitates the organizer assuming different roles. Six of the main roles will be briefly described.

Enabler. In this role the organizer helps people articulate their needs, clarify and identify their problems, and develop their capacities to deal with their own problems more effectively. This is the *classic* or traditional role of a community organizer. Considerable emphasis is placed on developing constructive relationships with community residents. The focus is to "help people organize to help themselves." The enabler makes extensive use of group dynamic principles. The enabler's role is simply to facilitate the community organization process.

In the enabler role, the organizer first helps to awaken and focus discontent about community conditions. In order to do this the organizer has to spend considerable time in getting acquainted with residents and in securing their trust and respect. After this respect is attained, the organizer encourages residents to verbalize their concerns.

The second function as enabler is to encourage organization. Apathy and passivity generally cause the community organization process to be painfully slow. Usually the time taken to identify problems and discontents will provide the motivation to organize. During this phase the organizer seeks to have residents with common concerns begin communicating with one another and to begin organizing to do something about their concerns. Even when the way has been well prepared, some communities falter at organizing. When this happens the reasons for the faltering need to be examined and dealt with.

The third function of an enabler is to nourish good interpersonal relations. This function is similar to the rapport a counselor seeks to establish with clients. The organizer seeks to have organizational meetings run smoothly. The objective is to have the physical and psychological conditions arranged in such a way that people feel comfortable, enjoy themselves, and feel free to verbalize their concerns.

The fourth function of the enabler is to facilitate effective planning. An organizer usually does this by asking relevant questions, such as, "What are some ways to resolve this?" and "What will be the effects if we try this?" The enabler does not lead, or provide answers. Instead s/he asks questions which stimulate insight, and supports and encourages members to develop plans to do something about their concerns.

Broker. A broker links individuals and groups who need help (and do not know where help is available) with community services. Today even moderate-sized communities have 200 or 300 social service agencies/organizations providing community services. Even human resource professionals are frequently only partially aware of the total service network in their community. As in the fields of finance and real estate, social service brokers serve the function of negotiating, for their clients, with a complex network of social institutions with which clients are uninformed and inexperienced at dealing with.

Often all that is required to perform this linkage function is to provide information that puts people in contact with resources. However, if difficulties arise, collective action (a community organization effort) may be needed to effect the exchange. (For example, a broker may suggest to elderly people that needed services—such as a community center—may be provided if they *collectively* request and document to the city council that such services are needed.) Through such brokerage activity, changes in policies and programs may occur which affect whole classes of persons.

A recent trend for a fairly large number of agencies (such as mental health clinics, neighborhood centers, community action

A block party sponsored by a neighborhood center to help foster a sense of "community"

agencies, agencies serving the elderly) is to employ "community outreach workers" whose function is to inform residents about available services, identify individuals and families with problems, and link such families with available services.

A number of governmental agencies (particularly in human services, education, health and housing) now employ one or more staff persons to work part- or full-time with citizens, educating citizens to the problems the agency is dealing with and eliciting citizens ideas to make changes in the delivery system to better serve customers. This broker function acts as a consciousness-raising device to show people what the system is really like and also makes the system more responsive to the needs of consumers.

Expert. As an expert, an organizer provides information and gives advice in a number of areas. An expert may suggest how an organization should be structured, including how subgroups should be represented. An expert may suggest different responsibilities for members to assume, including that of the leader. An expert may give advice on the goals and subgoals that a group should set. An expert may suggest tactics or strategies to accomplish goals that are set. An expert may give advice on how to do certain tasks, such as conducting a neighborhood survey. An expert should inform the organization about other relevant research and documents that exist and also inform the organization about other resources that may help them accomplish their goals. Also, an expert should give advice on how the organization can set up procedures to evaluate its activities and efforts.

It is important for an expert to remember not to insist on the acceptance of his/her advice. Advice given by an expert should only be viewed as being ideas offered for consideration, with the organization having

the responsibility to decide whether to accept these suggestions.

Social planner. A social planner gathers facts about a social problem, and analyzes the facts to arrive at the most rational course of action. The planner then develops a program, seeks funding sources, and strives to secure consensus among diverse interest groups about providing the program. Such consensus may or may not be obtained. If sufficient support is obtained (generally from the power structure), the planner's final task is facilitating the implementation of the plan. Social planners are generally employed, or at least sponsored, by the power structure; for example, city, county, and state governments, or the boards of influential private agencies such as the United Way or a community welfare council. Often, social planners are assigned to work with concerned community groups. Planners generally have graduate training in research or planning.

While the roles of expert and social planner overlap, an expert focuses more on giving advice, while a social planner focuses more on doing the tasks involved in developing and implementing programs.

Advocate. The role of an advocate has been borrowed from the law profession. It is an active directive role in which the organizer is an advocate for a client or for a citizen's group. When a client or a citizen's group is in need of help, and existing institutions are uninterested (and sometimes openly negative and hostile) in providing services, then the advocate's role is appropriate. In such a role, the advocate provides leadership for collecting information, for arguing the correctness of client's needs and requests, and for challenging the institution's decision not to provide services. The object is not to ridicule or censure a particular institution, but to modify or change one or more of the

Community meeting to prevent a fast-food franchise from locating in the neighborhood

service policies. In this role the advocate is a partisan who is extremely serving the interest of a client or of a citizen's group. The impartiality of the enabler and broker roles are absent here.

The activist. An activist seeks basic institutional change; often the objective involves a shift in power and resources to a disadvantaged group. An activist is concerned about social injustice, inequity, and deprivation. An activist seeks to stimulate a disadvantaged group to organize to take action against the existing power structure which is viewed as being the oppressor. Tactics involve conflict, confrontation, and negotiation. An effective activist is skilled at being an advocate, agitator, broker, and negotiator. Similar to an advocate, an activist takes a partisan role. The constituency of an activist is generally viewed as being a victim of the power structure.

Demonstration against ordinances regulating nude dancing

Reflections on these roles. The traditional neutrality role of the social work profession is often desirable. The enabler, expert, broker, and social planner are quite effective when such nonpartisan activity meets the needs of clients and client groups. When it does not, then the role of an advocate or of an activist may be warranted.

An advocate and an activist cannot be effective if they "blow their cool"; that is, let their actions and decisions be determined by emotion rather than rational thinking and planning. In order to be effective they must make decisions and plan strategy according to the following guideline: "Is what I'm doing going to be constructive (or destructive) in achieving the desired outcome, and is there an even better way to achieve the desired outcome?"

The remainder of this chapter will present two models of community organization/development: (1) The Biddles model, in which the organizer primarily has an "enabler" or "encourager" role, and (2) the "power confrontation" model developed by Saul Alinsky in which the organizer has primarily an "activist" role.

MODEL 1: THE BIDDLES MODEL— THE "ENCOURAGER" APPROACH TO COMMUNITY DEVELOPMENT/ ORGANIZATION

William and Loureide Biddle describe one approach to community development in *The Community Development Process: The Rediscovery of Local Initiative.* [5]

The Biddles note that many citizens have lost or are losing the sense of community. Often it is a community developer's role to move people from attitudes to despair about the community to those in which they realize their capacities to work together with their neighbors to help themselves.

The Biddles define community as "whatever sense of the local common good citizens can be helped to achieve."[6] Community development is defined as, "a social process by which human beings can become more competent to live with and gain some control over local aspects of a frustrating and changing world."[7] The term they feel that is most descriptive of the role of a community developer is that of an *encourager*.

Community development, according to the Biddles, can be summarized as having the following phases (each phase has several aspects that the community developer needs to give attention to):

Phase 1—Exploratory

Aspects needing attention:

a. History—When a community developer arrives upon a local scene, s/he needs to become informed about the population—their conflicts, their frustrations, and their hopes and fears. In particular s/he needs to be aware of recent events affecting the population, the present events that are taking place, and what is about to take place in the future.

b. Invitation—To legitimatize his/her role, an encourager should come to a local area only when s/he receives an invitation, generally from an organization or a small group that is discontented about present conditions. Often the developer has to tactfully invite such an invitation, by speaking to friends who will speak to others who will make it known that help is available for social improvement.

c. Introduction to people—When a developer arises, s/he is likely to be introduced as a representative of some employing program or agency. Often this identification with an organization will initially be a handicap as the local citizens are apt to have certain prejudices toward the organization or toward "bureaucrats." The manner of his/her introduction is important in minimizing prejudged conclusions about his/her purposes.

d. Informal conversation—Through talking informally with local citizens, often in their homes where people feel "at home," the developer builds rapport. Especially important is the skill to help people articulate their fears, concerns, and frustrations. Slowly and tactfully the conversation proceeds to exploring the interest in, and ideas for, cooperative self-help with others in the area. This phase may require several days, weeks or even months.

Phase 2—Organizational

a. Problem—Through informal conversations the developer seeks to find some common problem or concern that the local citizens are willing to try to resolve. The number of people who are willing to work at a problem is often very small at first, perhaps as small as two or three. But these few represent the beginning of a "nucleus." They become the means for involving others. A nucleus is defined as a small group of serious-minded citizens who should have the following characteristics: (1) know and trust each other, even when disagreements arise, (2) have a concern about local problems and a desire to improve conditions for all their neighbors, and (3) are conscious of standards of right and wrong.

b. Informal meetings—The few interested come together in periodic meetings to exchange thoughts about the problem under consideration. In these initial meetings an attempt is made to more precisely define and agree upon the area of interest. Often there will be many considerations, differing points of view, and long, long discussions. The initial few in the nucleus are encouraged to invite their friends and neighbors to these meetings to enlarge the size of the nucleus.

c. Structure—Informal meetings almost always lead to a recognition that the group needs to be organized to accomplish the proposed improvements. The formality of the structure that is decided upon may vary from a few officers (chair and secretary-treasurer) with perhaps a few subcommittees, to a formal structure with a constitution, bylaws, full slate of officers and a number of subcommittees. The Biddles have found that leaders can be expected to emerge from almost any population if the encourager is skillful.

d. Commitment—After a structure is agreed upon, it is important that the group members arrive at a commitment to work together for some time with a defined purpose. This commitment is often adopted in a form that can be circulated to potential new members and to the news media.

e. Discussional training—At times local participants become aware that they are lacking in some skill viewed as important to accomplishing their objective. Perhaps a need is recognized for training in record-keeping of events, meetings, and encounters with people. Or, perhaps a community survey is viewed as essential to accomplishing the purpose, and a need is felt for training in such research. When such a training need is agreed upon, a qualified and sympathetic outsider may be invited in to provide training or act as a resource discussant.

Phase 3—Discussional

a. Definitions—Members are encouraged to examine the problem that brought them together in order to choose some aspect that they can realistically hope to improve. Certain related aspects of the problem, because of their complexity, have to be postponed for later consideration. Narrowing the problem by selecting some aspect requires self-discipline among members. Often members need to learn the art of creative discussion. Some may need to learn that disagreeing with someone is not a personal attack, but an opportunity for broadening understanding. Others may have to learn to be more assertive in expressing their concerns, misgivings, and fears. Others may need to switch from talking about their discontentments to focusing on "doing" something to improve conditions.

b. Alternatives—After the problem is precisely defined, there is a listing of as many alternative ways of resolving a problem as the members can think of.

c. Study—The advantages and disadvantages of the proposed solutions are then carefully discussed, and weighed. The Biddles comment, "The attitude sought in nucleus participants is not the wild enthusiasm of the crusader, but the quiet conviction that develops in the thoughtful comparison of many points of view."[8]

d. Value basis—When the alternatives are being discussed, it is helpful to make decisions in terms of consciously accepted standards of value. At this time the encourager can and should ask questions about ultimate objectives to draw attention to the standards by which the rightness or wrongness of proposed alternatives are to be judged. The aim is to facilitate the process of developing a "value basis" for choosing.

e. Decision—A decision is arrived at to take certain specific steps to work toward resolving the agreed-upon problem.

Phase 4—Action

a. Work project—For people prone to blame others and lacking in self-confidence, a small project that requires little outside help is generally advisable. More complicated projects, involving interactions with the power structure, can come later. A wide variety of projects are possible, such as conducting a survey, circulating petitions, cleaning up the neighborhood, raising money, and so on. The project may be completed in a day, or be larger and perhaps run on for months.

b. Reporting—A report is made to the nucleus on the work done and on its effectiveness.

c. Analysis and evaluation—The members of the nucleus discuss and critically evaluate the results of the work project. Often, the encourager finds that the members will judge themselves harshly and be vigorous in self-criticism. Sometimes the encourager needs to soften the self-criticism, especially if certain participants react overly defensively. With such discussions participants and the nucleus frequently begin to make some revisions in their practical value systems.

Phase 5—New projects

a. Repeat—After the initial (usually simple) project the nucleus generally moves on to problems and interests of increasing complexity. For each new project the steps in the prior two phases (the discussional and action phases) are repeated. With increasing complexity of projects, participants' self-confidence increases.

b. Outside contacts—With projects increasing in number and complexity there is increased contact with decision makers and power figures in the community. With increased self-confidence, the nucleus members find they can meet and discuss their concerns with people in power, even though their requests may be turned down. Another set of contacts the nucleus is apt to make is with community service agencies.

c. Controversy increase—As the problems tackled become more complex, requests made to authority figures and to decision makers are more apt to be refused. Officials may prove to be "bureaucratically narrow" in determining whether to meet the request, or the nucleus may be given a "runaround." To obtain a favorable decision in making progress toward resolving a problem, it may be necessary to exert pressure.

d. Pressure action—Only when cooperative steps with power figures prove futile do the Biddles advise applying "pressure action." Prior to this time, the nucleus should be cooperative and act on the assumption that power figures will do whatever they can to help. If and when this fails, then the Biddles advise such pressure tactics as demonstrations and news media denunciations. The selection of a particular pressure tactic should be based upon what appears to be most constructive and effective.

e. Need for coalition—It is sometimes advantageous to form coalitions with nearby nuclei that are interested in working on similar problems. Forming coalitions also puts added pressure on uncooperative power figures.

Demonstration by tenants

Phase 6—Continuation

a. Permanent nucleus—If a nucleus' growth has been "healthy," it should result in the formation of an ongoing group with an indefinite continuation. One of the major goals of community development is establishing an ongoing group, in spite of occasional changes in the membership and in the leadership.

b. Withdrawal—After the nucleus has the self-confidence to continue on its own, the need for outside encouragement declines. At this point the encourager withdraws. The encourager may withdraw gradually, perhaps by attending fewer meetings and speaking less and less. The encourager may withdraw completely, except perhaps for friendly letters and an occasional visit. Or, perhaps the encourager will remain "on call" for complexities that arise. The nature, timing, and rapidity of the withdrawal are matters of judgment that should be based primarily on the needs of the nucleus.

c. Increasing responsibility—As the nucleus continues to grow in size and confidence, it is anticipated that the nucleus will take on increasing responsibility by tackling problems of increasing complexity.

In contrast to the Biddles' "encourager" model of community organization, is the "power confrontation" approach developed by Saul Alinsky. This latter theory has undoubtedly generated the most interest and controversy in recent years. This approach evolved through efforts to organize neighborhoods within inner cities to force the existing power structure to improve neighborhood living conditions. In the following article, Shel Trapp describes this approach. (It should be noted by the reader that most other theories of community organization are not as "militant," or social action oriented.)

MODEL 2: THE ALINSKY MODEL— THE "POWER CONFRONTATION" APPROACH TO COMMUNITY ORGANIZATION

POWER ANALYSIS*

Whenever an organizer approaches a new community or a new group, he/she should begin immediately to analyze the power structure in that community or group. All communities, churches, clubs, organizations have a power structure, real or assumed, out of which that group operates.

---

* This article by Shel Trapp is reprinted from a pamphlet "Dynamics of Organizing" (Chicago: National Training and Information Center, 1976). Permission to reprint has gratefully been received from Shel Trapp.

The National Training and Information Center has been providing assistance to developing and existing people's organizations since 1972. Founded by Shel Trapp and Gale Cincotta, pioneers in coalition and national network organizing, NTIC has served several

Who appears to have the power?

This is relatively easy to determine. Who is on the city council; who was honored at the "Good Citizen's Award Dinner"; who is on the board of directors of the hospital, bank, largest industry; whose name appears in the paper when an opinion is sought on an issue. Such person or persons may or may not be the real power in the community, but, at least on the surface, it appears so; and it may even be assumed by the group and observers that these people are the actual power structure. It is important for the organizer not to fall into this easy assumption. The task of analyzing the power structure is not complete at this point.

---

hundred organizations and trained as many organizers for grass-roots organizations. Trapp has assisted several hundred grass-roots organizations in developing action programs. Cincotta has emerged as a spokesperson for community organizations fighting for preservation of their neighborhoods.

Using as innovative models, the Metropolitan Area Housing Alliance (MAHA) of Chicago, Illinois, and the National People's Action (NPA), a national network of neighborhood-based organizations, NTIC has been successful in training people beyond the previously limited scope of community organizing. The National People's Action is the only neighborhood-based network that addresses itself to issues of regional and national impact.

Community leaders, workers, ministers, lawyers, organizers have participated in NTIC sessions or have received assistance through one or more of the NTIC programs. Neighborhood organizations, grass-roots organizations, citywide coalitions, churches, professional associations, national groups and unions have benefited from NTIC services. Some of these organzations are:

Buckeye-Woodland Community Congress-Cleveland, Ohio; Council on Municipal Performance-New York; Urban Reinvestment Task Force-Washington, D.C.; Metropolitan Area Housing Alliance-Chicago, Illinois; Citizens for community Improvement, Waterloo, Iowa; Center for Community Change-Washington, D.C.; Catholic Charities; United Methodist Church; Center for Urban Affairs-Northwestern University; Social Workers Alliance-Southern Illinois University; Neighborhood Housing and Information Center-St. Louis, Missouri; Chicago Metropolitan Area Senior Citizens Senate; National Urban Coalition; City of Pasadena, California; VISTA; National People's Action; People against Redlining-Salt Lake City, Utah.

Who has the power?

In a city, this is not that easy to determine. Much like an organizer, this person or persons prefers to remain a behind the scenes actor. He/she may well be a member of a family who at one time had great wealth or is respected because of their "name." Quite often this person turns up in the field of finances or organized crime. In a day when political campaign contributions are becoming public knowledge, that is a good place to begin ferreting out where the real power lies. Also, as the organizer talks with those who appear to have the power, a question such as, "Whose opinion do you really respect?" should be asked. This question may begin to uncover names that previously have not surfaced in the press or on the boards of directors.

Within a smaller organization or a community it is usually easier to determine whether those who appear to have the power in reality do have the power, because this person will surface at the time of a decision or when an opinion is required. Also, in the smaller group the person who has the real power usually does not have an ulterior motive for remaining behind the scenes. If those who appear to have the power—president, chairman, and so on are not the same as those who really make decisions, it is usually because the real power of the organization is temporarily out of office because of the constitution of the group.

Who has power in specific arenas?

If an organizer is going to use the churches in his* effort, he* had best be aware of who appears to have the power, as well as who has the real power in any kind of clergy group, whether it be officially organized or an informal network. In any small commu-

* Throughout the pamphlet, references to "he" should be understood as he/she.

nity as well, there are usually some people that the organizer must know about before making a move. If, in ringing door bells on a block, the name of "Mrs. Jones" comes up as a person that three or four people mention, then the wise organizer touches base with "Mrs. Jones" before he makes a move. Similarly, if the name of the reputed power figure rarely emerges, investigation into his/her actions ought to be pursued before false assumptions are made.

When and why does the organizer take on the existing power structure in a community?

A.   When the power structure no longer, if it ever did, represents the community.   A community organization discovered that there were 300 abandoned homes in their community and 50 more close to foreclosure. People on the streets were very concerned about the issue. However, the organization board of directors, made up of two clergymen, one city official, one county official, one individual who was running for office, and two people who had stopped coming to meetings, did not feel that this was a legitimate issue.

The organizer, without the sanction of the board, pulled 10 community people together and they scheduled a public meeting. Three hundred people showed up and they began to deal with the issue of abandonment and foreclosure. After the meeting, the board's position was, "Well, it probably is an issue, but it should have been handled a different way." The steering committee of the foreclosure issue has now become the real power of the organization although they hold no seats on the board. The organizer had read the issue correctly: there was a latent power base that could be mobilized quickly to override the unrepresentative position of the board of directors.

B. **When the power structure is incapable or unwilling to deal with real issues.** A community was faced with slum buildings, 70 children in a classroom at the public schools, racial tensions at the high school. The community organization held a Memorial Day Parade to increase community pride! Rather than dealing with the pressing issues of concern to many community people, the existing organization (reputed power structure) attempted to sidetrack reality. Community pride may be essential in maintaining neighborhood stability, but it could not change the hearts and minds of absentee landlords who were callous to the health and welfare of their inner-city tenants; it would not convince the Board of Education to ease crowded school facilities nor could it erase the causes of the racial tensions at the high school.

In this case, the organization "looked the other way" as the conditions became worse. The Memorial Day Parade, instead of installing pride, brought about cynicism and anger toward the people who supposedly had the power to improve the quality of life in the community.

The organizer did not have to destroy or take on the existing power structure, in this case. But its unwillingness to deal with the crucial issues in the community it brought about its own destruction when the rank-and-file community people became disenchanted with the existing organization.

How does the organizer take on the existing power base?

A. **Never by himself, only with a developed power base**

B. **By putting the existing power base into a position of reaction.** When the organizer finds a group of people who have an issue and the existing organization is not dealing with it, take that group into the meeting of the existing organization. The reaction of the existing organization is often, "We have been working on that for a long time. Why haven't you come to our meetings before?" To put it bluntly, quite often the newcomers get shit on. As they leave the meeting confused, they are fertile ground for the organizer to build a base. If the existing group accepts the newcomers and begins to move specifically on their issue, the organizer should have good access to the existing group because he has delivered new people into the existing organization. If he plays his cards right, the entire existing organization should soon be a power base.

C. **By avoiding the existing power base and the issues they are working on, moving so fast that the existing power base cannot keep up with the newly emerging group.** A local community had a very articulate group of people who dealt only with school issues. The Board of Education was happy to deal with this small group because they never held public meetings and the most people that this group could deliver was 12. This select, articulate group viewed itself as the spokespersons for the community and would not open up their group to participation by anyone else.

The organizer spent six months building 45 block clubs that dealt with housing and sanitation issues. Never did he attempt to move on education issues. At first, the education people attempted to disrupt his block club meetings, but within a month there were so many block club meetings every week that they could not keep up with all the activity. Since the block clubs did not deal with education issues, the school group soon lost interest in their existence and the efforts of the organizer. In a few months, the block clubs had developed some very strong articulate leadership.

The Board of Education announced that a new school was to be built in the community. The people who dealt with education issues said they wanted the school built in the "middle of the community." If that site was selected, it would mean that 75 homes would be razed to make room for the school. The block clubs could not take this seriously because, 1/4 mile away from this site, the Board of Education owned 8 acres of vacant land. Despite this, the Board of Education announced its plan to demolish the homes so the school could be in the "middle of the community."

The block clubs reacted: they invited the Board of Education out to the community and had 400 people at the meeting. The education people came to the meeting and spoke in favor of the "middle of the community site." The block clubs demanded the vacant land site. The Board of Education said that if the community couldn't get together, there would be no new school. The block club leaders requested that the Board of Education come out to another meeting in two weeks, at which time all the organizations in the community would testify as to their position on the school site, and they would abide by the decision of the majority. The Board of Education agreed.

At the follow-up meeting 600 people showed up. The blocks produced 43 of their clubs, two churches, a union and two other organizations in favor of the vacant land site. The education people produced themselves, one other group, and the owner of a large vacant building that would be razed if the "middle of the community" site was selected.

At the conclusion of the meeting, the leader of the block clubs announced to the Board of Education that the block clubs now had an education committee, and from now on the Board of Education would contact that committee about any plans they might have for the community. Today, a new school stands on what was once vacant land, without one home having been demolished.

One is not always so fortunate as to have an existing power base react in such a strong self-destructing manner as did this group. However, it is the organizer's job to force the existing power base, whether in the church, community or political arena, to react. Existing power bases make a habit of reacting against the people and the people's issues. At that point the organizer has the beginnings of a new *people's power base*.

D. Form a coalition under a new coalition name. Organizations with a history do not like to give up their history or their autonomy. If they can see a way that they can maintain their local base, the group may be more willing to give up its name when dealing with a specific issue. This is particularly true if the issue is one that the existing local power base has not dealt with or an issue too big for the existing group to handle. Thus, the organizer offers more participation through a coalition than the local group has ever had before, and the possibility of winning on a big issue. The only condition is that everyone flies under a new flag. That way all groups see that they are all giving up something to participate in the coalition.

When existing, but fragmented groups do not want to lose individual identity and autonomy, an alternative is to form a coalition around an issue common to all groups but too overwhelming for one group alone to challenge.

Taking on the existing power base often requires a united effort by diverse groups so that the people are not played off against each other by the structure threatened by the idea of relinquishing its "power."

Conclusion

It is important for the organizer to recognize that, once the analysis of a power structure is done, this analysis must be contin-

Farmworkers' demonstration

ually reevaluated and updated. Power is not static; it is continually changing and rearranging quite like the rearranging shape of a bean bag chair. The organizer must be aware of that, observe its shifts, anticipate the shifts, and, hopefully, force the shifts in favor of a people's organization. The organizer who cannot do this will find himself reading the want ads.

STRATEGY AND TACTICS

Deception is not enough—the enemy's leaders must be confused; if possible, driven insane.

Mao Tse-Tung

Strategy and tactics are a critical aspect of organizing. The issue can be sharp, the people angry and ready to go to battle; but, if the tactics are wrong or the strategy unclear, the entire battle can be lost. Therefore, in organizing it is important that the organizer, leaders and constituency be clear on the strategy. In developing strategy the organizer should ask these questions:

1. Will the people accept it?
2. Will it dramatize and build the issue?
3. Will it throw the enemy off balance?
4. Will it personalize the enemy?
5. Will it be fun for the people?
6. What alternatives must be planned?
7. Will it get us to the bargaining table?

1. Will the people accept it?

A new organizer eager to prove his ability in getting groups into action pushed the leadership very hard on a block that if the slumlord did not come to the meeting they would go out to his home and picket. The leadership was not ready for this move and thus reacted negatively not only to the strategy but also to the idea of having a meeting. The issue was lost because the people were pushed toward a strategy with which they did not feel comfortable.

It is important that there be a logical progression in the strategy. Thus, another organizer went into the same block and suggested a meeting of just the people on the block to talk about what they wanted to do about the slum building. At that meeting the residents decided that they would hold another meeting and invite the slumlord. When he did not come to the meeting, the people decided that they should hold another meeting and invite him again because, "It may not have been convenient for him to come tonight." When the slumlord did not come to the second meeting, the people decided that they would go to his house. Thus, the same group which initially had said "No" to going to the slumlord's house ended up doing that very thing because now it seemed to them a logical progression. People like to look upon themselves as being logical. Thus, the organizer will build the strategy in such a way that each escalation of activity seems very logical. This is particularly true with new groups. As groups get battle seasoned, they do not care as much about appearing logical as they do about winning the fight. The strategy with new groups has to build slowly and in a logical progression. This takes time, but if the organizer wants the people to participate in the strategy, then they must set their own pace and as they do so they will be a part of the development of the strategy.

2.   Will it dramatize and build the issue?

A community group could not get the alderman to respond to their demands on rat abatement. Several meetings were held, and the frustration of the community continued to mount. When the alderman refused to come to yet another meeting on the issue, 75 people went to his office and nailed a dead rat up on the door by its tail. Word quickly spread through the community, the alderman's office was besieged with calls threatening more rats, the press picked it up and did a series of articles on the rat issue in that community. Within one week, rat abatement crews had been through the community twice. In this case the issue was dramatized so well that there was not time to build the issue and it was won without further confrontation.

Strategy should be dramatic so that it is evident even to an outsider that people are upset and want something changed. Dramatization of the issue which gets the organization press makes it easier to build the organizational drive out on the streets, thus drawing more people in to the fight.

3.   Will it throw the enemy off balance?

A good tactic is one which the enemy is not expecting, something which takes him out of his usual sphere of operation and puts him in an unfamiliar situation. An organization had several very strong confrontations with a city agency. It was felt that the city officials were becoming too accustomed to the confrontational tactics so it was time to develop a different tactic. It was decided that a priest would open the meeting with prayer and in the prayer would speak of the concern of the city officials and their dedication and self-sacrificing for the community. This strategy so unnerved the city officials that the organization won its fight. The unexpected had thrown the enemy so off balance that they could not regain their composure throughout the entire meeting.

In another case, a Spanish group went to meet with the Board of Education about the need for more Spanish programs in the school system. They went into the meeting and only spoke Spanish, forcing the school administration to get an interpreter and carry on the entire meeting in Spanish. Again, the enemy was thrown so off balance that it acquiesced to the demands of the delegation.

Another means of throwing the enemy off balance is to fuse his worlds. The human animal likes to live in logic tight compartments: in the office he may be a tough businessman, but on Sunday morning he is an usher in the local church, or on Tuesday night he is the coach of a Little League team. The good organizer will develop strategy that will mix those worlds together.

A contractor had built some very poorly constructed homes and refused to make any of the needed repairs, despite the fact that under law he was responsible for those repairs. The organizer found that he was a highly respected member of his church and, in fact, had often preached when the minister was on vacation. The group went to the church with flyers that had a picture of the contractor, his name, the facts about the poor housing, and then several quotes from scripture, such as, "Thou shalt not steal," "Thou shalt not bear false witness." The builder's life was hopelessly mixed, no longer could he be the respected church man, for now his fellow church members knew that he had built poor homes.

When you mix the enemy's worlds, he is thrown off balance, giving the organization an advantage in the battle. "An army cannot be run by rules of etiquette." (Ts'ao Ts'ao). By not playing by the "rules of etiquette" the strategies developed fit the circumstances and are designed to hit the enemy when he least expects to be hit, thus giving the organization an advantageous position. Saul Alinsky included as a tactical rule: "Whenever possible go outside of the experience of the enemy," to cause confusion, frustration, and fear.

4. Will it personalize the enemy?

When an organization goes into battle, it is very important that they come to understand that the enemy they are fighting is a specific person. It is much easier to focus the issue and gain participation if the organization comes to understand that there is someone within the structure that they are fighting who can give what they want. It is the chairman of the board, the head of a department or a specific official. It is not all of city hall, or the entire banking industry. It is a specific person. For that reason, the strategies are developed to focus around one person, until that person says that someone else has the power to make the decision or gives the organization what they are seeking.

A Latin coalition was seeking jobs from the telephone company. They were fighting the personnel department of the phone com-

pany, then the training department of the phone company. It seemed that each new week brought a new enemy and they were going around in circles. Then the coalition decided that they would not deal with the entire phone company but would focus their entire efforts on its president. Cutting the issue simply: this man is president and he can give us what we want. The next two months saw a series of activities focusing on the president. Visits to his office, his home, his church, his private club, it even included 40 people following him around the golf course one Sunday morning. Needless to say, his game was somewhat off that day. After two months, the coalition won 2,700 jobs for latinos to be spread over a two-year period.

It is key to the organizing drive that the issue be cut and the strategies be developed to focus on specific personalities. That way, people see their problem as having its resolution not in some bureaucratic system, but in a specific individual.

5. Will it be fun for the people?

All of our lives are basically quite boring. That is why people watch so much TV, to live vicariously for a few hours in a different world. Thus, if at all possible, strategies should be fun for the people who are participating. That way, they will come back and in telling their friends and neighbors will become recruiters for the organizer for the next action.

The people had been trying to meet with a banker whom they were accusing of not making loans in their community (a practice known as "red lining"). Finally, they decided to go to his home in one of the affluent suburbs. In addition to passing out flyers to his neighbors, several people brought with them red streamers of crepe paper. This crepe paper was tossed over the roof of the banker's house, wrapped around the shrubs in the front yard. When the action was over, and despite the fact that at the front door the banker had agreed to meet with a group of neighborhood people the following week (which had been the purpose of the visit), the thing that the people talked about most in the following week was the fun they had had tossing the red crepe paper around the banker's yard. By the time the meeting came the following week, it was very easy to get people to the meeting because everyone wanted to come to see the banker who had been "redlined" by the community.

6. What alternatives must be planned?

Before going into a public meeting or an action it is imperative that the organizer has gone through with the leadership what their alternatives are going to be. What are we going to do if the enemy says "Yes" to demands one and two, but "No" to the third demand? What are we going to do if he says "Yes" to one and "No" to two and three? What are we going to do if he doesn't show up? What are we going to do if he walks out of the meeting? The initial strategy of the group mentioned earlier that nailed the rat to the alderman's door was to present the rat to the alderman in his office. Fortunately, they had thought through what they were going to do if he was not at his office. When they got there and the office was closed, the alternative plan of action was put into operation and the hammer and nail was gotten out of the car and with a great deal of ceremony the rat was nailed to the alderman's door. If they had not had an alternative strategy, someone may have thought of that on the spot, but it might also have resulted in the group deciding to go back home and come back at a later date, a sure way to kill an organizing drive.

Alternative strategies are key to an orga-

nizing effort so that even if the circumstances change, the leadership is prepared as far as possible with a variety of plans to meet the changing circumstances. It is the enemy that we want to catch off balance and keep off balance, not the leadership.

7. Will it get us to the bargaining table?

The purpose of all strategy is to get the organization to a bargaining table so that they can negotiate out their demands. Thus, strategy is not developed which will detract from the issue and take the focus off the main issue. In a battle over an overcrowded school, the leadership decided that they would stage a boycott to show their power. To increase the effectiveness of the boycott, it was decided to pass out flyers to the students the day before saying "No School Tomorrow." As the flyers were being passed out, a policeman drove up and said that he was going to arrest the group for contributing to the delinquency of minors. An attorney in the group wanted to protest the officer's right to make such an arrest. But immediately the organizer and top leader gathered all the flyers from the people and gave them to the policeman. This satisfied him and he drove off. Had someone been arrested, the battle of the overcrowded school would have been clouded by the arrest. At this time the police were not the issue, the school was; and thus nothing could come into the activity that would detract from the organizing drive on the school issue. The purpose of any strategy is to lead the organization to the bargaining table, not away from it.

Conclusion

Recognizing the amount of power the organization has and the amount of power it is going against, it is critical that sound strate-

Native American demonstration

gies be developed which will answer the above questions. In speaking of strategy Meng states: "Drive him crazy and bewilder him so that he disperses his forces in confusion." Thus, the organizer attempts to use strategy in such a way that the organization's power is maximized and the enemy's power minimized.

Having dealt with these questions in his own mind, the organizer then sits down with leadership and forces them to go through the same questions and works with them as to the strategy which they will select for the meeting or action. If carefully thought out and backed by enough power, there should be victory at the end of the battle.

DEVELOPING AN ISSUE GROUP

A. Identify an issue.
B. Test the issue.
C. Find a leader or leaders.

D. Hold a leadership meeting.
    Determine: 1. Meeting place. 2. Agenda and alternatives. 3. Assignments
E. Hold a meeting.
    Determine: 1. Action. 2. Needed follow-up. 3. Next meeting date.
F. Put the kill in.
G. Move the group to a new issue.

A. Identify an issue

This occurs in many ways. Someone may call the organization's office and complain of an abandoned car or a dead tree. As you are talking with people, whether it's in a laundromat, their front door or at an ice cream social, the good organizer is continually looking for issues. A casual gripe like, "Our streets haven't been cleaned in months." can be the seeds of an organizing drive. The organizer may see an abandoned house on a block and begin to talk with people in the area about the danger of that vacant building.

When probing for an issue, it is important to push to the point where people articulate a specific issue, not a glaring generality. An organizer doesn't accept a response of "I don't like all the slum buildings." The organizer at this point pushes, "Which one is the worst?" or "Would you say that that one across the street is the worst?"

The organizer is continually fishing for issues, when one seems to be hooked, it must be identified and made as specific and clear as possible so that when the organizer is testing the issue it is clear what is being tested and to what people are responding.

B. Test the issue

Just because one person brings up a problem or the organizer sees something that looks like an issue does not make it an issue. To an organizer an issue is that around which people can be mobilized. So that when something comes up, be it painting the garbage cans red or that there are rats in the alley, the issue is immediately tested. "Some of your neighbors are concerned about the rats in the alley; if we have a meeting, would you be interested in coming to the meeting?" If everyone in the area says, "There are no rats in the alley" then the organizer can be reasonably sure that a dead end on that issue has been reached. However, if several people respond that they are sick of seeing rats or afraid that children will be bitten, then it appears that an issue has been found and enough people are concerned that a meeting can be held.

C. Find a leader or leaders

Particularly with new groups, the organizer has to trust instinct and luck. Who brought up the issue? In talking with people who seemed to be the most angry about the issue, is there someone on the block or in the area whose name has come up several times as someone who knows the community?

When such a person (or persons) is found, the organizer attempts to get a couple of people together to discuss what they want to do. When talking to people at this point, the meeting is not billed as a leadership meeting—rather just a couple of people from the block are getting together to talk about what we can do about the rats in the alley.

D. Hold a leadership meeting

This is the first step in the training of leaders. The organizer must make the ground rules clear. Involve as many people as possible. The organizer doesn't speak for the group. The people make their own choices about how to move on the issues. We must move on issues, not just talk about them. The following quote of Alfred North

Whitehead reaffirms this point. "*We cannot think first and act afterwards. From the moment of birth we are immersed in action and can only fitfully guide it by taking thought.*"

After introductions are over and, if the organizer is lucky, a can of beer has been popped, it is time to get down to business.

What is the issue?

What are the things we can do about the issue?

Of these things, which one do we want to do first?

When and where do we have a meeting of more people so we can get support for this action?

Who is going to chair the meeting?

What is the agenda?

Who is going to pass out flyers or ring door bells?

Do we want to notify churches or other groups in the area about the meeting?

Do we want to notify the press?

With new groups and people who are not accustomed to community meetings, it is important that the leadership understand that this is their meeting and they have responsibility for making sure that it comes off. It is also important that the meeting be held as close physically to the issue as possible. A home, a church, an agency or lodge, or as was the case in one community, a vacant lot on the street. Whatever is easiest and most convenient and comfortable for the people.

E. Hold a meeting

When the notices for the meeting have gone out, phone calls made and door bells rung, the agenda made up, the organizer can only chew gum, smoke, pace and, in some rare cases, pray that people will show up.

If the prayers are answered and people begin to show up, the task of the organizer is to meet people as they come in and prepare them for the meeting. So that if the leadership has decided that after discussion of the issue they are going to suggest that the group sweep the trash out of the alley and take it to the front yard of a city official, the organizer tests the idea.

"What do you think we ought to do about the trash in the alley?"

"Gee, I don't know."

"Well, some people are talking about sweeping it up ourselves."

"Sounds good to me."

"You know, when we get all that trash together at the end of the alley, some people are even suggesting that we dump it in 'Jones's,' the commissioner of sanitation, front yard."

"Terrific idea!"

With several positive responses like this, the organizer keys in the leadership that it looks like the people are ready to accept the battle plan. If the organizer gets a negative reaction to all or part of the proposed strategy, the leadership is informed that the going may be rough and perhaps a fall back position would be to invite "Jones" to a follow-up meeting.

At this meeting, several things are very important.

1. Make sure you get a sign-in sheet.
2. Make sure that the leadership forces the group to make some decision about the issue. They are going to ask someone who can do something about the issue to come to the next meeting. They are going to write someone about the issue. It is critical that some step toward resolving the issue be taken, so that they don't decide to meet next week to decide what we are going to do about the issue. That was the purpose of this meeting.

3. Just before the meeting is over, there should be a recap of the decisions that have been made so everyone understands what the next steps will be. Also in the recap, the date, time, and place of the next meeting should be set.

F. Put the kill in

The issue has been cut, a meeting held, a course of action determined. Now the organizer's task is to continue to work with the leadership and group to win the issue.

G. Move the group to a new issue

As the group is celebrating its victory, the organizer is attempting to get them to take the next issues. This can be something that has come up at one of the meetings of something that the organizer has heard while on the street. Then the process starts over again.

Using this outline, let's take a case history and apply the previous outline to the case.

CASE STUDY

Identifying an issue

An organizer working in a changing neighborhood has found three homes that whites had sold for under $20,000 and within two weeks blacks had bought for over $30,000, the realtor walking off with the difference. A school built for 800, with an enrollment of 1,600 (one class was even meeting in the boys' lavatory). A slum building where a child had lead poisoning. All of these seemed like good issues to him. It was impossible to get people to buy into any of these issues. Finally, he began to ask people what they thought was the issue.

Finally, at one door the lady said that the thing that was wrong with the neighborhood was the shopping carts from the supermarket on the corner were being taken out of the store and left around the neighborhood. Children were playing with them in the street, scratching parked cars and someone almost hit a child last week. In addition, they were left out in the alley and you had to stop your car and get out to move the cart.

Testing the issue

The organizer could not believe that anyone would be interested in such a petty issue, particularly since he had identified so many major issues in the community. In talking with other people on the block, he mentioned that some of the neighbors were talking about the shopping carts which were out in the community. The response was unanimous—people wanted to do something about the issue and were willing to come to a meeting.

Finding a leader or leaders

The organizer went back to the woman who had originally brought up the issue and told her that several people were interested in coming to a meeting. He asked the woman if she and a couple of her friends and the organizer could sit down tomorrow night and talk about the meeting.

Leadership meeting

The organizer introduced himself and stated that a lot of people were concerned about the shopping carts and that they had to plan a meeting and an agenda for the meeting and a location for the meeting. It was decided that the meeting would be at the woman's home who had originally brought up the idea and that she and a neighbor would co-chair the meeting. They would try to get out of the meeting a committee to go up to the supermarket to talk with the man-

ager about the problem. The three people present agreed to bring two neighbors each and pass out flyers on their block.

Hold a meeting

Twelve people came to the meeting and spent a great deal of time discussing the fact that the Chicago Bears didn't have much of a team this year. Finally, the organizer had to say, "I thought we came to discuss the issue of the shopping carts." After much discussion, it was agreed that a committee would go to the supermarket the next Saturday morning to talk with the manager. It was agreed that only six people would go because they were sure that the manager was a nice guy who would be helpful in solving the problem. Six people signed up to go. They agreed to meet at the woman's home at 10:00 A.M. Saturday.

Put the kill in

Five people showed up Saturday morning so the group stopped by the sixth person's home on the way to the supermarket and picked him up. When they got to the supermarket, the manager kept them waiting for 20 minutes. Then, when they told him what they were there about, he looked at the blacks in the group and said, "I didn't have this problem until you people moved in." This triggered the group and they began to shout at the manager; he ordered them out of the store or he would call the police. Immediately, the organizer suggested that they go to someone's house and plan their next step. The people said they wanted a meeting on Tuesday night and they would suggest to the group that the next week they go to the supermarket and everyone would buy one item and take a shopping cart home with them.

The meeting was held, 21 people came.

The committee made its report of what had happened and suggested the battle plan. Someone volunteered their garage to store the shopping carts. It was also decided that everyone would meet the next Saturday morning to return the shopping carts to the store.

The group was so successful that by Saturday morning the supermarket had no shopping carts and the garage was full. Seventeen people showed up to return the carts. So a parade was held taking a very indirect route to the supermart. By the time the group reached the supermart, there were over 75 people—each one pushing a cart. The manager saw them coming and called the police.

When the police arrived, it was explained that they were law-abiding citizens and were returning this man's property to him and that if he couldn't figure out a way to keep the shopping carts in the store then they would have to do this every Saturday morning. Immediately, the police were on the side of the people and became an ally in the confrontation. The manager called the district office and obtained a promise that by Monday poles would be installed 18 inches apart so that carts could not leave the area in front of the supermarket.

Move on to the next issue

On Monday, the organizer drove by the supermarket and saw the poles going in. He bought a case of beer and went to the block and an impromptu victory party was had. After people had shared their victory stories, the organizer asked if there were any other issues that the group felt they should be working on. Someone suggested that the building on the corner was really looking bad and maybe they should have a meeting to decide what to do about it. A meeting date was set and the group was on to a new issue, the very building that the organizer had

tried, unsuccessfully, to force on the people in the first place.

Often times, issues which seem crucial to the organizer and a few people must be temporarily set aside because of "petty" issues. The shopping cart issue outlined above served as a training vehicle that introduced people to roles of leadership and the process of organizing and winning. Too often, organizers and some leaders try to reach for the stars too soon. Unless an organization is built gradually with steps of progression it may face an early death. In developing an issue group it is important to allow people independence in selecting initial issues so that when larger issues come up they are not totally dependent upon or controlled by the organizers or certain leaders.

COALITION ORGANIZING

Coalition—A temporary alliance of factions, parties, and so on, for some specific purpose.

Alliance—A close association for a common objective.

As the definitions state, it is the commonality of issues which pull various groups together who otherwise might not work together and in some cases may even be antagonistic to each other. Thus, the purpose of coalitions is to amass enough power to win an issue that could not be won by one group or organization alone.

Protecting integrity of coalition members

Community organizations increasingly find themselves in a position of facing issues which they cannot win by themselves and therefore must coalesce with other groups. This is difficult for an established power organization in that it means they must give up some of their local autonomy. There are several ways to overcome this problem.

First of all, it is necessary for every member of the coalition to be represented on the leadership or steering committee. This way, as strategy is developed, each group is participating in its planning. When the coalition is having a public meeting it is also good policy to have at the front table a representative from each of the member groups. Thus, members of each organization see that they are represented at the leadership table. Hopefully, each of the leaders have a demand to give or a statement to make. As these leaders identify themselves they say, "Mr. Smith, representing Roseland Organization of Citizens Coalition against Rent Increases."

In addition, many coalitions list their members on the agenda so that every organization sees its name. There are two dangers in this. First, you may reveal to your enemies your weakness, by only listing three groups when the enemy thought you had 20 (remember, the illusion of power is many times beneficial). Second, make sure that you list everyone or you will have some very angry people on your hands because the name of their organization did not appear.

In a coalition, those organizations which have staffed should have staff meetings concerning coalition efforts, in addition to leadership meetings so they are clear on the direction the coalition is going and who is resposible for what. Most problems occur in a coalition when leadership and/or staff is confused as to what the next steps of the coalition are to be. Touching base with each member of the coalition cannot be stressed enough.

Types of coalitions

Within an organization. This is the easiest type of coalition in that people and leaders are probably accustomed to working with each other. Several block clubs may band together and hold a slumlord compliance. Thus, each block club invites one slumlord and brings 15 people from the block. That way, the slumlord finds himself facing 100 people screaming about his bad building. He is not aware that perhaps only 10–15 people live on the block where his building is located. Because of the numbers of people he is more inclined to fix up his building. Thus, by forming a coalition, a block club stands a better chance of getting the slum building on their block fixed up.

Citywide coalition. This type of coalition is much harder to develop and maintain in that a variety of groups may be members all of which have varying amounts of experience. Also, in all likelihood, the leaders and the staff have not worked together in the past and thus are suspicious of each other. However, if all the members are concerned enough about the issue, they can overcome historical boundaries, race, geography and economic differences.

The Metropolitan Area Housing Alliance (MAHA) in Chicago had its birth when staff from eight organizations got together and discovered they all were having the same problem with Housing Court—no results. They decided to ask their leaders to come together and see if they wanted to work together on the issue. They sponsored a public meeting and won a monthly citywide day in court for member organizations. This day in court has been quite effective for the local organizations and they have seen real benefit in participation in MAHA. Through this experience leadership got to know each other and MAHA has gone on to win victories on a variety of other issues.

National coalitions. This is a very new and untested type of coalition for community groups. Fortunately, the first two national coalitions formed by community organizations have resulted in victories. A loose network of organizations around the country, National People's Action, (NPA) has created tremendous impetus. Two pieces of federal legislation have been passed, one requiring HUD to reimburse families who had bought sublending patterns. We see this effort as a creative and necessary step in the development of community organizations. Hopefully, the years ahead will hold many more coalitions of community organizations on a national level giving more input by community groups into national policy.

Building a coalition

There are no set rules in building a coalition. Some happen as MAHA did when several organizations decide out of necessity that they will band together. More often, one organization finds itself facing an issue which a few initial probes reveal to be too complex and that the organization must have more power if it is going to win the issue. Thus, the organization begins to look around for other groups with whom they can coalesce around that issue to win.

An organization in Pontiac, Michigan, learned that the local General Hospital was going to move and that there was a move to take it out of the hands of city control and make it a private hospital. Thus, there were two issues: (1) who would control the hospital, and (2) would the hospital move. After one public hearing in which they were not allowed to present their case, they immediately began to seek ways to expand their power base.

In this drive, they built a very interesting and diverse coalition. A large segment of Spanish were concerned that the hospital had no one in the emergency room who spoke Spanish. Thus, they came into the

coalition via the route of demanding a Spanish-speaking person in the emergency room. A welfare rights organization joined the coalition because, if the city lost control of the hospital and it became private, they feared that the hospital would no longer accept welfare recipients.

The organization did research and discovered that the plan of moving the hospital called for the city to pay for a large portion of the cost of relocation and construction. Thus, the middle-class homeowners came into the fight on the basis that their real estate taxes would go up if the hospital were allowed to move. The people who lived near the hospital did not want it to move because it was close to them and it was unclear what would happen to the vacant building once the hospital moved out. So they came into the fight. The organization's research showed that the proposed new hospital was to have a psychiatric ward. When the people who lived near the proposed new site learned that, they were opposed to the hospital moving into their community. The senior citizens joined the coalition because there was no transportation to the proposed new site.

By this time, the coalition was very strong and had several confrontations with the hospital and city. With this kind of exposure behind them, they approached the United Auto Workers to join and the UAW came into the fight. A politician running for a state office suddenly became very "interested" in the issue and came down on their side of the issue, thus giving the issue more exposure. Result: the victory was won.

The research and the organizer's ability to find the self interest of each group was key to the building of this coalition. Each group came from a different motivation and were able to be focused on the one issue of stopping the hospital from moving.

As one gets into organizing on broad based issues that require coalitions, research becomes a very important part of the organizing drive, first of all, because the issue is probably more complex than a block club issue. Second, the more research one has, the easier it is to determine ways that additional groups can be attracted into the coalition.

BUILDING POWER AND VICTORIES

The goal of every community organization is to build power, people power, so that the community can determine its needs, articulate them and fight for them. To build power there must be victories, only the masochist will stay on in a losing cause. For involvement in a community organization to make sense, community residents must see results or victories. Victories seem fairly easy to define, the football team with the most points wins, the golfer with the lowest score is victorious. In community organizing it is not quite so easy. Goals are changing, negotiations take place, a victory leads to another goal.

1. Definitions

A. Intermediate victories. These are the small victories along the road to the primary victory. They help build the organizing drive so that when the primary victory is reached the largest possible number of people are involved, feeling the victory is theirs.

B. Primary victories. These are the goals that have been set by the organization that have major meaning for the residents of the community, such as getting a new school built, stopping a rezoning by an outside developer.

C. No final victories. Just as intermediate victories lead to the primary victory, primary victories lead to a whole new set of organiz-

ing drives and a whole new set of intermediate and primary victories.

2. Illustration of a very local issue

An organization may set for itself the goal of cleaning up a slum building. The primary victory is not reached until the building is fixed up. Intermediate victories are usually achieved along the route, as for instance when the absentee owner agrees to a meeting with the residents after a picket line has been at his office.

Intermediate victories are very important because they keep the issue alive, and they are used as organizational tools in building toward the primary victory. The interpretation of these intermediate victories is very important to the people, so that they see that there is some movement in the issue and they are getting closer to the final goal.

An organizer had been working on a slum building and having little results. The owner refused to meet with the group even though they had been to his home and church with a large delegation. The leadership was discouraged, and the people were losing interest in the issue because they could see no movement in the issue. The organizer brought 10 members of the clergy from around the community to a leadership meeting. The leaders took them on a tour of the building so they could see first hand what the conditions of the building were. It was also arranged that when the clergy walked out of the building there was a reporter from the local neighborhood newspaper. The headline next week in the paper read "Local Clergy Pledge Support to Beleaguered Tenants." The article was duplicated and distributed throughout the neighborhood. People took hope from the fact that a new element was in the fight and there was new support for their fight. The clergy and members from their churches came to the next public meeting, and when the slumlord did not show up the group went again to the slumlord's home; the clergy went with them. With the added power of the clergy and more people, the leadership was more aggressive and there developed a strong confrontation on the slumlord's front porch which resulted in his agreeing to a timetable of fixing the building. The building was fixed up, and the primary victory was achieved. Yet it would never have been reached had there not been the intermediate victory of the tour of the clergy and their joining the fight. This intermediate victory was used to the utmost in building the issue and gaining exposure for the issue.

3. Illustration of a broad-based issue

A Chicago-based organization, Metropolitan Area Housing Alliance, set for itself the primary goal of getting all savings and loans regulated by the Federal Home Loan Bank to disclose their loans and deposits by zip code in the Chicago metropolitan area. A series of local meetings were held around the city and in neighboring suburbs. Each local group went to its local savings and loan association to request disclosure. The story was the same at each S&L. "We can't do it without authorization from the Federal Home Loan Bank." The question was then asked, "Would you be willing if the FHLB said to do it?" The answer was invariably "Yes."

The leaders of the local groups were pulled together and after reporting their experiences the decision was made to hold a meeting with the president of the Chicago Federal Home Loan Bank. He was invited to a meeting and refused to come. A large delegation went to his home and passed out flyers to his neighbors. The president agreed to a meeting. The first intermediate victory had been won. Word spread through the communities

that their efforts were having results, because the president of the Federal Home Loan Bank had agreed to meet to discuss disclosure.

At the meeting the president said that if all the local institutions had said what the people were reporting (i.e., that they would be willing to disclose if asked by the Federal Home Loan Bank), then he could see no problems with disclosure. But he wanted to check with his superiors in Washington, D.C. It was agreed that the following week officials from Washington would be at the meeting. Another intermediate victory! Washington was responding to the demands.

At the next meeting the officials from Washington said they felt a plot disclosure study would be of no value and that they could not authorize anything of the kind. After much shouting back and forth, it was decided that there would be another meeting with officers of local savings and loans and officials from the Chicago and Washington Federal Home Loan Banks. Another intermediate victory—"Washington officials are so frightened they are coming back to meet with us again."

Prior to the next meeting the local groups went back to their local savings and loans and reconfirmed that if asked by the Federal Home Loan Bank they would be willing to disclose. Some of them even went so far as to say they thought it would be good. So several local groups again scored intermediate victories.

When the meeting occurred, local officials of savings and loans faced with community residents were forced to say publicly what they had been saying in private to the community residents. The ranks of the bankers were hopelessly broken, and the leadership of MAHA stepped into the breach demanding a pilot program of disclosure. Since representatives of several larger local institutions had said they would not oppose such a pilot program, the officials of the Federal Home Loan Bank agreed that there would be such a study. The primary victory had been won! But in no way did that mean that the issue was over. MAHA leaders immediately demanded a meeting to work out the type of questionnaire to be used and the timetable for disclosure.

From that came a flurry of activity around local institutions who were not making loans, and on the basis of the pilot data, a city ordinance was enacted to require disclosure by any financial institution desiring to hold city funds. From there to a State and Federal Disclosure Law.

The important aspect is that as soon as the primary victory had been reached, the organization set new goals for itself and the primary victories developed into new issues and new organizing drives and eventually new victories. This means that there are no final victories.

The human animal is continually searching for the Holy Grail—that which when achieved will solve all problems and be the end of the struggle. People tend to view issues in that manner. "If we get a new school, then the kids will get a good education." "If we get disclosure, then red-lining will stop." Yet, the seasoned leader and organizer know that every victory leads to another organizing drive. So that when MAHA won a pilot disclosure program, that primary victory turned into an intermediate victory on the road to Federal Disclosure. Now that Federal Disclosure has been won, that victory has turned into an intermediate victory along the road to reinvestment which now has become the primary victory being sought. Thus it may appear to some that there is no end to organizing and that is true, not only about organizing but life itself. The football team that wins on Saturday is planning for the next game by Monday.

Conclusion

Since victories lead to new battles, that means that victories carry with them the responsibility to go on to new and perhaps uncharted areas. Thus victory scares some people. If you lose, then not much is expected of you and you don't have to take the next step. The organization that wins knows that victory will lead to new organizing lines and new fights, that with each new victory, come new responsibilities.

THE MYTH OF THE ORGANIZER

A myth is a way of pulling together the raw and contradictory evidence of life as it is known in any age. It lets people make patterns in their own lives, within the larger patterns.

Theodore H. White, *Breach of Faith*, 1975

Historically man has had myths by which he lived. These myths were the sign posts of his existence. They were his attempts to make sense out of nonsense and to give meaning to his life. Myths assisted him in dealing with a world that confused him, frightened him, and over which he had no control. Myths also fulfilled the role of calling upon members of the cult or community to extend themselves beyond their own estimation of themselves or their energies. Thus, initiation rites of pain, suffering or sacrifice and dedication.

Religion has fulfilled that need in man. Thus, the demands of most faiths for total commitment. Patriotism has met that need in others; thus, the right of the country to demand and receive the lives of its people in time of war. Movements have served that role for some. The early union organizers, under threat of death, faced each new day with the myth of the "one big strike" in which the balance of power would be shifted. The Freedom Movement of the 50s and 60s demanded and received full commitment from many for the myth of equal rights for all men.

All these and many more were and, in some cases, remain man's attempt to give meaning to his existence and drive him beyond his limitations. Participation in the myth will make me a better person, will make the world a better place to live, will make me part of a power structure which can bring about the changes that I want to see happen.

We find ourselves in a time in history when myths are hard to come by. Religion does not have appeal for us today that it had for our parents. In the wake of Watergate, few, if any, look upon politicians when it is called for by an elected official. The shaky economy and increasing shortages have destroyed the myth of a totally prosperous world that would be without want and need.

Myths, to give life meaning, have for a large segment of the population become the annual two- or three-week vacation, college education for the children, the mortgage paid off, a good pension plan. If these myths give meaning to an individual's life, all well and good, albeit rather boring myths to keep a person going.

A rather unromantic, but very pragmatic individual has stated, "Life is a shit sandwich without bread, and every day we take another bite." Is there a myth which can make any sense out of the shit sandwich?

The professional organizer is one who looks at the world the way it really is and deals with it. He sees the oppressed and the oppressor, those with power and those without power, and works toward the day when the roles shall be equalized or reversed—full

well knowing from history that when the powerless become powerful the process will have to begin again. He sees not only the viciousness of the oppressor, although cloaked in white collar and wrapped in a $500 suit. He sees also the smallness and pettiness of the oppressed. He sees the ruthlessness of the power and the submission of the powerless. He knows that if he is lucky or history is kind to him he will have, at best, two organizing campaigns in his life that will have social impact of any magnitude. What are some of the ingredients of the myth that keep the organizer going?

Life is to be exciting. The organizer's stock in trade is change. Change of the existing power structure of a precinct, ward, city, state. Change of the financial community. Change of the existing roles of oppressor and oppressed. Change of things as they are. Such change does not happen without excitement. Excitement for the organizer—excitement for the people he works for and the people he works against. In the movie *A Thousand Clowns,* Jason Robards, in talking about his adopted nephew, says, "I want him to give the world a goosing before he dies." A goosing is a very exciting experience, either negatively or positively for all involved. Thus, he is committed to the excitement of change in his own life and all the lives and structures with which he comes into contact.

This excitement can be at the level of organizing a group of welfare recipients to the point where they change roles with the welfare office and made demands that are honored. Or at the level of organizing a community so that it has enough power to say to the city planner, "Screw your plan. Here is our plan," and win. Or the excitement of seeing a person's image of himself change because of his involvement with the issue and organization.

An organizer who developed a senior citizens' coalition worked very hard with his leadership before the confrontation, in which they were demanding a special dial-a-bus program from the city. In the midst of the negotiation, it was obvious that his leaders were not going to win the fight. Just at the moment when it looked like the mayor had them so confused and bickering among themselves to the extent that the issue would be lost, a woman who had not previously been a strong leader stood up and shouted, "Mayor, you have a mother and father. Do you want them to have to walk six blocks with a bag of groceries or not go to the doctor because they don't want to spend the cab fare? You know this program is for your parents too, and some day it will be for you." This was the unifying battle cry which sparked the seniors and pulled them together, destroying all of the mayor's reasoned logic on why the program wouldn't be instituted. Fifteen minutes later the seniors walked out with a victory, and today the bus program is working in that community. The people elected the woman their permanent spokesperson. When she shows up with her constituents at a city office, they are immediately ushered in and their demands, more times than not, are met. When a new state or federal issue on aging comes up, the press calls her for a statement of the opinion of the senior coalition on the new proposal. She confided to the organizer, "You know, no one ever used to care what I thought or listen to my opinions, and now they do. This has been the most exciting two years of my life." It might be added that life was also not dull for those whom the senior coalition confronted during these two years. As he told the story, the organizer relieved the excitement of that organizing campaign. A big portion of the organizer's myth is that life is to be exciting.

A second major tenet in the myth of the organizer is his belief in and respect for people. This belief and respect is expressed in many ways. It is first exhibited when he enters the arena in which he is organizing. He samples as many opinions and ideas as possible from every economic, educational and ethnic strata of his arena. He does not judge the person who presents him with a concept contrary to his own, but accepts it as part of the mosaic that he is called upon to build. It is further exhibited in the selection of the issues to be worked on by the people. When a staff charges into the office saying, "I've got a great new issue," the lead organizer's immediate response is, "Did you check it out with people?" Once it has been determined by the people what issues will be worked on, then the organizer's job is to express his belief in and respect for people by allowing them to set the timetable, the tactics and the goals. He may lay out alternatives, *but in the end it is the people who make the decision on what course of action is to be taken.*

A white organizer working in a black community was continually told by his leadership, "We have to do something about the prostitutes in the community." He felt quite uneasy about the whole issue, but, finally, a meeting was organized with the police and a series of demands were made. The police promised to pick up all the prostitutes; however, they warned the people that the prostitutes would be back out on the street in three hours. The crowd decided to see what would happen and pushed the police to do their job, setting up a steering committee to meet in two weeks to see if they had gained any results. It didn't take two weeks for leadership to see that, indeed, the police were picking up the women; but that they were back from booking the same night in most cases, the next night in all cases. The organizer, desperate to come up with a solution of the issue, went to the police and talked with them about the problem. He was told by the police that over 90 percent of the patrons of the black prostitutes were whites from a nearby suburb. Since these people were from outside his arena, the organizer had his strategy: station people on the corners and, whenever you see a white male pick up one of the women, copy down his license number, trace the license number to registration, and send a letter to that residence addressed to Mrs. Smith asking if she knew where her husband was on such and such a night. Coupling this with a news release that this was going to happen, would cut the trade, and thereby get rid of the prostitutes.

Gleefully, he went to the leadership meeting with this strategy. For a variety of reasons, some of which were not too hard to see through, the strategy was turned down. The people decided instead to picket the prostitutes. As distasteful as this was to him personally, the organizer had chosen his arena and now was called upon to respect the people above his own feelings.

At this point, all kinds of rhetorical questions are thrown out. "How far do you let people go? Would you organize for segregation? Doesn't the organizer have a moral right to take a personal stand on issues?" On and on. Once the organizer has analyzed the arena in which he intends to organize, and, if he accepts that arena, then the myth by which he lives dictates that he is bound to respect the decisions of those people within the arena. For from his experience he has seen that when people are given the opportunity in a democratic arena to wrestle with their lives and the life of the community, the way in which people look at themselves and others changes, horizons broaden, self-interest expands beyond myself to my community and my city. He has seen homeowners fight for the right of the tenant; he has seen tenants fight for an issue that only benefits homeowners. He has seen people lose a day

of work to fight for issues that will not directly affect them.

A third basic ingredient in the organizer's myth is that no institution is to be trusted. This is easy for the novice to accept as he organizes an attack on city hall, or the bank, or the Board of Education. The professional knows that this applies also to the power base that he is organizing. Thus, he is constantly on the prowl for new ideas, new people, new segments of the community to bring into his organizing campaign. An institution that is not challenged with fresh people seeking leadership, with new issues to replace the old, soon becomes senile. Once senility starts, death is not far behind. Thus, the organizer knows that he cannot trust institutions; they must be challenged on every front, not only those that are attempting to oppress his arena, but his own arena as well.

An organizer was hired to direct an organization which was working in a multiethnic community. As he looked over the makeup of his executive board, he discovered that the ethnic group which made up 60 percent of the community only had 2 members on the 25-member board. Knowing that a reaction would result from the existing power structure, he used the constitution which said, if a board member missed three board meetings without excuse, he/she could be replaced. In six months nine new board members had been added to the board, all from the disenfranchised ethnic group. As a result, several other board members resigned because there were too many of "those people" on the board. Yet, the organizer knew he had to change or kill the arena in which he was working if he was to be true to his myth.

The myth of the organizer, that which pulls up out of bed in the morning to face another shit sandwich, is his belief in the excitement of life—that which he wants to create and that of which he wants to be a part. His belief in and respect for peoples' ability to make decisions about their lives and their ability to be cognizant of more than their limited self-interest in making those decisions. His distrust of all institutions and, thus, his drive to bring new ideas and new people to all institutions, thereby bringing excitement to those institutions.

SUMMARY

Community organization is the process of stimulating and assisting the local community to evaluate, plan, and coordinate its efforts to meet the needs of a community. Social work is one of several disciplines that provide training in community organizations.

There are several roles or models for community organization activities: including enabler, broker, expert, social planner, advocate, and activist. The model that is applied is generally determined by the task to be accomplished. Since a given community issue may involve several roles, there is overlap between the models used.

The enabler, broker, expert, and social planner roles are generally nonpartisan. If nonpartisan attempts are not successful in meeting the needs of individuals or groups of people, partisan activity (such as being an advocate or an activist) may be warranted.

For comparison and contrast purposes, two models of community organization/development were presented: (a) the Biddles model in which the developer is primarily an "encourager," and (b) the Alinsky "power confrontation" model in which the organizer plays more of an "activist" role. Among theories of community organization, the Alinsky model has generated the most interest and controversy in recent years.

NOTES

1. Alfred M. Stamm, "NASW Membership Characteristics, Deployment and Salaries," *Personnel Information* 12 (May 1969), p. 49.
2. Arnold Panitch, in *Contemporary Social Work*, ed. Donald Brieland, Lela Costin, and Charles Atherton, 2d ed. (New York: McGraw-Hill, 1980), pp. 124–25.
3. Neil Gilbert and Harry Specht, "Social Planning and Community Organization: Approaches," *Encyclopedia of Social Work*, 17th ed. (Washington, D.C.: National Association of Social Workers, 1977) pp. 1412–25.
4. Ibid.
5. William W. Biddle and Loureide J. Biddle, *The Community Development Process: The Rediscovery of Local Initiative* (New York: Holt, Rinehart & Winston, 1965).
6. Ibid., p. 77.
7. Ibid., p. 78.
8. Ibid., p. 98.

APPENDIX: The NASW Code of Ethics*

(The National Association of Social Workers, NASW, is the professional association which represents the social work profession in this country. Its Code of Ethics summarizes important practice ethics for social workers and is presented as follows:)

PREAMBLE

This code is intended to serve as a guide to the everyday conduct of members of the social work profession and as a basis for the adjudication of issues in ethics when the conduct of social workers is alleged to deviate from the standards expressed or implied in this code. It represents standards of ethical behavior for social workers in professional relationships with those served, with colleagues, with employers, with other individuals and professions, and with the community and society as a whole. It also embodies standards of ethical behavior governing individual conduct to the extent that such conduct is associated with an individual's status and identity as a social worker.

This code is based on the fundamental values of the social work profession that include the worth, dignity, and uniqueness of all persons as well as their rights and opportunities. It is also based on the nature of social work, which fosters conditions that promote these values.

In subscribing to and abiding by this code, the social worker is expected to view ethical responsibility in as inclusive a context as each situation demands and within which ethical judgement is required. The social worker is expected to take into consideration all the principles in this code that have a bearing upon any situation in which ethical judgement is to be exercised and professional intervention or conduct is planned. The course of action that the social worker chooses is expected to be consistent with the spirit as well as the letter of this code.

In itself, this code does not represent a set of rules that will prescribe all the behaviors of social workers in all the complexities of professional life. Rather, it offers general principles to guide conduct, and the judicious appraisal of conduct, in situations that have ethical implications. It provides the basis for making judgements about ethical actions before and after they occur. Frequently, the particular situation determines the ethical principles that apply and the manner of their application. In such cases, not only the particular ethical principles are taken into immediate consideration, but also the entire code and its spirit. Specific applications of ethical principles must be judged within the context in which they are being considered. Ethical behavior in a given situation must satisfy not only the judgement of the individual social worker, but also the judgement of an unbiased jury of professional peers.

* Reprinted by permission of the National Association of Social Workers: "NASW Code of Ethics," as revised by the 1979 Delegate Assembly. National Association of Social Workers, Inc., Washington, D.C.

This code should not be used as an instrument to deprive any social worker of the opportunity or freedom to practice with complete professional integrity; nor should any disciplinary action be taken on the basis of this code without maximum provision for safeguarding the rights of the social worker affected.

The ethical behavior of social workers results not from edict, but from a personal commitment of the individual. This code is offered to affirm the will and zeal of all social workers to be ethical and to act ethically in all that they do as social workers.

The following codified ethical principles should guide social workers in the various roles and relationships and at the various levels of responsibility in which they function professionally. These principles also serve as a basis for the adjudication by the National Association of Social Workers of issues in ethics.

In subscribing to this code, social workers are required to cooperate in its implementation and abide by any disciplinary rulings based on it. They should also take adequate measures to discourage, prevent, expose, and correct the unethical conduct of col-

---

NASW Code of Ethics

SUMMARY OF MAJOR PRINCIPLES

I. THE SOCIAL WORKER'S CONDUCT AND COMPORTMENT AS A SOCIAL WORKER
   A. *Propriety.* The social worker should maintain high standards of personal conduct in the capacity or identity as social worker.
   B. *Competence and Professional Development.* The social worker should strive to become and remain proficient in professional practice and the performance of professional functions.
   C. *Service.* The social worker should regard as primary the service obligation of the social work profession.
   D. *Integrity.* The social worker should act in accordance with the highest standards of professional integrity.
   E. *Scholarship and Research.* The social worker engaged in study and research should be guided by the conventions of scholarly inquiry.

II. THE SOCIAL WORKER'S ETHICAL RESPONSIBILITY TO CLIENTS
   F. *Primacy of Clients' Interests.* The social worker's primary responsibility is to clients.
   G. *Rights and Prerogatives of Clients.* The social worker should make every effort to foster maximum self-determination on the part of clients.
   H. *Confidentiality and Privacy.* The social worker should respect the privacy of clients and hold in confidence all information obtained in the course of professional service.
   I. *Fees.* When setting fees, the social worker should ensure that they are fair, reasonable, considerate, and commensurate with the service performed and with due regard for the client's ability to pay.

III. THE SOCIAL WORKER'S ETHICAL RESPONSIBILITY TO COLLEAGUES
   J. *Respect, Fairness, and Courtesy.* The social worker should treat colleagues with respect, courtesy, fairness, and good faith.
   K. *Dealing with Colleagues' Clients.* The social worker has the responsibility to relate to the clients of colleagues with full professional consideration.

IV. THE SOCIAL WORKER'S ETHICAL RESPONSIBILITY TO EMPLOYERS AND EMPLOYING ORGANIZATIONS
   L. *Commitments to Employing Organizations.* The social worker should adhere to commitments made to the employing organizations.

V. THE SOCIAL WORKER'S ETHICAL RESPONSIBILITY TO THE SOCIAL WORK PROFESSION
   M. *Maintaining the Integrity of the Profession.* The social worker should uphold and advance the values, ethics, knowledge, and mission of the profession.
   N. *Community Service.* The social worker should assist the profession in making social services available to the general public.
   O. *Development of Knowledge.* The social worker should take responsibility for identifying, developing, and fully utilizing knowledge for professional practice.

VI. THE SOCIAL WORKER'S ETHICAL RESPONSIBILITY TO SOCIETY
   P. *Promoting the General Welfare.* The social worker should promote the general welfare of society.

leagues. Finally, social workers should be equally ready to defend and assist colleagues unjustly charged with unethical conduct.

I. The social worker's conduct and comportment as a social worker

A. Propriety. The social worker should maintain high standards of personal conduct in the capacity or identity as social worker.

1. The private conduct of the social worker is a personal matter to the same degree as is any other person's, except when such conduct compromises the fulfillment of professional responsibilities.

2. The social worker should not participate in, condone, or be associated with dishonesty, fraud, deceit, or misrepresentation.

3. The social worker should distinguish clearly between statements and actions made as a private individual and as a representative of the social work profession or an organization or group.

B. Competence and professional development. The social worker should strive to become and remain proficient in professional practice and the performance of professional functions.

1. The social worker should accept responsibility or employment only on the basis of existing competence or the intention to acquire the necessary competence.

2. The social worker should not misrepresent professional qualifications, education, experience, or affiliations.

C. Service. The social worker should regard as primary the service obligation of the social work profession.

1. The social worker should retain ultimate responsibility for the quality and extent of the service that individual assumes, assigns, or performs.

2. The social worker should act to prevent practices that are inhumane or discriminatory against any person or group of persons.

D. Integrity. The social worker should act in accordance with the highest standards of professional integrity and impartiality.

1. The social worker should be alert to and resist the influences and pressures that interfere with the exercise of professional discretion and impartial judgement required for the performance of professional functions.

2. The social worker should not exploit professional relationships for personal gain.

E. Scholarship and research. The social worker engaged in study and research should be guided by the conventions of scholarly inquiry.

1. The social worker engaged in research should consider carefully its possible consequences for human beings.

2. The social worker engaged in research should ascertain that the consent of participants in the research is voluntary and informed, without any implied deprivation or penalty for refusal to participate, and with due regard for participants' privacy and dignity.

3. The social worker engaged in research should protect participants from unwarranted physical or mental discomfort, distress, harm, danger, or deprivation.

4. The social worker who engages in the evaluation of services or cases should discuss them only for professional purposes and only with persons directly and professionally concerned with them.

5. Information obtained about participants in research should be treated as confidential.

6. The social worker should take credit only for work actually done in connection

with scholarly and research endeavors and credit contributions made by others.

II. The social worker's ethical responsibility to clients

F. Primacy of client's interests. The social worker's primary responsibility is to clients.

1. The social worker should serve clients with devotion, loyalty, determination, and the maximum application of professional skill and competence.

2. The social worker should not exploit relationships with clients for personal advantage, or solicit the clients of one's agency for private practice.

3. The social worker should not practice, condone, facilitate or collaborate with any form of discrimination on the basis of race, color, sex, sexual orientation, age, religion, national origin, marital status, political belief, mental or physical handicap, or any other preference or personal characteristic, condition or status.

4. The social worker should avoid relationships or commitments that conflict with the interests of clients.

5. The social worker should under no circumstances engage in sexual activities with clients.

6. The social worker should provide clients with accurate and complete information regarding the extent and nature of the services available to them.

7. The social worker should apprise clients of their risks, rights, opportunities, and obligations associated with social service to them.

8. The social worker should seek advice and counsel of colleagues and supervisors whenever such consultation is in the best interest of clients.

9. The social worker should terminate service to clients, and professional relation-

ships with them, when such service and relationships are no longer required or no longer serve the clients' needs or interests.

10. The social worker should withdraw services precipitously only under unusual circumstances, giving careful consideration to all factors in the situation and taking care to minimize possible adverse effects.

11. The social worker who anticipates the termination or interruption of service to clients should notify clients promptly and seek the transfer, referral, or continuation of service in relation to the clients' needs and preferences.

G. Rights and prerogatives of clients. The social worker should make every effort to foster maximum self-determination on the part of clients.

1. When the social worker must act on behalf of a client who has been adjudged legally incompetent, the social worker should safeguard the interests and rights of that client.

2. When another individual has been legally authorized to act in behalf of a client, the social worker should deal with that person always with the clients' best interest in mind.

3. The social worker should not engage in any action that violates or diminishes the civil or legal rights of clients.

H. Confidentiality and privacy. The social worker should respect the privacy of clients and hold in confidence all information obtained in the course of professional service.

1. The social worker should share with others confidences revealed by clients, without their consent, only for compelling professional reasons.

2. The social worker should inform clients fully about the limits of confidentiality in a given situation, the purposes for which

information is obtained, and how it may be used.

3. The social worker should afford clients reasonable access to any official social work records concerning them.

4. When providing clients with access to records, the social worker should take due care to protect the confidences of others contained in those records.

5. The social worker should obtain informed consent of clients before taping, recording, or permitting third party observation of their activities.

I. Fees. When setting fees, the social worker should ensure that they are fair, reasonable, considerate, and commensurate with the service performed and with due regard for the clients' ability to pay.

1. The social worker should not divide a fee or accept or give anything of value for receiving or making a referral.

III. The social worker's ethical responsibility to colleagues

J. Respect, fairness, and courtesy. The social worker should treat colleagues with respect, courtesy, fairness, and good faith.

1. The social worker should cooperate with colleagues to promote professional interests and concerns.

2. The social worker should respect confidences shared by colleagues in the course of their professional relationships and transactions.

3. The social worker should create and maintain conditions of practice that facilitate ethical and competent professional performance by colleagues.

4. The social worker should treat with respect, and represent accurately and fairly, the qualifications, views, and findings of

colleagues and use appropriate channels to express judgements on these matters.

5. The social worker who replaces or is replaced by a colleague in professional practice should act with consideration for the interest, character, and reputation of that colleague.

6. The social worker should not exploit a dispute between a colleague and employers to obtain a position or otherwise advance the social worker's interest.

7. The social worker should seek arbitration or mediation when conflicts with colleagues require resolution for compelling professional reasons.

8. The social worker should extend to colleagues of other professions the same respect and cooperation that is extended to social work colleagues.

9. The social worker who serves as an employer, supervisor, or mentor to colleagues should make orderly and explicit arrangements, regarding the conditions of their continuing professional relationship.

10. The social worker who has the responsibility for employing and evaluating the performance of other staff members, should fulfill such responsibility in a fair, considerate, and equitable manner, on the basis of clearly enunciated criteria.

11. The social worker who has the responsibility for evaluating the performance of employees, supervisees, or students should share evaluations with them.

K. Dealing with colleagues' clients. The social worker has the responsibility to relate to the clients of colleagues with full professional consideration.

1. The social worker should not solicit the clients of colleagues.

2. The social worker should not assume professional responsibility for the clients of another agency or a colleague without appro-

priate communication with that agency or colleague.

3. The social worker who serves the clients of colleagues, during a temporary absence or emergency, should serve those clients with the same consideration as that afforded any client.

IV. The social worker's ethical responsibility to employers and employing organizations

L. Commitment to employing organization. The social worker should adhere to commitments made to the employing organization.

1. The social worker should work to improve the employing agency's policies and procedures, and the efficiency and effectiveness of its services.

2. The social worker should not accept employment or arrange student field placements in an organization which is currently under public sanction by NASW for violating personnel standards or imposing limitations on or penalties for professional actions on behalf of clients.

3. The social worker should act to prevent and eliminate discrimination in the employing organization's work assignments and in its employment policies and practices.

4. The social worker should use with scrupulous regard, and only for the purpose for which they are intended, the resources of the employing organization.

V. The social worker's ethical responsibility to the social work profession

M. Maintaining the integrity of the profession. The social worker should uphold and advance the values, ethics, knowledge, and mission of the profession.

1. The social worker should protect and enhance the dignity and integrity of the profession and should be responsible and vigorous in discussion and criticism of the profession.

2. The social worker should take action through appropriate channels against unethical conduct by any other member of the profession.

3. The social worker should act to prevent the unauthorized and unqualified practice of social work.

4. The social worker should make no misrepresentation in advertising as to qualifications, competence, service, or results to be achieved.

N. Community service. The social worker should assist the profession in making social services available to the general public.

1. The social worker should contribute time and professional expertise to activities that promote respect for the utility, the integrity, and the competence of the social work profession.

2. The social worker should support the formulation, development, enactment and implementation of social policies of concern to the profession.

O. Development of knowledge. The social worker should take responsibility for identifying, developing, and fully utilizing knowledge for professional practice.

1. The social worker should base practice upon recognized knowledge relevant to social work.

2. The social worker should critically examine, and keep current with, emerging knowledge relevant to social work.

3. The social worker should contribute to the knowledge base of social work and share research knowledge and practice wisdom with colleagues.

VI. The social worker's ethical responsibility to society

P. Promoting the general welfare. The social worker should promote the general welfare of society.

1. The social worker should act to prevent and eliminate discrimination against any person or group on the basis of race, color, sex, sexual orientation, age, religion, national origin, marital status, political belief, mental or physical handicap, or any other preference or personal characteristic, condition, or status.

2. The social worker should act to ensure that all persons have access to the resources, services, and opportunities which they require.

3. The social worker should act to expand choice and opportunity for all persons, with special regard for disadvantaged or oppressed groups and persons.

4. The social worker should promote conditions that encourage respect for the diversity of cultures which constitute American society.

5. The social worker should provide appropriate professional services in public emergencies.

6. The social worker should advocate changes in policy and legislation to improve social conditions and to promote social justice.

7. The social worker should encourage informed participation by the public in shaping social policies and institutions.

List of photo credits

Part three

Index

This book has been set VIP, in 10 and 9 point Palatino, leaded 2 points. Part numbers are 16 point Palatino bold and chapter numbers are 18 and 24 point Palatino bold. Part and chapter titles are 18 point Palatino bold. The size of the type page is 36 by 47 ½ picas.